T0320440

Ensemble Methods
Foundations and Algorithms

Ensemble methods that train multiple learners and then combine them to use, with *Boosting* and *Bagging* as representatives, are well-known machine learning approaches. It has become common sense that an ensemble is usually significantly more accurate than a single learner, and ensemble methods have already achieved great success in various real-world tasks.

Twelve years have passed since the publication of the first edition of the book in 2012 (Japanese and Chinese versions published in 2017 and 2020, respectively). Many significant advances in this field have been developed. First, many theoretical issues have been tackled, for example, the fundamental question of *why AdaBoost seems resistant to overfitting* gets addressed, so that now we understand much more about the essence of ensemble methods. Second, ensemble methods have been well developed in more machine learning fields, e.g., *isolation forest* in anomaly detection, so that now we have powerful ensemble methods for tasks beyond conventional supervised learning. Third, ensemble mechanisms have also been found helpful in emerging areas such as deep learning and online learning.

This edition expands on the previous one with additional content to reflect the significant advances in the field, and is written in a concise but comprehensive style to be approachable to readers new to the subject.

Zhi-Hua Zhou, Professor of Computer Science and Artificial Intelligence at Nanjing University, President of IJCAI trustee, Fellow of the ACM, AAAI, AAAS, IEEE, recipient of the IEEE Computer Society Edward J. McCluskey Technical Achievement Award, CCF-ACM Artificial Intelligence Award.

Chapman & Hall/CRC Machine Learning & Pattern Recognition

A First Course in Machine Learning
Simon Rogers, Mark Girolami

Statistical Reinforcement Learning: Modern Machine Learning Approaches
Masashi Sugiyama

Sparse Modeling: Theory, Algorithms, and Applications
Irina Rish, Genady Grabarnik

Computational Trust Models and Machine Learning
Xin Liu, Anwitaman Datta, Ee-Peng Lim

Regularization, Optimization, Kernels, and Support Vector Machines
Johan A.K. Suykens, Marco Signoretto, Andreas Argyriou

Machine Learning: An Algorithmic Perspective, Second Edition
Stephen Marsland

Bayesian Programming
Pierre Bessiere, Emmanuel Mazer, Juan Manuel Ahuactzin, Kamel Mekhnacha

Multilinear Subspace Learning: Dimensionality Reduction of Multidimensional Data
Haiping Lu, Konstantinos N. Plataniotis, Anastasios Venetsanopoulos

Data Science and Machine Learning: Mathematical and Statistical Methods
Dirk P. Kroese, Zdravko Botev, Thomas Taimre, Radislav Vaisman

Deep Learning and Linguistic Representation
Shalom Lappin

Artificial Intelligence and Causal Inference
Momiao Xiong

Introduction to Machine Learning with Applications in Information Security, Second Edition
Mark Stamp

Entropy Randomization in Machine Learning
Yuri S. Popkov, Alexey Yu. Popkov, Yuri A. Dubno

Transformers for Machine Learning
Uday Kamath, Kenneth Graham and Wael Emara

The Pragmatic Programmer for Machine Learning
Marco Scutari and Mauro Malvestio

Machine Learning, Animated
Mark Liu

Deep and Shallow: Machine Learning in Music and Audio
Shlomo Dubnov and Ross Greer

For more information on this series please visit: https://www.routledge.com/Chapman-HallCRC-Machine-Learning--Pattern-Recognition/book-series/CRCMACLEAPAT

Ensemble Methods

Foundations and Algorithms

Second Edition

Zhi-Hua Zhou

CRC Press is an imprint of the
Taylor & Francis Group, an **informa** business
A CHAPMAN & HALL BOOK

Designed cover image: Shutterstock_1117953086 and Shutterstock_145255999

Second edition published 2025
by CRC Press
2385 NW Executive Center Drive, Suite 320, Boca Raton FL 33431

and by CRC Press
4 Park Square, Milton Park, Abingdon, Oxon, OX14 4RN

CRC Press is an imprint of Taylor & Francis Group, LLC

Library of Congress Cataloging-in-Publication Data
Names: Zhou, Zhi-Hua (Computer scientist) author.
Title: Ensemble Methods : Foundations and Algorithms / Zhi-Hua Zhou.
Description: Second edition. | Boca Raton, FL : CRC Press, 2025. | Series: Chapman & Hall/CRC machine learning & pattern recognition | Includes bibliographical references and index. | Summary: "Ensemble methods that train multiple learners and then combine them to use, with ***undefined*** and ***undefined*** as representatives, are well-known machine learning approaches. It has become common sense that an ensemble is usually significantly more accurate than a single learner, and ensemble methods have already achieved great success in various real-world tasks. Twelve years have passed since the publication of the first edition of the book in 2012 (Japanese and Chinese versions published in 2017 and 2020, respectively). Many significant advances in this field have been developed. "-- Provided by publisher.
Identifiers: LCCN 2024041213 | ISBN 9781032960609 (hbk) | ISBN 9781032960616 (pbk) | ISBN 9781003587774 (ebk)
Subjects: LCSH: Multiple comparisons (Statistics) | Set theory. | Mathematical analysis.
Classification: LCC QA278.4 .Z47 2025 | DDC 006.3/1--dc23/eng/20241129
LC record available at https://lccn.loc.gov/2024041213

ISBN: 978-1-032-96060-9 (hbk)
ISBN: 978-1-032-96061-6 (pbk)
ISBN: 978-1-003-58777-4 (ebk)

DOI: 10.1201/9781003587774

Typeset in CMR10 font
by KnowledgeWorks Global Ltd.

Publisher's note: This book has been prepared from camera-ready copy provided by the authors.

Contents

Preface to the Second Edition

Ensemble methods that train multiple learners and then combine them to use, with *Boosting* and *Bagging* as representatives, are well-known machine learning approaches. It has become common sense that an ensemble is usually significantly more accurate than a single learner, and ensemble methods have already achieved great success in various real-world tasks.

Twelve years have passed since the publication of the first edition of the book in 2012 (Japanese and Chinese versions published in 2017 and 2020, respectively). Many significant advances in this field have been developed. First, many theoretical issues have been tackled, e.g., the fundamental question of *why AdaBoost seems resistant to overfitting* gets addressed, so that now we understand much more about the essence of ensemble methods. Second, ensemble methods have been well developed in more machine learning fields, e.g., *isolation forest* in anomaly detection, so that now we have powerful ensemble methods for tasks beyond conventional supervised learning. Third, ensemble mechanisms have also been found helpful in the phenomenon and emerging areas such as deep learning and online learning. Therefore, it is time to present the second edition of the book.

The book is intended to be written in a concise but comprehensive style, not to be too lengthy to make readers who just step into this field feel frightened. Due to the significantly increased amount of content, however, the current book is nearly half thicker than its anterior edition. It consists of twelve chapters that naturally constitute three parts:

Part I is composed of Chapter 1. Though this book is mainly written for readers with basic knowledge of machine learning, data mining, and pattern recognition, to enable readers who are unfamiliar with these fields to access the main contents, Chapter 1 tries to present some "background knowledge" of ensemble methods. It is impossible to provide a detailed introduction to all backgrounds in one chapter, and therefore, this chapter mainly serves as a guidance for further study. This chapter also serves to expose the use of terminologies in this book, for avoiding confusion caused by terminologies used differently in different but relevant fields.

Part II is composed of Chapters 2 to 6, which presents "core knowledge" of ensemble methods. Chapters 2 and 3 introduce *Boosting* and *Bagging*, respectively, including *Random Forest* which is a famous variant of *Bagging*. Chapter 4 focuses on ensemble diversity, the fundamental concept in ensemble methods. Chapter 5 introduces combination methods. In addition to various averaging and voting schemes, the *Stacking* method and relevant methods such as *Mixture of Experts* are introduced. Chapter 6 introduces ensemble pruning, which tries to prune a trained ensemble to get a better performance with smaller sizes.

Part III is composed of Chapters 7 to 12, which presents "advanced knowledge" of ensemble methods. Chapters 7 and 8 are about unsupervised learning, where Chapter 7 focuses on clustering ensemble which tries to generate a better clustering result by combining multiple clusterings, while Chapter 8 introduces ensemble methods for unsupervised anomaly detection, particularly the *Isolation Forest* method and its variants. Then, Chapter 9 presents ensemble methods for semi-supervised learning, where both unlabeled and labeled data are exploited. Chapter 10 introduces ensemble methods for handling class-imbalance and unequal misclassification costs that have to be coped with in real practice. Chapter 11 devotes to deep learning, including not only ensembles with/in deep neural networks, but also *Deep Forest* which builds deep models based on non-differentiable modules. Finally, Chapter 12 briefly discusses on ensemble methods in weakly supervised learning, open-environment learning, reinforcement learning, online learning, as well as understandability enhancement.

It is not the goal of the book to cover all relevant knowledge of ensemble methods. Ambitious readers may be interested in *Further Reading* sections for further exploration.

The book could not be written, at least could not be in the current form, without the help of many people. I am grateful to Wei Gao, Sheng-Jun Huang, Nan Li, Shen-Huan Lv, Chao Qian, Yang Yu, Min-Ling Zhang, and Peng Zhao for their helpful comments. I want to thank readers who sent me helpful comments and typo corrections of the first edition. I also want to thank Randi Slack and her colleagues at Chapman & Hall/CRC Press for their cooperation.

Last, but definitely not least, I am indebted to my family, friends, and students for their patience, support, and encouragement.

Zhi-Hua Zhou
@ Nanjing, China
August 2024

Preface to the First Edition

Ensemble methods that train multiple learners and then combine them to use, with Boosting and Bagging as representatives, are a kind of state-of-the-art learning approach. It is well-known that an ensemble is usually significantly more accurate than a single learner, and ensemble methods have already achieved great success in many real-world tasks.

It is difficult to trace the starting point of the history of ensemble methods since the basic idea of deploying multiple models has been in use in human society for a long time; however, it is clear that ensemble methods becomes a hot topic since 1990s, and researchers from various fields such as machine learning, pattern recognition, data mining, neural networks, and statistics have explored ensemble methods from different aspects.

This book tries to provide researchers, students, and practitioners with introductory material to ensemble methods. The book consists of eight chapters, which naturally constitute three parts.

Part I is composed of Chapter 1. Though this book is mainly written for readers with basic knowledge of machine learning and pattern recognition, to enable readers who are unfamiliar with these fields to access the main contents, Chapter 1 tries to present some "background knowledge" of ensemble methods. It is impossible to provide a detailed introduction to all backgrounds in one chapter, and therefore, this chapter mainly serves as a guidance for further study. This chapter also serves to expose the use of terminologies in this book, for avoiding confusion caused by terminologies used differently in different but relevant fields.

Part II is composed of Chapters 2 to 5, which presents "core knowledge" of ensemble methods. Chapters 2 and 3 introduce Boosting and Bagging, respectively. In addition to algorithms and theories, Chapter 2 introduces multi-class extension and noise tolerance, since classic Boosting algorithms are designed for binary classification and are usually hurt seriously by noise. Bagging is naturally a multi-class method and less sensitive to noise, and therefore, Chapter 3 does not discuss about these issues; instead, Chapter 3 devotes a section to Random Forest and some other random tree ensembles that can be viewed as variants of Bagging. Chapter 4 introduces combination methods. In addition to various averaging and voting schemes, the Stacking method and some other combination methods as well as relevant methods such as mixture of experts are introduced. Chapter 5 focuses on ensemble diversity.

After introducing the error-ambiguity and bias-variance decompositions, many diversity measures are presented, followed by recent advances in information theoretic diversity and diversity generation methods.

Part III is composed of Chapters 6 to 8, which presents "advanced knowledge" of ensemble methods. Chapter 6 introduces ensemble pruning, which tries to prune a trained ensemble to get a better performance. Chapter 7 introduces clustering ensemble, which tries to generate a better clustering result by combining multiple clusterings. Chapter 8 presents some developments of ensemble methods in semi-supervised learning, active learning, cost-sensitive learning, and class-imbalance learning, as well as comprehensibility enhancement.

It is not the goal of the book to cover all relevant knowledge of ensemble methods. Ambitious readers may be interested in *Further Reading* sections for further exploration.

There are two books [Kuncheva, 2004, Rokach, 2010] on ensemble methods before this one. To reflect the fast development of this field, I have attempted to present an updated and in-depth overview. However, when the book was writing, I found that this task is more challenging than what had been expected. Though there is abundant research work on ensemble methods, it is still far from a thorough understanding of many essentials and is even lack of thorough empirical comparisons of many technical developments. As a consequence, several chapters of the book just introduce a number of algorithms, while even for chapters with discussions on theoretical issues, there are still important yet unclear problems. On one hand, this reflects the unmatured situation of the ensemble methods field, while on the other hand, such a situation provides good chance for further research explorations.

The book could not be written, at least could not be in the current form, without the help of many people. I am grateful to Tom Dietterich who has carefully read the whole book and given very detailed and insightful comments and suggestions. I want to thank Songcan Chen, Nan Li, Xu-Ying Liu, Fabio Roli, Jianxin Wu, Yang Yu, and Min-Ling Zhang for their helpful comments. I also want to thank Randi Cohen and her colleagues at Chapman & Hall/CRC Press for their cooperation.

Last, but definitely not least, I am indebted to my family, friends, and students for their patience, support, and encouragement.

Zhi-Hua Zhou
@ Nanjing, China
March 2012

Notations

x	Scalar
$\boldsymbol{x}$	Vector
$\mathbf{A}$	Matrix
$\mathbf{I}$	Identity matrix
$\mathcal{X}, \mathcal{Y}$	Input and output spaces
$\mathcal{D}$	Probability distribution
D	Data set
$\mathcal{H}$	Hypothesis space
H	Hypothesis set
$\mathfrak{L}$	Learning algorithm
$(\cdot, \ \cdot, \ \cdot)$	Row vector
$(\cdot)^\top$	Transpose of vector or matrix
$\{\cdots\}$	Set
$\lvert\{\cdots\}\rvert$	Number of elements in set $\{\cdots\}$
$\lVert \cdot \rVert_p$	L_p-norm; L_2-norm when p is absent
$P(\cdot), \ P(\cdot \mid \cdot)$	Probability mass function, conditional probability mass function
$p(\cdot), \ p(\cdot \mid \cdot)$	Probability density function, conditional probability density function
$\mathbb{E}_{\cdot \sim \mathcal{D}}[f(\cdot)]$	Expectation of function $f(\cdot)$ with respect to $\cdot$ over distribution $\mathcal{D}$; $\mathcal{D}$ and/or $\cdot$ are omitted when context is clear
$\mathbb{I}(\cdot)$	Indicator function, returns 1 if $\cdot$ is true and 0 otherwise
$\mathtt{sign}(\cdot)$	Sign function, returns -1 if $\cdot < 0$, 0 if $\cdot = 0$, and 1 if $\cdot > 0$

Chapter 1

Introduction

1.1 Terminology

One major task of machine learning, data mining, and pattern recognition is to construct *good* **models** from **data sets**.

A "data set" generally consists of **feature vectors**, where each feature vector is a description of an object using a set of **features**. For example, take a look at the synthetic *three-Gaussians* data set as shown in Figure 1.1. Here, each object is a data point described by the features x-coordinate, y-coordinate, and shape, and a feature vector looks like (.5, .8, cross) or (.4, .5, circle). The number of features of a data set is called **dimension** or **dimensionality**; for example, the dimensionality of the above data set is three. Features are also called **attributes**, a feature vector is also called an **instance**, and sometimes a data set is called a **sample**.

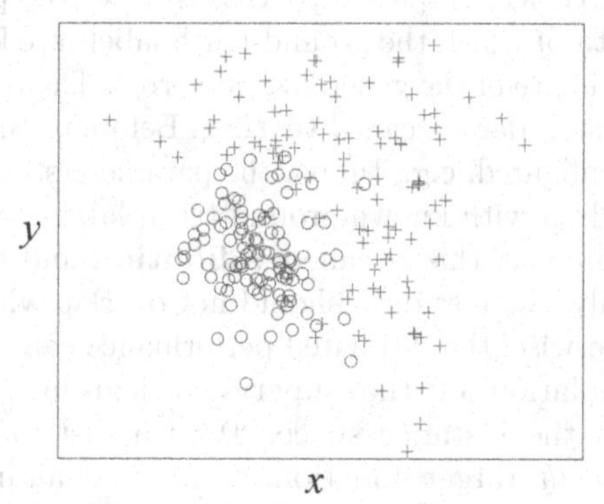

Figure 1.1: The synthetic *three-Gaussians* data set.

A "model" is usually a predictive model or a model of the structure of the data that we want to construct or discover from the data set, such as a decision tree, a neural network, a support vector machine, etc. The process

DOI: 10.1201/9781003587774-1

of generating models from data is called **learning** or **training**, which is accomplished by a **learning algorithm**. The learned model represents a **hypothesis** constructed or discovered from the data set, and in this book, it is also called a **learner**. There are different learning settings, while the most common one is **supervised learning**. Here, the goal is to predict the value of a target feature on *unseen* instances, and the learned model is also called a **predictor**. For example, if we want to predict the shape of the *three-Gaussians* data points, we call cross and circle **labels**, and the predictor should be able to predict the label of an instance for which the label information is unknown, e.g., (.2, .3). If the label is *categorical*, such as shape, the task is also called **classification** and the learner is also called **classifier**; if the label is *numerical*, such as x-coordinate, the task is also called **regression** and the learner is also called **regressor** or **fitted regression model**. For both cases, the training process is executed on data sets given label information, and an instance with known label is also called an **example. Binary classification** concerns about two classes generally called as "positive" and "negative", respectively, whereas **multi-class learning** concerns about more classes.

Basically, whether a model is *good* depends on whether its user is satisfied. Different users may have different requirements of the learning results, and it is difficult to know whether they can be satisfied before the concerned task has been tackled. A popular strategy is to evaluate and compare the performance of the models, and then let the user decide whether a model is acceptable, or choose the best available model from a set of candidates. The goal of learning is **generalization**, i.e., being capable of generalizing what has been learned from training data to handle *unseen* instances. A good learner should generalize well, i.e., have a small **generalization error**, also called the **prediction error**. It is infeasible, however, to estimate the generalization error directly since that requires knowing the **ground-truth** label information, which is unknown for unseen instances. A typical empirical process is to let the predictor make predictions on **test data** of which the ground-truth labels are known and take the **test error** as an estimate of the generalization error. The process of applying a learned model to unseen data is called **testing**. Before testing, a learned model often needs to be configured, e.g., tuning the parameters, and this process also involves the use of data with known ground-truth labels to evaluate and tune the learning performance; this is called **validation** and the data is **validation data**. Generally, the test data should not overlap with the training and validation data; otherwise, the estimated performance can be overly optimistic.

A formal formulation of the supervised learning process is as follows. Denote $\mathcal{X}$ as the instance space, $\mathcal{D}$ as a distribution over $\mathcal{X}$, and f as the *ground-truth* target function. Given a training data set $D = \{(\boldsymbol{x}_1, y_1), (\boldsymbol{x}_2, y_2), \ldots, (\boldsymbol{x}_m, y_m)\}$, where the instances $\boldsymbol{x}_i$ are drawn ***i.i.d.*** (independently and identically distributed) from $\mathcal{D}$ and $y_i = f(\boldsymbol{x}_i)$, taking classification as an example, the goal is to construct a learner h which minimizes the generalization error

$$\mathtt{err}(h) = \mathbb{E}_{\boldsymbol{x}\sim\mathcal{D}}[\mathbb{I}(h(\boldsymbol{x}) \neq f(\boldsymbol{x}))]. \tag{1.1}$$

Most of the book concerns about supervised learning; however, **unsupervised learning** will also be involved. Unsupervised learning does not rely on label information, the goal of which is to discover some inherent distribution information in the data. The most typical task is **clustering**, which attempts to discover the cluster structure of data points. **Density estimation** aiming to reconstruct the probability density function using a set of data points, and **anomaly detection** aiming to discover data points with abnormal characteristics, are also important unsupervised learning tasks.

We will briefly introduce popular learning algorithms and performance evaluation in Sections 1.2 and 1.3, respectively.

1.2 Popular Learning Algorithms

1.2.1 Decision Trees

Decision trees are very commonly used in ensemble methods, and thus, we introduce decision trees with more details. A decision tree consists of a set of tree-structured decision tests working in a *divide-and-conquer* way. Each non-leaf node is associated with a **feature test** also called a **split**; data points falling into the node will be split into different subsets according to their values on this feature test. Each leaf node is associated with a label, which will be assigned to instances falling into this node. In prediction, a series of feature tests is conducted starting from the root node, and the result is obtained when a leaf node is reached. Take Figure 1.2 as an example. The classification process starts by testing whether the value of the feature y-coordinate is larger than 0.73; if so, the instance is classified as cross, and otherwise the tree tests whether the feature value of x-coordinate is larger than 0.64; if so, the instance is classified as cross, and circle otherwise.

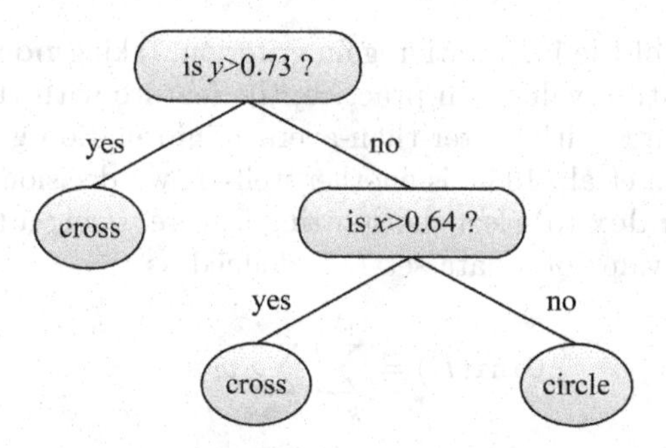

Figure 1.2: An example of a decision tree.

Decision tree learning algorithms are inherently recursive processes. In each step, a data set is given and a split is selected, and then, this split is used to divide the data set into subsets, where each subset is considered as the given data set for the next step. The key to a decision tree algorithm is how to select the features for split.

In the seminal ID3 algorithm [Quinlan, 1986], the **information gain** criterion is employed for split selection. Let p_k denote the proportion of instances belonging to the k-th class in training set D, where $k = 1, 2, \ldots, |\mathcal{Y}|$. The **entropy** of D is defined as

$$\texttt{Ent}(D) = -\sum_{k=1}^{|\mathcal{Y}|} p_k \log_2 p_k . \tag{1.2}$$

Suppose that the feature a is selected for split to v possible values $\{a^1, a^2, \ldots, a^v\}$. Therefore, the node holding D is divided into v child nodes. The i-th child node holds the subset D^i, which includes all instances in D taking the value a^i for feature a. A weight $|D^i|/|D|$ is assigned to reflect the importance of the i-th child node. The information gain of selecting a to split D is defined according to the amount of entropy reduction

$$\texttt{Gain}(D, a) = \texttt{Ent}(D) - \sum_{i=1}^{v} \frac{|D^i|}{|D|} \texttt{Ent}(D^i), \tag{1.3}$$

and the feature leading to the largest information gain is selected for split.

A deficiency of the information gain criterion lies in the fact that the split selection is biased towards features with more possible values. For example, suppose we are dealing with binary classification and each instance has a unique id. If id is considered as a feature, the information gain of taking this feature for split would be quite large because such a split will lead to child nodes that contain only one training instance each; however, it cannot generalize well on unseen instances. This deficiency is addressed in C4.5 [Quinlan, 1993] decision tree algorithm by employing **gain ratio**

$$\texttt{Gain\_ratio}(D, a) = \texttt{Gain}(D, a) \cdot \left(-\sum_{i=1}^{v} \frac{|D^i|}{|D|} \log_2 \frac{|D^i|}{|D|} \right)^{-1} , \tag{1.4}$$

which is a variant of the information gain criterion, taking **normalization** on the number of feature values. In practice, the feature with the highest gain ratio, among features with better-than-average information gains, is selected.

CART [Breiman et al., 1984] is another well-known decision tree algorithm, which uses **Gini index** to select the splitting feature. Using a notation similar to (1.2), the Gini value of a data set D is defined as

$$\begin{aligned} \texttt{Gini}(D) &= \sum_{k=1}^{|\mathcal{Y}|} \sum_{k' \neq k} p_k p_{k'} \\ &= 1 - \sum_{k=1}^{|\mathcal{Y}|} p_k^2 , \end{aligned} \tag{1.5}$$

and the Gini index of feature a is defined as

$$\texttt{Gini\_index}(D, a) = \sum_{i=1}^{v} \frac{|D^i|}{|D|} \texttt{Gini}(D^i) . \tag{1.6}$$

The feature with the lowest Gini index is selected for split.

It is often observed that a decision tree, which is perfect on the training set, will have a worse generalization ability than a tree which is not-so-good on the training set; this is called **overfitting**, which may be caused by the fact that some peculiarities of the training data, such as those caused by noise in collecting training examples, are misleadingly learned as the underlying truth. To decrease the risk of overfitting, a general strategy is to employ **pruning** to cut off some low-level tree branches because they are likely to be caused by noise or peculiarities of the training set. **Pre-pruning** tries to prune branches when the tree is being grown, while **post-pruning** re-examines fully grown trees to decide which branches should be removed. When a validation set is available, the tree can be pruned according to the validation error: for pre-pruning, a branch will not be grown if the validation error will increase by growing the branch; for post-pruning, a branch will be removed if the removal will decrease the validation error.

Early decision tree algorithms, such as ID3, can only deal with categorical features. Later ones, such as C4.5 and CART, are able to handle numerical features. The simplest way is to evaluate every possible split point on the numerical feature that divides the training set into two subsets, where one subset contains instances with the feature value smaller than the split point, whereas the other subset contains the remaining instances.

When the height of a decision tree is limited to 1, i.e., it takes only one feature test to make every prediction, the tree is called a **decision stump**. While decision trees are nonlinear classifiers in general, decision stumps are a kind of linear classifiers.

Figure 1.3 illustrates the decision boundary of the decision tree as shown in Figure 1.2.

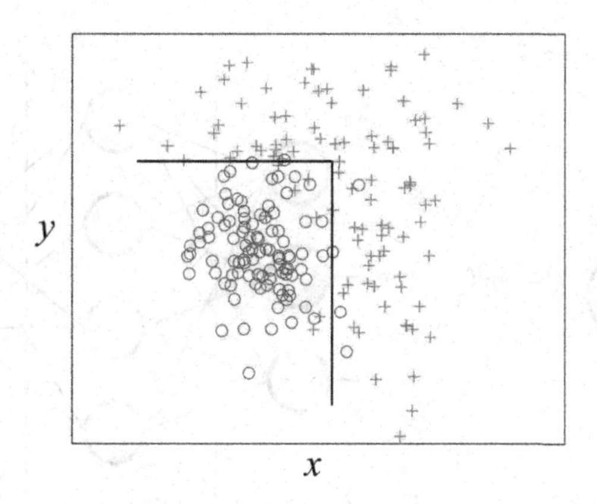

Figure 1.3: Decision boundary of a decision tree on *three-Gaussians*.

1.2.2 Neural Networks

Neural networks, also called **artificial neural networks**, are massively parallel interconnected networks of simple adaptive elements called **neuron**. The function of a neural network is determined by the model of neuron, the network structure, and the learning algorithm.

Neuron is also called **unit**, which is the basic computational component in neural networks. The most popular neuron model, i.e., the *McCulloch-Pitts* model (**M-P model**), is illustrated in Figure 1.4(a). In this model, input signals are multiplied with **connection weights**, and then, the aggregated signal is compared with a **threshold**. If the aggregated signal is larger than the threshold, the neuron will be activated and the output signal is generated by an **activation function**, also called *transfer function* or *squashing function.*

Neurons are linked by weighted connections to form a network. There are various network structures, among which the most common one is the **multi-layer feed-forward network**, as illustrated in Figure 1.4(b). Here the neurons are connected layer-by-layer, and there are neither in-layer connections nor cross-layer connections. There is an **input layer** which receives input feature vectors, where each neuron usually corresponds to one element of the feature vector. The activation function for input neurons is usually set as $f(x) = x$. There is an **output layer** which outputs labels, where each neuron usually corresponds to a possible label, or an element of a *label vector.* The layers between the input and output layers are called **hidden layers**. The hidden neurons and output neurons are **functional units**, and a popular activation function for them is the **sigmoid function**

$$f(x) = \frac{1}{1 + e^{-x}}. \tag{1.7}$$

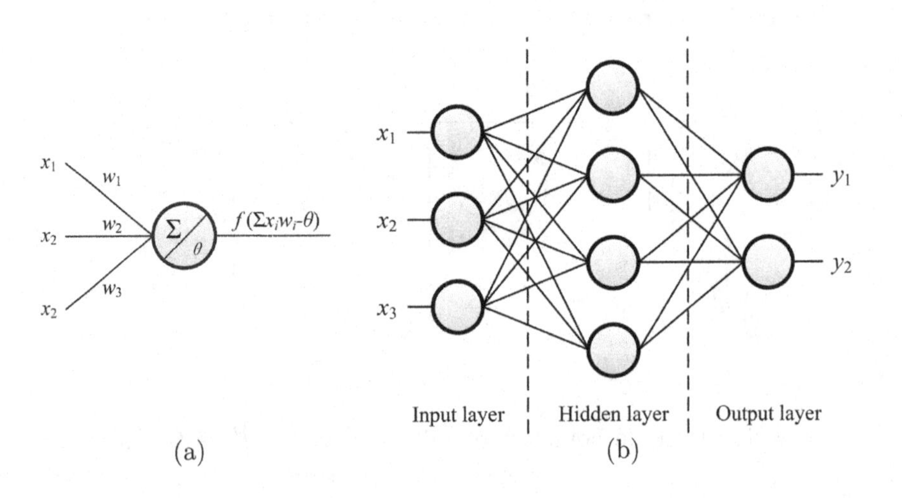

Figure 1.4: Illustration of (a) a neuron and (b) a neural network.

The goal of training a neural network is to determine the values of the connection weights and the thresholds of the neurons. A typical strategy for training a multi-layer feed-forward neural network is to regard the whole neural network as a differentiable function which can be optimized by the **gradient descent** method, given that the activation function is differentiable.

The most commonly used algorithm, **Backpropagation (BP)** [Werbos, 1974, Rumelhart et al., 1986], works as follows. At first, the inputs are feed-forwarded from the input layer via the hidden layer to the output layer, at which the error is calculated by comparing the network output with the ground-truth. Then, the error will be backpropagated to the hidden layer and the input layer, during which the connection weights and thresholds are adjusted to decrease the error. The process is accomplished by tuning towards the direction with the gradient. Such a process will be repeated in many rounds until the training error is minimized or the training process is terminated.

In theory, the *capacity* of neural networks will increase with the increase of the numbers of parameters and hidden layers, implying that they can handle more complicated learning tasks. Such models, however, often suffer from training inefficiency and overfitting when there are only small data for training. Note that the **gradient vanish** phenomenon occurs in networks trained by BP with more than five layers, leading to failure of training. Thus, *shallow* neural networks with less than five layers were generally used. During the past decade, with the use of big training data and powerful computational facilities, the overfiting risk and training inefficiency have got significantly relaxed. More importantly, many training tricks alleviating the phenomenon of gradient vanish, such as [Hinton and Salakhutdinov, 2006], have been developed. These advances enable the training of **deep neural networks (DNNs)** containing hundreds or even thousands of layers and billions of parameters, leading to the prosperous **deep learning** era [Goodfellow et al., 2016].

1.2.3 Naïve Bayes Classifier

To classify an instance $\boldsymbol{x}$, one approach is to formulate a probabilistic model to estimate the posterior probability $P(y \mid \boldsymbol{x})$ of different y's, and predict the one with the largest posterior probability; this is the ***maximum a posterior* (MAP)** rule. According to *Bayes' theorem*, we have

$$P(y \mid \boldsymbol{x}) = \frac{P(\boldsymbol{x} \mid y)P(y)}{P(\boldsymbol{x})}, \tag{1.8}$$

where $P(y)$ can be estimated by counting the proportion of training examples belonging to class y in the training set, and $P(\boldsymbol{x})$ can be ignored since we are comparing different y's on the same $\boldsymbol{x}$. Thus we only need to deal with $P(\boldsymbol{x} \mid y)$. An accurate estimate of $P(\boldsymbol{x} \mid y)$ leads to the best classifier in theory that can be obtained from the given training data, that is, the **Bayes optimal classifier** with the **Bayes error**, the lowest error rate in theory. Estimating $P(\boldsymbol{x} \mid y)$, however, is not straightforward because it involves the estimate of exponential numbers of joint probabilities of features. To make it tractable, some practical assumptions are needed.

The naïve Bayes classifier assumes that, given the class label, all the n features are independent of each other. Thus, we have

$$P(\boldsymbol{x} \mid y) = \prod_{i=1}^{n} P(x_i \mid y), \tag{1.9}$$

which implies that we only need to take into account each feature value in each class to estimate the conditional probability, and therefore, the calculation of joint probabilities is avoided.

In the training stage, the naïve Bayes classifier estimates the probabilities $P(y)$ for all classes $y \in \mathcal{Y}$, and $P(x_i \mid y)$ for all features $i = 1, \ldots, n$ and all feature values x_i from the training set. In the testing stage, an instance $\boldsymbol{x}$ will be predicted with label y, which leads to the maximal value of

$$P(y \mid \boldsymbol{x}) \propto P(y) \prod_{i=1}^{n} P(x_i \mid y) \tag{1.10}$$

among all the class labels.

1.2.4 k-Nearest Neighbor

The k-nearest neighbor (kNN) algorithm relies on the principle that objects similar in the input space are also similar in the output space. In contrast to most learning algorithms that attempt to build models once receiving training data (thus, they are called **eager learning** algorithms), k-nearest neighbor is a **lazy learning** algorithm since it does not have an explicit training process but simply stores the training set instead. For a test instance, a k-nearest neighbor learner identifies the k instances from the training set that are closest to the test instance. Then, for classification, the test instance will be classified to the majority class among the k instances, while for regression, the test instance will be assigned the average value of the k instances. Figure 1.5(a) illustrates how to classify an instance by a 3-nearest neighbor classifier. Figure 1.5(b) shows the decision boundary of a 1-nearest neighbor classifier, also called the **nearest neighbor classifier**.

1.2.5 Linear Discriminant Analysis

A **linear model** consists of a **weight vector** $\boldsymbol{w}$ and a **bias** b. Given an instance $\boldsymbol{x}$, the prediction y is obtained according to

$$y = \boldsymbol{w}^{\boldsymbol{T}}\boldsymbol{x} + b. \tag{1.11}$$

Linear Discriminant Analysis (LDA) is a classic classification method based on linear model, also known as *Fisher's Linear Discriminant* (FLD) since

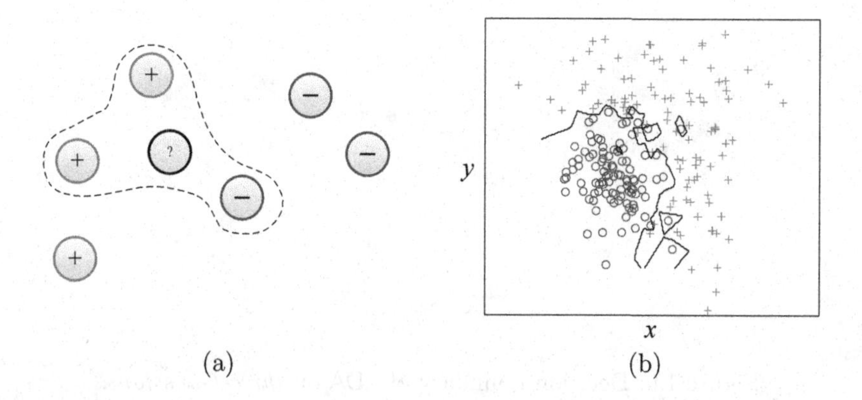

Figure 1.5: Illustration of (a) how a k-nearest neighbor classifier predicts on a test instance and (b) the decision boundary of the nearest neighbor classifier on *three-Gaussians.*

it was initially proposed by Fisher [1936] for binary classification problems, though strictly speaking, they are slightly different as LDA assumes equal and full-rank class covariances.

Briefly, the idea of LDA is to project the training data onto a line such that instances of different classes are far away from each other, whereas instances within the same class are close to each other. Test instances will be classified according to their projected locations on the same line.

Given a training set for binary classification, we consider all the positive instances and obtain their mean $\boldsymbol{\mu}_+$ and covariance matrix Σ_+; similarly, we consider all the negative instances and obtain their mean $\boldsymbol{\mu}_-$ and covariance matrix Σ_-. After projecting onto the line $\boldsymbol{w}$, the covariance of the two classes are $\boldsymbol{w}^{\boldsymbol{T}}\Sigma_+\boldsymbol{w}$ and $\boldsymbol{w}^{\boldsymbol{T}}\Sigma_-\boldsymbol{w}$, respectively, while the distance between the two class centers is $\|\boldsymbol{w}^{\boldsymbol{T}}\boldsymbol{\mu}_+ - \boldsymbol{w}^{\boldsymbol{T}}\boldsymbol{\mu}_-\|^2$. Thus, LDA attempts to maximize

$$J = \frac{\|\boldsymbol{w}^{\boldsymbol{T}}\boldsymbol{\mu}_+ - \boldsymbol{w}^{\boldsymbol{T}}\boldsymbol{\mu}_-\|^2}{\boldsymbol{w}^{\boldsymbol{T}}\Sigma_+\boldsymbol{w} + \boldsymbol{w}^{\boldsymbol{T}}\Sigma_-\boldsymbol{w}}, \tag{1.12}$$

from which the optimal solution can be solved [Zhou, 2021, Section 3.4].

Figure 1.6 illustrates the decision boundary of an LDA classifier.

1.2.6 Logistic Regression

For binary classification ($y \in \{0, 1\}$), logistic regression predicts the posterior $P(y = 1 \mid \boldsymbol{x})$ for instance $\boldsymbol{x}$ based on a linear function and logistic function, i.e.,

$$P(y = 1 \mid \boldsymbol{x}; \boldsymbol{w}, b) = \frac{1}{1 + e^{-(\boldsymbol{w}^{\boldsymbol{T}}\boldsymbol{x}+b)}}, \tag{1.13}$$

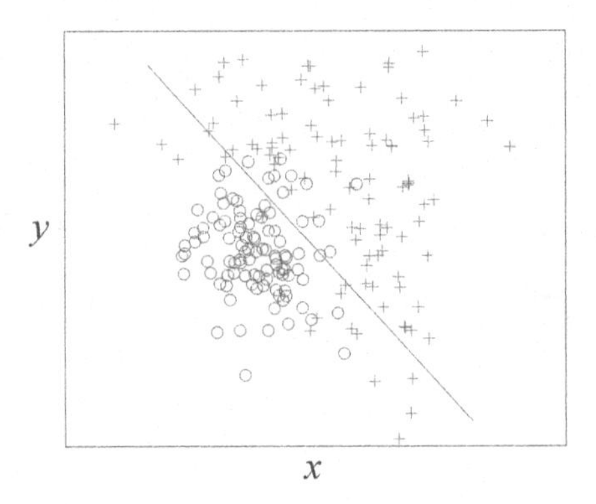

Figure 1.6: Decision boundary of LDA on *three-Gaussians.*

where $\boldsymbol{w}$ and b are parameters of the linear function. Similar with LDA, the classification process is accomplished by two steps: first, compute the linear function value $z = \boldsymbol{w}^T\boldsymbol{x} + b$; then, apply the logistic function $y = \frac{1}{1+e^{-z}}$ to get $P(y = 1 \mid \boldsymbol{x})$ and hereafter the class label.

Given training data set $\{(\boldsymbol{x}_i, y_i)\}_{i=1}^m$, logistic regression tries to find $\boldsymbol{w}$ and b that maximize the log-likelihood [Zhou, 2021, Section 3.3]

$$\begin{aligned} L(\boldsymbol{w}, b) &= \sum_{i=1}^{m} \ln P(y_i \mid \boldsymbol{x}_i; \boldsymbol{w}, b) \\ &= \sum_{i=1}^{m} \left(y_i(\boldsymbol{w}^T\boldsymbol{x}_i + b) - \ln\left(1 + e^{\boldsymbol{w}^T\boldsymbol{x}_i + b}\right)\right) . \end{aligned} \tag{1.14}$$

$L(\boldsymbol{w}, b)$ is convex and smooth of $\boldsymbol{w}$ and b, and therefore, classic convex optimization methods such as gradient descent method and Newton's method can be used to solve the optimal solution $\boldsymbol{w}^*$ and b^*.

1.2.7 Support Vector Machines and Kernel Methods

Support vector machines (SVMs) [Cristianini and Shawe-Taylor, 2000], originally designed for binary classification, are **large margin classifiers** that try to separate instances of different classes with the maximum margin hyperplane. The **margin** is defined as the minimum distance from instances of different classes to the classification hyperplane.

Given training data set $\{(\boldsymbol{x}_i, y_i)\}_{i=1}^m$, $y_i \in \{-1, +1\}$. A separating hyperplane in the sample space can be expressed as the linear equation $\boldsymbol{w}^T\boldsymbol{x} + b = 0$. Suppose this hyperplane can correctly classify the training examples, i.e., $y_i(\boldsymbol{w}^T\boldsymbol{x}_i + b) \geq 1$. As illustrated in Figure 1.7, the equality holds for feature vectors closet to the hyperplane; they are called **support vectors**. Note that the distance from any instance $\boldsymbol{x}$ in the sample space to the hyperplane can be written as $|\boldsymbol{w}^T\boldsymbol{x}_i + b|/\|\boldsymbol{w}\|$. Thus, the margin, i.e., the distance from two support vectors belonging to different classes to the hyperplane is $\gamma = \frac{2}{\|\boldsymbol{w}\|}$.

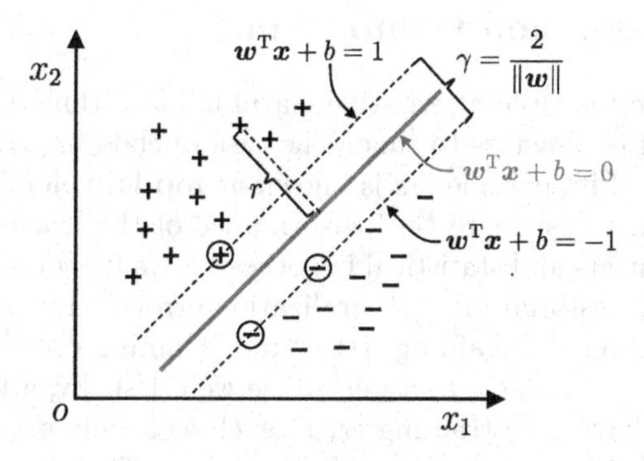

Figure 1.7: Illustration of SVM.

SVM attempts to find the hyperplane which maximizes the margin by solving the optimization problem

$$(\boldsymbol{w}^*, b^*) = \underset{\boldsymbol{w}, b, \xi_i}{\arg\min} \frac{\|\boldsymbol{w}\|^2}{2} + C\sum_{i=1}^{m} \xi_i \tag{1.15}$$

$$\text{s.t.} \quad y_i(\boldsymbol{w}^T\boldsymbol{x}_i + b) \geq 1 - \xi_i \ (\forall i = 1, \ldots, m)$$
$$\xi_i \geq 0 \ (\forall i = 1, \ldots, m) \ ,$$

where C is a parameter and ξ_i's are *slack variables* introduced to handle instances that cannot be perfectly separated [Zhou, 2021, Section 6.4].

Note that when data is intrinsically nonlinear, linear classifiers cannot separate the classes well. In such case, a general approach is to project the data points onto a higher-dimensional (or even infinite-dimensional) feature space where the data linearly non-separable in the original feature space become linearly separable. However, the learning process may become very slow and even intractable since inner product in the high-dimensional space can be hard to calculate.

Fortunately, there is a class of functions, **kernel functions** (also called **kernels**), can offer help. The feature space derived by kernel functions is called the **Reproducing Kernel Hilbert Space (RKHS)**. An inner product in the RKHS equals kernel mapping of inner product of instances in the original feature space. That is,

$$K(\boldsymbol{x}_i, \boldsymbol{x}_j) = \langle \phi(\boldsymbol{x}_i), \phi(\boldsymbol{x}_j) \rangle \tag{1.16}$$

for all $\boldsymbol{x}_i$'s, where ϕ is a mapping from the original feature space to a higher-dimensional space and K is a kernel. Thus, inner products in the high-dimensional space can be replaced by the kernel. Popular kernels include linear kernel, polynomial kernel, Gaussian kernel, etc.

The **kernel trick**, i.e., mapping the data points with a kernel and then accomplishing the learning task in the RKHS, is a general strategy that can be incorporated into any learning algorithm, such as LDA, that considers inner products between input feature vectors. Once the kernel trick is employed, a learning algorithm can be called a **kernel method**.

1.3 Evaluation and Comparison

Usually, we have multiple alternative learning algorithms to choose among, and a number of parameters to tune. The task of choosing the best algorithm and the settings of its parameters is known as **model selection**, and for this purpose we need to estimate the performance of the learner. This involves design of experiments and statistical hypothesis tests for comparing the models.

It is unwise to estimate the generalization error of a learner by **training error**, i.e., error on the training data, since training error prefers complex learners rather than learners that generalize well. Usually, a learner with high complexity can have zero training error, such as a fully grown decision tree; however, it is likely to perform poorly on unseen data due to overfitting. A proper process is to evaluate the performance on a validation set. Note that the labels in the training set and validation set are known, and should be used together to derive and tune the final learner once the model has been selected.

In fact, in most cases the training and validation sets are obtained by splitting a given training data set into different parts. While splitting, the properties of the original data set should be reserved as far as possible, and otherwise the validation set may provide misleading estimates; for an extreme example, the training set might contain only positive instances while the validation set contains only negative instances. In classification, when the original data set is split randomly, the class percentage should be maintained for both training and validation sets; this is called *stratification*, or **stratified sampling**.

A commonly used method is **cross-validation**. In *k-fold cross-validation*, the original data set D is partitioned by stratified split into k almost equal-size disjoint subsets, $D_1, \ldots, D_k$. Then, k runs of training-validation are performed. In the i-th run, D_i is used as the validation set while the union of all the other subsets, i.e., $\bigcup_{j \neq i} D_j$, is used as the training set. The average result of the k runs is taken as the result of the cross-validation. To reduce the influence of randomness introduced by data split, the k-fold cross-validation can be repeated t times, which is called **t-times k-fold cross-validation**. A commonly used configuration is *10-times 10-fold cross-validation (abbr. 10×10cv)*. Extremely, when k equals the number of instances in the original data set, there is only one instance in each validation set; this is called **leave-one-out (LOO)** validation.

After obtaining the estimated results, we can compare different learning algorithms. A simple comparison on average errors, however, is not reliable since the winning algorithm may occasionally perform well due to something such as randomness in data split. **Hypothesis tests** such as the Students' t-tests is usually employed to examine whether the difference is really significant.

In practice, there is often an overestimated probability for the hypothesis that there are significant difference to be true because the training and validation data are not really independent; for example, in 10×10cv the training and validation data are overlapped because D_i is used for validation in the i-th run but for training in other runs. To alleviate this issue, Dietterich [1998] presented an ingenious design, i.e., the **5 × 2 cv paired t-tests**.

As the name suggests, it repeats two-fold cross-validation five times, where the data is randomly shuffled before each two-fold cross-validation such that the data splitting is different in the five rounds of cross-validations. For example, after obtaining the validation error rates of two learners A and B in the i-th two-fold cross-validation, we calculate the difference between their error rates of the first fold, denoted by Δ_i^1, and the difference between their error rates of the second fold, denoted by Δ_i^2. To alleviate the violation of independence, we calculate the mean using only the first time of two-fold cross-validation, i.e.,

$$\mu = \frac{\Delta_1^1 + \Delta_1^2}{2} , \tag{1.17}$$

whereas the variance is still calculated based on all times of cross-validation, i.e.,

$$\sigma_i^2 = \left(\Delta_i^1 - \frac{\Delta_i^1 + \Delta_i^2}{2}\right)^2 + \left(\Delta_i^2 - \frac{\Delta_i^1 + \Delta_i^2}{2}\right)^2 \quad (i = 1, \dots, 5) . \tag{1.18}$$

Then the variable

$$\tau_t = \frac{\mu}{\sqrt{\frac{1}{5}\sum_{i=1}^{5}\sigma_i^2}} \tag{1.19}$$

follows a t-distribution with five degrees of freedom, where its two-tailed critical value $t_{\alpha/2,\,5}$ is 2.5706 when $\alpha = 0.05$, and 2.0150 when $\alpha = 0.1$.

The above process compares two algorithms on a single data set. In some cases, we want to compare multiple algorithms on multiple data sets. In this situation, we can use the ranking-based **Friedman test** [Demšar, 2006]. First, we sort the algorithms on each data set according to their average errors. On each data set, the best algorithm is assigned rank 1, the worse algorithms are assigned increased ranks, and average ranks are assigned in case of ties. Then, we average the ranks of each algorithm over all data sets, and after rejecting the hypothesis that *all algorithms' performance are the same* using F-test, we use the **Nemenyi post-hoc test** to further distinguish the algorithms. It calculates the *critical difference* value

$$CD = q_\alpha \sqrt{\frac{k(k+1)}{6N}} , \tag{1.20}$$

where k is the number of algorithms, N is the number of data sets and q_α is the *critical value*. A pair of algorithms are believed to be significantly different if the difference of their average ranks is larger than the critical difference.

The Friedman test results can be visualized by plotting the **critical difference diagram**, as illustrated in Figure 1.8, where each algorithm corresponds to a bar centered at the average rank with the width of critical difference value. Figure 1.8 discloses that the algorithm A is significantly better than all other algorithms, the algorithm D is significantly worse than all other algorithms, whereas the algorithms B and C are not significantly different, according to the given significance level.

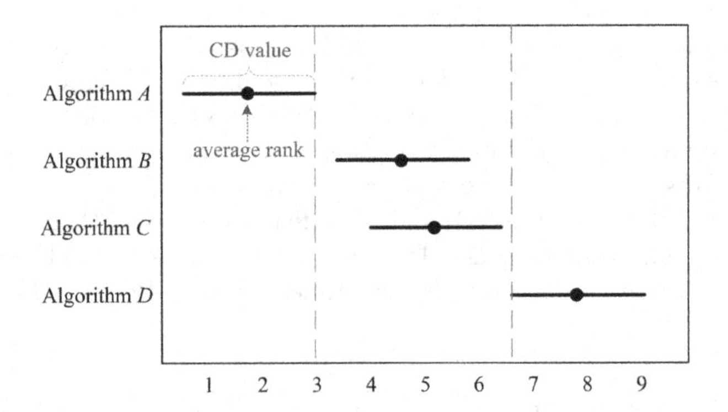

Figure 1.8: Illustration of critical difference diagram.

More information about Friedman and Nemenyi post-hoc tests as well as other commonly used hypothesis tests in machine learning can be found in Zhou [2021, Section 2.4.4].

1.4 Ensemble Methods

Ensemble methods train multiple learners to solve the same problem. In contrast to ordinary learning approaches that try to construct one learner from training data, ensemble methods try to construct and combine a set of learners. Ensemble learning was also called **committee-based learning**, or learning **multiple classifier systems**.

Figure 1.9 shows a common ensemble architecture. An ensemble contains a number of learners, called **individual learners** or **component learners**, generated from the given data set. In most commonly used ensemble methods, the individual learners are trained by the same learning algorithm. In other words, all learners in the ensemble are of the same type, e.g., all of them are decision trees. Such kind of ensembles are **homogeneous ensembles**. The learning algorithm used to generate the individual learners of a homogeneous ensemble is called the **base learning algorithm** of the ensemble, and the corresponding individual learners are called **base learners**. Ensembles can also be consisted of different types of individual learners; such kind of ensembles are **heterogeneous ensembles**. Since in heterogeneous ensembles the individual learners are generated by different learning algorithms, there is no base learning algorithm nor base learners.

The generalization ability of an ensemble is usually much stronger than that of individual learners. Actually, ensemble methods are appealing mainly because they are able to boost **weak learners** which are even just slightly better than random guess to **strong learners** which can make very accurate predictions. So, individual learners are also referred to as *weak learners*.

Generally, an ensemble is constructed in two steps, i.e., generating and then combining the individual learners. The key to building a strong ensemble is to

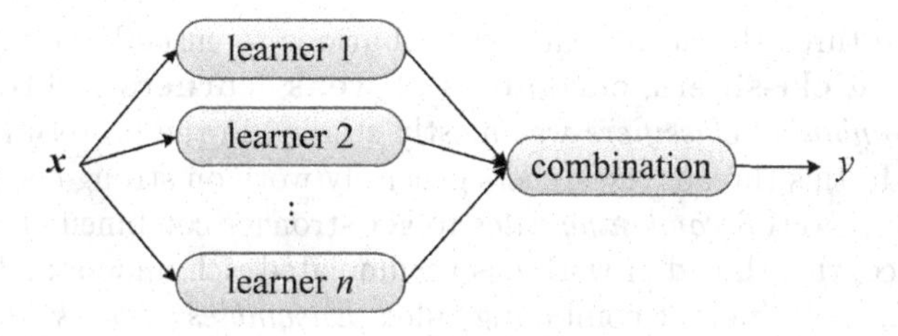

Figure 1.9: A common ensemble architecture.

generate **accurate but diverse** individual learners, as to be elaborated later in the book. As for homogeneous ensembles, how to maintain the **diversity** is a fundamental issue since all learners are generated from the same training data set. Commonly used ensemble methods, such as those introduced in Chapters 2 and 3, exploiting **unstable learners** (e.g., decision trees) whose prediction behaviors significantly change subject to minor perturbation of training data. The use of **stable learners** (e.g., SVMs) whose prediction behaviors do not significantly change subject to minor training data perturbation, requires other mechanisms for diversity enhancement as mentioned in Chapter 5. As for heterogeneous ensembles, the different types of individual learners inherently offers diversity, whereas how to combine the outputs of different types of learners remains a challenge because their outputs are generally incomparable, and there lacks theoretically sound solution though heuristic methods such as combination by learning are often effective. Homogeneous ensembles are usually with lower cost as they require implementing and maintaining only one base learning algorithm, and the use of same type of base learners endows the possibility of shared and compressed storage.

It is worth mentioning that, generally, the computational cost of constructing an ensemble is not much larger than using a single learner. This is because when we want to use a single learner, we usually need to generate multiple versions of the learner for model selection or parameter tuning; this is comparable to generating base learners in ensembles, while the computational cost for combining base learners is often small since most combination methods, as can be seen in Chapter 4, are simple. There are also techniques, as introduced in Chapter 6, that can not only decrease the number of individual learners, leading to reduced storage and prediction costs, but also improve generalization performance.

It is difficult to trace the starting point of the history of ensemble methods since the basic idea of deploying multiple models has been in use in human society for a long time. For example, even earlier than the introduction of **Occam's razor**, the common principle of scientific research which prefers simple hypotheses to complex ones when both are consistent with empirical observations, the Greek philosopher Epicurus (341–270 B.C.) introduced the **principle of multiple explanations** [Asmis, 1984] which advocated to keep all hypotheses that are consistent with empirical observations.

There are three threads of early contributions to ensemble methods; that is, **combining classifiers**, **ensembles of weak learners** and **mixture of experts**. *Combining classifiers* was mostly studied in the pattern recognition community. In this thread, researchers generally work on strong classifiers, and try to design powerful *combining rules* to get stronger combined classifiers. As a consequence, this thread of work has accumulated rich understanding on the design and use of different combining rules. *Ensembles of weak learners* was mostly studied in the machine learning community. In this thread, researchers often work on weak learners and try to design powerful algorithms to boost the performance from weak to strong. This thread of work has led to the birth of famous ensemble methods such as AdaBoost, Bagging, etc., and theoretical understanding on why and how weak learners can be boosted to strong ones. *Mixture of experts* was mostly studied in the neural networks community. In this thread, researchers generally consider a *divide-and-conquer* strategy, try to learn a mixture of parametric models jointly and use combining rules to get an overall solution. Later on, all these threads merged to form the current field of ensemble methods.

Ensemble methods received significant notice in early 1990s, with great promotion by two pieces of pioneering work. One is empirical [Hansen and Salamon, 1990], in which it was found that predictions made by the combination of a set of classifiers are often more accurate than predictions made by the best single classifier. A simplified illustration is shown in Figure 1.10. The other is theoretical [Schapire, 1990], in which it was proved that weak learners can be boosted to strong learners. Since weak learners are easy to obtain in real practice, whereas strong learners are desirable yet difficult to attain, this result opens a promising direction of generating strong learners by ensemble methods. Consequently, ensemble learning has been recognized as one of the major paradigms of machine learning since the 1990s. Note that most ensemble learning studies focused on prediction, but there are also studies concerning unsupervised learning, as can be seen in Chapters 7 to 8 of this book.

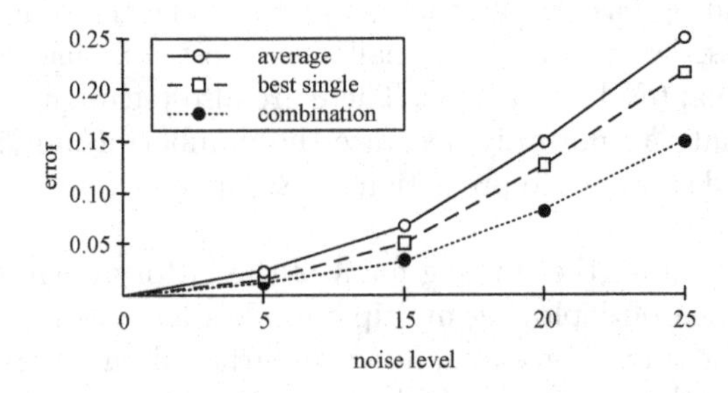

Figure 1.10: A simplified illustration of Hansen and Salamon [1990]'s observation: Ensemble is often better than the best single.

1.5 Applications of Ensemble Methods

The *KDD-Cup* [1] is a well-known data mining competition. Since 1997, it is held every year and attracts the interests of data mining teams all over the world. The competition problems cover a large variety of practical tasks, such as network intrusion detection (1999), molecular bioactivity & protein locale prediction (2001), pulmonary embolisms detection (2006), customer relationship management (2009), educational data mining (2010), music recommendation (2011), ads click-through estimation (2012), social network analysis (2016), de-biasing in e-commerce platform (2020), graph mining (2021), product search (2022), multilingual product recommendation (2023), etc. In the past KDD-Cup competitions, ensemble methods have drawn the most attention and can be found in nearly all the award-winning solutions.

Another competition, the *Netflix Prize*[2], is a little bit outdated but still worth mentioning since it boosted the rapid development of recommender systems. It was held by the online DVD-rental service Netflix and seeked to improve the accuracy of predictions about how much someone is going to enjoy a movie based on their preferences. If one participating team improves Netflix's own algorithm by 10% accuracy, they would win the grand prize of $1,000,000. On September 21, 2009, Nexflix awarded the $1M grand prize to the team *BellKor's Pragmatic Chaos*, whose solution was based on combining various classifiers including asymmetric factor models, regression models, restricted Boltzmann machines, matrix factorization, k-nearest neighbor, etc. Another team, which achieved the winning performance but was defeated because the result was submitted 20 minutes later, even used *The Ensemble* as the team name.

Kaggle[3], first launched in 2010, has become a major platform offering machine learning competitions. In winning solutions as well as their sharing and discussions, ensemble methods are well recognized as the most commonly used practical technique for generalization performance enhancement.

In addition to the impressive results in competitions, ensemble methods have been successfully applied to various areas and diverse tasks.

Computer vision has benefited much from ensemble methods. For example, Viola and Jones [2001, 2004] proposed a general object detection framework by combining AdaBoost with a cascade architecture, resulting in a face detector with comparable accuracy but almost 15 times faster than state-of-the-art techniques at that time, being recognized as the first real-time face detector. Huang et al. [2000] designed an ensemble architecture for pose-invariant face recognition, particularly for recognizing faces with in-depth rotations. The basic idea is to combine a number of view-specific neural networks with a specially designed combination module. In contrast to conventional techniques which require pose information as input, this framework does not need pose information and it can even output pose estimation in addition to the recognition result. Huang et al. [2000] reported that this framework even outperformed

[1] http://www.sigkdd.org/kddcup/.
[2] https://en.wikipedia.org/wiki/Netflix_Prize/.
[3] https://www.kaggle.com/.

conventional techniques facilitated with perfect pose information. A similar method was later applied to multi-view face detection [Li et al., 2001].

Even when deep learning becomes dominating, ensemble methods are still found helpful in computer vision. For example, Kazemi and Sullivan [2014] presented a general framework based on Gradient Boosting to address the problem of face alignment with single image, achieving super-realtime performance with high quality predictions. Bonettini et al. [2020] tackled the problem of detecting face manipulation in video by ensembling different convolutional neural networks, and achieved excellent results on publicly available data sets.

Ensemble methods have been found very useful to address **computer security** problems because each activity performed on computer systems can be observed at *multiple abstraction levels* and the relevant information may be collected from *multiple information sources* [Corona et al., 2009].

Giacinto et al. [2003] applied ensemble methods to intrusion detection. Considering that there are different types of features characterizing the connection, they constructed an ensemble from each type of features independently, and then combined the outputs from these ensembles to produce the final judgment. Giacinto et al. [2003] reported that, when detecting known attacks, ensemble methods lead to the best performance. Later, Giacinto et al. [2008] proposed an ensemble method for anomaly-based intrusion detection, which is able to detect intrusions never seen before. Mirsky et al. [2018] used an ensemble of autoencoders to collectively differentiate between normal and abnormal traffic patterns. Different from supervised learning methods, their proposed algorithm automatically constructs the ensemble of autoencoders in an unsupervised manner. Aburomman and Reaz [2017] gave a survey of intrusion detection systems based on ensemble methods.

Malicious executables are programs designed to perform a malicious function without the owner's permission, and they generally fall into three categories, i.e., viruses, worms, and Trojan horses. Schultz et al. [2001] proposed an ensemble method to detect previously unseen malicious executables automatically, based on representing the programs using binary profiling, string sequences and hex dumps. Kolter and Maloof [2006] represented programs using n-grams of byte codes, and reported that boosted decision trees achieved the best performance; they also suggested that this method could be used as the basis for an operational system for detecting new malicious executables never seen before. Idrees et al. [2017] employed ensemble methods to combine permissions and intents supplemented for identifying Android malware apps.

Ensemble methods have been found very useful in various tasks of **computer aided medical diagnosis**, particularly for increasing the diagnosis reliability.

Zhou et al. [2002b] designed a two-layered ensemble architecture for lung cancer cell identification, where the first layer predicts benign cases if and only if all component learners agree, and otherwise the case will be passed to the second layer to make a further decision among benign and different cancer types. Zhou et al. [2002b] reported that the two-layered ensemble results in a high identification rate with a low false-negative identification rate.

For early diagnosis of Alzheimer's disease, previous methods generally considered single channel data from the EEG (electroencephalogram). To make use of multiple data channels, Polikar et al. [2008] proposed an ensemble method where the component learners are trained on different data sources obtained from different electrodes in response to different stimuli and in different frequency bands, and their outputs are combined for the final diagnosis. Suk et al. [2017] proposed a novel method that combines two conceptually different models of sparse regression and deep neural networks for Alzheimer's disease/mild cognitive impairment diagnosis and prognosis. Specifically, they built multiple sparse regression models with different values of a regularization control parameter, and then devised a neural network by taking the predictions from the multiple regression models as input for final clinical decision making.

Ensemble methods are commonly used in **recommender systems** and **online advertising**. In this area, the most challenging task is to predict user responses, such as click on ads, user engagement or conversions [He et al., 2014]. On this topic, boosted decision trees achieve state-of-the-art performance and are the *de facto* industry standard, and off-the-shelf tools XGBoost [Chen and Guestrin, 2016] and LightGBM [Ke et al., 2017] are widely used.

Many recommendation and advertising tasks are inherently multi-task learning problems; for example, it is useful to simultaneously predict that whether a user will purchase a movie and what ratings she likes to give afterwards. Ma et al. [2018] proposed Multi-gate Mixture-of-Experts (MMoE), which adapts the Mixture-of-Experts (MoE) ensemble structure to multi-task learning by sharing the expert sub-models across all tasks, with a gating network trained to optimize each task. It has been successfully deployed in internet companies. Rajbhandari et al. [2022] presented *DeepSpeed-MoE*, an end-to-end MoE training and inference solution, including novel MoE architecture designs and model compression techniques that reduce MoE model size by up to 3.7x, and a highly optimized inference system that provides 7.3x better latency and cost compared to existing MoE inference solutions.

In addition to the aforementioned examples, ensemble methods have also been successfully deployed in other tasks such as credit card fraud detection [Chan et al., 1999, Panigrahi et al., 2009], bankruptcy prediction [West et al., 2005], protein structure classification [Tan et al., 2003, Shen and Chou, 2006, Cao et al., 2020], species distributions forecasting [Araújo and New, 2007], weather forecasting [Maqsood et al., 2004, Gneiting and Raftery, 2005, Wang et al., 2019a], electric load forecasting [Taylor and Buizza, 2002, Takeda et al., 2016], aircraft engine fault diagnosis [Goebel et al., 2000, Yan and Xue, 2008], musical genre and artist classification [Bergstra et al., 2006, Nanni et al., 2016], dialog system [Song et al., 2018], etc.

Overall, whenever and wherever machine learning techniques are launched, ensemble methods can be found useful.

1.6 Further Readings

[Kuncheva, 2014] and [Rokach, 2019] are books devoted to ensemble learning. [Kyriakides and Margaritis, 2019] introduces hands-on building ensemble methods using Python with scikit-learn and Keras. Reading materials about ensemble methods can also be found in introductory textbooks on machine learning [Alpaydin, 2020, Zhou, 2021], data mining [Han et al., 2022, Tan et al., 2018] and pattern recognition [Duda et al., 2000, Theodoridis and Koutroumbas, 2008], and intermediate level books [Hand et al., 2001, Bishop, 2006, Hastie et al., 2016]. Brief introduction to ensemble learning can also be found in various encyclopedias [Xu and Amari, 2009, Zhou, 2015, 2018b].

Decision trees can be mapped to a set of "if-then" rules [Quinlan, 1993]. Most decision trees use splits like "$\mathsf{x} \geq 1$" or "$\mathsf{y} \geq 2$", leading to axis-parallel partitions of instance space. There are also exceptions, e.g., **oblique decision trees** [Murthy et al., 1994] which use splits like "$\mathsf{x}+\mathsf{y} \geq 3$", leading to non-axis-parallel partitions. The BP algorithm is the most popular and most successful neural network learning algorithm. It has many variants, and can also be used to train neural networks whose structures are different from feed-forward networks, such as **recurrent neural networks** where there are cross-layer connections. Haykin [1998] provides an excellent introduction to shallow neural networks, whereas Goodfellow et al. [2016] offers a comprehensive introduction to deep neural networks. Though the nearest neighbor algorithm is very simple, it works well in most cases. The naïve Bayes classifier based on the conditional independence assumption works well in most cases [Domingos and Pazzani, 1997]; however, it is believed that the performance can be improved further by relaxing the assumption, and therefore many **semi-naïve Bayes classifiers** [Zhou, 2021, Section 7.4] have been developed, where a particularly successful one is the AODE [Webb et al., 2005] which incorporated ensemble mechanism. The error of the nearest neighbor classifier is guaranteed to be no worse than twice of the Bayes error rate on infinite data [Cover and Hart, 1967], and kNN approaches the Bayes error rate for some k value which is related to the amount of data. The distances between instances are not constrained to be calculated by the Euclidean distance, and the contributions from different neighbors can be weighted. More information on kNN can be found in [Dasarathy, 1991]. Linear discriminant analysis is closely related to **principal component analysis** (PCA) [Jolliffe, 2002], both looking for linear combination of features to represent the data. LDA is a supervised approach focusing on distinguishing between different classes, while PCA is an unsupervised approach generally used to identify the largest variability. Logistic regression is a classification method based on generalized linear regression model taking logistic function as link function, which can be understood as using linear regression to approximate log-odds. An extensive discussion about logistic regression can be found in [Hosmer et al., 2013]. SVMs are rooted in the **statistical learning theory** [Vapnik, 1998], and more introductory materials can be found in [Cristianini and Shawe-Taylor, 2000].

Introductory materials on hypothesis tests can be found in [Frost, 2020]. Different hypothesis tests are usually based on different assumptions, and should be applied in different situations. The 10-fold cross-validation t-test was popularly used; however, Dietterich [1998] disclosed that such a test underestimates the variability, and it is likely to incorrectly detect a difference when no difference exists, while the 5×2cv paired t-test is recommended instead.

The **No Free Lunch (NFL) Theorem** [Wolpert, 1996, Wolpert and Macready, 1997] implies that it is hopeless to dream for a learning algorithm which is consistently better than other learning algorithms on all possible learning tasks. In fact, whether a learning algorithm can work well on a task depends mostly on the fact that whether its **bias** matches with the characteristics of the concerning task [Zhou, 2021, Section 1.4].

Ensemble learning related research papers can be found in almost all journals and conferences in machine learning, data mining, pattern recognition, and their application areas.

Chapter 2

Boosting

2.1 A General Boosting Procedure

The term **Boosting** refers to a family of algorithms that are able to convert weak learners to strong learners. Intuitively, a weak learner is just slightly better than random guess, while a strong learner is very close to perfect performance. The birth of Boosting algorithms originated from the answer to an interesting theoretical question posed by Kearns and Valiant [1989]. That is, whether two complexity classes, *weakly learnable* and *strongly learnable* problems, are equavalent. This question is of fundamental importance, because if the answer is positive, any weak learner is potentially able to be boosted to a strong learner, particularly if we note that in real practice, it is generally very easy to obtain weak learners but difficult to get strong learners. Schapire [1990] proved that the answer is positive, and the proof is a construction, i.e., Boosting.

The general Boosting procedure is quite simple. Take binary classification as an example; that is, we are trying to classify instances as *positive* and *negative*. Suppose the weak learner will work on arbitrary data distribution. The training data in D are drawn *i.i.d.* from distribution $\mathcal{D}$, and the ground-truth function is f. Suppose $\mathcal{X}$ is composed of three parts $\mathcal{X}_1, \mathcal{X}_2$, and $\mathcal{X}_3$, each occupies $1/3$ amount of the distribution, and a learner working by random guess has 50% classification error on this problem. We want to get an accurate (e.g., zero error) classifier on the problem, but we are unlucky and only have a weak classifier at hand, which makes correct classifications in spaces $\mathcal{X}_1$ and $\mathcal{X}_2$ but wrong classifications in $\mathcal{X}_3$, thus, it has $1/3$ classification error. Let's denote this weak classifier by h_1. It is obvious that h_1 is far from a strong learner.

The idea of Boosting is to correct the mistakes made by h_1. We can try to derive a new distribution $\mathcal{D}'$ from $\mathcal{D}$, which makes the mistakes of h_1 more evident, e.g., it focuses more on the instances in $\mathcal{X}_3$. Then, we can train a classifier h_2 from $\mathcal{D}'$. Again, suppose we are unlucky and h_2 is also a weak classifier, which has correct classifications in $\mathcal{X}_1$ and $\mathcal{X}_3$ but wrong classifications in $\mathcal{X}_2$. By combining h_1 and h_2 in an adequate way (we will

DOI: 10.1201/9781003587774-2

Input: Sample distribution $\mathcal{D}$;
Base learning algorithm $\mathfrak{L}$;
Number of learning rounds T.

Process:
1. $\mathcal{D}_1 = \mathcal{D}$. % Initialize distribution
2. **for** $t = 1, \ldots, T$:
3. $h_t = \mathfrak{L}(\mathcal{D}_t)$; % Train a weak learner from distribution $\mathcal{D}_t$
4. $\epsilon_t = P_{\boldsymbol{x} \sim \mathcal{D}_t}(h_t(\boldsymbol{x}) \neq f(\boldsymbol{x}))$; % Evaluate the error of h_t
5. $\mathcal{D}_{t+1} = \mathit{Adjust\_Distribution}(\mathcal{D}_t, \epsilon_t)$
6. **end**

Output: $H(\boldsymbol{x}) = \mathit{Combine\_Outputs}(\{h_1(\boldsymbol{x}), \ldots, h_T(\boldsymbol{x})\})$

Figure 2.1: A general Boosting procedure.

explain how to combine them in the next section), the combined classifier will have correct classifications in $\mathcal{X}_1$, and maybe some errors in $\mathcal{X}_2$ and $\mathcal{X}_3$. Again, we derive a new distribution $\mathcal{D}''$ to make the mistakes of the combined classifier more evident, and train a classifier h_3 from the distribution, such that h_3 make correct classifications in $\mathcal{X}_2$ and $\mathcal{X}_3$. Then, by combining h_1, h_2, and h_3, we have a perfect classifier because in each space of $\mathcal{X}_1$, $\mathcal{X}_2$, and $\mathcal{X}_3$, at least two classifiers make correct classifications.

Briefly, Boosting works by training a set of learners sequentially and combining them for prediction, where the later learners focus more on the mistakes of the earlier learners. Figure 2.1 summarizes the general Boosting procedure.

2.2 AdaBoost

The general Boosting procedure described in Figure 2.1 is not a real algorithm since there are some unspecified parts such as *Adjust_Distribution* and *Combine_Outputs*. The most well-known Boosting algorithm, AdaBoost [Freund and Schapire, 1997], can be viewed as an instantiation of these parts as shown in Figure 2.2, where $y_i \in \{-1, +1\}$ and f is the ground-truth function.

There are multiple ways to derive the AdaBoost algorithm, while a straightforward one is based on using **additive model**, i.e., the linear combination of base learners

$$H(\boldsymbol{x}) = \sum_{t=1}^{T} \alpha_t h_t(\boldsymbol{x}) \tag{2.1}$$

to minimize the **exponential loss** [Friedman et al., 2000]

$$\ell_{\exp}(H \mid \mathcal{D}) = \mathbb{E}_{\boldsymbol{x} \sim \mathcal{D}} \left[e^{-f(\boldsymbol{x})H(\boldsymbol{x})} \right] . \tag{2.2}$$

The partial derivative of the exponential loss with respect to $H(\boldsymbol{x})$ is

$$\frac{\partial \ell_{\exp}(H \mid \mathcal{D})}{\partial H(\boldsymbol{x})} = -e^{-H(\boldsymbol{x})} P(f(\boldsymbol{x}) = 1 \mid \boldsymbol{x}) + e^{H(\boldsymbol{x})} P(f(\boldsymbol{x}) = -1 \mid \boldsymbol{x}) . \tag{2.3}$$

Input: Data set $D = \{(\boldsymbol{x}_1, y_1), (\boldsymbol{x}_2, y_2), \ldots, (\boldsymbol{x}_m, y_m)\}$;
Base learning algorithm $\mathfrak{L}$;
Number of learning rounds T.

Process:

1. $\mathcal{D}_1(\boldsymbol{x}) = 1/m$. % Initialize the weight distribution
2. **for** $t = 1, \ldots, T$:
3. $h_t = \mathfrak{L}(D, \mathcal{D}_t)$; % Train a classifier h_t from D under distribution $\mathcal{D}_t$
4. $\epsilon_t = P_{\boldsymbol{x}\sim\mathcal{D}_t}(h_t(\boldsymbol{x}) \neq f(\boldsymbol{x}))$; % Evaluate the error of h_t
5. **if** $\epsilon_t > 0.5$ **then break**
6. $\alpha_t = \frac{1}{2}\ln\left(\frac{1-\epsilon_t}{\epsilon_t}\right)$; % Determine the weight of h_t
7. $\mathcal{D}_{t+1}(\boldsymbol{x}) = \frac{\mathcal{D}_t(\boldsymbol{x})}{Z_t} \times \begin{cases} \exp(-\alpha_t) & \text{if } h_t(\boldsymbol{x}) = f(\boldsymbol{x}) \\ \exp(\alpha_t) & \text{if } h_t(\boldsymbol{x}) \neq f(\boldsymbol{x}) \end{cases}$
   $= \frac{\mathcal{D}_t(\boldsymbol{x})\exp(-\alpha_t f(\boldsymbol{x}) h_t(\boldsymbol{x}))}{Z_t}$ % Update the distribution, where
   % Z_t is a normalization factor which
   % enables $\mathcal{D}_{t+1}$ to be a distribution
8. **end**

Output: $\mathtt{sign}(H(\boldsymbol{x}))$ with $H(\boldsymbol{x}) = \sum_{t=1}^{T} \alpha_t h_t(\boldsymbol{x})$

Figure 2.2: The AdaBoost algorithm.

If $H(\boldsymbol{x})$ can minimize the exponential loss, the minimizer can be solved by setting (2.3) to zero, i.e.,

$$H(\boldsymbol{x}) = \frac{1}{2} \ln \frac{P(f(\boldsymbol{x}) = 1 \mid \boldsymbol{x})}{P(f(\boldsymbol{x}) = -1 \mid \boldsymbol{x})} \,. \tag{2.4}$$

We have

$$\begin{aligned} \mathtt{sign}(H(\boldsymbol{x})) &= \mathtt{sign}\left(\frac{1}{2}\ln\frac{P(f(\boldsymbol{x}) = 1 \mid \boldsymbol{x})}{P(f(\boldsymbol{x}) = -1 \mid \boldsymbol{x})}\right) \\ &= \begin{cases} 1, & P(f(\boldsymbol{x}) = 1 \mid \boldsymbol{x}) > P(f(\boldsymbol{x}) = -1 \mid \boldsymbol{x}) \\ -1, & P(f(\boldsymbol{x}) = 1 \mid \boldsymbol{x}) < P(f(\boldsymbol{x}) = -1 \mid \boldsymbol{x}) \end{cases} \\ &= \underset{y\in\{-1,1\}}{\arg\max}\, P(f(\boldsymbol{x}) = y \mid \boldsymbol{x}) \,, \end{aligned} \tag{2.5}$$

which implies that $\mathtt{sign}(H(\boldsymbol{x}))$ achieves the Bayes optimal error rate. In other words, the classification error rate is minimized when the exponential loss is minimized. Considering that the exponential loss has better mathematical properties, e.g., continuously differentiable, it is an adequate optimization target for replacing the original 0/1-loss function of classification. Note that in the above derivation we ignore the case $P(f(\boldsymbol{x}) = 1 \mid \boldsymbol{x}) = P(f(\boldsymbol{x}) = -1 \mid \boldsymbol{x})$.

In the AdaBoost algorithm, the base learning algorithm generates the first base classifier h_1 from the original training data and then iteratively generates the subsequent base classifiers h_t's and associated weights α_t's. Once the classifier h_t is generated from the distribution $\mathcal{D}_t$, its weight α_t is estimated by letting $\alpha_t h_t$ minimize the exponential loss

$$\begin{aligned}\ell_{\exp}(\alpha_t h_t \mid \mathcal{D}_t) &= \mathbb{E}_{\boldsymbol{x}\sim\mathcal{D}_t}[e^{-f(\boldsymbol{x})\alpha_t h_t(\boldsymbol{x})}] \\ &= \mathbb{E}_{\boldsymbol{x}\sim\mathcal{D}_t}\left[e^{-\alpha_t}\mathbb{I}(f(\boldsymbol{x}) = h_t(\boldsymbol{x})) + e^{\alpha_t}\mathbb{I}(f(\boldsymbol{x}) \neq h_t(\boldsymbol{x}))\right] \\ &= e^{-\alpha_t}P_{\boldsymbol{x}\sim\mathcal{D}_t}(f(\boldsymbol{x}) = h_t(\boldsymbol{x})) + e^{\alpha_t}P_{\boldsymbol{x}\sim\mathcal{D}_t}(f(\boldsymbol{x}) \neq h_t(\boldsymbol{x})) \\ &= e^{-\alpha_t}(1-\epsilon_t) + e^{\alpha_t}\epsilon_t\ , \end{aligned} \tag{2.6}$$

where $\epsilon_t = P_{\boldsymbol{x}\sim\mathcal{D}_t}(h_t(\boldsymbol{x}) \neq f(\boldsymbol{x}))$. The optimal α_t can be obtained by setting the derivative of the exponential loss

$$\frac{\partial \ell_{\exp}(\alpha_t h_t \mid \mathcal{D}_t)}{\partial \alpha_t} = -e^{-\alpha_t}(1-\epsilon_t) + e^{\alpha_t}\epsilon_t \tag{2.7}$$

to zero, that is,

$$\alpha_t = \frac{1}{2}\ln\left(\frac{1-\epsilon_t}{\epsilon_t}\right), \tag{2.8}$$

which is exactly the equation used in line 6 of Figure 2.2.

Once a sequence of base learners and their corresponding weights have been obtained, they are combined to form H_{t-1}. Then, AdaBoost adjusts the sample distribution such that the base learner h_t to be generated in the next round can correct some mistakes made by H_{t-1}. The ideal h_t, which can correct all mistakes of H_{t-1}, should minimize the exponential loss

$$\begin{aligned}\ell_{\exp}(H_{t-1} + h_t \mid \mathcal{D}) &= \mathbb{E}_{\boldsymbol{x}\sim\mathcal{D}}\left[e^{-f(\boldsymbol{x})(H_{t-1}(\boldsymbol{x})+h_t(\boldsymbol{x}))}\right] \\ &= \mathbb{E}_{\boldsymbol{x}\sim\mathcal{D}}\left[e^{-f(\boldsymbol{x})H_{t-1}(\boldsymbol{x})}e^{-f(\boldsymbol{x})h_t(\boldsymbol{x})}\right]. \end{aligned} \tag{2.9}$$

Using Taylor expansion of $e^{-f(\boldsymbol{x})h_t(\boldsymbol{x})}$, noticing $f^2(\boldsymbol{x}) = h_t^2(\boldsymbol{x}) = 1$, (2.9) can be approximated by

$$\begin{aligned}\ell_{\exp}(H_{t-1} + h_t \mid \mathcal{D}) &\simeq \mathbb{E}_{\boldsymbol{x}\sim\mathcal{D}}\left[e^{-f(\boldsymbol{x})H_{t-1}(\boldsymbol{x})}\left(1 - f(\boldsymbol{x})h_t(\boldsymbol{x}) + \frac{f^2(\boldsymbol{x})h_t^2(\boldsymbol{x})}{2}\right)\right] \\ &= \mathbb{E}_{\boldsymbol{x}\sim\mathcal{D}}\left[e^{-f(\boldsymbol{x})H_{t-1}(\boldsymbol{x})}\left(1 - f(\boldsymbol{x})h_t(\boldsymbol{x}) + \frac{1}{2}\right)\right]. \end{aligned} \tag{2.10}$$

Thus, the ideal base learner h_t is

$$\begin{aligned}h_t(\boldsymbol{x}) &= \arg\min_h \ell_{\exp}(H_{t-1} + h \mid \mathcal{D}) \\ &= \arg\min_h \mathbb{E}_{\boldsymbol{x}\sim\mathcal{D}}\left[e^{-f(\boldsymbol{x})H_{t-1}(\boldsymbol{x})}\left(1 - f(\boldsymbol{x})h(\boldsymbol{x}) + \frac{1}{2}\right)\right] \\ &= \arg\max_h \mathbb{E}_{\boldsymbol{x}\sim\mathcal{D}}\left[e^{-f(\boldsymbol{x})H_{t-1}(\boldsymbol{x})}f(\boldsymbol{x})h(\boldsymbol{x})\right] \\ &= \arg\max_h \mathbb{E}_{\boldsymbol{x}\sim\mathcal{D}}\left[\frac{e^{-f(\boldsymbol{x})H_{t-1}(\boldsymbol{x})}}{\mathbb{E}_{\boldsymbol{x}\sim\mathcal{D}}\left[e^{-f(\boldsymbol{x})H_{t-1}(\boldsymbol{x})}\right]}f(\boldsymbol{x})h(\boldsymbol{x})\right], \end{aligned} \tag{2.11}$$

by noticing that $\mathbb{E}_{\boldsymbol{x}\sim\mathcal{D}}[e^{-f(\boldsymbol{x})H_{t-1}(\boldsymbol{x})}]$ is a constant.

Let $\mathcal{D}_t$ denote the distribution

$$\mathcal{D}_t(\boldsymbol{x}) = \frac{\mathcal{D}(\boldsymbol{x})e^{-f(\boldsymbol{x})H_{t-1}(\boldsymbol{x})}}{\mathbb{E}_{\boldsymbol{x}\sim\mathcal{D}}\left[e^{-f(\boldsymbol{x})H_{t-1}(\boldsymbol{x})}\right]}. \tag{2.12}$$

Based on the definition of mathematical expectation, it is equivalent to rewrite (2.11) as

$$\begin{aligned} h_t(\boldsymbol{x}) &= \arg\max_h \mathbb{E}_{\boldsymbol{x}\sim\mathcal{D}}\left[\frac{e^{-f(\boldsymbol{x})H_{t-1}(\boldsymbol{x})}}{\mathbb{E}_{\boldsymbol{x}\sim\mathcal{D}}\left[e^{-f(\boldsymbol{x})H_{t-1}(\boldsymbol{x})}\right]}f(\boldsymbol{x})h(\boldsymbol{x})\right] \\ &= \arg\max_h \mathbb{E}_{\boldsymbol{x}\sim\mathcal{D}_t}[f(\boldsymbol{x})h(\boldsymbol{x})]. \end{aligned} \tag{2.13}$$

Since $f(\boldsymbol{x}), h(\boldsymbol{x}) \in \{-1, +1\}$, we have

$$f(\boldsymbol{x})h(\boldsymbol{x}) = 1 - 2\,\mathbb{I}(f(\boldsymbol{x}) \neq h(\boldsymbol{x}))\ . \tag{2.14}$$

Thus, the ideal base learner h_t is

$$h_t(\boldsymbol{x}) = \arg\min_h \mathbb{E}_{\boldsymbol{x}\sim\mathcal{D}_t}\left[\mathbb{I}(f(\boldsymbol{x}) \neq h(\boldsymbol{x}))\right]\ . \tag{2.15}$$

(2.15) implies that the ideal base learner h_t minimizes the classification error under the distribution $\mathcal{D}_t$. Therefore, the base learner in the t-th round is trained from $\mathcal{D}_t$, and its classification error should be less than 0.5 for $\mathcal{D}_t$. This idea can be viewed as a kind of **residue minimization** to some extent. Considering the relationship between $\mathcal{D}_t$ and $\mathcal{D}_{t+1}$, we have

$$\begin{aligned} \mathcal{D}_{t+1}(\boldsymbol{x}) &= \frac{\mathcal{D}_t(\boldsymbol{x})e^{-f(\boldsymbol{x})H_t(\boldsymbol{x})}}{\mathbb{E}_{\boldsymbol{x}\sim\mathcal{D}}\left[e^{-f(\boldsymbol{x})H_t(\boldsymbol{x})}\right]} \\ &= \frac{\mathcal{D}_t(\boldsymbol{x})e^{-f(\boldsymbol{x})H_{t-1}(\boldsymbol{x})}e^{-f(\boldsymbol{x})\alpha_t h_t(\boldsymbol{x})}}{\mathbb{E}_{\boldsymbol{x}\sim\mathcal{D}}\left[e^{-f(\boldsymbol{x})H_t(\boldsymbol{x})}\right]} \\ &= \mathcal{D}_t(\boldsymbol{x}) \cdot e^{-f(\boldsymbol{x})\alpha_t h_t(\boldsymbol{x})}\frac{\mathbb{E}_{\boldsymbol{x}\sim\mathcal{D}}\left[e^{-f(\boldsymbol{x})H_{t-1}(\boldsymbol{x})}\right]}{\mathbb{E}_{\boldsymbol{x}\sim\mathcal{D}}\left[e^{-f(\boldsymbol{x})H_t(\boldsymbol{x})}\right]}\ , \end{aligned} \tag{2.16}$$

which is used by AdaBoost to update sample distribution as in line 7 of Figure 2.2.

It is noteworthy that the AdaBoost algorithm described in Figure 2.2 requires the base learning algorithm to learn from specified distributions. This is often accomplished by **re-weighting**; that is, new weights are assigned to the training examples according to the new sample distribution in each round. For base learning algorithms that could not handle weighted training examples, **re-sampling** can be used; that is, a new training set is sampled according to the new sample distribution in each round.

For base learning algorithms that can be used with both re-weighting and re-sampling, generally there is no clear performance difference between these two implementations. However, re-sampling provides an option for **Boosting**

with restart [Kohavi and Wolpert, 1996]. Note that in each round, there is a *sanity check* to ensure that the current base learner satisfies some basic requirements (see line 5 of Figure 2.2). If the requirements are not met, the current base learner is discarded and the learning process terminates. In such cases, the number of rounds may be still far from the pre-specified number of rounds T, which may lead to unsatisfactory performance due to the small number of base learners in the ensemble. This occurs particularly often on multi-class tasks. If re-sampling is used, AdaBoost can avoid early termination by "restart". Specifically, a new training set is sampled according to the sample distribution again after discarding the current disqualified base learner, and then an alternative base learner is trained such that the learning process can continue to finish T rounds.

2.3 Illustrative Examples

It is helpful to gain an intuitive understanding of AdaBoost by observing its behavior. Consider an artificial data set in a two-dimensional space, plotted in Figure 2.3(a). There are only four instances, i.e.,

$$\left\{ \begin{array}{l} (\boldsymbol{x}_1 = (+1,0)\,, y_1 = +1) \\ (\boldsymbol{x}_2 = (-1,0)\,, y_2 = +1) \\ (\boldsymbol{x}_3 = (0,+1)\,, y_3 = -1) \\ (\boldsymbol{x}_4 = (0,-1)\,, y_4 = -1) \end{array} \right\},$$

where $y_i = f(\boldsymbol{x}_i)$ is the label of each instance. This is the XOR problem. As can be seen, there is no straight line that is able to separate positive instances (i.e., $\boldsymbol{x}_1$ and $\boldsymbol{x}_2$) from negative instances (i.e., $\boldsymbol{x}_3$ and $\boldsymbol{x}_4$); in other words, the two classes cannot be separated by a linear classifier.

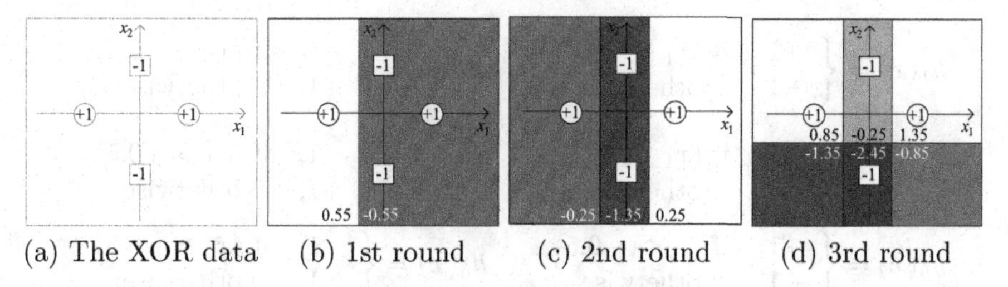

Figure 2.3: AdaBoost on the XOR problem.

Suppose we have a base learning algorithm which works as follows. It evaluates the eight basis functions h_1 to h_8 described in Figure 2.4 on the training data under a given distribution, and then outputs the one with the smallest error. If there are more than one basis functions with the smallest error, the algorithm selects one randomly. Note that none of these eight basis functions can separate the two classes.

Now we track how AdaBoost works:

1. The first step is to invoke the base learning algorithm on the original data. Since h_2, h_3, h_5, and h_8 all have the smallest classification error 0.25, suppose the base learning algorithm outputs h_2 as the classifier. After that, one instance, $\boldsymbol{x}_1$, is incorrectly classified, so the error is $1/4 = 0.25$. The weight of h_2 is $0.5 \ln 3 \approx 0.55$. Figure 2.3(b) visualizes the classification, where the shadow area is classified as negative (–1) and the weights of the classification, 0.55 and –0.55, are displayed.
2. The weight of $\boldsymbol{x}_1$ is increased, and the base learning algorithm is invoked again. Now h_3, h_5, and h_8 have the smallest error. Suppose h_3 is selected, of which the weight is 0.80. Figure 2.3(c) shows the combined classification of h_2 and h_3 with their weights, where different gray levels are used to distinguish the negative areas according to the combination weights.
3. The weight of $\boldsymbol{x}_2$ is increased. This time only h_5 and h_8 equally have the smallest error. Suppose h_5 is selected, of which the weight is 1.10. Figure 2.3(d) shows the combined classification of h_2, h_3, and h_5.

After the three steps, the sign of classification weights in each area can be examined in Figure 2.3(d). It can be observed that the sign of classification weights of $\boldsymbol{x}_1$ and $\boldsymbol{x}_2$ is "+", while that of $\boldsymbol{x}_3$ and $\boldsymbol{x}_4$ is "–". This means all the instances are correctly classified; thus, by combining the imperfect linear classifiers, AdaBoost has produced a non-linear classifier with zero error.

For a further understanding of AdaBoost, we visualize the decision boundaries of a single decision tree, AdaBoost and its component decision trees on the *three-Gaussians* data set, as shown in Figure 2.5. It can be observed that the decision boundary of AdaBoost is more flexible than that of a single decision

---

$$h_1(\boldsymbol{x}) = \begin{cases} +1, & \text{if } (x_1 > -0.5) \\ -1, & \text{otherwise} \end{cases} \qquad h_2(\boldsymbol{x}) = \begin{cases} -1, & \text{if } (x_1 > -0.5) \\ +1, & \text{otherwise} \end{cases}$$

$$h_3(\boldsymbol{x}) = \begin{cases} +1, & \text{if } (x_1 > +0.5) \\ -1, & \text{otherwise} \end{cases} \qquad h_4(\boldsymbol{x}) = \begin{cases} -1, & \text{if } (x_1 > +0.5) \\ +1, & \text{otherwise} \end{cases}$$

$$h_5(\boldsymbol{x}) = \begin{cases} +1, & \text{if } (x_2 > -0.5) \\ -1, & \text{otherwise} \end{cases} \qquad h_6(\boldsymbol{x}) = \begin{cases} -1, & \text{if } (x_2 > -0.5) \\ +1, & \text{otherwise} \end{cases}$$

$$h_7(\boldsymbol{x}) = \begin{cases} +1, & \text{if } (x_2 > +0.5) \\ -1, & \text{otherwise} \end{cases} \qquad h_8(\boldsymbol{x}) = \begin{cases} -1, & \text{if } (x_2 > +0.5) \\ +1, & \text{otherwise} \end{cases}$$

where $\boldsymbol{x} = (x_1, x_2)$, i.e., x_1 and x_2 are the values of $\boldsymbol{x}$ at the first and the second dimension, respectively.

Figure 2.4: The eight basis functions considered by the base learning algorithm.

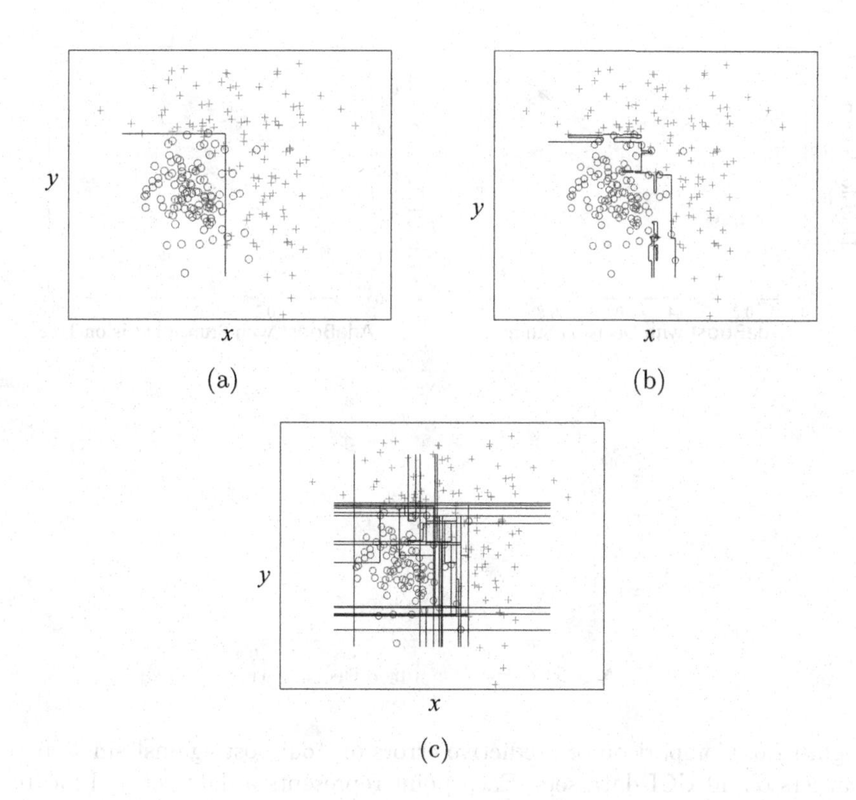

Figure 2.5: Decision boundaries of (a) a single decision tree, (b) AdaBoost, and (c) the 10 decision trees used by AdaBoost, on *three-Gaussians*.

tree, and this helps to reduce the error from 9.4% of the single decision tree to 8.3% of the boosted ensemble.

We also evaluate the AdaBoost algorithm on 40 data sets from the UCI Machine Learning Repository[1], which covers a broad range of tasks. The Weka[2] implementation of AdaBoost.M1 using re-weighting with 50 weak learners is evaluated. Almost all kinds of learning algorithms can be taken as base learning algorithms, such as decision trees, neural networks, etc. Here, we have tried three base learning algorithms: decision stumps, and pruned and unpruned J48 decision trees (Weka implementation of C4.5 decision trees). We plot the comparison results in Figure 2.6, from which it can be observed that AdaBoost usually outperforms its base learning algorithm, with only a few exceptions in which it hurts performance.

[1] `http://www.ics.uci.edu/~mlearn/MLRepository.html`

[2] `http://www.cs.waikato.ac.nz/ml/weka/`

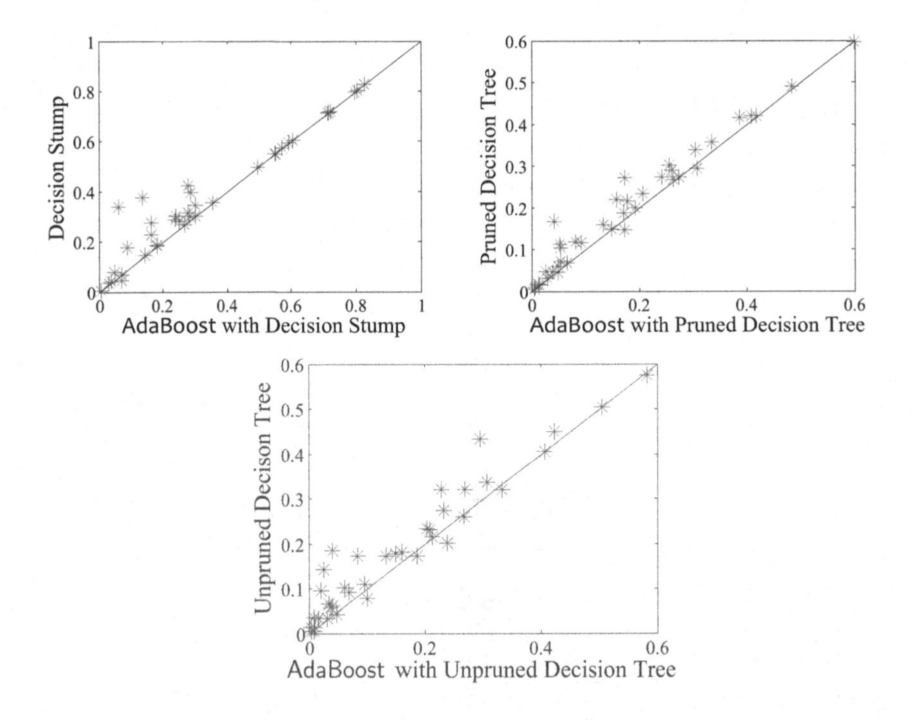

Figure 2.6: Comparison of predictive errors of AdaBoost against single base learners on 40 UCI data sets. Each point represents a data set and locates according to the predictive error of the two compared algorithms. The diagonal line indicates where the two compared algorithms have identical errors.

2.4 Theoretical Understanding

2.4.1 Training and Generalization

Freund and Schapire [1997] proved that, for binary classification, given a training set D, if the base learners of AdaBoost have errors ϵ_1, ϵ_2, ..., ϵ_T as shown in Figure 2.2, the training error of the final ensemble, ϵ_D, is upper bounded by

$$\begin{aligned}\epsilon_D &= \mathbb{E}_{\boldsymbol{x}\sim D}[\mathbb{I}[H(\boldsymbol{x}) \neq f(\boldsymbol{x})]] \\ &\leq 2^T \prod_{t=1}^{T} \sqrt{\epsilon_t(1-\epsilon_t)} \\ &\leq e^{-2\sum_{t=1}^{T}\gamma_t^2} , \end{aligned} \tag{2.17}$$

where $\gamma_t = 0.5 - \epsilon_t$ is called the **edge** of h_t. Note that the error of random guess in binary classification is 0.5, and thus, the edge expresses how much the base learner h_t is better than random guess.

(2.17) exhibits that AdaBoost reduces the training error exponentially fast. In particular, it can be derived that, to achieve a training error smaller than ϵ, the number of learning rounds T is upper bounded by

$$T \leq \left\lceil \frac{1}{2\gamma^2} \ln \frac{1}{\epsilon} \right\rceil , \tag{2.18}$$

where $\gamma \geq \gamma_t$ $(t \in \{1, \ldots, T\})$.

As for generalization error $\epsilon_{\mathcal{D}} = \mathbb{E}_{\boldsymbol{x} \sim \mathcal{D}} \mathbb{I}[H(\boldsymbol{x}) \neq f(\boldsymbol{x})]$, Freund and Schapire [1997] proved that it is upper bounded by

$$\epsilon_{\mathcal{D}} \leq \epsilon_D + \tilde{O}\left(\sqrt{\frac{dT}{m}}\right) \tag{2.19}$$

with probability at least $1 - \delta$, where d is the **VC-dimension** [Zhou, 2021, Section 12.4] of base learners, m is the number of training examples, T is the number of learning rounds, and $\tilde{O}(\cdot)$ is used instead of $O(\cdot)$ to hide logarithmic terms and constant factors.

(2.19) shows that increasing the size of training data helps decrease generalization error. More importantly, it suggests that, in order to achieve a nice generalization performance, it is necessary to constrain the complexity of base learners as well as the number of based learners; otherwise, AdaBoost will overfit, as increasing T can help decrease the training error ϵ_D in early rounds but hurt the generalization performance later, e.g., after training error reaches zero.

However, empirical studies show that AdaBoost often does *not* overfit; that is, the testing error often tends to decrease even after the training error reaches zero, even after a large number of rounds such as 1,000. For example, as can be observed from the typical performance of AdaBoost shown in Figure 2.7 [Schapire et al., 1998], zero training error is achieved in less than 10 rounds but after that, the generalization error keeps decreasing. This discloses that (2.19) does not offer a sound characterization about AdaBoost generalization performance.

This phenomenon seems to contradict with the fundamental principle in scientific research, i.e., Occam's razor, which prefers simple hypotheses to complex ones when both fit empirical observations well. In fact, as Figure 2.7 illustrated, the AdaBoosted ensembles comprising less than 10 base learners and comprising 1,000 learners are both consistent with empirical observations, i.e., both achieving zero error on training data, but by choosing the latter which is more complex, AdaBoost achieves better generalization performance. So, it is not strange that understanding why AdaBoost seems resistant to overfitting becomes the most fascinating fundamental theoretical issue, and the sound generalization characterization of AdaBoost can be obtained after this issue gets resolved. We will talk about this later in Section 2.4.3.

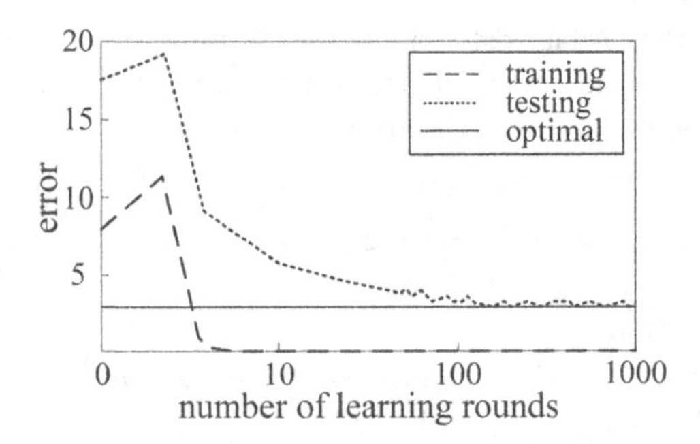

Figure 2.7: Training and testing error of AdaBoost on the UCI *letter* data set. (Plot based on a similar figure in [Schapire et al., 1998].)

2.4.2 Surrogate Loss and Optimization

The success of AdaBoost has drawn much attention, not only in the learning community, but also the statistics community. Statisticians have tried to understand AdaBoost from the perspective of statistical methods; in particular, what is the **surrogate loss function** of AdaBoost and how it is optimized.

It is well-known that the original classification 0/1-loss function is not a good target for optimization because its mathematical property is not good, e.g., it is not continuously differentiable. Thus, from the view of statistical methods, a surrogate loss function has to be used. Ideally, a surrogate loss function should be *consistent*, i.e., optimizing the surrogate loss will yield ultimately an optimal function with the Bayes optimal error rate for the original loss function, while the optimization of the surrogate loss is computationally more efficient. Note that, when [Freund and Schapire, 1997] proposed the AdaBoost algorithm, they did not explicitly mention surrogate loss function.

Friedman et al. [2000] showed that, AdaBoost algorithm can be interpreted as using an **additive model** (2.1) to optimize the exponential loss function (2.2) by a Newton-like stagewise estimation procedure; this is exactly how we derive the AdaBoost in Section 2.2. This understanding is called **statistical view** of AdaBoost . It inspired explorations of various AdaBoost variants by taking alternative surrogate loss functions and/or optimization procedures.

For example, the exponential loss function is a differentiable upper bound of the 0/1-loss function, while there are also other possible surrogate loss functions can be considered. Note that when the probability is estimated via

$$P(f(\boldsymbol{x}) = 1 \mid \boldsymbol{x}) = \frac{e^{H(\boldsymbol{x})}}{e^{H(\boldsymbol{x})} + e^{-H(\boldsymbol{x})}} , \tag{2.20}$$

the exponential loss function and the *log-loss* function (negative log-likelihood)

$$\ell_{log}(h \mid \mathcal{D}) = \mathbb{E}_{\boldsymbol{x} \sim \mathcal{D}} \left[\ln \left(1 + e^{-2f(\boldsymbol{x})h(\boldsymbol{x})} \right) \right] \tag{2.21}$$

Input: Data set $D = \{(\boldsymbol{x}_1, y_1), (\boldsymbol{x}_2, y_2), \ldots, (\boldsymbol{x}_m, y_m)\}$;
Least square base learning algorithm $\mathfrak{L}$;
Number of learning rounds T.

Process:

1. $y_0(\boldsymbol{x}) = f(\boldsymbol{x})$. % Initialize target
2. $H_0(\boldsymbol{x}) = 0$. % Initialize function
3. **for** $t = 1, \ldots, T$:
4. $p_t(\boldsymbol{x}) = \frac{1}{1+e^{-2H_{t-1}(\boldsymbol{x})}}$; %Calculate probability
5. $y_t(\boldsymbol{x}) = \frac{y_{t-1}(\boldsymbol{x}) - p_t(\boldsymbol{x})}{p_t(\boldsymbol{x})(1-p_t(\boldsymbol{x}))}$; % Update target
6. $D_t = \{(\boldsymbol{x}_i, y_t(\boldsymbol{x}_i))\}$ $(i \in \{1, \ldots, m\})$; % Update data
7. $\mathcal{D}_t(\boldsymbol{x}) = p_t(\boldsymbol{x})(1 - p_t(\boldsymbol{x}))$; % Update weight
8. $h_t = \mathfrak{L}(D_t, \mathcal{D}_t)$;
9. $H_t(\boldsymbol{x}) = H_{t-1}(\boldsymbol{x}) + \frac{1}{2} h_t(\boldsymbol{x})$; %Update ensemble
10. **end**

Output: $H(\boldsymbol{x}) = \textbf{sign}\left(\sum_{t=1}^{T} h_t(\boldsymbol{x})\right)$

Figure 2.8: The LogitBoost algorithm.

are minimized by the same minimizer (2.4). Thus, instead of taking the Newton-like updates in AdaBoost, Friedman et al. [2000] suggested to fit the additive model by optimizing the log-loss function via gradient decent with base regression models, leading to the LogitBoost algorithm shown in Figure 2.8.

In addition to LogitBoost, many other variants of AdaBoost have been developed by considering different surrogate loss functions, e.g., the L2Boost which considers the L_2-*loss* [Bühlmann and Yu, 2003].

On the other hand, if we just regard a Boosting procedure as an optimization of a loss function, an alternative way for this purpose is to use mathematical programming [Demiriz et al., 2002, Warmuth et al., 2008] to solve the weights of base learners. Consider an additive model $\sum_{h \in \mathcal{H}} \alpha_h h$ of a pool $\mathcal{H}$ of base learners, and let ξ_i be the loss of the model on instance $\boldsymbol{x}_i$. Demiriz et al. [2002] derived that, if the sum of coefficients and losses is bounded as

$$\sum_{h \in \mathcal{H}} \alpha_h + C \sum_{i=1}^{m} \xi_i \leq B , \tag{2.22}$$

where $C \geq 1$ and $\alpha_h \geq 0$, then it actually bounds the complexity (or **covering number**) of the model [Zhang, 1999]. The generalization error is therefore bounded by

$$\epsilon_{\mathcal{D}} \leq \tilde{O}\left(\frac{\ln m}{m} B^2 \ln(Bm) + \frac{1}{m} \ln \frac{1}{\delta}\right) , \tag{2.23}$$

where $\tilde{O}(\cdot)$ hides other variables and logarithmic terms. It is evident that minimizing B also minimizes this upper bound. Thus, considering T base learners, letting $y_i = f(\boldsymbol{x}_i)$ be the label of training instance $\boldsymbol{x}_i$ and $H_{i,j} = h_j(\boldsymbol{x}_i)$ be the output of the base learner h_j on $\boldsymbol{x}_i$, we have the optimization task

$$
\begin{aligned}
&\min_{\alpha_j,\xi_i} \sum_{j=1}^{T} \alpha_j + C\sum_{i=1}^{m} \xi_i \qquad (2.24)\\
\text{s.t.}\quad & y_i \sum\nolimits_{j=1}^{T} H_{i,j}\alpha_j + \xi_i \geq 1 \ , \ i \in \{1,\ldots,m\}\\
& \xi_i \geq 0 \ , \ i \in \{1,\ldots,m\}\\
& \alpha_j \geq 0 \ , \ j \in \{1,\ldots,T\} \ ,
\end{aligned}
$$

or equivalently,

$$
\begin{aligned}
&\max_{\alpha_j,\xi_i,\rho} \rho - C'\sum_{i=1}^{m} \xi_i \qquad (2.25)\\
\text{s.t.}\quad & y_i \sum\nolimits_{j=1}^{T} H_{i,j}\alpha_j + \xi_i \geq \rho \ , \ i \in \{1,\ldots,m\}\\
& \sum\nolimits_{j=1}^{T} \alpha_j = 1\\
& \xi_i \geq 0 \ , \ i \in \{1,\ldots,m\}\\
& \alpha_j \geq 0 \ , \ j \in \{1,\ldots,T\} \ ,
\end{aligned}
$$

of which the dual form is

$$
\begin{aligned}
&\min_{w_i,\beta} \beta \qquad (2.26)\\
\text{s.t.}\quad & \sum\nolimits_{i=1}^{m} w_i y_i H_{i,j} \leq \beta \ , \ j \in \{1,\ldots,T\}\\
& \sum\nolimits_{i=1}^{m} w_i = 1\\
& w_i \in [0, C'] \ , \ i \in \{1,\ldots,m\} \ .
\end{aligned}
$$

A difficulty for this optimization task is that T can be very large. Considering the final solution of the first linear programming, some α will be zero. One way to handle this problem is to find the smallest subset of all the columns; this can be done by *column generation* [Nash and Sofer, 1996]. Using the dual form, set $w_i = 1/m$ for the first column, and then find the j-th column that violates the following constraint to the most.

$$\sum_{i=1}^{m} w_i y_i H_{i,j} \leq \beta \qquad (2.27)$$

This is equivalent to maximizing $\sum_{i=1}^{m} w_i y_i H_{i,j}$; in other words, finding the base learner h_j with the smallest error under the weight distribution $\boldsymbol{w}$.

Input: Data set $D = \{(\boldsymbol{x}_1, y_1), (\boldsymbol{x}_2, y_2), \ldots, (\boldsymbol{x}_m, y_m)\}$;
Base learning algorithm $\mathfrak{L}$;
Parameter ν;
Number of learning rounds T.

Process:
1. $w_{1,i} = 1/m$, $(i \in \{1, \ldots, m\})$.
2. $\beta_1 = 0$.
3. **for** $t = 1, \ldots, T$:
4. $h_t = \mathfrak{L}(D, \boldsymbol{w})$; % Train a learner h_t from D under $\boldsymbol{w}$
5. **if** $\sum_{i=1}^{m} w_{t,i} y_i h_t(\boldsymbol{x}_i) \leq \beta_t$ **then** $T = t - 1$; **break**; % Check optimality
6. $H_{i,t} = h_t(\boldsymbol{x}_i)$ $(i \in \{1, \ldots, m\})$; % Fill a column
7. $(\boldsymbol{w}_{t+1}, \beta_{t+1}) = \arg\min_{\boldsymbol{w},\beta} \beta$

$$\text{s.t.} \quad \sum_{i=1}^{m} w_i y_i h_j(\boldsymbol{x}_i) \leq \beta \ (\forall j \leq t)$$
$$\sum_{i=1}^{m} w_i = 1$$
$$w_i \in \left[0, \frac{1}{m\nu}\right] \quad (i \in \{1, \ldots, m\})$$

8. **end**
9. solve $\boldsymbol{\alpha}$ from the dual solution $(\boldsymbol{w}_{T+1}, \beta_{T+1})$;

Output: $H(\boldsymbol{x}) = \mathbf{sign}\left(\sum_{t=1}^{T} \alpha_t h_t(\boldsymbol{x})\right)$

Figure 2.9: The LPBoost algorithm.

When the solved h_j does not violate any constraint, the optimality is reached and the column generation process terminates. The whole procedure forms the LPBoost algorithm [Demiriz et al., 2002] shown in Figure 2.9. The performance advantage of LPBoost against AdaBoost is not apparent [Demiriz et al., 2002], while it is observed that an improved version, entropy regularized LPBoost, often beats AdaBoost [Warmuth et al., 2008].

The statistical view inspired the development of many variants of AdaBoost, and many theoretical studies about specific statistical properties such as the *consistency* of Boosting with early stopping [Zhang and Yu, 2005], the consistency of exponential and logistic losses [Zhang and Yu, 2005, Bartlett et al., 2006], etc. However, there are contrary evidence suggesting that it failed to explain the behavior of AdaBoost; for example, the statistical view suggests that larger-size trees will lead to overfitting because of higher-level interaction, early stopping can be used to avoid overfitting, LogitBoost is better than AdaBoost for noisy data, etc., but all of them have been denied with contrary empirical results [Mease and Wyner, 2008]. Indeed, the AdaBoost algorithm is a classification algorithm with specially designed procedure for minimizing classification error, while the statistical view focuses on the minimization of the surrogate loss function (or equivalently, probability estimation); the subtle difference of these two problems might have led to significantly different algorithm behaviors. More importantly, the statistical view does not answer the fundamental question of why AdaBoost seems resistant to overfitting.

2.4.3 Why AdaBoost Resistant to Overfitting

Let $\mathcal{H}$ denote the hypothesis space, and $\mathcal{C}(\mathcal{H})$ denotes its convex hull, i.e., the ensemble model $H \in \mathcal{C}(\mathcal{H})$ is of the form

$$H(\boldsymbol{x}) = \sum_{t=1}^{T} \alpha_t h_t(\boldsymbol{x}), \tag{2.28}$$

where $\sum_{t=1}^{T} \alpha_t = 1$ and $\alpha_t \geq 0$. This ensemble model is a **voting classifier** because the base learners $h \colon \mathcal{X} \to \mathcal{Y}$ are combined via voting (also called *additive model* in statistical literatures). In the context of binary classification, i.e., $f(\boldsymbol{x}) \in \{-1, +1\}$, the **margin** of the base learner h on the instance $\boldsymbol{x}$, or intuitively, the distance of $\boldsymbol{x}$ to the classification hyperplane of h, is defined as $f(\boldsymbol{x})h(\boldsymbol{x})$. Similarly, the margin of the voting classifier (2.28) is

$$f(\boldsymbol{x})H(\boldsymbol{x}) = \sum_{t=1}^{T} \alpha_t f(\boldsymbol{x}) h_t(\boldsymbol{x}). \tag{2.29}$$

Based on the concept of margin, Schapire et al. [1998] proved the following margin theory for AdaBoost and upper bounded its generalization error, where $\theta > 0$ is a threshold of margin over the training sample D.

Theorem 2.1 ([Schapire et al., 1998]). *For any $\delta > 0$ and $\theta > 0$, with probability at least $1 - \delta$ over the random choice of sample D with size m, every voting classifier $H \in \mathcal{C}(\mathcal{H})$ satisfies the following bound:*

$$\epsilon_{\mathcal{D}} \leq P_{\boldsymbol{x} \sim D}(f(\boldsymbol{x})H(\boldsymbol{x}) \leq \theta) + O\left(\frac{1}{\sqrt{m}} \left(\frac{\ln m \ln |\mathcal{H}|}{\theta^2} + \ln \frac{1}{\delta}\right)^{1/2}\right). \tag{2.30}$$

Theorem 2.1 implies that, when other variables are fixed, the larger the margin over the training sample, the better the generalization performance of AdaBoost; this offers an intuitive explanation to why AdaBoost tends to be resistant to overfitting: It is able to increase margin even after training error reaches zero.

Note that the bound (2.30) depends heavily on the smallest margin, because $P_{\boldsymbol{x} \sim D}(f(\boldsymbol{x})H(\boldsymbol{x}) \leq \theta)$ will be small if the smallest margin is large. Based on this recognition, Breiman [1999] explicitly considered the **minimum margin**

$$\varrho = \min_{\boldsymbol{x} \in D} f(\boldsymbol{x})H(\boldsymbol{x}) \tag{2.31}$$

and proved the following theorem.

Theorem 2.2 ([Breiman, 1999]). *For any $\delta > 0$, if $\theta = \varrho > 4\sqrt{\frac{2}{|\mathcal{H}|}}$ and $R \leq 2m$, with probability at least $1-\delta$ over the random choice of sample D with size m, every voting classifier $H \in \mathcal{C}(\mathcal{H})$ satisfies the following bound:*

$$\epsilon_{\mathfrak{D}} \leq R\Big(\ln(2m) + \ln\frac{1}{R} + 1\Big) + \frac{1}{m}\ln\frac{|\mathcal{H}|}{\delta}, \tag{2.32}$$

where $R = \frac{32 \ln 2|\mathcal{H}|}{m\theta^2}$.

Breiman's minimum margin bound (2.32) is in $O(\ln m/m)$, sharper than Schapire et al.'s bound (2.30) that is in $O(\sqrt{\ln m/m})$. Thus, it was believed that the minimum margin is essential for margin theory. Based on this recognition, Breiman [1999] designed the arc-gv algorithm, a variant of AdaBoost. In each round, arc-gv updates α_t according to

$$\alpha_t = \frac{1}{2}\ln\left(\frac{1+\gamma_t}{1-\gamma_t}\right) - \frac{1}{2}\ln\left(\frac{1+\varrho_t}{1-\varrho_t}\right), \tag{2.33}$$

where γ_t is the edge of h_t, and ϱ_t is the minimum margin of the combined classifier up to the current round.

It is provable that arc-gv directly maximizes the minimum margin, and empirical results show that arc-gv does produce uniformly larger minimum margin than AdaBoost. The margin theory would appear to predict that arc-gv should perform better than AdaBoost. However, empirical results show that the generalization error of arc-gv is much larger than that of AdaBoost in almost every case. Thus, Breiman [1999] raised serious doubt about the margin-based explanation for AdaBoost, and almost sentenced the margin theory to death.

Seven years later, Reyzin and Schapire [2006] reported an interesting finding. The bounds of generalization error (2.30, 2.32) of AdaBoost are relevant to the margin θ, the sample size m, and $|\mathcal{H}|$ which is related to the number of learning rounds T and the complexity of base learners. To study the influence of margin, the other factors should be fixed. The sample size m and the number of learning rounds T are easy to be controlled. When comparing arc-gv and AdaBoost, Breiman [1999] tried to control the complexity of base learners by using decision trees with a fixed number of leaves. However, Reyzin and Schapire [2006] found that the trees generated by arc-gv tend to be deeper. Figure 2.10(a) depicts the difference of the depth of typical trees generated by the two algorithms. Though these trees have the same number of leaves, Reyzin and Schapire [2006] argued that trees with different depth may be with different model complexities. Then, they repeated Breiman's experiments using *decision stumps* which have only two leaves and therefore have a fixed complexity. They found that though the minimum margin of arc-gv is larger than that of AdaBoost, the **margin distribution** of AdaBoost is better than that of arc-gv, as illustrated in Figure 2.10(b). Thus, Reyzin and Schapire [2006] claimed that the minimum margin is not essential, while the margin distribution characterized by *average margin* or *median margin* may be essential.

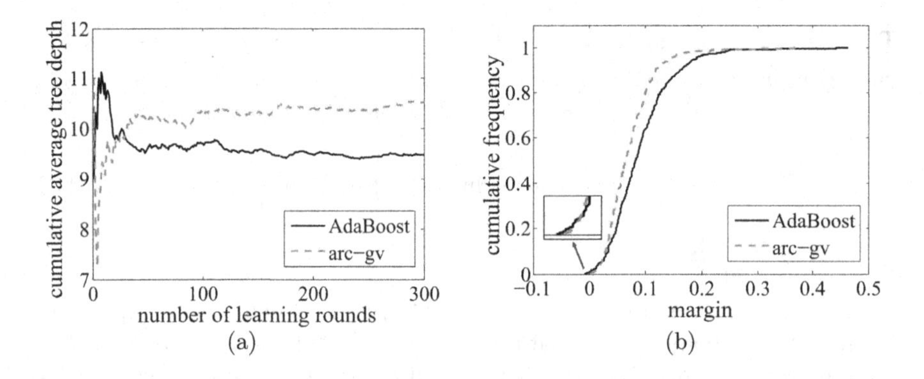

Figure 2.10: (a) Tree depth and (b) margin distribution of AdaBoost against arc-gv on the UCI *clean1* data set.

Though Reyzin and Schapire [2006] showed that the empirical attack of Breiman [1999] is not deadly, it is far from validating the soundness of margin theory. To enable the margin theory to get renascence, it is crucial to have a generalization bound based on margin distribution sharper than Breiman [1999]'s bound based on minimum margin. For this purpose, Wang et al. [2008] presented a sharper bound in term of *equilibrium margin*. However, it considered factors somewhat different from that considered by Schapire et al. [1998] and Breiman [1999]. Thus, it is unclear whether the sharpness owes to that equilibrium margin is more crucial, or the use of more information. Moreover, equilibrium margin is too un-intuitive to inspire algorithm design. Later, Gao and Zhou [2010b, 2013] proved that both minimum margin and equilibrium margin are just special cases of the *k-th margin*, all of them are *single margins* that could not measure margin distribution.

Fortunately, by considering exactly the same factors as in [Schapire et al., 1998, Breiman, 1999], Gao and Zhou [2013] proved a new margin theory:

Theorem 2.3 ([Gao and Zhou, 2013]). *For any $\delta > 0$, with probability at least $1 - \delta$ over the random choice of sample D with size $m \geq 5$, every voting classifier $H \in \mathcal{C}(\mathcal{H})$ satisfies the following bound:*

$$\epsilon_{\mathcal{D}} \leq \frac{2}{m} + \inf_{\theta \in (0,1]} \left[P_{\boldsymbol{x} \sim D}[f(\boldsymbol{x})H(\boldsymbol{x}) < \theta] + \frac{7\mu + 3\sqrt{3\mu}}{3m} + \sqrt{\frac{3\mu}{m} P_{\boldsymbol{x} \sim D}[f(\boldsymbol{x})H(\boldsymbol{x}) < \theta]} \right], \tag{2.34}$$

where $\mu = \frac{8}{\theta^2} \ln m \ln(2|\mathcal{H}|) + \ln \frac{2|\mathcal{H}|}{\delta}$.

The generalization bound (2.34) is uniformly sharper than both the bounds of Schapire et al. [1998] and Breiman [1999]. Reminding that all of them are generalization upper bounds, [Grønlund et al., 2019] proved that Gao and

Zhou [2013]'s bound nearly matches the lower bound, and they concluded that "*one cannot hope for much stronger upper bounds*". Thus, the generalization characterization of AdaBoost in terms of margins is finally resolved.

Gao and Zhou [2013]'s theory implies that both **margin-mean** and **margin-variance** are fundamentally crucial; this is the first time for the community to find that the margin theory does *not* rely on a *single* factor. The question of why AdaBoost seems resistant to overfitting gets finally answered: AdaBoost can improve margin-mean and decrease margin-variance even after its training error reaches zero, leading to its further improvement of generalization performance. However, this also implies that AdaBoost will finally overfit, when it could neither improve margin-mean nor decrease margin-variance further, though this appears very late in the training process.

2.5 Gradient Boosting and Implementations

2.5.1 Gradient Boosting

Gradient Boosting [Friedman, 2001] is a result from the statistical analysis of AdaBoost introduced in Section 2.4.2. In contrast to AdaBoost which is believed to optimize the exponential loss function, Gradient Boosting allows optimization of arbitrary differentiable loss functions, and can be used in both regression and classification tasks. It still runs in a stage-wise fashion. When decision trees are used as base learners, the algorithm is called GBDT (i.e., Gradient-Boosted Decision Trees).

From a statistical perspective, supervised learning can be viewed as finding a function $H^*(\boldsymbol{x})$ that best approximates the ground-truth real-valued output variable y from the input variable $\boldsymbol{x}$ *i.i.d.* sampled from distribution $\mathcal{D}$. By introducing a loss function ℓ, this can be formulated as

$$H^*(\boldsymbol{x}) = \arg\min_{H} \mathbb{E}_{\boldsymbol{x}\sim\mathcal{D}}\, \ell(y, H(\boldsymbol{x})). \tag{2.35}$$

Similar to additive model (2.1), H is a linear combination of base learners $h_i(\boldsymbol{x})$ from some function class $\mathcal{H}$, i.e.,

$$H(\boldsymbol{x}) = \sum_{t=1}^{T} \alpha_t h_t(\boldsymbol{x}) + c, \tag{2.36}$$

where T is the ensemble size and c is a constant.

Given training set $D = \{(\boldsymbol{x}_1, y_1), \ldots, (\boldsymbol{x}_m, y_m)\}$, Gradient Boosting follows the **empirical risk minimization** principle [Zhou, 2021, Section 12.4] and tries to find $H^*(\boldsymbol{x})$ which minimizes the empirical risk in a greedy fashion, i.e.,

$$H_t(\boldsymbol{x}) = H_{t-1}(\boldsymbol{x}) + \arg\min_{h_t\in\mathcal{H}} \left[\sum_{i=1}^{m} \ell\left(y_i - H_{t-1}\left(\boldsymbol{x}_i\right), h_t\left(\boldsymbol{x}_i\right)\right)\right], \tag{2.37}$$

Input: Data set $D = \{(\boldsymbol{x}_1, y_1), (\boldsymbol{x}_2, y_2), \ldots, (\boldsymbol{x}_m, y_m)\}$;
Differentiable loss function $\ell(y, H(\boldsymbol{x}))$;
Base learning algorithm $\mathfrak{L}$;
Number of learning rounds T.

Process:
1. $w_{1,i} = 1/m, \ (i \in \{1, \ldots, m\})$;
2. $H_0(\boldsymbol{x}) = \arg\min_c \sum_{i=1}^m \ell(y_i, c)$;
3. **for** $t = 1, \ldots, T$:
4. $\quad r_{it} = -\nabla_{H_{t-1}} \ell(y_i, H_{t-1}(\boldsymbol{x}_i)) \ (i \in \{1, \ldots, m\})$;
5. $\quad D_t = \{(\boldsymbol{x}_i, r_{it})\} \ (i \in \{1, \ldots, m\})$;
6. $\quad h_t = \mathfrak{L}(D_t, \boldsymbol{w})$;
7. $\quad \gamma_t = \arg\min_\gamma \sum_{i=1}^m \ell(y_i, H_{t-1}(\boldsymbol{x}_i) + \gamma h_t(\boldsymbol{x}_i))$;
8. $\quad H_t(\boldsymbol{x}) = H_{t-1}(\boldsymbol{x}) + \gamma_t h_t(\boldsymbol{x})$;
9. **end**

Output: $H_T(\boldsymbol{x})$.

Figure 2.11: The Gradient Boosting algorithm.

where H_0 is a constant that minimizes the empirical risk, i.e.,

$$H_0(\boldsymbol{x}) = \arg\min_c \sum_{i=1}^m \ell(y_i, c) \ . \tag{2.38}$$

Unfortunately, solving the minimization problem at each step is computationally infeasible. The basic idea of Gradient Boosting is to apply steepest descent. Note that the local maximum-descent direction of the loss function is the direction of negative gradient, we can have the linear approximation

$$H_t(\boldsymbol{x}) = H_{t-1}(\boldsymbol{x}) - \gamma \sum_{i=1}^m \nabla_{H_{t-1}} \ell(y_i, H_{t-1}(\boldsymbol{x}_i)) \ , \tag{2.39}$$

where $\gamma > 0$ is small. Then, we have

$$\gamma_t = \arg\min_\gamma \left[\sum_{i=1}^m \ell\left(y_i, H_{t-1}(\boldsymbol{x}_i) - \gamma \nabla_{H_{t-1}} \ell(y_i, H_{t-1}(\boldsymbol{x}_i))\right) \right] \ , \tag{2.40}$$

which is an one-dimensional optimization problem that can be efficiently solved via linear search. Figure 2.11 summarizes the process of the Gradient Boosting algorithm. GBDT is obtained when a decision tree learning algorithm is used as the base learning algorithm.

Various regularization techniques can be used to decrease the risk of overfitting. For example, the number of Boosting rounds T and tree depth in GBDT are natural regularization parameters. Increasing T may decrease training error, but may lead to overfitting; the deeper the trees, the larger the overfitting risk. Friedman [2002] proposed a minor modification which fits the base learners on subsamples of the training set drawn at random without replacement, and observed a substantial improvement in accuracy. Hastie et al. [2016] proposed to use **shrinkage** for regularization, and modified the update rule as

$$H_t(\boldsymbol{x}) = H_{t-1}(\boldsymbol{x}) + \nu \cdot \gamma_t \cdot h_t(\boldsymbol{x}), \tag{2.41}$$

where $0 \leq \nu \leq 1$ is the learning rate. Empirical studies show that using small learning rate (e.g., $\nu < 0.1$) leads to better generalization performance.

2.5.2 XGBoost and LightGBM

Gradient Boosting cannot become a widely used algorithm without the help of excellent implementations, particularly the off-the-shelf powerful tools XGBoost[3] [Chen and Guestrin, 2016] and LightGBM[4] [Ke et al., 2017].

Decision tree learning requires to scan all instances and features to find the best split for each node, making their computational workload proportional to both the number of features and the number of instances. XGBoost (eXtreme Gradient Boosting) is an open-source machine learning package, with a series of engineering innovations to make GBDT scalable and efficient.

The key of decision tree learning is to find the best split for each node. For this purpose, exact algorithms enumerate over all possible splits on all features; this is powerful but infeasible when data is too big to be held in memory entirely, or in distributed setting where the data is naturally distributed in different machines. Chen and Guestrin [2016] employed approximated mechanisms. Specifically, candidate splitting points are identified according to percentiles of feature distribution, and continuous features are then mapped into buckets split by these candidate points, and finally, the best split among the candidates are selected based on the aggregated statistics. Depending on the time for the candidates to be generated, there are two variants. The global method considers all possible candidate splits in the whole process, whereas the local method considers candidates after each split. It seems that the global method requires less effort for generating the candidates; in practice, however, it usually considers too many candidate splits than that are needed, whereas the local method is more appropriate for deeper trees. Using percentiles will lead to evenly distributed splits. To improve the split distribution, *quantile sketch* based on quantile summary data structure and merge/prune options can be used when every instance is equally important. A *weighted* quantile summary structure is designed to enable the use of weighted instances in Boosting.

Another major issue is about sparse pattern, which may be caused by missing values, or frequent zero entries, or artifacts of feature engineering such as one-hot encoding. To improve the efficiency, Chen and Guestrin [2016]

[3] https://github.com/dmlc/xgboost

[4] https://github.com/Microsoft/LightGBM/

proposed to add a default direction in each node. When a value is missing in a sparse instance, it is classified into the default direction. The optimal default directions are learned from the data, where the key is to visit the non-missing entries only. In this way, XGBoost provides a unified way to handle sparse patterns, and makes computation complexity linear to the number of non-missing entries.

XGBoost also utilizes out-of-core computation, data compression and sharding for scaling to large-scale data with the least amount of hardware resource.

LightGBM (Light Gradient Boosting Machine) is another open-source machine learning package based on Gradient Boosting. It shares many advantages of XGBoost, such as sparse optimization, parallel training, meanwhile it also improves the efficiency and scalability significantly when the feature dimension is high and data size is large. Specifically, the computational bottleneck of GBDT training lies in the fact that for each feature, it needs to scan all instances to compute information required to determine the candidate split. A straightforward idea is to reduce the number of data instances and the number of features by sampling, and there are some work that samples the data set according to instance weights to accelerate the training process. However, they could not be directly applied because GBDT does not use weighted instances at all. To tackle this problem, Ke et al. [2017] proposed two novel techniques.

The first is Gradient-based One-Side Sampling (GOSS). Though the instances are with equal weights, it is noteworthy that data instances with different gradients play different roles. Specifically, instances with larger gradients (i.e., under-trained instances) will contribute more to the information computation. Thus, Ke et al. [2017] proposed to keep instances with large gradients and only randomly downsample instances with small gradients.

The second is Exclusive Feature Bundling (EFB). Usually in real applications, though there are a large number of features, the feature space is generally sparse. Thus, it is possible to design a nearly lossless approach to reduce the number of effective features. Specifically, in a sparse feature space, many features are almost exclusive, i.e., they rarely take nonzero values simultaneously; such exclusive features can be safely bundled. To the end, Ke et al. [2017] designed an efficient greedy algorithm with a constant approximation ratio.

2.6 Extensions

2.6.1 Multi-Class Learning

The original proposal of AdaBoost focuses on binary classification, i.e., $\mathcal{Y} = \{+1, -1\}$. In many tasks, however, an instance belongs to one of many instead of two classes. For example, a handwritten digit belongs to one of the 10 classes, i.e., $\mathcal{Y} = \{0, \ldots, 9\}$. There are many alternative ways to extend AdaBoost to **multi-class learning**.

AdaBoost.M1 [Freund and Schapire, 1997] is a very straightforward extension, which is the same as the algorithm shown in Figure 2.2 except that the base learners now are multi-class learners instead of binary classifiers. This algorithm could not use binary classifiers, and has an overly strong constraint that every base learner has less than 1/2 multi-class 0/1-loss.

SAMME [Zhu et al., 2006] is an improvement over AdaBoost.M1, which replaces line 6 of AdaBoost.M1 in Figure 2.2 by

$$\alpha_t = \frac{1}{2}\ln\left(\frac{1-\epsilon_t}{\epsilon_t}\right) + \ln(|\mathcal{Y}|-1) \ . \tag{2.42}$$

This modification is derived from the minimization of multi-class exponential loss, and it was proved that, similar to the case of binary classification, optimizing the multi-class exponential loss approaches to the Bayes error rate, i.e.,

$$\mathtt{sign}(h^*(\boldsymbol{x})) = \arg\max_{y\in\mathcal{Y}} P(y \mid \boldsymbol{x}) \ , \tag{2.43}$$

where h^* is the optimal solution to the multi-class exponential loss.

A commonly used solution to the multi-class classification problem is to decompose the task into multiple binary classification problems. Popular decomposition schemes include **one-versus-rest** and **one-versus-one**. One-versus-rest decomposes a multi-class task of $|\mathcal{Y}|$ classes into $|\mathcal{Y}|$ binary classification tasks, where the i-th task is to classify whether an instance belongs to the i-th class or not. One-versus-one decomposes a multi-class task of $|\mathcal{Y}|$ classes into $\frac{|\mathcal{Y}|(|\mathcal{Y}|-1)}{2}$ binary classification tasks, where each task is to classify whether an instance belongs to, say, the i-th class or the j-th class.

AdaBoost.MH [Schapire and Singer, 1999] follows the one-versus-rest strategy. After training $|\mathcal{Y}|$ number of binary AdaBoost classifiers, the real-value output $H(\boldsymbol{x}) = \sum_{t=1}^{T} \alpha_t h_t(\boldsymbol{x})$ rather than the crisp classification of each AdaBoost classifier is used to identify the most probable class, that is,

$$H(\boldsymbol{x}) = \arg\max_{y\in\mathcal{Y}} H_y(\boldsymbol{x}) \ , \tag{2.44}$$

where H_y is the binary AdaBoost classifier classifying the y-th class from the rest.

AdaBoost.M2 [Freund and Schapire, 1997] follows the one-versus-one strategy, which minimizes a *pseudo-loss*. This algorithm is later generalized to AdaBoost.MR [Schapire and Singer, 1999] which minimizes a *ranking loss* motivated by the fact that the highest ranked class is more likely to be the correct class. Binary classifiers obtained by one-versus-one decomposition can also be aggregated by voting, pairwise coupling, directed acyclic graph, etc. [Hsu and Lin, 2002, Hastie and Tibshirani, 1998]. Voting and pairwise coupling are well-known, and thus, Figure 2.12 only illustrates the use of a directed acyclic graph.

Note that for binary classification, it is well-known that to guarantee the Boostability, the exact requirement for weak learners is to be better than

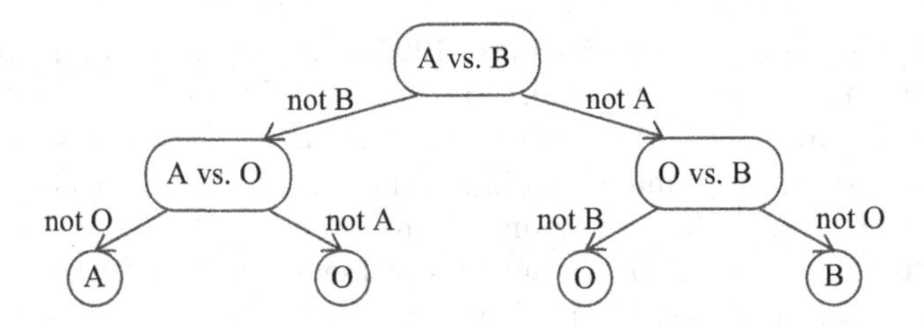

Figure 2.12: A directed acyclic graph that aggregates one-versus-one decomposition for classes of A, B, and O.

random guess [Freund and Schapire, 1997]. While for multi-class problems, it remains a mystery until the work by Mukherjee and Schapire [2010].

Mukherjee and Schapire [2010] adopted a game-theoretic view of Boosting between two players: Booster and Weak-Learner. For simplicity and better understanding, we introduce some different yet essentially equivalent notations as follows: Let $D = \{(\boldsymbol{x}_1, y_1), (\boldsymbol{x}_2, y_2), \ldots, (\boldsymbol{x}_m, y_m)\}$ be a training data set with $\boldsymbol{x}_i \in \mathcal{X}$ and $y_i \in \mathcal{Y}$. In each iteration for multi-class Boosting, the Booster creates a weight vector $\boldsymbol{w}$ over training data D, i.e., $\sum_{i\in[m]} \boldsymbol{w}_i = 1$ with $\boldsymbol{w}_i \geq 0$, as well as a cost matrix $\mathbf{C} = (C_{i,j})_{|\mathcal{Y}|\times|\mathcal{Y}|}$, where the cost $C_{i,j}$ denotes the cost of misclassifying an instance of the i-th class to the j-th class. See more details on *cost-sensitive learning* in Chapter 10. The Weak-Learner then returns a weak classifier $h(\boldsymbol{x})\colon \mathcal{X} \to \mathcal{Y}$ such that the total cost $\sum_{i=1}^{m} \boldsymbol{w}_i C_{y_i,h(\boldsymbol{x}_i)}$ is small.

Note that the weight vector $\boldsymbol{w}$ and cost matrix $\mathbf{C}$ should conform to certain constrains. By carefully choosing the weight vector and cost matrix in each round, Booster can minimize the total cost for the final result. Let's introduce a baseline matrix $\mathbf{B} = (B_{i,j})_{|\mathcal{Y}|\times|\mathcal{Y}|}$ to reflect a random guess in multi-class learning. For a weight vector space $\mathcal{W}$, cost matrix space $\mathcal{C}$ and baseline matrix $\mathbf{B}$, a weak classifier space $\mathcal{H}$ satisfies the condition $(\mathcal{W}, \mathcal{C}, \mathbf{B})$ if

$$\forall \boldsymbol{w} \in \mathcal{W}, \mathbf{C} \in \mathcal{C}, \exists h \in \mathcal{H}\colon \sum_{i=1}^{m} \boldsymbol{w}_i C_{y_i,h(\boldsymbol{x}_i)} \leq \sum_{i=1}^{m} \sum_{j=1}^{|\mathcal{Y}|} \boldsymbol{w}_i C_{y_i,j} B_{y_i,j} \,. \tag{2.45}$$

This condition states that a weak classifier should not exceed the average cost according to the baseline matrix $\mathbf{B}$. With different selections of $\boldsymbol{w}$, $\mathbf{C}$ and $\mathbf{B}$, it can reassemble the conditions used previously in AdaBoost.M1 [Freund and Schapire, 1997], AdaBoost.MH [Schapire and Singer, 1999], AdaBoost.MR [Freund and Schapire, 1997, Schapire and Singer, 1999], etc.

2.6.2 Multi-Label Learning

In contrast to multi-class classification where an instance will be assigned with a single label, in **multi-label learning** [Zhou and Zhang, 2017] an instance can be assigned with multiple labels simultaneously. Note that the evaluation of multi-label learning performance is much more complicated than classification; for example, there are various ways to measure which is more serious: misclassifying three labels of one instance or misclassifying one label each for three instances [Wu and Zhou, 2017].

There are different ways to extend AdaBoost for multi-label classification. A straightforward extension is to directly optimize multi-label losses. For examples, Schapire and Singer [1999] introduced AdaBoost.MH for *hamming loss*, and AdaBoost.MR for *ranking loss*. The training procedures of AdaBoost.MH and AdaBoost.MR for multi-label classification are as same as theirs for multi-class learning, but their prediction procedures are quite different. Namely, for multi-label learning, AdaBoost.MH chooses the predicted class labels based on each binary classifier independently, rather than choosing the most probable ones according to (2.44); AdaBoost.MR chooses more than one class labels based on its ranking list of class labels.

When there are large amount of labels, learning an independent learner for each label would become a computational issue. To tackle this issue, Yan et al. [2007] proposed MSSBoost (Model-Shared Subspace Boosting), which maintains a shared pool of base learners each trained from a random feature subspace with a random sample of the whole data set. In each Boosting round, it chooses the best learner from the pool and takes it as the base learner for all the labels.

Note that when every label has a sufficient amount of training examples, multi-label learning can be addressed by training a classifier per label. However, in practice, usually there are labels with insufficient amount of training data, and therefore, the key of multi-label learning lies in the exploitation of **label relationship**, such that labels with rare training data can get help from labels with rich amount of data.

Some approaches assume that the label relationship can be provided by external knowledge resources as prior knowledge, but unfortunately such prior knowledge is often unavailable in real-world applications. Some approaches try to model the label relationship, e.g., by considering label co-occurrence, but this kind of label relationship methods are easy to overfit the training data. Huang et al. [2012] proposed a multi-label Boosting approach named MAHR (Multi-lAbel Hypothesis Reuse), which is able to discover and exploit label relationship automatically in the learning process.

The basic idea is that, if two class labels are closely related, the hypothesis generated for one label could be helpful for the other. MAHR implements the idea with a Boosting approach with a hypothesis reuse mechanism. Specifically, denote by $D = \{(\boldsymbol{x}_1, \boldsymbol{y}_1), (\boldsymbol{x}_2, \boldsymbol{y}_2), \ldots, (\boldsymbol{x}_m, \boldsymbol{y}_m)\}$ a multi-label data set of m instances with L possible labels, where $\boldsymbol{x}_i$ is the i-th instance, and the corresponding $\boldsymbol{y}_i$ is a label vector of dimension L, whose l-th element, i.e., $y_i^l = 1$ if the l-th label is a proper label and -1 otherwise. As shown in Figure 2.13, MAHR maintains the general outline of Boosting. In each round t, it generates a base learner for each label. For the l-th label, it first trains a hypothesis $\hat{h}_{t,l}$ from its own hypothesis space (Step 4), and then use a *reuse function* R to generate another hypothesis $h_{t,l}$ from both $\hat{h}_{t,l}$ and the reuse

---

Input: Data set $D = \{(\boldsymbol{x}_1, \boldsymbol{y}_1), (\boldsymbol{x}_2, \boldsymbol{y}_2), \ldots, (\boldsymbol{x}_m, \boldsymbol{y}_m)\}$;
Base learning algorithm $\mathfrak{L}$;
Reuse function R;
Number of learning rounds T.

Process:
1. Initialize $D_{1,l} = \frac{1}{m}, Q_{1,l} = \varnothing$;
2. **for** $t = 1, \ldots, T$:
3. **for** $l = 1, \ldots, L$:
4. $\hat{h}_{t,l} = \mathfrak{L}(D, D_{t,l})$;
5. $h_{t,l} = R(\hat{h}_{t,l}, Q_{t,l})$ such that $h_{t,l}(\cdot) \in [-1, 1]$;
6. $\gamma_{t,l} = \frac{1}{2}\sum_i D_{t,l}(i) h_{t,l}(\boldsymbol{x}_i) y_i^l, \quad \alpha_{t,l} = \frac{1}{2}\ln(\frac{0.5+\gamma_{t,l}}{0.5-\gamma_{t,l}})$;
7. $D_{t+1,l}(i) = \left(1 + \exp\left(y_i^l \sum_{j=1}^t \alpha_{j,l} h_{j,l}(\boldsymbol{x}_i)\right)\right)^{-1}$;
8. $H_{t,l} = \sum_{j=1}^t \alpha_{j,l} h_{j,l}$;
9. $Q_{t+1,l} = \{H_{t,k} \mid k \neq l\} \cup \{-H_{t,k} \mid k \neq l\}$;
10. **end**
11. **end**

Output: $H_l(\boldsymbol{x}) = \sum_{t=1}^T \alpha_{t,l} h_{t,l} \qquad (l = 1, 2, \ldots, L)$

Figure 2.13: The MAHR algorithm.

of the hypotheses in the candidate set $Q_{t,l}$ (line 5). Then, based on Boosting framework, the combination weights and training set distribution are updated. Note that the candidate set for reuse in round $t+1$ on label l is defined as $Q_{t+1,l} = \{H_{t,k} \mid k \neq l\} \bigcup \{-H_{t,k} \mid k \neq l\}$ (Step 9), where $H_{t,k}$ is the combined hypothesis for label k up to round t, and $-H_{t,k}$ is included for the simplicity of optimization.

In MAHR, the reuse function R is employed to combine multiple hypotheses, and it can be implemented in different ways. Huang et al. [2012] implemented R via weighted linear combination. Formally, given a hypothesis pool $Q_{t,l}$ and a newly generated hypothesis $\hat{h}_{t,l}$ at the t-th round on the l-th label, the reuse function $R_{\boldsymbol{\beta}_{t,l}}$ is defined as

$$R_{\boldsymbol{\beta}_{t,l}}(\hat{h}_{t,l}, Q_{t,l}) = \boldsymbol{\beta}_{t,l}(\hat{h}_{t,l}) \cdot \hat{h}_{t,l} + \sum_{H \in Q_{t,l}} \boldsymbol{\beta}_{t,l}(H) \cdot H \;, \tag{2.46}$$

where $\boldsymbol{\beta}_{t,l}$ is the reuse weight vector and $\boldsymbol{\beta}_{t,l}(H)$ denotes the element of $\boldsymbol{\beta}_{t,l}$ corresponding to H. In practice, different methods can be employed to determine the parameter $\boldsymbol{\beta}$, for example, by minimizing different multi-label losses.

Since MAHR reuses hypotheses across labels, the amount of reuse can be considered as a measure of label relationship. If two labels are independent, the hypothesis for one label will be less useful to construct the hypothesis of the other label, and thus the reuse function will assign a very small weight to it; if two labels are strongly related, a large weight will be there. Therefore, by defining the *reuse score* from label j to i as

$$S(i,j) = \sum_{t=2}^{T} \alpha_{t,i}(\beta_{t,i}(H_{t-1,j}) - \beta_{t,i}(-H_{t-1,j})) \ , \tag{2.47}$$

where $\alpha_{t,i}$ is the weight of $h_{t,i}$, we can find that $S(i,j)$ assesses how much label j can help the learning of label i. It is worth noting that, unlike the commonly used relationship, such as label co-occurrence, the reuse score is not constrained to be symmetric, i.e., $S(i,j)$ does not necessarily equal $S(j,i)$.

2.6.3 Noise Tolerance

Real-world data are often noisy. The AdaBoost algorithm, however, was originally designed for clean data and has been observed to be very sensitive to noise. The noise sensitivity of AdaBoost is generally attributed to the exponential loss function (2.2) which specifies that if an instance were not classified to its given label, the weight of the instance will increase drastically. Consequently, when a training instance is associated with a noisy label, AdaBoost still tries to make the prediction according to it, and thus degenerates the performance.

MadaBoost [Domingo and Watanabe, 2000] improves AdaBoost by depressing large instance weights. It is almost the same as AdaBoost except for the weight updating rule. Recall the weight updating rule of AdaBoost, i.e.,

$$\begin{aligned} \mathcal{D}_{t+1}(\boldsymbol{x}) &= \tfrac{\mathcal{D}_t(\boldsymbol{x})}{Z_t} \times \begin{cases} e^{-\alpha_t}, & \text{if } h_t(\boldsymbol{x}) = f(\boldsymbol{x}) \\ e^{\alpha_t}, & \text{if } h_t(\boldsymbol{x}) \neq f(\boldsymbol{x}) \end{cases} \\ &= \tfrac{\mathcal{D}_t(\boldsymbol{x})}{Z_t} \times e^{-\alpha_t \cdot h_t(\boldsymbol{x}) \cdot f(\boldsymbol{x})} \\ &= \tfrac{\mathcal{D}_1(\boldsymbol{x})}{Z'_t} \times \textstyle\prod_{i=1}^{t} e^{-\alpha_i \cdot h_i(\boldsymbol{x}) \cdot f(\boldsymbol{x})} \ , \end{aligned} \tag{2.48}$$

where Z_t and Z'_t are the normalization terms. It can be seen that, if the prediction on an instance is different from its given label for a number of rounds, the term $\prod_{i=1}^{t} e^{-\alpha_i \cdot h_i(\boldsymbol{x}) \cdot f(\boldsymbol{x})}$ will grow very large, pushing the instance to be classified according to the given label in the next round. To reduce the undesired dramatic increase of instance weights caused by noise, MadaBoost sets an upper limit on the weights:

$$\mathcal{D}_{t+1}(\boldsymbol{x}) = \frac{\mathcal{D}_1(\boldsymbol{x})}{Z'_t} \times \min\left\{1, \prod_{i=1}^{t} e^{-\alpha_i \cdot h_i(\boldsymbol{x}) \cdot f(\boldsymbol{x})}\right\} \ , \tag{2.49}$$

where Z'_t is the normalization term. By using this weight updating rule, the instance weights will not grow too dramatically.

FilterBoost [Bradley and Schapire, 2007] does not employ the exponential loss function used in AdaBoost, but adopts the log loss function (2.21). Similar to the derivation of AdaBoost in Section 2.2, we consider fitting an additive model to minimize the log loss function. At round t, denote the combined learner as H_{t-1} and the classifier to be trained as h_t. Using the Taylor expansion of the loss function, we have

$$\begin{aligned}
\ell_{log}(H_{t-1} + h_t \mid \mathcal{D}) &= \mathbb{E}_{\boldsymbol{x}\sim\mathcal{D}}\left[-\ln \frac{1}{1+e^{-f(\boldsymbol{x})(H_{t-1}(\boldsymbol{x})+h_t(\boldsymbol{x}))}}\right] \\
&\approx \mathbb{E}_{\boldsymbol{x}\sim\mathcal{D}}\left[\ln(1+e^{-f(\boldsymbol{x})H_{t-1}(\boldsymbol{x})}) - \frac{f(\boldsymbol{x})h_t(\boldsymbol{x})}{1+e^{f(\boldsymbol{x})H_{t-1}(\boldsymbol{x})}} + \frac{e^{f(\boldsymbol{x})H_{t-1}(\boldsymbol{x})}}{2(1+e^{f(\boldsymbol{x})H_{t-1}(\boldsymbol{x})})^2}\right] \\
&\approx \mathbb{E}_{\boldsymbol{x}\sim\mathcal{D}}\left[-\frac{f(\boldsymbol{x})h_t(\boldsymbol{x})}{1+e^{f(\boldsymbol{x})H_{t-1}(\boldsymbol{x})}}\right], \qquad (2.50)
\end{aligned}$$

by noticing that $f(\boldsymbol{x})^2 = 1$ and $h_t(\boldsymbol{x})^2 = 1$. To minimize the loss function, h_t needs to satisfy

$$\begin{aligned}
h_t &= \arg\min_h \ell_{log}(H_{t-1} + h \mid \mathcal{D}) \\
&= \arg\max_h \mathbb{E}_{\boldsymbol{x}\sim\mathcal{D}}\left[\frac{f(\boldsymbol{x})h(\boldsymbol{x})}{1+e^{f(\boldsymbol{x})H_{t-1}(\boldsymbol{x})}}\right] \\
&= \arg\max_h \mathbb{E}_{\boldsymbol{x}\sim\mathcal{D}}\left[\frac{f(\boldsymbol{x})h(\boldsymbol{x})}{Z_t(1+e^{f(\boldsymbol{x})H_{t-1}(\boldsymbol{x})})}\right] \\
&= \arg\max_h \mathbb{E}_{\boldsymbol{x}\sim\mathcal{D}_t}\left[f(\boldsymbol{x})h(\boldsymbol{x})\right], \qquad (2.51)
\end{aligned}$$

where $Z_t = \mathbb{E}_{\boldsymbol{x}\sim\mathcal{D}}[\frac{1}{1+e^{f(\boldsymbol{x})H_{t-1}(\boldsymbol{x})}}]$ is the normalization factor, and the weight updating rule is

$$\mathcal{D}_t(\boldsymbol{x}) = \frac{\mathcal{D}(\boldsymbol{x})}{Z_t}\frac{1}{1+e^{f(\boldsymbol{x})H_{t-1}(\boldsymbol{x})}}. \qquad (2.52)$$

It is evident that with this updating rule, the increase of the instance weights is upper bounded by 1, similar to the weight depressing in MadaBoost, but smoother.

The BBM (Boosting-By-Majority) [Freund, 1995] algorithm was the first iterative Boosting algorithm. Though it is noise tolerant [Aslam and Decatur, 1993], it requires the user to specify mysterious parameters in advance. In fact, AdaBoost was motivated by removing the impractical requirement of specifying unknown parameters of BBM. BrownBoost [Freund, 2001] is another adaptive version of BBM, which inherits BBM's noise tolerance property. Derived from the loss function of BBM, which is an accumulated binomial distribution, the loss function of BrownBoost is corresponding to the *Brownian motion process* [Gardiner, 2004], i.e.,

$$\ell_{bmp}(H_{t-1} + h_t \mid \mathcal{D}) = \mathbb{E}_{\boldsymbol{x}\sim\mathcal{D}}\left[1 - erf\left(\frac{f(\boldsymbol{x})H_{t-1}(\boldsymbol{x}) + f(\boldsymbol{x})h_t(\boldsymbol{x}) + c - t}{\sqrt{c}}\right)\right], \qquad (2.53)$$

where the parameter c specifies the total *time* for the Boosting procedure, t is the current time which starts from zero and increases in each round, and $erf(\cdot)$ is the error function

$$erf(a) = \frac{1}{\pi}\int_{-\infty}^{a} e^{-x^2} dx \; . \tag{2.54}$$

The loss function (2.53) can be expanded as

$$\begin{aligned}\ell_{bmp}(H_{t-1} + h_t \mid \mathcal{D}) &\approx \mathbb{E}_{\boldsymbol{x}\sim\mathcal{D}}\left[\begin{array}{l}1 - erf(\frac{1}{\sqrt{c}}(f(\boldsymbol{x})H_{t-1}(\boldsymbol{x}) + c - t)) \\ -\frac{2}{c\pi}e^{-(f(\boldsymbol{x})H_{t-1}(\boldsymbol{x})+c-t)^2/c}f(\boldsymbol{x})h_t(\boldsymbol{x}) \\ -\frac{4}{c^2\pi}e^{-(f(\boldsymbol{x})H_{t-1}(\boldsymbol{x})+c-t)^2/c}f(\boldsymbol{x})^2h_t(\boldsymbol{x})^2\end{array}\right] \\ &\approx -\mathbb{E}_{\boldsymbol{x}\sim\mathcal{D}}\left[e^{-(f(\boldsymbol{x})H_{t-1}(\boldsymbol{x})+c-t)^2/c}f(\boldsymbol{x})h_t(\boldsymbol{x})\right] \; , \end{aligned} \tag{2.55}$$

and thus, the learner which minimizes the loss function is

$$\begin{aligned}h_t &= \arg\min_h \ell_{bmp}(H_{t-1} + h \mid \mathcal{D}) \\ &= \arg\max_h \mathbb{E}_{\boldsymbol{x}\sim\mathcal{D}}\left[e^{-(f(\boldsymbol{x})H_{t-1}(\boldsymbol{x})+c-t)^2/c}f(\boldsymbol{x})h(\boldsymbol{x})\right] \\ &= \arg\max_h \mathbb{E}_{\boldsymbol{x}\sim\mathcal{D}_t}\left[f(\boldsymbol{x})h(\boldsymbol{x})\right] \; , \end{aligned} \tag{2.56}$$

where the weight updating rule is

$$\mathcal{D}_t(\boldsymbol{x}) = \frac{\mathcal{D}(\boldsymbol{x})}{Z_t}e^{-(f(\boldsymbol{x})H_{t-1}(\boldsymbol{x})+c-t)^2/c} \; , \tag{2.57}$$

and Z_t is the normalization term. Note that the weighting function used at here, i.e., $e^{-(f(\boldsymbol{x})H_{t-1}(\boldsymbol{x})+c-t)^2/c}$ is quite different from that used in the Boosting algorithms introduced before. When the classification margin $f(\boldsymbol{x})H_{t-1}(\boldsymbol{x})$ equals the negative remaining time $-(c-t)$, the weight reaches the largest and will decrease as the margin goes whatever larger or smaller. This implies that BrownBoost/BBM "gives up" on some very hard training instances. With more learning rounds, $-(c-t)$ approaches 0. This implies that BrownBoost/BBM pushes the margin on most instances to be positive, whereas leaving alone the remaining hard instances that could be noise.

RobustBoost [Freund, 2009] is an improvement of BrownBoost, aiming at improving the noise tolerance ability by Boosting the normalized classification margin, which is believed to be related to their characterization of generalization error (see Section 2.4.3). Instead of minimizing the classification error, RobustBoost tries to minimize

$$\mathbb{E}_{\boldsymbol{x}\sim\mathcal{D}}\left[\mathbb{I}\left(\frac{\sum_{t=1}^{T}\alpha_t f(\boldsymbol{x})h_t(\boldsymbol{x})}{\sum_{t=1}^{T}\alpha_t} \leq \theta\right)\right] \; , \tag{2.58}$$

where θ is the goal margin. For this purpose, the Brownian motion process in BrownBoost is changed to the mean-reverting *Ornstein-Uhlenbeck process* [Gardiner, 2004], with the loss function

$$\ell_{oup}(H_{t-1} + h_t \mid \mathcal{D}) = \mathbb{E}_{\boldsymbol{x}\sim\mathcal{D}}\left[1 - erf\left(\frac{\tilde{m}(H_{t-1}(\boldsymbol{x}) + h_t(\boldsymbol{x})) - \mu(\frac{t}{c})}{\sigma(\frac{t}{c})}\right)\right] , \tag{2.59}$$

where $\tilde{m}(H)$ is the normalized margin of H, $0 \leq \frac{t}{c} \leq 1$, and

$$\mu(\frac{t}{c}) = (\theta - 2\rho)e^{1-\frac{t}{c}} + 2\rho , \tag{2.60}$$

$$\sigma(\frac{t}{c})^2 = (\sigma_f^2 + 1)e^{2(1-\frac{t}{c})} - 1 , \tag{2.61}$$

are respectively the mean and variance of the process, ρ, σ_f as well as θ are parameters of the algorithm. By a similar derivation as that of BrownBoost, the weight updating rule of RobustBoost is

$$\mathcal{D}_t(\boldsymbol{x}) = \frac{\mathcal{D}(\boldsymbol{x})}{Z_t} e^{-(f(\boldsymbol{x})H_{t-1}(\boldsymbol{x}) - \mu(\frac{t}{c}))^2/(2\sigma(\frac{t}{c})^2)} . \tag{2.62}$$

A major difference between the weighting functions (2.62) of RobustBoost and (2.57) of BrownBoost lies in the fact that $\mu(\frac{t}{c})$ approaches θ as t approaches the total time c. Thus, RobustBoost pushes the normalized classification margin to be larger than the goal margin θ, whereas BrownBoost just pushes the classification margin to be larger than zero.

2.7 Further Readings

Computational learning theory studies fundamental theoretical issues of learning. First introduced by Valiant [1984], the **Probably Approximately Correct (PAC)** framework models learning algorithms in a distribution free manner. Roughly speaking, for binary classification, a problem is *learnable* or *strongly learnable* if there exists an algorithm that outputs a learner h in polynomial time such that for all $0 < \delta, \epsilon \leq 0.5$, $P(\mathbb{E}_{\boldsymbol{x}\sim\mathcal{D}}[\mathbb{I}[h(\boldsymbol{x}) \neq f(\boldsymbol{x})]] < \epsilon) \geq 1 - \delta$, and a problem is *weakly learnable* if there exists an algorithm that outputs a learner with error $0.5 - 1/p$ where p is a polynomial in problem size and other parameters. [Anthony and Biggs, 1992, Kearns and Vazirani, 1994] provide nice introductions to computational learning theory.

In 1990, Schapire [1990] proved that the *strongly learnable* problem class equals the *weakly learnable* problem class, which was an open problem raised by Kearns and Valiant [1989]. The proof was a construction, i.e., the first Boosting algorithm. One year later, Freund developed the more efficient BBM algorithm, which was later published in [Freund, 1995]. Both algorithms, however, suffered from the practical deficiency that the error bounds of the base learners need to be known in advance. Later in 1995, Freund and Schapire [1995, 1997] developed the AdaBoost algorithm, which avoids the requirement on unknown parameters, thus named as *adaptive Boosting.* The AdaBoost paper [Freund and Schapire, 1997] won its authors the *Gödel Prize* in 2003 and the *ACM Paris Kanellakis Theory and Practice Award* in 2004.

Besides Breiman [1999]'s arc-gv, Harries [1999] also constructed an algorithm with empirical results showing that the minimum margin is not crucial for margin theory. Gao and Zhou [2013] proved their new theory based on the empirical Bernstein inequality [Maurer and Pontil, 2009], showing that it is crucial to pay attention to the maximization of margin-mean and minimization of margin-variance simultaneously. Note that the classic statistical learning algorithm, support vector machines, pay attention to just the maximization of minimum margin. Gao and Zhou [2013]'s result inspired the development of a series of Optimal margin Distribution Machines (ODMs) by replacing the optimization of minimum-margin in SVMs by the optimization of margin-mean and margin-variance simultaneously. Gao and Zhou [2013]'s result not only addresses the long-standing fundamental theoretical issue that why AdaBoost seems resistant to overfitting, but also implies that AdaBoost will finally overfit though very late in training process, confirmed with empirical observations reported in [Grove and Schuurmans, 1998]. Grønlund et al. [2019] proved that Gao and Zhou [2013]'s result about AdaBoost is nearly tight and one cannot hope for much stronger result. Later, Grønlund et al. [2020] tried to extend to Gradient Boosting, but assumed that every base learner is equally important, which is more close to Bagging and deviates from the running style of Boosting algorithms where different base learners are with unequal importance.

In addition to what have been introduced in Section 2.4, there are other theoretical studies about Boosting. For example, Breiman [2004a] proposed the population theory for Boosting, Bickel et al. [2006] considered Boosting as the Gauss-Southwell minimization of a loss function, etc. The **stability** of AdaBoost has also been studied [Kutin and Niyogi, 2002, Gao and Zhou, 2010a]. The **bias-variance decomposition** [Geman et al., 1992], which will be introduced in Section 5.2.2, has been employed to empirically study why AdaBoost achieves excellent performance, and it has been observed that AdaBoost primarily decreases the bias though it can also decrease the variance [Bauer and Kohavi, 1999, Breiman, 1996a, Zhou et al., 2002c].

Gradient Boosting has a variety of names in the literature. Friedman [2001] originally proposed it with the name of *Gradient Boosting Machine* (GBM), and later an advanced version *Multiple Additive Regression Trees* (MART) [Friedman and Meulman, 2003]. Mason et al. [1999] called this class of algorithms as *Functional Gradient Boosting*, while Elith et al. [2008] described it as *Boosted Regression Trees* (BRT). CatBoost[5] [Dorogush et al., 2018] is another off-the-shelf tool based on Gradient Boosting, particularly powerful for tasks involving lots of categorical features.

[5]https://github.com/catboost/catboost

Error Correcting Output Codes (ECOC) [Dietterich and Bakiri, 1995] is an important way to extend binary learners to multi-class learners, which will be introduced in Section 4.6.4. Among the alternative ways of characterizing noise in data and how a learning algorithm is resistant to noise, the **statistical query model** [Kearns, 1998] is a PAC compliant theoretical model, in which a learning algorithm learns from queries of noisy expectation values of hypotheses. We call a Boosting algorithm as a **SQ Boosting** if it efficiently boosts noise tolerant weak learners to strong learners. The noise tolerance of MadaBoost was proved by showing that it is a SQ Boosting, by assuming monotonic errors for the weak learners [Domingo and Watanabe, 2000]. Aslam and Decatur [1993] showed that BBM is also a SQ Boosting. In addition to algorithms introduced in Section 2.6, there are many other algorithms, such as GentleBoost [Friedman et al., 2000], trying to improve the robustness of AdaBoost. McDonald et al. [2003] reported an empirical comparison of AdaBoost, LogitBoost and BrownBoost on noisy data. Diakonikolas et al. [2021] studied the Boosting of weak learners in the PAC framework with **Massart noise**, where instance label has been flipped independently with probability $\eta(\boldsymbol{x}) \leq \eta < 1/2$.

Decision stumps (i.e., decision trees of depth one) are often used in AdaBoost as base learners. Considering that for some difficult tasks, simple Boosting stumps are usually insufficient to achieve a strong performance, Deep Boosting [Cortes et al., 2014] attempts to use more complicated base learners, e.g., the set of all decision trees with depth bounded by some relatively large number. In fact, in addition to decision trees and neural networks, Boosting can also be used with various other base learners, e.g., **Conditional Random Fields (CRFs)** [Dietterich et al., 2008], **latent variable models** [Hutchinson et al., 2011], **Generative Adversarial Networks (GANs)**[Tolstikhin et al., 2017].

Chapter 3

Bagging

3.1 Two Ensemble Paradigms

According to how the base learners are generated, roughly speaking, there are two paradigms of ensemble methods, that is, **sequential ensemble methods** where the base learners are generated sequentially, with AdaBoost as a representative, and **parallel ensemble methods** where the base learners are generated in parallel, with Bagging [Breiman, 1996d] as a representative.

The basic motivation of sequential methods is to exploit the *dependence* between the base learners, since the overall performance can be boosted in a *residual minimization* way, as seen in Chapter 2. The basic motivation of parallel ensemble methods is to exploit the *independence* between the base learners, since the error can be reduced dramatically by combining independent base learners.

Take binary classification on classes $\{-1, +1\}$ as an example. Suppose the ground-truth function is f, and each base learner has an independent generalization error ϵ, i.e., for base learner h_i,

$$P(h_i(\boldsymbol{x}) \neq f(\boldsymbol{x})) = \epsilon \ . \tag{3.1}$$

After combining T number of such base classifiers according to

$$H(\boldsymbol{x}) = \texttt{sign}\left(\sum_{i=1}^{T} h_i\left(\boldsymbol{x}\right)\right) , \tag{3.2}$$

the ensemble H makes an error only when at least half of its base classifiers make errors. Therefore, by **Hoeffding inequality**, the generalization error of the ensemble is

$$P\left(H\left(\boldsymbol{x}\right) \neq f(\boldsymbol{x})\right) = \sum_{k=0}^{\lfloor T/2 \rfloor} \binom{T}{k} (1-\epsilon)^k \epsilon^{T-k} \leq \exp\left(-\frac{1}{2}T\left(2\epsilon - 1\right)^2\right) \ . \tag{3.3}$$

(3.3) clearly shows that the generalization error reduces exponentially to the ensemble size T, and ultimately approaches to zero as T approaches to infinity.

DOI: 10.1201/9781003587774-3

Though it is practically impossible to get really independent base learners since they are generated from the same training data set, base learners with less dependence can be obtained by introducing randomness in the learning process, and a good generalization ability can be expected by the ensemble.

Another benefit of the parallel ensemble methods is that they are inherently favorable to parallel computing, and the training speed can be easily accelerated using multi-core computing processors or parallel computers. This is attractive as multi-core processors are commonly available nowadays.

3.2 Bagging

The name Bagging came from the abbreviation of *Bootstrap AGGregatING* [Breiman, 1996d]. As the name implies, the two key ingredients of Bagging are bootstrap and combination.

We know that the combination of independent base learners will lead to a dramatic decrease of errors and therefore, we want to get base learners as independent as possible. Given a training data set, one possibility seems to be sampling a number of non-overlapped data subsets and then training a base learner from each of the subsets. However, since we do not have infinite training data, such a process will produce very small and unrepresentative samples, leading to poor performance of base learners.

Bagging adopts the bootstrap distribution for generating different base learners. In other words, it applies **bootstrap sampling** [Efron and Tibshirani, 1993] to obtain the data subsets for training the base learners. In detail, given a training data set containing m number of training examples, a sample of m training examples will be generated by *sampling with replacement*. Some original examples appear more than once, while some original examples are not present in the sample. By applying the process T times, T samples of m training examples are obtained. Then, from each sample a base learner can be trained by applying the base learning algorithm.

Bagging adopts the most popular strategies for aggregating the outputs of the base learners, that is, *voting* for classification and *averaging* for regression. To predict a test instance, taking classification for example, Bagging feeds the instance to its base classifiers and collects all of their outputs, and then votes the labels and takes the winner label as the prediction, where ties are broken arbitrarily. Note that Bagging can deal with binary classification as well as multi-class classification. The Bagging algorithm is summarized in Figure 3.1.

It is worth mentioning that the bootstrap sampling also offers Bagging another advantage. As Breiman [1996d] indicated, given m training examples, the probability for the i-th training example to be selected $0, 1, 2, \ldots,$ times is approximately Poisson distributed with $\lambda = 1$, and thus, the probability for the i-th example to occur at least once is $1 - (1/e) \approx 0.632$. In other words, for each base learner in Bagging, there are about 36.8% original training examples unused in its training process. The goodness of the base learner can be estimated by using these **out-of-bag** examples, and thereafter the

---

Input: Data set $D = \{(\boldsymbol{x}_1, y_1), (\boldsymbol{x}_2, y_2), \ldots, (\boldsymbol{x}_m, y_m)\}$;
Base learning algorithm $\mathfrak{L}$;
Number of base learners T.

Process:
1. **for** $t = 1, \ldots, T$:
2. $\quad h_t = \mathfrak{L}(D, \mathcal{D}_{bs})$ % $\mathcal{D}_{bs}$ is the bootstrap distribution
3. **end**

Output: $H(\boldsymbol{x}) = \underset{y \in \mathcal{Y}}{\arg\max} \sum_{t=1}^{T} \mathbb{I}(h_t(\boldsymbol{x}) = y)$

Figure 3.1: The Bagging algorithm.

generalization error of the bagged ensemble can be estimated [Breiman, 1996c, Tibshirani, 1996, Wolpert and Macready, 1999].

To get the out-of-bag estimate, we need to record the training examples used for each base learner. Denote $H^{oob}(\boldsymbol{x})$ as the out-of-bag prediction on $\boldsymbol{x}$, where only the learners that have not been trained on $\boldsymbol{x}$ are involved, i.e.,

$$H^{oob}(\boldsymbol{x}) = \underset{y \in \mathcal{Y}}{\arg\max} \sum_{t=1}^{T} \mathbb{I}(h_t(\boldsymbol{x}) = y)\ \mathbb{I}(\boldsymbol{x} \notin D_t)\ . \tag{3.4}$$

Then, the out-of-bag estimate of the generalization error of Bagging is

$$err^{oob} = \frac{1}{|D|} \sum_{(\boldsymbol{x},y) \in D} \mathbb{I}(H^{oob}(\boldsymbol{x}) \neq y)\ . \tag{3.5}$$

The out-of-bag examples can also be used for many other purposes. For example, when decision trees are used as base classifiers, the *posterior* probability of each node of each tree can be estimated using the out-of-bag examples. If a node does not contain out-of-bag examples, it is marked "uncounted". For a test instance, its *posterior* probability can be estimated by averaging the *posterior* probabilities of non-uncounted nodes into which the instance falls.

3.3 Illustrative Examples

To get an intuitive understanding of Bagging, we visualize the decision boundaries of a single decision tree, Bagging and its component decision trees on the *three-Gaussians* data set, as shown in Figure 3.2. It can be observed that the decision boundary of Bagging is more flexible than that of a single decision tree, and this helps to decrease the error from 9.4% of the single decision tree to 8.3% of the Bagged ensemble.

We also evaluate the Bagging algorithm on 40 data sets from the UCI Machine Learning Repository. The Weka implementation of Bagging with 20 base classifiers is tested. We have tried three base learning algorithms: decision

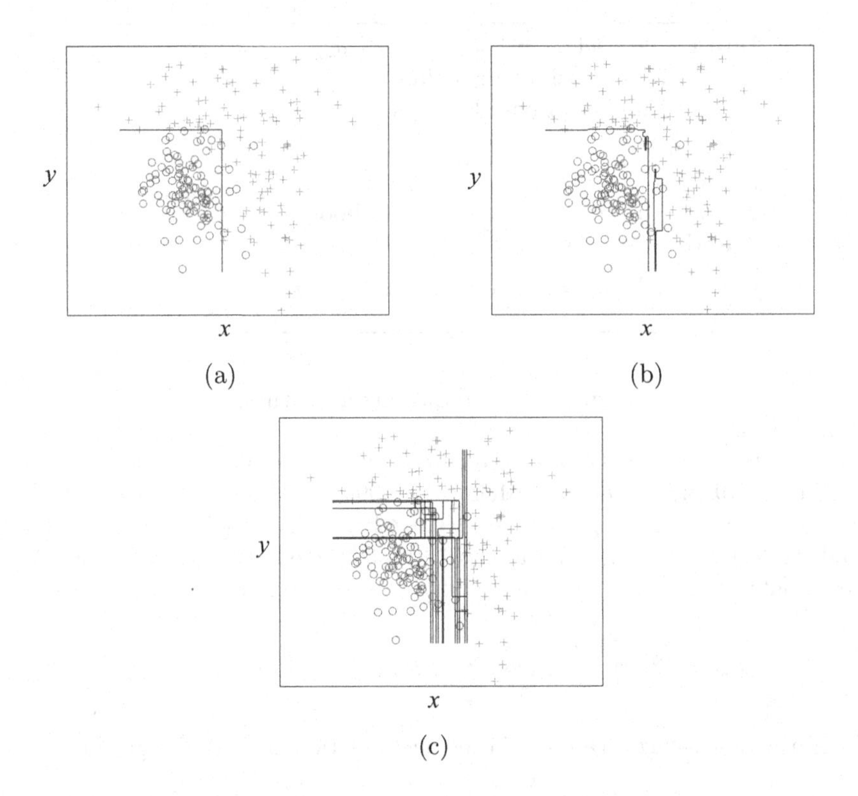

Figure 3.2: Decision boundaries of (a) a single decision tree, (b) Bagging, and (c) the 10 decision trees used by Bagging, on *three-Gaussians*.

stumps, pruned and unpruned J48 decision trees. We plot the comparison results in Figure 3.3, and it can be observed that Bagging often outperforms its base learning algorithm, and rarely hurts performance.

With a further observation on Figure 3.3, it can be found that Bagging using decision stumps is less powerful than Bagging using decision trees. This is easier to see in Figure 3.4.

Remember that Bagging adopts bootstrap sampling to generate different data samples, while all the data samples have large overlap, say, 63.2%, with the original data set. If a base learning algorithm is insensitive to perturbation on training samples, the base learners trained from the data samples may be quite similar, and thus combining them will not help improve the generalization performance; such learners are called **stable learners**. Decision trees are **unstable learners**, whereas decision stumps are more close to stable learners. On highly stable learners such as k-nearest neighbor classifiers, Bagging does not work. For example, Figure 3.5 shows the decision boundaries of a single 1-nearest neighbor classifier and Bagging of such classifiers. The difference

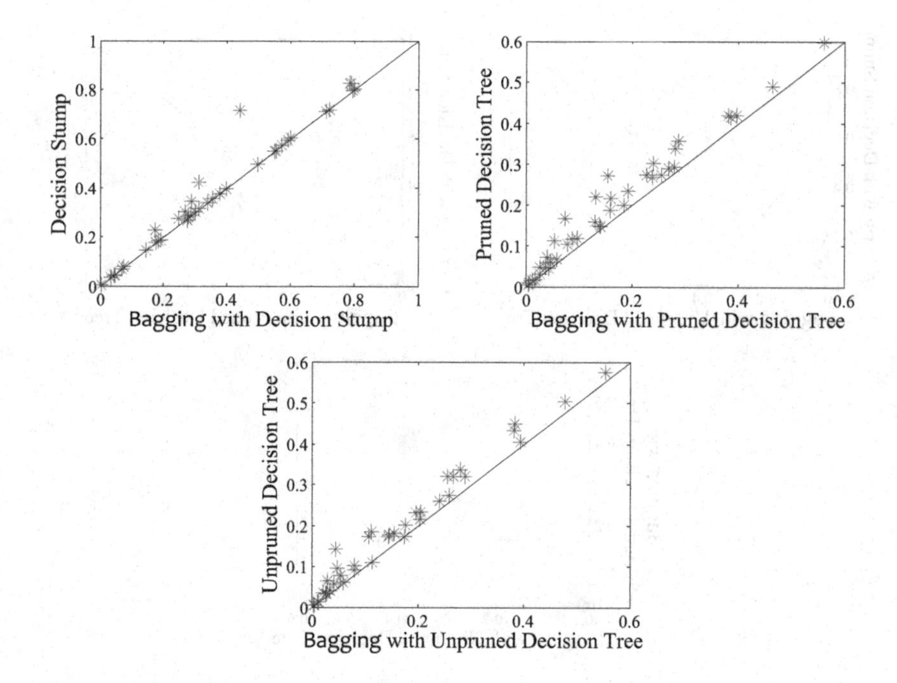

Figure 3.3: Comparison of predictive errors of Bagging against single base learners on 40 UCI data sets. Each point represents a data set and is located according to the predictive error of the two compared algorithms. The diagonal line indicates where the two compared algorithms have identical errors.

between the decision boundaries is hardly visible, and the predictive errors are both 9.1%.

Indeed, it is well-known that Bagging should be used with unstable learners, and generally, the more unstable, the larger the performance improvement. This explains why in Figure 3.4 the performance of Bagging with unpruned decision trees is better than with pruned decision trees, since unpruned trees are more unstable than pruned ones. This provides a good implication, that is, when we use Bagging, there is no need to do decision tree pruning.

With independent base learners, (3.3) shows that the generalization error decreases exponentially in the ensemble size T, and ultimately approaches zero as T approaches to infinity. In practice, we do not have infinite training data, and the base learners of Bagging are not independent since they are trained from bootstrap samples. However, it is worth mentioning that though the error might not drop to zero, the performance of Bagging converges as the **ensemble size**, i.e., the number of base learners, grows large, as illustrated in Figure 3.6.

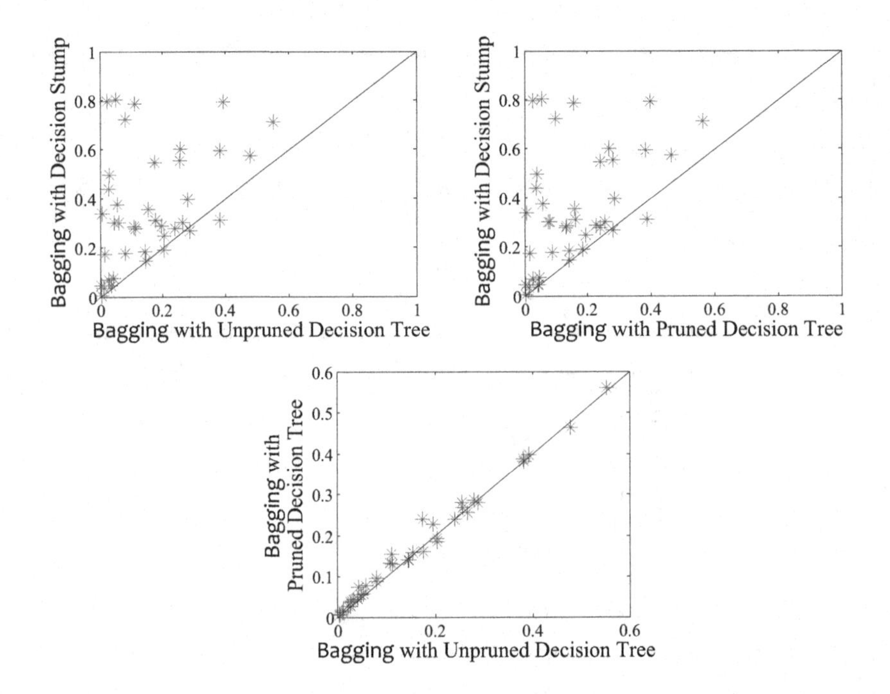

Figure 3.4: Comparison of predictive errors of Bagging using decision stumps, pruned decision trees and unpruned decision trees. Each point represents a data set and locates according to the predictive error of the two compared algorithms. The diagonal line indicates where two compared algorithms have identical errors.

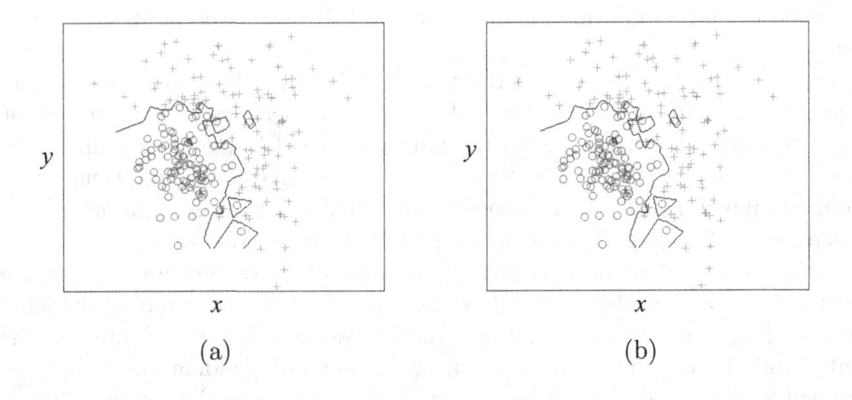

Figure 3.5: Decision boundaries of (a) 1-nearest neighbor classifier and (b) Bagging of 1-nearest neighbor classifiers, on *three-Gaussians*.

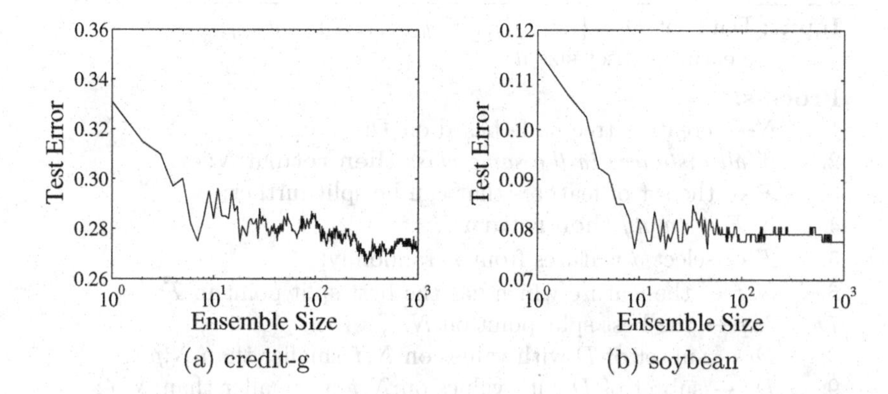

(a) credit-g (b) soybean

Figure 3.6: Impact of ensemble size on Bagging on two UCI data sets.

3.4 Random Subspace and Random Forest

Random Forest (RF) [Breiman, 2001] is a representative of the state-of-the-art ensemble methods. It is an extension of Bagging, where the major difference with Bagging is the incorporation of randomized feature selection.

The training data is usually described by a set of features. Different subsets of features, or called **subspaces**, provide different views on the data. Therefore, individual learners trained from different subspaces are usually diverse. The Random Subspace (RS) method [Ho, 1998] shown in Figure 3.7 is a powerful ensemble method which employs this mechanism. For data with a lot of redundant features, training a learner in a subspace is often not only effective but also efficient. Note that RS is not suitable to data with only a few features. Moreover, if there are lots of irrelevant features, it is usually better to filter out the most irrelevant features before generating the subspaces.

Input: Data set $D = \{(\boldsymbol{x}_1, y_1), (\boldsymbol{x}_2, y_2), \ldots, (\boldsymbol{x}_m, y_m)\}$;
Base learning algorithm $\mathfrak{L}$;
Number of base learners T;
Dimension of subspaces d.

Process:
1. **for** $t = 1, \ldots, T$:
2. $\mathcal{F}_t = \mathrm{RS}(D, d)$ % $\mathcal{F}_t$ is a set of d randomly selected features;
3. $D_t = \mathrm{Map}_{\mathcal{F}_t}(D)$ % D_t keeps only the features in $\mathcal{F}_t$
4. $h_t = \mathfrak{L}(D_t)$ % Train a learner
5. **end**

Output: $H(\boldsymbol{x}) = \arg\max_{y \in \mathcal{Y}} \sum_{t=1}^{T} \mathbb{I}\left(h_t\left(\mathrm{Map}_{\mathcal{F}_t}(\boldsymbol{x})\right) = y\right)$

Figure 3.7: The RS algorithm.

Input: Data set $D = \{(\boldsymbol{x}_1, y_1), (\boldsymbol{x}_2, y_2), \ldots, (\boldsymbol{x}_m, y_m)\}$;
Feature subset size d.

Process:
1. $N \leftarrow$ create a tree node based on D;
2. **if** *all instances in the same class* **then return** N;
3. $\mathcal{F} \leftarrow$ the set of features that can be split further;
4. **if** $\mathcal{F}$ *is empty* **then return** N;
5. $\tilde{\mathcal{F}} \leftarrow$ select d features from $\mathcal{F}$ randomly;
6. $N.f \leftarrow$ the feature which has the best split point in $\tilde{\mathcal{F}}$;
7. $N.p \leftarrow$ the best split point on $N.f$;
8. $D_l \leftarrow$ subset of D with values on $N.f$ smaller than $N.p$;
9. $D_r \leftarrow$ subset of D with values on $N.f$ no smaller than $N.p$;
10. $N_l \leftarrow$ call the process with parameters (D_l, d);
11. $N_r \leftarrow$ call the process with parameters (D_r, d);
12. **return** N

Output: A random decision tree

Figure 3.8: The random tree algorithm in RF.

The basic idea of RS has been exploited in Random Forest. During the construction of a component decision tree, at each step of split selection, RF first randomly selects a subset of features, and then carries out the conventional split selection procedure within the selected feature subset.

Figure 3.8 shows the random decision tree algorithm used in RF. The parameter d controls the incorporation of randomness. When d equals the total number of features, the constructed decision tree is identical to the traditional deterministic decision tree; when $d = 1$, a feature will be selected randomly. The suggested value of d is the logarithm of the number of features [Breiman, 2001]. Note that randomness is only introduced into the feature selection process, not into the choice of split points on the selected feature.

Figure 3.9 compares the decision boundaries of RF and Bagging as well as their base classifiers. It can be observed that the decision boundaries of RF and its base classifiers are more flexible, leading to a better generalization ability. On the *three-Gaussians* data set, the test error of RF is 7.85% while that of Bagging is 8.3%. Figure 3.10 compares the test errors of RF and Bagging on 40 UCI data sets. It is clear that RF is more preferable no matter whether pruned or unpruned decision trees are used.

The convergence property of RF is similar to that of Bagging. As illustrated in Figure 3.11, RF usually has a worse starting point, particularly when the ensemble size is one, owing to the performance degeneration of single base learners by the incorporation of randomized feature selection; however, it usually converges to lower test errors. It is worth mentioning that the training stage of RF is generally more efficient than Bagging. This is because in the tree construction process, Bagging uses deterministic decision trees that need

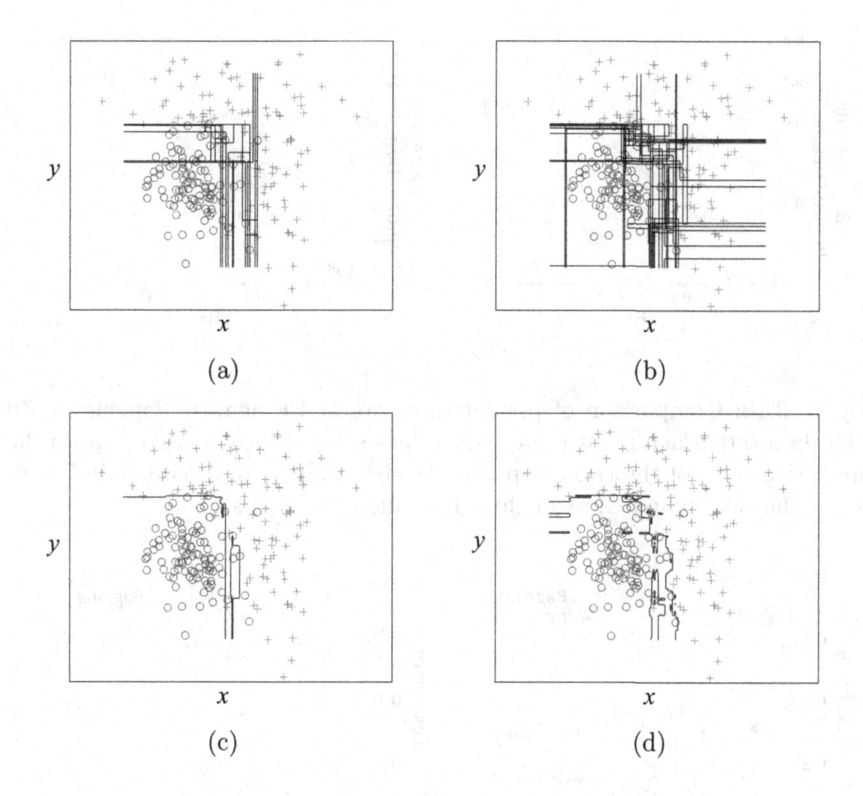

Figure 3.9: Decision boundaries on *three-Gaussians*: (a) the 10 base classifiers of Bagging; (b) the 10 base classifiers of RF; (c) Bagging; and (d) RF.

to evaluate all features for split selection, whereas RF uses random decision trees that only need to evaluate a subset of features.

3.5 Theoretical Understanding

3.5.1 About Bagging

Convergence with Ensemble Size

It is easy to understand that Bagging converges as the ensemble size grows. Given a training set, Bagging uses bootstrap sampling to generate a set of random samples to train the base learners. This process is equivalent to picking a set of base learners from a pool of all possible learners randomly according to the distribution implied by bootstrap sampling. Thus, given a test instance, the output of a base learner on the instance can be denoted as a random variable Y drawn from the distribution. Without loss of generality, let's consider binary classification where $Y \in \{-1, +1\}$. Bagging generally

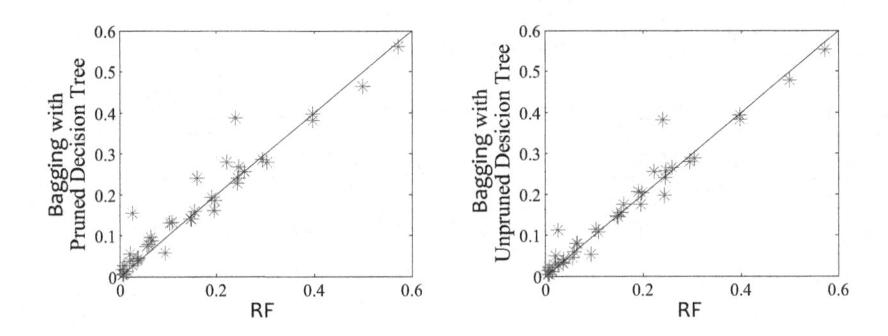

Figure 3.10: Comparison of predictive errors of RF against Bagging on 40 UCI data sets. Each point represents a data set and locates according to the predictive error of the two compared algorithms. The diagonal line indicates where the two compared algorithms have identical errors.

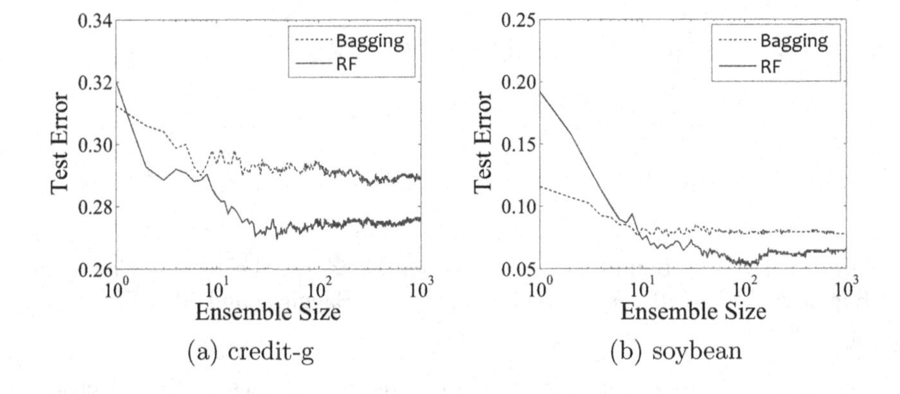

Figure 3.11: Impact of ensemble size on RF and Bagging on two UCI data sets.

employs voting to combine base classifiers, while we can consider averaging at first. Let $\bar{Y}_T = \frac{1}{T}\sum_{i=1}^{T} Y_i$ denote the average of the outputs of T drawn classifiers, and $\mathbb{E}[Y]$ denote the expectation. By the *law of large numbers*, we have

$$\lim_{T\to\infty} P(|\bar{Y}_T - \mathbb{E}[Y]| < \epsilon) = 1 . \tag{3.6}$$

Turning to voting then, we have

$$\lim_{T\to\infty} P\left(\mathtt{sign}\left(\bar{Y}_T\right) = \mathtt{sign}\left(\mathbb{E}[Y]\right)\right) = 1 , \tag{3.7}$$

unless $\mathbb{E}[Y] = 0$. Therefore, Bagging will converge to a steady error rate as the ensemble size grows, except for the rare case that Bagging equals random guess. Actually, this property is shared by all parallel ensemble methods.

Effectiveness with Unstable or Highly Nonlinear Learners

Breiman [1996d] presented an explanation when he proposed Bagging. Let's consider regression at first. Let f denote the ground-truth function and $h(\boldsymbol{x})$ denote a learner trained from the bootstrap distribution $\mathcal{D}_{bs}$. The ensemble learner generated by Bagging is

$$H(\boldsymbol{x}) = \mathbb{E}_{\mathcal{D}_{bs}}[h(\boldsymbol{x})] \ . \tag{3.8}$$

With simple algebra and the inequality $(\mathbb{E}[X])^2 \leq \mathbb{E}[X^2]$, we have

$$(f(\boldsymbol{x}) - H(\boldsymbol{x}))^2 \leq \mathbb{E}_{\mathcal{D}_{bs}}\left[(f(\boldsymbol{x}) - h(\boldsymbol{x}))^2\right] . \tag{3.9}$$

Thus, by integrating both sides over the distribution, we can get that the mean-squared error of $H(\boldsymbol{x})$ is smaller than that of $h(\boldsymbol{x})$ averaged over the bootstrap sampling distribution, and the difference depends on how unequal the following inequality is:

$$(\mathbb{E}_{\mathcal{D}_{bs}}[h(\boldsymbol{x})])^2 \leq \mathbb{E}_{\mathcal{D}_{bs}}\left[h(\boldsymbol{x})^2\right] . \tag{3.10}$$

This clearly discloses the importance of *unstability*. That is, if $h(\boldsymbol{x})$ does not change much with different bootstrap samples, the combination will not help, while if $h(\boldsymbol{x})$ changes much, the improvement provided by the combination will be great. This explains why Bagging is effective with **unstable learners**, and it reduces variance through the smoothing effect.

In the context of classification, suppose the classifier $h(\boldsymbol{x})$ predicts the class label $y \in \{y_1, y_2, \ldots, y_c\}$. Let $P(y \mid \boldsymbol{x})$ denote the probability of y being the ground-truth class label of $\boldsymbol{x}$. The probability of h correctly classifying $\boldsymbol{x}$ is

$$\sum_y P(h(\boldsymbol{x}) = y) P(y \mid \boldsymbol{x}) \ , \tag{3.11}$$

and the overall correct classification probability of h is

$$\int \sum_y P(h(\boldsymbol{x}) = y) P(y \mid \boldsymbol{x}) P(\boldsymbol{x}) d\boldsymbol{x} \ , \tag{3.12}$$

where $P(\boldsymbol{x})$ is the input probability distribution.

If the input probability of $\boldsymbol{x}$ with class label y is larger than any other classes, while h predicts class y for $\boldsymbol{x}$ more often, i.e.,

$$\arg\max_y P(h(\boldsymbol{x}) = y) = \arg\max_y P(y \mid \boldsymbol{x}) \ , \tag{3.13}$$

the predictor h is called **order-correct** at the input $\boldsymbol{x}$.

The ensemble classifier of Bagging is $H(\boldsymbol{x}) = \arg\max_y P(h(\boldsymbol{x}) = y)$. Its probability of correct classification at $\boldsymbol{x}$ is

$$\sum_y \mathbb{I}\left(\arg\max_z P(h(\boldsymbol{x}) = z) = y\right) P(y \mid \boldsymbol{x}) \ . \tag{3.14}$$

If h is order-correct at the input $\boldsymbol{x}$, the above probability equals $\max_y P(y \mid \boldsymbol{x})$. Thus, the correct classification probability of the ensemble classifier H is

$$\int_{\boldsymbol{x}\in C} \max_y P(y \mid \boldsymbol{x})P(\boldsymbol{x})d\boldsymbol{x} + \int_{\boldsymbol{x}\in C'} \left[\sum_y \mathbb{I}\left(H\left(\boldsymbol{x}\right)=y\right)P\left(y \mid \boldsymbol{x}\right)\right] P(\boldsymbol{x})d\boldsymbol{x} \ , \tag{3.15}$$

where C is the set of all inputs $\boldsymbol{x}$ where h is order-correct, and C' is the set of inputs at which h is not order-correct. It always holds that

$$\sum_y P\left(h\left(\boldsymbol{x}\right)=y\right)P(y \mid \boldsymbol{x}) \leq \max_y P(y \mid \boldsymbol{x}) \ . \tag{3.16}$$

Thus, the highest achievable accuracy of Bagging is

$$\int \max_y P(y \mid \boldsymbol{x})P(\boldsymbol{x})d\boldsymbol{x} \ , \tag{3.17}$$

which equals the Bayes optimal error rate.

Comparing (3.12) and (3.15), it can be found that if a predictor is order-correct at most instances, Bagging can transform it into a nearly optimal predictor. Note that if the base learner is unstable, the h's generated from different samples will be quite different, and will produce different predictions on $\boldsymbol{x}$, leading to a low probability of $P(h(\boldsymbol{x})=y)$. According to (3.11), the probability of correctly predicting $\boldsymbol{x}$ will be low. We know that, however, if h is order-correct at $\boldsymbol{x}$, Bagging will correctly classify $\boldsymbol{x}$ with high probability. This suggests that the performance improvement brought by Bagging is large when the base learner is unstable but order-correct.

Friedman and Hall [2007] studied Bagging through a decomposition of statistical predictors. They assumed that the learner $h(\boldsymbol{x};\gamma)$ is parameterized by a parameter vector γ, which can be obtained by solving an estimation function

$$\sum_{i=1}^{m} g\left(\left(\boldsymbol{x}_i, y_i\right), \gamma\right) = 0 \ , \tag{3.18}$$

where g is a smooth multivariate function, $(\boldsymbol{x}_i, y_i)$ is the i-th training example and m is the size of training set. Once γ is obtained, the learner h is decided.

Suppose γ^* is the solution of $\mathbb{E}_{\boldsymbol{x},y}[g((\boldsymbol{x}_i, y_i), \gamma)] = 0$. Based on the Taylor expansion of $g((\boldsymbol{x}_i, y_i), \gamma)$ around γ^*, (3.18) can be rewritten as

$$\sum_{i=1}^{m} \Bigg[g((\boldsymbol{x}_i, y_i), \gamma^*) + \sum_k g_k((\boldsymbol{x}_i, y_i), \gamma^*)(\gamma - \gamma^*)_k + \tag{3.19}$$
$$\sum_{k_1}\sum_{k_2} g_{k_1,k_2}((\boldsymbol{x}_i, y_i), \gamma^*)(\gamma - \gamma^*)_{k_1}(\gamma - \gamma^*)_{k_2} + \ldots, \Bigg] = 0 \ ,$$

where γ_k is the k-th component of γ, and g_k is the partial derivative of g with respect to γ_k. Suppose $\hat{\gamma}$ is a solution of (3.18), then from (3.19) it can be expressed as

$$\hat{\gamma} = \Gamma + \sum_{k_1}\sum_{k_2} \alpha_{k_1 k_2}(\bar{\Phi} - \phi)_{k_1}(\bar{\Phi} - \phi)_{k_2} + \sum_{k_1}\sum_{k_2}\sum_{k_3} \alpha_{k_1 k_2 k_3}(\bar{\Phi} - \phi)_{k_1}(\bar{\Phi} - \phi)_{k_2}(\bar{\Phi} - \phi)_{k_3} + \ldots, \quad (3.20)$$

with coefficients $\alpha_{k_1 k_2}, \alpha_{k_1 k_2 k_3}$,

$$\Gamma = \gamma^* + M^{-1}\frac{1}{m}\sum_{i=1}^{m} g((\boldsymbol{x}_i, y_i), \gamma^*) \ , \quad (3.21)$$

$$\bar{\Phi} = \frac{1}{m}\Phi_i \ , \qquad \phi = \mathbb{E}[\Phi_i] \ , \quad (3.22)$$

where M is a matrix whose k-th column is $\mathbb{E}_{\boldsymbol{x},y}[g_k((\boldsymbol{x}, y), \gamma^*)]$, and Φ_i is a vector of $g_k((\boldsymbol{x}_i, y_i), \gamma^*)$, $g_{k_1,k_2}((\boldsymbol{x}_i, y_i), \gamma^*), \ldots,$. It is obvious that $\hat{\gamma}$ can be decomposed into linear and high-order parts.

Suppose the learner generated from a bootstrap sample of the training data set D is parameterized by $\hat{\gamma}'$, and the sample size is m' ($m' \leq m$). According to (3.20), we have

$$\hat{\gamma}' = \Gamma' + \sum_{k_1}\sum_{k_2} \alpha_{k_1 k_2}(\bar{\Phi}' - \phi)_{k_1}(\bar{\Phi}' - \phi)_{k_2} + \sum_{k_1}\sum_{k_2}\sum_{k_3} \alpha_{k_1 k_2 k_3}(\bar{\Phi}' - \phi)_{k_1}(\bar{\Phi}' - \phi)_{k_2}(\bar{\Phi}' - \phi)_{k_3} + \ldots, \ . \quad (3.23)$$

The ensemble learner of Bagging is parameterized by

$$\hat{\gamma}_{bag} = \mathbb{E}[\hat{\gamma}' \mid D] \ . \quad (3.24)$$

If $\hat{\gamma}$ is linear in function of data, we have $\mathbb{E}[\Gamma' \mid D] = \Gamma$, and thus $\hat{\gamma}_{bag} = \hat{\gamma}$. This implies that Bagging does not improve linear components of $\hat{\gamma}$.

Now, let's consider higher-order components. Let

$$\rho_m = \frac{m}{m'} \ , \quad (3.25)$$

$$\hat{\sigma}_{k_1 k_2} = \frac{1}{m}\sum_{i=1}^{m}(\Phi_i - \Phi)_{k_1}(\Phi_i - \Phi)_{k_2} \ , \quad (3.26)$$

$$S = \sum_{k_1}\sum_{k_2} \alpha_{k_1 k_2}\hat{\sigma}_{k_1 k_2} \ . \quad (3.27)$$

Friedman and Hall [2007] showed that if $\rho_m \to \rho$ ($1 \leq \rho \leq \infty$) when $m \to \infty$, $\hat{\gamma}_{bag}$ can be expressed as

$$\hat{\gamma}_{bag} = \Gamma + \frac{1}{m}\rho_m S + \delta_{bag} \ , \quad (3.28)$$

where δ_{bag} represents the terms with orders higher than quadratic. From (3.26), it can be seen that the variance of $\hat{\sigma}_{k_1k_2}$ will decrease if the sample size m increases, and the dependence of the variance on the sample size is in the order $O(\frac{1}{m})$. Since S is linear in $\hat{\sigma}_{k_1k_2}$'s, the dependence of the variance of S on the sample size is also in the order of $O(\frac{1}{m})$. Thus, considering that ρ_m is asymptotic to a constant and the property of variance that $var(aX) = a^2 var(X)$, the dependence of the variance of $\frac{1}{m}\rho_m S$ on the sample size is in the order of $O(\frac{1}{m^3})$. If we rewrite (3.20) as $\hat{\gamma} = \Gamma + \Delta$, with a similar analysis, we can get the result that the dependence of the variance of Δ on sample size is asymptotically in the order of $O(\frac{1}{m^2})$. Therefore, Bagging reduce the variance of the quadratic terms of $\hat{\gamma}$ from $O(\frac{1}{m^2})$ to $O(\frac{1}{m^3})$. Similar effects can be found on terms with orders higher than quadratic.

Thus, Friedman and Hall [2007] concluded that Bagging can reduce the variance of higher-order components, yet not affect the linear components. This implies that Bagging is better applied to highly nonlinear learners. Since highly nonlinear learners tend to be unstable, i.e., their performance changes much with data sample perturbation, it is understandable that Bagging is effective with unstable base learners.

Variance Reduction

Friedman and Hall [2007] presented a theoretical results showing that Bagging can significantly reduce the variance, as introduced in the above section. Ghojogh and Crowley [2019] further presented a variance analysis. Let $h_1, h_2, \ldots, h_T$ denote T functions learned from T bootstrap samples, respectively, and the final ensemble $H(\boldsymbol{x}) = \sum_{i=1}^{T} h_i(\boldsymbol{x})/T$. Ghojogh and Crowley [2019] studied the variance of $H(\boldsymbol{x})$ from the view of individual correlations.

For $i \in [T]$, let ϵ_i denote the error of function h_i over the instance $\boldsymbol{x}$. Suppose that ϵ_i is a random variable with normal distribution of mean zero, i.e., $\epsilon_i \sim \mathcal{N}(0, \sigma^2)$. Let c denote the covariance of any two variables ϵ_i and ϵ_j for $i \neq j$, i.e., $cov(h_i, h_j) = c$. Hence, we have

$$var(H(\boldsymbol{x})) = \frac{1}{T^2}\sum_{i=1}^{T} var(h_i) + \frac{1}{T^2}\sum_{i \neq j} cov(h_i, h_j) = \frac{\sigma^2}{T} + \frac{T-1}{T}c \,. \quad (3.29)$$

(3.29) delivers an interesting interpretation: If two functions from two different bootstrap samples are very correlated, then we have $c \approx \sigma^2$ and

$$\lim_{c \to \sigma^2} var(H(\boldsymbol{x})) = \frac{1}{T}\sigma^2 + \frac{T-1}{T}\sigma^2 = \sigma^2 \,; \quad (3.30)$$

while if the two functions are very different (uncorrelated), then we have $c \approx 0$ and hence

$$\lim_{c \to 0} var(H(\boldsymbol{x})) = \frac{1}{T}\sigma^2 + \frac{T-1}{T}0 = \frac{\sigma^2}{T} \,. \quad (3.31)$$

This means that if the trained functions are very correlated in Bagging, there is no significant difference from using only one function; however, if the trained functions are very different, the variance improves significantly by a factor of T. This also implies that Bagging is never destructive, i.e., it either is ineffective or improves the estimate in terms of variance [Breiman, 1996d].

3.5.2 About Random Subspace

RS has been an attractive choice for learning tasks with a large number of features. Lim [2020] presented an explanation on random subspace from the view of data structure preservation; that is, RS can preserve the norm and dot-product between two vectors for high-dimensional data, similarly to **random projection**. Hence, RS can be applied with theoretical guarantees to some learning algorithms such as nearest neighbor, decision tree, and large margin methods, etc.

Let $\boldsymbol{x}_1, \boldsymbol{x}_2, \ldots, \boldsymbol{x}_m$ be m data points in $\mathbb{R}^d$ for large d. Let $\mathbf{P}$ denote the random subspace projection, where $\mathbf{P}$ is a $d \times d$ diagonal matrix with all entries zero except for k ($k \ll d$) diagonal entries set to 1 with their indices chosen by simple random sampling without replacement from $\{1, 2, \ldots, d\}$. Note that left-multiplying a $d \times m$ data matrix with $\mathbf{P}$ is equivalent to RS projection.

Lim [2020] showed that an RS projection implies a data-dependent **Johnson-Lindenstrauss Lemma** (JLL) type guarantee as follows.

Theorem 3.1 ([Lim, 2020]). *Let $\boldsymbol{x}_1, \ldots, \boldsymbol{x}_m$ be m points with $\|\boldsymbol{x}_i^2\|_\infty \leq c\|\boldsymbol{x}_i\|_2^2/d$ for constant $c \in [1, d]$. For every $i, j \in [m]$, the following holds with probability at least $1 - \delta$ over the random selection of matrix $\mathbf{P}$, where $\epsilon, \delta \in (0, 1]$, integer $k > c^2/2\epsilon^2 \ln(m^2/\delta)$, and $\mathbf{P}$ is a RS projection from $\mathbb{R}^d \mapsto \mathbb{R}^k$.*

$$(1 - \epsilon) \|\boldsymbol{x}_i - \boldsymbol{x}_j\|_2^2 \leq \frac{d}{k} \|\mathbf{P}\boldsymbol{x}_i - \mathbf{P}\boldsymbol{x}_j\|_2^2 \leq (1 + \epsilon) \|\boldsymbol{x}_i - \boldsymbol{x}_j\|_2^2 . \tag{3.32}$$

This theorem shows that Euclidean distance (i.e., L_2 norm) after RS projection is directly proportional to the original distance with the proportional factor k/d. Therefore, we can apply RS projection to some distance-based learning algorithms such as nearest neighbor, clustering, etc.

In comparison with random projection, RS is computationally far more efficient and more interpretable in practice. This is because RS merely involves selecting a subset of features randomly without replacement, and does not require a matrix-matrix multiplication. Empirically, RS can achieve indistinguishable performance with random projection on some data sets when RS dimension $k \geq 80$, as shown in [Lim, 2020].

For linear classifier $\boldsymbol{w} \in \mathbb{R}^d$, we can define the margin of an example $(\boldsymbol{x}, y)$ as $y\boldsymbol{x}^T\boldsymbol{w}$, and we have

$$(\mathbf{P}\boldsymbol{x})^T(\mathbf{P}\boldsymbol{w}) = (\|\mathbf{P}\boldsymbol{x} + \mathbf{P}\boldsymbol{w}\|_2^2 - \|\mathbf{P}\boldsymbol{x} - \mathbf{P}\boldsymbol{w}\|_2^2)/4 . \tag{3.33}$$

Based on Theorem 3.1, it holds that, with probability at least $1 - 2\delta$ over the random selection of matrix $\mathbf{P}$,

$$\boldsymbol{x}^T\boldsymbol{w} - \epsilon\|\boldsymbol{x}\|\|\boldsymbol{w}\| \leq \frac{d}{k}(\mathbf{P}\boldsymbol{x})^T(\mathbf{P}\boldsymbol{w}) \leq \boldsymbol{x}^T\boldsymbol{w} + \epsilon\|\boldsymbol{x}\|\|\boldsymbol{w}\| . \tag{3.34}$$

Hence, (3.34) guarantees that, for small $\epsilon > 0$, the RS projected margin $y(\mathbf{P}\boldsymbol{x})^T(\mathbf{P}\boldsymbol{w})$ is directly proportional to the original margin $y\boldsymbol{x}^T\boldsymbol{w}$ with the proportional factor k/d. This shows that the RS projection can be used for large margin methods with theoretical guarantee. For example, Lim [2020] extended the approach of Arriaga and Vempala [2006] on l-robust half-spaces to classification of RS-projected data in the presence of margin.

A half-space is said to be l-robust, if there is a probability of zero that any point is within an Euclidean distance l of the boundary of a linear threshold function separating the class supports. A key implication of this result is the (ϵ, δ)-learnability of a RS-projected robust half-space, that is, with probability $1 - \delta$, a hypothesis that is consistent with at least $1 - \epsilon$ of the data distribution is learnable. Lim [2020] derived the following theorem for robust half-spaces classification.

Theorem 3.2. *An l-robust half-space in $\mathbb{R}^d$ can be (ϵ, δ)-learned by projecting a set of m examples using RS projection to $\mathbb{R}^k$ when $k = 32c^2/l^2 \ln(8c/\epsilon l\delta)$ and $m \geq (8k\ln(48/\epsilon) + 4\ln(4/\epsilon))/\epsilon$.*

This result shows that the half-space in $\mathbb{R}^k$ defined by $\mathbf{P}\boldsymbol{w}$ can correctly classify all m examples after a RS projection from $\mathbb{R}^d \mapsto \mathbb{R}^k$, with probability at least $1 - \delta/2$ and the generalization error of this classifier can be upper bounded by ϵ with probability $1 - \delta$. Moreover, the margins remain at least $l/3$ after an RS projection.

Lim [2020] considered the RS classification using *flipping probability*, defined as the probability that the angular separation of two vectors in d-dimensions, changes from less than $\pi/2$ to larger than $\pi/2$, after projecting to a lower-dimensional space. They presented the following flipping probability upper bound for RS projection.

Theorem 3.3. *Let $\mathbf{P}$ be an RS projection chosen without replacement from $\mathbb{R}^d \mapsto \mathbb{R}^k$ with $0 < k < d/2$, and $\boldsymbol{w}, \boldsymbol{x} \in \mathbb{R}^d$ be two vectors with unit length and angle θ. If $\boldsymbol{w}^T\boldsymbol{x} \neq 0$, then*

$$P\left(\frac{(\mathbf{P}\boldsymbol{x})^T\mathbf{P}\boldsymbol{w}}{\boldsymbol{x}^T\boldsymbol{w}} \leq 0\right) \leq 2\exp\left(-\frac{2k\cos^2\theta}{d^2}\right) . \tag{3.35}$$

This upper bounds generalization error of classifiers trained through empirical risk minimization on an RS projected data set, by combining with [Durrant and Kabán, 2013, Theorem 3.1]. Details can be found in [Lim, 2020].

3.5.3 About Random Forest

Generalization

Breiman [2001] presented the generalization error bounds for RF. An RF is a classifier consisting of tree-structured classifiers $\{h(\boldsymbol{x}, \Theta_i), i = 1, 2, \ldots, \}$, where Θ_i are *i.i.d.* random vectors, and each tree casts a unit vote for the most popular class at instance $\boldsymbol{x}$.

Given an ensemble of classifiers $h_1(\boldsymbol{x}), h_2(\boldsymbol{x}), \ldots, h_T(\boldsymbol{x})$, and with training set drawn at random from the distribution $\mathcal{D}$, define the margin function as

$$\theta(\boldsymbol{x}, y) = \frac{1}{T}\sum_{i=1}^{T} \mathbb{I}(h_i(\boldsymbol{x}) = y) - \max_{j \neq y} \left\{ \frac{1}{T}\sum_{i=1}^{T} \mathbb{I}(h_i(\boldsymbol{x}) = j) \right\} . \tag{3.36}$$

The margin measures the extent to which the average number of votes at $(\boldsymbol{x}, y)$ for the correct class exceeds any other class. The larger the margin, the larger the confidence in classification. The generalization error for RF is given by

$$\epsilon_{\mathcal{D}} = P_{(\boldsymbol{x},y)\sim\mathcal{D}}(\theta(\boldsymbol{x}, y) < 0) . \tag{3.37}$$

For RF, an upper bound can be derived for the generalization error in terms of two parameters measuring the accuracy of individual classifiers and the dependence between them. The interplay between these two gives the foundation for understanding the workings of random forests. The basis of the analysis is [Amit and Geman, 1997].

Definition 3.1. *The margin function for a random forest is*

$$\bar{\theta}(\boldsymbol{x}, y) = P_{\Theta}(h(\boldsymbol{x}, \Theta) = y) - \max_{j \neq y} P_{\Theta}(h(\boldsymbol{x}, \Theta) = j) , \tag{3.38}$$

and the strength of the set of classifiers $\{h(\boldsymbol{x}, \Theta)\}$ *is*

$$s = \mathbb{E}_{(\boldsymbol{x},y)\sim\mathcal{D}}[\bar{\theta}(\boldsymbol{x}, y)] . \tag{3.39}$$

Assuming $s \geq 0$, Chebychev's inequality gives

$$\epsilon_{\mathcal{D}} \leq var(\bar{\theta})/s^2 . \tag{3.40}$$

Denote by $\hat{\jmath}(\boldsymbol{x}, y) = \arg\max_{j \neq y} P_{\Theta}(h(\boldsymbol{x}, \Theta) = j)$. A more revealing expression for the variance of $\bar{\theta}$ is

$$\begin{aligned} \bar{\theta}(\boldsymbol{x}, y) &= P_{\Theta}(h(\boldsymbol{x}, \Theta) = y) - P_{\Theta}(h(\boldsymbol{x}, \Theta) = \hat{\jmath}(\boldsymbol{x}, y)) \\ &= \mathbb{E}_{\Theta}[\mathbb{I}(h(\boldsymbol{x}, \Theta) = y) - \mathbb{I}(h(\boldsymbol{x}, \Theta) = \hat{\jmath}(\boldsymbol{x}, y))] . \end{aligned} \tag{3.41}$$

Definition 3.2. *The raw margin function is*

$$\theta_r(\Theta, \boldsymbol{x}, y) = \mathbb{I}(h(\boldsymbol{x}, \Theta) = y) - \mathbb{I}(h(\boldsymbol{x}, \Theta) = \hat{\jmath}(\boldsymbol{x}, y)) . \tag{3.42}$$

Thus, $\bar{\theta}(\boldsymbol{x}, y)$ is the expectation of $\theta_r(\Theta, \boldsymbol{x}, y)$ with respect to Θ. We have

$$\bar{\theta}(\boldsymbol{x}, y)^2 = \mathbb{E}_{\Theta,\Theta'}[\theta_r(\Theta, \boldsymbol{x}, y) \cdot \theta_r(\Theta', \boldsymbol{x}, y)] , \tag{3.43}$$

where Θ and Θ' are independent with the same distribution. Using (3.43) gives

$$\begin{aligned} var(\bar{\theta}) &= \mathbb{E}_{\Theta,\Theta'}\left[cov_{(\boldsymbol{x},y)}\langle\theta_r(\Theta, \boldsymbol{x}, y), \theta_r(\Theta', \boldsymbol{x}, y)\rangle\right] \\ &= \mathbb{E}_{\Theta,\Theta'}[\rho(\Theta, \Theta')\sigma(\Theta)\sigma(\Theta')] , \end{aligned} \tag{3.44}$$

where $\rho(\Theta, \Theta')$ is the correlation between $\theta_r(\Theta, \boldsymbol{x}, y)$ and $\theta_r(\Theta', \boldsymbol{x}, y)$, and $\sigma(\Theta)$ is the standard deviation of $\theta_r(\Theta, \boldsymbol{x}, y)$. Then,

$$var(\bar{\theta}) = \bar{\rho}(\mathbb{E}_\Theta[\sigma(\Theta)])^2 \leq \bar{\rho}\mathbb{E}_\Theta[var(\Theta)] \ , \tag{3.45}$$

where $\bar{\rho}$ is the mean value of the correlation, that is,

$$\bar{\rho} = \mathbb{E}_{\Theta,\Theta'}\left[\rho(\Theta, \Theta')\sigma(\Theta)\sigma(\Theta')\right] / \mathbb{E}_{\Theta,\Theta'}\left[\sigma(\Theta)\sigma(\Theta')\right] \ . \tag{3.46}$$

We have

$$\mathbb{E}_\Theta[var(\Theta)] \leq \mathbb{E}_\Theta\left[\mathbb{E}_{(\boldsymbol{x},y)\sim\mathcal{D}}[\theta_r(\Theta, \boldsymbol{x}, y)]\right]^2 - s^2 \leq 1 - s^2 \ . \tag{3.47}$$

Putting (3.40), (3.45), and (3.47) together yields:

Theorem 3.4 ([Breiman, 2001]). *An upper bound for the generalization error of RF is given by*

$$\epsilon_\mathcal{D} \leq \bar{\rho}(1 - s^2)/s^2 \ . \tag{3.48}$$

Although the bound is likely to be loose, it suggests that the generalization error of RF is dependent on the strength of the individual classifiers in the forest, and the correlation between them in terms of the raw margin functions.

Consistency

Given the instance space $\mathcal{X}$, let $\mathcal{D}$ be a distribution over $\mathcal{X} \times \{-1, +1\}$. For a classifier $h\colon \mathcal{X} \to \{-1, +1\}$, we define the classification error as

$$\epsilon_\mathcal{D}(h) = P_{(\boldsymbol{x},y)\sim\mathcal{D}}(h(\boldsymbol{x}) \neq y) \ . \tag{3.49}$$

The **Bayes optimal classifier** $h^* = \arg\min_h\{\epsilon_\mathcal{D}(h)\}$ has the **Bayes error** $\epsilon^*_\mathcal{D} = \min_h\{\epsilon_\mathcal{D}(h)\}$, where the minimum takes over all measure functions. For any classifier h,

$$\epsilon_\mathcal{D}(h) \geq \epsilon^*_\mathcal{D} = \epsilon_\mathcal{D}(h^*) \ . \tag{3.50}$$

In other words, h^* is the best classifier and $\epsilon_\mathcal{D}(h^*)$ is the minimum error over distribution $\mathcal{D}$.

Let $D = \{(\boldsymbol{x}_1, y_1), (\boldsymbol{x}_2, y_2), \ldots, (\boldsymbol{x}_m, y_m)\}$ be a training data set of size m, where each element is drawn *i.i.d.* from distribution $\mathcal{D}$. Let $H(\boldsymbol{x})$ be the random forest classifier trained from D. We say that random forest is consistent if

$$\mathbb{E}[\epsilon_\mathcal{D}(H)] \to \epsilon^*_\mathcal{D} \quad \text{as} \quad m \to +\infty \ , \tag{3.51}$$

i.e., the random forest H approaches to the optimal classifier h^*. The consistent property guarantees that it is sufficient to learn the optimal classifier by taking more training data, despite of the unknown distribution $\mathcal{D}$. This is because $\epsilon_\mathcal{D}(H)$ can be pushed as close to the desired optimal error $\epsilon^*_\mathcal{D}$.

It is rather difficult to directly analyze the consistency of Bremain's original random forest [Breiman, 2001], because of the correlation between randomization process and data-dependent structure during the construction of random forest. Some simplifications and assumptions have been introduced for the consistency analysis of random forests. For example, Biau et al. [2008] studied purely RF [Breiman, 2000a], which randomly selects the splitting leaf, the splitting feature and splitting point during the construction of random tree, and presented the following theorem which states that purely RF is consistent.

Theorem 3.5 ([Biau et al., 2008]). *Assume that $\mathcal{D}$ is supported over instance space $\mathcal{X} = [0,1]^d$, and let $H(\boldsymbol{x})$ be the classifier by applying purely RF of k leaves to training data D of size m. We have $\mathbb{E}[\epsilon_{\mathcal{D}}(H)] \to \epsilon_{\mathcal{D}}^*$ whenever $k \to +\infty$ and $k/m \to 0$ as $k \to +\infty$.*

Convergence Rate

Given the instance space $\mathcal{X}$, let $\mathcal{D}$ be a distribution over $\mathcal{X} \times \{-1,+1\}$. We further denote by conditional distribution $\eta(\boldsymbol{x}) = P(y = +1 \mid \boldsymbol{x})$ and marginal distribution $\mathcal{D}_{\mathcal{X}}$ over instance space $\mathcal{X}$. We say that $\eta(\boldsymbol{x})$ is L-Lipschitz if

$$|\eta(\boldsymbol{x}_1) - \eta(\boldsymbol{x}_2)| \leq L\|\boldsymbol{x}_1 - \boldsymbol{x}_2\| \quad \text{for} \quad \boldsymbol{x}_1, \boldsymbol{x}_2 \in \mathcal{X}. \tag{3.52}$$

Gao et al. [2022] studied the convergence rate of purely RF [Breiman, 2000a] and presented the following theorem.

Theorem 3.6 ([Gao et al., 2022]). *Let $H(\boldsymbol{x})$ be the classifier by applying purely RF of k leaves to training data D of size m. Under the L-Lipschitz assumption over conditional probability, we have*

$$\mathbb{E}[\epsilon_{\mathcal{D}}(H)] - \epsilon_{\mathcal{D}}^* \leq \frac{4\sqrt{2e}Ld^{3/2}}{k^{1/8d}} + 2\sqrt{\frac{k}{m}} + \frac{6k}{m}\,. \tag{3.53}$$

This theorem exhibits the gap between the purely RF classifier $H(\boldsymbol{x})$ and the Bayes optimal classifier $h^*(\boldsymbol{x})$ according to data size, dimensionality, number of leaves, etc. By setting $k = O(m^{4d/(4d+1)})$, it can be obtained that

$$\mathbb{E}[\epsilon_{\mathcal{D}}(H)] - \epsilon_{\mathcal{D}}^* \leq O(1/m^{8d+2})\,. \tag{3.54}$$

Different splitting mechanisms will yield different convergence rates for random forest, which is helpful to understand the influence of different splitting mechanisms on random forest construction. For example, Gao et al. [2022] derived better convergence rate $O(1/m^{3.87d+2})$ for purely RF with midpoint splits, and reached the minimax convergence rate $O(m^{-1/(d+2)}(\ln m)^{1/(d+2)})$ (except for a factor $(\ln m)^{1/(d+2)}$) under the Lipschitz assumption, by considering different selections of splitting leaves, features and points.

Though nice results have been obtained for purely RF [Breiman, 2000a], it remains open problems to fully understand the consistency and convergence rate of the original random forest for classification Breiman [2001].

3.6 Spectrum of Randomization

RF generates random decision trees by selecting a feature subset randomly at each node, while the split selection within the selected feature subset is still deterministic. Liu et al. [2008a] described the VR-Tree ensemble method, which generates random decision trees by randomizing both the feature selection and split selection processes.

The base learners of VR-Tree ensembles are VR-Trees. At each node of the tree, a coin is tossed with α probability heads up. If a head is obtained, a deterministic node is constructed; that is, the best feature split point among all possible split points is selected in the same way as traditional decision trees. Otherwise, a random node is constructed; that is, a feature is selected randomly and a split point is selected on the feature randomly. Figure 3.12 shows the VR-Tree algorithm.

Input: Data set $D = \{(\boldsymbol{x}_1, y_1), (\boldsymbol{x}_2, y_2), \ldots, (\boldsymbol{x}_m, y_m)\}$;
Probability of using deterministic split selection α.

Process:
1. $N \leftarrow$ create a tree node based on D;
2. **if** *all instances in the same class* **then return** N;
3. $\mathcal{F} \leftarrow$ the set of features that can be split further;
4. **if** $\mathcal{F}$ *is empty* **then return** N;
5. $r \leftarrow$ a random number in interval $[0, 1]$;
6. **if** $r < \alpha$
7. **then** $N.f \leftarrow$ a feature selected from $\mathcal{F}$ deterministically;
8. $N.p \leftarrow$ a split point selected on $N.f$ deterministically;
9. **else** $N.f \leftarrow$ a feature selected from $\mathcal{F}$ randomly;
10. $N.p \leftarrow$ a split point selected on $N.f$ randomly;
11. $D_l \leftarrow$ subset of D with values on $N.f$ smaller than $N.p$;
12. $D_r \leftarrow$ subset of D with values on $N.f$ no smaller than $N.p$;
13. $N_l \leftarrow$ call the process with parameters (D_l, α);
14. $N_r \leftarrow$ call the process with parameters (D_r, α);
15. **return** N

Output: A VR-tree

Figure 3.12: The VR-Tree algorithm.

The parameter α controls the degree of randomness. When $\alpha = 1$, the produced VR-trees are identical to deterministic decision trees, while when $\alpha = 0$, the produced VR-trees are completely random trees. By adjusting the parameter value, we can observe a spectrum of randomization [Liu et al., 2008a], as illustrated in Figure 3.13. This provides a way to study the influence of randomness on the ensemble performance. The spectrum has two ends, i.e., the random end (α close to 0) and the deterministic end (α close to 1). In the

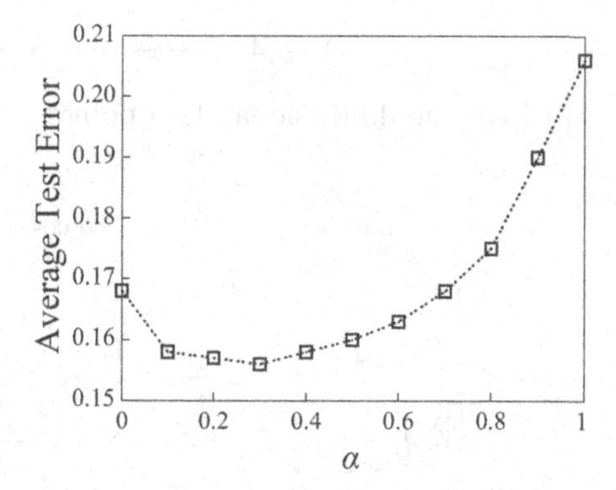

Figure 3.13: Illustration of the spectrum of randomization [Liu et al., 2008a]. The x-axis shows the α values, and the y-axis shows the predictive error of VR-Tree ensembles averaged over 45 UCI data sets.

random end, the trees are more diverse and of larger sizes; in the deterministic end, the trees are with higher accuracy and of smaller sizes. While the two ends have different characteristics, classifier ensembles can be improved by shifting toward the middle part of the spectrum. In practice, it is generally difficult to know which middle point is a really good choice. Liu et al. [2008a] suggested the Coalescence method which aggregates VR-trees with the parameter α being randomly chosen from $[0, 0.5]$, and it was observed in experiments that Coalescence often achieves better performance than RF and VR-Tree ensemble with fixed α's.

Note that the **completely random tree** lying at the random end (when $\alpha = 0$) does not require label information, and can be used in unsupervised learning, e.g., **density estimation** [Fan et al., 2003, Fan, 2004, Liu et al., 2005]. A completely random tree does not test whether the instances belong to the same class; instead, it can grow until every leaf node contains only one instance or indistinguishable instances. The construction algorithm can be obtained by replacing the condition "*all instances in the same class*" in the 2nd step of Figure 3.12 by "*only one instance*", and removing the 5th to 8th steps.

Figure 3.14 illustrates how completely random tree ensembles estimate data density. Figure 3.14(a) plots five one-dimensional data points, labeled as 1, 2, …,, 5, respectively. The completely random tree grows until every instance falls into a sole leaf node. First, we randomly choose a split point in between points 1 and 5, to divide the data into two groups. With a dominating probability, the split point falls either in between the points 1 and 2, or in between the points 4 and 5, since the gaps between these pairs of points are large. Suppose the split point adopted is in between the points 1 and 2, and thus, the point 1 is in a sole leaf node. Then, the next split point will be picked in between the points 4 and 5 with a large probability, and this will make

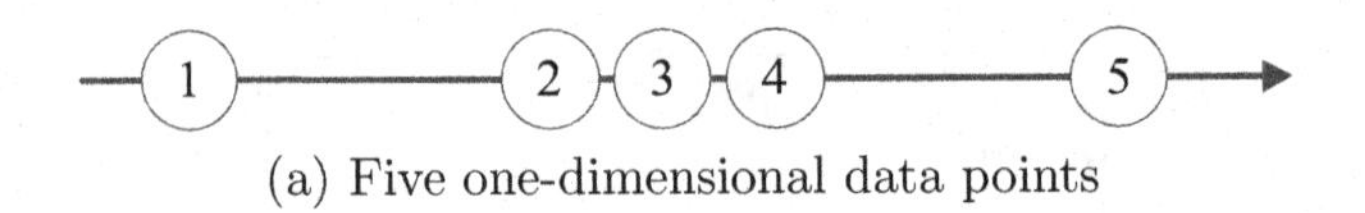

(a) Five one-dimensional data points

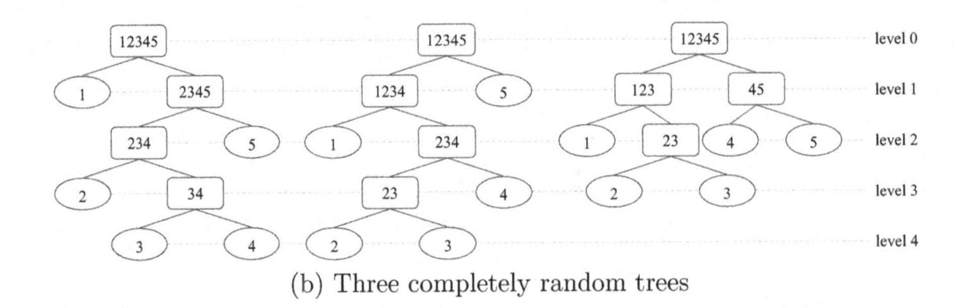

(b) Three completely random trees

(c) The depth of leaves on the one-dimensional data, each corresponding to a random tree in the sub-figure (b)

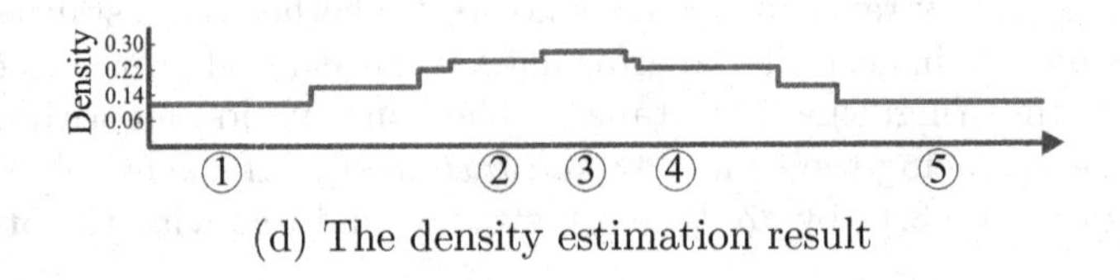

(d) The density estimation result

Figure 3.14: Illustration of density estimation by completely random tree ensemble.

the point 5 be put into a sole leaf node. It is clear that the points 1 and 5 are more likely to be put into "shallow" leaf nodes, while the points 2 to 4 are more likely to be put into "deep" leaf nodes. Figure 3.14(b) plots three completely random trees generated from the data. We can count the average depth of each data point: 1.67 for the points 1 and 5, 3.33 for the point 2, 3.67

for the point 3, and 3 for the point 4. Even though there are just three trees, we can conclude that the points 1 and 5 are located in a relatively sparse area, while the points 2 to 4 are located in relatively dense area. Figure 3.14(d) plots the density estimation result, where the density values are calculated as, e.g., $1.67/(1.67 \times 2 + 3.33 + 3.67 + 3)$ for the point 1.

The principle illustrated on one-dimensional data above also holds for higher-dimensional data and for more complex data distributions. It is easy to extend to tasks where the ensembles are constructed incrementally, such as in *online learning* or on streaming data. Note that the construction of a completely-random tree is quite efficient, since all it has to do is picking random numbers. Overall, the data density can be estimated through generating an ensemble of completely random trees and then calculating the average depth of each data point; this provides a practical and efficient tool for density estimation.

Completely random trees are also key components in **isolation forest**, a well-known ensemble method for anomaly detection (see Section 8.4), and **deep forest**, the first deep model based on non-differentiable modules (see Section 11.2).

3.7 Further Readings

Constructing ensembles of stable learners is difficult not only for Bagging but also for AdaBoost and other ensemble methods relying on **data sample manipulation**. The reason is that the pure data sample perturbation could not enable the base learners to have sufficiently large diversity. Chapter 5 will introduce diversity and discuss more on ensembles of stable learners.

Bagging typically adopts *majority voting* for classification and *simple averaging* for regression. If the base learners are able to output confidence values, *weighted voting* or *weighted averaging* are often used. Chapter 4 will introduce combination methods.

Bühlmann and Yu [2002] theoretically showed that Bagging tends to smooth crisp decisions, and the smoothing operation results in the variance reduction effect. Buja and Stuetzle [2000a,b, 2006] analyzed Bagging by using U-statistics, and found that the leading effect of Bagging on variance is at the second order. They also extended Bagging from statistics to statistical functional, and found that a Bagged functional is also smooth.

The term *forest* was first used to refer ensembles of decision trees by Ho [1995]. There are many other random decision tree ensemble methods, in addition to the ones introduced in this chapter, e.g., Dietterich [2000b], Cutler and Zhao [2001], Robnik-Šikonja [2004], Rodriguez et al. [2006], Geurts et al. [2006], Meinshausen and Ridgeway [2006]. There are discussion whether RF is the best classifier Fernández-Delgado et al. [2014], Wainberg et al. [2016]. Actually, even in the deep learning era, a practical routine for improving classification performance of deep neural networks is to replace the last layer of the neural network, after training, by a random forest [Kong and Yu, 2018].

Although the algorithm of RF [Breiman, 2001] looks simple, it is not easy for theoretical analysis. Breiman [2004b] presented consistency analysis of a simplified random forest, and Lin and Jeon [2006] showed that random forest can be viewed as an adaptive nearest neighbor algorithm. While most studies focused on random forest for regression [Biau, 2012, Denil et al., 2014, Scornet et al., 2015, Tang et al., 2018, Klusowski and Tian, 2024], Biau et al. [2008] made a significant progress on the consistency analysis of simplified random forest for classification. Gao et al. [2022] presented the first convergence rate of random forest for classification, while the first non-trivial convergence rate $O(m^{-1/(d+2)})$ for heuristic tree learning algorithms was obtained later in [Zheng et al., 2023]. Note that most theoretical studies were made on simplified random forest, and there is still a long way to fully understand random forest.

Chapter 4

Combination Methods

4.1 Benefits of Combination

After generating a set of base learners, rather than trying to find the best single learner, ensemble methods resort to combination to achieve a strong generalization ability, where the combination method plays a crucial role. Dietterich [2000a] attributed the benefit from combination to the following three fundamental reasons:

- *Statistical issue*: It is often the case that the hypothesis space is too large to explore for limited training data, and that there may be several different hypotheses giving the same accuracy on the training data. If the learning algorithm chooses one of these hypotheses, there is a risk that a mistakenly chosen hypothesis could not predict the future data well. As shown in Figure 4.1(a), by combining the hypotheses, the risk of choosing a wrong hypothesis can be reduced.

- *Computational issue*: Many learning algorithms perform some kind of local search that may get stuck in local optima. Even if there are enough training data, it may still be very difficult to find the best hypothesis. By running the local search from many different starting points, the combination may provide a better approximation to the true unknown hypothesis. As shown in Figure 4.1(b), by combining the hypotheses, the risk of choosing a wrong local minimum can be reduced.

- *Representational issue*: In many machine learning tasks, the true unknown hypothesis could not be represented by any hypothesis in the hypothesis space. As shown in Figure 4.1(c), by combining the hypotheses, it may be possible to expand the space of representable functions, and thus the learning algorithm may be able to form a more accurate approximation to the true unknown hypothesis.

DOI: 10.1201/9781003587774-4

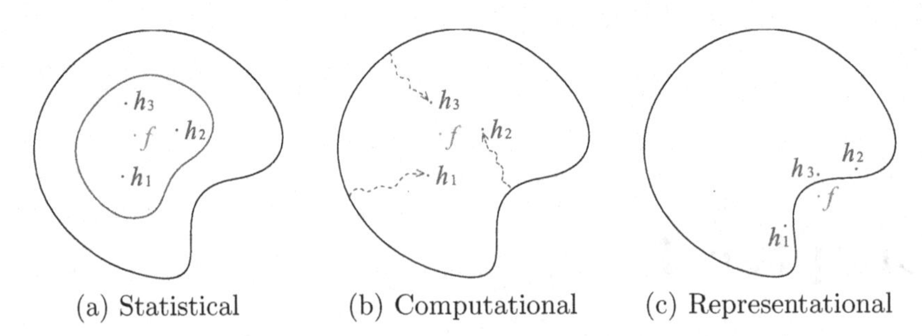

(a) Statistical (b) Computational (c) Representational

Figure 4.1: Three fundamental reasons for combination: (a) the statistical issue, (b) the computational issue, and (c) the representational issue. The outer curve represents the hypothesis space, and the inner curve in (a) represents the hypotheses with the same accuracy on the training data. The point label f is the true hypothesis, and h_i's are the individual hypotheses. (Plot based on a similar figure in [Dietterich, 2000a].)

These three issues are among the most important factors for which the traditional learning approaches fail. A learning algorithm that suffers from the statistical issue is generally said to have a high "*variance*", a learning algorithm that suffers from the computational issue can be described as having a high "*computational variance*", and a learning algorithm that suffers from the representational issue is generally said to have a high "*bias*". Therefore, through combination, the variance as well as the bias of learning algorithms may be reduced; this has been confirmed by many empirical studies [Xu et al., 1992, Bauer and Kohavi, 1999, Opitz and Maclin, 1999].

4.2 Averaging and Voting

4.2.1 Averaging

Averaging is the most popular and fundamental combination method for numeric outputs. In this section we take regression as an example to explain how averaging works. Suppose we are given a set of T individual learners $\{h_1, \ldots, h_T\}$ and the output of h_i for the instance $\boldsymbol{x}$ is $h_i(\boldsymbol{x}) \in \mathbb{R}$, our task is to combine h_i's to attain the final prediction on the real-valued variable.

Simple Averaging

Simple averaging obtains the combined output by averaging the outputs of individual learners directly. Specifically, simple averaging gives the combined output $H(\boldsymbol{x})$ as

$$H(\boldsymbol{x}) = \frac{1}{T}\sum_{i=1}^{T} h_i(\boldsymbol{x}). \tag{4.1}$$

Suppose the underlying true function we try to learn is $f(\boldsymbol{x})$, and $\boldsymbol{x}$ is sampled according to a distribution $p(\boldsymbol{x})$. The output of each learner can be written as the true value plus an error item, i.e.,

$$h_i(\boldsymbol{x}) = f(\boldsymbol{x}) + \epsilon_i(\boldsymbol{x}), \quad i = 1, \ldots, T. \tag{4.2}$$

Then, the mean squared error of h_i can be written as

$$\int (h_i(\boldsymbol{x}) - f(\boldsymbol{x}))^2 p(\boldsymbol{x}) d\boldsymbol{x} = \int \epsilon_i(\boldsymbol{x})^2 p(\boldsymbol{x}) d\boldsymbol{x} , \tag{4.3}$$

and the averaged error made by the individual learners is

$$\overline{err}(h) = \frac{1}{T} \sum_{i=1}^{T} \int \epsilon_i(\boldsymbol{x})^2 p(\boldsymbol{x}) d\boldsymbol{x} . \tag{4.4}$$

Similarly, it can be derived that the expected error of the combined learner (i.e., the ensemble) is

$$err(H) = \int \left(\frac{1}{T} \sum_{i=1}^{T} h_i(\boldsymbol{x}) - f(\boldsymbol{x}) \right)^2 p(\boldsymbol{x}) d\boldsymbol{x} = \int \left(\frac{1}{T} \sum_{i=1}^{T} \epsilon_i(\boldsymbol{x}) \right)^2 p(\boldsymbol{x}) d\boldsymbol{x}. \tag{4.5}$$

It can be seen that

$$err(H) \leq \overline{err}(h) . \tag{4.6}$$

That is, the expected ensemble error will be no larger than the averaged error of the individual learners.

Moreover, if we assume that the errors ϵ_i's have zero mean and are uncorrelated, i.e.,

$$\int \epsilon_i(\boldsymbol{x}) p(\boldsymbol{x}) d\boldsymbol{x} = 0 \quad \text{and} \quad \int \epsilon_i(\boldsymbol{x}) \epsilon_j(\boldsymbol{x}) p(\boldsymbol{x}) d\boldsymbol{x} = 0 \quad (\text{for } i \neq j) , \tag{4.7}$$

it is not difficult to get

$$err(H) = \frac{1}{T} \overline{err}(h) , \tag{4.8}$$

which suggests that the ensemble error is smaller by a factor of T than the averaged error of the individual learners.

Owing to its simplicity and effectiveness, simple averaging is among the most popularly used methods and represents the first choice in many real applications. It is worth noting, however, that the error reduction shown in (4.8) is derived based on the assumption that the errors of the individual learners are uncorrelated, while in ensemble learning the errors are typically highly correlated since the individual learners are trained on the same problem. Therefore, the error reduction shown in (4.8) is generally hard to achieve.

Weighted Averaging

Weighted averaging obtains the combined output by averaging the outputs of individual learners with different weights implying different importance. Specifically, weighted averaging gives the combined output $H(\boldsymbol{x})$ as

$$H(\boldsymbol{x}) = \sum_{i=1}^{T} w_i h_i(\boldsymbol{x}) \ , \tag{4.9}$$

where w_i is the weight for h_i, and the weights w_i's are usually assumed to be constrained by

$$w_i \geq 0 \quad \text{and} \quad \sum_{i=1}^{T} w_i = 1 \ . \tag{4.10}$$

Similarly as in Section 4.2.1, suppose the underlying true function we try to learn is $f(\boldsymbol{x})$, and $\boldsymbol{x}$ is sampled according to a distribution $p(\boldsymbol{x})$. The output of each learner can be written as (4.2). Then the ensemble error can be written as [Perrone and Cooper, 1995]

$$\begin{aligned} err(H) &= \int \left(\sum_{i=1}^{T} w_i h_i(\boldsymbol{x}) - f(\boldsymbol{x}) \right)^2 p(\boldsymbol{x}) d\boldsymbol{x} \\ &= \int \left(\sum_{i=1}^{T} w_i h_i(\boldsymbol{x}) - f(\boldsymbol{x}) \right) \left(\sum_{j=1}^{T} w_j h_j(\boldsymbol{x}) - f(\boldsymbol{x}) \right) p(\boldsymbol{x}) d\boldsymbol{x} \\ &= \sum_{i=1}^{T} \sum_{j=1}^{T} w_i w_j C_{ij} \ , \end{aligned} \tag{4.11}$$

where

$$C_{ij} = \int \left(h_i\left(\boldsymbol{x}\right) - f\left(\boldsymbol{x}\right) \right) \left(h_j\left(\boldsymbol{x}\right) - f\left(\boldsymbol{x}\right) \right) p(\boldsymbol{x}) d\boldsymbol{x} \ . \tag{4.12}$$

It is evident that the optimal weights can be solved by

$$\boldsymbol{w} = \arg\min_{\boldsymbol{w}} \sum_{i=1}^{T} \sum_{j=1}^{T} w_i w_j C_{ij} \ . \tag{4.13}$$

By applying the famous *Lagrange multiplier* method, it can be obtained that [Perrone and Cooper, 1995]

$$w_i = \frac{\sum_{j=1}^{T} [C^{-1}]_{ij}}{\sum_{k=1}^{T} \sum_{j=1}^{T} [C^{-1}]_{kj}} \ . \tag{4.14}$$

This provides a closed-form solution to the optimal weights. It is worth noticing, however, that this solution requires the correlation matrix C to be invertible, yet in ensemble learning such a matrix is usually singular or ill-conditioned, since the errors of the individual learners are typically highly correlated and many individual learners may be similar since they are trained on the same problem. Therefore, the solution shown in (4.14) is generally infeasible, and moreover, it does not guarantee non-negative solutions.

Simple averaging, which can be regarded as taking equal weights for all individual learners, is a special case of weighted averaging. Other combination methods, such as voting, are also special cases or variants of weighted averaging. Indeed, given a set of individual learners, the weighted averaging formulation [Perrone and Cooper, 1995] provides a fundamental motivation for ensemble methods, since any ensemble method can be regarded as trying a specific way to decide the weights for combining the individual learners, and different ensemble methods can be regarded as different implementations of weighted averaging. From this aspect it discloses that there is no ensemble method which is consistently the best, since deciding the weights is a computationally hard problem.

Note that though simple averaging is a special case of weighted averaging, it does not mean that weighted averaging is definitely better than simple averaging. In fact, experimental results reported in the literature do not show that weighted averaging is clearly superior to simple averaging [Xu et al., 1992, Ho et al., 1994, Kittler et al., 1998]. One important reason is that the data in real tasks are usually noisy and insufficient, and thus the estimated weights are often unreliable. In particular, with a large ensemble, there are a lot of weights to learn, and this can easily lead to overfitting; simple averaging does not have to learn any weights, and so suffers little from overfitting. In general, it is widely accepted that simple averaging is appropriate for combining learners with similar performances, whereas if the individual learners exhibit non-identical strength, weighted averaging with unequal weights may achieve a better performance.

4.2.2 Voting

Voting is the most popular and fundamental combination method for nominal outputs. In this section we take classification to explain how voting works. Suppose we are given a set of T individual classifiers $\{h_1, \ldots, h_T\}$ and our task is to combine h_i's to predict the class label from a set of l possible class labels $\{c_1, \ldots, c_l\}$. It is generally assumed that for an instance $\boldsymbol{x}$, the outputs of the classifier h_i are given as an l-dimensional label vector $(h_i^1(\boldsymbol{x}), \ldots, h_i^l(\boldsymbol{x}))^{\boldsymbol{T}}$, where $h_i^j(\boldsymbol{x})$ is the output of h_i for the class label c_j. The $h_i^j(\boldsymbol{x})$ can take different types of values according to the information provided by the individual classifiers, e.g.,

- Crisp label: $h_i^j(\boldsymbol{x}) \in \{0, 1\}$, which takes value one if h_i predicts c_j as the class label and zero otherwise.

- Class probability: $h_i^j(\boldsymbol{x}) \in [0, 1]$, which can be regarded as an estimate of the posterior probability $P(c_j \mid \boldsymbol{x})$.

For classifiers that produce un-normalized margins, such as SVMs, **calibration** methods such as Platt scaling [Platt, 2000] or Isotonic Regression [Zadrozny and Elkan, 2001] can be used to convert such an output to a probability. Note that the class probabilities estimated by most classifiers are poor; however, combination methods based on class probabilities are often highly competitive with those based on crisp labels, especially after a careful calibration.

Majority Voting

Majority voting is the most popular voting method. Here, every classifier votes for one class label, and the final output class label is the one that receives more than half of the votes; if none of the class labels receives more than half of the votes, a *rejection option* will be given and the combined classifier makes no prediction. That is, the output class label of the ensemble is

$$H(\boldsymbol{x}) = \begin{cases} c_j & \text{if } \sum_{i=1}^{T} h_i^j(\boldsymbol{x}) > \frac{1}{2} \sum_{k=1}^{l} \sum_{i=1}^{T} h_i^k(\boldsymbol{x}) , \\ \text{rejection} & \text{otherwise} . \end{cases} \tag{4.15}$$

If there are a total of T classifiers for a binary classification problem, the ensemble decision will be correct if at least $\lfloor T/2 + 1 \rfloor$ classifiers choose the correct class label. Assume that the outputs of the classifiers are independent and each classifier has an accuracy p, implying that each classifier makes a correct classification at probability p. The probability of the ensemble for making a correct decision can be calculated using a binomial distribution; specifically, the probability of obtaining at least $\lfloor T/2 + 1 \rfloor$ correct classifiers out of T is [Hansen and Salamon, 1990]:

$$P_{mv} = \sum_{k=\lfloor T/2+1 \rfloor}^{T} \binom{T}{k} p^k (1-p)^{T-k} . \tag{4.16}$$

The accuracy of the ensemble with different values of p and T is illustrated in Figure 4.2.

Lam and Suen [1997] showed that

- If $p > 0.5$, then P_{mv} is monotonically increasing in T, and

$$\lim_{T \to +\infty} P_{mv} = 1;$$

- If $p < 0.5$, then P_{mv} is monotonically decreasing in T, and

$$\lim_{T \to +\infty} P_{mv} = 0;$$

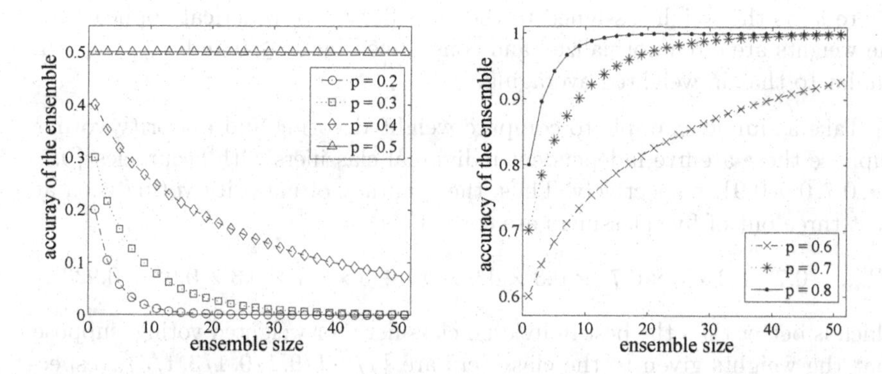

Figure 4.2: Ensemble accuracy of majority voting of T independent classifiers with accuracy p for binary classification.

- If $p = 0.5$, then $P_{mv} = 0.5$ for any T.

Note that this result is obtained based on the assumption that the individual classifiers are statistically independent, yet in practice the classifiers are generally highly correlated since they are trained on the same problem. Therefore, it is impractical to expect the majority voting accuracy to reach 1 as the number of individual classifiers increases.

Plurality Voting

In contrast to majority voting which requires the final winner to take at least half of votes, plurality voting takes the class label which receives the largest number of votes as the final winner. That is, the output class label of the ensemble is

$$H(\boldsymbol{x}) = c_{\arg\max_j \sum_{i=1}^{T} h_i^j(\boldsymbol{x})} , \tag{4.17}$$

and ties are broken arbitrarily. It is obvious that plurality voting does not have a reject option, since it can always find a label receiving the largest number of votes. Moreover, in the case of binary classification, plurality voting indeed coincides with majority voting.

Weighted Voting

If the individual classifiers are with unequal performance, intuitively, it is reasonable to give more power to the stronger classifiers in voting; this is realized by weighted voting. The output class label of the ensemble is

$$H(\boldsymbol{x}) = c_{\arg\max_j \sum_{i=1}^{T} w_i h_i^j(\boldsymbol{x})} , \tag{4.18}$$

where w_i is the weight assigned to the classifier h_i. In practical applications, the weights are often normalized and constrained by $w_i \geq 0$ and $\sum_{i=1}^{T} w_i = 1$, similar to that in weighted averaging.

Take a simple example to compare weighted voting and majority voting. Suppose there are five independent individual classifiers with accuracies $\{0.7, 0.7, 0.7, 0.9, 0.9\}$, respectively. Thus, the accuracy of majority voting (i.e., at least three out of five classifiers are correct) is

$$P_{mv} = 0.7^3 + 2 \times 3 \times 0.7^2 \times 0.3 \times 0.9 \times 0.1 + 3 \times 0.7 \times 0.3 \times 0.9^2 \approx 0.933 ,$$

which is better than the best individual classifier. For weighted voting, suppose that the weights given to the classifiers are $\{1/9, 1/9, 1/9, 1/3, 1/3\}$, respectively, and then the accuracy of weighted voting (i.e, the total weight of correct classifiers is larger than that of wrong classifiers) is

$$P_{wv} = 0.9^2 + 2 \times 3 \times 0.9 \times 0.1 \times 0.7^2 \times 0.3 + 2 \times 0.9 \times 0.1 \times 0.7^3 \approx 0.951 .$$

This shows that, with adequate weight assignments, weighted voting can be better than both the best individual classifier and majority voting. Similar to weighted averaging, the key is how to obtain the weights.

Let $\boldsymbol{\ell} = (\ell_1, \ldots, \ell_T)^{\boldsymbol{T}}$ denote the outputs of the individual classifiers, where ℓ_i is the class label predicted for the instance $\boldsymbol{x}$ by the classifier h_i, and let p_i denote the accuracy of h_i. There is a Bayes optimal discriminant function for the combined output on class label c_j, i.e.,

$$H^j(\boldsymbol{x}) = \log\left(P\left(c_j\right) P\left(\boldsymbol{\ell} \mid c_j\right)\right) . \tag{4.19}$$

Assuming that the outputs of the individual classifiers are conditionally independent, i.e., $P(\boldsymbol{\ell} \mid c_j) = \prod_{i=1}^{T} P(\ell_i \mid c_j)$, then it follows that

$$\begin{aligned} H^j(\boldsymbol{x}) &= \log P(c_j) + \sum_{i=1}^{T} \log P(\ell_i \mid c_j) \\ &= \log P(c_j) + \log\left(\prod_{i=1,\ell_i=c_j}^{T} P(\ell_i \mid c_j) \prod_{i=1,\ell_i\neq c_j}^{T} P(\ell_i \mid c_j)\right) \\ &= \log P(c_j) + \log\left(\prod_{i=1,\ell_i=c_j}^{T} p_i \prod_{i=1,\ell_i\neq c_j}^{T} (1-p_i)\right) \\ &= \log P(c_j) + \sum_{i=1,\ell_i=c_j}^{T} \log\frac{p_i}{1-p_i} + \sum_{i=1}^{T} \log(1-p_i) . \end{aligned} \tag{4.20}$$

Since $\sum_{i=1}^{T} \log(1-p_i)$ does not depend on the class label c_j, and $\ell_i = c_j$ can be expressed by the result of $h_i^j(\boldsymbol{x})$, the discriminant function can be reduced to

$$H^j(\boldsymbol{x}) = \log P(c_j) + \sum_{i=1}^{T} h_i^j(\boldsymbol{x}) \log \frac{p_i}{1 - p_i}. \tag{4.21}$$

The first term at the right-hand side of (4.21) does not rely on the individual learners, while the second term discloses that the optimal weights for weighted voting satisfy

$$w_i \propto \log \frac{p_i}{1 - p_i}, \tag{4.22}$$

which shows that the weights should be in proportion to the performance of the individual learners.

Note that (4.22) is obtained by assuming independence among the outputs of individual classifiers, yet this does not hold since all the individual classifiers are trained on the same problem and they are usually highly correlated. Moreover, it requires the estimation of ground-truth accuracies of individual classifiers, and does not take the class priors into account. Therefore, in real practice, (4.22) does not always lead to a performance better than majority voting.

Soft Voting

For individual classifiers which produce crisp class labels, majority voting, plurality voting and weighted voting can be used, while for individual classifiers which produce class probability outputs, soft voting is generally the choice. Here, the individual classifier h_i outputs a l-dimensional vector $(h_i^1(\boldsymbol{x}), \ldots, h_i^l(\boldsymbol{x}))^T$ for the instance $\boldsymbol{x}$, where $h_i^j(\boldsymbol{x}) \in [0, 1]$ can be regarded as an estimate of the posterior probability $P(c_j \mid \boldsymbol{x})$.

If all the individual classifiers are treated equally, the *simple soft voting* method generates the combined output by simply averaging all the individual outputs, and the final output for class c_j is given by

$$H^j(\boldsymbol{x}) = \frac{1}{T} \sum_{i=1}^{T} h_i^j(\boldsymbol{x}). \tag{4.23}$$

If we consider combining the individual outputs with different weights, the *weighted soft voting* method can be any of the following three forms:

- A classifier-specific weight is assigned to each classifier, and the combined output for class c_j is

$$H^j(\boldsymbol{x}) = \sum_{i=1}^{T} w_i h_i^j(\boldsymbol{x}), \tag{4.24}$$

  where w_i is the weight assigned to the classifier h_i.

- A class-specific weight is assigned to each classifier per class, and the combined output for class c_j is

$$H^j(\boldsymbol{x}) = \sum_{i=1}^{T} w_i^j h_i^j(\boldsymbol{x}), \tag{4.25}$$

where w_i^j is the weight assigned to the classifier h_i for the class c_j.

- A weight is assigned to each example of each class for each classifier, and the combined output for class c_j is

$$H^j(\boldsymbol{x}) = \sum_{i=1}^{T} \sum_{k=1}^{m} w_{ik}^j h_i^j(\boldsymbol{x}), \tag{4.26}$$

where w_{ik}^j is the weight of the instance $\boldsymbol{x}_k$ of the class c_j for the classifier h_i.

In real practice, the third type is not often used since it may involve a large number of weight coefficients. The first type is similar to weighted averaging or weighted voting, and so, in the following, we focus on the second type, i.e., class-specific weights. Since $h_i^j(\boldsymbol{x})$ can be regarded as an estimate of $P(c_j \mid \boldsymbol{x})$, it follows that

$$h_i^j(\boldsymbol{x}) = P(c_j \mid \boldsymbol{x}) + \epsilon_i^j(\boldsymbol{x}) \ , \tag{4.27}$$

where $\epsilon_i^j(\boldsymbol{x})$ is the approximation error. In classification, the target output is given as a class label. If the estimation is unbiased, the combined output $H^j(\boldsymbol{x}) = \sum_{i=1}^{T} w_i^j h_i^j(\boldsymbol{x})$ is also unbiased, and we can obtain a variance-minimized unbiased estimation $H^j(\boldsymbol{x})$ for $P(c_j \mid \boldsymbol{x})$ by setting the weights. Minimizing the variance of the combined approximation error $\sum_{i=1}^{T} w_i^j \epsilon_i^j(\boldsymbol{x})$ under the constraints $w_i^j \geq 0$ and $\sum_{i=1}^{T} w_i^j = 1$, we can get the optimization problem

$$\boldsymbol{w}^j = \arg\min_{\boldsymbol{w}^j} \sum_{k=1}^{m} \left(\sum_{i=1}^{T} w_i^j h_i^j(\boldsymbol{x}_k) - \mathbb{I}(f(\boldsymbol{x}_k) = c_j) \right)^2 , \quad j = 1, \ldots, l, \tag{4.28}$$

from which the weights can be solved.

Note that soft voting is generally used for *homogeneous ensembles*. For *heterogeneous ensembles*, the class probabilities generated by different types of learners usually cannot be compared directly without careful calibration. In such situations, the class probability outputs are often converted to class label outputs by setting $h_i^j(\boldsymbol{x})$ to 1 if $h_i^j(\boldsymbol{x}) = \max_j\{h_i^j(\boldsymbol{x})\}$ and 0 otherwise, and then the voting methods for crisp labels can be applied.

4.2.3 Theoretical Explanations

In Section 4.2, theoretical analysis shows that averaging can reduce the expected ensemble error. Here, we will introduce theoretical explanations of voting.

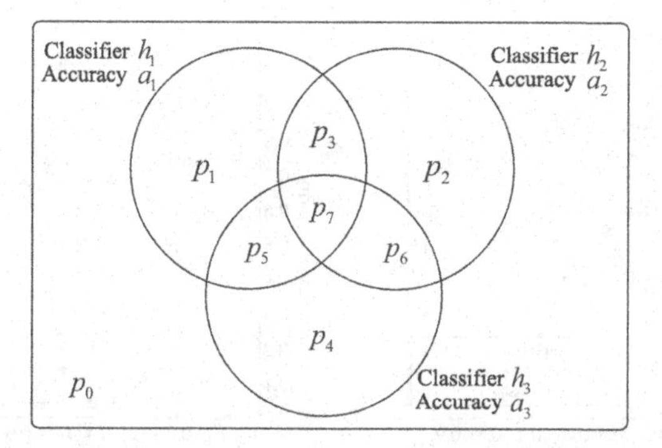

Figure 4.3: Venn diagram showing joint statistics of three classifiers. The regions marked with different p_i's correspond to different bit combinations, and p_i is the probability associated with the corresponding region. (Plot based on a similar figure in [Narasimhamurthy, 2003].)

Theoretical Bounds of Majority Voting

Narasimhamurthy [2003, 2005] analyzed the theoretical bounds of majority voting. In this section we focus on the introduction of this analysis.

Consider the binary classification problem, given a set of T classifiers, $h_1, \ldots, h_T$, with accuracies $a_1, \ldots, a_T$, respectively, and for simplicity, assuming that T is an odd number (similar results for an even number can be found in [Narasimhamurthy, 2005]). The joint statistics of classifiers can be represented by **Venn diagrams**, and an example of three classifiers is illustrated in Figure 4.3. Here, each classifier is represented by a bit (i.e., 1 or 0) with 1 indicating that the classifier is correct and 0 otherwise. The regions in the Venn diagram correspond to the bit combinations. For example, the region marked with p_3 corresponds to the bit combination "110", i.e., it corresponds to the event that both h_1 and h_2 are correct while h_3 is incorrect, and p_3 indicates the probability associated with this event. Now, let $\boldsymbol{p} = [p_0, \ldots, p_{2^T-1}]^{\boldsymbol{T}}$ denote the vector of joint probabilities, $bit(i, T)$ denotes the T-bit binary representation of integer i, and $\boldsymbol{f}_{mv}$ denotes a bit vector of length 2^T where the entry at the i-th position is

$$\boldsymbol{f}_{mv}(i) = \begin{cases} 1 & \text{if the number of 1's in } bit(i, T) > T/2, \\ 0 & \text{otherwise.} \end{cases} \tag{4.29}$$

Then, the probability of correct classification of majority voting can be represented as $\boldsymbol{f}_{mv}^{\mathrm{T}} \boldsymbol{p}$. This is the objective to be maximized/minimized subject to certain constraints [Narasimhamurthy, 2003, 2005].

Note that the accuracy of classifier h_i is a_i, that is, the probability of h_i being correct is a_i. This can be represented as T constraints in the form of

$$\boldsymbol{b}_i^{\mathrm{T}} \boldsymbol{p} = a_i \ (1 \le i \le T) \ , \tag{4.30}$$

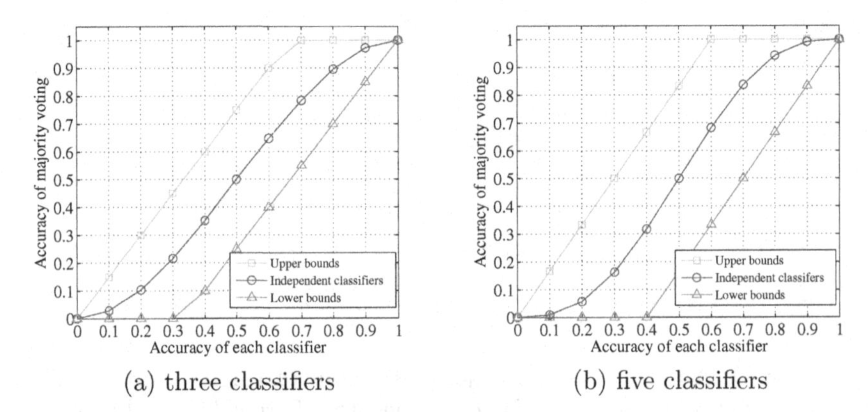

(a) three classifiers (b) five classifiers

Figure 4.4: Theoretical lower and upper bounds of majority voting, and the accuracy of individual independent classifiers when there are (a) three classifiers and (b) five classifiers. (Plot from a similar figure in [Narasimhamurthy, 2003].)

and it can be found that

$$\begin{aligned}
\boldsymbol{b}_1 &= (0,1,\ldots,0,1)^{\mathrm{T}} \\
\boldsymbol{b}_2 &= (0,0,1,1,\ldots,0,0,1,1)^{\mathrm{T}} \\
&\vdots \\
\boldsymbol{b}_T &= (\overbrace{0,0,\ldots,0,0}^{2^{T-1}},\ldots,\overbrace{1,1,\ldots,1,1}^{2^{T-1}})^{\mathrm{T}}.
\end{aligned}$$

Let $\mathbf{B} = (\boldsymbol{b}_1,\ldots,\boldsymbol{b}_T)^{\mathrm{T}}$ and $\boldsymbol{a} = (a_1,\ldots,a_T)^{\mathrm{T}}$. Considering the constraints $\sum_{i=0}^{2^T-1} p_i = 1$ and $0 \leq p_i \leq 1$, the lower and upper bounds of majority voting can be solved from linear programming problems [Narasimhamurthy, 2003, 2005]:

$$\begin{aligned}
&\min / \max{}_{\boldsymbol{p}} \ \boldsymbol{f}_{mv}^{\mathrm{T}}\boldsymbol{p} \\
\text{s.t.} \quad &\mathbf{B}\boldsymbol{p} = \boldsymbol{a} \\
&\mathbf{1}^{\mathrm{T}}\boldsymbol{p} = 1 \\
&0 \leq p_i \leq 1 \quad (\forall i = 0,1,\ldots,2^T-1).
\end{aligned} \tag{4.31}$$

The theoretical lower and upper bounds of majority voting for three and five classifiers are respectively illustrated in Figure 4.4(a) and (b). For the purpose of illustration, all classifiers are assumed to have the same accuracy. The accuracy varies from 0 to 1 and the corresponding lower and upper bounds of majority voting are determined for each value. The accuracy of the individual classifiers is also plotted, and it is obvious that the accuracy curves locate inside the region bounded by the lower and upper bounds.

As for the role of the ensemble size T, we can find that the number of constraints is linear in T, whereas the dimension of the vector $\boldsymbol{p}$ is exponential in T. In other words, the "degrees of freedom" increase exponentially as T increases. Hence, for a particular accuracy of the classifiers, increasing the ensemble size will lead to a lower theoretical minimum (lower bound) and a higher theoretical maximum (upper bound). This trend can be found by comparing Figure 4.4(a) and (b). It is worth noting, however, that this conclusion is drawn based on the assumption that the individual classifiers are independent, while this assumption usually does not hold in real practice.

Theoretical Bounds of Weighted Majority Voting

In this section, we consider the majority voting from a weighted distribution Q over a (finite) set of voters $\mathcal{H}$. For an instance $\boldsymbol{x} \in \mathcal{X}$, the output $B_Q(\boldsymbol{x})$ of a Q-weighted majority voting classifier B_Q is given by

$$B_Q(\boldsymbol{x}) = \mathtt{sign}\left(\mathbb{E}_{h\sim Q}[h(\boldsymbol{x})]\right) . \tag{4.32}$$

This section focuses on binary classification $y \in \{-1, +1\}$, and we have the classification error of majority vote classifier B_Q over data distribution $\mathfrak{D}$ as

$$\epsilon_{\mathfrak{D}}(B_Q) = \underset{(\boldsymbol{x},y)\sim\mathfrak{D}}{P}\left(B_Q(\boldsymbol{x}) \neq y\right) = \underset{(\boldsymbol{x},y)\sim\mathfrak{D}}{P}\left(\underset{h\sim Q}{\mathbb{E}}[yh(\boldsymbol{x})] \leq 0\right) . \tag{4.33}$$

The output of majority vote classifier B_Q is closely related to the output of a stochastic classifier called the *Gibbs classifier*. To classify an instance $\boldsymbol{x}$, the Gibbs classifier G_Q randomly chooses a voter h according to the weighted distribution Q, and then returns the prediction $h(\boldsymbol{x})$. Note that the outputs may be different even for the same instance $\boldsymbol{x}$ according to the stochasticity of the Gibbs classifier. We define the Gibbs error of classifier G_Q as

$$\epsilon_{\mathfrak{D}}(G_Q) = \underset{\substack{h\sim Q\\(\boldsymbol{x},y)\sim\mathfrak{D}}}{P}\left(h(\boldsymbol{x}) \neq y\right) = \underset{(\boldsymbol{x},y)\sim\mathfrak{D}}{\mathbb{E}}\ \underset{h\sim Q}{\mathbb{E}}\left[\mathbb{I}(h(\boldsymbol{x}) \neq y)\right] . \tag{4.34}$$

For binary classification $y \in \{-1, +1\}$ and $h(\boldsymbol{x}) \in \{-1, +1\}$, it can be derived that

$$\epsilon_{\mathfrak{D}}(G_Q) = \frac{1}{2}\left(1 - \underset{(\boldsymbol{x},y)\sim\mathfrak{D}}{\mathbb{E}}\ \underset{h\sim Q}{\mathbb{E}}[yh(\boldsymbol{x})]\right) . \tag{4.35}$$

For Q-weighted classifier B_Q and Gibbs classifier G_Q, we have, from (4.33),

$$\begin{aligned}
\epsilon_{\mathfrak{D}}(B_Q) &= \underset{(\boldsymbol{x},y)\sim\mathfrak{D}}{P}\left(\underset{h\sim Q}{\mathbb{E}}[yh(\boldsymbol{x})] \leq 0\right)\\
&= \underset{(\boldsymbol{x},y)\sim\mathfrak{D}}{P}\left(1 - \underset{h\sim Q}{\mathbb{E}}[yh(\boldsymbol{x})] \geq 1\right)\\
&\leq \underset{(\boldsymbol{x},y)\sim\mathfrak{D}}{\mathbb{E}}\left(1 - \underset{h\sim Q}{\mathbb{E}}[yh(\boldsymbol{x})]\right)\\
&= 1 - \underset{(\boldsymbol{x},y)\sim\mathfrak{D}}{\mathbb{E}}\ \underset{h\sim Q}{\mathbb{E}}[yh(\boldsymbol{x})] = 2\epsilon_{\mathfrak{D}}(G_Q) ,
\end{aligned}$$

where the inequality and last equality hold from Markov's inequality and (4.35), respectively. This gives the following theorem:

Theorem 4.1 ([Langford and Shawe-Taylor, 2002, Germain et al., 2015]). *For any weighted distribution Q on a set of voters $\mathcal{H}$, and for any data distribution $\mathcal{D}$ on $\mathcal{X} \times \{-1, 1\}$, we have*

$$\epsilon_{\mathcal{D}}(B_Q) \leq 2\epsilon_{\mathcal{D}}(G_Q). \tag{4.36}$$

This theorem shows that the classification error of weighted majority voting classifier B_Q is bounded by twice the Gibbs error of classifier G_Q. Langford and Shawe-Taylor [2002] proved that this bound (i.e., the factor 2) is almost tight, which presents a possible limitation of majority voting in the worst case. Also, the factor 2 can be improved to $1 + \delta$ for some small $\delta \in (0, 1)$ under some circumstances, as shown in [Langford and Shawe-Taylor, 2002].

Theorem 4.1 presents upper bound for $\epsilon_{\mathcal{D}}(B_Q)$ by considering the first moment of $\mathbb{E}_{(\boldsymbol{x},y)\sim\mathcal{D}}\mathbb{E}_{h\sim Q}[yh(\boldsymbol{x})]$ based on Markov's inequality. Germain et al. [2015] further considered its second moments and Chebyshev's inequality to present the better $\mathcal{C}$-bound, which is originally introduced by Lacasse et al. [2006] but some different variants.

For weighted probability distribution Q on a set of voters $\mathcal{H}$, the *expected disagreement* $d_Q^{\mathcal{D}}$ relative to $\mathcal{D}$ is defined as

$$\begin{aligned} d_Q^{\mathcal{D}} &= \mathbb{E}_{\boldsymbol{x}\sim D_{\mathcal{X}}} P_{h_1,h_2\sim Q}[h_1(\boldsymbol{x}) \neq h_2(\boldsymbol{x})] \\ &= 1/2 - \mathbb{E}_{\boldsymbol{x}\sim D_{\mathcal{X}}}\mathbb{E}_{h_1,h_2\sim Q}[h_1(\boldsymbol{x})h_2(\boldsymbol{x})]/2 \\ &= 1/2 - \mathbb{E}_{\boldsymbol{x}\sim D_{\mathcal{X}}}\left[\mathbb{E}_{h\sim Q}[h(\boldsymbol{x})]\right]^2/2\,, \end{aligned} \tag{4.37}$$

where $\mathcal{D}_{\mathcal{X}}$ denotes the marginal distribution over the instance space $\mathcal{X}$ from data distribution $\mathcal{D}$. Note that the expected disagreement $d_Q^{\mathcal{D}}$ does not depend on the label y of example $(x, y) \sim D'$, and we can estimate it with unlabeled data.

From (4.33), we have

$$\begin{aligned} \epsilon_{\mathcal{D}}(B_Q) &= \underset{(\boldsymbol{x},y)\sim\mathcal{D}}{P}\left(\underset{h\sim Q}{\mathbb{E}}[yh(\boldsymbol{x})] \leq 0\right) \\ &= \underset{(\boldsymbol{x},y)\sim\mathcal{D}}{P}\left(\underset{(\boldsymbol{x},y)\sim\mathcal{D}}{\mathbb{E}}\left[\underset{h\sim Q}{\mathbb{E}}[yh(\boldsymbol{x})]\right] - \underset{h\sim Q}{\mathbb{E}}[yh(\boldsymbol{x})] \geq \underset{(\boldsymbol{x},y)\sim\mathcal{D}}{\mathbb{E}}\left[\underset{h\sim Q}{\mathbb{E}}[yh(\boldsymbol{x})]\right]\right) \\ &\leq \frac{var_{(\boldsymbol{x},y)\sim\mathcal{D}}\left(\mathbb{E}_{h\sim Q}[yh(\boldsymbol{x})]\right)}{var_{(\boldsymbol{x},y)\sim\mathcal{D}}\left(\mathbb{E}_{h\sim Q}[yh(\boldsymbol{x})]\right) + \left(\mathbb{E}_{(\boldsymbol{x},y)\sim\mathcal{D}}\left[\mathbb{E}_{h\sim Q}[yh(\boldsymbol{x})]\right]\right)^2}\,, \end{aligned} \tag{4.38}$$

where the inequality holds from one-sided Chebyshev inequality. This follows that, by using $var(X) = \mathbb{E}[X^2] - (E[X])^2$,

$$\epsilon_{\mathcal{D}}(B_Q) \leq 1 - \frac{\left(\mathbb{E}_{(\boldsymbol{x},y)\sim\mathcal{D}}\left[\mathbb{E}_{h\sim Q}[yh(\boldsymbol{x})]\right]\right)^2}{\mathbb{E}_{(\boldsymbol{x},y)\sim\mathcal{D}}\left[\mathbb{E}_{h\sim Q}[yh(\boldsymbol{x})]\right]^2}\,. \tag{4.39}$$

Combining with (4.35) and (4.37) gives the $\mathcal{C}$-bounds as follows:

Theorem 4.2 ([Germain et al., 2015]). *For any weighted distribution Q on a set of voters $\mathcal{H}$, and for any data distribution $\mathcal{D}$ on $\mathcal{X} \times \{-1, 1\}$, if $\epsilon_{\mathcal{D}}(G_Q) < 1/2$ then we have*

$$\epsilon_{\mathcal{D}}(B_Q) \leq 1 - \frac{(1 - 2\epsilon_{\mathcal{D}}(G_Q))^2}{1 - 2d_Q^{\mathcal{D}}} . \tag{4.40}$$

This theorem shows that the error of the majority voting classifier decreases when the Gibbs error $\epsilon_{\mathcal{D}}(G_Q)$ decreases or when the disagreement $d_Q^{\mathcal{D}}$ increases. This new bound therefore suggests that a majority vote should perform a trade-off between the Gibbs error and the disagreement in order to achieve a low error. This is more informative than the bound in Theorem 4.1, which focuses solely on the minimization of the Gibbs error. Germain et al. [2015] also showed the optimality of the $\mathcal{C}$-bounds, and the $\mathcal{C}$-bounds can be arbitrarily small, even for large Gibbs error.

Decision Boundary Analysis

Tumer and Ghosh [1996] developed the *decision boundary analysis* framework. Later, Fumera and Roli [2005] analyzed the simple as well as weighted soft voting methods based on this framework. In this section we focus on the introduction of this framework and the main results in [Tumer and Ghosh, 1996, Fumera and Roli, 2005].

For simplicity, we consider one-dimensional feature space as in [Tumer and Ghosh, 1996, Fumera and Roli, 2005], while it is known that the same results hold for multi-dimensional feature spaces [Tumer, 1996]. According to Bayesian decision theory, an instance x should be assigned to class c_i for which the posterior probability $P(c_i \mid x)$ is the maximum. As shown in Figure 4.5, the ideal decision boundary between the classes c_i and c_j is the point x^* such that

$$P(c_i \mid x^*) = P(c_j \mid x^*) > \max_{k \neq i,j} P(c_k \mid x^*) . \tag{4.41}$$

In practice, the classifier can only provide an estimate $h^j(x)$ of the true posterior probability $P(c_j \mid x)$, that is,

$$h^j(x) = P(c_j \mid x) + \epsilon_j(x) , \tag{4.42}$$

where $\epsilon_j(x)$ denotes the error term, which is regarded as a random variable with mean β_j (named "bias") and variance σ_j^2. Thus, when Bayesian decision rule is applied, misclassification occurs if

$$\arg\max_i h^i(x) \neq \arg\max_i P(c_i \mid x) . \tag{4.43}$$

The decision boundary obtained from the estimated posteriors, denoted as x_b, is characterized by

$$h^i(x_b) = h^j(x_b) , \tag{4.44}$$

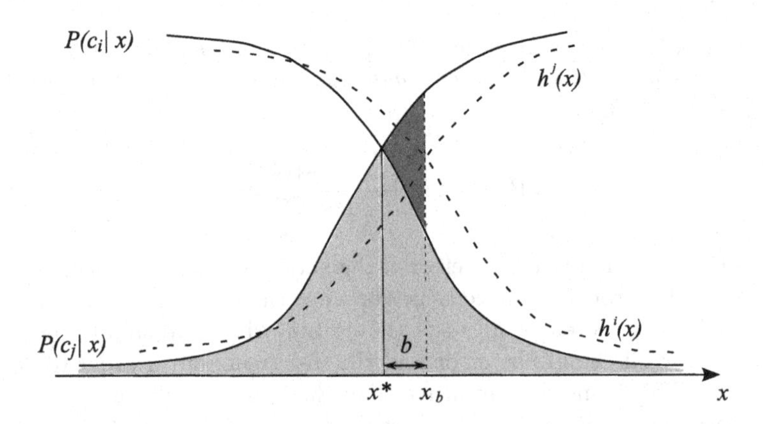

Figure 4.5: True posteriors $P(c_i \mid x)$ and $P(c_j \mid x)$ (solid lines) around the boundary x^*, and the estimated posteriors $h^i(x)$ and $h^j(x)$ (dashed lines) leading to the boundary x_b. Lightly and darkly shaded areas represent *Bayes error* and *added error*, respectively. (Plot from a similar figure in [Fumera and Roli, 2005].)

and it may differ from the ideal boundary by an offset

$$b = x_b - x^* \ . \tag{4.45}$$

As shown in Figure 4.5, this leads to an additional misclassification error term over Bayes error, named *added error* [Tumer and Ghosh, 1996].

In the following, we focus on the case of unbiased and uncorrelated errors (detailed analysis on other cases can be found in [Tumer and Ghosh, 1996, Fumera and Roli, 2005]). Thus, for any given x, the mean of every error item $\epsilon_j(x)$ is zero, i.e., $\beta_j = 0$, and the error items on different classes, $\epsilon_i(x)$ and $\epsilon_j(x)$, $i \neq j$, are uncorrelated.

Without loss of generality, assume $b > 0$. From Figure 4.5, it can be seen that the added error depends on the offset b and is given by

$$\int_{x^*}^{x^*+b} \left[P\left(c_j \mid x\right) - P\left(c_i \mid x\right) \right] p(x) dx \ , \tag{4.46}$$

where $p(x)$ is the probability distribution of x. Assuming that the shift $b = x_b - x^*$ is small, a linear approximation can be used around x^*, that is,

$$P(c_k \mid x^* + b) = P(c_k \mid x^*) + bP'(c_k \mid x^*) \ . \tag{4.47}$$

Moreover, $p(x)$ is approximated by $p(x^*)$. Therefore, the added error becomes $p(x^*)tb^2/2$, where $t = P'(c_j \mid x^*) - P'(c_i \mid x^*)$. Based on (4.42) and (4.44), it can be obtained that

$$b = \frac{\epsilon_i(x_b) - \epsilon_j(x_b)}{t} \ . \tag{4.48}$$

Since $\epsilon_i(x)$ and $\epsilon_j(x)$ are unbiased and uncorrelated, the bias and variance of b are given by $\beta_b = 0$ and $\sigma_b^2 = \frac{\sigma_i^2+\sigma_j^2}{t^2}$. Consequently, the expected value of the added error with respect to b, denoted by err_{add}, is then given by [Tumer and Ghosh, 1996]

$$err_{add}(h) = \frac{p(x^*)t}{2}(\beta_b^2 + \sigma_b^2) = \frac{p(x^*)}{2t}(\sigma_i^2 + \sigma_j^2) \ . \tag{4.49}$$

Now, consider the simplest form of weighted soft voting, which assigns a non-negative weight w_i to each individual learner. Based on (4.42), the averaged estimate for the j-th class is

$$h_{wsv}^j(x) = \sum_{i=1}^{T} w_i h_i^j(x) = P(c_j \mid x) + \epsilon_j^{wsv}(x) \ , \tag{4.50}$$

where $\epsilon_j^{wsv}(x) = \sum_{i=1}^{T} w_i \epsilon_j^i(x)$ and "wsv" denotes "weighted soft voting". Analogous to that in Figure 4.5, the decision boundary $x_{b_{wsv}}$ is characterized by $h_{wsv}^i(x) = h_{wsv}^j(x)$, and it has an offset b_{wsv} from x^*. Following the same steps as above, the expected added error of weighted soft voting can be obtained as

$$err_{add}^{wsv}(H) = \frac{p(x^*)}{2t}\sum_{k=1}^{T} w_k^2 \left[(\sigma_i^k)^2 + (\sigma_j^k)^2\right] = \sum_{k=1}^{T} w_k^2 err_{add}(h_k) \ , \tag{4.51}$$

where, from (4.49),

$$err_{add}(h_k) = \frac{p(x^*)}{2t}\left[(\sigma_i^k)^2 + (\sigma_j^k)^2\right] \tag{4.52}$$

is the expected added error of the individual classifier h_k. Thus, the performance of soft voting methods can be analyzed based on the expected added errors of individual classifiers, instead of the biases and variances.

Minimizing $err_{add}^{wsv}(H)$ under the constraints $w_k \geq 0$ and $\sum_{k=1}^{T} w_k = 1$, the optimal weights can be obtained as

$$w_k = \left(\sum_{i=1}^{T} \frac{1}{err_{add}(h_i)}\right)^{-1} \frac{1}{err_{add}(h_k)} \ . \tag{4.53}$$

This shows that the optimal weights are inversely proportional to the expected added error of the corresponding classifiers. This provides a theoretical support to the argument that different weights should be used for classifiers of different strengths [Tumer and Ghosh, 1996].

Substituting (4.53) into (4.51), the value of $err_{add}^{wsv}(H)$ corresponding to the optimal weights is

$$err_{add}^{wsv}(H) = \frac{1}{\frac{1}{err_{add}(h_1)} + \cdots + \frac{1}{err_{add}(h_T)}} \ . \tag{4.54}$$

On the other hand, if simple soft voting is used, an equal weight $w_i = 1/T$ is applied to (4.51), and the expected added error is

$$err_{\text{add}}^{ssv}(H) = \frac{1}{T^2} \sum_{k=1}^{T} err_{add}(h_k) , \tag{4.55}$$

where "ssv" denotes "simple soft voting".

When the individual classifiers exhibit identical expected added errors, i.e., $err_{add}(h_i) = err_{add}(h_j)$ $(\forall i, j)$, it follows that $err_{\text{add}}^{wsv}(H) = err_{\text{add}}^{ssv}(H)$, and the expected added error is reduced by a factor T over each individual classifier.

When the individual classifiers exhibit non-identical added errors, it follows that $err_{\text{add}}^{wsv}(H) < err_{\text{add}}^{ssv}(H)$. Without loss of generality, denote the smallest and largest expected added errors as

$$err_{\text{add}}^{best}(H) = \min_i \{err_{add}(h_i)\} \quad \text{and} \quad err_{\text{add}}^{worst}(H) = \max_i \{err_{add}(h_i)\} , \tag{4.56}$$

and the corresponding classifiers are called the "best" and "worst" classifiers, respectively. From (4.55), the error reduction achieved by simple soft voting over the k-th classifier is

$$\frac{err_{\text{add}}^{ssv}(H)}{err_{add}(h_k)} = \frac{1}{T^2} \left(1 + \sum_{i \neq k} \frac{err_{add}(h_i)}{err_{add}(h_k)} \right) . \tag{4.57}$$

It follows that the reduction factors over the best and worst classifiers are respectively in the ranges

$$\frac{err_{\text{add}}^{ssv}(H)}{err_{\text{add}}^{best}(H)} \in \left(\frac{1}{T}, +\infty \right), \quad \frac{err_{\text{add}}^{ssv}(H)}{err_{\text{add}}^{worst}(H)} \in \left(\frac{1}{T^2}, \frac{1}{T} \right) . \tag{4.58}$$

From (4.54), the reduction factor of weighted soft voting is

$$\frac{err_{\text{add}}^{wsv}(H)}{err_{add}(h_k)} = \left(1 + \sum_{i \neq k} \frac{err_{add}(h_k)}{err_{add}(h_i)} \right)^{-1} , \tag{4.59}$$

and consequently

$$\frac{err_{\text{add}}^{wsv}(H)}{err_{\text{add}}^{best}(H)} \in \left(\frac{1}{T}, 1 \right), \quad \frac{err_{\text{add}}^{wsv}(H)}{err_{\text{add}}^{worst}(H)} \in \left(0, \frac{1}{T} \right) . \tag{4.60}$$

From (4.58) and (4.60) it can be seen that, if the individual classifiers have non-identical added errors, both the simple and weighted soft voting achieve an error reduction smaller than a factor of T over the best classifier, and larger than a factor of T over the worst classifier. Moreover, weighted soft voting always performs better than the best individual classifier, while when the performances of individual classifiers are quite poor, the added error of simple soft voting may become arbitrarily larger than that of the best individual classifier. Furthermore, the reduction achieved by weighted soft voting over the worst individual classifier can be arbitrarily large, while the maximum reduction achievable by simple soft voting over the worst individual classifier is $1/T^2$. It is worth noting that all these conclusions are obtained based on the assumptions that the individual classifiers are uncorrelated and that the optimal weights for weighted soft voting can be solved, yet real situations are more complicated.

4.3 Combining by Learning

4.3.1 Stacking

Stacking [Wolpert, 1992, Breiman, 1996b, Smyth and Wolpert, 1998] is a general procedure where a learner is trained to combine the individual learners. Here, the individual learners are called the *first-level learners*, while the combiner is called the *second-level learner*, or **meta-learner**.

The basic idea is to train the first-level learners using the original training data set, and then generate a new data set for training the second-level learner, where the outputs of the first-level learners are regarded as input features while the original labels are still regarded as labels of the new training data. The first-level learners are often generated by applying different learning algorithms, and so, stacked ensembles are often heterogeneous, though it is also possible to construct homogeneous stacked ensembles. The pseudo-code of a general stacking procedure is summarized in Figure 4.6.

On one hand, stacking is a general framework which can be viewed as a generalization of many ensemble methods. On the other hand, it can be viewed as a specific combination method which combines by learning, and this is the reason why we introduce Stacking in this chapter.

In the training phase of stacking, a new data set needs to be generated from the first-level classifiers. If the exact data that are used to train the first-level learner are also used to generate the new data set for training the second-level learner, there will be a high risk of overfitting. Hence, it is suggested that the instances used for generating the new data set are excluded from the training examples for the first-level learners, and a cross-validation or leave-one-out procedure is often recommended.

Take k-fold cross-validation for example. Here, the original training data set D is randomly split into k almost equal parts $D_1, \ldots, D_k$. Define D_j and $D_{(-j)} = D \setminus D_j$ to be the test and training sets for the j-th fold. Given T learning algorithms, a first-level learner $h_t^{(-j)}$ is obtained by invoking the t-th learning algorithm on $D_{(-j)}$. For each $\boldsymbol{x}_i$ in D_j, the test set of the j-th fold, let $\boldsymbol{z}_{it}$ denote the output of the learner $h_t^{(-j)}$ on $\boldsymbol{x}_i$. Then, at the end of the entire cross-validation process, the new data set is generated from the T individual

Input: Data set $D = \{(\boldsymbol{x}_1, y_1), (\boldsymbol{x}_2, y_2), \ldots, (\boldsymbol{x}_m, y_m)\}$;
First-level learning algorithms $\mathfrak{L}_1, \ldots, \mathfrak{L}_T$;
Second-level learning algorithm $\mathfrak{L}$.

Process:

1. **for** $t = 1, \ldots, T$: % Train a first-level learner by applying the
2. $h_t = \mathfrak{L}_t(D)$; % first-level learning algorithm $\mathfrak{L}_t$
3. **end**
4. $D' = \emptyset$; % Generate a new data set
5. **for** $i = 1, \ldots, m$:
6. **for** $t = 1, \ldots, T$:
7. $z_{it} = h_t(\boldsymbol{x}_i)$;
8. **end**
9. $D' = D' \cup ((z_{i1}, \ldots, z_{iT}), y_i)$;
10. **end**
11. $h' = \mathfrak{L}(D')$; % Train the second-level learner h' by applying % the second-level learning algorithm $\mathfrak{L}$ to the % new data set $\mathcal{D}'$.

Output: $H(\boldsymbol{x}) = h'(h_1(\boldsymbol{x}), \ldots, h_T(\boldsymbol{x}))$

Figure 4.6: A general Stacking procedure.

learners as

$$D' = \{(z_{i1}, \ldots, z_{iT}, y_i)\}_{i=1}^{m} , \tag{4.61}$$

on which the second-level learning algorithm will be applied, and the resulting learner h' is a function of $(\boldsymbol{z}_1, \ldots, \boldsymbol{z}_T)$ for y. After generating the new data set, generally, the final first-level learners are re-generated by training on the whole training data.

Breiman [1996b] demonstrated the success of stacked regression. He used regression trees of different sizes or linear regression models with different numbers of variables as the first-level learners, and least-square linear regression model as the second-level learner under the constraint that all regression coefficients are non-negative. This non-negativity constraint was found to be crucial to guarantee that the performance of the stacked ensemble would be better than selecting the single best learner.

For stacked classification, Wolpert [1992] indicated that it is crucial to consider the types of features for the new training data, and the types of learning algorithms for the second-level learner.

Ting and Witten [1999] recommended to use *class probabilities* instead of crisp class labels as features for the new data, since this makes it possible to take into account not only the predictions but also the confidences of the individual classifiers. For first-level classifiers that can output class probabilities, the output of the classifier h_k on an instance $\boldsymbol{x}$ is $(h_{k1}(\boldsymbol{x}), \ldots, h_{kl}(\boldsymbol{x}))$, which is a probability distribution over all the possible class labels $\{c_1, \dots, c_l\}$, and $h_{kj}(\boldsymbol{x})$ denotes the probability predicted by h_k for the instance $\boldsymbol{x}$ belonging to class c_j. Though h_k predicts only the class c_j with the largest class probability $h_{kj}(\boldsymbol{x})$ as the class label, the probabilities it obtained for all classes contain helpful information. Thus, the class probabilities from all first-level classifiers on $\boldsymbol{x}$ can be used along with the true class label of $\boldsymbol{x}$ to form a new training example for the second-level learner.

Ting and Witten [1999] also recommended to use **multi-response linear regression** (MLR), which is a variant of the least-square linear regression algorithm [Breiman, 1996b], as the second-level learning algorithm. Any classification problem with real-valued features can be converted into a multi-response regression problem. For a classification problem with l classes $\{c_1, \dots, c_l\}$, l separate regression problems are formed as follows: for each class c_j, a linear regression model is constructed to predict a binary variable, which equals one if c_j is the correct class label and zero otherwise. The linear regression coefficients are determined based on the least-squares principle. In the prediction stage, given an instance $\boldsymbol{x}$ to classify, all the trained linear regression models will be invoked, and the class label corresponding to the regression model with the largest value will be output. It was found that the non-negativity constraints that are necessary in regression [Breiman, 1996b] are irrelevant to the performance improvement in classification [Ting and Witten, 1999]. Later, Seewald [2002] suggested to use different sets of features for the l linear regression problems in MLR. That is, only the probabilities of class c_j predicted by the different classifiers, i.e., $h_{kj}(\boldsymbol{x})$ $(k = 1, \dots, T)$, are used to construct the linear regression model corresponding to c_j. Consequently, each of the linear regression problems has T instead of $l \times T$ features. The Weka implementation of Stacking provides both the standard Stacking algorithm and the StackingC algorithm which implements Seewald [2002]'s suggestion.

Clarke [2003] provided a comparison between Stacking and **Bayesian Model Averaging** (BMA) which assigns weights to different models based on posterior probabilities. In theory, if the correct *data generating model* is among the models under consideration, and if the noise level is low, BMA is never worse and often better than Stacking. However, in practice, it is usually not the case since the correct data generating model is often not in the models under consideration and may even be difficult to be approximated well by the considered models. Clarke [2003]'s empirical results showed that stacking is more robust than BMA, and BMA is quite sensitive to model approximation error.

4.3.2 Infinite Ensemble

Most ensemble methods exploit only a small finite subset of hypotheses, while Lin and Li [2008] developed an infinite ensemble framework that constructs ensembles with infinite hypotheses. This framework can be regarded as learning the combination weights for all possible hypotheses. It is based on support vector machines, and by embedding infinitely many hypotheses into a kernel, it can be found that the learning problem reduces to an SVM training problem with specific kernels.

Let $\mathcal{H} = \{h_\alpha : \alpha \in \mathcal{C}\}$ denote the hypothesis space, where $\mathcal{C}$ is a measure space. The kernel that embeds $\mathcal{H}$ is defined as

$$K_{\mathcal{H},r}(\boldsymbol{x}_i, \boldsymbol{x}_j) = \int_{\mathcal{C}} \Phi_{\boldsymbol{x}_i}(\alpha)\Phi_{\boldsymbol{x}_j}(\alpha)d\alpha \ , \tag{4.62}$$

where $\Phi_{\boldsymbol{x}}(\alpha) = r(\alpha)h_\alpha(\boldsymbol{x})$, and $r : \mathcal{C} \mapsto \mathbb{R}^+$ is chosen such that the integral exists for all $\boldsymbol{x}_i$, $\boldsymbol{x}_j$. Here, α denotes the parameter of the hypothesis h_α, and the notation $Z(\alpha)$ indicates that this variable depends on α. In the following we denote $K_{\mathcal{H},r}$ by $K_{\mathcal{H}}$ when r is clear from the context. It can be proved that (4.62) defines a valid kernel [Schölkopf and Smola, 2002].

Following SVM, the framework formulates the following (primal) problem:

$$\begin{aligned} \min_{w\in\mathcal{L}_2(\mathcal{C}), b\in\mathbb{R}, \xi\in\mathbb{R}^m} \quad & \frac{1}{2}\int_{\mathcal{C}} w^2(\alpha)d\alpha + C\sum_{i=1}^{m} \xi_i \\ \text{s.t.} \quad & y_i\left(\int_{\mathcal{C}} w(\alpha)r(\alpha)h_\alpha(\boldsymbol{x})d\alpha + b\right) \geq 1 - \xi_i \\ & \xi_i \geq 0 \qquad (\forall i = 1, \ldots, m). \end{aligned} \tag{4.63}$$

The final classifier obtained from this optimization problem is

$$g(\boldsymbol{x}) = \texttt{sign}\left(\int_{\mathcal{C}} w(\alpha)r(\alpha)h_\alpha(\boldsymbol{x})d\alpha + b\right) . \tag{4.64}$$

Obviously, if $\mathcal{C}$ is uncountable, it is possible that each hypothesis h_α takes an infinitesimal weight $w(\alpha)r(\alpha)d\alpha$ in the ensemble. Thus, the obtained final classifier is very different from those obtained with other ensemble methods. Suppose $\mathcal{H}$ is negation complete, that is, $h \in \mathcal{H} \Leftrightarrow -h \in \mathcal{H}$. Then, every linear combination over $\mathcal{H}$ has an equivalent linear combination with only non-negative weights. By treating b as a constant hypothesis, the classifier in (4.64) can be seen as an ensemble of infinite hypotheses.

By using the *Lagrangian multiplier* method and the kernel trick, the dual problem of (4.63) can be obtained, and the final classifier can be written in terms of the kernel $K_{\mathcal{H}}$ as

$$g(\boldsymbol{x}) = \texttt{sign}\left(\sum_{i=1}^{m} y_i\lambda_i K_{\mathcal{H}}(\boldsymbol{x}_i, \boldsymbol{x}) + b\right) , \tag{4.65}$$

where $K_{\mathcal{H}}$ is the kernel embedding the hypothesis set $\mathcal{H}$, and λ_i's are the *Lagrange multipliers*. (4.65) is equivalent to (4.64) and hence it is also an infinite ensemble over $\mathcal{H}$. In practice, if a kernel $K_{\mathcal{H}}$ can be constructed according to (4.62) with a proper embedding function r, such as the *stump kernel* and the *perceptron kernel* in [Lin and Li, 2008], the learning problem can be reduced to solve an SVM with the kernel $K_{\mathcal{H}}$, and thus, the final ensemble can be obtained by applying typical SVM solvers.

4.4 Dynamic Classifier Selection

Dynamic Classifier Selection (DCS) is a specific method for exploiting multiple learners. After training multiple individual learners, DCS dynamically selects one learner for each test instance. In contrast to classic learning methods which select the "best" individual learner and discard other individual learners, DCS needs to keep all the individual learners; in contrast to typical ensemble methods which combine individual learners to make predictions, DCS makes predictions by using one individual learner. Considering that DCS keeps all the individual learners for prediction, it can be regarded as a "soft combination" method.

Ho et al. [1994] were the first to introduce DCS. They briefly outlined the DCS procedure and proposed a selection method based on a partition of training examples. The individual classifiers are evaluated on each partition so that the best-performing one for each partition is determined. In the testing stage, the test instance will be categorized into a partition and then classified by the corresponding best classifier.

Woods et al. [1997] proposed a DCS method called DCS-LA. The basic idea is to estimate the accuracy of each individual classifier in local regions surrounding the test instance, and then the most locally accurate classifier is selected to make the classification. In DCS-LA, the local regions are specified in terms of *k-nearest neighbors* in the training data, and the local accuracy can be estimated by *overall local accuracy* or *local class accuracy*. The overall local accuracy is simply the percentage of local examples that are correctly classified; the local class accuracy is the percentage of local examples belonging to the same class that are correctly classified. Giacinto and Roli [1997] developed a similar DCS method based on local accuracy. They estimated the class posterior and calculated a "confidence" for the selection. Didaci et al. [2005] studied the performance bounds of DCS-LA and showed that the upper bounds of DCS-LA are realistic and can be attained by accurate parameter tuning in practice. Their experimental results clearly showed the effectiveness of DCS based on local accuracy estimates.

Giacinto and Roli [2000a,b] placed DCS in the framework of Bayesian decision theory and found that, under the assumptions of *decision regions complementarity* and *decision boundaries complementarity*, the optimal Bayes classifier can be obtained by the selection of non-optimal classifiers. This provides theoretical support for the power of DCS. Following the theoretical analysis, they proposed the *a prior selection* and *a posterior selection* methods which directly exploit probabilistic estimates.

4.5 Mixture of Experts

Mixture of experts (MoE) [Jacobs et al., 1991, Xu et al., 1994] is an effective approach to exploit multiple learners. In contrast to typical ensemble methods where individual learners are trained for the same problem, MoE works in

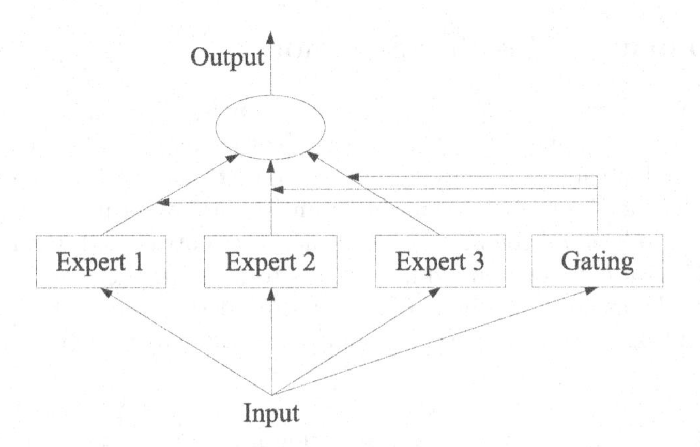

Figure 4.7: An illustrative example of mixture of experts. (Plot based on a similar figure in [Jacobs et al., 1991].)

a **divide-and-conquer** strategy where a complex task is broken up into several simpler and smaller subtasks, and individual learners (called *experts*) are trained for different subtasks. **Gating** is usually employed to combine the experts. Figure 4.7 illustrates an example for MoE which consists of three experts.

Note that the keys of MoE are different from those of typical ensemble methods. In typical ensemble methods, since the individual learners are trained for the same problem, particularly from the same training data set, they are generally highly correlated and a key problem is how to make the individual learners diverse, while in MoE, the individual learners are generated for different subtasks and there is no need to devote to diversity. Typical ensemble methods do not divide the task into subtasks, while in MoE, a key problem is how to find the natural division of the task and then derive the overall solution from sub-solutions. In literature on MoE, much emphasis was given to make the experts local, and this is thought to be crucial to the performance. A basic method for this purpose is to target each expert to a distribution specified by the gating function, rather than the whole original training data distribution.

Without loss of generality, assume that an MoE architecture is comprised of T experts, and the output y is a discrete variable with possible values 0 and 1 for binary classification. Given an input $\boldsymbol{x}$, each local expert h_i tries to approximate the distribution of y and obtains a local output $h_i(y \mid \boldsymbol{x}; \boldsymbol{\theta_i})$, where $\boldsymbol{\theta}_i$ is the parameter of the i-th expert h_i. The gating function provides a set of coefficients $\pi_i(\boldsymbol{x}; \boldsymbol{\alpha})$ that weigh the contributions of experts, and $\boldsymbol{\alpha}$ is the parameter of the gating function. Thus, the final output of the MoE is a weighted sum of all the local outputs produced by the experts, i.e.,

$$H(y \mid \boldsymbol{x}; \Psi) = \sum_{i=1}^{T} \pi_i(\boldsymbol{x}; \boldsymbol{\alpha}) \cdot h_i(y \mid \boldsymbol{x}; \boldsymbol{\theta_i}) \ , \tag{4.66}$$

where Ψ includes all unknown parameters. The output of the gating function is often modeled by the **softmax function** as

$$\pi_i(\boldsymbol{x};\boldsymbol{\alpha}) = \frac{\exp(\boldsymbol{v}_i^T\boldsymbol{x})}{\sum_{j=1}^{T}\exp(\boldsymbol{v}_j^T\boldsymbol{x})}, \tag{4.67}$$

where $\boldsymbol{v}_i$ is the weight vector of the i-th expert in the gating function, and $\boldsymbol{\alpha}$ contains all the elements in $\boldsymbol{v}_i$'s. In the training stage, $\pi_i(\boldsymbol{x};\boldsymbol{\alpha})$ states the probability of the instance $\boldsymbol{x}$ appearing in the training set of the i-th expert h_i, while in the test stage, it defines the contribution of h_i to the final prediction.

In general, the training procedure tries to achieve two goals: for given experts, to find the optimal gating function; for given gating function, to train the experts on the distribution specified by the gating function. The unknown parameters are usually estimated by the **Expectation Maximization (EM)** algorithm [Jordan and Xu, 1995, Xu et al., 1994, Xu and Jordan, 1996].

The MoE architecture can be used not only for single output, but also for multiple outputs, which falls into the multi-task learning area. Specifically, multi-task learning aims to build an model that learns multiple goals and tasks simultaneously, and it is important to study the modeling tradeoffs between task-specific objectives and inter-task relationships. Ma et al. [2018] proposed Multi-gate Mixture-of-Experts (MMoE) which explicitly learns to model task relationships from data, and exploits the MoE architecture by sharing the expert submodels across all tasks while also having a gating network trained to optimize each task. MMoE has been employed in many web-scale applications, including many industrial recommender systems, personalized search engines and online advertising systems.

In recent years, the MoE mechanism has been successfully applied in some *large models* such as GPT-4, where the MoE is composed of a number of small expert systems, and takes the divide-and-conquer strategy to solve the users' problems by one or some small expert systems.

4.6 Other Combination Methods

There are many other combination methods in addition to averaging, voting and combining by learning. In this section we briefly introduce the *algebraic* methods, *BKS method* and *decision template method*.

4.6.1 Algebraic Methods

Since the class probabilities output from individual classifiers can be regarded as an estimate of the posterior probabilities, it is straightforward to derive combination rules under the probabilistic framework [Kittler et al., 1998].

Denote $h_i^j(\boldsymbol{x})$, the class probability of c_j output from h_i, as h_i^j. According to Bayesian decision theory, given T classifiers, the instance $\boldsymbol{x}$ should be assigned to the class c_j which maximizes the posteriori probability $P(c_j \mid h_1^j, \ldots, h_T^j)$. From the Bayes' theorem, it follows that

$$P(c_j \mid h_1^j, \ldots, h_T^j) = \frac{P(c_j)P(h_1^j, \ldots, h_T^j \mid c_j)}{\sum_{i=1}^{l} P(c_i)P(h_1^j, \ldots, h_T^j \mid c_i)}, \tag{4.68}$$

where $P(h_1^j, \ldots, h_T^j \mid c_j)$ is the joint probability distribution of the outputs from the classifiers.

Assume that the outputs are conditionally independent, i.e.,

$$P(h_1^j, \ldots, h_T^j \mid c_j) = \prod_{i=1}^{T} P(h_i^j \mid c_j). \tag{4.69}$$

Then, from (4.68), it follows that

$$\begin{aligned} P(c_j \mid h_1^j, \ldots, h_T^j) &= \frac{P(c_j)\prod_{i=1}^{T} P(h_i^j \mid c_j)}{\sum_{i=1}^{l} P(c_i)\prod_{k=1}^{T} P(h_k^j \mid c_i)} \\ &\propto P(c_j)^{-(T-1)} \prod_{i=1}^{T} P(c_j \mid h_i^j). \end{aligned} \tag{4.70}$$

Thus, if all classes are with equal prior, we get the *product rule* [Kittler et al., 1998] for combination, i.e.,

$$H^j(\boldsymbol{x}) = \prod_{i=1}^{T} P(c_j \mid h_i^j). \tag{4.71}$$

Similarly, Kittler et al. [1998] derived the soft voting method, as well as the *maximum/minimum/median rules*. Briefly speaking, these rules choose the maximum/minimum/median of the individual outputs as the combined output. For example, the *median rule* generates the combined output according to

$$H^j(\boldsymbol{x}) = \operatorname*{med}_i(P(c_j \mid h_i^j)), \tag{4.72}$$

where $\mathrm{med}(\cdot)$ denotes the median statistic.

4.6.2 Behavior Knowledge Space Method

The Behavior Knowledge Space (BKS) method was proposed by Huang and Suen [1995]. Let $\boldsymbol{\ell} = (\ell_1, \ldots, \ell_T)^T$ denote the class labels assigned by the individual classifiers $h_1, \ldots, h_T$ to the instance $\boldsymbol{x}$, where $\ell_i = h_i(\boldsymbol{x})$. If we consider $\boldsymbol{\ell}$ as a T-dimensional random variable, the task can be reduced to estimate $P(c_j \mid \boldsymbol{\ell})$. For this, every possible combination of class labels (i.e., every possible value of $\boldsymbol{\ell}$) can be regarded as an index to a cell in the BKS table [Huang and Suen, 1995]. This table is filled using a data set D, and each example $(\boldsymbol{x}_i, y_i)$ is placed in the cell indexed by $(h_1(\boldsymbol{x}_i), \ldots, h_T(\boldsymbol{x}_i))$. The number of examples in each cell are counted; then, the most representative class label is selected for this cell, where ties are broken arbitrarily and the empty cells are labeled at random or by majority. In the testing stage, the BKS method labels $\boldsymbol{x}$ to the class of the cell indexed by $(h_1(\boldsymbol{x}), \ldots, h_T(\boldsymbol{x}))$.

The BKS method performs well if large and representative data sets are available. It suffers from the *small sample size* problem, in which case overfitting may be serious. To deal with this problem, Raudys and Roli [2003] analyzed the generalization error of the BKS method, and obtained an analytical model which relates error to sample size. Based on the model, they proposed to use linear classifiers in "ambiguous" cells of the BKS table, and this strategy was reported to strongly improve the BKS performance [Raudys and Roli, 2003].

4.6.3 Decision Template Method

The Decision Template method was developed by Kuncheva et al. [2001]. In this method, the outputs of the classifiers on an instance $\boldsymbol{x}$ are organized in a *decision profile* as the matrix

$$DP(\boldsymbol{x}) = \begin{pmatrix} h_1^1(\boldsymbol{x}) & \cdots & h_1^j(\boldsymbol{x}) & \cdots & h_1^l(\boldsymbol{x}) \\ \vdots & \ddots & \vdots & \ddots & \vdots \\ h_i^1(\boldsymbol{x}) & \cdots & h_i^j(\boldsymbol{x}) & \cdots & h_i^l(\boldsymbol{x}) \\ \vdots & \ddots & \vdots & \ddots & \vdots \\ h_T^1(\boldsymbol{x}) & \cdots & h_T^j(\boldsymbol{x}) & \cdots & h_T^l(\boldsymbol{x}) \end{pmatrix}. \tag{4.73}$$

Based on the training data set $D = \{(\boldsymbol{x}_1, y_1), \ldots, (\boldsymbol{x}_m, y_m)\}$, the decision templates are estimated as the expected $DP(\boldsymbol{x})$, i.e.,

$$DT_k = \frac{1}{m_k} \sum_{i: y_i = c_k} DP(\boldsymbol{x}_i), \quad k = 1, \ldots, l \tag{4.74}$$

where m_k is the number of training examples in the class c_k.

The testing stage of this method works like a nearest neighbor algorithm. That is, the similarity between $DP(\boldsymbol{x})$, i.e., the decision profile of the test instance $\boldsymbol{x}$, and the decision templates DT_k's are calculated based on some similarity measure [Kuncheva et al., 2001], and then the class label of the most similar decision template is assigned to $\boldsymbol{x}$.

4.6.4 Error-Correcting Output Codes

Error-Correcting Output Codes (ECOC) is a simple yet powerful approach to deal with a multi-class problem based on the combination of binary classifiers [Dietterich and Bakiri, 1995, Allwein et al., 2000]. In general, the ECOC approach works in two steps:

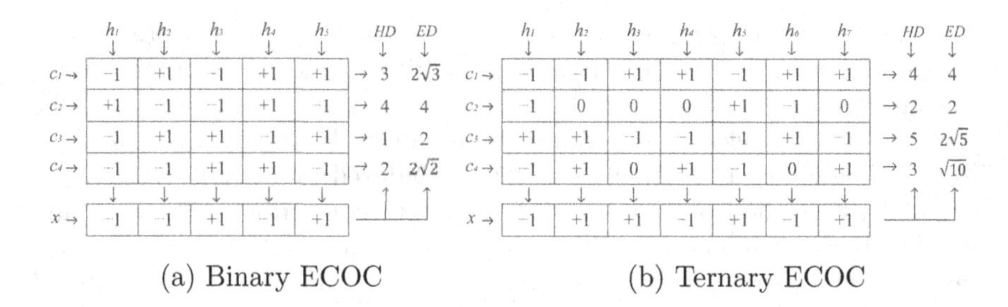

(a) Binary ECOC (b) Ternary ECOC

Figure 4.8: ECOC examples. (a) Binary ECOC for a 4-class problem. An instance $\boldsymbol{x}$ is classified to class c_3 using the Hamming or the Euclidean decoding; (b) Ternary ECOC example, where an instance $\boldsymbol{x}$ is classified to class c_2 according to the Hamming or the Euclidean decoding.

1. **The coding step**. In this step, a set of B different bipartitions of the class label set $\{c_1, \ldots, c_l\}$ are constructed, and subsequently B binary classifiers $h_1, \ldots, h_B$ are trained over the partitions.
2. **The decoding step**. In this step, given an instance $\boldsymbol{x}$, a **codeword** is generated by using the outputs of B binary classifiers. Then, the codeword is compared to the *base codeword* of each class, and the instance is assigned to the class with the most similar codeword.

Typically, the partitions of class set are specified by a **coding matrix M**, which can appear in different forms, e.g., binary form [Dietterich and Bakiri, 1995] and ternary form [Allwein et al., 2000].

In the binary form, $\mathbf{M} \in \{-1, +1\}^{l \times B}$ [Dietterich and Bakiri, 1995]. Figure 4.8(a) provides an example of a binary coding matrix, which transforms a four-class problem into five binary classification problems. In the figure, regions coded by $+1$ are considered as a class, while regions coded by -1 are considered as the other class. Consequently, binary classifiers are trained based on these bipartitions. For example, the binary classifier h_2 is trained to discriminate $\{c_1, c_3\}$ against $\{c_2, c_4\}$, that is,

$$h_2(\boldsymbol{x}) = \begin{cases} +1 & \text{if } \boldsymbol{x} \in \{c_1, c_3\} \\ -1 & \text{if } \boldsymbol{x} \in \{c_2, c_4\}. \end{cases} \tag{4.75}$$

In the decoding step, by applying the five binary classifiers, a codeword can be generated for the instance $\boldsymbol{x}$. Then, the codeword is compared with the base codewords defined in the rows of $\mathbf{M}$. For example, in Figure 4.8(a), the instance $\boldsymbol{x}$ is classified to c_3 according to either Hamming distance or Euclidean distance.

In the ternary form, $\mathbf{M} \in \{-1, 0, 1\}^{l \times B}$ [Allwein et al., 2000]. Figure 4.8(b) provides an example of a ternary coding matrix, which transforms a four-class classification problem into seven binary problems. Here, "zero" indicates that the corresponding class is excluded from training the binary classifier. For example, the classifier h_4 is trained to discriminate c_3 against $\{c_1, c_4\}$ without taking into account c_2. Note that the codeword of a test instance cannot contain zeros since the output of each binary classifier is either -1 or $+1$. In Figure 4.8(b), the instance $\boldsymbol{x}$ is classified to c_2 according to either Hamming distance or Euclidean distance.

Popular binary coding schemes mainly include the **one-versus-rest** scheme and **dense random** scheme [Allwein et al., 2000]. In the one-versus-rest scheme, each binary classifier is trained to discriminate one class against all the other classes. Obviously, the codeword is of length l if there are l classes. In the dense random scheme, each element in the code is usually chosen with a probability of $1/2$ for $+1$ and $1/2$ for -1. Allwein et al. [2000] suggested an optimal codeword length of $10 \log l$. Among a set of dense random matrices, the optimal one is with the largest Hamming decoding distance among each pair of codewords.

Popular ternary coding schemes mainly include the **one-versus-one** scheme and **sparse random** scheme [Allwein et al., 2000]. The one-versus-one scheme considers all pairs of classes, and each classifier is trained to discriminate between two classes. Thus, the codeword length is $l(l-1)/2$. The sparse random scheme is similar to the dense random scheme, except that it includes the zero value in addition to $+1$ and -1. Generally, each element is chosen with probability of $1/2$ for 0, a probability of $1/4$ for $+1$ or -1, and the codeword length is set to $15 \log l$ [Allwein et al., 2000].

The central task of decoding is to find the base codeword $\boldsymbol{w}_i$ (corresponding to class c_i) which is the closest to the codeword $\boldsymbol{v}$ of the given test instance. Popular binary decoding schemes mainly include:

- **Hamming decoder**. This scheme is based on the assumption that the learning task can be modeled as an error-correcting communication problem [Nilsson, 1965]. The measure is given by

$$HD(\boldsymbol{v}, \boldsymbol{w}_i) = \frac{\sum_j (1 - \mathbf{sign}(v^j \cdot w_i^j))}{2} . \tag{4.76}$$

- **Euclidean decoder**. This scheme is directly based on Euclidean distance [Pujol et al., 2006]. The measure is given by

$$ED(\boldsymbol{v}, \boldsymbol{w}_i) = \sqrt{\sum_j (v^j - w_i^j)^2} . \tag{4.77}$$

- **Inverse Hamming decoder**. This scheme is based on the matrix Δ which is composed of the Hamming decoding measures between the codewords of $\mathbf{M}$, and $\Delta_{ij} = HD(\boldsymbol{w}_i, \boldsymbol{w}_j)$ [Windeatt and Ghaderi, 2003]. The measure is given by

$$IHD(\boldsymbol{v}, \boldsymbol{w}_i) = \max(\Delta^{-1} \boldsymbol{D}^T) , \tag{4.78}$$

where $\boldsymbol{D}$ denotes the vector of Hamming decoder values of $\boldsymbol{v}$ for each of the base codewords $\boldsymbol{w}_i$.

Popular ternary decoding schemes mainly include:

- **Attenuated Euclidean decoder**. This is a variant of the Euclidean decoder, which has been redefined to ensure the measure to be unaffected by the positions of the codeword $\boldsymbol{w}_i$ containing zeros [Pujol et al., 2008]. The measure is given by

$$AED(\boldsymbol{v}, \boldsymbol{w}_i) = \sqrt{\sum\nolimits_j |\boldsymbol{w}_i^j| \cdot (\boldsymbol{v}^j - \boldsymbol{w}_i^j)^2} \ . \tag{4.79}$$

- **Loss-based decoder**. This scheme chooses the class c_i that minimizes a particular loss function [Allwein et al., 2000]. The measure is given by

$$LB(\boldsymbol{x}, \boldsymbol{w}_i) = \sum\nolimits_j L(h_j(\boldsymbol{x}), \boldsymbol{w}_i^j) \ , \tag{4.80}$$

where $h_j(\boldsymbol{x})$ is the real-valued prediction on $\boldsymbol{x}$, and L is the loss function. In practice, the loss function has many choices, while two commonly used ones are $L(h_j(\boldsymbol{x}), \boldsymbol{w}_i^j) = -h_j(\boldsymbol{x}) \cdot \boldsymbol{w}_i^j$ and $L(h_j(\boldsymbol{x}), \boldsymbol{w}_i^j) = \exp(-h_j(\boldsymbol{x}) \cdot \boldsymbol{w}_i^j)$.

- **Probabilistic-based decoder**. This is a probabilistic scheme based on the real-valued output of the binary classifiers [Passerini et al., 2004]. The measure is given by

$$PD(\boldsymbol{v}, \boldsymbol{w}_i) = -\log\left(\prod\nolimits_{j:\boldsymbol{w}_i^j \neq 0} P(\boldsymbol{v}^j = \boldsymbol{w}_i^j \mid h_j(\boldsymbol{x})) + C\right) \ , \tag{4.81}$$

where C is a constant, and $P(\boldsymbol{v}^j = \boldsymbol{w}_i^j \mid h_j(\boldsymbol{x}))$ is estimated by

$$P(\boldsymbol{v}^j = \boldsymbol{w}_i^j \mid h_j(\boldsymbol{x})) = \frac{1}{1 + \exp(\boldsymbol{w}_i^j(a^j \cdot h_j(\boldsymbol{x}) + b^j))} \ , \tag{4.82}$$

where a and b are obtained by solving an optimization problem [Passerini et al., 2004].

4.7 Further Readings

Van ErP et al. [2002] categorized ensemble combinations methods into three classes according to the combined outputs of the component classifiers, i.e., vote-based methods where each component classifier only provides a single class label, rank-based methods where each component classifier provides a list of class labels in the order the classifier finds to be the most likely, and score-based methods where each component classifier provides a list of class labels with "confidence" scores or estimated probabilities. Considering that many combination methods, such as combining by learning, can be applied to almost all kinds of outputs, and combination methods are used in tasks not limited to classification, this book presents them according to different operation mechanisms.

Weighted averaging was shown effective in ensemble learning by [Perrone and Cooper, 1995]. This method is quite basic and was used for combining multiple evidences long time ago, e.g., (4.14) was well-known in **portfolio selection** in the 1950s [Markowitz, 1952]. In its early formulation there was no constraint on the weights. Later, it was found that the weights in practice may take large negative and positive values, and hence giving extreme predictions even when the individual learners provide reasonable predictions; moreover, since the training data are used for training the individual learners as well as estimating the weights, the process is very easy to suffer from overfitting. So, Breiman [1996b] suggested considering the constraints as shown in (4.10), which has become a standard setting.

The expression of majority voting accuracy, (4.16), was first shown by de Concorcet [1785] and later re-developed by many authors. The relation between the majority voting accuracy P_{mv}, the individual accuracy p and the ensemble size T was also given at first by de Concorcet [1785], but for odd sizes only; Lam and Suen [1997] generalized the analysis to even cases, leading to the overall result shown in Section 4.2.2.

Though the effectiveness of plurality voting has been validated by empirical studies, theoretical analysis on plurality voting is somewhat difficult and there are only a few works [Lin et al., 2003, Mu et al., 2009]. In particular, Lin et al. [2003] theoretically compared the recognition/error/rejection rates of plurality voting and majority voting under different conditions, and showed that plurality voting is more efficient to achieve tradeoff between the rejection and error rates.

Kittler et al. [1998], Kittler and Alkoot [2003] showed that voting can be regarded as a special case of averaging, while the averaging rule is more resilient to estimation errors than other combination methods. Kuncheva [2002] theoretically studied six simple classifier combination methods under the assumption that the estimates are independent and identically distributed. Kuncheva et al. [2003] empirically studied majority voting, and showed that dependent classifiers can offer improvement over independent classifiers for majority voting.

The **Dempster-Shafer (DS) theory** [Dempster, 1967, Shafer, 1976] is a theory on evidence aggregation, which is able to represent uncertainties and ignorance (lack of evidence). Several combination methods have been inspired by the DS theory, e.g., [Xu et al., 1992, Rogova, 1994, Al-Ani and Deriche, 2002, Ahmadzadeh and Petrou, 2003, Bi et al., 2008].

Utschick and Weichselberger [2004] proposed to improve the process of binary coding by optimizing a maximum-likelihood objective function; however, they found that the one-versus-rest scheme is still the optimal choice for many multi-class problems. General coding schemes could not guarantee that the coded problems are most suitable for a given task. Crammer and Singer [2002] were the first to design problem-dependent coding schemes, and proved that the problem of finding the optimal discrete coding matrix is NP-complete. Later, several other problem-dependent designs were developed based on exploiting the problem by finding representative binary problems that increase the generalization performance while keeping the code length small. Discriminant ECOC (DECOC) [Pujol et al., 2006] is based on the embedding of discriminant tree structures derived from the problem. Forest-ECOC [Escalera et al., 2007] extends DECOC by including additional classifiers. ECOC-ONE [Pujol et al., 2008] uses a coding process that trains the binary problems guided by a validation set. For binary decoding, Allwein et al. [2000] reported that the practical behavior of the Inverse Hamming decoder is quite similar to the Hamming decoder. For ternary decoding, Escalera et al. [2010b] found that the zero symbol introduces two kinds of biases, and to overcome these problems, they proposed the *Loss-Weighted decoder* (LW) and the *Pessimistic Beta Density Distribution decoder* (β-DEN). An open source ECOC library developed by Escalera et al. [2010a] can be found at `http://mloss.org`.

The application of Dynamic Classifier Selection is not limited to classification. For example, Zhu et al. [2004] showed that DCS has promising performance in mining data streams with concept drifting or with significant noise. The idea of DCS has even been generalized to *dynamic ensemble selection* by Ko et al. [2008].

Hierarchical mixture of experts (HME) [Jordan and Jacobs, 1991] extends mixture of experts (MoE) into a tree structure. In contrast to MoE which builds the experts on the input directly, in HME the experts are built from multiple levels of experts and gating functions. The EM algorithm still can be used to train HME. Waterhouse and Robinson [1995] described how to grow the tree structure of HME gradually. Bayesian frameworks for inferring the parameters of ME and HME were developed by Waterhouse et al. [1995] and Bishop and Svensén [2003], respectively.

Chapter 5

Diversity

5.1 Ensemble Diversity

Ensemble diversity, that is, the difference among the individual learners, is a fundamental issue in ensemble methods.

Intuitively, it is easy to understand that to gain from combination, the individual learners must be different, and otherwise there would be no performance improvement if identical individual learners were combined. Tumer and Ghosh [1995] analyzed the performance of *simple soft voting* ensemble using the decision boundary analysis introduced in Section 4.2.3, by introducing a term θ to describe the overall correlation among the individual learners. They showed that the expected *added error* of the ensemble is

$$err_{add}^{ssv}(H) = \frac{1 + \theta(T-1)}{T} \overline{err}_{add}(h) \ , \tag{5.1}$$

where $\overline{err}_{add}(h)$ is the expected added error of the individual learners (for simplicity, all individual learners were assumed to have equal error), and T is the ensemble size. (5.1) discloses that if the learners are independent, i.e., $\theta = 0$, the ensemble will achieve a factor of T of error reduction than the individual learners; if the learners are totally correlated, i.e., $\theta = 1$, no gains can be obtained from the combination. This analysis clearly shows that the diversity is crucial to ensemble performance. A similar conclusion can be obtained for other combination methods.

Generating diverse individual learners, however, is not easy. The major obstacle lies in the fact that the individual learners are trained for the same task from the same training data, and thus they are usually highly correlated. Many theoretically plausible approaches, e.g., the optimal solution of weighted averaging (4.14), do not work in practice simply because they are based on the assumption of independent or less correlated learners. The real situation is even more difficult. For example, the derivation of (5.1), though it considers high correlation between individual learners, is based on the assumption that the

DOI: 10.1201/9781003587774-5

individual learners produce independent estimates of the posterior probabilities; this is actually not the case in practice.

In fact, the problem of generating diverse individual learners is even more challenging if we consider that the individual learners must not be very poor, and otherwise their combination would not improve and could even worsen the performance. For example, it can be seen from (4.58) that when the performance of individual classifiers is quite poor, the added error of simple soft voted ensemble may become arbitrarily large; similar analytical results can also be obtained for other combination methods.

So, it is desired that the individual learners should be *accurate and diverse.* Combining only accurate learners is often worse than combining some accurate ones together with some relatively weak ones, since complementarity is more important than pure accuracy. Ultimately, the success of ensemble learning lies in achieving a good tradeoff between the individual performance and diversity.

Unfortunately, though diversity is crucial, we still do not have a full understanding of diversity. There is no doubt that understanding diversity is the holy grail in the field of ensemble learning.

5.2 Error Decomposition

It is important to see that the generalization error of an ensemble depends on a term related to diversity. For this purpose, this section introduces two well-known error decomposition schemes for ensemble methods, that is, the error-ambiguity decomposition and the bias-variance decomposition.

5.2.1 Error-Ambiguity Decomposition

The error-ambiguity decomposition was proposed by Krogh and Vedelsby [1994]. Assume that the task is to use an ensemble of T individual learners $h_1, \ldots, h_T$ to approximate a function $f : R^d \mapsto R$, and the final prediction of the ensemble is obtained through weighted averaging, i.e.,

$$H(\boldsymbol{x}) = \sum_{i=1}^{T} w_i h_i(\boldsymbol{x})$$

where w_i is the weight for the learner h_i, and the weights are constrained by $w_i \geq 0$ and $\sum_{i=1}^{T} w_i = 1$.

Given an instance $\boldsymbol{x}$, the *ambiguity* of the individual learner h_i is defined as [Krogh and Vedelsby, 1994]

$$ambi(h_i \mid \boldsymbol{x}) = (h_i(\boldsymbol{x}) - H(\boldsymbol{x}))^2 , \tag{5.2}$$

and the *ambiguity* of the ensemble is

$$\overline{ambi}(h \mid \boldsymbol{x}) = \sum_{i=1}^{T} w_i \cdot ambi(h_i \mid \boldsymbol{x}) = \sum_{i=1}^{T} w_i (h_i(\boldsymbol{x}) - H(\boldsymbol{x}))^2 . \tag{5.3}$$

Obviously, the ambiguity term measures the disagreement among the individual learners on instance $\boldsymbol{x}$. If we use the squared error to measure the performance, then the error of the individual learner h_i and the ensemble H are respectively

$$err(h_i \mid \boldsymbol{x}) = (f(\boldsymbol{x}) - h_i(\boldsymbol{x}))^2 \;, \tag{5.4}$$

$$err(H \mid \boldsymbol{x}) = (f(\boldsymbol{x}) - H(\boldsymbol{x}))^2 \;. \tag{5.5}$$

Then, we have

$$\overline{ambi}(h \mid \boldsymbol{x}) = \sum_{i=1}^{T} w_i err(h_i \mid \boldsymbol{x}) - err(H \mid \boldsymbol{x}) = \overline{err}(h \mid \boldsymbol{x}) - err(H \mid \boldsymbol{x}) \;, \tag{5.6}$$

where $\overline{err}(h \mid \boldsymbol{x}) = \sum_{i=1}^{T} w_i \cdot err(h_i \mid \boldsymbol{x})$ is the weighted average of the individual errors. Since (5.6) holds for every instance $\boldsymbol{x}$, after averaging over the input distribution, it still holds that

$$\begin{aligned} &\sum_{i=1}^{T} w_i \int ambi(h_i \mid \boldsymbol{x}) p(\boldsymbol{x}) d\boldsymbol{x} \\ &= \sum_{i=1}^{T} w_i \int err(h_i \mid \boldsymbol{x}) p(\boldsymbol{x}) d\boldsymbol{x} - \int err(H \mid \boldsymbol{x}) p(\boldsymbol{x}) d\boldsymbol{x} \;, \end{aligned} \tag{5.7}$$

where $p(\boldsymbol{x})$ is the input distribution from which the instances are sampled. The generalization error and the ambiguity of the individual learner h_i can be written respectively as

$$err(h_i) = \int err(h_i \mid \boldsymbol{x}) p(\boldsymbol{x}) d\boldsymbol{x} \;, \tag{5.8}$$

$$ambi(h_i) = \int ambi(h_i \mid \boldsymbol{x}) p(\boldsymbol{x}) d\boldsymbol{x} \;. \tag{5.9}$$

Similarly, the generalization error of the ensemble can be written as

$$err(H) = \int err(H \mid \boldsymbol{x}) p(\boldsymbol{x}) d\boldsymbol{x} \;. \tag{5.10}$$

Based on the above notations and (5.6), we can get the error-ambiguity decomposition [Krogh and Vedelsby, 1994]

$$err(H) = \overline{err}(h) - \overline{ambi}(h), \tag{5.11}$$

where $\overline{err}(h) = \sum_{i=1}^{T} w_i \cdot err(h_i)$ is the weighted average of individual generalization errors, and $\overline{ambi}(h) = \sum_{i=1}^{T} w_i \cdot ambi(h_i)$ is the weighted average of ambiguities that is also referred to as the ensemble ambiguity.

On the right-hand side of (5.11), the first item $\overline{err}(h)$ is the average error of the individual learners, depending on the generalization ability of individual learners; the second item $\overline{ambi}(h)$ is the ambiguity, which measures the variability among the predictions of individual learners, depending on the ensemble diversity. Since the second term is always positive, and it is subtracted from the first term, it is clear that the error of the ensemble will never be larger than the average error of the individual learners. More importantly, (5.11) shows that the more accurate and the more diverse the individual learners, the better the ensemble.

Note that (5.11) was derived for the regression setting. It is difficult to get similar results for classification. Furthermore, it is difficult to estimate $\overline{ambi}$ empirically. Usually, the estimate of $\overline{ambi}$ is obtained by subtracting the estimated value of $\overline{err}$ from the estimated value of err, and thus this estimated value just shows the difference between the ensemble error and individual error, not really showing the physical meaning of diversity; moreover, such an estimate often violates the constraint that $\overline{ambi}$ should be positive. Thus, (5.11) does not provide a unified formal formulation of ensemble diversity, though it does offer some important insights.

5.2.2 Bias-Variance-Covariance Decomposition

The **bias-variance-covariance decomposition** [Geman et al., 1992], or popularly called as **bias-variance decomposition**, is an important general tool for analyzing the performance of learning algorithms. Given a learning target and the size of training set, it divides the generalization error of a learner into three components, i.e., **intrinsic noise**, **bias** and **variance**. The intrinsic noise is a lower bound on the expected error of any learning algorithm on the target; the bias measures how closely the average estimate of the learning algorithm is able to approximate the target; the variance measures how much the estimate of the learning approach fluctuates for different training sets of the same size.

Since the intrinsic noise is difficult to estimate, it is often subsumed into the bias term. Thus, the generalization error is broken into the bias term which describes the error of the learner in expectation, and the variance term which reflects the sensitivity of the learner to variations in the training samples.

Let f denote the target and h denote the learner. For squared loss, the decomposition is

$$\begin{aligned} err(h) &= \mathbb{E}\left[(h-f)^2\right] \\ &= (\mathbb{E}[h]-f)^2 + \mathbb{E}\left[(h-\mathbb{E}[h])^2\right] \\ &= bias(h)^2 + variance(h), \end{aligned} \tag{5.12}$$

where the bias and variance of the learner h is respectively

$$bias(h) = \mathbb{E}[h] - f, \tag{5.13}$$

$$variance(h) = \mathbb{E}\left[h - \mathbb{E}[h]\right]^2. \tag{5.14}$$

The key of estimating the bias and variance terms empirically lies in how to simulate the variation of training samples with the same size. Kohavi and Wolpert [1996]'s method, for example, works in a two-fold cross validation style, where the original data set is split into a training set D_1 and a test set D_2. Then, T training sets are sampled from D_1; the size of these training sets is roughly half of that of D_1 for ensuring that there are not many duplicate training sets in these T training sets even for small D. After that, the learning algorithm is trained on each of those training sets and tested on D_2, from which the bias and variance are estimated. The whole process can be repeated several times to improve the estimates.

For an ensemble of T learners $h_1, \ldots, h_T$, the decomposition of (5.12) can be further expanded, yielding the *bias-variance-covariance decomposition* [Ueda and Nakano, 1996]. Without loss of generality, suppose that the individual learners are combined with equal weights. The averaged bias, averaged variance, and averaged **covariance** of the individual learners are defined respectively as

$$\overline{bias}(H) = \frac{1}{T}\sum_{i=1}^{T}(\mathbb{E}[h_i] - f), \tag{5.15}$$

$$\overline{variance}(H) = \frac{1}{T}\sum_{i=1}^{T}\mathbb{E}[h_i - \mathbb{E}[h_i]]^2, \tag{5.16}$$

$$\overline{covariance}(H) = \frac{1}{T(T-1)}\sum_{i=1}^{T}\sum_{\substack{j=1 \\ j\neq i}}^{T}\mathbb{E}[h_i - \mathbb{E}[h_i]]\,\mathbb{E}[h_j - \mathbb{E}[h_j]]. \tag{5.17}$$

The bias-variance-covariance decomposition of squared error of ensemble is

$$err(H) = \overline{bias}(H)^2 + \frac{1}{T}\overline{variance}(H) + \left(1 - \frac{1}{T}\right)\overline{covariance}(H) \ . \tag{5.18}$$

(5.18) shows that the squared error of the ensemble depends heavily on the covariance term, which models the correlation between the individual learners. The smaller the covariance, the better the ensemble. It is obvious that if all the learners make similar errors, the covariance will be large, and therefore it is preferred that the individual learners make different errors. Thus, through the covariance term, (5.18) shows that the diversity is important for ensemble performance. Note that the bias and variance terms are constrained to be positive, while the covariance term can be negative. Also, (5.18) was derived under regression setting, and it is difficult to obtain similar results for classification. So, (5.18) does not provide a formal formulation of ensemble diversity either.

Brown et al. [2005a,b] disclosed the connection between the error-ambiguity decomposition and the bias-variance-covariance decomposition. For simplicity, assume that the individual learners are combined with equal weights. Considering that the left-hand side of (5.11) is the same as the left-hand side of (5.18), by putting the right-hand sides of (5.11) and (5.18) together, it follows that

$$\begin{aligned}\overline{err}(h) - \overline{ambi}(h) &= \mathbb{E}\left[\frac{1}{T}\sum_{i=1}^{T}(h_i - f)^2 - \frac{1}{T}\sum_{i=1}^{T}(h_i - H)^2\right] \\ &= \overline{bias}(H)^2 + \frac{1}{T}\overline{variance}(H) + \left(1 - \frac{1}{T}\right)\overline{covariance}(H) .\end{aligned} \tag{5.19}$$

After some derivations [Brown et al., 2005a,b], we get

$$\overline{err}(h) = \mathbb{E}\left[\frac{1}{T}\sum_{i=1}^{T}(h_i - f)^2\right] = \overline{bias}^2(H) + \overline{variance}(H) , \tag{5.20}$$

$$\begin{aligned}\overline{ambi}(h) &= \mathbb{E}\left[\frac{1}{T}\sum_{i=1}^{T}(h_i - H)^2\right] \\ &= \overline{variance}(H) - variance(H) \\ &= \overline{variance}(H) - \frac{1}{T}\overline{variance}(H) - \left(1 - \frac{1}{T}\right)\overline{covariance}(H) .\end{aligned} \tag{5.21}$$

Thus, we can see that the term $\overline{variance}$ appears in both the averaged squared error term and the average ambiguity term, and it cancels out if we subtract the ambiguity from the error term. Moreover, the fact that the term $\overline{variance}$ appears in both $\overline{err}$ and $\overline{ambi}$ terms indicates that it is hard to maximize the ambiguity term without affecting the bias term, implying that generating diverse learners is a challenging problem.

Wood et al. [2023] revealed that diversity is a hidden dimension in bias-variance decomposition of an ensemble, and presented new decomposition for squared loss as follows

$$err(H) = \underbrace{\frac{1}{T}\sum_{i=1}^{T}(\mathbb{E}[h_i]-f)^2}_{\text{average bias}} + \underbrace{\frac{1}{T}\sum_{i=1}^{T}\mathbb{E}\left[(h_i-\mathbb{E}[h_i])^2\right]}_{\text{average variance}} - \underbrace{\frac{1}{T}\sum_{i=1}^{T}\mathbb{E}\left[(h_i-H)^2\right]}_{\text{diversity or ambiguity}} . \tag{5.22}$$

Compared with (5.18), the ensemble diversity can be understood as a term accompanying bias and variance, which is helpful to decrease the influence of intrinsic noise because of ensemble averaging, but it remains unknown how to encourage the diversity in practical ensemble methods. Similar decomposition can be made for other loss functions such as entropy loss for classification and Poisson loss for regression.

5.3 Diversity Measures

5.3.1 Pairwise Measures

To measure ensemble diversity, a classical approach is to measure the pairwise similarity/dissimilarity between two learners, and then average all the pairwise measurements for the overall diversity.

Given a data set $D = \{(\boldsymbol{x}_1, y_1), \ldots, (\boldsymbol{x}_m, y_m)\}$, for binary classification (i.e., $y_i \in \{-1, +1\}$), we have the following **contingency table** for two classifiers h_i and h_j, where $a + b + c + d = m$ are non-negative variables showing the numbers of examples satisfying the conditions specified by the corresponding rows and columns. We will introduce some representative pairwise measures based on these variables.

	$h_i = +1$	$h_i = -1$
$h_j = +1$	a	c
$h_j = -1$	b	d

Disagreement Measure [Skalak, 1996, Ho, 1998] between h_i and h_j is defined as the proportion of examples on which two classifiers make different predictions, that is,

$$dis_{ij} = \frac{b + c}{m} \, . \tag{5.23}$$

The value dis_{ij} is in $[0, 1]$; the larger the value, the larger the diversity.

Q-Statistic [Yule, 1900] of h_i and h_j is defined as

$$Q_{ij} = \frac{ad - bc}{ad + bc}. \tag{5.24}$$

It can be seen that Q_{ij} takes value in the range of $[-1, 1]$. Q_{ij} is zero if h_i and h_j are independent; Q_{ij} is positive if h_i and h_j make similar predictions; Q_{ij} is negative if h_i and h_j make different predictions.

Correlation Coefficient [Sneath and Sokal, 1973] of h_i and h_j is defined as

$$\rho_{ij} = \frac{ad - bc}{\sqrt{(a + b)(a + c)(c + d)(b + d)}}. \tag{5.25}$$

This is a classic statistic for measuring the correlation between two binary vectors. It can be seen that ρ_{ij} and Q_{ij} have the same sign, and $|\rho_{ij}| \geq |Q_{ij}|$.

Kappa-Statistic [Cohen, 1960] is also a classical measure in statistical literature, and it was first used to measure the diversity between two classifiers by [Margineantu and Dietterich, 1997, Dietterich, 2000b]. It is defined as [1]

$$\kappa_p = \frac{\Theta_1 - \Theta_2}{1 - \Theta_2}, \tag{5.26}$$

[1] The notation κ_p is used for pairwise kappa-statistic, and the interrater agreement measure κ (also called non-pairwise kappa-statistic) will be introduced later.

where Θ_1 and Θ_2 are the probabilities that the two classifiers agree and *agree by chance*, respectively. The probabilities for h_i and h_j can be estimated on the data set D according to

$$\Theta_1 = \frac{a+d}{m}, \tag{5.27}$$

$$\Theta_2 = \frac{(a+b)(a+c)+(c+d)(b+d)}{m^2}. \tag{5.28}$$

$\kappa_p = 1$ if the two classifiers totally agree on D; $\kappa_p = 0$ if the two classifiers agree by chance; $\kappa_p < 0$ is a rare case where the agreement is even less than what is expected by chance.

The above measures do not require to know the classification correctness. If the correctness of classification is known, the following measure can be used:

Double-Fault Measure [Giacinto and Roli, 2001] is defined as the proportion of examples that have been misclassified by both the classifiers h_i and h_j, i.e.,

$$df_{ij} = \frac{e}{m} , \tag{5.29}$$

where $e = \sum_{k=1}^{m} \mathbb{I}\left(h_i(\boldsymbol{x}_k) \neq y_k \wedge h_j(\boldsymbol{x}_k) \neq y_k\right)$.

5.3.2 Non-Pairwise Measures

Non-pairwise measures try to assess the ensemble diversity directly, rather than by averaging pairwise measurements. Given a set of individual classifiers $\{h_1, \ldots, h_T\}$ and a data set $D = \{(\boldsymbol{x}_1, y_1), \ldots, (\boldsymbol{x}_m, y_m)\}$ where $\boldsymbol{x}_i$ is an instance and $y_i \in \{-1, +1\}$ is class label, in the following we will introduce some representative non-pairwise measures.

Kohavi-Wolpert Variance was proposed by Kohavi and Wolpert [1996], and originated from the bias-variance decomposition of the error of a classifier. On an instance $\boldsymbol{x}$, the variability of the predicted class label y is defined as

$$var_{\boldsymbol{x}} = \frac{1}{2}\left(1 - \sum_{y \in \{-1,+1\}} P(y \mid \boldsymbol{x})^2\right) . \tag{5.30}$$

Kuncheva and Whitaker [2003] modified the variability to measure diversity by considering two classifier outputs: *correct* (denoted by $\tilde{y} = +1$) and *incorrect* (denoted by $\tilde{y} = -1$), and estimated $P(\tilde{y} = +1 \mid \boldsymbol{x})$ and $P(\tilde{y} = -1 \mid \boldsymbol{x})$ over individual classifiers, that is,

$$\hat{P}(\tilde{y} = 1 \mid \boldsymbol{x}) = \frac{\rho(\boldsymbol{x})}{T} \quad \text{and} \quad \hat{P}(\tilde{y} = -1 \mid \boldsymbol{x}) = 1 - \frac{\rho(\boldsymbol{x})}{T} , \tag{5.31}$$

where $\rho(\boldsymbol{x})$ is the number of individual classifiers that classify $\boldsymbol{x}$ correctly. By substituting (5.31) into (5.30) and averaging over the data set D, the following kw measure is obtained:

$$kw = \frac{1}{mT^2} \sum_{k=1}^{m} \rho(\boldsymbol{x}_k)(T - \rho(\boldsymbol{x}_k)) . \tag{5.32}$$

The larger the kw measurement, the larger the diversity.

Interrater agreement is a measure of interrater (inter-classifier) reliability [Fleiss, 1981]. Kuncheva and Whitaker [2003] used it to measure the level of agreement within a set of classifiers. This measure is defined as

$$\kappa = 1 - \frac{\frac{1}{T}\sum_{k=1}^{m} \rho(\boldsymbol{x}_k)(T - \rho(\boldsymbol{x}_k))}{m(T-1)\bar{p}(1-\bar{p})} , \tag{5.33}$$

where $\rho(\boldsymbol{x}_k)$ is the number of classifiers that classify $\boldsymbol{x}_k$ correctly, and

$$\bar{p} = \frac{1}{mT} \sum_{i=1}^{T} \sum_{k=1}^{m} \mathbb{I}(h_i(\boldsymbol{x}_k) = y_k) \tag{5.34}$$

is the average accuracy of individual classifiers. Similarly with κ_p, $\kappa = 1$ if the classifiers totally agree on D, and $\kappa \leq 0$ if the agreement is even less than what is expected by chance.

Entropy is motivated by the fact that for an instance $\boldsymbol{x}_k$, the disagreement will be maximized if a tie occurs in the votes of individual classifiers. Cunningham and Carney [2000] directly calculated the Shannon's entropy on every instance and averaged them over D for measuring diversity, that is,

$$Ent_{cc} = \frac{1}{m} \sum_{k=1}^{m} \sum_{y \in \{-1,+1\}} -P(y \mid \boldsymbol{x}_k) \log P(y \mid \boldsymbol{x}_k) , \tag{5.35}$$

where $P(y \mid \boldsymbol{x}_k) = \frac{1}{T}\sum_{i=1}^{T} \mathbb{I}(h_i(\boldsymbol{x}_k) = y)$ can be estimated by the proportion of individual classifiers that predict y as the label of $\boldsymbol{x}_k$. The calculation of Ent_{cc} does not require to know the correctness of individual classifiers.

Shipp and Kuncheva [2002] assumed to know the correctness of the classifiers, and defined their entropy measure as

$$Ent_{sk} = \frac{1}{m} \sum_{k=1}^{m} \frac{\min(\rho(\boldsymbol{x}_k), T - \rho(\boldsymbol{x}_k))}{T - \lceil T/2 \rceil} , \tag{5.36}$$

where $\rho(\boldsymbol{x})$ is the number of individual classifiers that classify $\boldsymbol{x}$ correctly. The Ent_{sk} value is in the range of $[0, 1]$, where 0 indicates no diversity and 1 indicates the largest diversity. Note that (5.36) is not a classical entropy, since it does not use the logarithm function. Though it can be transformed into classical form by using a nonlinear transformation, (5.36) is preferred in practice because it is easier to handle and faster to calculate [Shipp and Kuncheva, 2002].

Difficulty was originally proposed by Hansen and Salamon [1990] and explicitly formulated by Kuncheva and Whitaker [2003]. Let a random variable X taking values in $\{0, \frac{1}{T}, \frac{2}{T}, \ldots, 1\}$ denote the proportion of classifiers that correctly classify a randomly drawn instance $\boldsymbol{x}$. The probability mass function of X can be estimated by running the T classifiers on the data set D. Considering the distribution shape, if the same instance is *difficult* for all classifiers, and the other instances are *easy* for all classifiers, the distribution shape is with two separated peaks; if the instances that are difficult for some classifiers are easy for other classifiers, the distribution shape is with one off-centered peak; if all instances are equally difficult for all classifiers, the distribution shape is without clear peak. So, by using the variance of X to capture the distribution shape, the difficulty measure is defined as

$$\theta = variance(X). \tag{5.37}$$

The smaller the θ value, the larger the diversity.

Generalized Diversity [Partridge and Krzanowski, 1997] was motivated by the argument that the diversity is maximized when the failure of one classifier is accompanied by the correct prediction of the other. The measure is defined as

$$gd = 1 - \frac{p(2)}{p(1)}, \tag{5.38}$$

where

$$p(1) = \sum_{i=1}^{T} \frac{i}{T} p_i, \tag{5.39}$$

$$p(2) = \sum_{i=1}^{T} \frac{i}{T} \frac{i-1}{T-1} p_i, \tag{5.40}$$

and p_i denotes the probability of i randomly chosen classifiers failed on a randomly drawn instance $\boldsymbol{x}$. The gd value is in the range of $[0, 1]$, and the diversity is minimized when $gd = 0$.

Coincident Failure [Partridge and Krzanowski, 1997] is a modified version of the generalized diversity, defined as

$$cfd = \begin{cases} 0, & p_0 = 1 \\ \frac{1}{1-p_0} \sum_{i=1}^{T} \frac{T-i}{T-1} p_i, & p_0 < 1\ . \end{cases} \tag{5.41}$$

$cfd = 0$ if all classifiers give the same predictions simultaneously, and $cfd = 1$ if each classifier makes mistakes on unique instances.

Table 5.1: Summary of ensemble diversity measures, where ↑ (↓) indicates that the larger (smaller) the measurement, the larger the diversity ("Known" indicates whether it requires to know the correctness of individual classifiers).

Diversity Measure	Symbol	↑/↓	Pairwise	Known	Symmetric
Disagreement	dis	↑	Yes	No	Yes
Q-statistic	Q	↓	Yes	No	Yes
Correlation coefficient	ρ	↓	Yes	No	Yes
Kappa-statistic	κ_p	↓	Yes	No	Yes
Double-fault	df	↓	Yes	Yes	No
Interrater agreement	κ	↓	No	Yes	Yes
Kohavi-Wolpert variance	kw	↑	No	Yes	Yes
Entropy (C&C's)	Ent_{cc}	↑	No	No	Yes
Entropy (S&K's)	Ent_{sk}	↑	No	Yes	Yes
Difficulty	θ	↓	No	Yes	No
Generalized diversity	gd	↑	No	Yes	No
Coincident failure	cfd	↑	No	Yes	No

5.3.3 Summary and Visualization

Table 5.1 provides a summary of the 12 diversity measures introduced above. The table shows whether a measure is pairwise or non-pairwise, whether it requires to know the correctness of classifiers, and whether it is symmetric or non-symmetric. A **symmetric measure** will keep the same when the values of 0 (incorrect) and 1 (correct) in binary classification are swapped [Ruta and Gabrys, 2001].

Kuncheva and Whitaker [2003] showed that the Kohavi-Wolpert variance (kw), the averaged disagreement (dis_{avg}) and the kappa-statistic (κ) are closely related as

$$kw = \frac{T-1}{2T} dis_{avg}, \tag{5.42}$$

$$\kappa = 1 - \frac{T}{(T-1)\bar{p}(1-\bar{p})} kw, \tag{5.43}$$

where $\bar{p}$ is in (5.34). Moreover, Kuncheva and Whitaker [2003]'s empirical study disclosed that these diversity measures exhibited reasonably strong relationships.

One advantage of pairwise measures lies in the fact that they can be visualized in two-dimensional plots. This was first shown by Margineantu and Dietterich [1997]'s **kappa-error diagram**, a scatter-plot where each point corresponds to a pair of classifiers, with the x-axis denoting the value of κ_p for the two classifiers, and the y-axis denoting the average error rate of these two classifiers. Figure 5.1 provides some examples of the kappa-error diagram.

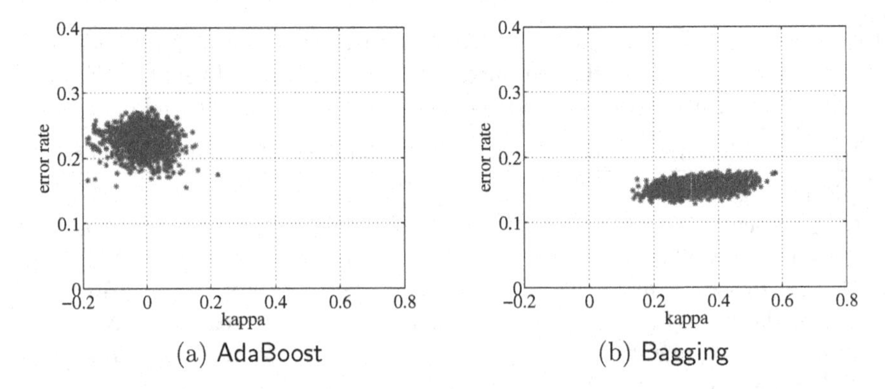

Figure 5.1: Examples of kappa-error diagrams on *credit-g* data set, where each ensemble comprises 50 C4.5 decision trees.

It can be seen that the kappa-error diagram visualizes the accuracy-diversity tradeoff of different ensemble methods. The higher the point clouds, the less accurate the individual classifiers; the more right-hand the point clouds, the less diverse the individual classifiers. Other pairwise diversity measures can be visualized in a similar way.

5.3.4 Limitation of Diversity Measures

Kuncheva and Whitaker [2003] presented possibly the first doubt on diversity measures. Through a broad range of experiments, they showed that the effectiveness of existing diversity measures are discouraging, because it seems that there is no clear relation between those diversity measurements and the ensemble performance.

Tang et al. [2006] theoretically analyzed six diversity measures and showed that if the average accuracy of individual learners is fixed and the maximum diversity is achievable, maximizing the diversity among the individual learners is equivalent to maximizing the minimum margin of the ensemble on the training examples. They showed empirically, however, that the maximum diversity is usually not achievable, and the minimum margin of an ensemble is not monotonically increasing with respect to existing diversity measures.

In particular, Tang et al. [2006] showed that, compared to algorithms that seek diversity implicitly, exploiting the above diversity measures explicitly is ineffective in constructing consistently stronger ensembles. On one hand, the change of existing diversity measurements does not provide consistent guidance on whether an ensemble achieves good generalization performance. On the other hand, the measurements are closely related to the average individual accuracies, which is undesirable since it is not expected that the diversity measure becomes another estimate of accuracy.

Note that it is still well accepted that the motivation of generating diverse individual learners is right. However, the *right* formulation and measures for diversity are unsolved yet, and understanding ensemble diversity remains a holy grail problem for this field.

5.4 Theoretical Exploration

5.4.1 PAC Understanding

Diversity is critical to ensemble methods, and understanding diversity is fundamental in the theoretical studies of ensemble methods. Li et al. [2012] presented a theoretical study about the effect of diversity on the generalization ability of ensemble in the **Probably Approximately Correct (PAC)** framework [Valiant, 1984].

Specifically, considering binary classification, suppose the ensemble result is obtained by taking an average of T trained classifiers $\{h_1(\boldsymbol{x}), h_2(\boldsymbol{x}), \dots, h_T(\boldsymbol{x})\}$, where each classifier $h_i \colon \mathcal{X} \mapsto \{-1, +1\}$ is a mapping from the input space $\mathcal{X}$ to output space $\{-1, +1\}$, i.e.,

$$H(\boldsymbol{x}) = \frac{1}{T}\sum_{i=1}^{T} h_i(\boldsymbol{x}) \ , \tag{5.44}$$

and it predicts the class label of $\boldsymbol{x}$ as $\texttt{sign}[H(\boldsymbol{x})]$. Obviously, it makes wrong prediction on example $(\boldsymbol{x}, y)$ only if $yH(\boldsymbol{x}) \leq 0$, and $yH(\boldsymbol{x})$ is called the **margin** of H at $(\boldsymbol{x}, y)$.

Let $\mathcal{D}$ be an underlying distribution over $\mathcal{X} \times \{-1, +1\}$, and $D = \{(\boldsymbol{x}_1, y_1), \dots, (\boldsymbol{x}_m, y_m)\}$ is a set of examples drawn *i.i.d.* from distribution $\mathcal{D}$. The *generalization error* and *empirical error* with margin θ on D are defined as

$$\epsilon_{\mathcal{D}}(H) = P_{(\boldsymbol{x},y)\sim\mathcal{D}}[yH(\boldsymbol{x}) \leq 0], \tag{5.45}$$

$$\epsilon_D^{\theta}(H) = \frac{1}{m}\sum_{i=1}^{m} \mathbb{I}[y_i H(\boldsymbol{x}_i) \leq \theta] \ , \tag{5.46}$$

respectively. The diversity is measured based on pairwise difference defined as

$$\texttt{div}(h_1, h_2, \dots, h_T) = 1 - \frac{1}{T^2 - T}\sum_{1\leq i\neq j\leq T} \texttt{diff}(h_i, h_j) \ , \tag{5.47}$$

where $\texttt{diff}(\cdot,\cdot)$ measures the pairwise difference between two classifiers as

$$\texttt{diff}(h_i, h_j) = \frac{1}{m}\sum_{k=1}^{m} h_i(\boldsymbol{x}_k) h_j(\boldsymbol{x}_k) \ . \tag{5.48}$$

The difference $\texttt{diff}(h_i, h_j)$ falls into the interval $[-1, 1]$, and $\texttt{diff}(h_i, h_j)$ equals to 1 (or -1) only if two classifiers h_i and h_j always make the same (or opposite) predictions on D. The smaller the value $\texttt{diff}(h_i, h_j)$, the larger the difference between h_i and h_j. Note that the diversity is based on the average of pairwise differences. Consequently, the larger the value $\texttt{div}(h_1, h_2, \ldots, h_T)$, the larger the diversity of the classifier set $\{h_i(\boldsymbol{x})\}_{i=1}^T$.

This diversity measure is closely related with the disagreement measure [Kuncheva and Whitaker, 2003]. Moreover, different from [Yu et al., 2011] which defines the diversity in the parameter space of classifiers, here this diversity measure is defined in the output space, thus can cover various kinds of individual classifiers.

In learning theory, it is known that the generalization error of a learning algorithm can be bounded by its empirical error and the complexity of feasible hypothesis space [Valiant, 1984, Bartlett, 1998]. Since the hypothesis space is uncountable for many learning methods, the hypothesis space complexity is often described by a quantity called **covering number**, as defined below.

Let B be a metric space with metric ρ. Given a set of m examples $D = \{\boldsymbol{x}_1, \ldots, \boldsymbol{x}_m\}$ and a function space $\mathcal{F}$, characterize every $f \in \mathcal{F}$ with a vector $\boldsymbol{v}_D(f) = [f(\boldsymbol{x}_1), \ldots, f(\boldsymbol{x}_m)]^{\boldsymbol{T}} \in B^m$. The covering number in p-norm $\mathcal{N}_p(\mathcal{F}, \epsilon, D)$ is the minimum number l of vectors $\boldsymbol{u}_1, \ldots, \boldsymbol{u}_l \in B^m$ such that, for all $f \in \mathcal{F}$ there exists $j \in \{1, \ldots, l\}$,

$$\|\rho(\boldsymbol{v}_D(f), \boldsymbol{u}_j)\|_p = \left(\sum_{i=1}^m \rho(f(\boldsymbol{x}_i), u_{j,i})^p\right)^{1/p} \leq m^{1/p}\epsilon\ , \tag{5.49}$$

and $\mathcal{N}_p(\mathcal{F}, \epsilon, m) = \sup_{D:|D|=m} \mathcal{N}_p(\mathcal{F}, \epsilon, D)$.

Denote by $\mathbf{f} = [H(\boldsymbol{x}_1), \ldots, H(\boldsymbol{x}_m)]^{\boldsymbol{T}}$, where $H(\cdot)$ is defined by (5.44). If $\texttt{div}(h_1, h_2, \ldots, h_T) \geq q$, then it follows that

$$\|\mathbf{f}\|_1 \leq m\sqrt{1/T + (1 - 1/T)(1 - q)}\ . \tag{5.50}$$

(5.50) holds from $\|\mathbf{f}\|_1 \leq \sqrt{m}\|\mathbf{f}\|_2$ and

$$\begin{aligned} \|\mathbf{f}\|_2^2 &= \sum_{i=1}^m \left(\frac{1}{T}\sum_{t=1}^T h_t(\boldsymbol{x}_i)\right)^2 = \sum_{i=1}^m \left(\frac{1}{T} + \frac{1}{T^2}\sum_{1\leq j\neq k\leq T} h_j(\boldsymbol{x}_i)h_k(\boldsymbol{x}_i)\right) \\ &= m\left(1/T + (1 - \texttt{div}(h_1, h_2, \ldots, h_T)(1 - 1/T)\right) \geq 0\ , \end{aligned} \tag{5.51}$$

where the quantity $1/T + (1 - q)(1 - 1/T)$ is always non-negative.

Li et al. [2012] showed the effect of ensemble diversity on the generalization performance based on its influence on hypothesis space complexity.

Theorem 5.1 ([Li et al., 2012]). *Let $\mathcal{F}$ denote the function space such that for every $H \in \mathcal{F}$, there exists a set of T classifiers $\{h_i(\boldsymbol{x})\}_{i=1}^T$ satisfying $H(\boldsymbol{x}) = \sum_{i=1}^T h_i(\boldsymbol{x})/T$ and $\texttt{div}(h_1, h_2, \ldots, h_T) \geq q$ for any i.i.d. sample D of size m, then for any ϵ, it holds that*

$$\begin{aligned} \log_2 \mathcal{N}_\infty(\mathcal{F}, \epsilon, m) &\leq 36(1 + \ln T)/\epsilon^2 \\ &\quad \times \log_2\left(2m\lceil 4\sqrt{1/T + (1 - 1/T)(1 - q)}/\epsilon + 2\rceil + 1\right). \end{aligned} \tag{5.52}$$

This theorem follows a similar strategy with [Zhang, 2002, Theorems 4 and 5]. Here, we present the sketch and focus on the main difference. (5.52) holds obviously for $\epsilon \geq 1$, and it remains to assume $\epsilon \leq 1$.

First, the interval $[-1-\epsilon/2, 1+\epsilon/2]$ is divided into $n = \lceil 4/\epsilon + 2 \rceil$ sub-intervals, and θ_j be the boundaries of the sub-intervals so that $\theta_j - \theta_{j-1} \leq \epsilon/2$ for all j. Let $j_l(i)$ denote the maximum index of θ_j such that $H(\boldsymbol{x}_i) - \theta_{j_l(i)} \geq \epsilon/2$ and $j_r(i)$ the maximum index of θ_j such that $H(\boldsymbol{x}_i) - \theta_{j_r(i)} \leq -\epsilon/2$. Let $\boldsymbol{h}_i = [h_1(\boldsymbol{x}_i), \ldots, h_T(\boldsymbol{x}_i)]^{\boldsymbol{T}}$, $\boldsymbol{h}'_i = [\boldsymbol{h}_i, -\theta_{j_l(i)}]^{\boldsymbol{T}}$ and $\boldsymbol{h}''_i = [-\boldsymbol{h}_i, \theta_{j_r(i)}]^{\boldsymbol{T}}$.

Based on similar steps in Zhang [2002], the covering number $\mathcal{N}_\infty(\mathcal{F}, \epsilon, D)$ is no more than the number of possible values of the vector β, which is defined as

$$\beta = g_p\left(\sum_{i=1}^m a_i \boldsymbol{h}'_i + \sum_{i=1}^m b_i \boldsymbol{h}''_i\right) \quad , \tag{5.53}$$

where $g_p(\boldsymbol{u})$ is a component-wise function mapping each component u_i of $\boldsymbol{u}$ to $p \cdot \mathtt{sign}(u_i)|u_i|^{p-1}$ with $p \geq 2$, and a_i's and b_i's are non-negative integers under

$$\sum_{i=1}^m (a_i + b_i) \leq 36(1+\ln n)/\epsilon^2 \ . \tag{5.54}$$

There is an one-to-one mapping between $\boldsymbol{h}'_i$ and $\boldsymbol{h}''_i$, so the number of possible values of $\boldsymbol{h}'_i$ and $\boldsymbol{h}''_i$ equals to that of $\boldsymbol{h}'_i$.

From 5.50, it holds that $\|[H(\boldsymbol{x}_1), \ldots, H(\boldsymbol{x}_m)]\|_1 \leq m\sqrt{1/T + (1-1/T)(1-q)}$. From the definition of $\theta_{j_l(i)}$, the number of possible values of $\boldsymbol{h}'_i$ is no more than $m\lceil 4\sqrt{1/T + (1-1/T)(1-q)}/\epsilon + 2\rceil$. By (5.53) and (5.54), the number of values of (β, z) is upper-bounded by

$$\left(2m\lceil 4\sqrt{1/T + (1-1/T)(1-q)}/\epsilon + 2\rceil + 1\right)^{36(1+\ln T)/\epsilon^2} \quad , \tag{5.55}$$

and this completes the proof of Theorem 5.1.

Based on [Bartlett, 1998, Lemma 4], it holds that

$$\epsilon_{\mathcal{D}}(H) \leq \epsilon_D^\theta(H) + \sqrt{\frac{2}{m}\left(\ln \mathcal{N}_\infty(\mathcal{F}, \epsilon/2, 2m) + \ln\frac{2}{\delta}\right)} \ . \tag{5.56}$$

By considering Theorem 5.1 and (5.56), the following result can be obtained:

Corollary 5.1 ([Li et al., 2012]). *Under the assumptions of Theorem 5.1, with probability at least* $1-\delta$*, for any* $\theta > 0$*, every function* $H \in \mathcal{F}$ *satisfies*

$$\epsilon_{\mathcal{D}}(H) \leq \epsilon_D^\theta(H) + \frac{C}{\sqrt{m}}\left(\frac{\ln T \ln\left(m\sqrt{1/T + (1-1/T)(1-q)}\right)}{\theta^2} + \ln\frac{1}{\delta}\right)^{1/2} \quad , \tag{5.57}$$

where C is a constant.

The above result shows that, when other factors are fixed, encouraging larger diversity among individual classifiers (i.e., a larger value of q in Corollary 5.1) will make the hypothesis space complexity smaller, and thus, better generalization performance can be expected. In other words, the diversity has a direct impact on hypothesis space complexity; this implies that encouraging diversity can be understood as a kind of regularization for ensemble methods from the view of statistical learning.

5.4.2 Information Theoretic Diversity

Information theoretic diversity [Brown, 2009, Zhou and Li, 2010b] attempts to understand ensemble diversity from the view of information theory.

The fundamental concept of information theory is the **entropy**, which is a measure of uncertainty. The entropy of a random variable X is defined as

$$Ent(X) = \sum_{x} -p(x) \log p(x), \tag{5.58}$$

where x is the value of X and $p(x)$ is its probability. Based on the concept of entropy, the dependence between two variables X_1 and X_2 can be measured by the **mutual information** [Cover and Thomas, 1991]

$$I(X_1; X_2) = \sum_{x_1, x_2} p(x_1, x_2) \log \frac{p(x_1, x_2)}{p(x_1)p(x_2)}, \tag{5.59}$$

or if given another variable Y, measured by the **conditional mutual information** [Cover and Thomas, 1991]

$$I(X_1; X_2 \mid Y) = \sum_{y, x_1, x_2} p(y)p(x_1, x_2 \mid y) \log \frac{p(x_1, x_2 \mid y)}{p(x_1 \mid y)p(x_2 \mid y)}. \tag{5.60}$$

In the context of information theory, suppose a message Y is sent through a communication channel and the value X is received, the goal is to recover the correct Y by decoding the received value X; that is, a decoding operation $\hat{Y} = g(X)$ is needed. In machine learning, Y is the ground-truth class label, X is the input, and g is the predictor. For ensemble methods, the goal is to recover Y from a set of T classifiers $\{X_1, \ldots, X_T\}$ by a combination function g, and the objective is to minimize the probability of error prediction $p\left(g\left(X_{1:T}\right) \neq Y\right)$, where $X_{1:T}$ denotes T variables $X_1, \ldots, X_T$. Based on information theory, Brown [2009] bounded the probability of error by two inequalities [Fano, 1961, Hellman and Raviv, 1970] as

$$\frac{Ent(Y) - I(X_{1:T}; Y) - 1}{\log(|Y|)} \leq p\left(g\left(X_{1:T}\right) \neq Y\right) \leq \frac{Ent(Y) - I(X_{1:T}; Y)}{2}. \tag{5.61}$$

Thus, to minimize the prediction error, the mutual information $I(X_{1:T}; Y)$ should be maximized. By considering different expansions of the mutual information term, different formulations of information theoretic diversity can be obtained, as will be introduced in the next sections.

Interaction Information Diversity

Interaction information [McGill, 1954] is a multivariate generalization of mutual information for measuring the dependence among multiple variables. The interaction information $I(X_{1:n})$ and the **conditional interaction information** $I(\{X_{1:n}\} \mid Y)$ are respectively defined as

$$I(\{X_{1:n}\}) = \begin{cases} I(X_1; X_2) & \text{for } n = 2 \\ I(\{X_{1:n-1}\} \mid X_n) - I(\{X_{1:n-1}\}) & \text{for } n \geq 3, \end{cases} \tag{5.62}$$

$$I(\{X_{1:n}\} \mid Y) = \mathbb{E}_Y[I(\{X_{1:n}\}) \mid Y]. \tag{5.63}$$

Based on interaction information, Brown [2009] presented the following expansion of $I(X_{1:T}; Y)$:

$$I(X_{1:T}; Y) = \underbrace{\sum_{i=1}^{T} I(X_i; Y)}_{\text{relevancy}} + \underbrace{\sum_{k=2}^{T} \sum_{S_k \subseteq S} I(\{S_k \cup Y\})}_{\text{interaction information diversity}} \tag{5.64}$$

$$= \underbrace{\sum_{i=1}^{T} I(X_i; Y)}_{\text{relevancy}} - \underbrace{\sum_{k=2}^{T} \sum_{S_k \subseteq S} I(\{S_k\})}_{\text{redundancy}} + \underbrace{\sum_{k=2}^{T} \sum_{S_k \subseteq S} I(\{S_k\} \mid Y)}_{\text{conditional redundancy}}, \tag{5.65}$$

where $S = \{X_1, X_2, \ldots, X_T\}$ and S_k is a set of size k. (5.65) shows that the mutual information $I(X_{1:T}; Y)$ can be expanded into three terms.

The first term, $\sum_{i=1}^{T} I(X_i; Y)$, is the sum of the mutual information between each classifier and the target. It is referred to as *relevancy*, which actually gives a bound on the accuracy of the individual classifiers. Since it is additive to the mutual information, a large relevancy is preferred.

The second term, $\sum_{k=2}^{T} \sum_{S_k \subseteq S} I(\{S_k\})$, measures the dependency among all possible subsets of classifiers, and it is independent to the class label Y. This term is referred to as *redundancy*. Note that it is subtractive to the mutual information. A large $I(\{S_k\})$ indicates strong correlations among classifiers without considering the target Y, which reduces the value of $I(X_{1:T}; Y)$, and hence a small value is preferred.

The third term, $\sum_{k=2}^{T} \sum_{S_k \subseteq S} I(\{S_k\} \mid Y)$, measures the dependency among the classifiers given the class label. It is referred to as *conditional redundancy*. Note that it is additive to the mutual information, and a large conditional redundancy is preferred.

It is evident that the relevancy term corresponds to the accuracy, while both the redundancy and the conditional redundancy describe the correlations among classifiers. Thus, the interaction information diversity naturally emerges as (5.64). The interaction information diversity discloses that the correlations among classifiers are not necessarily helpful to ensemble performance, because there are different kinds of correlations and the helpful ones are those which have considered the learning target. Moreover, the diversity exists at multiple orders of correlations, not simply pairwise.

One limitation of the interaction information diversity lies in the fact that the expression of the diversity terms, especially the involved interaction information, are quite complicated and there lacks effective process to estimate them at multiple orders in practice.

Multi-Information Diversity

Multi-information [Watanabe, 1960, Studeny and Vejnarova, 1998, Slonim et al., 2006] is another multivariate generalization of mutual information. The multi-information $\mathbb{I}(X_{1:n})$ and **conditional multi-information** $\mathbb{I}(X_{1:n} \mid Y)$ are respectively defined as

$$\mathbb{I}(X_{1:n}) = \sum_{x_{1:n}} p(x_1, \ldots, x_n) \log \frac{p(x_1, \ldots, x_n)}{p(x_1)p(x_2)\cdots p(x_n)}, \tag{5.66}$$

$$\mathbb{I}(X_{1:n} \mid Y) = \sum_{y, x_{1:n}} p(y)p(x_{1:n} \mid y) \log \frac{p(x_{1:n} \mid y)}{p(x_1 \mid y)\cdots p(x_n \mid y)}. \tag{5.67}$$

When $n = 2$ the (conditional) multi-information is reduced to (conditional) mutual information. Moreover,

$$\mathbb{I}(X_{1:n}) = \sum_{i=2}^{n} I(X_i; X_{1:i-1}); \tag{5.68}$$

$$\mathbb{I}(X_{1:n} \mid Y) = \sum_{i=2}^{n} I(X_i; X_{1:i-1} \mid Y). \tag{5.69}$$

Based on multi-information and conditional multi-information, Zhou and Li [2010b] presented the following expansion of $I(X_{1:T}; Y)$:

$$\begin{aligned} I(X_{1:T}; Y) &= \underbrace{\sum_{i=1}^{T} I(X_i; Y)}_{\text{relevance}} + \underbrace{\mathbb{I}(X_{1:T} \mid Y) - \mathbb{I}(X_{1:T})}_{\text{multi-information diversity}} \\ &= \underbrace{\sum_{i=1}^{T} I(X_i; Y)}_{\text{relevance}} - \underbrace{\sum_{i=2}^{T} I(X_i; X_{1:i-1})}_{\text{redundancy}} + \underbrace{\sum_{i=2}^{T} I(X_i; X_{1:i-1} \mid Y)}_{\text{conditional redundancy}} . \end{aligned} \tag{5.70}$$

Zhou and Li [2010b] proved that (5.64) and (5.70) are mathematically equivalent, though the formulation of (5.70) is much simpler. One advantage of (5.70) is that its terms are *decomposable* over individual classifiers. Take the redundancy term for example. Given an ensemble of size k, its redundancy is $\mathbb{I}(X_{1:k}) = \sum_{i=2}^{k} I(X_i; X_{1:i-1})$. Then, if a new classifier X_{k+1} is added, the new redundancy becomes $\mathbb{I}(X_{1:k+1}) = \sum_{i=2}^{k+1} I(X_i; X_{1:i-1})$, where the only difference is the adding of the mutual information $I(X_{k+1}; X_{1:k})$.

Estimation Method

The interaction information diversity (5.64) consists of both low-order and high-order components. If we only consider the pairwise components, the following can be obtained:

$$I(X_{1:T}; Y) \approx \sum_{i=1}^{T} I(X_i; Y) - \sum_{i=1}^{T} \sum_{j=i+1}^{T} I(X_i; X_j) + \sum_{i=1}^{T} \sum_{j=i+1}^{T} I(X_i; X_j \mid Y). \tag{5.71}$$

This estimation could not be accurate since it omits higher-order components. If we want to consider higher-order components, however, we need to estimate higher-order interaction information, which is quite difficult and currently there lacks effective approach.

For the multi-information diversity (5.70), Zhou and Li [2010b] presented an approximate estimation approach. Take the redundancy term in (5.70) for example. It is needed to estimate $I(X_i; X_{1:i-1})$ for all i's. Rather than calculating it directly, $I(X_i; X_{1:i-1})$ is approximated by

$$I(X_i; X_{1:i-1}) \approx \max_{\Omega_k \subseteq \Omega} I(X_i; \Omega_k) \ , \tag{5.72}$$

where $\Omega = \{X_{i-1}, \ldots, X_1\}$, Ω_k is a subset of size k $(1 \leq k \leq i-1)$. For an illustrative example, Figure 5.2 depicts a Venn diagram for four variables, where the ellipses represent the entropies of variables, while mutual information can be represented by the combination of regions in the diagram. As shown in the right-side of the figure, the high-order component $I(X_4; X_3, X_2, X_1)$ shares a large intersection with the low-order component $I(X_4; X_2, X_1)$, where the only difference is region e. Note that if X_1, X_2, and X_3 are strongly correlated, it is very likely that the uncertainty of X_3 is covered by X_1 and X_2; that is, the regions c and e are very small. Thus, $I(X_4; X_2, X_1)$ provides an approximation to $I(X_4; X_3, X_2, X_1)$. Such a scenario often happens in ensemble construction, since the individual classifiers generally have strong correlations.

Similarly, the conditional redundancy term can be approximated as

$$I(X_i; X_{1:i-1} \mid Y) \approx \max_{\Omega_k \subseteq \Omega} I(X_i; \Omega_k \mid Y). \tag{5.73}$$

Thus, the multi-information diversity can be estimated by

$$I(X_i; X_{1:i-1} \mid Y) - I(X_i; X_{1:i-1}) \approx \max_{\Omega_k \subseteq \Omega} \left[I(X_i; \Omega_k \mid Y) - I(X_i; \Omega_k) \right] . \tag{5.74}$$

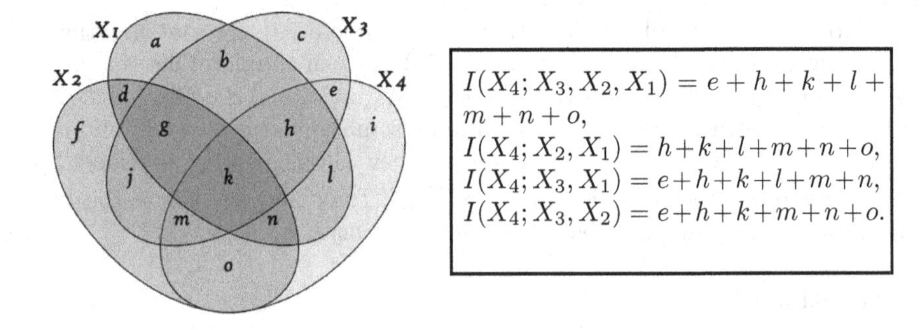

Figure 5.2: Venn diagram of an illustrative example of Zhou and Li [2010b]'s approximation method.

It is proved that this estimation provides a lower-bound of the information theoretic diversity.

To accomplish the estimation, an enumeration over all Ω_k's is desired. In this way, however, for every i it needs to estimate $I(X_i; \Omega_k)$ and $I(X_i; \Omega_k \mid Y)$ for C_{i-1}^k number of different Ω_k's. When k is near $(i-1)/2$, the number will be large, and the estimation of $I(X_i; \Omega_k)$ and $I(X_i; \Omega_k \mid Y)$ will become difficult. Hence, a trade-off is needed, and Zhou and Li [2010b] showed that a good estimation can be achieved even when k is restricted to be small values such as 1 or 2.

5.5 Diversity Enhancement

Though there is no generally accepted formal formulation or measures for ensemble diversity, there are effective heuristic mechanisms for diversity generation in ensemble construction. The common basic idea is to inject some randomness into the learning process. Popular mechanisms include manipulating the data samples, input features, learning parameters, and output representations.

Data Sample Manipulation. This is the most popularly used mechanism. Given a data set, multiple different data samples can be generated, and then the individual learners are trained from different data samples. Generally, the data sample manipulation is based on *sampling* approaches, e.g., Bagging adopts *bootstrap sampling* [Efron and Tibshirani, 1993], AdaBoost adopts *sequential sampling*, etc.

Input Feature Manipulation. The training data is usually described by a set of features. Different subsets of features, or called **subspaces**, provide different views on the data. Therefore, individual learners trained from different subspaces are usually diverse. The Random Subspace method [Ho, 1998] introduced in Section 3.4 is a representative which employs this mechanism. For data with a lot of redundant features, training a learner in a subspace will be not only effective but also efficient.

Learning Parameter Manipulation. This mechanism tries to generate diverse individual learners by using different parameter settings for the base learning algorithm. For example, different initial weights can be assigned to individual neural networks [Kolen and Pollack, 1990], different split selections can be applied to individual decision trees [Kwok and Carter, 1988, Liu et al., 2008a], different candidate rule conditions can be applied to individual FOIL rule inducers [Ali and Pazzani, 1996], etc. The Negative Correlation method [Liu and Yao, 1999] explicitly constrains the parameters of individual neural networks to be different by a *regularization* term.

Output Representation Manipulation. This mechanism tries to generate diverse individual learners by using different output representations. For example, the ECOC approach [Dietterich and Bakiri, 1995][Zhou, 2021, Section 3.5] employs error-correcting output codes, the Flipping Output method [Breiman, 2000b] randomly changes the labels of some training instances, the Output Smearing method [Breiman, 2000b] converts multi-class outputs to multivariate regression outputs to construct individual learners, etc.

In addition to the above popular mechanisms, there are some other attempts. For example, Melville and Mooney [2005] tried to encourage diversity by using artificial training data. They constructed an ensemble in an iterative way. In each round, a number of artificial instances were generated from the data distribution. These artificial instances were then assigned the labels that disagree with the current ensemble prediction to the most. After that, a new learner is trained from the original training data together with the artificial training data. If adding the new learner to the current ensemble increases training error, the new learner will be discarded and another learner will be generated with another set of artificial examples; otherwise, the new learner will be accepted into the current ensemble.

Note that different mechanisms for diversity enhancement can be used together. For example, Random Forest [Breiman, 2001] adopts both the mechanisms of data sample manipulation and input feature manipulation.

Most existing ensemble methods can only improve the predictive performance of unstable learners, such as decision trees and neural networks. To improve the performance of stable learns, such as naïve Bayes and kNN, Davidson [2004] proposed to create a number of bootstrap samples from the training data, build a model from each and then aggregate their predictions; Zhou and Yu [2005] proposed FASBIR (Filtered Attribute Subspace based Bagging with Injected Randomness), which utilizes multimodal perturbation to help generate accurate but diverse component learners; Ting et al. [2011] introduced Feating (Feature-Subspace Aggregating), which builds local models instead of global models.

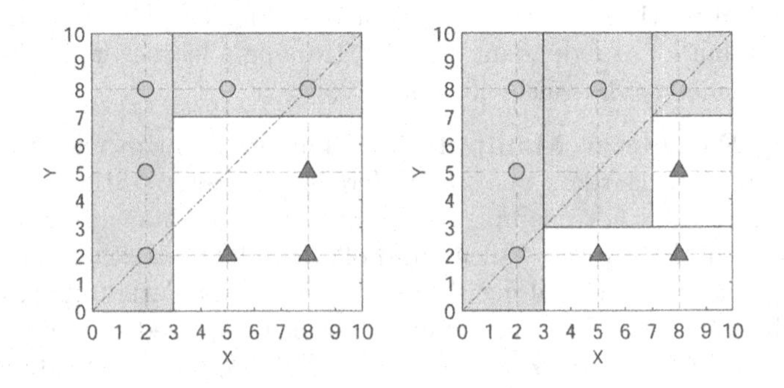

Figure 5.3: Decision regions of two decision trees for the task of predicting if $Y \geq X$. Green circles denote positive instances while magenta triangles denote negative instances. Red lines indicate ground-truth decision boundaries. Grey shaded regions are predicted as positive. The two decision trees are obviously different even though making exactly the same predictions on the eight instances.

5.6 Structural Diversity

The deficiency of previous diversity measures might lie in the fact that they consider only **behavioral diversity**, i.e., how the classifiers behave when making predictions, neglecting the fact that classifiers may be potentially different even when they make the same predictions. Consider the simple task of predicting whether $Y \geq X$, where X and Y are two components of an instance and both lie in $[0, 10]$. Figure 5.3 plots the decision regions of two decision trees. The two classifiers make the same predictions on the eight instances; however, they use totally different partitions of the feature space and are obviously different. For another example, suppose that there are redundancy in the features, and therefore, two classifiers can make exactly the same predictions while using different features. Consequently, they may have different capability of handling missing and drifting features.

Sun and Zhou [2018] advocated to consider **structural diversity** as a complement to behavioral diversity. The structure of a learner embeds some inherent properties, such as tendency to overfit, thus is quite important. Unlike behavioral diversity, structural diversity does not rely on specific data. Take decision tree as an example: deeper trees make predictions based on a longer sequence of tests and therefore intuitively tend to be more specialized than shallow trees that tend to be more general. Besides, the similarity in local structure of decision trees corresponds to the similarity in their partitions of feature space. Thus, it could be beneficial to encourage diversity in the structure.

The term *structure*, however, is not so apparent as it sounds. Turing Award recipient Frederick P. Brooks, Jr. summarized three great challenges for half-century-old computer science in the 50th anniversary of *Journal of the ACM* [Brooks, 2003], where the first challenge is *quantification of structural information.* We have no theory that gives a metric for the information embedded in structure, and this remains a fundamental issue and needs further insights.

For the seminal study of structural diversity, Sun and Zhou [2018] focused on ensembles of decision trees. A decision tree consists of a set of nodes and branches. Each non-leaf node is associated with a feature to split and each leaf node is associated with a class label. The structure of a decision tree is quite important. Deep trees and shallow trees may have totally different properties. Besides, the order of nodes matters a lot as instances are passed from root to leaf through nodes and branches sequentially. However, to give an appropriate metric of the structural difference between two decision trees is really hard. Sun and Zhou [2018] proposed the *tree matching diversity* (TMD) measure, which is simple to implement and easy to understand as follows.

The *pairwise* tree matching diversity measure is defined as the minimum number of node operations to match the structure of two decision trees, where three node operations are considered, including inserting a node, deleting a node and replacing the associated feature of a node. The value is no larger than the total number of nodes of the two decision trees. It is closely related to **tree edit distance**, which can be calculated using strategies like dynamic programming or more efficient decomposition strategies [Pawlik and Augsten, 2016]. The TMD measure is symmetric for the two decision trees. The larger the value, the larger their structural difference. The overall diversity of an ensemble consists of more than two decision trees is defined as the average of all pairwise TMD values, and it can be normalized by the maximum pairwise value inside the ensemble.

Figure 5.4 presents an illustration, where five decision trees are trained on the *Breast Cancer Winsconsin* data set [Wolberg and Mangasarian, 1990] which has nine attributes, i.e., Clump Thickness (CT), Cell Size Uniformity (CSI), Cell Shape Uniformity (CSH), Marginal Adhesion (MA), Single Epithelial Cell Size (SE), Bare Nuclei (BN), Bland Chromatin (BC), Normal Nucleoli (NN) and Mitoses (MI). The task is to predict whether the tumor is Benign (B) or Malignant (M). Pairwise TMD's are listed in the figure. The TMD between T_1 and T_2 is 1 as only one node Insertion/Deletion is needed to match the two trees. The TMD between T_3 and T_4 is also 1 as only one node Relabel is needed. All the four trees have a large TMD with T_5. Hence, it is expected that T_1 and T_2 would perform similarly, T_3 and T_4 would perform similarly, while all four would perform differently from T_5. The TMD of the ensemble would be the average of 10 pairwise TMD's, i.e., 5.4. Furthermore, the pairwise TMD can be normalized by the maximum pairwise measure of 10.

Now consider the task of predicting whether $Y \geq X$ mentioned at the beginning of this section. Figure 5.5 plots three decision trees, where the decision regions of Tree 1 and Tree 2 are as same as those in Figure 5.3, respectively. Suppose that we have already got two decision trees, Tree 1 and

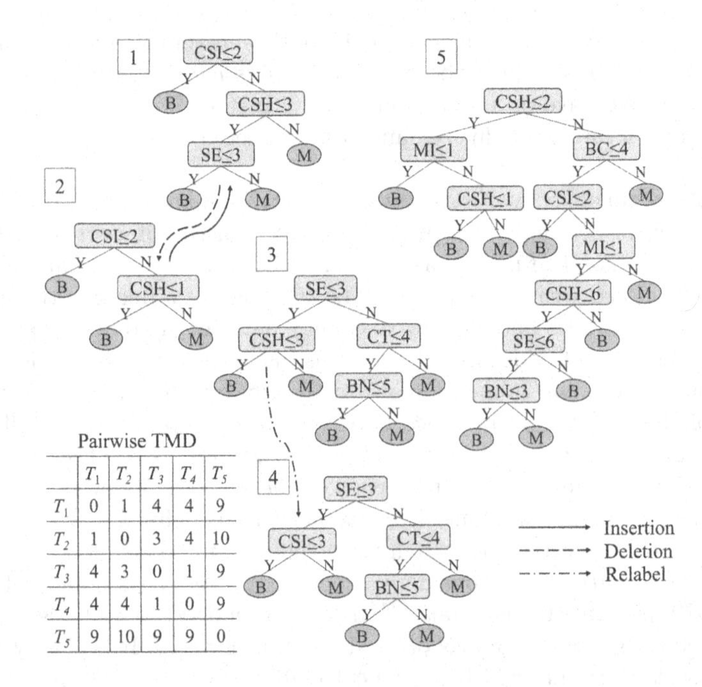

	T_1	T_2	T_3	T_4	T_5
T_1	0	1	4	4	9
T_2	1	0	3	4	10
T_3	4	3	0	1	9
T_4	4	4	1	0	9
T_5	9	10	9	9	0

Figure 5.4: Five decision trees. The arrows indicate the node operations needed to match the two trees. Pairwise TMD values are listed.

Tree 3, and we have eight instances as indicated in Figure 5.3. Now we want to add another decision tree from Tree 1 and Tree 2 to ensemble. None of the existing behavioral diversity measures can tell the difference between Tree 1 and Tree 2, because they predict the same on the eight instances. In contrast, TMD favors Tree 2 with a different structure rather than a duplicate of Tree 1. In fact, if X and Y are uniformly sampled from $[0, 10]$, the expected majority voting error by adding Tree 1 is 0.17 while that by adding Tree 2 is only 0.13. In practice, classifiers may predict quite differently, thus both structural and behavioral diversities should be considered together to attain a good ensemble.

Though the TMD measure is simple, significant improvements have been observed when it is used to enhance the behavioral diversity measures, showing the helpfulness of considering structural diversity. Note that TMD is specially designed for decision trees, and it remains an open problem how to design structural diversity measures for other kinds of base learners. It is also worthwhile to investigate how to exploit behavioral and structural diversities together.

5.7 Further Readings

In addition to [Kohavi and Wolpert, 1996], there are a number of practically effective bias-variance decomposition approaches, e.g., [Kong and Dietterich,

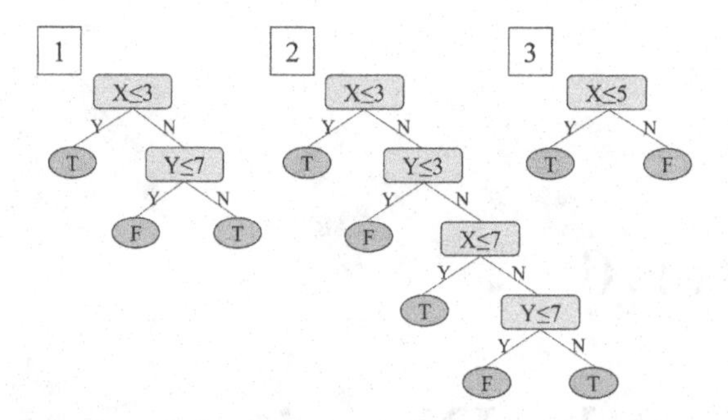

Figure 5.5: Three decision trees for the task of predicting if $Y \geq X$. $X, Y \in [0, 10]$. Given Tree 1, Tree 3 and the eight instances in Figure 5.3, TMD (based on structural diversity) suggests to include Tree 2 rather than another Tree 1, whereas existing diversity measures (based on behavioral diversity) could not exhibit the difference between Tree 1 and Tree 2.

1995, Breiman, 1996a]. Most approaches focus solely on 0/1-loss and produce quite different definitions. James [2003] proposed a framework which accommodates the essential characteristics of bias and variance, and their decomposition can be generalized to any symmetric loss function.

Stable learners, e.g., naïve Bayes and k-nearest neighbor classifiers, which are insensitive to small perturbations on training data, are usually difficult to improve through typical ensemble methods. Zhou and Yu [2005] proposed the FASBIR approach and showed that **multimodal perturbation**, which combines multiple mechanisms of diversity generation, provides a practical way to construct ensembles of stable learners.

A comprehensive survey on diversity enhancement approaches can be found in [Brown et al., 2005a]. Current ensemble methods generally try to generate diverse individual learners from *labeled* training data. Zhou [2009] advocated to try to exploit *unlabeled* training data to enhance diversity, which will be discussed in Section 9.6.

Though at least seventy-six diversity measures have been proposed [Kuncheva, 2016], and there are some new understandings such as [Wood et al., 2023], the *right* formulation and measures for diversity are unsolved yet, and understanding ensemble diversity remains a holy grail problem for ensemble learning field. Considering structural information of the learners rather than considering only behavior information like [Sun and Zhou, 2018] seems worthwhile to be explored.

Chapter 6

Ensemble Pruning

6.1 What is Ensemble Pruning

Given a set of trained individual learners, rather than combining all of them, **ensemble pruning** tries to select a subset of individual learners to comprise the ensemble.

An apparent advantage of ensemble pruning is to obtain ensembles with smaller sizes; this reduces the storage resources required for holding the ensembles and the computational resources required for calculating outputs of individual learners, and thus improves efficiency. There is another benefit, that is, the generalization performance of the pruned ensemble may be even better than the ensemble consisting of all the given individual learners.

The first study on ensemble pruning is possibly [Margineantu and Dietterich, 1997] which tried to prune Boosted ensembles. Tamon and Xiang [2000], however, showed that Boosting pruning is intractable even to approximate. Instead of pruning ensembles generated by sequential methods, Zhou et al. [2002c] tried to prune ensembles generated by parallel methods such as Bagging, and first showed that the pruning can lead to smaller ensembles with better generalization performance. Later, most ensemble pruning studies switched from sequential ensembles to parallel ensembles. Caruana et al. [2004] showed that pruning parallel heterogeneous ensembles comprising different types of individual learners is better than taking the original heterogeneous ensembles. In [Zhou et al., 2002c] the pruning of parallel ensembles was called **selective ensemble**, while in [Caruana et al., 2004], the pruning of parallel heterogeneous ensembles was called **ensemble selection**. In this chapter we put all of them under the umbrella of *ensemble pruning*.

Originally, ensemble pruning was defined for the setting where *the individual learners have already been generated*, and no more individual learners will be generated from training data during the pruning process. Note that conventional **sequential ensemble methods** will discard some individual learners during their training process, but that is *not* ensemble pruning. These

DOI: 10.1201/9781003587774-6

methods typically generate individual learners one by one; once an individual learner is generated, a *sanity check* is applied and the individual learner will be discarded if it cannot pass the check. Such a sanity check is important to ensure the validity of sequential ensembles and prevent them from growing infinitely. For example, in AdaBoost, an individual learner will be discarded if its accuracy is below 0.5; however, AdaBoost is not an ensemble pruning method, and Boosting pruning [Margineantu and Dietterich, 1997] tries to reduce the number of individual learners after the Boosting procedure terminated and no more individual learners will be generated. It is noteworthy that some recent studies have extended ensemble pruning to all steps of ensemble construction, and individual learners may be pruned even before all individual learners have been generated. Nevertheless, an essential difference between ensemble pruning and sequential ensemble methods remains: for sequential ensemble methods, an individual learner would *not* be excluded once it is added into the ensemble, while for ensemble pruning methods, any individual learners can be excluded, even for the ones which have been kept in the ensemble for a long time.

Ensemble pruning can be viewed as a special kind of **Stacking**. As introduced in Section 4.3.1, Stacking tries to apply a meta-learner to combine the individual learners, while the ensemble pruning procedure can be viewed as a special meta-learner. Also, recall that as mentioned in Chapter 4, if we do not consider how the individual learners are generated, then different ensemble methods can be regarded as different implementations of weighted combination; from this aspect, ensemble pruning can be regarded as a procedure which sets the weights of some base learners to zero.

6.2 Many Could Be Better Than All

To show that it is possible to get an ensemble with smaller size but better generalization performance through pruning, this section presents Zhou et al. [2002c]'s analyses.

We start from the regression setting on which the analysis is easier. Suppose there are N individual learners $h_1, \ldots, h_N$ available, and thus the final ensemble size $T \leq N$. Without loss of generality, assume that the learners are combined via weighted averaging according to (4.9) and the weights are constrained by (4.10). For simplicity, assume that equal weights are used, and thus, from (4.11) we have the generalization error of the ensemble as

$$err = \sum_{i=1}^{N} \sum_{j=1}^{N} C_{ij}/N^2, \tag{6.1}$$

where C_{ij} is defined in (4.12) and measures the correlation between h_i and h_j. If the k-th individual learner is excluded from the ensemble, the generalization error of the pruned ensemble is

$$err' = \sum_{\substack{i=1 \\ i \neq k}}^{N} \sum_{\substack{j=1 \\ j \neq k}}^{N} C_{ij}/(N-1)^2. \tag{6.2}$$

By comparing (6.1) and (6.2), we get the condition under which err is no smaller than err', implying that the generalization performance of the pruned ensemble is better than the all-member ensemble, that is,

$$(2N-1) \sum_{i=1}^{N} \sum_{j=1}^{N} C_{ij} \leq 2N^2 \sum_{\substack{i=1 \\ i \neq k}}^{N} C_{ik} + N^2 C_{kk}. \tag{6.3}$$

(6.3) usually holds in practice since the individual learners are often highly correlated. For an extreme example, when all individual learners are duplicates, (6.3) indicates that the ensemble size can be reduced without sacrificing generalization ability. This simple analysis exhibits that in regression, given a number of individual learners, ensembling some instead of all of them may be better.

It is interesting to study the difference between ensemble pruning and *sequential ensemble methods* based on (6.3). As above, let N denote the upper bound of the final ensemble size. Suppose the sequential ensemble method employs the sanity check that the new individual learner h_k $(1 < k \leq N)$ will be kept if the ensemble consisting of $h_1, \ldots, h_k$ is better than the ensemble consisting of $h_1, \ldots, h_{k-1}$ on mean squared error. Then, h_k will be discarded if [Perrone and Cooper, 1995]

$$(2k-1) \sum_{i=1}^{k-1} \sum_{j=1}^{k-1} C_{ij} \leq 2(k-1)^2 \sum_{i=1}^{k-1} C_{ik} + (k-1)^2 C_{kk}. \tag{6.4}$$

Comparing (6.3) and (6.4), one can get the following observations. Firstly, ensemble pruning methods consider the correlation among *all* the individual learners while sequential ensemble methods consider only the correlation between the new individual learner and previously generated ones. For example, assume $N = 100$ and $k = 10$; sequential ensemble methods consider only the correlation between $h_1, \ldots, h_{10}$, while ensemble pruning methods consider the correlations between $h_1, \ldots, h_{100}$. Secondly, when (6.4) holds, sequential ensemble methods will only discard h_k, but $h_1, \ldots, h_{k-1}$ won't be discarded, while any classifier in $h_1, \ldots, h_N$ may be discarded by ensemble pruning methods when (6.3) holds.

Note that the analysis from (6.1) to (6.4) only applies to regression. Since supervised learning includes regression and classification, analysis of classification settings is needed for a unified result. Again, let N denote the number of available individual classifiers, and thus the final ensemble size $T \leq N$.

Without loss of generality, consider binary classification with labels $\{-1,+1\}$, and assume that the learners are combined via majority voting introduced in Section 4.2.2 and ties are broken arbitrarily. Given m training instances, the expected output on these instances is $(f_1,\ldots,f_m)^T$ where f_j is the ground-truth of the j-th instance, and the prediction made by the i-th classifier h_i on these instances is $(h_{i1},\ldots,h_{im})^T$ where h_{ij} is the prediction on the j-th instance. Since $f_j, h_{ij} \in \{-1,+1\}$, it is obvious that h_i correctly classifies the j-th instance when $h_{ij}f_j = +1$. Thus, the error of the i-th classifier on these m instances is

$$err(h_i) = \frac{1}{m}\sum_{j=1}^{m} \eta(h_{ij}f_j) , \tag{6.5}$$

where $\eta(\cdot)$ is a function defined as

$$\eta(x) = \begin{cases} 1 & \text{if } x = -1, \\ 0.5 & \text{if } x = 0, \\ 0 & \text{if } x = 1. \end{cases} \tag{6.6}$$

Let $\boldsymbol{s} = (s_1,\ldots,s_m)^T$ where $s_j = \sum_{i=1}^{N} h_{ij}$. The output of the all-member ensemble on the j-th instance is

$$H_j = \mathtt{sign}(s_j) . \tag{6.7}$$

It is obvious that $H_j \in \{-1,0,+1\}$. The prediction of the all-member ensemble on the j-th instance is correct when $H_jf_j = +1$ and wrong when $H_jf_j = -1$, while $H_jf_j = 0$ corresponds to a tie. The error of the all-member ensemble is

$$err = \frac{1}{m}\sum_{j=1}^{m} \eta(H_jf_j) . \tag{6.8}$$

Now, suppose the k-th individual classifier is excluded from the ensemble. The prediction made by the pruned ensemble on the j-th instance is

$$H'_j = \mathtt{sign}(s_j - h_{kj}) , \tag{6.9}$$

and the error of the pruned ensemble is

$$err' = \frac{1}{m}\sum_{j=1}^{m} \eta(H'_jf_j) . \tag{6.10}$$

Then, by comparing (6.8) and (6.10), we get the condition under which err is no smaller than err', implying that the pruned ensemble is better than the all-member ensemble; that is,

$$\sum_{j=1}^{m} \left(\eta\left(\mathtt{sign}\left(s_j\right) f_j\right) - \eta\left(\mathtt{sign}\left(s_j - h_{kj}\right) f_j\right)\right) \geq 0 . \tag{6.11}$$

Since the exclusion of the k-th individual classifier will not change the output of the ensemble if $|s_j| > 1$, and

$$\eta(\mathtt{sign}(x)) - \eta(\mathtt{sign}(x - y)) = -\frac{1}{2}\mathtt{sign}(x + y) , \tag{6.12}$$

the condition for the k-th individual classifier to be pruned is

$$\sum_{j:\ |s_j| \leq 1} \mathtt{sign}((s_j + h_{kj})f_j) \leq 0 . \tag{6.13}$$

(6.13) usually holds in practice since the individual classifiers are often highly correlated. For an extreme example, when all the individual classifiers are duplicates, (6.13) indicates that the ensemble size can be reduced without sacrificing generalization ability.

Through combining the analyses on both regression and classification (i.e., (6.3) and (6.13)), we get the MCBTA ("*many could be better than all*") theorem [Zhou et al., 2002c], which indicates that for supervised learning, given a set of individual learners, it may be better to ensemble some instead of all of these individual learners.

6.3 Categorization of Pruning Methods

Note that simply pruning individual learners with poor performance may not lead to a good pruned ensemble. Generally, it is better to keep some accurate individuals together with some not-that-good but complementary individuals. Furthermore, note that neither (6.3) nor (6.13) provides practical solutions to ensemble pruning since the required computation is usually intractable. Indeed, the central problem of ensemble pruning research is how to design practical algorithms leading to smaller ensembles without sacrificing or even improving the generalization performance contrasting to all-member ensembles.

Many effective ensemble pruning methods have been developed. Roughly speaking, they can be classified into three categories [Tsoumakas et al., 2009]:

- **Ordering-based pruning.** Those methods try to order the individual learners according to some criterion, and only the learners in the front-part will be put into the final ensemble. Though they work in a sequential style, it is noteworthy that they are quite different from sequential ensemble methods (e.g., AdaBoost) since all the available individual learners are given in advance and no more individual learners will be generated in the pruning process; moreover, any individual learner, not just the latest generated one, may be pruned.

- **Clustering-based pruning.** Those methods try to identify a number of representative *prototype* individual learners to constitute the final ensemble. Usually, a clustering process is employed to partition the individual learners into a number of groups, where individual learners in the same group behave similarly while different groups have large diversity. Then, the prototypes of clusters are put into the final ensemble.

- **Optimization-based pruning.** Those methods formulate the ensemble pruning problem as an optimization problem which aims to find the subset of individual learners that optimizes an objective related to the generalization ability as well as the size of the final ensemble. This school of methods has become the mainstream in ensemble pruning, and various optimization techniques have been used.

It is obvious that the boundaries between different categories are not crisp, and there are methods that can be put into more than one category. In particular, though there are many early studies on *pure* ordering-based or clustering-based pruning methods, along with the explosively increasing exploitation of optimization techniques in machine learning, recent ordering-based and clustering-based pruning methods become closer to optimization-based methods.

6.4 Ordering-Based Pruning

Ordering-based pruning originated from the work of Margineantu and Dietterich [1997] on pruning sequential ensemble methods. After the work of Zhou et al. [2002c], most ensemble pruning efforts were turned to pruning ensembles generated by parallel ensemble methods.

Given N individual learners $h_1, \ldots, h_N$, suppose they are combined sequentially in a random order, the generalization error of the ensemble generally decreases monotonically as the ensemble size increases, and approaches an asymptotic constant error. It has been found that [Martínez-Muñoz and Suárez, 2006], however, if an appropriate ordering is devised, the ensemble error generally reaches a minimum with intermediate ensemble size and this minimum is often lower than the asymptotic error, as shown in Figure 6.1. Hence, ensemble

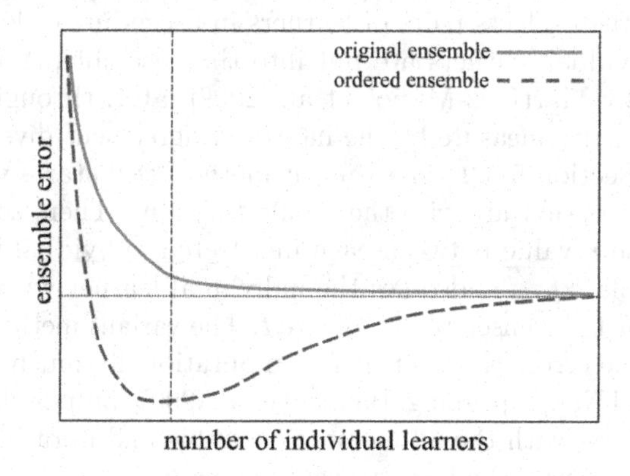

Figure 6.1: Illustration of error curves of the original ensemble (aggregated in random order) and ordered ensemble.

pruning can be realized by ordering the N individual learners and then putting the front T individual learners into the final ensemble.

It is generally hard to decide the best T value, but fortunately there are usually many T values that will lead to excellent performance, and at least the T value can be tuned on training data. A more crucial problem is how to order the individual learners appropriately, for which many ordering strategies have been developed. Most of them consider both the accuracy and diversity of individual learners, and a validation data set V with size $|V|$ is usually used (when there are not sufficient data, the training data set D or its sub-samples can be used for validation). In the following, we introduce some representative ordering-based pruning methods.

Reduce-Error Pruning [Margineantu and Dietterich, 1997]. This method starts with the individual learner whose validation error is the smallest. Then, the remaining individual learners are sequentially put into the ensemble such that the validation error of the resulting ensemble is as small as possible in each round. This procedure is greedy, and therefore, after obtaining the top T individual learners, Margineantu and Dietterich [1997] used Backfitting [Freidman and Stuetzle, 1981] search to improve the ensemble. In each round, it tries to replace one of the already selected individual learners with an unselected individual learner which could reduce the ensemble error. This process repeats until none of the individual learners can be replaced, or the pre-set maximum number of learning rounds is reached. It can be seen that Backfitting is time-consuming. Moreover, it was reported [Martínez-Muñoz and Suárez, 2006] that Backfitting could not improve the generalization ability significantly for parallel ensemble methods such as Bagging.

Kappa Pruning [Margineantu and Dietterich, 1997]. This method assumes that all the individual learners have similar performance, and uses the κ_p diversity measure introduced in Section 5.3.1 to calculate the diversity of every pair of individual learners on the validation set. It starts with the pair with the smallest κ_p (i.e., the largest diversity among the given individual learners), and then selects pairs of learners in ascending order of κ_p. Finally, the top T individual learners are put into the ensemble. A variant method was proposed by Martínez-Muñoz et al. [2009] later, through replacing the pairwise κ_p diversity measure by the interrater agreement diversity measure κ introduced in Section 5.3.2. The variant method still starts with the pair of individual learners that are with the smallest κ value. Then, at the t-th round, it calculates the κ value between each unselected individual learner and the current ensemble H_{t-1}, and takes the individual learner with the smallest κ value to construct the ensemble H_t of size t. The variant method often leads to smaller ensemble error. However, it is computationally much more expensive than the original Kappa pruning. Banfield et al. [2005] proposed another variant method that starts with the all-member ensemble and iteratively removes the individual learner with the largest average κ value.

Kappa-Error Diagram Pruning [Margineantu and Dietterich, 1997]. This method is based on the **kappa-error diagram** introduced in Section 5.3.3. It constructs the *convex hull* of the points in the diagram, which can be regarded as a summary of the entire diagram and includes both the most accurate and the most diverse pairs of individual learners. The pruned ensemble consists of any individual learner that appears in a pair corresponding to a point on the convex hull. From the definition of the kappa-error diagram, it can be seen that this pruning method simultaneously considers the accuracy as well as diversity of individual learners.

Complementariness Pruning [Martínez-Muñoz and Suárez, 2004]. This method favors the inclusion of individual learners that are complementary to the current ensemble. It starts with the individual learner of the smallest validation error. Then, at the t-th round, given the ensemble H_{t-1} of size $t-1$, the complementariness pruning method adds the individual learner h_t which satisfies

$$h_t = \arg\max_{h_k} \sum_{(\boldsymbol{x},y)\in V} \mathbb{I}\left(h_k(\boldsymbol{x}) = y \text{ and } H_{t-1}(\boldsymbol{x}) \neq y\right), \tag{6.14}$$

where V is the validation data set, and h_k is picked up from the unselected individual learners.

Margin Distance Pruning [Martínez-Muñoz and Suárez, 2004]. This method defines a *signature vector* for each individual learner. For example, the signature vector $\boldsymbol{c}^{(k)}$ of the k-th individual learner h_k is a $|V|$-dimensional vector where the i-th element is

$$c_i^{(k)} = 2\mathbb{I}\left(h_k\left(\boldsymbol{x}_i\right) = y_i\right) - 1, \tag{6.15}$$

where $(\boldsymbol{x}_i, y_i) \in V$. Obviously, $c_i^{(k)} = 1$ if and only if h_k classifies $\boldsymbol{x}_i$ correctly and -1 otherwise. The performance of the ensemble can be characterized by the average of $\boldsymbol{c}^{(k)}$'s, i.e., $\bar{\boldsymbol{c}} = \frac{1}{N}\sum_{k=1}^{N} \boldsymbol{c}^{(k)}$. The i-th instance is correctly classified by the ensemble if the i-th element of $\bar{\boldsymbol{c}}$ is positive, and the value of $|\bar{c}_i|$ is the *margin* on the i-th instance. If an ensemble correctly classifies all the instances in V, the vector $\bar{\boldsymbol{c}}$ will lie in the first-quadrant of the $|V|$-dimensional hyperspace, that is, every element of $\bar{\boldsymbol{c}}$ is positive. Consequently, the goal is to select the ensemble whose signature vector is near an objective position in the first-quadrant. Suppose the objective position is the point $\boldsymbol{o}$ with equal elements, i.e., $o_i = p$ $(i = 1, \ldots, |V|; 0 < p < 1)$. In practice, the value of p is usually a small value (e.g., $p \in (0.05, 0.25)$). The individual learner to be selected is the one which can reduce the distance between $\bar{\boldsymbol{c}}$ and $\boldsymbol{o}$ to the most.

Orientation Pruning [Martínez-Muñoz and Suárez, 2006]. This method uses the signature vector defined as above. It orders the individual learners increasingly according to the angles between the corresponding signature vectors and the *reference direction*, denoted as $\boldsymbol{c}_{ref}$, which is the projection of the first-quadrant diagonal onto the hyperplane defined by the signature vector $\bar{\boldsymbol{c}}$ of the all-member ensemble.

Boosting-Based Pruning [Martínez-Muñoz and Suárez, 2007]. This method uses AdaBoost to determine the order of the individual learners. It is similar to the AdaBoost algorithm except that in each round, rather than generating a base learner from the training data, the individual learner with the lowest weighted validation error is selected from the given individual learners. When the weighted error is larger than 0.5, the **Boosting with restart** strategy is used, that is, the weights are reset and another individual learner is selected. Note that the weights are used in the ordering process, while Martínez-Muñoz and Suárez [2007] reported that there is no significant difference for the pruned ensemble to make prediction with/without the weights.

Reinforcement Learning Pruning [Partalas et al., 2009]. This method models the ensemble pruning problem as an episodic task. Given N individual learners, it assumes that there is an agent which takes N sequential actions each corresponding to either including the individual learner h_k in the final ensemble or not. Then, the Q-learning algorithm [Watkins and Dayan, 1992], a famous **reinforcement learning** technique, is applied to solve an optimal policy of choosing the individual learners.

Diversity Regularized Pruning [Li et al., 2012]. This method iteratively selects individual classifiers based on both accuracy and diversity explicitly. By considering majority voting introduced in Section 4.2.2 and measuring the diversity by the average pairwise difference (similar to the disagreement measure introduced in Section 5.3.1) between individual classifiers, Li et al. [2012] gave a PAC theoretical analysis on the effect of diversity on the generalization performance (see Section 5.4.1). Inspired by the understanding that diversity plays a regularization role for ensemble methods, the diversity regularized pruning method starts with the individual classifier with the smallest validation error. At the t-th round, given the ensemble H_{t-1} of size $t-1$, it first sorts the unselected individual classifiers in the descending order of their differences with H_{t-1}, and then from the top ρ fraction of sorted list it selects h_t which can reduce the error of H_{t-1} to the most on validation set. It can be seen that the parameter ρ trades off empirical error and diversity, i.e., a large value of ρ implies more emphasis on the empirical error, while a small ρ pays more attention to the diversity.

Banzhaf Power Index Pruning [Ykhlef and Bouchaffra, 2017]. This method regards each classifier as a player and formulates the ensemble pruning problem as a non-monotone simple coalitional game [Osborne and Rubinstein, 1994]. Each coalition in this game is a subset of individual classifiers and a coalition wins if the average pairwise diversity is large. It then uses the Banzhaf power index [Banzhaf, 1964] to evaluate the contribution of each h_i for winning, i.e.,

$$Bz(h_i) = \frac{1}{2^{N-1}} \sum_{S \subseteq H \setminus \{h_i\}} (v(S \cup \{h_i\}) - v(S)),$$

where H is the ensemble of N classifiers, and function $v(\cdot)$ returns 1 if the input coalition wins, and 0 otherwise. The players with higher Banzhaf power index will be picked up and compose the final ensemble.

Mutual Information Pruning [Bian et al., 2019]. This method uses the mutual information introduced in Section 5.4.2 to measure both accuracy and diversity. Let $\boldsymbol{h}_i = (h_i(\boldsymbol{x}_1), \ldots, h_i(\boldsymbol{x}_m))^{\boldsymbol{T}}$ denote the prediction vector of the individual classifier h_i on the validation data $V = \{(\boldsymbol{x}_1, y_1), \ldots, (\boldsymbol{x}_m, y_m)\}$, and $\boldsymbol{y} = (y_1, \ldots, y_m)^{\boldsymbol{T}}$ denote the true class label vector. The normalized mutual information between $\boldsymbol{h}_i$ and $\boldsymbol{y}$, i.e., $I(\boldsymbol{h}_i; \boldsymbol{y})/\sqrt{Ent(\boldsymbol{h}_i) \cdot Ent(\boldsymbol{y})}$, reflects their relevancy, which is used to measure the accuracy of the individual classifier h_i. Note that $Ent(\cdot)$ and $I(\cdot;\cdot)$ denote the entropy and mutual information, respectively, as defined in (5.58) and (5.59). The normalized variation of information between the two individual classifiers $\boldsymbol{h}_i$ and $\boldsymbol{h}_j$, i.e., $1 - I(\boldsymbol{h}_i; \boldsymbol{h}_j)/Ent(\boldsymbol{h}_i, \boldsymbol{h}_j)$, is used to measure their diversity, where $I(\boldsymbol{h}_i; \boldsymbol{h}_j)$ can be viewed as the redundancy between $\boldsymbol{h}_i$ and $\boldsymbol{h}_j$, and a smaller value of $I(\boldsymbol{h}_i; \boldsymbol{h}_j)$ implies a larger diversity. Then, Bian et al. [2019] measures the goodness of an ensemble H by

$$\frac{\lambda}{2} \sum_{h_i, h_j \in H} \left(1 - \frac{I(\boldsymbol{h}_i; \boldsymbol{h}_j)}{Ent(\boldsymbol{h}_i, \boldsymbol{h}_j)}\right) + \frac{(1-\lambda)(n-1)}{2} \sum_{h_i \in H} \frac{I(\boldsymbol{h}_i; \boldsymbol{y})}{\sqrt{Ent(\boldsymbol{h}_i) \cdot Ent(\boldsymbol{y})}}, \tag{6.16}$$

where λ trades off the diversity of the ensemble H and the overall accuracy of the individual classifiers in H. (6.16) is used to guide the ordering of individual classifiers. That is, the mutual information pruning method starts from an arbitrary individual classifier, and then iteratively adds one unselected individual classifier with the largest marginal gain on the criterion (6.16).

6.5 Clustering-Based Pruning

An intuitive idea for ensemble pruning is to identify some *prototype* individual learners that are representative yet diverse among the given individual learners, and then use only these prototypes to constitute the ensemble. This category of methods is known as clustering-based pruning because the most straightforward way to identify the prototypes is to use clustering techniques.

Generally, clustering-based pruning methods work in two steps. In the first step, the individual learners are grouped into a number of clusters. Different clustering techniques have been exploited for this purpose. For example, Giacinto et al. [2000] used **hierarchical agglomerative clustering** and regarded the probability that the individual learners do not make coincident validation errors as the distance; Lazarevic and Obradovic [2001] used **k-means clustering** based on Euclidean distance; Bakker and Heskes [2003] used **deterministic annealing** for clustering; etc.

In the second step, prototype individual learners are selected from clusters. Different strategies have been developed. For examples, Giacinto et al. [2000] selected from each cluster the learner which is the most distant to other clusters;

Lazarevic and Obradovic [2001] iteratively removed individual learners from the least to the most accurate inside each cluster until the ensemble accuracy starts to decrease; Bakker and Heskes [2003] selected the centroid of each cluster; etc.

6.6 Optimization-Based Pruning

Optimization-based pruning originated from [Zhou et al., 2002c] which employs a **genetic algorithm** [Goldberg, 1989] to select individual learners. Later, many other optimization techniques, including evolutionary optimization, mathematical programming, probabilistic methods, and *Pareto optimization* have been exploited. This section introduces several representative methods.

6.6.1 Heuristic Optimization Pruning

Recognizing that the theoretically optimal solution to weighted combination in (4.14) is infeasible in practice, Zhou et al. [2002c] regarded the ensemble pruning problem as an optimization task and proposed a practical method GASEN.

The basic idea is to associate each individual learner with a weight that can characterize the goodness of including the individual learner in the final ensemble. Given N individual learners, the weights can be organized as an N-dimensional weight vector, where small elements in the weight vector suggest that the corresponding individual learners could be excluded. Thus, one weight vector corresponds to one solution to ensemble pruning. In GASEN, a set of weight vectors are randomly initialized at first. Then, a genetic algorithm is applied to the *population* of weight vectors, where the *fitness* of each weight vector is calculated based on the corresponding ensemble performance on validation data. The pruned ensemble is obtained by decoding the optimal weight vector evolved from the genetic algorithm, and then excluding individual learners associated with small weights.

There are different GASEN implementations, by using different coding schemes or different genetic operators. For example, Zhou et al. [2002c] used a *floating coding* scheme, while Zhou and Tang [2003] used a *bit coding* scheme which directly takes 0–1 weights and avoids the problem of setting an appropriate threshold to decide which individual learner should be excluded.

In addition to genetic algorithms [Coelho et al., 2003], many other heuristic optimization techniques have been used in ensemble pruning; for example, greedy hill-climbing [Caruana et al., 2004], artificial immune algorithms [Castro et al., 2005, Zhang et al., 2005], case similarity search [Coyle and Smyth, 2006], etc.

6.6.2 Mathematical Programming Pruning

One deficiency of heuristic optimization is the lack of solid theoretical foundations. Along with the great success of using mathematical programming in machine learning, ensemble pruning methods based on mathematical programming optimization have been proposed.

SDP Relaxation

Zhang et al. [2006] formulated ensemble pruning as a quadratic integer programming problem. Since finding the optimal solution to this problem is computationally infeasible, they provided an approximate solution by **Semi-Definite Programming** (SDP).

First, given N individual classifiers and m training instances, Zhang et al. [2006] recorded the errors in the matrix $\mathbf{P}$ as

$$P_{ij} = \begin{cases} 0 & \text{if } h_j \text{ classifies } \boldsymbol{x}_i \text{ correctly} \\ 1 & \text{otherwise.} \end{cases} \tag{6.17}$$

Let $\mathbf{G} = \mathbf{P}^T\mathbf{P}$. Then, the diagonal element G_{ii} is the number of mistakes made by h_i, and the off-diagonal element G_{ij} is the number of co-occurred mistakes of h_i and h_j. The matrix elements are normalized according to

$$\tilde{G}_{ij} = \begin{cases} \frac{G_{ij}}{m} & i = j \\ \frac{1}{2}\left(\frac{G_{ij}}{G_{ii}} + \frac{G_{ji}}{G_{jj}}\right) & i \neq j\ . \end{cases} \tag{6.18}$$

Thus, $\sum_{i=1}^{N} \tilde{G}_{ii}$ measures the overall performance of the individual classifiers, $\sum_{i,j=1;i\neq j}^{N} \tilde{G}_{ij}$ measures the diversity, and a combination of these two terms $\sum_{i,j=1}^{N} \tilde{G}_{ij}$ is a good approximation of the ensemble error.

Consequently, the ensemble pruning problem is formulated as the quadratic integer programming problem

$$\min_{\boldsymbol{z}} \ \boldsymbol{z}^T\tilde{\mathbf{G}}\boldsymbol{z} \quad \text{s.t.} \sum_{i=1}^{N} z_i = T,\ z_i \in \{0,1\}\ , \tag{6.19}$$

where the binary variable z_i represents whether the i-th classifier h_i is included in the ensemble, and T is the size of the pruned ensemble.

(6.19) is a standard 0–1 optimization problem, which is generally NP-hard. However, let $v_i = 2z_i - 1 \in \{-1, 1\}$,

$$\mathbf{V} = \boldsymbol{v}\boldsymbol{v}^T, \quad \mathbf{H} = \begin{pmatrix} \mathbf{1}^T\tilde{\mathbf{G}}\mathbf{1} & \mathbf{1}^T\tilde{\mathbf{G}} \\ \tilde{\mathbf{G}}\mathbf{1} & \tilde{\mathbf{G}} \end{pmatrix}, \text{ and } \mathbf{D} = \begin{pmatrix} N & \mathbf{1}^T \\ \mathbf{1} & \mathbf{I} \end{pmatrix}, \tag{6.20}$$

where $\mathbf{1}$ is all-one column vector and $\mathbf{I}$ is identity matrix, then (6.19) can be rewritten as the equivalent formulation [Zhang et al., 2006]

$$\begin{aligned} \min_{\mathbf{V}} \quad & \mathbf{H} \otimes \mathbf{V} \\ \text{s.t.} \quad & \mathbf{D} \otimes \mathbf{V} = 4T,\ \operatorname{diag}(\mathbf{V}) = \mathbf{1},\ \mathbf{V} \succeq 0 \\ & \operatorname{rank}(\mathbf{V}) = 1\ , \end{aligned} \tag{6.21}$$

where $\mathbf{A}\otimes\mathbf{B} = \sum_{ij} A_{ij}B_{ij}$. Then, by dropping the rank constraint, it is relaxed to the following convex SDP problem which can be solved in polynomial time [Zhang et al., 2006]

$$\begin{aligned} \min_{\mathbf{V}} \quad & \mathbf{H}\otimes\mathbf{V} \\ \text{s.t.} \quad & \mathbf{D}\otimes\mathbf{V} = 4T,\ \operatorname{diag}(\mathbf{V}) = \mathbf{1},\ \mathbf{V}\succeq 0\ . \end{aligned} \tag{6.22}$$

ℓ_1-Norm Regularization

Li and Zhou [2009] proposed a regularized selective ensemble method RSE which reduces the ensemble pruning task to a **Quadratic Programming** (QP) problem.

Given N individual classifiers and considering weighted combination, RSE determines the weight vector $\boldsymbol{w} = [w_1, \ldots, w_N]^{\boldsymbol{T}}$ by minimizing the regularized risk function

$$R(\boldsymbol{w}) = \lambda V(\boldsymbol{w}) + \Omega(\boldsymbol{w})\ , \tag{6.23}$$

where $V(\boldsymbol{w})$ is the empirical loss which measures the misclassification on training data $D = \{(\boldsymbol{x}_1, y_1), \ldots, (\boldsymbol{x}_m, y_m)\}$, $\Omega(\boldsymbol{w})$ is the *regularization* term which tries to make the final classifier smooth and simple, and λ is a *regularization* parameter which trades off the minimization of $V(\boldsymbol{w})$ and $\Omega(\boldsymbol{w})$.

By using the *hinge loss* and *graph Laplacian* regularizer as the empirical loss and *regularization* term, respectively, the problem is formulated as

$$\begin{aligned} \min_{\boldsymbol{w}} \quad & \boldsymbol{w}^{\boldsymbol{T}}\mathbf{P}\mathbf{L}\mathbf{P}^{\boldsymbol{T}}\boldsymbol{w} + \lambda\sum_{i=1}^{m}\max(0, 1 - y_i\boldsymbol{p}_i^{\boldsymbol{T}}\boldsymbol{w}) \\ \text{s.t.} \quad & \mathbf{1}^{\boldsymbol{T}}\boldsymbol{w} = 1, \quad \boldsymbol{w}\geq\mathbf{0} \end{aligned} \tag{6.24}$$

where $\boldsymbol{p}_i = (h_1(\boldsymbol{x}_i), \ldots, h_N(\boldsymbol{x}_i))^{\boldsymbol{T}}$ encodes the predictions of individual classifiers on $\boldsymbol{x}_i$, $\mathbf{P} \in \{-1, +1\}^{N\times m}$ is the *prediction matrix* which collects predictions of all individual classifiers on all training instances, where $P_{ij} = h_i(\boldsymbol{x}_j)$. $\mathbf{L}$ is the *normalized graph Laplacian* of the neighborhood graph G of the training data. Denote the weighted adjacency matrix of G by $\mathbf{W}$, and $\mathbf{D}$ is a diagonal matrix where $D_{ii} = \sum_{j=1}^{m} W_{ij}$. Then, $\mathbf{L} = \mathbf{D}^{-1/2}(\mathbf{D}-\mathbf{W})\mathbf{D}^{-1/2}$.

By introducing slack variables $\boldsymbol{\xi} = (\xi_1, \ldots, \xi_m)^{\boldsymbol{T}}$, (6.24) can be rewritten as

$$\begin{aligned} \min_{\boldsymbol{w}} \quad & \boldsymbol{w}^{\boldsymbol{T}}\mathbf{P}\mathbf{L}\mathbf{P}^{\boldsymbol{T}}\boldsymbol{w} + \lambda\ \mathbf{1}^{\boldsymbol{T}}\boldsymbol{\xi} \\ \text{s.t.} \quad & y_i\boldsymbol{p}_i^{\boldsymbol{T}}\boldsymbol{w} + \xi_i \geq 1, \quad (\forall i = 1, \ldots, m) \\ & \mathbf{1}^{\boldsymbol{T}}\boldsymbol{w} = 1, \quad \boldsymbol{w}\geq\mathbf{0}, \quad \boldsymbol{\xi}\geq\mathbf{0}\ . \end{aligned} \tag{6.25}$$

Obviously, (6.25) is a standard QP problem that can be efficiently solved by existing optimization packages.

Note that $\mathbf{1}^{\boldsymbol{T}}\boldsymbol{w} = 1, \boldsymbol{w}\geq\mathbf{0}$ is a ℓ_1-norm constraint on the weights $\boldsymbol{w}$. The ℓ_1-norm is a sparsity-inducing constraint which will force some w_i's to be zero, and thus, RSE favors an ensemble with small sizes and only a subset of the given individual learners will be included in the final ensemble.

Another advantage of RSE is that it naturally fits the **semi-supervised learning** setting due to the use of the graph Laplacian regularizer, hence it can exploit *unlabeled data* to improve ensemble performance. More information on semi-supervised learning will be introduced in Chapter 9.

Constrained Eigen-Optimization

Xu et al. [2012] also considered ensemble pruning problem as the quadratic integer programming problem (6.19), but relaxed it as a constrained eigenvector problem with an efficient algorithm of globally convergent guarantees.

Recall the quadratic integer programming problem (6.19) as

$$\min_{\boldsymbol{z}} \ \boldsymbol{z}^T\tilde{\mathbf{G}}\boldsymbol{z} \quad \text{s.t.} \sum_{i=1}^{N} z_i = T,\ z_i \in \{0,1\}\ , \tag{6.26}$$

where $\tilde{\mathbf{G}}$ is given by (6.18). $\sum_{i=1}^{N} \tilde{G}_{ii}$ measures the overall performance of the individual classifiers, $\sum_{i,j=1;i\neq j}^{N} \tilde{G}_{ij}$ measures the diversity.

Xu et al. [2012] introduced an efficient method to solve (6.26) after some reformulation and relaxations. First rewrite the problem (6.26) as

$$\min_{\boldsymbol{w}} \ (\boldsymbol{w}+\mathbf{1})^T\tilde{\mathbf{G}}(\boldsymbol{w}+\mathbf{1})/4 \quad \text{s.t.} \sum_{i=1}^{N} w_i = 2T-N,\ w_i \in \{-1,+1\}\ , \tag{6.27}$$

by using $\boldsymbol{w} = 2\boldsymbol{z} - \mathbf{1}$, where $\mathbf{1}$ is all-one column vector of size N. Let

$$\hat{\boldsymbol{w}}_{(N+1)\times 1} = \begin{bmatrix} 1 \\ \boldsymbol{w} \end{bmatrix} \quad \text{and} \quad \tilde{\mathbf{G}}'_{(N+1)\times(N+1)} = \begin{bmatrix} \mathbf{1}^T\tilde{\mathbf{G}}\mathbf{1} & \mathbf{1}^T\tilde{\mathbf{G}} \\ \tilde{\mathbf{G}}\mathbf{1} & \tilde{\mathbf{G}} \end{bmatrix}, \tag{6.28}$$

and then write problem (6.27) in a more concise form as follows:

$$\min_{\hat{\boldsymbol{w}}} \ \hat{\boldsymbol{w}}^T\tilde{\mathbf{G}}'\hat{\boldsymbol{w}} \quad \text{s.t.} \sum_{i=1}^{N+1} w_i = 2T-N+1,\ \hat{w}_i \in \{-1,+1\},\ \hat{w}_1 = +1\ . \tag{6.29}$$

Introduce a normalized vector $\boldsymbol{v} = \hat{\boldsymbol{w}}/\sqrt{N+1}$, and it can be observed that $\|\boldsymbol{v}\| = 1$ and $\boldsymbol{v} \in \{+1,-1\}^{N+1}/\sqrt{N+1}$. Xu et al. [2012] removed the discrete constraints $\boldsymbol{v} \in \{+1,-1\}^{N+1}/\sqrt{N+1}$ and only constrain $\|\mathbf{v}\| = 1$. This gives

$$\min_{\boldsymbol{v}} \ \boldsymbol{v}^T\tilde{\mathbf{G}}'\boldsymbol{v} \quad \text{s.t.} \sum_{i=1}^{N+1} v_i = \frac{2T-N+1}{\sqrt{N+1}},\ \|\boldsymbol{v}\| = 1,\ v_1 = \frac{1}{\sqrt{N+1}}\ . \tag{6.30}$$

The linear constraints above on vector $\mathbf{v}$ can be written in a more compact way as $A\mathbf{v} = \mathbf{b}$, where

$$\mathbf{A} = \begin{bmatrix} 1 & 0 & \cdots & 0 \\ 1 & 1 & \cdots & 1 \end{bmatrix} \quad \text{and} \quad \boldsymbol{b} = \frac{1}{\sqrt{N+1}} \begin{bmatrix} 1 \\ 2T-N+1 \end{bmatrix}. \tag{6.31}$$

Problem (6.30) is still non-convex, but it can be solved exactly and efficiently. Switch the minimization formulation in problem (6.30) to a maximization problem without affecting the solution:

$$\min_{\boldsymbol{v}} \ \boldsymbol{v}^T(\alpha\mathbf{I} - \tilde{\mathbf{G}}')\boldsymbol{v} \qquad \text{s.t. } \|\boldsymbol{v}\| = 1, \ \mathbf{A}\boldsymbol{v} = \boldsymbol{b} \ , \tag{6.32}$$

where $\mathbf{I}$ denotes the identity matrix of size $(N+1)\times(N+1)$, and α is sufficiently large such that $\alpha\mathbf{I} - \tilde{\mathbf{G}}'$ is a semidefinite positive matrix.

Now the problem (6.32) is similar to a maximum eigenvalue computation, except for some additional inhomogeneous linear constraints, which complicate the optimization problem. Fortunately, projected power method [Xu et al., 2009] can be applied here to find the exact solution to problem (6.32) through an iterative procedure with convergence to the global solution guaranteed.

6.6.3 Probabilistic Pruning

Chen et al. [2006, 2009] proposed a probabilistic pruning method under the Bayesian framework by introducing a sparsity-inducing prior over the combination weights, where the *maximum a posteriori* (MAP) estimation of the weights is obtained by **Expectation Maximization** (EM) [Chen et al., 2006] and **Expectation Propagation** (EP) [Chen et al., 2009], respectively. Due to the sparsity-inducing prior, many of the posteriors of the weights are sharply distributed at zero, and thus many individual learners are excluded from the final ensemble.

Given N individual learners $h_1, \ldots, h_N$, the output vector of the individual learners on the instance $\boldsymbol{x}$ is $\boldsymbol{h}(\boldsymbol{x}) = (h_1(\boldsymbol{x}), \ldots, h_N(\boldsymbol{x}))^T$. The output of the all-member ensemble is $H(\boldsymbol{x}) = \boldsymbol{w}^T\boldsymbol{h}(\boldsymbol{x})$, where $\boldsymbol{w} = [w_1, \ldots, w_N]^T$ is a non-negative weight vector, $w_i \geq 0$.

To make the weight vector $\boldsymbol{w}$ sparse and non-negative, a left-truncated *Gaussian prior* is introduced to each weight w_i [Chen et al., 2006], that is,

$$p(\boldsymbol{w} \mid \boldsymbol{\alpha}) = \prod_{i=1}^{N} p(w_i \mid \alpha_i) = \prod_{i=1}^{N} \mathcal{N}_t(w_i \mid 0, \alpha_i^{-1}), \tag{6.33}$$

where $\boldsymbol{\alpha} = [\alpha_1, \ldots, \alpha_N]^T$ is the inverse variance of weight vector $\boldsymbol{w}$ and $\mathcal{N}_t(w_i \mid 0, \alpha_i^{-1})$ is a left-truncated Gaussian distribution defined as

$$\mathcal{N}_t(w_i \mid 0, \alpha_i^{-1}) = \begin{cases} 2\mathcal{N}(w_i \mid 0, \alpha_i^{-1}) & \text{if } w_i \geq 0 \ , \\ 0 & \text{otherwise} \ . \end{cases} \tag{6.34}$$

For regression, it is assumed that the ensemble output is corrupted by a Gaussian noise $\epsilon_i \sim \mathcal{N}(0, \sigma^2)$ with mean zero and variance σ^2. That is, for each training instance $(\boldsymbol{x}_i, y_i)$, it holds that

$$y_i = \boldsymbol{w}^T\boldsymbol{h}(\boldsymbol{x}_i) + \epsilon_i \ . \tag{6.35}$$

Assuming *i.i.d.* training data, the likelihood can be expressed as

$$p(\boldsymbol{y} \mid \boldsymbol{w}, \mathbf{X}, \sigma^2) = (2\pi\sigma^2)^{-m/2} \exp\left\{-\frac{1}{2\sigma^2}\|\boldsymbol{y}^{\boldsymbol{T}} - w^{\boldsymbol{T}}\mathbf{H}\|^2\right\} , \tag{6.36}$$

where $\boldsymbol{y} = [y_1, \ldots, y_m]^{\boldsymbol{T}}$ is the ground-truth output vector, and $\mathbf{H} = [\boldsymbol{h}(\boldsymbol{x}_1), \ldots, \boldsymbol{h}(\boldsymbol{x}_m)]$ is an $N \times m$ matrix which collects all the predictions of individual learners on all the training instances. Consequently, the posterior of $\boldsymbol{w}$ can be written as

$$p(\boldsymbol{w} \mid \mathbf{X}, \boldsymbol{y}, \boldsymbol{\alpha}) \propto \prod_{i=1}^{N} p(w_i \mid \alpha_i) \prod_{i=1}^{m} p(y_i \mid \boldsymbol{x}_i, \boldsymbol{w}) . \tag{6.37}$$

As defined in (6.34), the prior over $\boldsymbol{w}$ is a left-truncated Gaussian, and therefore, exact Bayesian inference is intractable. However, the EM algorithm or EP algorithm can be employed to generate an MAP solution, leading to an approximation of the sparse weight vector [Chen et al., 2006, 2009].

For classification, the ensemble output is formulated as

$$H(\boldsymbol{x}) = \Phi\left(\boldsymbol{w}^{\boldsymbol{T}}\boldsymbol{h}(\boldsymbol{x})\right) , \tag{6.38}$$

where $\Phi(x) = \int_{-\infty}^{x} \mathcal{N}(t \mid 0, 1)dt$ is the Gaussian cumulative distribution function. The class label of $\boldsymbol{x}$ is $+1$ if $H(\boldsymbol{x}) \geq 1/2$ and 0 otherwise. As above, the posterior of $\boldsymbol{w}$ can be derived as

$$p(\boldsymbol{w} \mid \mathbf{X}, \boldsymbol{y}, \boldsymbol{\alpha}) \propto \prod_{i=1}^{N} p(w_i \mid \alpha_i) \prod_{i=1}^{m} \Phi(y_i \boldsymbol{w}^{\boldsymbol{T}}\boldsymbol{h}(\boldsymbol{x}_i)) , \tag{6.39}$$

where both the prior $p(w_i \mid \alpha_i)$ and the likelihood $\Phi(y_i \boldsymbol{w}^{\boldsymbol{T}}\boldsymbol{h}(\boldsymbol{x}_i))$ are non-Gaussian, and thus, the EM algorithm or the EP algorithm is used to obtain an MAP estimation of the sparse weight vector [Chen et al., 2006, 2009].

6.6.4 Pareto Optimization Pruning

Note that ensemble pruning naturally bears two goals simultaneously, that is, maximizing the generalization performance and minimizing the ensemble size. Qian et al. [2015a] formulated ensemble pruning as a bi-objective optimization problem explicitly, and proposed the PEP (Pareto Ensemble Pruning) approach. PEP solves the bi-objective optimization of ensemble pruning by Pareto optimization combined with a local search operator.

Given N individual learners $h_1, \ldots, h_N$, let $H_{\boldsymbol{s}}$ denote a pruned ensemble with the selector vector $\boldsymbol{s} \in \{0,1\}^N$, where $\forall i \in \{1, 2, \ldots, N\}$, $s_i = 1$ and $s_i = 0$ mean that the individual learner h_i is selected and unselected, respectively. The ensemble pruning problem is formulated as a bi-objective optimization problem

$$\arg\max_{\boldsymbol{s} \in \{0,1\}^N} \left(f(H_{\boldsymbol{s}}), -|\boldsymbol{s}|\right) , \tag{6.40}$$

where $f(H_{\boldsymbol{s}})$ is some objective related to the generalization performance of the pruned ensemble $H_{\boldsymbol{s}}$, and $|\boldsymbol{s}| = \sum_{i=1}^{N} s_i$ is the number of selected individual learners, i.e., the size of $H_{\boldsymbol{s}}$. That is, the generalization performance and the ensemble size are to be optimized simultaneously.

In the bi-objective formulation, any candidate solution $\boldsymbol{s}$ has an objective vector rather than a scalar objective value. For example, a solution which results in value 0.2 of the employed f function and 10 individual learners will have the objective vector $(0.2, -10)$. Unlike single-objective optimization, the objective vector makes the comparison between two solutions less straightforward, because it is possible that one solution is better on the first dimension, whereas the other is better on the second dimension. More generally, for comparing two solutions in multi-objective optimization where the number n of objectives is at least 2, the domination relationship is usually used. Given n objective functions $f_1, f_2, \ldots, f_n$ to be maximized, a solution $\boldsymbol{s}$ *weakly dominates* another solution $\boldsymbol{s}'$, denoted as $\boldsymbol{s} \succeq \boldsymbol{s}'$, if $\forall i \in \{1, 2, \ldots, n\} : f_i(\boldsymbol{s}) \geq f_i(\boldsymbol{s}')$; $\boldsymbol{s}$ *dominates* $\boldsymbol{s}'$, denoted as $\boldsymbol{s} \succ \boldsymbol{s}'$, if $\boldsymbol{s} \succeq \boldsymbol{s}'$ and $\exists i \in \{1, 2, \ldots, n\} : f_i(\boldsymbol{s}) > f_i(\boldsymbol{s}')$; they are *incomparable*, if neither $\boldsymbol{s} \succeq \boldsymbol{s}'$ nor $\boldsymbol{s}' \succeq \boldsymbol{s}$. Consequently, a multi-objective optimization problem may not have a single optimal solution, but instead have a set of *Pareto optimal* solutions. A solution is Pareto optimal if there is no other solution that dominates it.

PEP employs Pareto optimization to solve the bi-objective ensemble pruning problem in (6.40). It firstly generates a random solution, and puts it into the population; it then follows a cycle to improve the solutions in the population iteratively. In each iteration, a solution $\boldsymbol{s}$ is selected randomly from the population and then *mutated* to generate a new *offspring* solution $\boldsymbol{s}'$; if $\boldsymbol{s}'$ is not dominated by any solution in the population, $\boldsymbol{s}'$ will be added into the population and meanwhile those solutions in the population that are weakly dominated by $\boldsymbol{s}'$ will get removed. As Pareto optimization is inspired by evolutionary algorithms, which usually focus on global exploration but may utilize local information less well, a local search operator is incorporated to improve the quality of the new offspring solution $\boldsymbol{s}'$ in order to improve the efficiency. After a set of Pareto optimal solutions has been generated, one final solution can be selected according to the users' preference, i.e., the final solution selection can be task-dependent.

Different from single-objective heuristic optimization pruning methods, PEP can have theoretical guarantees [Qian et al., 2015a]. Theoretical results disclose the advantage of PEP over ordering-based and single-objective heuristic optimization pruning methods. In particular, for any pruning task and any generalization performance measure f, PEP is proved to be able to efficiently produce at least an equally good solution as that by the ordering-based pruning method in both the performance f and the ensemble size; for some specific cases, PEP can be strictly better than the ordering-based pruning method as well as a single-objective heuristic optimization pruning method.

PEP can have different implementations by choosing different generalization performance measures f. Qian et al. [2015a] directly used the validation error as f. However, as introduced in Section 2.4.3, the generalization performance depends on not only the error on a sampled data set, but also the **margin distribution**. Wu et al. [2022] thus measured the generalization performance of a pruned ensemble $H_{\boldsymbol{s}}$, by combining the error and margin distribution of $H_{\boldsymbol{s}}$ on the validation data. As it is hard to trade off the validation error and margin distribution directly, these two terms are also viewed as two explicit objectives to optimize. That is, the ensemble pruning problem is formulated as a three-objective optimization problem that optimizes the validation error, margin distribution, and ensemble size simultaneously. Wu et al. [2022] characterized the margin distribution by margin ratio [Lyu et al., 2019], defined by the standard deviation of margin over margin mean. The smaller the margin ratio, the better the margin distribution. Empirical results show that optimizing the margin distribution additionally brings further improvement.

6.7 Further Readings

Tsoumakas et al. [2009] provided a brief review on ensemble pruning methods. Hernández-Lobato et al. [2011] reported an empirical study which shows that optimization-based and ordering-based pruning methods, at least for pruning parallel regression ensembles, generally outperform ensembles generated by AdaBoost.R2, Negative Correlation and several other approaches.

In addition to clustering, there are also other approaches for selecting the prototype individual learners, e.g., Tsoumakas et al. [2004, 2005] picked prototype individual learners by using statistical tests to compare their individual performance. Hernández-Lobato et al. [2008] proposed the *instance-based pruning* method, where the individual learners selected for making prediction are determined for each instance separately. Soto et al. [2010] applied the instance-based pruning to pruned ensembles generated by other ensemble pruning methods, yielding the *double pruning* method. A similar idea has been described by Fan et al. [2002]. Liu and Mazumder [2023] pruned tree ensembles by trimming depth layers from individual trees instead of selecting a subset of individual trees.

Many optimization algorithms, such as the genetic algorithm mentioned in Section 6.6.1 and the pareto optimization utilized in PEP in Section 6.6.4, are **evolutionary algorithms**, where Section 6.6.1 mainly exploits single-objective ones, whereas Section 6.6.4 utilizes multi-objective ones. Evolutionary algorithms were regarded as almost pure heuristics, but recently there have been tremendous efforts trying to establish theoretical foundations for evolutionary algorithms used in machine learning [Zhou et al., 2019], enabling the analysis of theoretical property of PEP mentioned in Section 6.6.4.

Durrant and Lim [2020] empirically showed that the generalization performance of a majority-voting ensemble can be accurately modeled using a Polya-Eggenberger distribution [Sen and Mishra, 1996], whose dispersion parameter is estimated by the pairwise diversity measure, correlation coefficient introduced in Section 5.3.1. Such a way of predicting the generalization performance can be used as the ordering criterion of ordering-based pruning methods as well as the objective function of optimization-based pruning methods. Also, based on this way of prediction, Durrant and Lim [2020] discussed the desired ensemble size under different ranges of the average correlation coefficient.

If each individual learner is viewed as a fancy feature extractor [Kuncheva, 2008, Brown, 2010], ensemble pruning has close relation to **feature selection** [Guyon and Elisseeff, 2003] and new ensemble pruning methods can get inspiration from feature selection techniques. It is worth noting, however, that the different natures of ensemble pruning and feature selection must be considered. For example, in ensemble pruning the individual learners predict the same target and thus have the same physical meaning, while in feature selection the features usually have different physical meanings; the individual learners in ensemble pruning are usually highly correlated, while this may not be the case for features in feature selection. The well-known *Viola-Jones face detector* [Viola and Jones, 2004] in computer vision actually can be viewed as a pruning of Harr-feature-based decision stump ensemble, or selection of Harr features by AdaBoost with a cascade architecture.

Ensemble pruning is also closely related to the general **subset selection** problem [Qian et al., 2015b, 2017], which aims to select a subset with limited size from a ground set for optimizing some given objective function. By setting the ground set as the set of all individual learners, subset selection is actually instantiated to ensemble pruning. Thus, new ensemble pruning methods can also get inspiration from subset selection techniques, e.g., Bian et al. [2019] proposed a distributed framework for ensemble pruning by using the two-round divide-and-conquer strategy from distributed subset selection [Mirzasoleiman et al., 2016].

Chapter 7

Clustering Ensemble

7.1 Clustering

Clustering aims to find the inherent structure of the unlabeled data by grouping them into clusters of objects [Jain et al., 1999]. A good clustering will produce high quality clusters where the **intra-cluster similarity** is maximized while the **inter-cluster similarity** is minimized. Clustering can be used as a stand-alone exploratory tool to gain insights on the nature of the data, and it can also be used as a preprocessing stage to facilitate subsequent learning tasks. Formally, given the data $D = \{\boldsymbol{x}_1, \boldsymbol{x}_2, \ldots, \boldsymbol{x}_m\}$ where the i-th instance $\boldsymbol{x}_i = (x_{i1}, x_{i2}, \ldots, x_{id})^{\boldsymbol{T}} \in \mathcal{R}^d$ is a d-dimensional feature vector, the task of clustering is to group D into k disjoint clusters $\{C_j \mid j = 1, \ldots, k\}$ with $\bigcup_{j=1}^{k} C_j = D$ and $C_i \bigcap_{i \neq j} C_j = \emptyset$. The clustering results returned by a clustering algorithm $\mathfrak{L}$ can be represented as a label vector $\lambda \in \mathcal{N}^m$, with the i-th element $\lambda_i \in \{1, \ldots, k\}$ indicating the *cluster assignment* of $\boldsymbol{x}_i$.

7.1.1 Clustering Methods

A lot of clustering methods have been developed, and various taxonomies can be defined from different perspectives, such as different data types the algorithms can deal with, different assumptions the methods have adopted, etc. Here, we adopt Han et al. [2022]'s taxonomy, which roughly divides clustering methods into the following five categories.

Partitioning Methods. A partitioning method organizes D into k partitions by optimizing an objective partitioning criterion. The most well-known partitioning method is **k-means clustering** [Lloyd, 1982], which minimizes the *squared-error*

$$err = \sum_{j=1}^{k} \sum_{\boldsymbol{x} \in C_j} dis(\boldsymbol{x}, \bar{\boldsymbol{x}}_j)^2 \ , \tag{7.1}$$

DOI: 10.1201/9781003587774-7

where $\bar{\boldsymbol{x}}_j = \frac{1}{|C_j|}\sum_{\boldsymbol{x}\in C_j} \boldsymbol{x}$ is the mean of the partition C_j, and $dis(\cdot,\cdot)$ measures the distance between two instances (e.g., Euclidean distance). Note that finding the optimal partitioning which minimizes err would require exhaustive search of all the possible solutions and is obviously computationally prohibitive due to the combinatorial nature of the search space. To circumvent this difficulty, k-means adopts an *iterative relocation* technique to find the desired solution heuristically. First, it randomly selects k instances from D as the initial cluster centers. Then, every instance in D is assigned to the cluster whose center is the nearest. After that, the cluster centers are updated and the instances are re-assigned to their nearest clusters. The above process will be repeated until convergence.

Hierarchical Methods. A hierarchical method creates a hierarchy of clusterings on D at various granular levels, where a specific clustering can be obtained by thresholding the hierarchy at a specified level of granule. An early attempt toward hierarchical clustering is the SAHN method [Anderberg, 1973, Day and Edelsbrunner, 1984], which forms the hierarchy of clusterings in a *bottom-up* manner. Initially, each data point is placed into a cluster of its own, and an $m \times m$ dissimilarity matrix $\mathbf{D}$ among clusters is set with elements $\mathbf{D}(i,j) = dis(\boldsymbol{x}_i, \boldsymbol{x}_j)$. Two closest clusters C_i and C_j are identified based on $\mathbf{D}$ and replaced by the agglomerated cluster C_h. The dissimilarity matrix $\mathbf{D}$ is then updated to reflect the deletion of C_i and C_j, as well as the new dissimilarities between C_h and all remaining clusters C_k $(k \neq i,j)$ according to

$$\mathbf{D}(h,k) = \alpha_i \mathbf{D}(i,k) + \alpha_j \mathbf{D}(j,k) + \beta \mathbf{D}(i,j) + \gamma |\mathbf{D}(i,k) - \mathbf{D}(j,k)|, \quad (7.2)$$

where α_i, α_j, β and γ are parameters whose setting leads to different implementations. The above merging process is repeated until all the data points fall into a single cluster. Typical implementations of SAHN are named as *single-linkage* $(\alpha_i = 1/2; \alpha_j = 1/2; \beta = 0; \gamma = -1/2)$, *complete-linkage* $(\alpha_i = 1/2; \alpha_j = 1/2; \beta = 0; \gamma = 1/2)$ and *average-linkage* $(\alpha_i = |C_i|/(|C_i| + |C_j|); \alpha_j = |C_j|/(|C_i| + |C_j|); \beta = 0; \gamma = 0)$.

Density-Based Methods. A density-based method constructs clusters from D based on the notion of *density*, where regions with high density of instances are regarded as clusters to be separated from regions with low density. DBSCAN [Ester et al., 1996] is a representative density-based clustering method, which characterizes the density of the data space with a pair of parameters $(\varepsilon, MinPts)$. Given an instance $\boldsymbol{x}$, its neighborhood within a radius ε is called the ε-neighborhood of $\boldsymbol{x}$. $\boldsymbol{x}$ is called a *core object* if its ε-neighborhood contains at least $MinPts$ number of instances. An instance $\boldsymbol{p}$ is *directly density-reachable* to a core object $\boldsymbol{x}$ if $\boldsymbol{p}$ is within the ε-neighborhood of $\boldsymbol{x}$. First, DBSCAN identifies core objects which satisfy the requirement imposed by the $(\varepsilon, MinPts)$ parameters. Then, it forms clusters by iteratively connecting the directly density-reachable instances starting from those core objects. The connecting process terminates when no new data point can be added to any cluster.

Grid-Based Methods. A grid-based method quantizes D into a finite number of cells forming a grid structure, where the quantization process is usually performed in a multi-resolution style. STING [Wang et al., 1997] is a representative grid-based method, which divides the data space into a number of rectangular cells. Each cell stores statistical information of the instances falling into this cell, such as *count*, *mean*, *standard deviation*, *minimum*, *maximum*, *type of distribution*, etc. There are several levels of rectangular cells, each corresponding to a different level of resolution. Here, each cell at a higher level is partitioned into a number of cells at the next lower level, and statistical information of higher-level cells can be easily inferred from its lower-level cells with simple operations such as elementary algebraic calculations.

Model-Based Methods. A model-based method assumes a mathematical model characterizing the properties of D, where the clusters are formed to optimize the fit between the data and the underlying model. The most well-known model-based method is **GMM-based clustering** [Redner and Walker, 1984], which works by utilizing the **Gaussian Mixture Model (GMM)**

$$p(\boldsymbol{x} \mid \boldsymbol{\Theta}) = \sum_{j=1}^{k} \alpha_j \mathcal{N}(\boldsymbol{x} \mid \boldsymbol{\mu}_j, \boldsymbol{\Sigma}_j) , \tag{7.3}$$

where each mixture component $\mathcal{N}(\boldsymbol{x} \mid \boldsymbol{\mu}_j, \boldsymbol{\Sigma}_j)$ $(j = 1, \ldots, k)$ employs Gaussian distribution with mean $\boldsymbol{\mu}_j$ and covariance $\boldsymbol{\Sigma}_j$, and participates in constituting the whole distribution $p(\boldsymbol{x} \mid \boldsymbol{\Theta})$ with non-negative coefficient α_j, $\sum_{j=1}^{k} \alpha_j = 1$ and $\boldsymbol{\Theta} = \{\alpha_j, \boldsymbol{\mu}_j, \boldsymbol{\Sigma}_j \mid j = 1, \ldots, k\}$. The cluster assignment λ_i for the instance $\boldsymbol{x}_i \in D$ is specified according to

$$\lambda_i = \mathop{\arg\max}_{1 \leq l \leq k} \frac{\alpha_l \mathcal{N}(\boldsymbol{x}_i \mid \boldsymbol{\mu}_l, \boldsymbol{\Sigma}_l)}{\sum_{j=1}^{k} \alpha_j \mathcal{N}(\boldsymbol{x}_i \mid \boldsymbol{\mu}_j, \boldsymbol{\Sigma}_j)} . \tag{7.4}$$

The GMM parameters $\boldsymbol{\Theta}$ are learned from D by employing the EM algorithm [Dempster et al., 1977] to maximize the following *log-likelihood* function in an iterative manner:

$$p(D \mid \boldsymbol{\Theta}) = \sum_{i=1}^{m} \ln \left(\sum_{j=1}^{k} \alpha_j \mathcal{N}(\boldsymbol{x}_i \mid \boldsymbol{\mu}_j, \boldsymbol{\Sigma}_j) \right) . \tag{7.5}$$

Details of the iterative optimization procedure can be found in [Jain and Dubes, 1988, Bilmes, 1998, Jain et al., 1999, Duda et al., 2000].

7.1.2 Clustering Evaluation

The task of evaluating the quality of clustering results is commonly referred to as **cluster validity analysis** [Jain and Dubes, 1988, Halkidi et al., 2001].

Existing cluster validity indices for clustering quality assessment can be roughly categorized into two types: **external indices** and **internal indices**.

The external indices evaluate the clustering results by comparing the identified clusters to a pre-specified structure, e.g., the ground-truth clustering. Given the data set $D = \{\boldsymbol{x}_1, \ldots, \boldsymbol{x}_m\}$, let $\mathcal{C} = \{C_1, \ldots, C_k\}$ denote the identified clusters with label vector $\lambda \in \mathcal{N}^m$. Suppose that $\mathcal{C}^* = \{C_1^*, \ldots, C_s^*\}$ is the pre-specified clustering structure with label vector λ^*. Then, four complementary terms can be defined to reflect the relationship between $\mathcal{C}$ and $\mathcal{C}^*$:

$$\begin{cases} a = |SS|, & SS = \{(\boldsymbol{x}_i, \boldsymbol{x}_j) \mid \lambda_i = \lambda_j,\, \lambda_i^* = \lambda_j^*,\, i < j\}, \\ b = |SD|, & SD = \{(\boldsymbol{x}_i, \boldsymbol{x}_j) \mid \lambda_i = \lambda_j,\, \lambda_i^* \neq \lambda_j^*,\, i < j\}, \\ c = |DS|, & DS = \{(\boldsymbol{x}_i, \boldsymbol{x}_j) \mid \lambda_i \neq \lambda_j,\, \lambda_i^* = \lambda_j^*,\, i < j\}, \\ d = |DD|, & DD = \{(\boldsymbol{x}_i, \boldsymbol{x}_j) \mid \lambda_i \neq \lambda_j,\, \lambda_i^* \neq \lambda_j^*,\, i < j\}, \end{cases} \tag{7.6}$$

where SS contains pairs of instances which belong to the same cluster in both $\mathcal{C}$ and $\mathcal{C}^*$; the meanings of SD, DS and DD can be inferred similarly based on the above definitions. It is evident that $a + b + c + d = m(m-1)/2$.

A number of popular external cluster validity indices are defined as follows [Jain and Dubes, 1988, Halkidi et al., 2001]:

- *Jaccard Coefficient* (JC):

$$\mathrm{JC} = \frac{a}{a+b+c}\ , \tag{7.7}$$

- *Fowlkes and Mallows Index* (FMI):

$$\mathrm{FMI} = \sqrt{\frac{a}{a+b} \cdot \frac{a}{a+c}}\ , \tag{7.8}$$

- *Rand Index* (RI):

$$\mathrm{RI} = \frac{2(a+d)}{m(m-1)}\ . \tag{7.9}$$

All these cluster validity indices take values between 0 and 1, and the larger the index value, the better the clustering quality.

The internal indices evaluate the clustering results by investigating the inherent properties of the identified clusters without resorting to a reference structure. Given the data set $D = \{\boldsymbol{x}_1, \ldots, \boldsymbol{x}_m\}$, let $\mathcal{C} = \{C_1, \ldots, C_k\}$ denote the identified clusters. The following terms are usually employed:

$$f(C) = \frac{2}{|C|(|C|-1)} \sum_{i=1}^{|C|-1} \sum_{j=i+1}^{|C|} dis(\boldsymbol{x}_i, \boldsymbol{x}_j), \tag{7.10}$$

$$diam(C) = \max_{\boldsymbol{x}_i, \boldsymbol{x}_j \in C} dis(\boldsymbol{x}_i, \boldsymbol{x}_j), \tag{7.11}$$

$$d_{min}(C_i, C_j) = \min_{\boldsymbol{x}_i \in C_i, \boldsymbol{x}_j \in C_j} dis(\boldsymbol{x}_i, \boldsymbol{x}_j), \tag{7.12}$$

$$d_{cen}(C_i, C_j) = dis(\mathbf{c}_i, \mathbf{c}_j), \tag{7.13}$$

where $dis(\cdot,\cdot)$ measures the distance between two data points and $\boldsymbol{c}_i$ denotes the centroid of cluster C_i. Therefore, $f(C)$ is the average distance between the instances in cluster C, $diam(C)$ is the diameter of cluster C, $d_{min}(C_i, C_j)$ measures the distance between the two nearest instances in C_i and C_j, and $d_{cen}(C_i, C_j)$ measures the distance between the centroids of C_i and C_j.

A number of popular internal cluster validity indices are defined as follows [Jain and Dubes, 1988, Halkidi et al., 2001]:

- *Davies-Bouldin Index* (DBI):

$$\mathrm{DBI} = \frac{1}{k}\sum_{i=1}^{k} \max_{1\le j\le k, j\ne i}\left(\frac{f(C_i)+f(C_j)}{d_{cen}(C_i,C_j)}\right), \tag{7.14}$$

- *Dunn Index* (DI):

$$\mathrm{DI} = \min_{1\le i\le k}\left\{\min_{1\le j\le k}\left(\frac{d_{min}(C_i,C_j)}{\max_{1\le l\le k} diam(C_l)}\right)\right\}, \tag{7.15}$$

- *Silhouette Index* (SI):

$$\mathrm{SI} = \frac{1}{k}\sum_{i=1}^{k}\left(\frac{1}{|C_i|}\sum_{p=1}^{|C_i|} S_p^i\right), \tag{7.16}$$

where

$$S_p^i = \frac{a_p^i - b_p^i}{\max\left\{a_p^i, b_p^i\right\}}, \tag{7.17}$$

$$a_p^i = \min_{j\ne i}\left\{\frac{1}{|C_j|}\sum_{q=1}^{|C_j|} dis(\boldsymbol{x}_p, \boldsymbol{x}_q)\right\}, \tag{7.18}$$

$$b_p^i = \frac{1}{|C_i|-1}\sum_{q\ne p} dis(\boldsymbol{x}_p, \boldsymbol{x}_q). \tag{7.19}$$

For DBI, the smaller the index value, the better the clustering quality; for DI and SI, the larger the index value, the better the clustering quality.

7.1.3 Why Clustering Ensemble

Clustering ensembles, also called **cluster ensembles** or **consensus clustering**, are a kind of ensemble whose base learners are *clusterings*, also called *clusters*, generated by clustering methods.

There are several general motivations for investigating clustering ensembles [Fred and Jain, 2002, Strehl and Ghosh, 2002]:

To Improve Clustering Quality. As we can see in previous chapters, strong generalization ability can be obtained with ensemble methods for supervised learning tasks, as long as the base learners in the ensemble are accurate and diverse. Hence, it is not surprising that better clustering quality can be anticipated if ensemble methods are also applied for the unsupervised learning scenario.

For this purpose, a diverse ensemble of *good* base clusterings should be generated. It is interesting to note that in clustering, it is less difficult to generate diverse clusterings, since clustering methods have inherent randomness. Diverse clusterings can be obtained by, for example, running clustering methods with different parameter configurations, with different initial data points, or with different data samples, etc. An ensemble is then derived by combining the outputs of the base clusterings, such that useful information encoded in each base clustering is fully leveraged to identify the final clustering with high quality.

To Improve Clustering Robustness. As introduced in Section 7.1.1, a clustering method groups the instances into clusters by assuming a specific structure on the data. Therefore, no single clustering method is guaranteed to be robust across all clustering tasks as the ground-truth structures of different data may vary significantly. Furthermore, due to the inherent randomness of many clustering methods, the clustering results may also be unstable if a single clustering method is applied to the same clustering task several times.

Therefore, it is intuitive to utilize clustering ensemble techniques to generate robust clustering results. Given any data set for clustering analysis, multiple base clusterings can be generated by running diverse clustering methods to accommodate various clustering assumptions, or invoking the same clustering method with different settings to compensate for the inherent randomness. Then, the derived ensemble may play more stably than a single clustering method.

To Enable Knowledge Reuse and Distributed Computing. In many applications, a variety of *legacy* clusterings for the data may already exist and can serve as the knowledge bases to be reused for future data exploration. It is also a common practice that the data are gathered and stored in distributed locations as a result of organizational or operational constraints, while performing clustering analysis by merging them into a centralized location is usually infeasible due to communication, computational and storage costs.

In such situations, it is rather natural to apply clustering ensemble techniques to exploit the multiple base clusterings. The legacy clusterings can directly serve as the base clusterings for further combination. While in the distributed setting, a base clustering can be generated from each distributed data sample, and then the base clustering rather than the original data can be sent to a centralized location for a further exploitation.

7.2 Categorization of Clustering Ensemble Methods

Given data set $D = \{\boldsymbol{x}_1, \boldsymbol{x}_2, \ldots, \boldsymbol{x}_m\}$ where the i-th instance $\boldsymbol{x}_i = (x_{i1}, x_{i2}, \ldots, x_{id})^{\boldsymbol{T}} \in \mathcal{R}^d$ is a d-dimensional feature vector, like ensemble methods in supervised learning setting, clustering ensemble methods also work in two steps:

1. **Clustering generation**: In this step, each base clusterer $\mathfrak{L}^{(q)}$ $(1 \leq q \leq r)$ groups D into $k^{(q)}$ clusters $\{C_j^{(q)} \mid j = 1, 2, \ldots, k^{(q)}\}$. Equivalently, the clustering results returned by $\mathfrak{L}^{(q)}$ can be represented by a label vector $\boldsymbol{\lambda}^{(q)} \in \mathcal{N}^m$, where the i-th element $\lambda_i^{(q)} \in \{1, 2, \ldots, k^{(q)}\}$ indicates the cluster assignment of $\boldsymbol{x}_i$.

2. **Clustering combination**: In this step, given the r base clusterings $\{\boldsymbol{\lambda}^{(1)}, \boldsymbol{\lambda}^{(2)}, \ldots, \boldsymbol{\lambda}^{(r)}\}$, a combination function $\Gamma(\cdot)$ is used to consolidate them into the final clustering $\boldsymbol{\lambda} = \Gamma(\{\boldsymbol{\lambda}^{(1)}, \boldsymbol{\lambda}^{(2)}, \ldots, \boldsymbol{\lambda}^{(r)}\}) \in \mathcal{N}^m$ with k clusters, where $\lambda_i \in \{1, \ldots, k\}$ indicates the cluster assignment of $\boldsymbol{x}_i$ in the final clustering. For example, suppose four base clusterings of seven instances have been generated as follows,

$$\boldsymbol{\lambda}^{(1)} = (1,1,2,2,2,3,3)^{\boldsymbol{T}} \qquad \boldsymbol{\lambda}^{(2)} = (2,3,3,2,2,1,1)^{\boldsymbol{T}}$$

$$\boldsymbol{\lambda}^{(3)} = (3,3,1,1,1,2,2)^{\boldsymbol{T}} \qquad \boldsymbol{\lambda}^{(4)} = (1,3,3,4,4,2,2)^{\boldsymbol{T}}$$

where $\boldsymbol{\lambda}^{(1)}$, $\boldsymbol{\lambda}^{(2)}$ and $\boldsymbol{\lambda}^{(3)}$ each groups the seven instances into three clusters, while $\boldsymbol{\lambda}^{(4)}$ results in a clustering with four clusters. Furthermore, though $\boldsymbol{\lambda}^{(1)}$ and $\boldsymbol{\lambda}^{(3)}$ look very different at the first glance, they actually yield the identical clustering results, i.e., $\{\{\boldsymbol{x}_1, \boldsymbol{x}_2\}, \{\boldsymbol{x}_3, \boldsymbol{x}_4, \boldsymbol{x}_5\}, \{\boldsymbol{x}_6, \boldsymbol{x}_7\}\}$. Then, a reasonable consensus (with three clusters) could be $(1,1,2,2,2,3,3)^{\boldsymbol{T}}$, or any of its six equivalent labelings such as $(2,2,2,1,1,3,3)^{\boldsymbol{T}}$, which shares *as much information as possible* with the four base clusterings in the ensemble [Strehl and Ghosh, 2002].

Generally speaking, clustering generation is relatively easier since any data partition generates a clustering, while the major difficulty of clustering ensembles lies in clustering combination. Specifically, for m instances with k clusters, the number of possible clusterings is $\frac{1}{k!}\sum_{j=1}^{k}\binom{k}{j}(-1)^{(k-j)}j^m$, or approximately $k^m/k!$ for $m \gg k$ [Jain and Dubes, 1988]. For example, there will be 171,798,901 ways to form four groups of only 16 instances [Strehl and Ghosh, 2002]. Therefore, a brute-force search over all the possible clusterings to find the optimal combined clustering is apparently infeasible and smart strategies are needed.

Most studies on clustering ensembles focus on the complicated clustering combination part. To successfully derive the clustering ensemble, the key lies in how the information embodied in each base clustering is *expressed* and *aggregated*. During the past two decades, many clustering ensemble methods have been proposed. Roughly speaking, these methods can be classified into the following four categories:

- **Similarity-Based Methods**: A similarity-based method expresses the base clustering information as *similarity matrices* and then aggregates multiple clusterings via *matrix averaging*. Examples include [Fred and Jain, 2002, 2005, Strehl and Ghosh, 2002, Fern and Brodley, 2003].
- **Graph-Based Methods**: A graph-based method expresses the base clustering information as an *undirected graph* and then derives the clustering ensemble via *graph partitioning*. Examples include [Ayad and Kamel, 2003, Fern and Brodley, 2004, Strehl and Ghosh, 2002].
- **Relabeling-Based Methods**: A relabeling-based method expresses the base clustering information as *label vectors* and then aggregates via *label alignment*. Examples include [Long et al., 2005, Zhou and Tang, 2006].
- **Transformation-Based Methods**: A transformation-based method expresses the base clustering information as *features for re-representation* and then derives the clustering ensemble via *meta-clustering*. Examples include [Topchy et al., 2003, 2004a].

7.3 Similarity-Based Methods

The basic idea of similarity-based clustering ensemble methods is to exploit the base clusterings to form an $m \times m$ consensus **similarity matrix M**, and then generate the final clustering result based on the consensus similarity matrix. Intuitively, the matrix element $\mathbf{M}(i,j)$ characterizes the similarity (or closeness) between the pair of instances $\boldsymbol{x}_i$ and $\boldsymbol{x}_j$. The general procedure of similarity-based methods is shown in Figure 7.1.

Input: Data set $D = \{\boldsymbol{x}_1, \boldsymbol{x}_2, \ldots, \boldsymbol{x}_m\}$;
Base clusterer $\mathfrak{L}^{(q)}$ $(q = 1, \ldots, r)$;
Consensus clusterer $\mathfrak{L}$ on similarity matrix.

Process:
1. **for** $q = 1, \ldots, r$:
2. $\lambda^{(q)} = \mathfrak{L}^{(q)}(D)$; % Form a base clustering from D with $k^{(q)}$ clusters
3. Derive an $m \times m$ base similarity matrix $\mathbf{M}^{(q)}$ based on $\lambda^{(q)}$;
4. **end**
5. $\mathbf{M} = \frac{1}{r}\sum_{q=1}^{r} \mathbf{M}^{(q)}$; % Form the consensus similarity matrix
6. $\lambda = \mathfrak{L}(\mathbf{M})$; % Form the clustering ensemble based on consensus
% similarity matrix $\mathbf{M}$

Output: Clustering ensemble λ

Figure 7.1: General procedure of similarity-based clustering ensemble methods.

A total of r base similarity matrices $\mathbf{M}^{(q)}$ $(q = 1, \ldots, r)$ are firstly obtained based on the clustering results of each base clusterer $\mathfrak{L}^{(q)}$ and then *averaged* to form the consensus similarity matrix. Generally, the base similarity matrix $\mathbf{M}^{(q)}$ can be instantiated in two different ways according to how $\mathfrak{L}^{(q)}$ returns the clustering results, i.e., *crisp clustering* and *soft clustering*.

Crisp Clustering. In this setting, $\mathfrak{L}^{(q)}$ works by partitioning the data set D into $k^{(q)}$ *crisp* clusters, such as k-means [Strehl and Ghosh, 2002, Fred and Jain, 2002, 2005]. Here, each instance belongs to exactly one cluster. The base similarity matrix $\mathbf{M}^{(q)}$ can be set as $\mathbf{M}^{(q)}(i, j) = 1$ if $\lambda_i^{(q)} = \lambda_j^{(q)}$ and 0 otherwise. In other words, $\mathbf{M}^{(q)}$ corresponds to a binary matrix specifying whether each pair of instances co-occurs in the same cluster.

Soft Clustering. In this setting, $\mathfrak{L}^{(q)}$ works by grouping the data set D into $k^{(q)}$ *soft* clusters, such as GMM-based clustering [Fern and Brodley, 2003]. Here, the probability of $\boldsymbol{x}_i$ belonging to the l-th cluster can be modeled as $P(l \mid i)$ with $\sum_{l=1}^{k^{(q)}} P(l \mid i) = 1$. The base similarity matrix $\mathbf{M}^{(q)}$ can be set as $\mathbf{M}^{(q)}(i, j) = \sum_{l=1}^{k^{(q)}} P(l \mid i) \cdot P(l \mid j)$. In other words, $\mathbf{M}^{(q)}$ corresponds to a real-valued matrix specifying the probability for each pair of instances to co-occur in any of the clusters.

After obtaining the consensus similarity matrix $\mathbf{M}$, the clustering ensemble λ can be derived from $\mathbf{M}$ by $\mathfrak{L}$ in a number of ways, such as running the single-linkage [Fred and Jain, 2002, 2005], complete-linkage [Fern and Brodley, 2003] or average-linkage [Fred and Jain, 2005] agglomerative clustering over D by taking $1 - \mathbf{M}(i, j)$ as the distance between $\boldsymbol{x}_i$ and $\boldsymbol{x}_j$, or invoking partitioning clustering method [Strehl and Ghosh, 2002] over a similarity graph with $\boldsymbol{x}_i$ being the vertex and $\mathbf{M}(i, j)$ being the edge weight between vertices.

The most prominent advantage of similarity-based methods lies in their conceptual simplicity since the similarity matrices are easy to instantiate and aggregate. The consensus similarity matrix also offers much flexibility for subsequent analysis, where many existing clustering methods which operate on the similarity matrix can be applied to produce the final clustering ensemble.

The major deficiency of similarity-based methods lies in their efficiency. The computational and storage complexities are both quadratic in m, i.e., the number of instances. Therefore, similarity-based methods are more suitable for small or medium-scale problems.

7.4 Graph-Based Methods

The basic idea of graph-based clustering ensemble methods is to construct a graph $\mathcal{G} = (V, E)$ to integrate the clustering information conveyed by the base clusterings, and then identify the clustering ensemble by performing graph partitioning of the graph. Intuitively, the intrinsic grouping characteristics among all the instances are implicitly encoded in $\mathcal{G}$.

Input: Data set $D = \{\boldsymbol{x}_1, \boldsymbol{x}_2, \ldots, \boldsymbol{x}_m\}$;
Clusters in all the base clusterings $\mathcal{C} = \{C_j \mid 1 \leq j \leq k^*\}$.

Process:
1. $V = D$; % Set vertices v_i as instances $\boldsymbol{x}_i$ in D
2. $E = \emptyset$;
3. **for** $j = 1, \ldots, k^*$:
4. $E = E \bigcup \{C_j\}$;
5. **end**
6. $\mathcal{G} = (V, E)$;
7. $\lambda =$ HMETIS($\mathcal{G}$); % Invoke HMETIS package [Karypis et al., 1997] on $\mathcal{G}$

Output: Clustering ensemble λ

Figure 7.2: The HGPA algorithm.

Given an ensemble of r base clusterings $\{\lambda^{(q)} \mid 1 \leq q \leq r\}$, where each $\lambda^{(q)}$ imposes $k^{(q)}$ clusters over the data set D, let $\mathcal{C} = \{C_l^{(q)} \mid 1 \leq q \leq r,\ 1 \leq l \leq k^{(q)}\}$ denote the set consisting of all the clusters in the base clusterings. Furthermore, let $k^* = |\mathcal{C}| = \sum_{q=1}^{r} k^{(q)}$ denote the size of $\mathcal{C}$, i.e., the total number of clusters in all base clusterings. Without loss of generality, clusters in $\mathcal{C}$ can be re-indexed as $\{C_j \mid 1 \leq j \leq k^*\}$. There are three alternative ways to construct the graph $\mathcal{G} = (V, E)$ based on how the vertex set V is configured, that is, $V = D$, $V = \mathcal{C}$ and $V = D \cup \mathcal{C}$.

$\boldsymbol{V = D}$. In this setting, each vertex in V corresponds to a single data point $\boldsymbol{x}_i \in D$ [Ayad and Kamel, 2003, Strehl and Ghosh, 2002]. HGPA (HyperGraph-Partitioning Algorithm) [Strehl and Ghosh, 2002] is a representative method within this category, whose pseudo-code is given in Figure 7.2.

Here, $\mathcal{G}$ is a **hypergraph** with equally weighted vertices. Given $\mathcal{C}$, HGPA regards each cluster $C \in \mathcal{C}$ as a **hyperedge** (connecting a set of vertices) and adds it into E. In this way, high-order (≥ 3) rather than only pairwise relationships between instances are incorporated in the hypergraph $\mathcal{G}$. The clustering ensemble λ is obtained by applying the HMETIS hypergraph partitioning package [Karypis et al., 1997] on $\mathcal{G}$, where a cut over a hyperedge C is counted if and only if the vertices in C fall into two or more groups as the partitioning process terminates, and the hyperedge-cut is minimized subject to the constraint that comparable-sized partitioned groups are favored.

$\boldsymbol{V = \mathcal{C}}$. In this setting, each vertex in V corresponds to a set of data points $C \in \mathcal{C}$, i.e., one cluster in the base clusterings. Each edge in E is an ordinary edge connecting two vertices from different base clusterings. MCLA (Meta-CLustering Algorithm) [Strehl and Ghosh, 2002] is a representative method within this category, whose pseudo-code is given in Figure 7.3.

Here, MCLA constructs $\mathcal{G}$ as a r-partite graph, where r is the number of base clusterings. Each edge is assigned with weight w_{ij} specifying the degree

---

Input: Data set $D = \{\boldsymbol{x}_1, \boldsymbol{x}_2, \ldots, \boldsymbol{x}_m\}$;
Clusters in all the base clusterings $\mathcal{C} = \{C_j \mid 1 \leq j \leq k^*\}$.
Process:
1. $V = \mathcal{C}$; % Set vertices v_i as clusters C_i in $\mathcal{C}$
2. $E = \emptyset$;
3. **for** $i = 1, \ldots, k^*$:
4. **for** $j = 1, \ldots, k^*$:
5. **if** C_i and C_j belong to different base clusterings
6. **then** $E = E \cup \{e_{ij}\}$; % Add edge $e_{ij} = (v_i, v_j)$
7. $w_{ij} = |C_i \cap C_j| / (|C_i| + |C_j| - |C_i \cap C_j|)$; % Set weight for e_{ij}
8. **end**
9. **end**
10. $\mathcal{G} = (V, E)$;
11. $\{C_1^{(M)}, C_2^{(M)}, \ldots, C_k^{(M)}\} = \mathsf{METIS}(\mathcal{G})$;
% Invoke METIS package [Karypis and Kumar, 1998] on
% $\mathcal{G}$ to induce meta-clusters $C_p^{(M)}$ $(p = 1, \ldots, k)$
12. **for** $p = 1, \ldots, k$:
13. **for** $i = 1, \ldots, m$:
14. $h_{pi}^{(M)} = \sum_{C \in C_p^{(M)}} \mathbb{I}(\boldsymbol{x}_i \in C) / |C_p^{(M)}|$;
15. **end**
16. **end**
17. **for** $i = 1, \ldots, m$:
18. $\lambda_i = \arg\max_{p \in \{1, \ldots, k\}} h_{pi}^{(M)}$;
19. **end**

Output: Clustering ensemble λ

Figure 7.3: The MCLA algorithm.

of overlap between two connecting clusters. The METIS package [Karypis and Kumar, 1998] is used to partition $\mathcal{G}$ into k balanced meta-clusters $C_p^{(M)}$ $(p = 1, \ldots, k)$, each characterized by an m-dimensional *indicator vector* $\boldsymbol{h}_p^{(M)} = (h_{p1}^{(M)}, h_{p2}^{(M)}, \ldots, h_{pm}^{(M)})^{\boldsymbol{T}}$ expressing the level of association between instances and the meta-cluster. The clustering ensemble λ is then formed by assigning each instance to the meta-cluster mostly associated with it. Note that it is not guaranteed that every meta-cluster can win for at least one instance, and ties are broken arbitrarily [Strehl and Ghosh, 2002].

$\boldsymbol{V = D \cup \mathcal{C}}$. In this setting, each vertex in V corresponds to either a single data point $\boldsymbol{x}_i \in D$ or a set of data points $C \in \mathcal{C}$. Each edge in E is an ordinary edge connecting two vertices with one from D and another from $\mathcal{C}$. HBGF (Hybrid Bipartite Graph Formulation) [Fern and Brodley, 2003] is a representative method within this category, whose pseudo-code is given in Figure 7.4.

Input: Data set $D = \{\boldsymbol{x}_1, \boldsymbol{x}_2, \ldots, \boldsymbol{x}_m\}$;
Clusters in all the base clusterings $\mathcal{C} = \{C_j \mid m+1 \leq j \leq m+k^*\}$;
Graph partitioning package $\mathcal{L}$ (SPEC [Shi and Malik, 2000] or METIS [Karypis and Kumar, 1998]).

Process:
1. $V = D \bigcup \mathcal{C}$; % Set vertices v_i as instances $\boldsymbol{x}_i$ in D or clusters C_i in $\mathcal{C}$
2. $E = \emptyset$;
3. **for** $i = 1, \ldots, m$:
4. **for** $j = m+1, \ldots, m+k^*$:
5. **if** $v_i \in v_j$ % v_i being an instance in D; v_j being a cluster in $\mathcal{C}$
6. **then** $E = E \bigcup \{e_{ij}\}$; % Add edge $e_{ij} = (v_i, v_j)$
7. $w_{ij} = 1$; % Set equal weight for e_{ij}
8. **end**
9. **end**
10. $\mathcal{G} = (V, E)$;
11. $\lambda = \mathcal{L}(\mathcal{G})$; % Invoke the specified graph partitioning package on $\mathcal{G}$

Output: Clustering ensemble λ

Figure 7.4: The HBGF algorithm.

Here, HBGF constructs $\mathcal{G}$ as a bi-partite graph with equally weighted edges. The clustering ensemble λ is obtained by applying the SPEC [Shi and Malik, 2000] or the METIS [Karypis and Kumar, 1998] graph partitioning package [Karypis et al., 1997] on $\mathcal{G}$. Here, the partitioning of the bi-partite graph groups the instance vertices as well as the cluster vertices simultaneously. Therefore, the partitions of the individual instances are returned as the final clustering results.

An appealing advantage of graph-based methods lies in their linear computational complexity in m, the number of instances. Thus, this category of methods provides a practical choice for clustering analysis on large-scale data. In addition, graph-based methods are able to handle more complicated interactions between instances beyond pairwise relationships, e.g., the high-order relationship encoded by hyperedges in HGPA.

The major deficiency of graph-based methods lies in the fact that the performance heavily relies on the graph partitioning method that is used to produce the clustering ensemble. Since graph partitioning techniques are not designed for clustering tasks and the partitioned clusters are just by-products of the graph partitioning process, the quality of the clustering ensemble can be impaired. Moreover, most graph partitioning methods such as HMETIS [Karypis et al., 1997] have the constraint that each cluster contains approximately the same number of instances, and thus, the final clustering ensemble would become inappropriate if the intrinsic data clusters are highly imbalanced.

Input: Data set $D = \{\boldsymbol{x}_1, \boldsymbol{x}_2, \ldots, \boldsymbol{x}_m\}$;
Base clusterings $\Lambda = \{\lambda^{(1)}, \lambda^{(2)}, \ldots, \lambda^{(r)}\}$ each with k clusters.

Process:

1. Randomly select $\lambda^{(b)} = \{C_l^{(b)} \mid l = 1, \ldots, k\}$ in Λ as *reference* clustering;
2. $\Lambda = \Lambda - \{\lambda^{(b)}\}$;
3. **repeat**
4. Randomly select $\lambda^{(q)} = \{C_l^{(q)} \mid l = 1, \ldots, k\}$ in Λ to *align* with $\lambda^{(b)}$;
5. Initialize $k \times k$ matrix $\mathbf{O}$ with $\mathbf{O}(u, v) = \left|C_u^{(b)} \cap C_v^{(q)}\right|$ $(1 \leq u, v \leq k)$;
   % Count instances shared by clusters in $\lambda^{(b)}$ and $\lambda^{(q)}$
6. $\mathcal{I} = \{(u, v) \mid 1 \leq u, v \leq k\}$;
7. **repeat**
8. $(u', v') = \arg\max_{(u,v) \in \mathcal{I}} \mathbf{O}(u, v)$;
9. Relabel $C_{v'}^{(q)}$ as $C_{u'}^{(q)}$;
10. $\mathcal{I} = \mathcal{I} - \{(u', w) \mid (u', w) \in \mathcal{I}\} \cup \{(w, v') \mid (w, v') \in \mathcal{I}\}$;
11. **until** $\mathcal{I} = \emptyset$
12. $\Lambda = \Lambda - \{\lambda^{(q)}\}$;
13. **until** $\Lambda = \emptyset$;

Output: Relabeled clusterings $\{\lambda^{(q)} \mid 1 \leq q \leq r\}$ with aligned cluster labels

---

Figure 7.5: The relabeling process for crisp label correspondence [Zhou and Tang, 2006].

7.5 Relabeling-Based Methods

The basic idea of relabeling-based clustering ensemble methods is to *align* or *relabel* the cluster labels of all base clusterings, such that the same label denotes similar clusters across the base clusterings, and then derive the final clustering ensemble based on the aligned labels.

Note that unlike supervised learning where the class labels represent specific classes, in unsupervised learning the cluster labels only express grouping characteristics of the data and are not directly comparable across different clusterings. For example, given two clusterings $\lambda^{(1)}$ and $\lambda^{(2)}$, where the corresponding clustering label vector is $(1, 1, 2, 2, 3, 3, 1)^{\boldsymbol{T}}$ and $(2, 2, 3, 3, 1, 1, 2)^{\boldsymbol{T}}$, respectively, though the cluster labels for each instance differ across the two clusterings, $\lambda^{(1)}$ and $\lambda^{(2)}$ are in fact identical. It is obvious that the labels of different clusterings should be aligned, or relabeled, based on label correspondence. Relabeling-based methods have two alternative settings according to the type of label correspondence to be established, i.e., crisp label correspondence and soft label correspondence.

Crisp Label Correspondence. In this setting, each base clustering is assumed to group data set $D = \{\boldsymbol{x}_1, \boldsymbol{x}_2, \ \ldots, \boldsymbol{x}_m\}$ into an equal number of clusters, i.e., $k^{(q)} = k$ $(q = 1, \ldots, r)$. As a representative, the method described in [Zhou and Tang, 2006] aligns cluster labels as shown in Figure 7.5.

In [Zhou and Tang, 2006], clusters in different clusterings are iteratively aligned based on the recognition that similar clusters should contain similar instances. The task of matching two clusterings, e.g., $\lambda^{(q)}$ and $\lambda^{(b)}$, can also be accomplished by formulating it as a standard *assignment problem* [Kuhn, 1955], where the cost of assigning cluster $C_v^{(q)} \in \lambda^{(q)}$ to cluster $C_u^{(b)} \in \lambda^{(b)}$ can be set as $m - |C_u^{(b)} \cap C_v^{(q)}|$. Then, the *minimum cost* one-to-one assignment problem can be solved by the popular *Hungarian algorithm* [Topchy et al., 2004b, Hore et al., 2009].

After the labels of different base clusterings have been relabeled, strategies for combining classifiers can be applied to derive the final clustering ensemble λ. Let $\lambda_i^{(q)} \in \{1, \ldots, k\}$ denote the cluster label of $\boldsymbol{x}_i$ $(i = 1, \ldots, m)$ in the *aligned* base clustering $\lambda^{(q)}$ $(q = 1, \ldots, r)$, four strategies are described in [Zhou and Tang, 2006] to derive λ:

- *Simple Voting*: The ensemble clustering label λ_i of $\boldsymbol{x}_i$ is simply given by

$$\lambda_i = \operatorname*{arg\,max}_{l \in \{1, \ldots, k\}} \sum_{q=1}^{r} \mathbb{I}(\lambda_i^{(q)} = l). \tag{7.20}$$

- *Weighted Voting*: The mutual information between a pair of clusterings [Strehl et al., 2000] is employed to derive the weight for each $\lambda^{(q)}$. Given two base clusterings $\lambda^{(p)}$ and $\lambda^{(q)}$, let $m_u = |C_u^{(p)}|$, $m_v = |C_v^{(q)}|$ and $m_{uv} = |C_u^{(p)} \cap C_v^{(q)}|$. The [0,1]-normalized mutual information Φ^{NMI} between $\lambda^{(p)}$ and $\lambda^{(q)}$ can be defined as

$$\Phi^{\mathrm{NMI}}(\lambda^{(p)}, \lambda^{(q)}) = \frac{2}{m} \sum_{u=1}^{k} \sum_{v=1}^{k} m_{uv} \log_{k^2} \left(\frac{m_{uv} \cdot m}{m_u \cdot m_v} \right). \tag{7.21}$$

Other kinds of definitions can be found in [Strehl and Ghosh, 2002, Fred and Jain, 2005]. Then, for each base clustering, the average mutual information can be calculated as

$$\beta^{(q)} = \frac{1}{r-1} \sum_{p=1, p \neq q}^{r} \Phi^{\mathrm{NMI}}(\lambda^{(p)}, \lambda^{(q)}) \quad (q = 1, \ldots, r). \tag{7.22}$$

Intuitively, the larger the $\beta^{(q)}$ value, the less statistical information contained in $\lambda^{(q)}$ while not contained in other base clusterings [Zhou and Tang, 2006]. Thus, the weight for $\lambda^{(q)}$ can be defined as

$$w^{(q)} = \frac{1}{Z \cdot \beta^{(q)}} \quad (q = 1, \ldots, r), \tag{7.23}$$

where Z is a normalizing factor such that $\sum_{q=1}^{r} w^{(q)} = 1$. Finally, the ensemble clustering label λ_i of $\boldsymbol{x}_i$ is determined by

$$\lambda_i = \arg\max_{l \in \{1,\ldots,k\}} \sum_{q=1}^{r} w^{(q)} \cdot \mathbb{I}(\lambda_i^{(q)} = l). \tag{7.24}$$

- *Selective Voting*: This is a strategy which incorporates **ensemble pruning** (see Chapter 6). In [Zhou and Tang, 2006], the mutual information weights $\{w^{(q)} \mid q = 1, \ldots, r\}$ are used to select the base clusterings for combination, where the base clusterings with weights smaller than a threshold w_{thr} are excluded from the ensemble. Zhou and Tang [2006] simply set $w_{thr} = \frac{1}{r}$. Let $\mathcal{Q} = \{q \mid w^{(q)} \geq \frac{1}{r}, 1 \leq q \leq r\}$, then the ensemble clustering label λ_i of $\boldsymbol{x}_i$ is determined by

$$\lambda_i = \arg\max_{l \in \{1,\ldots,k\}} \sum_{q \in \mathcal{Q}} \mathbb{I}(\lambda_i^{(q)} = l). \tag{7.25}$$

- *Selective Weighted Voting*: This is a weighted version of selective voting, where the ensemble clustering label λ_i of $\boldsymbol{x}_i$ is determined by

$$\lambda_i = \arg\max_{l \in \{1,\ldots,k\}} \sum_{q \in \mathcal{Q}} w^{(q)} \cdot \mathbb{I}(\lambda_i^{(q)} = l). \tag{7.26}$$

It was reported in [Zhou and Tang, 2006] that the selective weighted voting leads to the best empirical results, where the weighted voting and selective voting both contribute to performance improvement.

Soft Label Correspondence. In this setting, each base clustering is assumed to group the data set D into an *arbitrary* number of clusters, i.e., $k^{(q)} \in \mathcal{N}$ $(q = 1, \ldots, r)$. Each base clustering $\lambda^{(q)} = \{C_l^{(q)} \mid l = 1, 2, \ldots, k^{(q)}\}$ can be represented as an $m \times k^{(q)}$ matrix $\mathbf{A}^{(q)}$, where $\mathbf{A}^{(q)}(i, l) = 1$ if $\boldsymbol{x}_i \in C_l^{(q)}$ and 0 otherwise. Given two base clusterings $\lambda^{(p)}$ and $\lambda^{(q)}$, a $k^{(p)} \times k^{(q)}$ *soft correspondence* matrix $\mathbf{S}$ is assumed to model the correspondence relationship between clusters of each clustering. Here, $\mathbf{S} \succeq 0$ and $\sum_{v=1}^{k^{(q)}} \mathbf{S}(u, v) = 1$ $(u = 1, 2, \ldots, k^{(p)})$. Intuitively, with the help of $\mathbf{S}$, the membership matrix $\mathbf{A}^{(p)}$ for $\lambda^{(p)}$ can be mapped to the membership matrix $\mathbf{A}^{(q)}$ for $\lambda^{(q)}$ by $\mathbf{A}^{(p)}\mathbf{S}$. The quality of this mapping can be measured by the **Frobenius matrix norm** between $\mathbf{A}^{(q)}$ and $\mathbf{A}^{(p)}\mathbf{S}$, i.e., $\|\mathbf{A}^{(q)} - \mathbf{A}^{(p)}\mathbf{S}\|_F^2$. The smaller the Frobenius norm, the more precisely the soft correspondence matrix $\mathbf{S}$ captures the relation between $\mathbf{A}^{(p)}$ and $\mathbf{A}^{(q)}$.

Given r base clusterings with membership matrices $\mathbf{A}^{(1)} \in \mathcal{R}^{m \times k^{(1)}}, \ldots, \mathbf{A}^{(r)} \in \mathcal{R}^{m \times k^{(r)}}$ and the number of k, as a representative, the SCEC (Soft Correspondence Ensemble Clustering) method [Long et al., 2005] aims to find the final clustering ensemble $\mathbf{A} \in \mathcal{R}^{m \times k}$ together with r soft correspondence matrices $\mathbf{S}^{(1)} \in \mathcal{R}^{k^{(1)} \times k}, \ldots, \mathbf{S}^{(r)} \in \mathcal{R}^{k^{(r)} \times k}$ by minimizing the objective function

$$\min \sum_{q=1}^{r} \|\mathbf{A} - \mathbf{A}^{(q)}\mathbf{S}^{(q)}\|_F^2 \tag{7.27}$$

$$\text{s.t. } \mathbf{S}^{(q)}(u,v) \geq 0 \text{ and } \sum_{v=1}^{k} \mathbf{S}^{(q)}(u,v) = 1 \quad \forall\, q,u,v.$$

This optimization problem can be solved by the **alternating optimization** strategy, i.e., optimizing $\mathbf{A}$ and each $\mathbf{S}^{(q)}$ one at a time by fixing the others. Rather than directly optimizing (7.27), SCEC chooses to make two modifications to the above objective function. First, as the minimizer of (7.27) may converge to a final clustering ensemble $\mathbf{A}$ with unreasonably small number of clusters (i.e., resulting in many all-zero columns in $\mathbf{A}$), a *column-sparseness* constraint is enforced on each $\mathbf{S}^{(q)}$ to help produce an $\mathbf{A}$ with as many clusters as possible. Specifically, the sum of the variation of each column of $\mathbf{S}^{(q)}$ is a good measure of its column-sparseness [Long et al., 2005], i.e., the larger the value of $\|\mathbf{S}^{(q)} - \frac{1}{k^{(q)}}\mathbf{1}_{k^{(q)}k^{(q)}}\mathbf{S}^{(q)}\|_F^2$, the more column-sparse the $\mathbf{S}^{(q)}$. Here, $\mathbf{1}_{k^{(q)}k^{(q)}}$ is a $k^{(q)} \times k^{(q)}$ matrix with all ones. Second, as it is hard to handle the normalization constraint $\sum_{v=1}^{k} \mathbf{S}^{(q)}(u,v) = 1$ efficiently, it is transformed into a soft constraint by adding a penalty term to (7.27) with $\sum_{q=1}^{r} \|\mathbf{S}^{(q)}\mathbf{1}_{kk} - \mathbf{1}_{k^{(q)}k}\|_F^2$. Now, the objective function of SCEC becomes

$$\min \sum_{q=1}^{r} \|\mathbf{A} - \mathbf{A}^{(q)}\mathbf{S}^{(q)}\|_F^2 \tag{7.28}$$

$$-\alpha\|\mathbf{S}^{(q)} - \frac{1}{k^{(q)}}\mathbf{1}_{k^{(q)}k^{(q)}}\mathbf{S}^{(q)}\|_F^2 + \beta\|\mathbf{S}^{(q)}\mathbf{1}_{kk} - \mathbf{1}_{k^{(q)}k}\|_F^2$$

$$\text{s.t. } \mathbf{S}^{(q)}(u,v) \geq 0 \quad \forall\, q,u,v,$$

where α and β are coefficients balancing different terms. Like (7.27), the modified objective (7.28) can be solved by the alternative optimization process [Long et al., 2005] in Figure 7.6. Specifically (step 8), the division between two matrices is performed in an element-wise manner, and $\odot$ denotes the *Hadamard product* of two matrices. It has been proved that (7.28) is guaranteed to reach a local minimum based on the given alternative optimization process [Long et al., 2005].

An advantage of relabeling-based methods is that they offer the possibility of investigating the connections between different base clusterings, which may be helpful in studying the implications of the clustering results. In particular, in crisp label correspondence, the reference clustering can be viewed as a profiling structure of the data set, while in soft label correspondence, the learned correspondence matrices provide intuitive interpretations to the relations between the clustering ensemble and each base clustering.

A deficiency of relabeling-based methods lies in the fact that if there is no reasonable correspondence among the base clusterings, they may not work

Input: Data set $D = \{\boldsymbol{x}_1, \boldsymbol{x}_2, \ldots, \boldsymbol{x}_m\}$;
Base clusterings $\Lambda = \{\lambda^{(1)}, \lambda^{(2)}, \ldots, \lambda^{(r)}\}$ each with $k^{(q)}$ clusters;
Integer k, coefficients α, β, small positive constant ϵ.

Process:

1. **for** $q = 1, \ldots, r$:
2. Form an $m \times k^{(q)}$ membership matrix $\mathbf{A}^{(q)}$, where $\mathbf{A}^{(q)}(i,l) = 1$ if $\boldsymbol{x}_i \in C_l^{(q)}$ and 0 otherwise; % $\lambda^{(q)} = \{C_l^{(q)} \mid l = 1, 2, \ldots, k^{(q)}\}$
3. Randomly initialize a $k^{(q)} \times k$ soft correspondence matrix $\mathbf{S}^{(q)}$ with $\mathbf{S}^{(q)} \succeq 0$;
4. **end**
5. **repeat**
6. $\mathbf{A} = \frac{1}{r}\sum_{q=1}^{r} \mathbf{A}^{(q)}\mathbf{S}^{(q)}$; % By setting $\frac{\partial f}{\partial \mathbf{A}} = 0$ with f being the % objective function in (7.28)
7. **for** $q = 1, \ldots, r$:
8. $\mathbf{S}^{(q)} = \mathbf{S}^{(q)} \odot \frac{(\mathbf{A}^{(q)})^{\boldsymbol{T}}\mathbf{A} + \beta k \mathbf{1}_{k^{(q)}k}}{\mathbf{B} + \epsilon \cdot \mathbf{1}_{k^{(q)}k}}$, where $\mathbf{B} = (\mathbf{A}^{(q)})^{\boldsymbol{T}}\mathbf{A}^{(q)}\mathbf{S}^{(q)} - \alpha\mathbf{S}^{(q)} + \frac{\alpha}{k^{(q)}}\mathbf{1}_{k^{(q)}k^{(q)}}\mathbf{S}^{(q)} + \beta k \mathbf{S}^{(q)}\mathbf{1}_{kk}$
9. **end**
10. **until** convergence;

Output: Membership matrix $\mathbf{A}$ for clustering ensemble

Figure 7.6: The SCEC method.

well. Moreover, the crisp label correspondence methods require each base clustering to have identical number of clusters, and it may result in a final clustering ensemble with fewer clusters than the base clusterings. The soft label correspondence methods need to solve an optimization problem involving numerous variables, and this is prone to get stuck in local minimum far from the optimal solution.

7.6 Transformation-Based Methods

The basic idea of transformation-based clustering ensemble methods is to re-represent each instance as an r-tuple, where r is the number of base clusterings and the q-th element indicates its cluster assignment given by the q-th base clustering, and then derive the final clustering ensemble by performing clustering analysis over the transformed r-tuples.

For example, suppose there are four base clusterings over five instances, and the corresponding clustering label vectors are $\boldsymbol{\lambda}^{(1)} = (1,1,2,2,3)^{\boldsymbol{T}}$, $\boldsymbol{\lambda}^{(2)} = (1,2,2,2,3)^{\boldsymbol{T}}$, $\boldsymbol{\lambda}^{(3)} = (2,2,3,1,3)^{\boldsymbol{T}}$ and $\boldsymbol{\lambda}^{(4)} = (3,1,3,2,3)^{\boldsymbol{T}}$. Then, based on the transformation process, $\boldsymbol{x}_i$ will be transformed into the r-tuple $\varphi(\boldsymbol{x}_i)$ ($r = 4$) as: $\varphi(\boldsymbol{x}_1) = (\varphi_1(\boldsymbol{x}_1), \varphi_2(\boldsymbol{x}_1), \varphi_3(\boldsymbol{x}_1), \varphi_4(\boldsymbol{x}_1))^{\boldsymbol{T}} = (1,1,2,3)^{\boldsymbol{T}}$, and similarly, $\varphi(\boldsymbol{x}_2) = (1,2,2,1)^{\boldsymbol{T}}$, $\varphi(\boldsymbol{x}_3) = (2,2,3,3)^{\boldsymbol{T}}$, $\varphi(\boldsymbol{x}_4) = (2,2,1,2)^{\boldsymbol{T}}$ and $\varphi(\boldsymbol{x}_5) = (3,3,3,3)^{\boldsymbol{T}}$.

Each transformed r-tuple $\varphi(\boldsymbol{x}) = (\varphi_1(\boldsymbol{x}), \varphi_2(\boldsymbol{x}), \ldots, \varphi_r(\boldsymbol{x}))^{\boldsymbol{T}}$ can be regarded as a categorical vector, where $\varphi_q(\boldsymbol{x}) \in \mathcal{K}^{(q)} = \{1, 2, \ldots, k^{(q)}\}$ $(q = 1, \ldots, r)$. Any categorical clustering technique can then be applied to group the transformed r-tuples to identify the final clustering ensemble. For example, one can define a similarity function $sim(\cdot, \cdot)$ between the transformed r-tuples, e.g.,

$$sim(\varphi(\boldsymbol{x}_i), \varphi(\boldsymbol{x}_j)) = \sum_{q=1}^{r} \mathbb{I}(\varphi_q(\boldsymbol{x}_i) = \varphi_q(\boldsymbol{x}_j)), \tag{7.29}$$

and then use traditional clustering methods such as k-means to identify the final clustering ensemble [Topchy et al., 2003].

The task of clustering categorical data can also be equivalently transformed into the task of creating a clustering ensemble, where the q-th categorical feature with $k^{(q)}$ possible values can naturally give rise to a base clustering with $k^{(q)}$ clusters [He et al., 2005].

Besides resorting to categorical clustering techniques, the task of clustering the transformed r-tuples can also be tackled directly in a probabilistic framework [Topchy et al., 2004a], as introduced in the following.

Given r base clusterings $\lambda^{(q)}$ $(q = 1, \ldots, r)$ over the data set D, let $\boldsymbol{y} = (y_1, y_2, \ldots, y_r)^{\boldsymbol{T}} \in \mathcal{K}^{(1)} \times \mathcal{K}^{(2)} \cdots \times \mathcal{K}^{(r)}$ denote the r-dimensional *random vector*, and $\boldsymbol{y}_i = \varphi(\boldsymbol{x}_i) = (y_1^i, y_2^i, \ldots, y_r^i)^{\boldsymbol{T}}$ denote the transformed r-tuple for $\boldsymbol{x}_i$. The random vector $\boldsymbol{y}$ is modeled by a mixture of *multinomial distributions*, i.e.,

$$P(\boldsymbol{y} \mid \boldsymbol{\Theta}) = \sum_{j=1}^{k} \alpha_j P_j(\boldsymbol{y} \mid \boldsymbol{\theta}_j), \tag{7.30}$$

where k is the number of mixture components which also corresponds to the number of clusters in the final clustering ensemble. Each mixture component is parameterized by $\boldsymbol{\theta}_j$ and $\boldsymbol{\Theta} = \{\alpha_j, \boldsymbol{\theta}_j \mid j = 1, \ldots, k\}$. Assume that the components of $\boldsymbol{y}$ are conditionally independent, i.e.,

$$P_j(\boldsymbol{y} \mid \boldsymbol{\theta}_j) = \prod_{q=1}^{r} P_j^{(q)}(y_q \mid \boldsymbol{\theta}_j^{(q)}) \ \ (1 \leq j \leq k). \tag{7.31}$$

Moreover, the conditional probability $P_j^{(q)}(y_q \mid \boldsymbol{\theta}_j^{(q)})$ is viewed as the outcome of one multinomial try, i.e.,

$$P_j^{(q)}(y_q \mid \boldsymbol{\theta}_j^{(q)}) = \prod_{l=1}^{k^{(q)}} \vartheta_{qj}(l)^{\delta(y_q, l)}, \tag{7.32}$$

where $k^{(q)}$ is the number of clusters in the q-th base clustering and $\delta(\cdot, \cdot)$ represents the Kronecker delta function. The probabilities of the $k^{(q)}$ multinomial outcomes are defined as $\vartheta_{qj}(l)$ with $\sum_{l=1}^{k^{(q)}} \vartheta_{qj}(l) = 1$, and thus, $\boldsymbol{\theta}_j = \{\vartheta_{qj}(l) \mid 1 \leq q \leq r,\ 1 \leq l \leq k^{(q)}\}$.

Input: Data set $D = \{\boldsymbol{x}_1, \boldsymbol{x}_2, \ldots, \boldsymbol{x}_m\}$;
Base clusterings $\Lambda = \{\lambda^{(1)}, \lambda^{(2)}, \ldots, \lambda^{(r)}\}$ each with $k^{(q)}$ clusters;
Integer k.

Process:

1. **for** $i = 1, \ldots, m$:
2. **for** $q = 1, \ldots, r$:
3. $y_q^i = \lambda_i^{(q)}$;
4. **end**
5. $\varphi(\boldsymbol{x}_i) = (y_1^i, y_2^i, \ldots, y_r^i)^{\boldsymbol{T}}$; % Set the transformed r-tuple for $\boldsymbol{x}_i$
6. **end**
7. Initialize α_j $(1 \leq j \leq k)$ with $\alpha_j \geq 0$ and $\sum_{j=1}^k \alpha_j = 1$;
8. **for** $j = 1, \ldots, k$:
9. **for** $q = 1, \ldots, r$:
10. Initialize $\vartheta_{qj}(l)$ $(1 \leq l \leq k^{(q)})$ with $\vartheta_{qj}(l) \geq 0$ and $\sum_{l=1}^{k^{(q)}} \vartheta_{qj}(l) = 1$;
11. **end**
12. **end**
13. **repeat**
14. $\mathbb{E}[z_{ij}] = \frac{\alpha_j \prod_{q=1}^r \prod_{l=1}^{k^{(q)}} (\vartheta_{qj}(l))^{\delta(y_q^i, l)}}{\sum_{j=1}^k \alpha_j \prod_{q=1}^r \prod_{l=1}^{k^{(q)}} (\vartheta_{qj}(l))^{\delta(y_q^i, l)}}$; % E-step
15. $\alpha_j = \frac{\sum_{i=1}^m \mathbb{E}[z_{ij}]}{\sum_{i=1}^m \sum_{j=1}^k \mathbb{E}[z_{ij}]}$; $\vartheta_{qj}(l) = \frac{\sum_{i=1}^m \delta(y_q^i, l)\mathbb{E}[z_{ij}]}{\sum_{i=1}^m \sum_{l=1}^{k^{(q)}} \delta(y_q^i, l)\mathbb{E}[z_{ij}]}$; % M-step
16. **until** convergence;
17. $\lambda_i = \arg\max_{1 \leq j \leq k} \alpha_j P_j(\varphi(\boldsymbol{x}_i) \mid \boldsymbol{\theta}_j)$; % c.f.: (7.30)–(7.32)

Output: Clustering ensemble λ

Figure 7.7: The EM procedure for the transformation-based method [Topchy et al., 2004a] within probabilistic framework.

Based on the above assumptions, the optimal parameter $\boldsymbol{\Theta}^*$ is found by maximizing the log-likelihood function with regard to the m transformed r-tuples $\boldsymbol{Y} = \{\boldsymbol{y}_i \mid 1 \leq i \leq m\}$, i.e.,

$$\begin{aligned} \boldsymbol{\Theta}^* &= \arg\max_{\boldsymbol{\Theta}} \log L(\boldsymbol{Y} \mid \boldsymbol{\Theta}) = \arg\max_{\boldsymbol{\Theta}} \log \left(\prod_{i=1}^m P(\boldsymbol{y}_i \mid \boldsymbol{\Theta}) \right) \\ &= \arg\max_{\boldsymbol{\Theta}} \sum_{i=1}^m \log \left(\sum_{j=1}^k \alpha_j P_j(\boldsymbol{y}_i \mid \boldsymbol{\theta}_j) \right) . \end{aligned} \tag{7.33}$$

The EM algorithm is used to solve (7.33). To facilitate the EM procedure, the hidden variables $\mathbf{Z} = \{z_{ij} \mid 1 \leq i \leq m, \ 1 \leq j \leq k\}$ are introduced, where $z_{ij} = 1$ if $\boldsymbol{y}_i$ belongs to the j-th mixture component and 0 otherwise. Figure 7.7 illustrates the detailed EM procedure given in [Topchy et al., 2004a].

An advantage of transformation-based methods is that they are easy to implement, since the re-representation of the instances using the base clustering information is rather direct, and any off-the-shelf categorical clustering techniques can be applied to the transformed tuples to compute the final clustering ensemble.

A deficiency of these methods lies in the fact that when re-representing each instance into a categorical tuple, it is possible that the transformed data could not fully encode the information embodied in the original data representation. Therefore, it is by no means guaranteed that the clustering results obtained from the transformed data resemble exactly the desired clustering ensemble from the original base clusterings.

7.7 Further Readings

In the literature, a lot of clustering methods have been developed. In addition to k-means, well-known partitioning methods include k-medoids [Kaufman and Rousseeuw, 1990] whose cluster centers are exactly training instances, k-modes [Huang, 1998] for categorical data, CLARANS [Ng and Han, 1994] for large-scale data, etc. In addition to SAHN, well-known hierarchical clustering methods include AGNES [Kaufman and Rousseeuw, 1990] which can be regarded as a special case of SAHN, DIANA [Kaufman and Rousseeuw, 1990] which forms the hierarchy in a *top-down* manner, BIRCH [Zhang et al., 1996] which integrates hierarchical clustering with other clustering methods, ROCK [Guha et al., 1999] which was designed for categorical data, etc. In addition to DBSCAN, well-known density-based methods include OPTICS [Ankerst et al., 1999] which augments DBSCAN with an ordering of clusters, DENCLUE [Hinneburg and Keim, 1998] which utilizes density distribution functions, etc. In addition to STING, well-known grid-based methods include WaveCluster [Sheikholeslami et al., 1998] which exploits wavelet transformation, CLIQUE [Agrawal et al., 1998] which was designed for high-dimensional data, etc. In addition to GMM-based clustering, well-known model-based methods include SOM [Kohonen, 1989] which forms clusters by mapping from high-dimensional space into lower-dimensional (two-dimensional or three-dimensional) space with the neural network model of *self-organizing maps*, COBWEB [Fisher, 1987] which clusters categorical data incrementally, etc. There are so many clustering methods partially because users may have different motivations to cluster the same data, where there is no unique objective, and therefore, once a new criterion is given, a new clustering method can be proposed [Estivill-Castro, 2002].

In addition to the cluster quality indices introduced in Section 7.1.2, Jain and Dubes [1988] and Halkidi et al. [2001] also provide introduction to many other indices such as the external indices *adjusted Rand index*, *Huberts* Γ *statistic* and the internal indices *C index* and *Hartigan index*. In contrast to classification where *accuracy* has a clear meaning, in clustering there is no unique equivalent concept. Therefore, the study of the accuracy-diversity relation of clustering ensemble is rather difficult. Kuncheva and Hadjitodorov [2004], Kuncheva et al. [2006], Hadjitodorov et al. [2006], Hadjitodorov and Kuncheva [2007] presented attempts towards this direction.

Clustering ensemble methods have been applied to various tasks such as image segmentation [Zhang et al., 2008] and gene expression data analysis [Avogadri and Valentini, 2009, Hu et al., 2009, Yu and Wong, 2009]. There are also studies on clustering ensemble pruning [Fern and Lin, 2008, Hong et al., 2009], scalable clustering ensemble [Hore et al., 2006, 2009], multi-view clustering ensemble [Tao et al., 2020], deep clustering ensemble [Affeldt et al., 2020], soft clustering ensemble via discrete Wasserstein Barycenter [Qin et al., 2021], etc.

Topchy et al. [2004c] provided a theoretical justification for the usefulness of clustering ensemble under strong assumptions. Kuncheva and Vetrov [2006] studied the stability of clustering ensemble with k-means. Li et al. [2019] proposed a clustering ensemble algorithm based on sample stability. Berikov and Pestunov [2017] presented error bound and convergence properties for clustering ensemble based on weighted co-association matrices. Indeed, only a few works have been devoted to theoretical aspects of clustering ensemble, and many important theoretical issues are to be explored in the future.

Chapter 8

Anomaly Detection and Isolation Forest

8.1 Anomaly Detection

Anomalies are data points which do not conform to the general or expected behavior of the majority of data, and the task of anomaly detection is to separate anomaly points from normal ones in a given data set [Hodge and Austin, 2004, Chandola et al., 2009]. Generally, the terms *anomalies* and **outliers** are used interchangeably, and anomalies are also referred to as *discordant observations*, *exceptions*, *peculiarities* or *contaminants* in different domains. Anomaly detection finds extensive applications in a wide variety of domains such as fraud detection for credit cards, insurance or health care, intrusion detection for cyber-security, fault detection in safety-critical systems, etc.

At an abstract level, an anomaly is defined as a data point in a region that does not conform to expected normal behavior, and thus, a straightforward approach is to define a region that represents normal behaviors and declare any data point that does not belong to this region as an anomaly. However, this is not practical because it is often difficult to define a normal region which encompasses every possible normal data point, and the boundary between normal and anomalous points is often not very precise, particularly when data noise often tends to appear like anomalies. The task is even more challenging as the normal behavior often keeps evolving and a current notion of normal behavior might not be sufficiently representative in the future, and the anomalies often correspond to malicious behaviors, whereas some malicious adversaries often make them appear like normal. Furthermore, the concept of anomaly is quite different for different application domains, and therefore, it is not easy for anomaly detection to solve in the most general form. Existing techniques for this problem usually consider various factors such as the nature of data, availability of labeled data, types of malicious anomalies, and so on.

 DOI: 10.1201/9781003587774-8

There are various supervised and unsupervised approaches for anomaly detection. Supervised approaches require a set of data points labeled as normal or anomalous, on which a classifier can be trained to distinguish normal and anomalous data points, e.g., one-class SVM [Schölkopf and Smola, 2002]. Such approaches could achieve nice performance when there are sufficient amounts of data points labeled accurately as normal or anomalous. In addition to such a discriminative model, it is also possible to fit a generative model based on normal data, and then data points with low probability generated from the model can be declared as anomalies [Eskin, 2000, Yeung and Chow, 2002]. Such approaches can perform well if the generative model assumption fits the true normal data distribution.

In more situations, it is difficult to collect a sufficient amount of labeled data points, particularly hard for some important but rare anomalous ones. In such cases, unsupervised anomaly detection has been at the core of anomaly detection research. Unsupervised anomaly detection approaches are generally based on the concepts of **distance** or **density**. Specifically, normal data points are believed to occur in dense neighbors far from anomalies, where the anomaly score can be derived from *distance* [Ramaswamy et al., 2000, Eskin et al., 2002, Otey et al., 2006], or *density* [Breunig et al., 2000, Tang et al., 2002, Hautamaki et al., 2004]. The calculation can be realized in ways of nearest-neighbor or clustering [Ester et al., 1996, Yu et al., 2002]. However, the unsolved problems include how to define an adequate distance and how to detect relatively dense anomalous data points. The **isolation** concept presented in Section 8.4 offers a new perspective on anomaly detection, leading to many effective and efficient unsupervised anomaly detection approaches.

Though ensemble methods have been studied for decades, there were only a few studies about ensemble methods for unsupervised anomaly detection. Zimek et al. [2014] attributed this phenomenon to three factors: First, it is not clear for performance evaluation for anomaly detection; second, it is unknown how to use the measure of ensemble diversity in anomaly detection; and third, new combination mechanisms are needed for combining anomaly detection results, e.g., anomalous rankings of data points.

During the past decade, many ensemble methods have been developed for unsupervised anomaly detection [Zimek et al., 2014, Aggarwal and Sathe, 2017]. In what follows, we will introduce ensemble methods for unsupervised anomaly detection, with an emphasis on **isolation forest** [Liu et al., 2008b, 2012], which has been widely used in various domains.

8.2 Sequential Ensemble Methods

This category of ensemble methods works by applying base anomaly detectors to the whole or portions of the data set in a sequential manner. Representative methods include OUTRES, HiCS and CARE.

OUTRES [Müller et al., 2011]: This method measures the anomaly score of a data point by recursively identifying its set of relevant subspaces based on tailored statistical analyses, and then aggregates its degree of anomaly in each identified subspace. Given the d-dimensional feature space $\mathcal{X} = \mathcal{F}_1 \times \mathcal{F}_2, \cdots \times \mathcal{F}_d$ and a set of unlabeled data points $D = \{\boldsymbol{x}_1, \boldsymbol{x}_2, \ldots, \boldsymbol{x}_m\}$ in $\mathcal{X}$, OUTRES measures the anomaly score $s(\boldsymbol{x}_i)$ for each data point $\boldsymbol{x}_i \in D$ based on a set of relevant subspaces $RS(\boldsymbol{x}_i)$ identified for $\boldsymbol{x}_i$. The choice of relevant subspace S depends on whether there is a *high contrast* between $\boldsymbol{x}_i$ and its neighboring data points. Specifically, let $\mathcal{N}(\boldsymbol{x}_i, S)$ denote the adaptive neighborhood of $\boldsymbol{x}_i$ with ε_S-distance to $\boldsymbol{x}_i$ in subspace S:

$$\mathcal{N}(\boldsymbol{x}_i, S) = \{\boldsymbol{z} \mid \mathrm{dist}_S(\boldsymbol{x}_i, \boldsymbol{z}) \leq \varepsilon_S,\ \boldsymbol{z} \in D\} . \tag{8.1}$$

Here, $\mathrm{dist}_S(\cdot,\cdot)$ calculates the distance between two data points within the subspace S. Furthermore, the neighborhood threshold ε_S is chosen in an adaptive manner so as to account for the dimensionality of subspace S [Silverman, 1986, Müller et al., 2011]:

$$\varepsilon_S = \varepsilon \cdot \frac{h_{opt}(|S|)}{h_{opt}(2)} , \tag{8.2}$$

where ε is the initial neighborhood threshold specified for 2-dimensional feature space, and based on the gamma function $\Gamma(\cdot)$, function $h_{opt}(\cdot)$ is given by

$$h_{opt}(r) = \left(\frac{8 \cdot \Gamma(\frac{r}{2}+1)}{\pi^{\frac{r}{2}}} \cdot (r+4) \cdot (2\sqrt{\pi})^r\right) \cdot m^{\frac{-1}{r+4}} . \tag{8.3}$$

To determine whether the subspace S is relevant for anomaly score measurement, the null hypothesis H_0 that the neighborhood size is uniformly distributed according to a *Binomial* distribution is taken, i.e.,

$$|\mathcal{N}(\boldsymbol{x}_i, S)| \sim \mathcal{B}(m, vol(\mathcal{N}(\boldsymbol{x}_i, S))) , \tag{8.4}$$

where m is the number of data points in D and $vol(\mathcal{N}(\boldsymbol{x}_i, S))$ is the volume of the neighborhood with each feature being normalized into $[0,1]$ [Silverman, 1986, Müller et al., 2011]. Then, the subspace S is regarded to be relevant if H_0 is rejected at a 0.01 significance level based on the Kolmogorov-Smirnov goodness-of-fit test for uniform distribution [Stephens, 1970], i.e.,

$$RS(\boldsymbol{x}_i) = \{S \in \mathcal{P}(\{\mathcal{F}_1, \mathcal{F}_2, \ldots, \mathcal{F}_d\}) \mid H_0 \text{ is rejected w.r.t. } S,\ |S| \geq 2\} , \tag{8.5}$$

where $\mathcal{P}(\cdot)$ corresponds to the powerset operator.

Accordingly, the anomaly score $s(\boldsymbol{x}_i)$ is measured by aggregating its degree of anomaly in each relevant subspace, that is,

$$s(\boldsymbol{x}_i) = \prod_{S \in RS(\boldsymbol{x}_i)} o(\boldsymbol{x}_i, S) . \tag{8.6}$$

Conceptually, the degree of anomaly $o(\boldsymbol{x}_i, S)$ depends on the local density $den(\boldsymbol{x}_i, S)$ of $\boldsymbol{x}_i$ w.r.t. S. In OUTRES, the local density is calculated by employing the Epanechnikov kernel [Silverman, 1986] to instantiate the Parzen window density function

$$den(\boldsymbol{x}_i, S) = \frac{1}{m} \sum_{\boldsymbol{z} \in \mathcal{N}(\boldsymbol{x}_i, S)} K_e \left(\frac{\text{dist}_S(\boldsymbol{x}_i, \boldsymbol{z})}{\varepsilon_S} \right) , \tag{8.7}$$

where

$$K_e(t) = 1 - t^2, \ \ t < 1 . \tag{8.8}$$

Accordingly, let μ and σ denote the mean and standard deviation of $den(\boldsymbol{z}, S)$ over all neighboring data points $\boldsymbol{z} \in \mathcal{N}(\boldsymbol{x}_i, S)$. Then, the degree of anomaly $o(\boldsymbol{x}_i, S)$ is calculated as

$$o(\boldsymbol{x}_i, S) = \begin{cases} \frac{den(\boldsymbol{x}_i, S)}{dev(\boldsymbol{x}_i, S)}, & \text{if } dev(\boldsymbol{x}_i, S) \geq 1 \\ 1, & \text{otherwise} , \end{cases} \tag{8.9}$$

where

$$dev(\boldsymbol{x}_i, S) = \frac{\mu - den(\boldsymbol{x}_i, S)}{2\sigma} . \tag{8.10}$$

The OUTRES algorithm is summarized in Figure 8.1.

HiCS [Keller et al., 2012]: This method measures the anomaly score of a data point by exploiting subspaces with high contrast and then averages the degree of anomaly computed in each high contrast subspace with density-based anomaly detection techniques. It is assumed that anomalies are usually hidden in multiple high contrast subspaces, where the contrast score of subspace is measured by considering the conditional dependence among the subspace features.

Without loss of generality, let $S \in \mathcal{P}(\{\mathcal{F}_1, \mathcal{F}_2, \ldots, \mathcal{F}_d\})$ be a feature subspace with s features $\mathcal{F}_{a_1}, \mathcal{F}_{a_2}, \ldots, \mathcal{F}_{a_s}$ $(s \leq d)$. For the feature $\mathcal{F}_{a_j} \in S$ $(1 \leq j \leq s)$ in the subspace, HiCS computes the contrast score of subspace by considering the discrepancy between the marginal probability distribution $p(\mathcal{F}_{a_j})$ and the conditional probability distribution $p(\mathcal{F}_{a_j} \mid S_{a_j}^{\perp})$, where $S_{a_j}^{\perp}$ represents all features in S except $\mathcal{F}_{a_j}$. As the ground-truth information on the probability distributions is generally unknown, the discrepancy computation between $p(\mathcal{F}_{a_j})$ and $p(\mathcal{F}_{a_j} \mid S_{a_j}^{\perp})$ is instantiated by performing statistical tests over two samples of one-dimensional data w.r.t. the considered probability distributions, i.e.,

$$A_{a_j} = \{x_{ia_j} \mid \boldsymbol{x}_i = [x_{i1}, x_{i2}, \ldots, x_{id}]^{\boldsymbol{T}} \in D\} , \tag{8.11}$$

$$A_{a_j}^{\perp} = \{x_{ia_j} \mid \boldsymbol{x}_i \in D, \ \forall \mathcal{F}_{a_k} \in S_{a_j}^{\perp} : x_{ia_k} \in [l_{a_k}, u_{a_k}]\} . \tag{8.12}$$

Let $\mathcal{I}_{a_j} = \prod_{\mathcal{F}_{a_k} \in S_{a_j}^{\perp}} [l_{a_k}, u_{a_k}]$ denote the $(s-1)$-dimensional axis-parallel *subspace slice* with each edge in $\mathcal{F}_{a_k}$ defined by an interval $[l_{a_k}, u_{a_k}]$. Let $\alpha \in (0, 1)$ be the pre-specified parameter, which controls the expected fraction

---

Input: Unlabeled data set $D = \{\boldsymbol{x}_1, \boldsymbol{x}_2, \ldots, \boldsymbol{x}_m\}$;
Initial neighborhood threshold ε.

Process:
1. **for** $i = 1, \ldots, m$:
2. $s(\boldsymbol{x}_i) = 1$;
3. **for** $j = 1, \ldots, d$:
4. $S = \{\mathcal{F}_j\}$; % initialize S with the j-th feature
5. $s(\boldsymbol{x}_i) =$ **OUTRES_RECUR**$(\boldsymbol{x}_i, D, S, s(\boldsymbol{x}_i))$;
% recursively update $s(\boldsymbol{x}_i)$ w.r.t. identified relevant subspaces
6. **end**
7. **end**

Output: Anomaly score $s(\boldsymbol{x}_i)$ $(1 \leq i \leq m)$

OUTRES_RECUR$(\boldsymbol{x}_i, D, S, s(\boldsymbol{x}_i))$
1. $s = s(\boldsymbol{x}_i)$;
2. **for** each $\mathcal{F}_j \in \{\mathcal{F}_1, \mathcal{F}_2, \ldots, \mathcal{F}_d\} \setminus S$:
3. $S = S \bigcup \{\mathcal{F}_j\}$;
4. **if** S is relevant % refer to (8.5)
5. **then** Calculate the degree of anomaly $o(\boldsymbol{x}_i, S)$ according to(8.9);
6. $s = s \cdot o(\boldsymbol{x}_i, S)$;
7. $s =$ **OUTRES_RECUR**$(\boldsymbol{x}_i, D, S, s)$;
8. **end**
9. **return** s

Figure 8.1: The OUTRES algorithm.

of remaining data points after slicing D along each dimension of S. Conceptually, any interval in $\mathcal{F}_{a_j}$ with $m\sqrt[s]{\alpha}$ data points in D can be used to instantiate $[l_{a_j}, u_{a_j}]$. The discrepancy between $p(\mathcal{F}_{a_j})$ and $p(\mathcal{F}_{a_j} \mid S_{a_j}^{\perp})$, namely $\text{dis}_{\mathcal{I}_{a_j}}(p(\mathcal{F}_{a_j}), p(\mathcal{F}_{a_j} \mid S_{a_j}^{\perp}))$, is computed by performing statistical tests over two samples A_{a_j} and $A_{a_j}^{\perp}$ based on the Welch's t-test [Silverman, 1986] or the Kolmogorov-Smirnov test [Stephens, 1970]. For Welch's t-test, the two-tailed p-value, w.r.t. the resulting t-distribution derived from sample means and variances, is used to yield the discrepancy. For Kolmogorov-Smirnov test, the maximal difference between two empirical cumulated distributions derived from both samples is used to yield the discrepancy. Accordingly, HiCS computes the contrast score of subspace by invoking the discrepancy computation for a number of times as

$$C(S) = \frac{1}{M} \sum_{a_j \in \psi_M} \text{dis}_{\mathcal{I}_{a_j}}(p(\mathcal{F}_{a_j}), p(\mathcal{F}_{a_j} \mid S_{a_j}^{\perp})) \ , \tag{8.13}$$

where the index multiset ψ_M is given by randomly sampling from $\{a_1, a_2, \ldots, a_s\}$ with replacement for M times.

Based on the contrast score measurement, the subspace generation process of HiCS works in a sequential expansion manner. In each iteration, all eligible

s-dimensional subspaces are generated and sorted in descending order w.r.t. their contrast scores. Then, a maximum of T subspaces with top contrast scores are retained and then generate $(s+1)$-dimensional subspaces in the next iteration. A $(s+1)$-dimensional subspace is eligible if it contains one of the s-dimensional subspaces retained in the previous iteration. As the subspace generation process terminates, a pruning step is further taken to remove any generated s-dimensional subspace S, whose contrast score is lower than its $(s+1)$-dimensional encompassing subspace, leading to a **selective ensemble**. Note that an anomaly detector is built in each of the remaining subspace by invoking a base anomaly detection algorithm $\mathcal{A}(D, S)$, e.g., LOF [Breunig et al., 2000], and the final anomaly score $s(\boldsymbol{x}_i)$ is obtained by aggregation as

$$s(\boldsymbol{x}_i) = \frac{1}{|RS|} \sum_{S \in RS} s_S(\boldsymbol{x}_i) \ , \tag{8.14}$$

where RS denotes the set of the remained high contrast subspaces. The HiCS algorithm is summarized in Figure 8.2.

CARE [Rayana et al., 2016]: This method performs unsupervised anomaly detection from the perspective of bias-variance reduction, where weighted aggregation is employed over feature-bagged base anomaly detectors in each iteration to reduce variance, and a cumulative sampling strategy is employed across the results of previous iterations to reduce bias.

Specifically, CARE follows a sequential ensemble generation procedure to measure the anomaly score $s(\boldsymbol{x}_i)$ for each data point. In the ℓ-th iteration, a set of B base anomaly detectors $\{h_b,\ 1 \leq b \leq B\}$ are created by invoking the given kNN-based anomaly detection algorithm $\mathcal{A}(D, N_\ell, S_b, k)$, such as AvgKNN [Rayana et al., 2016] or LOF [Breunig et al., 2000]. Here, $N_\ell \subseteq D$ is a subsample of normal data points ($N_1 = D$) to calculate the degree of anomaly $h_b(\boldsymbol{x}_i)$, which is measured by considering $\boldsymbol{x}_i$'s k nearest neighbors identified in N_ℓ. Furthermore, the distance between two data points is computed within a feature subspace $S_b \in \mathcal{P}(\{\mathcal{F}_1, \mathcal{F}_2, \ldots, \mathcal{F}_d\})$ generated from a bootstrap sampling process over the whole feature space.

For each base anomaly detector h_b, the Cantelli's inequality [Grimmett and Stirzaker, 2020] is utilized to estimate a cutoff threshold $-th_b$ which separates each data point $\boldsymbol{x}_i$ in D into either an inlier ($h_b(\boldsymbol{x}_i) < th_b$) or an outlier ($h_b(\boldsymbol{x}_i) \geq th_b$). Then, let U be the union of outliers across all base anomaly detectors, and an unsupervised agreement rate is estimated for each pair of base anomaly detectors h_a and h_b [Platanios et al., 2014] as

$$r_{ab} = \frac{1}{|U|} \sum_{\boldsymbol{x} \in U} \mathbb{I}\left((h_a(\boldsymbol{x}) - th_a)(h_b(\boldsymbol{x}) - th_b) > 0\right) \ . \tag{8.15}$$

Then, the error rate e_b (or, e_{ab}) is estimated for an individual base anomaly detector (or, a pair of base anomaly detectors), by solving the following constrained optimization problem [Platanios et al., 2014]:

Input: Unlabeled data set $D = \{\boldsymbol{x}_1, \boldsymbol{x}_2, \ldots, \boldsymbol{x}_m\}$;
Number of sampling rounds M for computing contrast score;
Expected fraction of remaining data points α after subspace slicing;
Number of maximally retained subspaces T in each iteration;
Anomaly detection algorithm $\mathcal{A}$.

Process:
1. $RS = \emptyset$;
2. Initialize $ES = \{S \mid S \in \mathcal{P}(\{\mathcal{F}_1, \mathcal{F}_2, \ldots, \mathcal{F}_d\}),\ |S| = 2\}$, i.e., the set of eligible 2-dimensional subspaces;
3. **for** $s = 2, \ldots, d$:
4. **for** every $S \in ES$
5. Initialize the index multiset $\psi_M = \emptyset$;
6. **for** $j = 1, \ldots, M$:
7. Randomly select one feature a_j from the subspace S;
8. $\psi_M = \psi_M \bigcup \{a_j\}$;
9. Construct the $(s-1)$-dimensional axis-parallel subspace slice $\mathcal{I}_{a_j}$ by randomly choosing an interval in each $\mathcal{F}_{a_k} \in S_{a_j}^{\perp}$ with $m \cdot \sqrt[s]{\alpha}$ data points in D to instantiate $[l_{a_k}, u_{a_k}]$;
10. **end**
11. Compute the contrast score $C(S)$ according to (8.13) by using the Welch's t-test or Kolmogorov-Smirnov test;
12. **end**
13. Update ES by retaining $\min(|ES|, T)$ subspaces with top $C(S)$ scores;
14. $RS = RS \bigcup ES$, $\widehat{ES} \leftarrow ES$;
15. **if** $(\widehat{ES} = \emptyset) \vee (s = d)$ **then break**;
17. $ES = \{S \mid S \in \mathcal{P}(\{\mathcal{F}_1, \mathcal{F}_2, \ldots, \mathcal{F}_d\}), |S| = s+1, \exists \widehat{S} \in \widehat{ES} : \widehat{S} \subset S\}$;
18. **end**
19. Prune RS by removing every $S \in RS$, whose contrast score is lower than its $(|S|+1)$-dimensional encompassing subspace;
20. **for** each $S \in RS$
21. Compute the anomaly score $s_S(\boldsymbol{x}_i)$ w.r.t. S for each data point $\boldsymbol{x}_i$ by invoking $\mathcal{A}(D, S)$;
22. **end**
23. Obtain the anomaly score $s(\boldsymbol{x}_i)$ according to (8.14);

Output: Anomaly score $s(\boldsymbol{x}_i)$ $(1 \leq i \leq m)$

Figure 8.2: The HiCS algorithm.

$$\begin{aligned}
\min_{\{e_b, e_{ab}, \xi_b, \xi_{ab} \mid 1 \leq a < b \leq B\}} \quad & \sum_{1 \leq b \leq B} (e_b^2 + \xi_b) + \sum_{1 \leq a < b \leq B} (e_{ab}^2 + \xi_{ab}) \\
\text{s.t.} \quad & r_{ab} = 1 - e_a - e_b + 2e_{ab} \ (1 \leq a < b \leq B) \\
& 0 \leq e_b \leq 0.5 + \xi_b, \ 0 \leq \xi_b \ (1 \leq b \leq B) \\
& 0 \leq e_{ab} \leq 0.5 + \xi_{ab}, \ 0 \leq \xi_{ab} \ (1 \leq a < b \leq B) \, .
\end{aligned} \tag{8.16}$$

To make the outputs from base anomaly detectors comparable to each other, the **Gaussian scaling** [Kriegel et al., 2011] is used to convert the degree of anomaly $h_b(\boldsymbol{x}_i)$ into probability estimate $P_b^i \in [0, 1]$. Then, the anomaly score $s_\ell(\boldsymbol{x}_i)$, yielded in the ℓ-th iteration, is measured by weighted aggregation across all base anomaly detectors according to

$$s_\ell(\boldsymbol{x}_i) = \frac{\sum_{b=1}^{B} w_b \cdot \mathbb{I}(e_b < 0.5) \cdot P_b^i}{\sum_{b=1}^{B} w_b \cdot \mathbb{I}(e_b < 0.5)} \quad (1 \le i \le m) \ , \tag{8.17}$$

where

$$w_b = \frac{1}{2} \cdot \log\left(\frac{2}{e_b} - 1\right) \quad (1 \le b \le B). \tag{8.18}$$

For the next iteration, the subsample N_ℓ will be updated to $N_{\ell+1}$ by applying FVPS (Filtered Variable Probability Sampling) [Rayana et al., 2016] over the cumulative average anomaly score $\bar{s}_\ell(\boldsymbol{x}_i) = \frac{1}{\ell}\sum_{l=1}^{\ell} s_l(\boldsymbol{x}_i)$. Specifically, by applying the Cantelli's inequality [Grimmett and Stirzaker, 2020] based on $\bar{s}_\ell(\boldsymbol{x}_i)$, data points in D identified as anomalies will be discarded so as to generate the filtered data set D'. Then, a sampling ratio $\gamma \in [0, 1]$ is randomly selected from the uniform distribution between $\min\left(1, \frac{50}{m}\right)$ and $\min\left(1, \frac{1000}{m}\right)$. Accordingly, $N_{\ell+1}$ is updated by sub-sampling $\lfloor \gamma \cdot |D'| \rfloor$ data points from D' based on the probability of $\boldsymbol{x}_i$ being normal, i.e., $1 - \bar{s}_\ell(\boldsymbol{x}_i)$.

Thereafter, CARE proceeds to the next iteration and the sequential ensemble generation procedure terminates when the pre-specified stopping criterion or the maximum number of iterations is reached. The cumulative average anomaly score $\bar{s}_L(\boldsymbol{x}_i)$ at the terminating iteration L is returned as the final anomaly score $s(\boldsymbol{x}_i)$ for each data point.

8.3 Parallel Ensemble Methods

This category of ensemble methods works by applying base anomaly detectors to full or portions of the data set in a parallel manner. Representative methods include Itemsets Bootstrap, Feature Bagging, and SELECT.

Itemsets Bootstrap [Barbará et al., 2003]: This method was originally designed for intrusion detection where the instances are described by discrete-valued features, and it can be regarded as a parallel ensemble method for unsupervised anomaly detection. It involves a two-phase procedure. In the first phase, normal data points are identified by partitioning the data set into parallel subsets with the help of **association rule** techniques in data mining [Agrawal et al., 1993, Han et al., 2022]. In the second phase, anomaly scores are obtained based on clustering analysis over the identified normal data points.

Specifically, this method deals with data points $\boldsymbol{x}_i = [x_{i1}, x_{i2}, \ldots, x_{id}]^T$ in discrete-valued feature space, where the j-th feature x_{ij} takes value in $E_j = \{e_j^1, e_j^2, \ldots, e_j^{l_j}\}$ with l_j number of possible elements. From the view of association rule mining, every possible feature value e_j^k $(1 \leq k \leq l_j)$ in E_j can be viewed as an *item*, and hence a data point $\boldsymbol{x}_i$ can be viewed as an **itemset** of d items.

In the first phase, the set of unlabeled data points D is partitioned into T non-overlapping subsets $\{D_1, D_2, \ldots, D_T\}$ in parallel, where $\bigcup_{t=1}^{T} D_t = D$ and $D_s \bigcap D_t = \emptyset$ $(\forall s \neq t)$. The partition can be performed in various ways such as time frames [Barbará et al., 2003]. Let $G_t = \{IS \mid IS \text{ is a frequent itemset in } D_t\}$ denote the set of **frequent itemsets** mined from D_t by invoking a given association rule mining algorithm. In other words, based on the support threshold *supp* of the association rule mining algorithm, IS $(|IS| \leq d)$ is a specific combination of feature values that occur in at least *supp*% data points in D_t. Then, the method proceeds to filter the set of itemsets presented in at least k $(k \geq 2)$ sets out of $G_1, G_2, \ldots, G_T$ as

$$E_t^k = \{IS \mid IS \in G_t, c_{IS} \geq k\} \text{ with } c_{IS} = |\{t \mid IS \in G_t,\ 1 \leq t \leq T\}| \ . \tag{8.19}$$

Thereafter, the set of presumed normal data points $\widetilde{D}_t$ are identified by mapping back the frequent itemsets in E_t^k to D_t as

$$\widetilde{D}_t = \{\boldsymbol{x}_i \mid \boldsymbol{x}_i \in D_t,\ \exists IS \in E_t^k : IS \subseteq \boldsymbol{x}_i\} \ . \tag{8.20}$$

In the second phase, a clustering is performed on the presumed normal data points $\bigcup_{t=1}^{T} \widetilde{D}_t$ by invoking a categorical clustering algorithm such as COOLCAT [Barbará et al., 2002, 2003]. Then, the anomaly score of each of the remaining point $\boldsymbol{x}_i \in D \setminus \bigcup_{t=1}^{T} \widetilde{D}_t$ can be measured w.r.t. clusters [Barbará et al., 2003].

Feature Bagging [Lazarevic and Kumar, 2005]: This method measures the anomaly score of a data point by invoking a sampling procedure over feature space, and then combines the detection results yielded by each base anomaly detector built on randomly selected feature subset. The size of the feature subset in the t-th feature sampling round, i.e., n_t $(1 \leq t \leq T)$, is randomly chosen between $\lfloor d/2 \rfloor$ and $d - 1$. A feature subset S_t is then created by randomly selecting n_t features from $\mathcal{X}$ without replacement, based on which a base anomaly detector f_t is built by invoking given anomaly detection algorithm $\mathcal{A}(D, S_t)$, such as LOF [Breunig et al., 2000, Lazarevic and Kumar, 2005]. It can be seen that the procedure does not invoke bootstrap sampling of data, which is the core of Bagging (see Chapter 3); instead, it is based on random sampling of feature subsets, actually more relevant to RS (see Section 3.5.2).

Based on the assumption that the degrees of anomalous $f_t(\boldsymbol{x}_i)$'s returned by different anomaly detectors can be comparable to each other, the final anomaly score $s(\boldsymbol{x}_i)$ can be obtained by combining the results of f_t $(1 \leq t \leq T)$ by *Breadth-First Scheme* (BFS) or Sum. For BFS, the anomaly detectors are traversed in turn w.r.t. descending order of their sorted degree of anomaly. For Sum, the degree of anomaly of each anomaly detector is summed up to yield the final anomaly score. The Feature Bagging algorithm is summarized in Figure 8.3.

Input: Unlabeled data set $D = \{\boldsymbol{x}_1, \boldsymbol{x}_2, \ldots, \boldsymbol{x}_m\}$;
Number of feature-bagged base detectors T;
Anomaly detection algorithm $\mathcal{A}$;
The mode α for combining outlier detectors ($\alpha = 1$: BFS; $\alpha = 2$: Sum).

Process:
1. **for** $t = 1, \ldots, T$:
2. Randomly choose the size n_t of feature subset between $\lfloor d/2 \rfloor$ and $d - 1$;
3. Construct a feature subset S_t by randomly selecting n_t features from $\mathcal{X}$ without replacement;
4. Build outlier detector f_t by invoking $\mathcal{A}(D, S_t)$;
5. **end**
6. **if** $\alpha = 1$
7. **then** $Z = \emptyset$;
8. **for** $i = 1, \ldots, m$:
9. **for** $t = 1, \ldots, T$:
10. Let $\boldsymbol{z}_{it}$ be the data point in D with i-th largest degree of anomalous as ranked by f_t;
11. **if** $\boldsymbol{z}_{it} \notin Z$
12. **then** $s(\boldsymbol{z}_{it}) = f_t(\boldsymbol{z}_{it})$ and $Z = Z \bigcup \{\boldsymbol{z}_{it}\}$;
13. **end**
14. **end**
15. **else** **for** $i = 1, \ldots, m$:
16. $s(\boldsymbol{x}_i) = \sum_{t=1}^{T} f_t(\boldsymbol{x}_i)$
17. **end**

Output: Anomaly score $s(\boldsymbol{x}_i)$ for $i = 1, \ldots, m$

Figure 8.3: The Feature Bagging algorithm.

SELECT [Rayana and Akoglu, 2016]: This method employs a two-phase meta-strategy, which selectively combines the results of base anomaly detectors as well as different aggregation alternatives for better and robust performance, exhibiting the power of **selective ensemble** [Zhou et al., 2002c] in anomaly detection. In its first phase, SELECT constructs a selective ensemble of base anomaly detectors by invoking a number of heterogenous anomaly detection algorithms. In the second phase, different aggregated anomaly detectors are generated from the selected base anomaly detectors, where a selective ensemble of aggregated anomaly detectors is further constructed to yield the final anomaly score for each data point. By treating either the base anomaly detector or the aggregated anomaly detector as constituent components, SELECT proposes to apply the *vertical* or *horizontal* selection strategy to construct the selective ensemble [Rayana and Akoglu, 2016].

Without loss of generality, let $\{h_1, h_2, \ldots, h_T\}$ be the set of T components for a selective ensemble with $h_t(\boldsymbol{x}_i)$ being the anomaly score returned by h_t. For the vertical selection strategy, the basic idea is to progressively add constituent component into the selective ensemble by maximizing weighted Pearson correlation with the pseudo target of averaged Unification probability score [Kriegel et al., 2011] over h_t $(1 \leq t \leq T)$. For the horizontal selection strategy, the basic idea is to statistically filter out constituent component from the selective ensemble by thresholding $h_t(\boldsymbol{x}_i)$ with Mixture Modeling probability score [Gao and Tan, 2006] to identify pseudo anomalies, on which the constituent component has insufficient detection performance. After the selective ensemble phases for both base anomaly detectors and aggregated anomaly detectors, the final anomaly score $s(\boldsymbol{x}_i)$ for each data point is obtained by combining the results of the selected aggregated anomaly detectors using inverse rank aggregation.

8.4 Isolation Forest

Most unsupervised anomaly detection approaches are based on **density** or **distance** assumptions explicitly or implicitly. The former assumes that "*normal points occur in dense regions, while anomalies occur in sparse regions*", whereas the latter assumes that "*normal point is close to its neighbors and anomaly is far away from its neighbors*" [Chandola et al., 2009]. However, high density and short distance do not always imply normal instances, likewise low density and long distance do not always imply anomalies.

Liu et al. [2008b, 2012] claimed that anomalies are born with two essential properties simultaneously, i.e., (1) the minority consisting of few instances, and (2) different attribute values from those of normal distances. In other words, anomalies are "*few and different*", which makes them more susceptible to a mechanism called **isolation**.

The term *isolation* means "separating a data point from the rest of the data points". In general, isolation-based methods measure individual data point's susceptibility to be isolated, and anomalies are those that have the highest susceptibility. Isolation can be implemented by any means that separates instances. Liu et al. [2008b, 2012] proposed to exploit a kind of **completely-random tree**, called **isolation tree** (iTree) . It recursively partitions the instance space, where anomalies are generally located with notable shorter paths because they are more likely to be isolated early in the partitioning process. Then, when a forest of trees collectively produces shorter path lengths for some particular data points, those points are highly likely to be anomalies. Figure 8.4 illustrates the idea of anomaly detection via completely random trees. It can be observed that a normal data point $\boldsymbol{x}$ generally requires more partitions to be isolated, while an anomaly data point $\boldsymbol{x}^*$ is much easier to be isolated with many fewer partitions.

Liu et al. [2008b, 2012] described the iForest (Isolation Forest) method for anomaly detection. In the *training stage*, isolation trees are constructed by recursively partitioning a subsample $D' \subset D$ of the full unlabeled data set with subsampling size ψ. Specifically, an isolation tree is a *proper binary tree* where each node in the tree is either an *internal* node with two child nodes or

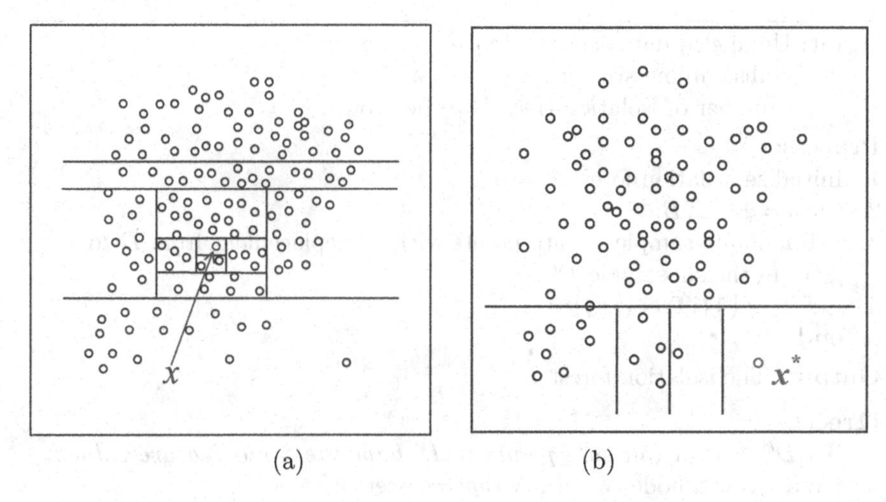

Figure 8.4: Illustration of anomaly detection by completely random trees: (a) a normal point $\boldsymbol{x}$ requires eleven random tree partitions to be isolated and (b) an anomaly point $\boldsymbol{x}^*$ requires only four random tree partitions to be isolated.

an *external* node without child nodes. A partition test at a node N consists of a randomly selected feature $\mathcal{F}$ and a randomly selected split value a between the minimum and maximum values of $\mathcal{F}$ at N, which determines the traversal of a data point to either the left child $N.l$ or the right child $N.r$. The recursive partition procedure terminates until only one data point resides in the node or all data points in the node have the same feature values. The training stage of iForest is summarized in Figure 8.5.

For the subsampling size ψ, the anomaly detection performance of iForest is found to become stable when ψ increases to a desired value. In this case, there is no need to further increase the value of ψ, which will not bring any gain in anomaly detection performance while unnecessarily leading to higher time and space consumption. It is assumed that anomalies are "few and different", and accordingly normal data points are assumed to be "many and similar". Therefore, a small subsampling size will suffice for iForest to isolate anomalies from normal data points. Empirically, setting $\psi = 256$ (2^8) generally yields satisfactory performance across a wide range of anomaly detection tasks for iForest. For the number of isolation trees B, the resulting anomaly score usually converges well before $B = 100$, which is thus used as the default value for iForest. After completing the training stage, an ensemble of isolation trees is generated and ready for anomaly score evaluation. As shown in Figure 8.5, the worst-case time and space complexity correspond to $O(B\psi^2)$ and $O(B\psi)$, respectively, in the training stage of iForest.

In the *evaluation stage*, each data point $\boldsymbol{x}_i$ is passed through isolation trees to obtain the anomaly score. For each isolation tree, the number of partitions, required to isolate a data point, can be measured by the path length $h(\boldsymbol{x}_i)$

Input: Unlabeled data set $D = \{\boldsymbol{x}_1, \boldsymbol{x}_2, \ldots, \boldsymbol{x}_m\}$;
Subsampling size ψ;
Number of isolation trees B to be grown.

Process:
1. Initialize isolation forest $F = \emptyset$;
2. **for** $b = 1, \ldots, B$:
3. Randomly sample ψ data points without replacement from D to form the subsample D';
4. $F = F \bigcup \{\textbf{iTree}(D')\}$;
5. **end**

Output: The isolation forest F

iTree(D')
1. **if** $(|D'| = 1)$ or (*all data points in* D' *have the same feature values*)
2. **then** Grow a node N with $N.type =$ external;
3. $N.size = |D'|$;
4. **else** Randomly select a feature $\mathcal{F}_j$ from the feature set $\{\mathcal{F}_1, \mathcal{F}_2, \ldots, \mathcal{F}_d\}$;
5. Randomly select a split value $a \in (\min_{\boldsymbol{x}_i \in D'} x_{ij}, \max_{\boldsymbol{x}_i \in D'} x_{ij})$;
6. $D'_l = \{\boldsymbol{x}_i \mid \boldsymbol{x}_i \in D',\ x_{ij} < a\}$;
7. $D'_r = \{\boldsymbol{x}_i \mid \boldsymbol{x}_i \in D',\ x_{ij} \geq a\}$;
8. Grow a node N with $N.type =$ internal;
9. $N.size = |D'|$;
10. $N.splitFeature = \mathcal{F}_j$;
11. $N.splitValue = a$;
12. $N.leftNode = \textbf{iTree}(D'_l)$;
13. $N.rightNode = \textbf{iTree}(D'_r)$;
14. **return** N

Figure 8.5: The training stage of iForest.

from the root node to the external node containing the data point. The fewer the required partitions, the easier the data point to be isolated. It is obvious that only the data points with short path lengths are of interest. Thus, to reduce unnecessary computation, the isolation trees in iForest are set with a height limit *hlim*, that is, a limit on the tree depth. Given the subsampling size ψ, the height limit of iForest can be set as $\lceil \log_2(\psi) \rceil$ or $\psi - 1$, which is approximately the average tree height [Knuth, 1997] or the maximum tree height, respectively.

To calculate the anomaly score $s(\boldsymbol{x}_i)$ of instance $\boldsymbol{x}_i$, the expected path length $\mathbb{E}[h(\boldsymbol{x}_i)]$ is derived by passing $\boldsymbol{x}_i$ through every isolation tree in the ensemble. The path length at each isolation tree is divided by an adjustment term $c(\psi)$ to account for the ungrown branch beyond the tree height limit. Given a subsample of ψ data points, $c(\psi)$ is set as the average path length [Preiss, 1999]

Input: Unlabeled data set $D = \{\boldsymbol{x}_1, \boldsymbol{x}_2, \ldots, \boldsymbol{x}_m\}$;
Subsampling size ψ;
Isolation forest F containing B isolation trees;
Height limit *hlim* for tree traversal.
Process:
1. **for** $i = 1, \ldots, m$:
2. $L = 0$;
3. **for** each isolation tree $N \in F$
4. $L = L +$ **PathLength**$(\boldsymbol{x}_i, N, hlim, 0)$;
5. **end**
6. $\mathbb{E}[h(\boldsymbol{x}_i)] = L/B$;
7. Calculate anomaly score $s(\boldsymbol{x}_i)$ according to (8.22);
8. **end**
Output: Anomaly score $s(\boldsymbol{x}_i)$ $(1 \le i \le m)$

PathLength$(\boldsymbol{x}_i, N, hlim, h)$
1. **if** $N.type =$ external or $h \ge hlim$
2. **then return** $h + c(N.size)$;
3. **else** $\mathcal{F}_j = N.splitFeature$;
4. $a = N.splitValue$;
5. **if** $x_{ij} < a$
6. **then return PathLength**$(\boldsymbol{x}_i, N.leftNode, hlim, h+1)$;
7. **else return PathLength**$(\boldsymbol{x}_i, N.rightNode, hlim, h+1)$.

Figure 8.6: The evaluation stage of iForest.

$$c(\psi) = \begin{cases} 2H(\psi - 1) - 2(\psi - 1)/\psi, & \psi > 2 \\ 1, & \psi = 2 \\ 0, & \text{otherwise} \end{cases} \quad (8.21)$$

where $H(x)$ is the harmonic number estimated by

$$H(x) \approx \ln(x) + 0.5772156649 \text{ (Euler's constant)} .$$

Then, the anomaly score $s(\boldsymbol{x}_i)$ is calculated according to [Liu et al., 2012]

$$s(\boldsymbol{x}_i) = 2^{-\frac{\mathbb{E}[h(\boldsymbol{x}_i)]}{c(\psi)}} , \quad (8.22)$$

where $c(\psi)$ serves as a normalization factor corresponding to the average path length of traversing an isolation tree constructed from a subsample with size ψ. Finally, if $s(\boldsymbol{x}_i)$ is very close to 1, $\boldsymbol{x}_i$ is definitely an anomaly; if $s(\boldsymbol{x}_i)$ is much smaller than 0.5, $\boldsymbol{x}_i$ is quite safe to be regarded as a normal data point, while if $s(\boldsymbol{x}_i) \approx 0.5$ for all $\boldsymbol{x}_i$'s, there is no distinct anomaly [Liu et al., 2012]. The evaluation stage of iForest is summarized in Figure 8.6.

8.5 Isolation Forest Extensions

Clustered anomalies are anomalies which form clusters outside the range of normal data points. Liu et al. [2010] proposed the SCiForest approach (SC means "with Split selection Criterion"), a variant of iForest, to detect clustered anomalies. In contrast to iForest with only axis-parallel splits of original features in the construction of isolation trees, SCiForest tries to get smoother decision boundaries, somewhat similar to **oblique decision trees** [Zhou, 2021, Section 4.5], by considering hyperplane splits derived from the combination of original features. Furthermore, a split selection criterion is defined to facilitate the selection of appropriate hyperplanes at each node to reduce the risk of falling into poor sub-optimal solutions, rather than working with a completely random manner, since the hypothesis space is more complicated by considering hyperplanes.

Following SCiForest, Hariri et al. [2021] proposed the EIF (Extended Isolation Forest) approach by employing hyperplane with random slope for recursive node splitting. At each internal node, the splitting hyperplane is specified by choosing a normal vector $\boldsymbol{p} \in \mathbb{R}^d$ and an intercept point $\boldsymbol{q} \in \mathbb{R}^d$. Here, each coordinate of $\boldsymbol{p}$ is randomly drawn from the standard Gaussian distribution $\mathcal{N}(0, 1)$ and $\boldsymbol{q}$ is randomly drawn from a uniform distribution over the enclosing hyper-rectangle over all data points in the node. Then, any data point $\boldsymbol{x}_i$ will move to either side of the splitting hyperplane based on whether $(\boldsymbol{x}_i - \boldsymbol{q})^{\boldsymbol{T}} \cdot \boldsymbol{p} \leq 0$ holds. Correspondingly, an *extension level* l can be controlled by the number of free coordinates in $\boldsymbol{p}$ to l and setting the values of other coordinates to zero. Hence, it is obvious that EIF will have the same splitting strategy as iForest as $l = 1$. The evaluation stage of EIF is the same as iForest by calculating the average traversal path length over all isolation trees in ensemble. The training and evaluation stages of EIF are summarized in Figures 8.7 and 8.8 respectively.

The existence of multiple clusters of normal data points may bring difficulties for anomaly detection, where clustered anomalies are prone to be masked by normal clusters of similar densities. For this situation, Aryal et al. [2014] proposed another variant of iForest named ReMass-iForest. In contrast to iForest which uses the traversal path length of isolation tree to measure anomaly score, ReMass-iForest takes local data distribution into account by exploiting the **data mass** estimation techniques [Ting et al., 2013]. The ratio of data mass is calculated for each isolation tree between the external node containing the data point and that of its immediate parent internal node, which is then normalized by subsampling size ψ and averaged across the tree ensemble to yield the final anomaly score.

By incorporating expert feedback into the anomaly detection process, AAD (Active Anomaly Discovery) [Das et al., 2016] aims to exploit the knowledge of human analyst to help improve the precision of true anomalies in high-ranking anomalous data points. Das et al. [2017] extended isolation forest by incorporating expert feedback and proposed the IF-AAD approach (IF denotes "Isolation Forest"). Specifically, each node of the component isolation tree is assigned with a weight, and the sum of weights over all traversed paths

---

Input: Unlabeled data set $D = \{\boldsymbol{x}_1, \boldsymbol{x}_2, \ldots, \boldsymbol{x}_m\}$;
Subsampling size ψ;
Extension level $l \geq 1$;
Number of isolation trees B to be grown.

Process:
1. Initialize isolation forest $F = \emptyset$;
2. **for** $b = 1, \ldots, B$:
3. Randomly sample ψ data points without replacement from D to form the subsample D';
4. $F = F \bigcup \{\mathbf{iTree}(D')\}$;
5. **end**

Output: The isolation forest F

iTree(D')
1. **if** $(|D'| = 1)$ or (*all data points in* D' *have the same feature values*)
2. **then** Grow a node N with $N.type$ = external;
3. $N.size = |D'|$;
4. **else** Choose a normal vector $\boldsymbol{p}$ with each coordinate randomly drawn from the standard Gaussian distribution $\mathcal{N}(0, 1)$;
5. Choose the intercept point $\boldsymbol{q}$ by randomly drawn from a uniform distribution over the enclosing hyper-rectangle of D';
6. Set the values of $(d - l)$ coordinates of $\boldsymbol{p}$ to 0;
7. $D'_l = \{\boldsymbol{x}_i \mid \boldsymbol{x}_i \in D',\ (\boldsymbol{x}_i - \boldsymbol{q})^{\boldsymbol{T}} \cdot \boldsymbol{p} \leq 0\}$;
8. $D'_r = \{\boldsymbol{x}_i \mid \boldsymbol{x}_i \in D',\ (\boldsymbol{x}_i - \boldsymbol{q})^{\boldsymbol{T}} \cdot \boldsymbol{p} > 0\}$;
9. Grow a node N with $N.type$ = internal;
10. $N.size = |D'|$;
11. $N.normalVector = \boldsymbol{p}$;
12. $N.interceptPoint = \boldsymbol{q}$;
13. $N.leftNode = \mathbf{iTree}(D'_l)$;
14. $N.rightNode = \mathbf{iTree}(D'_r)$;
15. **return** N

Figure 8.7: The training stage of EIF.

in the tree ensemble is used to yield the anomaly score. In each feedback iteration, the data point with top-ranked anomaly score receives ground-truth "anomalous/normal" label from human analyst. A maximum margin formulation is utilized to refine the weight values by employing pairwise ranking constraints on data points with anomalous and normal human labels.

Most anomaly detection methods deal with data points (i.e., observations) in a finite dimensional feature space. Staerman et al. [2019] proposed the FIF (Functional Isolation Forest) approach for anomaly detection in potentially infinite dimensional context, such as **functional data**, rather than the common value-based data. Specifically, a functional Hilbert space $\mathcal{H}$ with scalar product

---

Input: Unlabeled data set $D = \{\boldsymbol{x}_1, \boldsymbol{x}_2, \ldots, \boldsymbol{x}_m\}$;
Subsampling size ψ;
Isolation forest F containing B isolation trees;
Height limit $hlim$ for tree traversal.

Process:
1. **for** $i = 1, \ldots, m$:
2. $L = 0$;
3. **for** each isolation tree $N \in F$
4. $L = L + \textbf{PathLength}(\boldsymbol{x}_i, N, hlim, 0)$;
5. **end**
6. $\mathbb{E}[h(\boldsymbol{x}_i)] = L/B$;
7. Calculate anomaly score $s(\boldsymbol{x}_i)$ according to (8.22);
8. **end**

Output: Anomaly score $s(\boldsymbol{x}_i)$ $(1 \le i \le m)$

PathLength$(\boldsymbol{x}_i, N, hlim, h)$
1. **if** $N.type$ = external or $h \ge hlim$
2. **then return** $h + c(N.size)$;
3. **else** $\vec{\boldsymbol{n}} = N.normalVector$;
4. $\vec{\boldsymbol{p}} = N.interceptPoint$;
5. **if** $(\boldsymbol{x}_i - \boldsymbol{q})^{\boldsymbol{T}} \cdot \boldsymbol{p} \le 0$
6. **then return PathLength**$(\boldsymbol{x}_i, N.leftNode, hlim, h+1)$;
7. **else return PathLength**$(\boldsymbol{x}_i, N.rightNode, hlim, h+1)$.

Figure 8.8: The evaluation stage of EIF.

$\langle .,. \rangle_{\mathcal{H}}$ is assumed where each observation $\boldsymbol{x}_i \in \mathcal{H}$ corresponds to a curve defined by a real-valued function over $[0, 1]$. To instantiate the recursive partition procedure as iForest, FIF chooses to project each observation on a dictionary $\mathcal{D} \subset \mathcal{H}$ where the product $\langle \boldsymbol{x}_i, \boldsymbol{r} \rangle_{\mathcal{H}}$ $(\boldsymbol{r} \in \mathcal{D})$ gives a feature description of observation $\boldsymbol{x}_i$. The split variable $\boldsymbol{r}$ in each internal node is chosen based on a probability distribution defined on $\mathcal{D}$, and the corresponding split value is chosen uniformly from the interval by projecting observations in the current node on $\boldsymbol{r}$.

Online anomaly detection deals with streaming data which necessitates timely update of detection models; this is relevant to **online learning** to be discussed in Section 12.4. To endow iForest with the ability of online anomaly detection, Ma et al. [2020] proposed the iMForest (isolation Mondrian Forests) approach by introducing the Mondrian process [Roy and Teh, 2008, Lakshminarayanan et al., 2014] to enable online update of isolation Mondrian trees (iMTree) in the ensemble. In addition to the information of split feature and its split value as an iTree node embodies, each node in the iMTree also holds a hyper-rectangular block enclosing all data points in the node as well as a split time controlled by a block-based exponential distribution. Given a new streaming data point, each iMTree in the ensemble is extended recursively starting from the root, by adjusting the block bounds of internal nodes, and adding new nodes if the split time of child node is much greater than the split time of parent nodes. The anomaly score is evaluated in the same way as iForest based on the average traversal path length over all component trees.

Each isolation tree in the iForest ensemble takes the form of a proper binary tree, which can be extended to more generic form such as N-ary trees. Following this idea, Karczmarek et al. [2020] proposed the k-Means IF approach by instantiating the node split operation with k-means clustering. Given the randomly chosen split feature at each internal node, k-means clustering is performed on the set of values at the chosen split feature over all data points in the node. The number of clusters is determined with the elbow rule [Ketchen Jr and Shook, 1996] by identifying the joint cluster number yielding stable clustering performance afterwards, and each splitting branch is grown recursively consisting of data points belonging to one cluster. Accordingly, the anomaly score is evaluated by considering the membership of each data point to the cluster of traversed paths. A direct variant is proposed in [Karczmarek et al., 2021] by replacing the k-means clustering by fuzzy k-means clustering.

The iForest can also be extended by considering alternative ways for anomaly score evaluation. For example, Mensi and Bicego [2021] proposed to extend the evaluation procedure of iForest in two different ways. The first way works at the tree level by exploiting additional information along the traversal path of an isolation tree rather than only using the depth of the traversed path. A path-weighted anomaly score is defined as the weight which can be instantiated for each node along the traversed path based on different information, such as the number of data points passed to the node, the *one-class proxy function* [Goix et al., 2017] measuring the information loss after split, or the depth of the *least common ancestor* of the evaluated data point and each training data point. The second one works at forest level by replacing the multiplicative aggregation of path length $h(\boldsymbol{x}_i)$ (i.e., $\prod_{h\in F} 2^{-\frac{h(\boldsymbol{x}_i)}{|F|c(\psi)}}$ according to (8.22) to the additive aggregation counterpart (i.e., $\frac{1}{|F|}\sum_{h\in F} 2^{-\frac{h(\boldsymbol{x}_i)}{c(\psi)}}$).

The mechanism of isolation can be implemented in alternative ways. For example, Bandaragoda et al. [2018] proposed the iNNE (isolation using Nearest Neighbor Ensemble) approach by exploiting the nearest neighbor calculation. Let $D' \subset D$ be a subsample of size ψ. For each data point $\boldsymbol{z} \in D'$, let $\eta_{\boldsymbol{z}}$ be $\boldsymbol{z}$'s nearest neighbor identified in D', and let $S(\boldsymbol{z})$ denote the *largest hypersphere* centered at $\boldsymbol{z}$, which can separate $\boldsymbol{z}$ from the other data points in D' with radius $\tau(\boldsymbol{z}) = \|\boldsymbol{z} - \eta_{\boldsymbol{z}}\|_2$. Correspondingly, let $\mathcal{S} = \bigcup_{\boldsymbol{z}\in D'} S(\boldsymbol{z})$ denote the union of separating hyperspheres of all data points in D'. As anomalies are likely to reside in locally sparse areas, the radius $\tau(\boldsymbol{z})$ can be naturally used as a measure of isolation with a larger value implying a larger degree of isolation. Given a data point $\boldsymbol{x}_i$, denote by $\kappa(\boldsymbol{x}_i) = \arg\min_{\{\boldsymbol{z}\in D',\ \boldsymbol{x}_i\in S(\boldsymbol{z})\}} \tau(\boldsymbol{z})$ the data point in D', whose separating hypersphere contains $\boldsymbol{x}_i$ but with the minimum radius. Then, the isolation score for $\boldsymbol{x}_i$ with regard to D' is defined as

---

Input: Unlabeled data set $D = \{\boldsymbol{x}_1, \boldsymbol{x}_2, \ldots, \boldsymbol{x}_m\}$;
Subsampling size ψ;
Ensemble size B.

Process:
1. Initialize the ensemble $E = \emptyset$;
2. **for** $b = 1, \ldots, B$:
3. Randomly sample ψ data points without replacement from D to form the subsample D';
4. Initialize $\mathcal{S} = \emptyset$;
5. **for** each $\boldsymbol{z} \in D'$
6. Identify $\boldsymbol{z}$'s nearest neighbor $\eta_{\boldsymbol{z}}$ in D' and then calculate the radius $\tau(\boldsymbol{z}) = \|\boldsymbol{z} - \eta_{\boldsymbol{z}}\|_2$ for separating hypersphere $S(\boldsymbol{z})$;
7. $\mathcal{S} = \mathcal{S} \bigcup \{S(\boldsymbol{z})\}$;
8. **end**
9. $E = E \bigcup \{\mathcal{S}\}$;
10. **end**
11. **for** $i = 1, \ldots, m$:
12. Set $s(\boldsymbol{x}_i) = \frac{1}{B} \sum_{\mathcal{S} \in E} I_{\mathcal{S}}(\boldsymbol{x}_i)$ according to (8.23);
13. **end**

Output: Anomaly score $s(\boldsymbol{x}_i)$ $(1 \leq i \leq m)$

Figure 8.9: The iNNE algorithm.

$$I_{\mathcal{S}}(\boldsymbol{x}_i) = \begin{cases} 1 - \frac{\tau(\eta_{\kappa(\boldsymbol{x}_i)})}{\tau(\kappa(\boldsymbol{x}_i))}, & \text{if } \boldsymbol{x}_i \in \mathcal{S} \\ 1, & \text{otherwise}. \end{cases} \tag{8.23}$$

According to the above definition, it is obvious that the isolation score $I_{\mathcal{S}}(\boldsymbol{x}_i)$ takes values in $[0, 1]$. The iNNE algorithm is summarized in Figure 8.9.

Isolation can also be realized with bounding boxes [Xu et al., 2021b]. Given a data set D, an initial bounding box $\mathbf{B}$ is defined as the smallest hyper-rectangle covering all data points in D. Here, the lower bound L_j and upper bound U_j on the j-th feature A_j correspond to $L_j = \min\{x_{ij} \mid \boldsymbol{x}_i \in D,\ 1 \leq i \leq m\}$ and $U_j = \max\{x_{ij} \mid \boldsymbol{x}_i \in D,\ 1 \leq i \leq m\}$, respectively. For any internal node with split feature A_j and split value a, the upper bound U_j of $\mathbf{B}$ will be refined to $\min\{U_j, a\}$ by traversing along the left branch, while the lower bound L_j of $\mathbf{B}$ will be refined to $\max\{L_j, a\}$ by traversing along the right branch. For an isolation tree f, the resulting bounding box $\mathbf{B}_f(\boldsymbol{x}_i)$ for data point $\boldsymbol{x}_i$ corresponds to the one obtained by refining $\mathbf{B}$ along the traversal path of $\boldsymbol{x}_i$ in f till the external node. Then, the bounding box $\mathbf{B}_F(\boldsymbol{x}_i)$ yielded by an iForest ensemble F is given by the intersections of all isolation tree bounding boxes, i.e., $\mathbf{B}_F(\boldsymbol{x}_i) = \bigcap_{f \in F} \mathbf{B}_f(\boldsymbol{x}_i)$. A reconstructed data point $\boldsymbol{x}_i^{\text{rec}}$ can be defined as the center of bounding box $\mathbf{B}_F(\boldsymbol{x}_i)$, where the anomaly score $s(\boldsymbol{x}_i)$ is calculated based on the reconstruction error $s(\boldsymbol{x}_i) = \|\boldsymbol{x}_i^{\text{rec}} - \boldsymbol{x}_i\|_2^2$.

In addition to anomaly detection, the mechanism of isolation can also be utilized to help develop techniques for other learning tasks. For example, Ting et al. [2018] employed the structural information of isolation partitions yielded by iForest to design **data-dependent kernels**. Specifically, let $\mathcal{H}_\psi(D)$ denote the space of all possible axis-parallel external node partitions of all isolation trees grown from a subsample of D with size ψ. For two data points $\boldsymbol{x}$ and $\boldsymbol{z}$ in $\mathbb{R}^d$, an **isolation kernel** $K_\psi(\cdot,\cdot)$ is defined as the expectation over the (unknown) probability distribution $P_\psi(\cdot)$ of $\mathcal{H}_\psi(D)$, where both $\boldsymbol{x}$ and $\boldsymbol{z}$ fall into the same axis-parallel partition $H \in \mathcal{H}_\psi(D)$, i.e.,

$$K_\psi(\boldsymbol{x},\boldsymbol{z}) = \mathbb{E}_{H\sim P_\psi}\ \mathbb{I}((\boldsymbol{x}\in H)\wedge(\boldsymbol{z}\in H)) \ . \tag{8.24}$$

It is evident that $K_\psi(\cdot,\cdot)$ is a valid kernel, and it can be estimated from a finite number of partitions $\Omega \subset \mathcal{H}_\psi(D)$ as

$$\widehat{K}_\psi(\boldsymbol{x},\boldsymbol{z}\mid\Omega) = \frac{1}{|\Omega|}\sum_{H\in\Omega}\mathbb{I}((\boldsymbol{x}\in H)\wedge(\boldsymbol{z}\in H)) \ . \tag{8.25}$$

Under uniform distribution over the feature space, the isolation kernel $K_\psi(\cdot,\cdot)$ is equivalent to the data-independent kernel proposed by [Breiman, 2000b] based on completely random trees. $K_\psi(\cdot,\cdot)$ can also well approximate the popular Laplacian kernel and make two data points with the same Euclidean distance to be more similar in sparse regions yet less similar in dense regions. It has been shown that SVMs facilitated with isolation kernel can yield excellent predictive performance on data sets with varied densities between classes [Ting et al., 2018].

Xu et al. [2019] extended the isolation kernel defined at instance-level to the *isolation set-kernel* (ISK) defined at set-level. Following the above notations, given two sets of data points $X = \{\boldsymbol{x}_1,\ldots,\boldsymbol{x}_a\}$ and $Z = \{\boldsymbol{z}_1,\ldots,\boldsymbol{z}_b\}$, an ISK $K_\psi^{ISK}(\cdot,\cdot)$ is defined as the expectation over $P_\psi(\cdot)$ that each pair of data points $\boldsymbol{x}\in X$ and $\boldsymbol{z}\in Z$ fall into the same axis-parallel partition, i.e.,

$$K_\psi^{ISK}(\boldsymbol{x},\boldsymbol{z}) = \mathbb{E}_{H\sim P_\psi}\ \mathbb{I}((\boldsymbol{x}\in H)\wedge(\boldsymbol{z}\in H)\ \ \forall(\boldsymbol{x},\boldsymbol{z})\in X\times Z) \ . \tag{8.26}$$

For a finite number of partitions $\Omega \subset \mathcal{H}_\psi(D)$, the ISK can be estimated by

$$\widehat{K}_\psi^{ISK}(X,Z\mid\Omega) = \frac{1}{|X||Z|}\sum_{(\boldsymbol{x},\boldsymbol{z})\in X\times Z}\widehat{K}_\psi(\boldsymbol{x},\boldsymbol{z}\mid\Omega) \ . \tag{8.27}$$

Let $\Omega_N \subset \mathcal{H}_\psi(D)$ denote the ψ external node partitions of an isolation tree f, and a feature map $\Phi : 2^{\mathcal{X}} \to \mathbb{R}^{B\times\psi}$ can be defined for any set X based on an isolation forest F, i.e., $\Phi_F(X) = \operatorname{concat}\left[\boldsymbol{v}(X\mid f)\right]_{f\in F}$. Here, the j-th feature $v_j(X\mid f)$ of the ψ-dimensional vector $\boldsymbol{v}(X\mid f)$ corresponds to the proportion of data points in X falling into the j-th partition $H_j\in\Omega_f$: $v_j(X\mid f) = \frac{1}{|X|}\sum_{\boldsymbol{x}\in X}\mathbb{I}(\boldsymbol{x}\in H_j)$. With the above feature mapping from a set to a feature vector with fixed length $B\times\psi$, it is natural to apply ISK to tackle **multi-instance learning** (Section 12.1.2) with set-level (i.e., *bag* of instances) representation.

8.6 Learning with Emerging New Class

Conventional machine learning studies generally assume that the class label of any unseen instance $\hat{\boldsymbol{x}}$ must be a member of the given label set known in advance, i.e., $\hat{y} \in \mathcal{Y}$. Unfortunately, this does not always hold in some applications. For example, let's consider a forest disease monitor aided by a machine learning model trained with signals sending from sensors deployed in the forest. It is evident that one can hardly enumerate all possible class labels in advance, because some forest diseases can be totally novel, such as those caused by invasive insect pests never encountered in this region before. To be able to handle $\hat{y} \notin \mathcal{Y}$ is a basic requirement for **open-environment learning**, which will be discussed in Section 12.2.

It might be thought that one can artificially generate some virtual training examples for the new classes, just like popular training tricks employed in adversarial deep neural networks. Here, the difficulty lies in the fact that one can hardly imagine what unknown class (called *NewClass* in the following) might occur, and training a model accommodating *all possible classes* is impossible or unbearably expensive.

Technically, if *all data* is at hand, especially including the unlabeled instances to be predicted, then handling NewClass can be treated as a special semi-supervised learning [Zhou, 2018a] task, e.g., by establishing the semi-supervised large margin separator corresponding to the tightest contour for each known class, and then regarding unlabeled instances falling outside all contours as NewClass instances [Da et al., 2014]. Actually, the distribution of NewClass can be approximated by separating the distribution of known classes for that of the unlabeled data [Zhang et al., 2020]. Such strategies, however, are not directly applicable when data are accumulated with time.

Consider the following setting of *learning with emerging new class.* A machine learning model is trained from some initial training data and then deployed to handle unseen instances coming like a stream. For incoming instances of known classes, the trained model should be able to make correct predictions. For incoming instances of unknown class, the model should be able to report that a NewClass instance is encountered; the user can then create a new label for the NewClass. After encountering a few instances of this NewClass, the trained model should be able to be refined/updated such that the NewClass becomes a known class whose incoming instances can be accurately predicted. Ideally, it is desired that the whole process does not require retraining based on storage of *all data* received, since this would be terribly expensive or even infeasible in real big data tasks. Evidently, the above describes an unsupervised/supervised mixing task with human in the loop.

In the first glance, learning with emerging new class seems relevant to **zero-shot learning**, a topic in image classification, aiming to classify visual classes that did not occur in training data set [Socher et al., 2013, Xian et al., 2019, Chen et al., 2021a]. Note that zero-shot learning is assumed to work with **side information**, i.e., external knowledge such as class

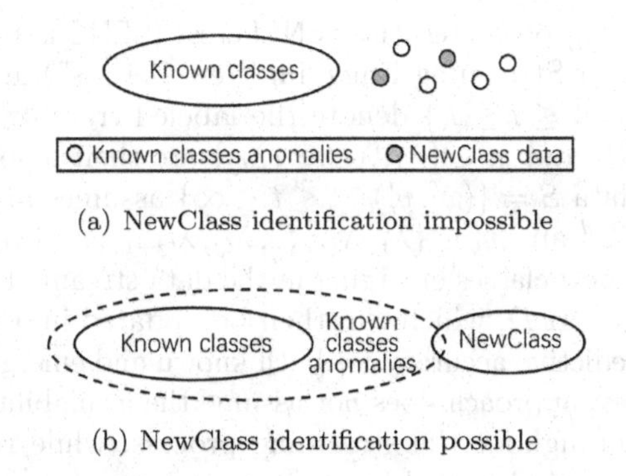

Figure 8.10: NewClass identification not always possible.

definitions/descriptions/properties, that can help associate the seen and unseen classes, and thus, it can be treated as a kind of **transfer learning** [Pan and Yang, 2009]; in contrast, learning with emerging new class is a general learning setting which does not assume such external knowledge. In other words, zero-shot learning assumes that the unseen classes are known, though they did not occur in training data, whereas learning with emerging new class are tackling the grand challenge that the unseen classes are unknown. Thus, approaches for learning with emerging new class can be more general, and can be converted and applied to zero-shot learning.

Mu et al. [2017a] presented a general solution for learning with emerging new class. The first phase, NewClass identification, is realized by anomaly detection. Here, the challenge is to distinguish the NewClass data from anomalies of known classes. In general, this is not always possible; for example, Figure 8.10(a) provides an illustration where the NewClass and anomalies of known classes can hardly be distinguished. Fortunately, in many real tasks, it is reasonable to assume that *NewClass instances are more 'abnormal' than anomalies of known classes*, as illustrated in Figure 8.10(b). If this assumption does not hold in the original feature space, we can try to identify an adequate feature space by kernel mapping or representation learning. After that, the identification of NewClass instances reduces to anomaly detection from streams, which can be tackled by approaches such as isolation forest.

A major challenge is to refine/update a trained model to accommodate NewClass without sacrificing performance on known classes. For models like neural networks, a retraining based on all data (or at least, on smartly selected subsamples) would be required to avoid *catastrophic forgetting*, with huge computational and storage costs. It would be ideal to do local refinement only for accommodating NewClass rather than make global changes that may seriously affect known classes. An appealing solution is to exploit the advantage of tree/forest models through refining only tree leaves involving NewClass in an incremental way, which does not even need any storage for known class data.

Mu et al. [2017a] presented the SENCForest (SENC is the abbreviation of "classification under Streaming Emerging New Classes") approach. Formally, let $D = \{(\boldsymbol{x}_i, y_i) \mid 1 \leq i \leq L\}$ denote the labeled training set with training instances $\boldsymbol{x}_i \in \mathbb{R}^d$, and $y_i \in \{\lambda_1, \lambda_2, \ldots, \lambda_Q\}$ are their associated class label. The streaming data $S = \{(\boldsymbol{x}'_t, y'_t) \mid 1 \leq t < \infty\}$ assumes an augmented label space with $\boldsymbol{x}'_t \in \mathbb{R}^d$ and $y'_t \in \{\lambda_1, \lambda_2, \ldots, \lambda_Q, \lambda_{Q+1}, \ldots, \lambda_M\}$ such that there might be $M - Q$ new classes emerging in the data stream. The task is to learn an initial model from D, which can then be updated in a timely manner to maintain high predictive accuracy for both known and emerging new classes on S. The SENCForest approach does not assume the availability of ground-truth class labels y'_t throughout the streaming process, while relaxations of this condition can be easily handled by the approach.

The model training, deployment, and update stages of SENCForest are summarized in Figures 8.11 to 8.13, respectively.

For the model training stage, the iForest approach replaces the component tree structure of iTree with SENCTree to accommodate both anomaly detection and classification. The key is to enrich the information embodied in external node of the component tree including: a) the center $\boldsymbol{c}$ and radius r of a ball V, which subdivides the axis-parallel partition H of an external node into *anomaly subregion* (i.e., $H \wedge V$, anomalies of known classes) and *outlying anomaly subregion* (i.e., $H \setminus V$, anomalies of emerging new classes); and b) the frequency distribution $\boldsymbol{\alpha} = [\alpha_1, \alpha_2, \ldots, \alpha_P]^{\boldsymbol{T}}$ ($Q \leq P \leq M$), where each element α_j records the number of instances of the j-th currently known class ($1 \leq j \leq P$) falling into the external node. Once a SENCTree N is grown, a threshold τ_N is found to determine whether H should be regarded as anomaly region and thus amenable to further ball subdivision. Let O denote the list of path lengths in ascending order of all external nodes in N, which can be bi-partitioned by any threshold τ into left sublist O^l_τ and right sublist O^r_τ. Then, the anomaly regions are determined to be those axis-parallel partitions of external nodes whose path lengths are less than

$$\tau_N = \arg\min_\tau \left|\sigma(O^l_\tau) - \sigma(O^r_\tau)\right| \ . \tag{8.28}$$

Here, $\sigma(\cdot)$ corresponds to the standard deviation operator.

For the model deployment stage, the ensemble F of SENCTrees trained in previous stage is employed to make prediction on the test instance $\boldsymbol{x}'_t$ in the data stream. Let P be the number of currently known classes, and each SENCTree N yields a class label $y'_t \in \{\lambda_1, \ldots, \lambda_P, \lambda_{P+1}\}$ on $\boldsymbol{x}'_t$, where λ_{P+1} corresponds to the emerging new class. Specifically, the class label λ_{P+1} will be yielded if $\boldsymbol{x}'_t$ falls into the *outlying anomaly subregion* of an external node of N whose path length is less than τ_N; otherwise, the class label λ_j will be yielded of highest external node frequency α_j among all the currently known classes. Correspondingly, the majority class label yielded by the B SENCTrees in the ensemble F is taken as the prediction on $\boldsymbol{x}'_t$. For a test instance $\boldsymbol{x}'_t$ predicted with the class label λ_{P+1} by F, it will be placed in buffer Δ which

---

Input: Labeled training set $D = \{(\boldsymbol{x}_i, y_i) \mid 1 \leq i \leq L\}$;
Subsampling size ψ;
Minimum internal node size ξ;
Number of SENCTrees B to be grown.

Process:
1. Initialize SENCForest $F = \emptyset$;
2. **for** $b = 1, \ldots, B$:
3. Randomly sample ψ labeled training instances without replacement from D to form the subsample D';
4. $F = F \bigcup \{$**SENCTree**$(D', \xi, Q)\}$;
5. **end**

Output: The SENCForest F

SENCTree(D', ξ, Q)
1. **if** $|D'| \leq \xi$
2. **then** Grow a node N with $N.type$ = external;
3. $N.size = |D'|$;
4. $N.centre = \mathbf{c}$ with ball V's centre $\mathbf{c} = \frac{1}{|D'|} \sum_{\boldsymbol{x} \in D'} \boldsymbol{x}$;
5. $N.radius = r$ with ball V's radius $r = \max_{(\boldsymbol{x},y) \in D'} \|\boldsymbol{x} - \mathbf{c}\|_2$;
6. $N.freqDis = \boldsymbol{\alpha}$ with the j-th element $\alpha_j = |\{(\boldsymbol{x}, y) \mid (\boldsymbol{x}, y) \in D', y = \lambda_j\}|$ $(1 \leq j \leq Q)$;
7. **else** Randomly select a feature $\mathcal{F}_j$ from the feature set $\{\mathcal{F}_1, \mathcal{F}_2, \ldots, \mathcal{F}_d\}$;
8. Randomly select a split value $a \in (\min_{(\boldsymbol{x}_i,y_i) \in D'} x_{ij}, \max_{(\boldsymbol{x}_i,y_i) \in D'} x_{ij})$;
9. $D'_l = \{(\boldsymbol{x}_i, y_i) \mid (\boldsymbol{x}_i, y_i) \in D', x_{ij} < a\}$;
10. $D'_r = \{(\boldsymbol{x}_i, y_i) \mid (\boldsymbol{x}_i, y_i) \in D', x_{ij} \geq a\}$;
11. Grow a node N with $N.type$ = internal;
12. $N.size = |D'|$;
13. $N.splitFeature = \mathcal{F}_j$;
14. $N.splitValue = a$;
15. $N.leftNode =$ **SENCTree**(D'_l, ξ, Q);
16. $N.rightNode =$ **SENCTree**(D'_r, ξ, Q);
17. **return** N

Figure 8.11: The model training stage of SENCForest.

stores candidates of emerging new class. When the buffer size reaches δ, all candidates in Δ will be used to update the ensemble F.

For the model update stage, each SENCTree in the ensemble F is updated by incorporating ψ instances randomly selected from the buffer Δ.

When the number of known classes in F reaches a pre-specified threshold θ, SENCForest will stop updating SENCTrees in current ensemble. Instead, a new ensemble of SENCTrees will be grown for the next θ emerging new classes.

Input: Streaming (unlabeled) data $S = \{\boldsymbol{x}'_t \mid 1 \leq t < \infty\}$;
The SENCForest F;
Number of currently known classes P;
Buffer size δ.

Process:
1. Initialize buffer $\Delta = \emptyset$;
2. **for** each $\boldsymbol{x}'_t \in S$
3. $y'_t =$ **SENCForestPred**$(F,\ \boldsymbol{x}'_t,\ P)$;
4. **if** $y'_t = \lambda_{P+1}$;
5. **then** $\Delta = \Delta \bigcup \{\boldsymbol{x}'_t\}$;
6. **if** $|\Delta| = \delta$
7. **then** Update F with Δ according to the model update process given in Figure 8.13;
8. $\Delta = \emptyset$;
9. $P = P + 1$;
10. **end**

Output: The predicted class label y'_t $(1 \leq t < \infty)$

SENCForestPred$(F,\ \boldsymbol{x}'_t,\ P)$
1. Initialize counting vector $\boldsymbol{\eta} = [\eta_1, \ldots, \eta_{P+1}]^{\boldsymbol{T}}$ with all-zero elements;
2. **for** each SENCTree $N \in F$
3. Find the threshold τ_N according to (8.28);
4. Traverse $\boldsymbol{x}'_t$ along N to identify the external node N^e which contains $\boldsymbol{x}'_t$ with path length h, ball V's centre $\mathbf{c} = N^e.centre$, ball V's radius $r = N^e.radius$, and frequency distribution $\boldsymbol{\alpha} = N^e.freqDis$;
5. **if** $(h < \tau_N) \wedge (r < \|\boldsymbol{x}'_t - \mathbf{c}\|_2)$
6. **then** $idx = P + 1$;
7. **else** $idx = \arg\max_{1 \leq j \leq P} \alpha_j$;
8. $\eta_{idx} = \eta_{idx} + 1$;
9. **end**
10. $idx = \arg\max_{1 \leq j \leq P+1} \eta_j$;
11. $y'_t = \lambda_{idx}$;
12. **return** Predicted class label y'_t.

Figure 8.12: The model deployment stage of SENCForest.

A retirement mechanism is designed to cope with streaming data scenario where an ensemble F is eliminated for future usage if: a) F has not been used to predict known classes for a certain period; or b) the number of ensembles reaches a pre-specified limit ρ and F is the least used once in the last period.

8.7 Further Readings

There are many studies about anomaly detection performance measures during the past decade [Clémençon and Jakubowicz, 2013, Zimek et al., 2014, Goix

---

Input: The SENCForest F;
Subsampling size ψ;
Minimum internal node size ξ;
Number of currently known classes P;
The buffer Δ.

Process:
1. Augment Δ by replacing each unlabeled instance $\boldsymbol{x}'_t \in \Delta$ with its labeled counterpart $(\boldsymbol{x}'_t, \lambda_{P+1})$;
2. **for** each SENCTree $N \in F$
3. Randomly sample ψ labeled instances without replacement from Δ to form the subsample Δ';
4. **for** each external node N^e in T
5. Retrieve ball V's centre $\boldsymbol{c} = N^e.centre$, and frequency distribution $\boldsymbol{\alpha} = N^e.freqDis$ of N^e;
6. X' = labeled instances of Δ' which fall into N^e;
7. **if** $|X'| > 0$
8. **then** Initialize the set of pseudo labeled instances $X = \emptyset$;
9. **for** $j = 1, \ldots, P$
10. $X = X \bigcup \{(\boldsymbol{c}_k, \lambda_j) \mid \boldsymbol{c}_k = \boldsymbol{c},\ 1 \leq k \leq \alpha_j\}$;
11. **end**
12. $N^e = \textbf{SENCTree}(X' \bigcup X,\ \xi,\ P+1)$;
13. **else** Augment $\boldsymbol{\alpha}$ with one additional element $\alpha_{P+1} = 0$;
14. $N^e.freqDis = \boldsymbol{\alpha}$;
15. **end**
16. **end**

Output: The updated SENCForest F

Figure 8.13: The model update stage of SENCForest.

et al., 2015]. Zimek et al. [2013] enhanced ensemble diversity for anomaly detection by using subsampling .

An ensemble of one-class SVMs has been successfully applied to anomaly detection [Perdisci et al., 2006]. Shoemaker and Hall [2011] studied the distributed anomaly detection and showed similar performance in contrast to non-distributed anomaly detection, by using random forests and the distance-based anomaly partitioning with ensemble voting. Recently, neural network ensembles such as Autoencoder ensembles and GAN ensembles have also been presented for anomaly detection [Chen et al., 2017, Kieu et al., 2019, Han et al., 2021].

Many anomaly detection approaches are based on distance measures. There are studies about learning adequate distance measures from data under the umbrella of **distance metric learning** [Zhou, 2021, Section 10.6]. Ensemble methods have been exploited in distance metric learning, e.g., Tu et al. [2012]

proposed a *cross-diffusion process* to generate an enhanced similarity measure by combing multiple given metrics, and Ye et al. [2019] proposed a *unified multi-metric learning* framework to exploit multiple types of metrics.

There are other variations of **isolation kernel** in addition to ISK. For example, Ting et al. [2020, 2023] proposed the IDK (*Isolation Distributional Kernel*) to measure the similarity between distributions, aiming to define a distributional kernel which is data-dependent with finite-dimensional feature map, rather than popular *kernel mean embedding* [Smola et al., 2007, Muandet et al., 2017] techniques with data independent kernelization and infinite-dimensional feature map. Xu et al. [2021a] proposed the IGK (*Isolation Graph Kernel*) to measure the similarity between attributed graphs for graph classification.

Learning with emerging new classes is actually a kind of **incremental learning**, which emphasizes that a trained model requires only slight modification to accommodate new information. There is a long history of studies on incremental learning [Utgoff, 1989, Giraud-Carrier, 2000, He et al., 2011], mostly concerning increment of training examples, i.e., E-IL (example-incremental learning) defined in [Zhou and Chen, 2002]. In addition to E-IL, Zhou and Chen [2002] also defined A-IL (attribute-incremental learning) and C-IL (class-incremental learning), where C-IL concerns about class increment, closely related to learning with emerging new class, though previous studies concerned little about the identification of new class and generally assumed that the incremental class is known [Masana et al., 2023].

Classification with reject option [Fumera et al., 2000, Bartlett and Wegkamp, 2008, Geifman and El-Yaniv, 2019] aims to avoid unconfident predictions that are likely to be incorrect, assuming all classes known in advance. **Open set recognition/classification** [Scheirer et al., 2013, Geng et al., 2020] extends reject option to consider the possibility that unknown class may occur in testing phase, with the goal of recognizing known classes and reject NewClass. Neither of them attempts to enable the trained model to accommodate NewClass. Some generalized open set recognition studies try to recognize unknown class, by assuming the availability of *side information*, i.e., external knowledge such as class definitions/descriptions/properties, that can help associate the known and unknown classes [Geng et al., 2020], whereas learning with emerging new class is a general learning setting without such external knowledge assumption.

Besides tree/forest models, there are some other models, such as those based on global and local sketching [Mu et al., 2017b], that can localize the influence of NewClass such that changes according to NewClass won't significantly affect known classes. If there are multiple emerging NewClasses, the clustering structure of NewClass data can be exploited [Zhu et al., 2017b]. To reduce the gap between the moments when a NewClass is detected for the first time and when the model has been refined, some efforts have been devoted to enabling the model update based on fewer NewClass data [Zhu et al., 2017a].

Chapter 9

Semi-Supervised Ensemble

9.1 Semi-Supervised Learning

In many practical applications, we are given a small amount of labeled data which is insufficient to train a good learner, while abundant unlabeled data are available. For example, in web page classification the ground-truth labels are given by human annotators; it is easy to get a huge number of web pages from the internet, whereas only a small subset of web pages can be annotated due to the human cost. **Semi-supervised learning** attempts to exploit the abundant unlabeled data along with the limited labeled data to help improve generalization performance [Chapelle et al., 2006, Zhu, 2006, Zhou and Li, 2010a].

Formally, taking binary classification as an example, given the feature space $\mathcal{X}$ and label space $\mathcal{Y} = \{+1, -1\}$, the task of semi-supervised learning is to learn $f : \mathcal{X} \mapsto \mathcal{Y}$ from a training data set $D = \{(\boldsymbol{x}_1, y_1), \ldots, (\boldsymbol{x}_l, y_l), \boldsymbol{x}_{l+1}, \ldots, \boldsymbol{x}_m\}$. There are l labeled training examples $(\boldsymbol{x}_i, y_i)$ $(i \in \{1, \ldots, l\})$ with $\boldsymbol{x}_i \in \mathcal{X}$ being associated with label $y_i \in \mathcal{Y}$, and $u = m - l$ unlabeled instances $\boldsymbol{x}_j$ $(j \in \{l+1, \ldots, m\})$ with $\boldsymbol{x}_j \in \mathcal{X}$. It is assumed that each training example $(\boldsymbol{x}_i, y_i)$, no matter y_i being given or not, is an *i.i.d.* sample generated according to an unknown distribution $\mathcal{D}$ over $\mathcal{X} \times \mathcal{Y}$.

One might be curious about why unlabeled data can help construct predictive models. For a simple explanation [Miller and Uyar, 1996], assume that the data comes from a **Gaussian mixture model** with n mixture components, i.e.,

$$P(\boldsymbol{x} \mid \Theta) = \sum_{j=1}^{n} \alpha_j \mathcal{N}(\boldsymbol{x} \mid \theta_j) \ , \tag{9.1}$$

where $\alpha_j > 0$ is the mixture coefficient with $\sum_{j=1}^{n} \alpha_j = 1$, and $\Theta = \{\theta_j \mid 1 \leq j \leq n\}$ are the model parameters. In this case, given a labeled example $(\boldsymbol{x}_i, y_i)$, the class label y_i can be considered as a random variable whose distribution $P(y_i \mid \boldsymbol{x}_i, g_i)$ is determined by the feature vector $\boldsymbol{x}_i$ and the mixture component $g_i \in \{1, \ldots, n\}$. According to the *maximum a posterior* criterion, we have the

DOI: 10.1201/9781003587774-9

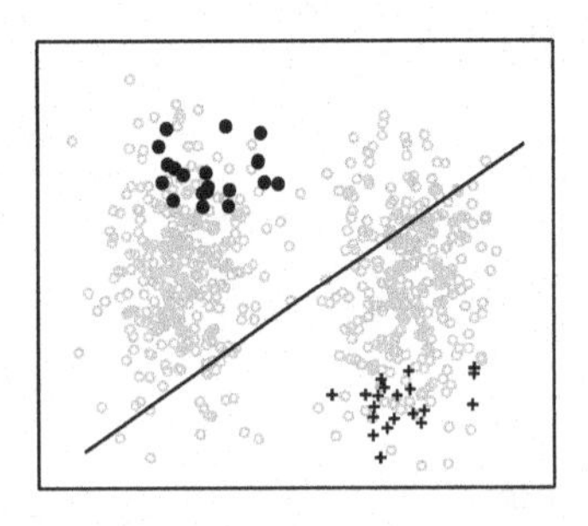

(a) Without unlabeled data

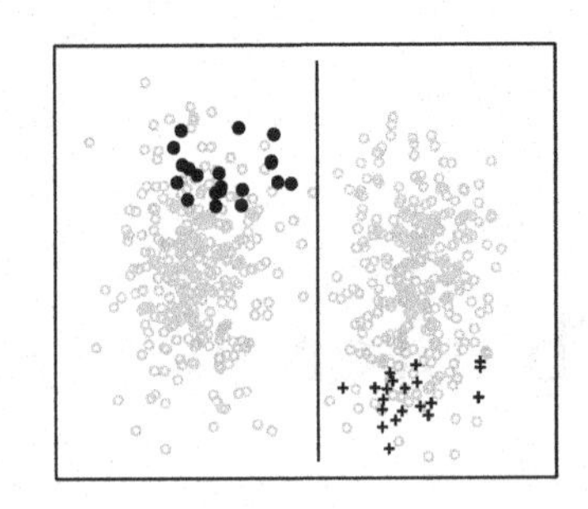

(b) With unlabeled data

Figure 9.1: Illustration of the usefulness of unlabeled data. The optimal classification boundary without/with considering unlabeled data are plotted, respectively.

predictive model

$$h(\boldsymbol{x}) = \underset{c\in\{+1,-1\}}{\arg\max} \sum_{j=1}^{n} P\left(y_i = c \mid g_i = j, \boldsymbol{x}_i\right) P\left(g_i = j \mid \boldsymbol{x}_i\right) , \tag{9.2}$$

where

$$P\left(g_i = j \mid \boldsymbol{x}_i\right) = \frac{\alpha_j \mathcal{N}(\boldsymbol{x}_i \mid \theta_j)}{\sum_{k=1}^{n} \alpha_k \mathcal{N}(\boldsymbol{x}_i \mid \theta_k)} . \tag{9.3}$$

The objective can be accomplished by estimating the terms $P\left(y_i = c \mid g_i = j, \boldsymbol{x}_i\right)$ and $P\left(g_i = j \mid \boldsymbol{x}_i\right)$ from the training data. It is evident that only the first term requires label information, while unlabeled data can be used to help estimate the second term and thus improve the performance of the learned predictive model.

Figure 9.1 gives an illustration of the usefulness of unlabeled data. It can be observed that though both the classification boundaries are perfectly consistent with the labeled data, the boundary obtained by considering unlabeled data has better classification performance. In fact, since both the unlabeled data and the labeled data are drawn from the same distribution $\mathcal{D}$, unlabeled data can disclose some information on data distribution, which is helpful for constructing a model with good generalization ability.

Actually, in semi-supervised learning, there are two basic assumptions, i.e., the **cluster assumption** and **manifold assumption**, both of them are about data distribution. The former assumes that data have inherent cluster structure, and thus, instances falling into the same cluster have the same class label. The latter assumes that data lie on a manifold, and thus, nearby instances have similar predictions. The essence of both assumptions lies in the belief that similar data points should have similar outputs, whereas unlabeled data can be helpful to disclose which data points are similar.

There are four major categories of semi-supervised learning approaches, i.e., generative methods, graph-based methods, low-density separation methods and disagreement-based methods.

Generative methods [Miller and Uyar, 1996, Nigam et al., 2000] assume that both labeled and unlabeled data are generated from the same inherent model. Thus, labels of unlabeled instances can be treated as missing values of model parameters, and estimated by approaches such as the EM (Expectation-Maximization) algorithm [Dempster et al., 1977]. These methods differ in fitting data using different generative models, and one usually needs domain knowledge to determine adequate generative model in achieving good performance. There are also attempts to combine advantages of generative and discriminative approaches [Fujino et al., 2005] to learn from both labeled and unlabeled data.

Graph-based methods [Blum and Chawla, 2001, Zhu et al., 2003, Zhou et al., 2002a] construct a graph, where the nodes correspond to training instances and the edges correspond to relation (usually some kind of similarity or distance) between instances, and then propagate label information on the graph according to certain criteria; for example, labels can be propagated inside different subgraphs separated by minimum cut [Blum and Chawla, 2001]. The performance will heavily depend on how the graph is constructed [Carreira-Perpinan and Zemel, 2004, Wang and Zhang, 2006, Hein and Maier, 2006]. Note that for m data points, these approaches generally require about $O(m^2)$ storage and almost $O(m^3)$ computational complexity. Thus, they suffer seriously from scalability; in addition, they are inherently *transductive* [Zhou, 2021, Section 13.1], because it is difficult to accommodate new instances without graph reconstruction.

Low-density separation methods enforce the classification boundary to go across the less dense regions in input space. The most well-known representatives are S3VMs (**Semi-Supervised Support Vector Machines**) [Joachims, 1999, Chapelle and Zien, 2005, Li et al., 2013c] that try to identify a classification boundary which goes across the less dense region while correctly classifying the labeled data. Such a goal can be accomplished by trying different label assignments for unlabeled data points in different ways, leading to complicated optimization problems. Thus, much effort in this line of research is devoted to design efficient approaches for the resulting optimization problems.

Disagreement-based methods [Blum and Mitchell, 1998, Zhou and Li, 2005, 2010a] generate multiple learners and let them collaborate to exploit unlabeled data, where the disagreement among the learners is crucial to ensure the learning process to continue. The most well-known representative, co-training [Blum and Mitchell, 1998], works by training two learners from two different feature sets (or called two *views*). In each iteration, each learner picks its most confidently predicted unlabeled instances, and assigns its predictions as pseudo-labels for the training of its peer learner. Such approaches can be further enhanced by combining learners to ensemble [Zhou, 2009]. Note that disagreement-based methods offer a natural way to combine semi-supervised learning with active learning: In addition to let the learners teach each other, some unlabeled instances, on which the learners are all unconfident or highly confident but contradictive, can be selected to query [Zhou et al., 2006].

9.2 Semi-Supervised and Ensemble Mutually Helpful

Constructing learning systems with strong generalization ability is one of the fundamental goals of machine learning. Semi-supervised learning tries to achieve strong generalization by exploiting unlabeled data, while ensemble learning tries to achieve strong generalization by combining multiple learners. It is noteworthy that, however, these two paradigms were developed almost in parallel. This phenomenon has been attributed by Zhou [2009] to the fact that the semi-supervised learning community and the ensemble learning community have different philosophies: From the view of the semi-supervised learning community, it seems that using unlabeled data to boost the learning performance is good enough, and so there is no need to involve multiple learners, while from the view of the ensemble learning community, it seems that using multiple learners can do all the things and therefore no need to consider unlabeled data.

It has been advocated in Zhou [2009] that semi-supervised learning and ensemble learning are indeed beneficial to each other, and stronger learning machines can be generated by leveraging unlabeled data and learner combination. In this section, we will take *disagreement-based semi-supervised learning* [Zhou and Li, 2010a] as an example to present the arguments in Zhou [2009] on why it is good to leverage unlabeled data and learner combination.

9.2.1 Learner Combination Helpful to Semi-Supervised Learning

For feature space $\mathcal{X}$ and label space $\mathcal{Y} = \{-1, +1\}$, data set $D = L \cup U$ with labeled data $L = \{(\boldsymbol{x}_1, y_1), \ldots, (\boldsymbol{x}_l, y_l)\} \subset \mathcal{X} \times \mathcal{Y}$ and unlabeled data $U = \{\boldsymbol{x}_{l+1}, \ldots, \boldsymbol{x}_m\} \subset \mathcal{X}$. Let $\mathfrak{D}$ be an unknown distribution over $\mathcal{X}$, and $\mathcal{H} = \{h : \mathcal{X} \to \mathcal{Y}\}$ is a hypothesis space. Assume that $|\mathcal{H}|$ is finite, and L is generated by the ground-truth hypothesis $h^* \in \mathcal{H}$. For a finite sample, it is hard to achieve h^* over D. Suppose we obtain a learner $h^i \in \mathcal{H}$ from D, which is somewhat different from h^*. Let $d(h^i, h^*)$ denote the disagreement between h^i and h^*, then

$$d(h^i, h^*) = P_{\boldsymbol{x} \in \mathfrak{D}}[h^i(\boldsymbol{x}) \neq h^*(\boldsymbol{x})] \ . \tag{9.4}$$

Let ϵ be the generalization error bound of the learner which we wish to achieve finally. That is, if $d(h^i, h^*) = P_{\boldsymbol{x} \in \mathfrak{D}}[h^i(\boldsymbol{x}) \neq h^*(\boldsymbol{x})] < \epsilon$, we say that we have obtained a desired learner; otherwise, we say that the learner h^i is unsatisfactory. Generally, we wish to have a high probability to achieve a good learner. The learning process is said to do PAC (probably approximately correct) learning of h^* if and only if $P[d(h^i, h^*) \geq \epsilon] \leq \delta$, i.e., the disagreement between the ground-truth hypothesis h^* and the learned hypothesis h^i should be small (less than ϵ) with high probability (larger than $1 - \delta$).

Consider the following disagreement-based semi-supervised learning process:

Process: *At first, train two initial learners h_1^0 and h_2^0 using L which contains l labeled examples. Then, h_1^0 selects u unlabeled instances from U to label, and puts these newly labeled examples into the data set σ_2 which contains all*

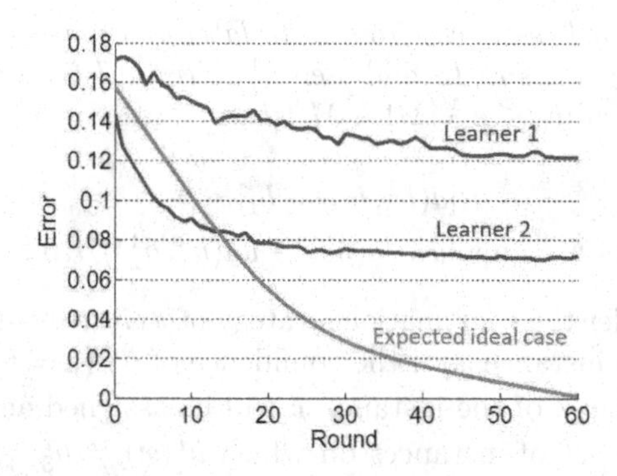

Figure 9.2: An illustration of typical empirical observation.

the examples in L; at the same time, h_2^0 selects u unlabeled instances from U to label, and puts these newly labeled examples into the data set σ_1 which contains all the examples in L. Then, h_1^1 and h_2^1 are trained from σ_1 and σ_2, respectively. After that, h_1^1 selects u unlabeled instances to label, and uses these newly labeled examples to update σ_2, while h_2^1 also selects u unlabeled instances to label, and uses these newly labeled examples to update σ_1. Such a process is repeated for a pre-set number of learning rounds.

If the above process is able to boost the performance to arbitrarily high by using unlabeled data, as believed previously, then there is surely no need to exploit learner combination. However, contrary to previous believes, a typical empirical observation looks like Figure 9.2, where the errors of the two learners could not drop further after a number of learning rounds, far from the expected ideal case where the error was expected to drop to arbitrarily low.

Wang and Zhou [2007] proved that such a phenomenon is not occasional, because the key condition for disagreement-based learning process to continue is that the two learners have a large **diversity**, while during the learning process, the two learners will become more and more similar since they keep on teaching each other. As a result, after some rounds the diversity between them could not allow the learning process to continue effectively.

Thus, we know that it is hard to improve the performance to arbitrarily high by using unlabeled data, and so we are interested in whether the use of learner combination can be helpful for further performance improvement. It is provable that even when the individual learners could not improve the performance any more, learner combination is still possible to improve generalization further. We start by Theorem 9.1 which bounds the error of individual learners.

Theorem 9.1. *Given an initial labeled and clean data set L, assume that the size of L is sufficient to learn two learners h_1^0 and h_2^0 whose upper bound of the generalization error is $a_0 < 0.5$ and $b_0 < 0.5$, respectively, with high probability (more than $1 - \delta$) in the PAC model, i.e., $l \geq max[\frac{1}{a_0} ln\frac{|\mathcal{H}|}{\delta}, \frac{1}{b_0} ln\frac{|\mathcal{H}|}{\delta}]$. Then,*

h_1^0 selects u unlabeled instances from U to label and puts them into σ_2 which contains all the examples in L, and then h_2^1 is trained from σ_2 by minimizing the empirical risk. If $lb_0 \leq e\sqrt[M]{M!} - M$, then

$$P[d(h_2^1, h^*) \geq b_1] \leq \delta \ . \tag{9.5}$$

Here, $M = ua_0$ and $b_1 = \max[b_0 + (ua_0 - ud(h_1^0, h_2^1))/l, 0]$.

Here, we consider the combination strategy of *weighted voting* for simplicity. In detail, for some instance $\boldsymbol{x}$, if the confidence of h_j^i $(j = 1, 2)$ is larger than that of h_{3-j}^i, the label of the instance $\boldsymbol{x}$ will be assigned according to $h_j^i(\boldsymbol{x})$. Let S^i denote the set of instances on which $h_j^i(\boldsymbol{x}) \neq h_{3-j}^i(\boldsymbol{x})$ and let h_{com}^i denote the combination of the learners h_j^i and h_{3-j}^i. For the convenience of analysis, we assume that $P_{\boldsymbol{x}\in S^i}[h_{com}^i(\boldsymbol{x}) \neq h^*(\boldsymbol{x})] = \gamma_i$. Therefore, γ_i indicates the probability of h_{com}^i in the disagreement region of the individual learners. Thus the error rate of the combination h_{com}^i can be expressed as

$$\begin{aligned} P[h_{com}^i(\boldsymbol{x}) \neq h^*(\boldsymbol{x})] &= P[h_1^i(\boldsymbol{x}) \neq h^*(\boldsymbol{x})]/2 \\ &+ P[h_2^i(\boldsymbol{x}) \neq h^*(\boldsymbol{x})]/2 + (\gamma_i - 1/2)P[h_1^i(\boldsymbol{x}) \neq h_2^i(\boldsymbol{x})] \ . \end{aligned} \tag{9.6}$$

Suppose that the decrease of the diversity between the two learners can be expressed as a non-negative function τ with parameters of the learner h_j^i $(j = 1, 2)$ and the set of u newly labeled instances $S_{h_j^i}^u$ provided by h_j^i. This implies that

$$d(h_1^{i-1}, h_2^{i-1}) - d(h_1^{i-1}, h_2^i) = \tau(h_1^{i-1}, S_{h_1^{i-1}}^u) \ , \tag{9.7}$$

$$d(h_1^{i-1}, h_2^{i-1}) - d(h_1^i, h_2^{i-1}) = \tau(h_2^{i-1}, S_{h_2^{i-1}}^u) \ , \tag{9.8}$$

$$d(h_1^{i-1}, h_2^{i-1}) - d(h_1^i, h_2^i) = \tau(h_1^{i-1}, S_{h_1^{i-1}}^u) + \tau(h_2^{i-1}, S_{h_2^{i-1}}^u) \ . \tag{9.9}$$

It can be seen that $d(h_1^{i-1}, h_2^i) + d(h_1^i, h_2^{i-1}) = d(h_1^{i-1}, h_2^{i-1}) + d(h_1^i, h_2^i)$. For the convenience of discussion, suppose $\gamma_i = \gamma$ in the i-th round. This gives the performance of the learner combination as follows.

Theorem 9.2. *If $d(h_1^1, h_2^1) > \frac{ua_0 + ub_0 + \left(l(1-2\gamma) - u\right)d(h_1^0, h_2^0)}{u + l(1-2\gamma)}$ and $u > l$, then*

$$P[h_{com}^1(\boldsymbol{x}) \neq h^*(\boldsymbol{x})] < P[h_{com}^0(\boldsymbol{x}) \neq h^*(\boldsymbol{x})]. \tag{9.10}$$

Based on Theorems 9.1 and 9.2, we have the following theorem which indicates that even when the performance of both individual learners are no longer improved, the performance of the combination of the individual learners could still be improved further.

Theorem 9.3. *If $d(h_1^0, h_2^0) > a_0 > b_0$ and $\gamma \geq \frac{1}{2} + \frac{u(a_0 + b_0 - d(h_1^0, h_2^0))}{2ld(h_1^0, h_2^0)}$, even when $P[h_j^1(\boldsymbol{x}) \neq h^*(\boldsymbol{x})] \geq P[h_j^0(\boldsymbol{x}) \neq h^*(\boldsymbol{x})]$ $(j = 1, 2)$, $P[h_{com}^1(\boldsymbol{x}) \neq h^*(\boldsymbol{x})]$ is still less than $P[h_{com}^0(\boldsymbol{x}) \neq h^*(\boldsymbol{x})]$.*

Second, it is provable that using learner combination can be better than using the individual learners in prediction. Without loss of generality, assume that $a_0 > b_0$ and for any instance $\boldsymbol{x}$, let $\phi_j^i(\boldsymbol{x}) : \mathcal{X} \rightarrow [0,1]$ $(j = 1, 2)$ denote the confidence of the prediction $h_j^i(\boldsymbol{x})$. Therefore, learner combination h_{com}^i of the individual learners according to *weighted voting* can be formulated as

$$h_{com}^i(\boldsymbol{x}) = \begin{cases} h_1^i(\boldsymbol{x}) & \text{if } \phi_1^i(\boldsymbol{x}) > \phi_2^i(\boldsymbol{x}) \\ h_2^i(\boldsymbol{x}) & \text{otherwise} . \end{cases} \tag{9.11}$$

We define confidence risk $CR(\cdot)$ and confidence gain $CG(\cdot)$ of h_j^i, respectively, as

$$CR(h_j^i) = \frac{\int_{h_j^i(\boldsymbol{x}) \neq h^*(\boldsymbol{x})} \phi_j^i(\boldsymbol{x}) p(\boldsymbol{x}) d\boldsymbol{x}}{\int_{h_j^i(\boldsymbol{x}) \neq h^*(\boldsymbol{x})} p(\boldsymbol{x}) d\boldsymbol{x}} , \tag{9.12}$$

$$CG(h_j^i) = \frac{\int_{h_j^i(\boldsymbol{x}) = h^*(\boldsymbol{x})} \phi_j^i(\boldsymbol{x}) p(\boldsymbol{x}) d\boldsymbol{x}}{\int_{h_j^i(\boldsymbol{x}) = h^*(\boldsymbol{x})} p(\boldsymbol{x}) d\boldsymbol{x}} . \tag{9.13}$$

It is not difficult to see that if $CR(h_1^i) < CG(h_2^i)$ and $CR(h_2^i) < CG(h_1^i)$ hold, then h_{com}^i in (9.11) will correctly classify the instances in the disagreement region with high probability.

Suppose that distribution $\mathcal{D}$ over the feature space $\mathcal{X}$ is a uniform distribution. Assume that $\phi_1^0(\boldsymbol{x})$ is uniformly distributed over $[CR(h_1^0) - \alpha_1, CR(h_1^0) + \alpha_1]$ for the instance set in which $h_1^0(\boldsymbol{x}) \neq h^*(\boldsymbol{x})$, and $\phi_1^0(\boldsymbol{x})$ is uniformly distributed over $[CG(h_1^0) - \beta_1, CG(h_1^0) + \beta_1]$ for the instance set in which $h_1^0(\boldsymbol{x}) = h^*(\boldsymbol{x})$; similarly, suppose that $\phi_2^0(\boldsymbol{x})$ is uniformly distributed over $[CR(h_2^0) - \alpha_2, CR(h_2^0) + \alpha_2]$ for the instance set in which $h_2^0(\boldsymbol{x}) \neq h^*(\boldsymbol{x})$, and $\phi_2^0(\boldsymbol{x})$ is uniformly distributed over $[CG(h_2^0) - \beta_2, CG(h_2^0) + \beta_2]$ for the instance set in which $h_2^0(\boldsymbol{x}) = h^*(\boldsymbol{x})$. Without loss of generality, assume $CR(h_1^0) + \alpha_1 > CG(h_2^0) - \beta_2$ and $CR(h_2^0) + \alpha_2 > CG(h_1^0) - \beta_1$.

We have the following theorem which indicates that the learner combination can be better than individual learners in prediction.

Theorem 9.4. *Suppose the combination* $h_{com}^0(\cdot)$ *of the individual learners* $h_1^0(\cdot)$ *and* $h_2^0(\cdot)$ *is generated according to (9.11). If*

$$\begin{aligned} a_0\alpha_2\big(CR(h_1^0) - CG(h_2^0)\big) + b_0\alpha_1\big(CR(h_2^0) - CG(h_1^0)\big) \\ < \alpha_1\alpha_2\big(d(h_1^0, h_2^0) - 2a_0\big) - a_0\alpha_2\beta_2 - b_0\alpha_1\beta_1 , \end{aligned} \tag{9.14}$$

then the error rate of $h_{com}^0(\cdot)$ *is less than* $\min\{a_0, b_0\}$.

9.2.2 Unlabeled Data Helpful to Ensemble Learning

Generally, a lot of labeled training examples are needed for constructing a strong ensemble. In some real applications, however, the number of labeled training examples may be too few to launch a successful ensemble learning. Under such situations, unlabeled data can be helpful for enabling ensemble learning.

Zhou et al. [2007] showed that, under the classical assumption of co-training for disagreement-based semi-supervised learning, exploiting unlabeled data possibly helps enrich the labeled training examples. This is feasible even when there is only one labeled example. After such a process, standard ensemble methods can be applied. In the following, we briefly introduce the method presented in [Zhou et al., 2007].

Let $\mathcal{X}$ and $\mathcal{Y}$ denote the two **sufficient and redundant views**, that is, two independent attribute sets each containing sufficient information for constructing a strong learner. Let $((\boldsymbol{x}, \boldsymbol{y}), c)$ denote a labeled example where $\boldsymbol{x} \in \mathcal{X}$ and $\boldsymbol{y} \in \mathcal{Y}$ are the two attribute portions of the example, and c is the associated label. To simplify the discussion, assume that $c \in \{0, 1\}$ where 0 and 1 denote negative and positive classes, respectively. Given $((\boldsymbol{x}_0, \boldsymbol{y}_0), 1)$ and a large number of unlabeled instances $\mathcal{U} = \{((\boldsymbol{x}_i, \boldsymbol{y}_i), c_i)\}$ $(i = 1, \ldots, l-1;$ c_i is unknown), we hope to exploit $\mathcal{U}$ to enrich the labeled examples.

Because the two views are sufficient and independent, some projections on these two views should have strong correlation with the ground-truth. If the correlated projections of these two views can be identified, they can help induce the labels of some unlabeled instances.

The correlation between the projections on the two views can be identified by the **canonical correlation analysis** [Hotelling, 1936] or its kernel extension [Hardoon et al., 2004], and a number of correlated pairs of projections can be identified. If the two views are really conditionally independent given the class label, the most strongly correlated pair of projections should be in accordance with the ground-truth. In real applications, however, the conditional independence rarely holds and therefore, information conveyed by the other pairs of correlated projections should not be omitted. The OLTV method [Zhou et al., 2007] takes a simple strategy as follows to use these information.

Let n denote the number of pairs of correlated projections which have been identified, an instance $(\boldsymbol{x}^*, \boldsymbol{y}^*)$ can be projected into $\langle P_j(\boldsymbol{x}^*), P_j(\boldsymbol{y}^*)\rangle$ $(j = 1, 2, \ldots, n)$. Then, in the j-th projection, the similarity $sim_{i,j}$ can be measured between an original unlabeled instance $(\boldsymbol{x}_i, \boldsymbol{y}_i)$ $(i = 1, 2, \ldots, l-1)$ and the original labeled instance $(\boldsymbol{x}_0, \boldsymbol{y}_0)$. Considering that $(\boldsymbol{x}_0, \boldsymbol{y}_0)$ is a positive instance, $\rho_i = \sum_{j=1}^{n} \lambda_j sim_{i,j}$ delivers the confidence of $(\boldsymbol{x}_i, \boldsymbol{y}_i)$ being a positive instance. Here, λ_j is a coefficient reflecting the strength of the correlation solved by the projection identification method. Thus, several unlabeled instances with the largest and smallest ρ values can be selected as the additional positive and negative examples, respectively. In this way, the number of labeled training examples is increased.

The quality of the additional labeled training examples derived by the OLTV method is much better than that derived by using strategies such as k nearest neighbors in the original feature space (e.g., using the k unlabeled instances nearest to $(\boldsymbol{x}_0, \boldsymbol{y}_0)$ as additional positive examples while the k farthest

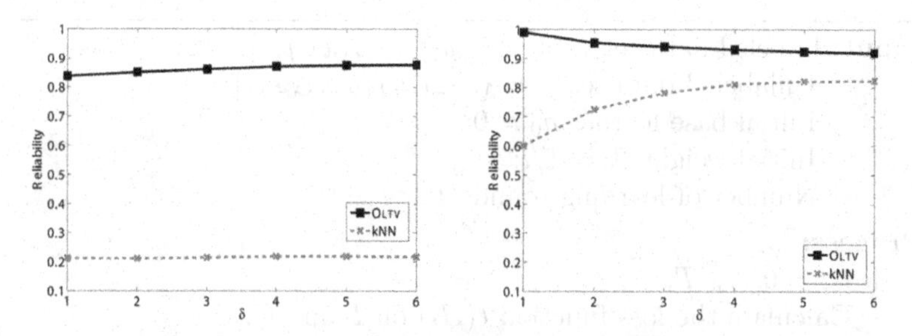

Figure 9.3: The reliability of OLTV and kNN on two data sets.

unlabeled instances as additional negative ones). Let *reliability* be b/a if the labels for a unlabeled instances have been induced, among which b of them are correct. As shown in Figure 9.3 [Zhou et al., 2007], where δ is a coefficient related to the number of additional labeled examples induced, the reliability of the kNN strategy is far worse than that of OLTV. On all experimental data sets, the reliability of OLTV is always higher than 80% and even often higher than 90%.

Thus, the labeled training data can be significantly enriched by exploiting unlabeled data, and thus ensemble learning can be enabled.

Another important, even more fundamental, issue showing the helpfulness of unlabeled data to ensemble learning lies in the finding that unlabeled data can help enhance ensemble diversity [Zhou, 2009], and a new diversity enhancement mechanism is thereafter invented [Zhang and Zhou, 2010a]. This is relevant to Chapter 5, and we will give more introduction in Section 9.6.

9.3 Semi-Supervised Sequential Ensemble Methods

Semi-supervised sequential ensemble methods mainly include Boosting-style methods, such as SSMBoost, ASSEMBLE, SemiBoost, and RegBoost.

SSMBoost [d'Alché-Buc et al., 2001]. This method extends the *margin* definition to unlabeled data and employs gradient descent to construct an ensemble which minimizes the margin loss function on both labeled and unlabeled data. Here, Boosting is generalized as a linear combination of hypotheses, that is,

$$H(\boldsymbol{x}) = \sum_{t=1}^{T} \beta_t h_t(\boldsymbol{x}) \ , \tag{9.15}$$

where the output of each base learner h_t is in $[-1, 1]$. The overall loss function is defined with any decreasing function ℓ of the margin γ as

$$\ell(H) = \sum_{i=1}^{l} \ell\left(\gamma\left(H\left(\boldsymbol{x}_i\right), y_i\right)\right) \ , \tag{9.16}$$

where $\gamma(H(\boldsymbol{x}_i), y_i) = y_i H(\boldsymbol{x}_i)$ is the margin of the hypothesis H on the labeled example $(\boldsymbol{x}_i, y_i)$. Apparently, the margin measures the confidence of

---

Input: Labeled data set $L = \{(\boldsymbol{x}_1, y_1), \ldots, (\boldsymbol{x}_l, y_l)\}$;
Unlabeled data set $U = \{\boldsymbol{x}_{l+1}, \boldsymbol{x}_{l+2} \ldots, \boldsymbol{x}_m\}$;
Initial base learner $h_0 = 0$;
Initial weight $\beta_0 = 1/l$;
Number of learning rounds T.

Process:
1. **for** $t = 0, \ldots, T$:
2. Calculate the loss function $\ell(H_t)$ on L and U:
$\ell(H_t) = \sum_{i=1}^{l} \ell(\gamma(H_t(\boldsymbol{x}_i), y_i)) + \sum_{i=l+1}^{m} \ell(\gamma_u(H_t(\boldsymbol{x}_i)))$;
% refer to (9.20)
3. Use Boosting algorithm to find h_{t+1} and β_{t+1} minimizing the loss function;
4. Build $H_{t+1}(\boldsymbol{x}) = \sum_{i=1}^{t+1} \beta_i h_i(\boldsymbol{x})$;
5. **end**

Output: H_{T+1}

Figure 9.4: The SSMBoost algorithm.

the classification for labeled data. For unlabeled data, however, the margin can not be calculated, because we do not know the ground-truth labels. One alternative is to use the expected margin

$$\gamma_u\left(H\left(\boldsymbol{x}\right)\right) = \mathbb{E}_y\big(\gamma(H(\boldsymbol{x}), y)\big) \; . \tag{9.17}$$

Using the output $(H(\boldsymbol{x}) + 1)/2$ as threshold for an estimate of the posterior probability $P(y = +1 \mid \boldsymbol{x})$, the expected margin for unlabeled data in U becomes

$$\gamma_u\left(H\left(\boldsymbol{x}\right)\right) = \frac{H(\boldsymbol{x}) + 1}{2} H(\boldsymbol{x}) + \left(1 - \frac{H\left(\boldsymbol{x}\right) + 1}{2}\right)\left(-H\left(\boldsymbol{x}\right)\right) = \left(H(\boldsymbol{x})\right)^2 . \tag{9.18}$$

Another way is to use the *maximum a posteriori* probability of y directly, and thus,

$$\gamma_u\left(H\left(\boldsymbol{x}\right)\right) = H(\boldsymbol{x})\mathtt{sign}\big(H(\boldsymbol{x})\big) = |H(\boldsymbol{x})| \; . \tag{9.19}$$

Note that the margins in both (9.18) and (9.19) require the outputs of the learner on unlabeled data, which can be regarded as the *pseudo-label* assigned by the ensemble. With the definition of margin for unlabeled data, the overall loss function of SSMBoost at the t-th round is defined as

$$\ell(H_t) = \sum_{i=1}^{l} \ell\big(\gamma(H_t(\boldsymbol{x}_i), y_i)\big) + \sum_{i=l+1}^{m} \ell\big(\gamma_u(H_t(\boldsymbol{x}_i))\big) \; . \tag{9.20}$$

Then, in the t-th round, SSMBoost tries to create a new base learner h_{t+1} and the corresponding weight β_{t+1} to minimize $\ell(H_t)$. The final ensemble H is obtained when the number of rounds T is reached. Note that rather than standard AdaBoost, SSMBoost uses the MarginBoost, which is a variant of AnyBoost [Mason et al., 2000] to attain base learners in each round. The SSMBoost algorithm is summarized in Figure 9.4.

ASSEMBLE [Bennett et al., 2002]. This method is similar to SSMBoost. It also constructs ensembles in the form of (9.15), and alternates between assigning pseudo-labels to unlabeled data using the existing ensemble and generating the next base learner to maximize the margin on both labeled and unlabeled data, where the margin on unlabeled data is calculated according to (9.19). The main difference between SSMBoost and ASSEMBLE lies in the fact that SSMBoost requires the base learning algorithm be a semi-supervised learning method, while Bennett et al. [2002] enabled ASSEMBLE to work with any weight-sensitive learner for both binary and multi-class problems.

SemiBoost [Mallapragada et al., 2009]. Recall that in SSMBoost and ASSEMBLE, in each round the pseudo-labels are assigned to some unlabeled data with high confidence, and the pseudo-labeled data along with the labeled data is used together to train a new base learner in the next round. In this way, the pseudo-labeled data may be only helpful to increase the classification margin, because much of the high-confidence unlabeled data may have already been learned well by the current ensemble. To make the pseudo-labeled data more informative, Mallapragada et al. [2009] proposed the SemiBoost algorithm, which uses pairwise similarity measurements to guide the selection of unlabeled data to assign pseudo-labels. They imposed the constraint that similar unlabeled instances must be assigned the same label, and if an unlabeled instance is similar to a labeled instance then it must be assigned the label of the labeled instance. With these constraints, the SemiBoost algorithm is closely related to graph-based semi-supervised learning approaches exploiting the manifold assumption.

Specifically, let S_{ij} be the similarity between the unlabeled instance $\boldsymbol{x}_i$ and the labeled instance $\boldsymbol{x}_j$, and S_{ik} be the similarity between unlabeled instances $\boldsymbol{x}_i$ and $\boldsymbol{x}_k$ for $j \in \{1, \ldots, l\}$, $i, k \in \{l+1, \ldots, m\}$. According to the bound optimization procedure employed by SemiBoost Mallapragada et al. [2009], define the positive and negative prediction confidence p_i and q_i, respectively, for each unlabeled instance $\boldsymbol{x}_i$ as

$$p_i = \sum_{j=1}^{l} S_{ij} e^{-2H(\boldsymbol{x}_i)} \mathbb{I}(y_j = +1) + \frac{C}{2} \sum_{k=l+1}^{m} S_{ik} e^{H(\boldsymbol{x}_k) - H(\boldsymbol{x}_i)} , \quad (9.21)$$

$$q_i = \sum_{j=1}^{l} S_{ij} e^{2H(\boldsymbol{x}_i)} \mathbb{I}(y_j = -1) + \frac{C}{2} \sum_{k=l+1}^{m} S_{ik} e^{H(\boldsymbol{x}_i) - H(\boldsymbol{x}_k)} . \quad (9.22)$$

Here, C is used to balance the importance between labeled and unlabeled instances. The combination weight β of base learner in each iteration is set to

$$\beta = \frac{1}{4} \ln \frac{\sum_{i=l+1}^{m} p_i \mathbb{I}(z_i = +1) + \sum_{i=l+1}^{m} q_i \mathbb{I}(z_i = -1)}{\sum_{i=l+1}^{m} p_i \mathbb{I}(z_i = -1) + \sum_{i=l+1}^{m} q_i \mathbb{I}(z_i = +1)} , \quad (9.23)$$

Input: Labeled data set $L = \{(\boldsymbol{x}_1, y_1), \ldots, (\boldsymbol{x}_l, y_l)\}$;
Unlabeled data set $U = \{\boldsymbol{x}_{l+1}, \boldsymbol{x}_{l+2} \ldots, \boldsymbol{x}_m\}$;
Initial ensemble $H_0(\boldsymbol{x}) = 0$;
Balance parameter C;
Similarity matrix $\mathbf{S} = [S_{ab}]_{m \times m}$;
A supervised learning algorithm $\mathfrak{L}$;
Number of learning rounds T.

Process:
1. **for** $t = 0, \ldots, T$:
2. Calculate p_i and q_i for each unlabeled instance $\boldsymbol{x}_i$ based on (9.21) and (9.22), respectively;
3. Randomly select 10 percent unlabeled instances from U with $\boldsymbol{x}_i$ being sampled with probability $|p_i - q_i| / \sum_{i=l+1}^{m} |p_i - q_i|$, and assigned with pseudo-label $z_i = \mathtt{sign}(p_i - q_i)$;
4. Combine L with the sampled pseudo-labeled instances and train base learner h_{t+1} using the supervised learning algorithm $\mathfrak{L}$;
5. Set the combination weight β_{t+1} according to (9.23);
6. Build $H_{t+1}(\boldsymbol{x}) = \sum_{i=1}^{t+1} \beta_i h_i(\boldsymbol{x})$;
7. **end**

Output: H_{T+1}

Figure 9.5: The SemiBoost algorithm.

where $z_i = \mathtt{sign}(p_i - q_i)$ is the pseudo-label of $\boldsymbol{x}_i$. The SemiBoost algorithm is summarized in Figure 9.5. It has been generalized to multi-class learning by Valizadegan et al. [2008].

RegBoost [Chen and Wang, 2011]. This method is similar to SemiBoost, which also constructs the ensemble by utilizing the similarity information among instances. Given the labeled data set L and unlabeled data set U, RegBoost defines the Boosting cost functional $\mathcal{C}(H)$ consisting of the classification margin cost on labeled data and the pseudo-label margin cost on unlabeled data with kNN regularization

$$\mathcal{C}(H) = \frac{1}{l} \sum_{i=1}^{l} \alpha_i \ell(y_i H(\boldsymbol{x}_i)) + \frac{1}{u} \sum_{i=l+1}^{m} \beta_i |N(i)|^{-1} \sum_{j \in N(i)} \omega_{ij} \ell(\hat{y}_j H(\boldsymbol{x}_i)) \ , \quad (9.24)$$

where $N(i)$ is index set for the k nearest neighbors of unlabeled instance $\boldsymbol{x}_i$ identified in $L \cup U$. Correspondingly, $\hat{y}_j = y_j$ if $\boldsymbol{x}_j \in L$, and $\hat{y}_j = H(\boldsymbol{x}_j)$ if $\boldsymbol{x}_j \in U$. The parameter α_i is used to weight the importance of labeled data, and β_i is set to be proportional to the density of unlabeled data. Furthermore, ω_{ij} corresponds to the pairwise similarity between $\boldsymbol{x}_i$ and $\boldsymbol{x}_j$ as calculated by Gaussian kernel. In each iteration, the new base learner h is found by minimizing the inner product between the gradient of cost functional $\nabla\mathcal{C}(H)$ and h, i.e. $\langle\nabla\mathcal{C}(H), h\rangle$, and then the combination weight w is solved by minimizing the cost functional $\mathcal{C}(H + wh)$.

9.4 Semi-Supervised Parallel Ensemble Methods

Semi-supervised parallel ensemble methods are usually *disagreement-based methods*, such as Tri-Training, Co-Forest, and Asymmetric Tri-Training.

Tri-Training [Zhou and Li, 2005]. This method can be viewed as an extension of the Co-Training method [Blum and Mitchell, 1998]. Co-Training trains two learners from different feature sets, and in each round, each learner labels some unlabeled data for the other learner to refine. Co-Training works well on data with two *independent* feature sets both containing *sufficient* information for constructing a strong learner. Most data sets in real-world tasks contain only a single feature set, and it is difficult to judge which learner should be trusted when they disagree. To address this issue, Zhou and Li [2005] proposed to train three learners, and in each round, the unlabeled data are used in a *majority teaching minority* way; that is, for an unlabeled instance, if the predictions of two learners agree yet the third learner disagrees, then the unlabeled instance will be labeled by the agreed two learners for the third learner. To reduce the risk of "correct minority" being misled by "incorrect majority", a sanity check mechanism was designed in [Zhou and Li, 2005], which is examined in each round. In the testing phase, the prediction is obtained by majority voting. The Tri-Training method can work with any base learners and is easy to implement. Note that, like ensembles in supervised learning, the three learners need to be diverse. Zhou and Li [2005] generated the initial learners using *bootstrap sampling*, similar to the strategy used in Bagging. Other strategies for augmenting diversity can also be applied, and there is no doubt that Tri-Training can work well with multiple views since different views will provide natural diversity.

Specifically, let h_1, h_2, and h_3 denote the three learners to be trained by Tri-Training. Furthermore, let e_i denote the classification error rate yielded by $h_j \& h_k$ for $j, k \neq i$, which is measured through dividing the number of examples in L on which both h_j and h_k make incorrect classification by the number of examples in L on which h_j and h_k agree on the classification. The Tri-Training algorithm is summarized in Figure 9.6.

Co-Forest [Li and Zhou, 2007]. This method is an extension of Tri-Training to include more base learners. In each round, each learner is refined with unlabeled instances labeled by its *concomitant ensemble*, which comprises all the other learners. The **concomitant ensembles** used in Co-Forest are usually more accurate than the three learners used in Tri-Training. However, by using more learners, it is noteworthy that, during the "majority teaching minority" procedure the behaviors of the learners will become more and more similar, and thus the diversity of the learners decreases rapidly. This problem can be

Input: Labeled data set $L = \{(\boldsymbol{x}_1, y_1), \ldots, (\boldsymbol{x}_l, y_l)\}$;
Unlabeled data set $U = \{\boldsymbol{x}_{l+1}, \boldsymbol{x}_{l+2} \ldots, \boldsymbol{x}_m\}$;
A supervised learning algorithm $\mathfrak{L}$.

Process:

1. Train h_1, h_2, h_3 by applying $\mathfrak{L}$ over a bootstrapped sample of L;
2. Initialize $e'_i = 0.5$ and $l'_i = 0$;
3. **repeat**
4. **for** $i = 1, \ldots, 3$:
5. Set $L_i = \emptyset$ and $Update_i$ = FALSE;
6. Measure the classification error e_i yielded by $h_j \& h_k$ $(j, k \neq i)$ based on L;
7. **if** $e_i < e'_i$ **then**
8. **for** $u = l + 1, \ldots, m$:
9. **if** $h_j(\boldsymbol{x}_u) = h_k(\boldsymbol{x}_u)$ for $j, k \neq i$ **then**
10. Add $(\boldsymbol{x}_u, h_j(\boldsymbol{x}_u))$ into L_i;
11. **end**
12. **if** $l'_i = 0$ **then** % h_i has not been updated before
13. Set $l'_i = \left\lfloor \frac{e_i}{e'_i - e_i} + 1 \right\rfloor$;
14. **if** $l'_i < |L_i|$ **then**
15. **if** $e_i|L_i| < e'_i l'_i$ **then**
16. $Update_i$ = TRUE;
17. **else if** $l'_i > \frac{e_i}{e'_i - e_i}$ **then**
18. Subsample $\left\lceil \frac{e'_i l'_i}{e_i} - 1 \right\rceil$ examples from L_i;
19. $Update_i$ = TRUE;
20. **end**
21. **for** $i = 1, \ldots, 3$:
22. **if** $Update_i$ = TRUE **then**
23. Train h_i by applying $\mathfrak{L}$ over $L \bigcup L_i$, update e'_i with e_i, and update l'_i with $|L_i|$;
24. **end**
25. **until** none of h_1, h_2, h_3 changes;

Output: An ensemble consisting of three learners h_1, h_2, h_3

Figure 9.6: The Tri-Training algorithm.

reduced to some extent by injecting randomness into the learning process. In [Li and Zhou, 2007], a random forest was used to realize the ensemble, and in each round, different subsets of unlabeled instances were sampled from the unlabeled data for different learners. This strategy is not only helpful for augmenting diversity, but also helpful for reducing the risk of being trapped into poor local minima.

Asymmetric Tri-Training [Saito et al., 2017]. This method is an extension of Tri-Training for deep unsupervised domain adaptation [Ganin and Lempitsky,

Input: Data set $D = \{\boldsymbol{x}_1, \boldsymbol{x}_2 \ldots, \boldsymbol{x}_m\}$;
Must-link constraints set $\mathcal{M}$;
Cannot-link constraints set $\mathcal{C}$;
Number of clusters k.
Process:
1. Randomly select k samples from D to form the initial mean vectors $\{\boldsymbol{\mu}_1, \boldsymbol{\mu}_2, \ldots, \boldsymbol{\mu}_k\}$;
2. **repeat**
3. Set $C_j = \emptyset$ for $j \in \{1, \ldots, k\}$;
4. **for** $i = 1, \ldots, m$:
5. Calculate the distance $d_{ij} = \|\boldsymbol{x}_i - \boldsymbol{\mu}_j\|_2$ between $\boldsymbol{x}_i$ and each mean vector $\boldsymbol{\mu}_j$ $(j \in \{1, \ldots, k\})$;
6. Set $\mathcal{K} = \{1, 2, \ldots, k\}$ and $Merged$ = FALSE;
7. **while** $\neg Merged$ **do**
8. Identify the cluster which is nearest to $\boldsymbol{x}_i$: $r = \arg\min_{j \in \mathcal{K}} d_{ij}$;
9. Set $Violated$ = TRUE if any constraint in $\mathcal{M}$ and $\mathcal{C}$ is violated by merging $\boldsymbol{x}_i$ into C_r; Otherwise, set $Violated$ = FALSE;
10. **if** $\neg Violated$ **then**
11. $C_r = C_r \cup \{\boldsymbol{x}_i\}$, $Merged$ = TRUE;
12. **else**
13. $\mathcal{K} = \mathcal{K} \setminus \{r\}$;
14. *Break and report erroneous termination if* $\mathcal{K} = \emptyset$;
15. **end**
16. **end**
17. **for** $j = 1, \ldots, k$:
18. $\boldsymbol{\mu}_j = \frac{1}{|C_j|} \sum_{\boldsymbol{x} \in C_j} \boldsymbol{x}$;
19. **end**
20. **until** none of the mean vectors $\boldsymbol{\mu}_j$ $(j \in \{1, \ldots, k\})$ changes;

Output: Clusters $\{C_1, C_2, \ldots, C_k\}$

Figure 9.7: The Constrained k-means algorithm.

2015]. Three neural networks are employed in an *asymmetric* manner where two of them are trained with labeled data from the source domain and used to provide pseudo-labels on unlabeled data from target domain, while the remaining neural network is trained with the pseudo-labeled target domain data. In each round, in order to pick up reliable pseudo-labels, an unlabeled data is assigned with a pseudo-label only if the two neural networks trained from source domain agree with the prediction on the unlabeled data and at least one of the two neural networks has high predictive confidence. Furthermore, in order to augment the diversity of the two source domain neural networks, a constraint term is enforced to their loss functions which maximizes the difference of the weights of their fully connected layer.

9.5 Semi-Supervised Clustering Ensemble

Clustering is a typical unsupervised learning problem, in which we do not rely on supervision information. In practice, however, we often have access to some additional supervision information, which can be utilized to obtain better clustering results via **semi-supervised clustering**.

Typically, there are two kinds of supervision information in clustering tasks. The first kind is **must-link** and **cannot-link** constraints, where must-link means the samples must belong to the same cluster, and cannot-link means the samples must not belong to the same cluster. The second kind of supervision information refers to a small number of labeled samples.

Constrained k-means [Wagstaff et al., 2001]. This method is a representative semi-supervised clustering algorithm that utilizes supervision information in the form of must-link and cannot-link constraints. Given a data set $D = \{\boldsymbol{x}_1, \boldsymbol{x}_2, \ldots, \boldsymbol{x}_m\}$, a must-link set $\mathcal{M}$, and a cannot-link set $\mathcal{C}$, where $(\boldsymbol{x}_i, \boldsymbol{x}_j) \in \mathcal{M}$ means $\boldsymbol{x}_i$ and $\boldsymbol{x}_j$ must be in the same cluster and $(\boldsymbol{x}_i, \boldsymbol{x}_j) \in \mathcal{C}$ means $\boldsymbol{x}_i$ and $\boldsymbol{x}_j$ must not be in the same cluster. Constrained k-means, which is an extension of k-means, ensures that the constraints in $\mathcal{M}$ and $\mathcal{C}$ are satisfied during the clustering process; otherwise, it will return an error when the constraints are violated. The Constrained k-means algorithm is summarized in Figure 9.7.

Constrained Seed k-means [Basu et al., 2002]. This method makes use of supervision information which exists in the form of a small number of labeled samples (the labels here refer to *cluster labels* rather than *class labels*). Given a data set $D = \{\boldsymbol{x}_1, \boldsymbol{x}_2, \ldots, \boldsymbol{x}_m\}$ and a small set of labeled samples $S = \bigcup_{j=1}^{k} S_j \subset D$, where $S_j \neq \varnothing$ is the set of samples in the j-th cluster. It is straightforward to use such supervision information: We can use the labeled samples as the *seeds* to initialize the k centroids of the k-means algorithm, and these seeds are retained in their clusters during the learning process. The Constrained Seed k-means algorithm is summarized in Figure 9.8.

Constrained Complete-Link [Klein et al., 2002]. This method is an extension of Constrained k-means. It works on the *complete-linkage* clustering algorithm [Kaufman and Rousseeuw, 1990] and an initial proximity matrix $\mathbf{D}$ between the samples. $\mathbf{D}$ is adjusted by taking the *imposing constraints* that samples known to be in the same cluster should be nearby while sample known to be in different clusters should be far away, and the *propagating constraints* that samples near to those in the same (different) cluster should also be in the same (different) cluster. The metric of the adjusted proximity matrix is restored using a modified Floyd-Warshall algorithm [Cormen et al., 1990], which can also be fulfilled by directly employing a metric learning procedure [Xing et al., 2002, Bilenko et al., 2004]. The Constrained Complete-Link algorithm is summarized in Figure 9.9.

Input: Data set $D = \{\boldsymbol{x}_1, \boldsymbol{x}_2 \ldots, \boldsymbol{x}_m\}$;
A small set of labeled samples $S = \bigcup_{j=1}^{k} S_j \subset D$;
Number of clusters k.

Process:
1. **for** $j = 1, \ldots, k$:
2. $\quad \boldsymbol{\mu}_j = \frac{1}{|S_j|} \sum_{\boldsymbol{x} \in S_j} \boldsymbol{x}$;
3. **end**
4. **repeat**
5. $\quad$ Set $C_j = S_j$ for $j \in \{1, \ldots, k\}$;
6. $\quad$ **for** $\boldsymbol{x}_i \in D \setminus S$:
7. $\quad\quad$ Calculate the distance $d_{ij} = \|\boldsymbol{x}_i - \boldsymbol{\mu}_j\|_2$ between $\boldsymbol{x}_i$ and each mean vector $\boldsymbol{\mu}_j$ for $j \in \{1, \ldots, k\}$;
6. $\quad\quad$ Identify the cluster which is nearest to $\boldsymbol{x}_i$: $r = \arg\min_{j \in \{1,\ldots,k\}} d_{ij}$;
7. $\quad\quad$ Merge $\boldsymbol{x}_i$ into C_r: $C_r = C_r \bigcup \{\boldsymbol{x}_i\}$;
16. $\quad$ **end**
17. $\quad$ **for** $j = 1, \ldots, k$:
18. $\quad\quad \boldsymbol{\mu}_j = \frac{1}{|C_j|} \sum_{\boldsymbol{x} \in C_j} \boldsymbol{x}$;
19. $\quad$ **end**
20. **until** none of the mean vectors $\boldsymbol{\mu}_j$ $(j \in \{1, \ldots, k\})$ changes;

Output: Clusters $\{C_1, C_2, \ldots, C_k\}$

Figure 9.8: The Constrained Seed k-means algorithm.

9.6 Semi-Supervised Diversity Enhancement

Ensemble methods working in supervised setting attempts to achieve a high accuracy and high diversity for individual learners by using the labeled training data. It is noteworthy, however, that pursuing high accuracy and high diversity on the same labeled training data can suffer from a dilemma; that is, the increase of diversity may require the sacrifice of individual accuracy. For an extreme example, if all learners are nearly perfect on training data, to increase diversity, the training accuracy of some learners needs to be decreased.

From the aspect of diversity augmentation, using unlabeled data makes a big difference. For example, given two sets of learners, $H = \{h_1, \ldots, h_T\}$ and $G = \{g_1, \ldots, g_T\}$, if we know that all of the learners are 100% accurate on labeled training data, there is no basis for choosing between ensemble H and ensemble G. However, if we find that the g_i's make the same predictions on unlabeled data while the h_i's make different predictions on the same set of unlabeled data, we know that the ensemble H would have good chance to be better than G, because it is more diverse while still being equally accurate on the training data.

Note that most semi-supervised ensemble methods, as introduced in Section 9.3, exploit unlabeled data to improve the individual accuracy by assigning

---

Input: Data set $D = \{\boldsymbol{x}_1, \boldsymbol{x}_2 \ldots, \boldsymbol{x}_m\}$;
Must-link constraints set $\mathcal{M}$;
Cannot-link constraints set $\mathcal{C}$;
Number of clusters k;
Proximity matrix $\mathbf{D}$;
Complete-linkage clustering algorithm $\mathcal{A}$.

Process:
1. **for** $(\boldsymbol{x}_i, \boldsymbol{x}_j) \in \mathcal{M}$:
2. $\quad \mathbf{D}(i,j) = 0$, $\mathbf{D}(j,i) = 0$;
3. **end**
4. Set $I = \{i \mid \exists j \neq i, (\boldsymbol{x}_i, \boldsymbol{x}_j) \in \mathcal{M}\}$;
5. **for** $k \in I$ and $i, j \in \{1, \ldots, m\}$: % modified Floyd-Warshall procedure
6. $\quad \mathbf{D}(i,j) = \min\{\mathbf{D}(i,j), \mathbf{D}(i,k) + \mathbf{D}(k,j)\}$;
7. **end**
8. **for** (i,j) s.t. $\mathbf{D}(i,j) = 0$:
9. $\quad \mathcal{M} = \mathcal{M} \cup \{(\boldsymbol{x}_i, \boldsymbol{x}_j)\}$;
10. **end**
11. **for** $(\boldsymbol{x}_i, \boldsymbol{x}_j) \in \mathcal{C}$ and $(\boldsymbol{x}_j, \boldsymbol{x}_k) \in \mathcal{M}$:
12. $\quad \mathbf{D}(i,j) = \infty$, $\mathbf{D}(i,k) = \infty$;
13. **end**
14. $\{C_1, C_2, \ldots, C_k\} = \mathcal{A}(\mathbf{D}, k)$;

Output: Clusters $\{C_1, C_2, \ldots, C_k\}$

Figure 9.9: The Constrained Complete-Link algorithm.

pseudo-labels to unlabeled data and then using the pseudo-labeled examples together with the original labeled examples to train the individual learners. Zhou [2009] indicated that it is possible to design new ensemble methods by using unlabeled data to help enhance diversity, and Zhang and Zhou [2010a] proposed the UDEED method along this direction.

Following the same notations used in Section 9.2, let $L_u = \{\boldsymbol{x}_1, \boldsymbol{x}_2, \ldots, \boldsymbol{x}_l\}$ denote the unlabeled data set derived from L by neglecting the label information. Assume that the ensemble comprises T component learners $\{h_1, h_2, \ldots, h_T\}$, each taking the form $h_k : \mathcal{X} \to [-1, +1]$. Furthermore, assume that the value $|h_k(\boldsymbol{x})|$ can be regarded as the confidence of $\boldsymbol{x}$ being positive or negative. As before, the output $(h_k(\boldsymbol{x}) + 1)/2$ is used as a threshold for an estimate of the posterior probability $P(y = +1 \mid \boldsymbol{x})$.

The basic idea of the UDEED method is to maximize the *fit* of the learners on the labeled data, while maximizing the *diversity* of the learners on the unlabeled data. Therefore, UDEED generates the ensemble $H = \{h_1, h_2, \ldots, h_T\}$ by minimizing the loss function

$$V(H, L, D) = V_{emp}(H, L) + \alpha \cdot V_{div}(H, D) , \tag{9.25}$$

where $V_{emp}(H, L)$ corresponds to the *empirical loss* of H on L, $V_{div}(H, D)$ corresponds to the *diversity loss* of H on a data set D (e.g., $D = U$), and α is a parameter to balance between these two terms.

Indeed, (9.25) provides a general framework which can be realized with different choices of the loss functions. In [Zhang and Zhou, 2010a], $V_{emp}(H, L)$ and $V_{div}(H, D)$ are realized, respectively, by

$$V_{emp}(H, L) = \frac{1}{T} \cdot \sum_{k=1}^{T} l(h_k, L) , \tag{9.26}$$

$$V_{div}(H, D) = \frac{2}{T(T-1)} \cdot \sum_{p=1}^{T-1} \sum_{q=p+1}^{T} d(h_p, h_q, D) . \tag{9.27}$$

Here, $l(h_k, L)$ measures the empirical loss of h_k on L, and

$$d(h_p, h_q, D) = \frac{1}{|D|} \sum_{\boldsymbol{x} \in D} h_p(\boldsymbol{x}) h_q(\boldsymbol{x}) \tag{9.28}$$

represents the *prediction difference* between individual learners h_p and h_q on D. Note that the prediction difference is calculated based on the real output $h(\boldsymbol{x})$ instead of the signed output $\texttt{sign}(h(\boldsymbol{x}))$.

Thus, UDEED aims to find the target model H^* that minimizes the loss function (9.25), that is,

$$H^* = \arg\min_H V(H, L, D) . \tag{9.29}$$

In [Zhang and Zhou, 2010a], logistic regression learners were used as the component learners, and the minimization of the loss function was realized by gradient descent optimization. By instantiating the ensemble with $D = U$ and $D = L_u$, the resulting implementations of UDEED are referred to as LcUd and Lcd, respectively. Figure 9.10 gives the scatter plots between LcUD (using U for diversity enhancement) and its counterpart implementation (without using U for diversity enhancement) on two data sets. In each plot, the classification accuracy of LcUd is plotted against that of the counterpart implementation with a marker '+' out of 50 runs. Obviously, using unlabeled data in the way of UDEED is quite helpful in achieving better performance. Moreover, various ensemble diversity measures were evaluated in [Zhang and Zhou, 2010a], and the results verified that the use of unlabeled data in the way of UDEED significantly augmented the ensemble diversity and improved the prediction accuracy.

Based on the same idea of UDEED, Chen et al. [2018b] proposed the SemiNCL method by adapting the *negative correlation learning* strategy [Liu and Yao, 1999] for diversity enhancement with unlabeled data. Given the ensemble of learners $H = \{h_1, h_2, \ldots, h_T\}$, a negative correlation term p_k is defined over data set D as the diversity penalty of h_k

$$\begin{aligned} p_k(D) &= \sum_{\boldsymbol{x} \in D} (h_k(\boldsymbol{x}) - H(\boldsymbol{x})) \sum_{j \neq k} (h_j(\boldsymbol{x}) - H(\boldsymbol{x})) \\ &= -\sum_{\boldsymbol{x} \in D} (h_k(\boldsymbol{x}) - H(\boldsymbol{x}))^2 , \end{aligned} \tag{9.30}$$

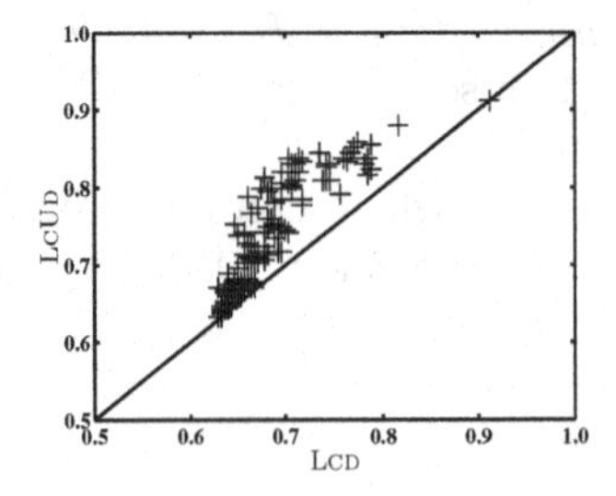

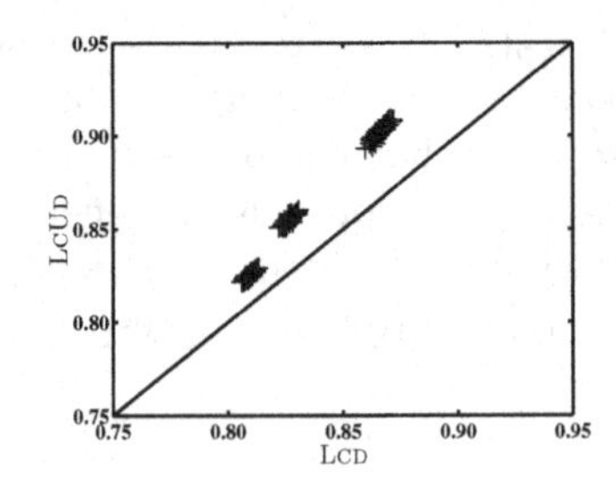

Figure 9.10: Scatter plots of classification accuracy between LcUd and Lcd on two data sets out of 50 runs.

where $H(\boldsymbol{x}) = \frac{1}{T}\sum_{k=1}^{T} h_k(\boldsymbol{x})$ corresponds to the ensemble output on $\boldsymbol{x}$. Then, SemiNCL generates the ensemble H by minimizing the loss function

$$\begin{aligned} V(H, L, U) &= V_{emp}(H, L) + \alpha_1 V_{div}(H, L) + \alpha_2 V_{div}(H, U) \\ &= \frac{1}{Tl}\sum_{i=1}^{l}\sum_{k=1}^{T}(f_k(\boldsymbol{x}_i) - y_i)^2 + \frac{\alpha_1}{Tl}\sum_{k=1}^{T} p_k(L) + \frac{\alpha_2}{Tu}\sum_{k=1}^{T} p_k(U) \\ &= \frac{1}{Tl}\sum_{i=1}^{l}\sum_{k=1}^{T}(f_k(\boldsymbol{x}_i) - y_i)^2 - \frac{\alpha_1}{Tl}\sum_{i=1}^{l}\sum_{k=1}^{T}(h_k(\boldsymbol{x}_i) - H(\boldsymbol{x}_i))^2 \\ &\quad - \frac{\alpha_2}{Tu}\sum_{i=l+1}^{m}\sum_{k=1}^{T}(h_k(\boldsymbol{x}_i) - H(\boldsymbol{x}_i))^2 . \end{aligned} \tag{9.31}$$

Thus, SemiNCL aims to find the target model H^* minimizing the loss function (9.31), that is,

$$H^* = \arg\min_H V(H, L, U) . \tag{9.32}$$

In [Chen et al., 2018b], radial basis functions (RBF) networks are employed as the base learners with closed-form solutions whose model parameters can be efficiently solved via block coordinate descent [Friedman et al., 2010].

9.7 Further Readings

Semi-supervised learning is a branch of **weakly supervised learning** which involves learning with *incomplete*, *inexact*, and *inaccurate* supervision [Zhou, 2018a]. In particular, both semi-supervised learning and **active learning** attempts to handle incomplete supervision, though the latter assumes human intervention, whereas the former does not. More discussion about weakly supervised learning will be given in Section 12.1.

It is worth mentioning that although the learning performance is expected to be improved by exploiting unlabeled data, in some cases the performance may become worse. This issue has been raised and studied for two decades Cozman and Cohen [2002]. Now we have the understanding that the exploitation of unlabeled data naturally leads to rich model options, whereas inadequate choice may lead to poor performance. Li and Zhou [2015] disclosed that the fundamental strategy to make semi-supervised learning *safe* is to optimize the worst-case performance among choosing different options, while their S4VM (Safe Semi-Supervised SVM) approach employs ensemble mechanisms implicitly by letting the final model rely on multiple low-density separators rather than a single separator.

There are abundant theoretical studies about semi-supervised learning [Zhu, 2006], some even earlier than the name of semi-supervised learning being coined [Castelli and Cover, 1995]. Wang and Zhou [2007] showed that the co-training process can succeed if two learners have large diversity, and Wang and Zhou [2010] further provided the sufficient and necessary condition for co-training to succeed. Darnstädt et al. [2014] gave (almost tight) upper and lower bounds of sample complexity for co-training PAC-learners in realizable case under conditional independence assumption. Wang and Zhou [2017] presented a thorough study about disagreement-based approaches.

Various deep ensemble methods have been developed for semi-supervised learning, e.g., Chen et al. [2018a] proposed the deep neural network Tri-Net to use massive unlabeled data to help the learning with limited labeled data; Qiao et al. [2018] introduced the Deep Co-Training method to exploit multiple deep neural networks and adversarial examples for different views; Yang et al. [2021a] presented deep co-training with task decomposition for semi-supervised domain adaptation; Pagliardini et al. [2023] introduced a disagreement-based semi-supervised deep ensemble method for better transferability.

Zhou [2009] indicated that it is possible to design new ensemble methods by using unlabeled data to help augment diversity for semi-supervised learning, and Zhang and Zhou [2010a] proposed the UDEED method. Along this direction, Ross et al. [2020] built ensembles of locally independent prediction models by encouraging disagreement on unlabeled extrapolated patches on data manifold. It has also been applied to out-of-distribution problems, e.g., Lee et al. [2022] exploited the mutual information of learners' predictions on unlabeled data; Pagliardini et al. [2023] presented D-BAT (Diversity By-disAgreement Training) which enforces the agreement of learners on training data, but encourages disagreement on out-of-distribution data.

Chapter 10

Class-Imbalance and Cost-Sensitive Ensemble

10.1 Class-Imbalance and Cost-Sensitive Learning

In real-world applications, data sets are often imbalanced; that is, one class has much more examples than other classes. Considering binary classification for simplicity, we call the big class as **majority class** and the other **minority class**. This problem is prevalent in many applications, such as fraud/intrusion detection, medical diagnosis/monitoring, etc. The **imbalance level**, i.e., the number of majority class examples divided by that of minority class examples, can be 10^6 or even larger. Learning algorithms that do not consider the special characteristics of **class-imbalance learning** tend to be overwhelmed by the majority class and ignore the minority one.

Conventional learning approaches generally try to minimize the *number of mistakes* they will make in predicting unseen instances. However, it is often meaningless to achieve high accuracy when there is class imbalance; e.g., even when the imbalance level is just 1,000, which is very common in fraud detection tasks, a trivial solution $\mathsf{Trv}_{1,000}$ which simply predicts all unseen instances to belong to the majority class will achieve an accuracy of 99.9%, while the solution is useless because no fraud will be detected.

Note that the primary interest of class-imbalance learning is on the minority class. If the minority class is not much more important than the majority class, it would not be a problem for the minority class to be overwhelmed by majority class. In fact, even when there is no class imbalance, different classes are generally with different importance, expressed by their different costs. For example, in medical diagnosis, the cost of mistakenly diagnosing a patient to be healthy may be much larger than that of mistakenly diagnosing a healthy person as being sick, because the former type of mistake may result in the loss of a life that could have been saved. **Cost-sensitive learning** attempts to

 DOI: 10.1201/9781003587774-10

handle such kind of unequal costs. As it has been stated in the Technological Roadmap of the MLnetII project (European Network of Excellence in Machine Learning) [Saitta and Lavrac, 2000], the inclusion of costs into learning is one of the most important topics of machine learning research. In fact, the learning process may involve many kinds of costs, such as the *test cost*, *teacher cost*, *intervention cost* [Turney, 1994], *feature extraction cost* [Liu et al., 2008c], etc. Here we are concerning about the **misclassification cost**.

Misclassification cost can be further categorized into two types, i.e., **example-dependent cost** [Zadrozny and Elkan, 2001, Brefeld et al., 2003] and **class-dependent cost** [Domingos, 1999, Margineantu, 2001]. The former assumes that the costs are associated with examples; that is, every example has its own misclassification cost. The latter assumes that the costs are associated with classes; that is, every class has its own misclassification cost. It is noteworthy that in most real tasks, it is feasible to request a domain expert to specify the cost of misclassifying a class to another class, yet only in special cases it is convenient to get the cost for every training example. We will focus on class-dependent costs and hereafter *class-dependent* will not be mentioned explicitly.

Class-imbalance learning and cost-sensitive learning can be handled by a general Rescaling approach, as will be introduced in Section 10.3. Before that we shall introduce how to evaluate the performance of learning with class imbalance and unequal misclassification costs.

10.2 Performance Evaluation

We consider binary classification where $y \in \{-1, +1\}$ for simplicity. Given data set $D = \{(\boldsymbol{x}_1, y_1), (\boldsymbol{x}_2, y_2), \ldots, (\boldsymbol{x}_m, y_m)\}$, suppose that the positive class is the minority class of m_+ examples, and the negative class is the majority class of m_- examples, and $m_+ \ll m_-$ with $m_+ + m_- = m$. The **confusion matrix** of a classifier h is given by

	Ground-truth "+"	Ground-truth "−"
Predicted as "+"	*TP (true positive)*	*FP (false positive)*
Predicted as "−"	*FN (false negative)*	*TN (true negative)*

where

$$\begin{cases} TP &= \sum_{i=1}^{m} \mathbb{I}(y_i = +1)\mathbb{I}(h(\boldsymbol{x}_i) = +1) \\ FP &= \sum_{i=1}^{m} \mathbb{I}(y_i = -1)\mathbb{I}(h(\boldsymbol{x}_i) = +1) \\ TN &= \sum_{i=1}^{m} \mathbb{I}(y_i = -1)\mathbb{I}(h(\boldsymbol{x}_i) = -1) \\ FN &= \sum_{i=1}^{m} \mathbb{I}(y_i = +1)\mathbb{I}(h(\boldsymbol{x}_i) = -1) \;. \end{cases} \tag{10.1}$$

It can be derived that

$$TP + FN = m_+, \;\; TN + FP = m_- \;\text{ and }\; TP + FN + TN + FP = m \;. \tag{10.2}$$

Then, the **accuracy** and **error rate** can be written, respectively, as

$$acc = \frac{TP + TN}{m} \quad \text{and} \quad err = \frac{FP + FN}{m} . \tag{10.3}$$

We have $acc + err = 1$.

It is evident that accuracy and error rates treat two classes equally, and therefore, they are inadequate to evaluate the performance of learning with imbalanced class and unequal costs. Subsequently, we introduce several commonly used evaluation measures for learning with imbalanced class and unequal costs.

10.2.1 G-Mean, F-Measure, and P-R Curve

G-mean is the geometric mean of the accuracy of every class, i.e.,

$$G\text{-}mean = \sqrt{\frac{TP}{m_+} \times \frac{TN}{m_-}} , \tag{10.4}$$

where the different sizes of different classes have already been taken into account, and therefore, it can be used for evaluating the performance of class-imbalance learning. Back to the example mentioned in Section 10.1, the G-mean of the trivial solution $\mathsf{Trv}_{1,000}$ is zero, disclosing that it is not a good solution though it achieves an accuracy of 99.9%.

Precision and **recall** are defined, respectively, as

$$Precision = \frac{TP}{TP + FP} , \tag{10.5}$$

$$Recall = \frac{TP}{TP + FN} . \tag{10.6}$$

Note that if all examples are negative and correctly predicted as negative, then the precision becomes $\frac{0}{0+0}$, which is defined as one (i.e., 100%) in this scenario. It is evident that the precision measures how many samples classified as positive are really positive, whereas the recall measures how many positive samples are correctly classified as positive. Neither provides a complete evaluation of learning performance, and they are complementary to each other. As for the aforementioned $\mathsf{Trv}_{1,000}$, its precision is one but recall is zero, disclosing that $\mathsf{Trv}_{1,000}$ is not a good solution for the task.

Though a high precision and a high recall are both desired, there are often conflicts to achieve the two goals together since FP usually becomes larger when TP increases. Being a tradeoff, the **F-measure** is defined as the harmonic mean of precision and recall as [van Rijsbergen, 1979]

$$F_\alpha = \left(\alpha \frac{1}{Recall} + (1 - \alpha) \frac{1}{Precision} \right)^{-1} , \tag{10.7}$$

where α is a parameter to weight the relative importance of precision and recall. By default, α is set to 0.5 to regard the precision and recall as equally important.

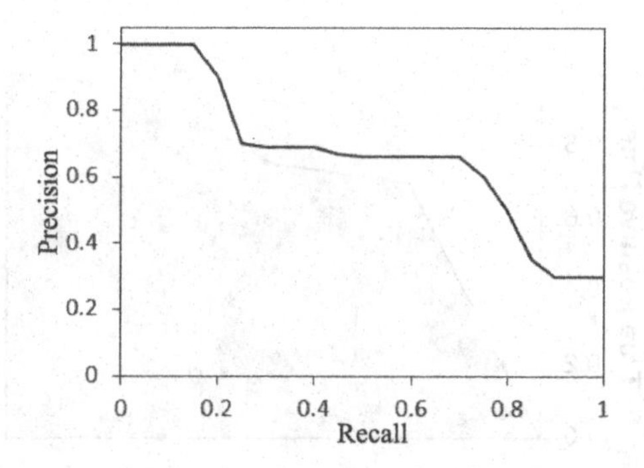

Figure 10.1: Illustration of PR curve.

To evaluate a learning method in various situations, e.g., with different class distributions, a single pair of (*Precision, Recall*) or a single choice of α for the F-measure is not enough. For this purpose, the **Precision-Recall (PR) curve** can be used, where recall and precision are plotted on x- and y-axis, respectively, as illustrated in Figure 10.1.

A classifier corresponds to a point in the PR space. If it classifies all examples correctly, $Precision = 1$ and $Recall = 1$; if it classifies all examples as positive, $Recall = 1$ and $Precision = m_+/m$; if it classifies all examples as negative, $Recall = 0$ and $Precision = 1$. To compare two classifiers, the one located on the upper right is better. A functional hypothesis $h : \mathcal{X} \rightarrow R$ corresponds to a curve, on which a series of (*Precision, Recall*) points can be generated by applying different thresholds on the outputs of h to separate different classes.

10.2.2 ROC Curve and AUC

ROC curve [Green and Swets, 1966, Spackman, 1989] can be used to evaluate learning performance under unknown class distributions or misclassification costs. ROC is the abbreviation for *Receiver Operating Characteristic*, which was originally used in radar signal detection in World War II. As illustrated in Figure 10.2, the ROC curve plots how the true positive rate *tpr* on the y-axis changes with the false positive rate fpr on the x-axis, where

$$tpr = \frac{TP}{TP + FN} = \frac{TP}{m_+} , \tag{10.8}$$

$$fpr = \frac{FP}{FP + TN} = \frac{FP}{m_-} . \tag{10.9}$$

A classifier corresponds to a point in the ROC space. If it classifies all examples as positive, $tpr = 1$ and $fpr = 1$; if it classifies all examples as negative, $tpr = 0$ and $fpr = 0$; if it classifies all examples correctly, $tpr = 1$ and $fpr = 0$. When the *tpr* increases, the fpr will be unchanged or increase. To compare two classifiers, the one located to the upper left is better. A functional hypothesis

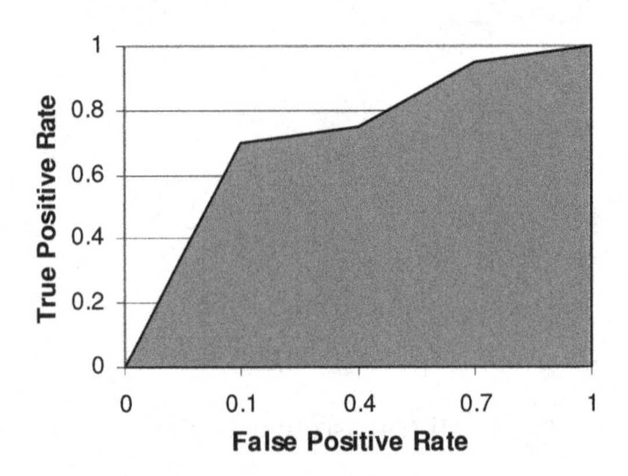

Figure 10.2: Illustration of ROC curve. AUC is the area of the dark region.

$h : \mathcal{X} \to R$ corresponds to a curve with $(0, 0)$ being the start point and $(1, 1)$ being the end point, on which a series of (fpr, tpr) points can be generated by applying different thresholds on the outputs of h to separate different classes.

The **AUC** (Area Under ROC Curve) [Metz, 1978, Hanley and McNeil, 1983] is defined as the Area under the ROC Curve, as shown in Figure 10.2. This criterion integrates the performances of a classifier over all possible values of fpr to represent the overall performance. The statistical interpretation of AUC is the probability of the functional hypothesis $h : \mathcal{X} \to R$ assigning a higher score to a positive example than to a negative example, i.e.,

$$AUC(h) = P\big(h(\boldsymbol{x}_+) > h(\boldsymbol{x}_-)\big) . \tag{10.10}$$

The *normalized Wilcoxon-Mann-Whitney statistic* gives the maximum likelihood estimate of the AUC as [Yan et al., 2003]

$$W = \frac{\sum_{\boldsymbol{x}_+} \sum_{\boldsymbol{x}_-} \mathbb{I}\big(h(\boldsymbol{x}_+) > h(\boldsymbol{x}_-)\big)}{m_+ m_-} . \tag{10.11}$$

Therefore, the AUC measures the ranking quality of h. Maximizing the AUC is equivalent to maximizing the number of the pairs satisfying $h(\boldsymbol{x}_+) > h(\boldsymbol{x}_-)$. In fact, the **ranking loss** ℓ_{rank} corresponds to the area above the ROC curve, and there is a relation [Zhou, 2021, Section 2.3]

$$\text{AUC} = 1 - \ell_{\text{rank}} . \tag{10.12}$$

10.2.3 Total Cost and Cost Curve

For learning with unequal misclassification cost, we no longer want to minimize the *number of mistakes* but the **total cost**, i.e., the total misclassification cost. Consider binary classification for simplicity. Let $\texttt{cost}_+$ be the cost of

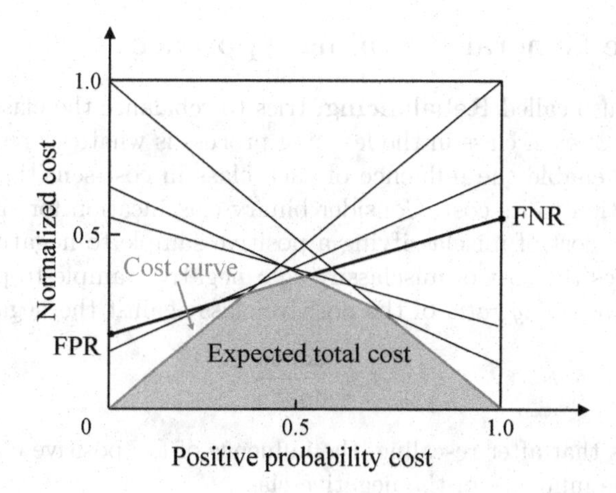

Figure 10.3: Illustration of Cost curve. The expected total cost is the area of the dark region.

misclassifying a positive sample to negative class, and $\texttt{cost}_-$ denotes the cost of misclassifying a negative sample to positive class. Then, the normalized total cost can be calculated as

$$\texttt{total\_cost} = \frac{\texttt{cost}_+ \cdot FN + \texttt{cost}_- \cdot FP}{m}. \tag{10.13}$$

Cost curve [Drummond and Holte, 2006] plots at the x-axis the positive probability cost, i.e., the probability cost of positive class is given by

$$P(+)\texttt{cost} = \frac{p \times \texttt{cost}_+}{p \times \texttt{cost}_+ + (1-p) \times \texttt{cost}_-}, \tag{10.14}$$

where $p \in [0, 1]$ is the probability of a sample being positive. The y-axis is the normalized cost which takes values from $[0, 1]$, defined by

$$\texttt{cost} = \frac{fnr \times p \times \texttt{cost}_+ + fpr \times (1-p) \times \texttt{cost}_-}{p \times \texttt{cost}_+ + (1-p) \times \texttt{cost}_-}, \tag{10.15}$$

where fpr is the false positive rate defined in (10.9), and $fnr = 1 - tpr$ is the false negative rate with tpr defined in (10.8). The cost curve can be drawn as follows: Since every point (fpr, tpr) on the ROC curve corresponds to a line segment on the cost plane, we can calculate the fnr and draw a line segment from $(0, fpr)$ to $(1, fnr)$. Then, the area under the line segment represents the expected total cost for the given p, fpr, and tpr. By converting all points on the ROC curve to line segments on the cost plane, the expected total cost is given by the area under the lower bound of all line segments, as shown in Figure 10.3.

10.3 The General Rescaling Approach

Rescaling, also called **Rebalancing**, tries to rebalance the classes such that the influence of each class in the learning process is whatever required by the task; e.g., to enable the influence of each class in cost-sensitive learning to be in proportion to its cost. Consider binary classification for simplicity. Let $\texttt{cost}_+$ be the cost of misclassifying a positive sample to negative class, and $\texttt{cost}_-$ denotes the cost of misclassifying a negative sample to positive class. The *optimal rescaling ratio* of the positive class against the negative class is

$$\tau = \frac{\texttt{cost}_+}{\texttt{cost}_-} , \tag{10.16}$$

which implies that after rescaling, the influence of the positive class should be τ times of the influence of the negative class.

For learning with imbalanced class, let $\texttt{size}_+$ be the size of positive class which is the minority class, and $\texttt{size}_-$ denotes the size of negative class which is the majority class. Intuitively, if the ground-truth *imbalance level* $\texttt{size}_-/\texttt{size}_+$ is known, then the rescaling ratio of the positive class against the negative class should be

$$\tau = \frac{\texttt{size}_-}{\texttt{size}_+} , \tag{10.17}$$

which implies that after rescaling, the influence of a positive example should be τ times of the influence of a negative example.

(10.17) becomes (10.16) by treating the misclassification cost of the majority class example as 1 whereas that of the minority class example as $\texttt{size}_-/\texttt{size}_+$. Thus, they can be unified in the same framework and we will discuss based on (10.16) in the follows.

Note that **Rescaling** is a general framework, which can be implemented in different ways, and can be realized either as a stand-alone pre-processing process or an embedded in-processing in learning algorithms. For example, it can be implemented by **re-weighting**, i.e., assigning different weights to training examples of different classes, and then passing the re-weighted training examples to any common learning algorithms that can handle weighted examples; or by **re-sampling**, i.e., extracting a sample from the training data according to the proportion specified by (10.16), and then passing the re-sampled data to any common learning algorithms; or by **threshold-moving**, i.e., moving the decision threshold toward the cheaper class according to (10.16). In particular, the threshold-moving strategy has been incorporated into many learning methods to generate their cost-sensitive variants. For example, for decision trees, the tree splits can be selected based on a moved decision threshold [Schiffers, 1997], and the tree pruning can be executed based on a moved decision threshold [Drummond and Holte, 2000]; for neural networks, the learning objective can be biased towards the high-cost class based on a moved decision threshold [Kukar and Kononenko, 1998]; for support vector machines, the corresponding optimization problem can be written as [Lin et al., 2002]

$$\begin{aligned} \min_{\boldsymbol{w},b,\xi} \quad & \frac{1}{2}\|\boldsymbol{w}\|_{\mathcal{H}}^2 + C\sum_{i=1}^{m} cost(\boldsymbol{x}_i)\xi_i \\ \text{s.t.} \quad & y_i(\boldsymbol{w}^T\boldsymbol{\phi}(\boldsymbol{x}_i) + b) \geq 1 - \xi_i \\ & \xi_i \geq 0 \quad (\forall i = 1, \ldots, m) \end{aligned} \tag{10.18}$$

where $\boldsymbol{\phi}$ is the feature induced from a kernel function and $cost(\boldsymbol{x}_i)$ is the example-dependent cost for misclassifying $\boldsymbol{x}_i$. It is clear that the classification boundary is moved according to the rescaling ratio specified by the cost terms.

For class-imbalance learning, the use of resampling strategies require special attention. These strategies can be further categorized into **under-sampling** which decreases the majority class examples, and **over-sampling** which increases the minority class examples. Either method can be implemented by random sampling with or without replacement. However, randomly duplicating the minority class examples may increase the risk of overfitting, while randomly removing the majority class examples may lose useful information. To relax those problems, many advanced resampling methods have been developed.

To improve under-sampling, some methods selectively remove the majority class examples such that more informative examples are kept. For example, the one-sided sampling method [Kubat and Matwin, 1997] tries to find a *consistent* subset D' of the original data D in the sense that the 1-NN rule learned from D' can correctly classify all examples in D. Initially, D' contains all the minority class examples and one randomly selected majority class example. Then, an 1-NN classifier is constructed on D' to classify the examples in D. The misclassified majority examples are added into D'. After that, the *Tomek link* [Tomek, 1976] is employed to remove borderline or noisy examples in the majority class in D'. Let $d(\boldsymbol{x}_i, \boldsymbol{x}_j)$ denote the distance between $\boldsymbol{x}_i$ and $\boldsymbol{x}_j$. A pair of examples $(\boldsymbol{x}_i, \boldsymbol{x}_j)$ is called a **Tomek Link** if their class labels are different, and no example $\boldsymbol{x}_k$ exists such that $d(\boldsymbol{x}_i, \boldsymbol{x}_k) < d(\boldsymbol{x}_i, \boldsymbol{x}_j)$ or $d(\boldsymbol{x}_j, \boldsymbol{x}_k) < d(\boldsymbol{x}_j, \boldsymbol{x}_i)$. Examples participating in Tomek links are usually either borderline or noisy.

To improve over-sampling, some methods use synthetic examples instead of exact copies to reduce the risk of overfitting. SMOTE [Chawla et al., 2002] is a representative. Specifically, it generates *synthetic* examples by randomly interpolating between a minority class example and one of its neighbors from the same class. This causes the selection of a random point along the line segment between two specific features. This approach effectively forces the decision region of the minority class to become more general. Data cleaning techniques such as the Tomek link can be applied further to remove the possible noise introduced in the interpolation process.

In this chapter we mainly discuss purely class-imbalance learning or purely cost-sensitive learning, and consider the imbalance-only rescaling ratio for the former, whereas the cost-only rescaling ratio for the latter. When they occur together, the situation becomes more complicated, and the optimal rescaling ratio is not that easy to be derived, especially when take into account the fact that the imbalance level observed in training data set may not be the ground-truth imbalance level. Liu and Zhou [2006] empirically disclosed that, for non-seriously imbalanced data, considering cost-only rescaling ratio is enough, while for seriously imbalanced data, a good rescaling ratio should be larger than the sum of the two ratios (cost-only and imbalance-only rescaling ratio), but far smaller than their product.

10.4 Theoretical Understanding

Let $cost_{ij}$ $(i, j \in \{1...c\}, cost_{ii} = 0)$ denote the cost of misclassifying an example of the i-th class to the j-th class, where c is the number of classes. These costs can be organized into a **cost matrix** where the element at the i-th row and the j-th column is $cost_{ij}$. Let m denote the total number of training examples, and $m_i = m/c$ denotes the number of training examples of the i-th class, i.e., assuming we are only handling unequal misclassification cost and there is no class imbalance for simplicity of discussion.

The principle of **Rescaling** is to enable the influence of the higher-cost classes to be larger than that of the lower-cost classes in proportion to their costs. For binary classification, the optimal prediction is the first class if and only if the expected cost of this prediction is no larger than that of predicting the second class, i.e.,

$$p \times cost_{11} + (1-p) \times cost_{21} \leq p \times cost_{12} + (1-p) \times cost_{22} \ , \tag{10.19}$$

where $p = P(class = 1 \mid \boldsymbol{x})$. If the equality holds in (10.19), predicting either class is optimal. Hence, the threshold p^* for making optimal decision satisfies

$$p^* \times cost_{11} + (1-p^*) \times cost_{21} = p^* \times cost_{12} + (1-p^*) \times cost_{22} \ . \tag{10.20}$$

When the classifier is not biased to any class, the threshold p_0 is 0.5. Considering (10.20), we have the following theorem:

Theorem 10.1 ([Elkan, 2001]). *For binary classification, to make a target probability threshold p^* correspond to a given probability threshold p_0, the number of the second class examples in the training set should be multiplied by* $\frac{p^*}{1-p^*}\frac{1-p_0}{p_0}$.

Theorem 10.1 tells that the second class should be rescaled against the first class according to $\frac{p^*}{(1-p^*)} = \frac{cost_{21}}{cost_{12}}$ (remind that $cost_{11} = cost_{22} = 0$), implying that the influence of the first class should be $\frac{cost_{12}}{cost_{21}}$ times that of the second class. Generally speaking, the optimal rescaling ratio of the i-th class against the j-th class can be defined as

$$\tau_{opt}(i, j) = \frac{cost_{ij}}{cost_{ji}} \ , \tag{10.21}$$

which indicates that the classes should be rescaled in the way that the influence of the i-th class is $\tau_{opt}(i, j)$ times of that of the j-th class. For example, assuming reweighting is employed to implement **Rescaling**, if the weight assigned to the training examples of the j-th class after rescaling is w_j, then that of the i-th class will be $w_i = \tau_{opt}(i,j) \times w_j$ ($w_i > 0$).

In conventional studies of rescaling [Breiman et al., 1984, Domingos, 1999, Ting, 2002], a quantity $cost_i$ is derived by

$$cost_i = \sum_{j=1}^{c} cost_{ij} \ . \tag{10.22}$$

Again, assuming reweighting is employed, a weight w_i is assigned to the i-th class after rescaling, which is computed according to

$$w_i = \frac{(m \times cost_i)}{\sum_{k=1}^{c} (m_k \times cost_k)} \ . \tag{10.23}$$

When $m_i = m/c$, (10.23) becomes

$$w_i = \frac{(c \times cost_i)}{\sum_{k=1}^{c} cost_k} \ . \tag{10.24}$$

Thus, it is evident that in the conventional rescaling approach, the rescaling ratio of the i-th class against the j-th class is

$$\tau_{old}(i,j) = \frac{w_i}{w_j} = \frac{(c \times cost_i) \,/\, \sum_{k=1}^{c} cost_k}{(c \times cost_j) \,/\, \sum_{k=1}^{c} cost_k} = \frac{cost_i}{cost_j} \ . \tag{10.25}$$

When $c = 2$,

$$\begin{aligned} \tau_{old}(i,j) &= \frac{cost_i}{cost_j} = \frac{\sum_{k=1}^{2} cost_{ik}}{\sum_{k=1}^{2} cost_{jk}} = \frac{cost_{11} + cost_{12}}{cost_{21} + cost_{22}} \\ &= \frac{cost_{12}}{cost_{21}} = \frac{cost_{ij}}{cost_{ji}} = \tau_{opt}(i,j) \ , \end{aligned}$$

which is exactly the equation in (10.16). This explains why the conventional rescaling approach can be effective in dealing with the unequal misclassification costs in binary classification, as shown by previous research [Breiman et al., 1984, Domingos, 1999, Ting, 2002].

Unfortunately, as Zhou and Liu [2006b] disclosed, when $c > 2$, it holds that

$$\tau_{old}(i,j) = \frac{cost_i}{cost_j} = \frac{\sum_{k=1}^{c} cost_{ik}}{\sum_{k=1}^{c} cost_{jk}} \ , \tag{10.26}$$

which is usually unequal to $\tau_{opt}(i,j)$. This explains why the conventional rescaling approach is often ineffective in handling unequal misclassification costs on multi-class problems.

Suppose each class can be assigned with a weight w_i ($w_i > 0$) after rescaling (again, assuming that reweighting is employed). In order to adequately rescale all the classes simultaneously, according to the above analysis, it is desired that the weights satisfy $\frac{w_i}{w_j} = \tau_{opt}(i,j)$ $(i,j \in \{1..c\})$, implying the following $\binom{c}{2}$ number of constraints

$$\begin{array}{llll} \frac{w_1}{w_2} = \frac{cost_{12}}{cost_{21}}, & \frac{w_1}{w_3} = \frac{cost_{13}}{cost_{31}}, & \ldots, & \frac{w_1}{w_c} = \frac{cost_{1c}}{cost_{c1}} \\ & \frac{w_2}{w_3} = \frac{cost_{23}}{cost_{32}}, & \ldots, & \frac{w_2}{w_c} = \frac{cost_{2c}}{cost_{c2}} \\ & \ldots & \ldots & \ldots \\ & & & \frac{w_{c-1}}{w_c} = \frac{cost_{c-1,c}}{cost_{c,c-1}} . \end{array}$$

These constraints can be transformed into the equations

$$\mathbf{M}\boldsymbol{w} = 0 , \tag{10.27}$$

where $\boldsymbol{w} = [w_1, w_2, \ldots, w_c]^{\boldsymbol{T}}$ and

$$\mathbf{M} = \begin{bmatrix} cost_{21} & -cost_{12} & 0 & \cdots & 0 \\ cost_{31} & 0 & -cost_{13} & \cdots & 0 \\ \cdots & \cdots & \cdots & \cdots & 0 \\ cost_{c1} & 0 & 0 & \cdots & -cost_{1c} \\ 0 & cost_{32} & -cost_{23} & \cdots & 0 \\ \cdots & \cdots & \cdots & \cdots & 0 \\ 0 & cost_{c2} & 0 & \cdots & -cost_{2c} \\ \cdots & \cdots & \cdots & \cdots & \cdots \\ \cdots & \cdots & \cdots & \cdots & \cdots \\ 0 & \cdots & 0 & \cdots & -cost_{c-1,c} \end{bmatrix} . \tag{10.28}$$

If non-trivial solution $\boldsymbol{w}$ can be solved from (10.27) (the solution will be unique, up to a multiplicative factor), then the classes can be adequately rescaled simultaneously, implying that the multi-class cost-sensitive learning problem can be solved as before. It is evident that (10.27) has a non-trivial solution if and only if the rank of its $\frac{c(c-1)}{2} \times c$ coefficient matrix $\mathbf{M}$ is smaller than c, which is equivalent to the condition that the determinant of any $c \times c$ sub-matrix of $\mathbf{M}$ is zero. Note that the rank of $\mathbf{M}$ is at most c. Unit vector can be solved from (10.27) as a non-trivial solution of $\boldsymbol{w}$ when all classes with equal costs, and thus the classes should be equally rescaled (in this case the problem degenerates to a common equal-cost multi-class learning problem).

Thus, we have the following theorem:

Theorem 10.2 ([Zhou and Liu, 2006b]). *For multi-class problem with c classes, if the rank of the coefficient matrix $\mathbf{M}$ is smaller than c, the classes can be rescaled simultaneously according to $w_1, w_2, \ldots, w_c$ solved from (10.27); otherwise, the classes cannot be adequately rescaled simultaneously.*

From (10.16) and (10.17), it can be seen that both Theorems 10.1 and 10.2 are applicable not only to learning with unequal cost but also imbalanced class. When the rank of the coefficient matrix is c, (10.27) does not have non-trivial solution, which implies that there will be no proper weight assignment for rescaling all the classes simultaneously. Therefore, rescaling could not work well if applied directly, and in order to use rescaling, the multi-class problem has to be decomposed into a series of two-class problems to address, and the final prediction will be made by ensemble voting.

Based on the above analysis, Zhou and Liu [2006b] proposed a new Rescale approach which becomes common sense in machine learning and data mining now. For a given cost matrix, the coefficient matrix in the form of (10.28) is generated at first. If the rank of the coefficient matrix is smaller than c (in this case, the cost matrix is called as a *consistent* cost matrix), $\boldsymbol{w}$ is solved from (10.27) and used to rescale the classes simultaneously, and the rescaled data set is then passed to any common learning algorithm; otherwise (the cost matrix is called as an *inconsistent* cost matrix), the multi-class problem is decomposed into $\binom{c}{2}$ number of binary classification problems, and each binary classification data set is rescaled and passed to any common learning algorithm, while the final prediction is made by voting the class labels predicted by the binary classifiers. In other words, it is finally addressed by ensemble.

10.5 Cost-Sensitive Ensemble

As mentioned in Section 10.3, many cost-sensitive learning approaches have been developed based on **Rescaling**. Actually, the reweighting and resampling can be realized as a pre-processing process, and then the pre-processed data can be input to common ensemble methods for constructing a cost-sensitive ensemble. Thus, this section focuses on representative cost-sensitive ensemble methods realized by threshold-moving.

10.5.1 Bagging-Based Methods

MetaCost [Domingos, 1999]. This method constructs a decision tree ensemble by Bagging to estimate the posterior probability $p(y \mid \boldsymbol{x})$. Then, it relabels each training example to the class with the minimum expected risk according to the moved decision threshold. Finally, the relabeled data are used to train a learner to minimize the error rate. Thus, MetaCost also employs a pre-processing process, though it is based on threshold-moving rather than reweighting and resampling. The MetaCost algorithm is summarized in Figure 10.4.

Note that, the probability estimates generated by different learning methods are usually different, and therefore, it might be more reliable to use the same learner in both steps of MetaCost. However, the probability estimates produced by classifiers are usually not trustworthy, because they are just by-product of classification. Needless to say, many classifiers do not provide probability estimates. Therefore, Bagging is used in MetaCost. Though MetaCost was proposed based on Bagging, other ensemble methods can also be used to obtain the probability estimates actually.

Input: Training data set $D = \{(\boldsymbol{x}_1, y_1), (\boldsymbol{x}_2, y_2), \ldots, (\boldsymbol{x}_m, y_m)\}$;
Base learning algorithm $\mathfrak{L}$;
Cost matrix cost $= (cost_{ij})_{c \times c}$, where $cost_{ij}$ is the cost of misclassifying examples of the i-th class to the j-th class;
Number of subsamples in Bagging T_b;
Number of examples in each subsample m;
pb is $True$ *iff* $\mathfrak{L}$ produces class probabilities;
all is $True$ *iff* all subsamples are to be used for each example.

Process:
1. **for** $i = 1, \ldots, T_b$:
2. D_i is a subsample of D with m examples;
3. $M_i = \mathfrak{L}(D_i)$;
4. **end**
5. **for** each example $\boldsymbol{x}$ in D:
6. **for** each class j:
7. $p(j \mid \boldsymbol{x}) = \frac{1}{\sum_i 1} \sum_i p(j \mid x, M_i)$;
8. where
9. **if** pb **then**
10. $p(j \mid \boldsymbol{x}, M_i)$ is produced by M_i;
11. **else**
12. $p(j \mid \boldsymbol{x}, M_i) = \begin{cases} 1 & \text{for the class predicted by } M_i \text{ for } \boldsymbol{x}, \\ 0 & \text{for all other classes.} \end{cases}$
13. **end**
14. **if** all **then**
15. i ranges over all M_i's;
16. **else**
17. i ranges over all M_i's such that $\boldsymbol{x} \notin D_i$;
18. **end**
19. **end**
20. Assign $\boldsymbol{x}$'s class label to be $\arg\min_i \sum_j p(j \mid \boldsymbol{x}) cost_{ji}$;
21. **end**
22. Build a model M by applying $\mathfrak{L}$ on data set D with new labels;

Output: M

Figure 10.4: The MetaCost algorithm.

10.5.2 Boosting-Based Methods

Asymmetric Boosting [Masnadi-Shirazi and Vasconcelos, 2007]. This method directly modifies the AdaBoost algorithm such that the cost-sensitive solution is consistent with the Bayes optimal risk. In detail, according to threshold-moving, Asymmetric Boosting modify the exponential loss function

---

Input: Training data set $D = \{(\boldsymbol{x}_1, y_1), (\boldsymbol{x}_2, y_2), \ldots, (\boldsymbol{x}_m, y_m)\}$;
Base learning algorithm $\mathfrak{L}$;
Cost of misclassifying positive/negative examples $cost_+/cost_-$;
Number of learning trails T;
Number of iterations in gradient descent N_{gd}.

Process:
1. $\mathcal{I}_+ = \{i \mid y_i = +1\}$ and $\mathcal{I}_- = \{i \mid y_i = -1\}$;
2. Initialize weights as $w_1(i) = \frac{1}{2|\mathcal{I}_+|}, \forall i \in \mathcal{I}_+$ and $w_1(i) = \frac{1}{2|\mathcal{I}_-|}, \forall i \in \mathcal{I}_-$;
3. **for** $t = 1$ to T:
4. $k = 1$;
5. Initialize β_k as a random number in $[0, 1]$;
6. Using gradient descent to solve f_k from
$$f_k(x) = \arg\min_f [(e^{cost_+\beta_k} - e^{-cost_+\beta_k}) \cdot b + e^{-cost_+\beta_k} T_+ + (e^{cost_-\beta_k} - e^{-cost_-\beta_k}) \cdot d + e^{-cost_-\beta_k} T_-]$$
where
$$T_+ = \textstyle\sum_{i \in \mathcal{I}_+} w_t(i), \quad T_- = \sum_{i \in \mathcal{I}_-} w_t(i),$$
$$b = \textstyle\sum_{i \in \mathcal{I}_+} w_t(i) \mathbb{I}(y_i \neq f_{k-1}(\boldsymbol{x}_i)),$$
$$d = \textstyle\sum_{i \in \mathcal{I}_-} w_t(i) \mathbb{I}(y_i \neq f_{k-1}(\boldsymbol{x}_i));$$
7. **for** $k = 2$ to N_{gd}:
8. Solve β_k from
$$2 \cdot cost_+ \cdot b \cdot \cosh(cost_+\beta_k) + 2 \cdot cost_- \cdot d \cdot \cosh(cost_-\beta_k) - cost_+ T_+ e^{-cost_+\beta_k} - cost_- T_- e^{-cost_-\beta_k} = 0;$$
9. Use gradient descent to solve f_k from
$$f_k(x) = \arg\min_f [(e^{cost_+\beta_k} - e^{-cost_+\beta_k}) \cdot b + e^{-cost_+\beta_k} T_+ + (e^{cost_-\beta_k} - e^{-cost_-\beta_k}) \cdot d + e^{-cost_-\beta_k} T_-];$$
10. **end**
11. Let (h_t, α_t) to be (f_k, β_k) with the smallest loss;
12. Update weights as $w_{t+1}(i) = w_t(i) e^{-cost_{y_i} \alpha_t y_i h_t(\boldsymbol{x}_i)}$;
13. **end**

Output: $H(x) = \mathbf{sign}(\sum_{t=1}^{T} \alpha_t h_t(\boldsymbol{x}))$

Figure 10.5: The Asymmetric Boosting algorithm.

(2.2) to

$$\ell_{cost}(h \mid \mathcal{D}) = \mathbb{E}_{\boldsymbol{x} \sim \mathcal{D}}[e^{-yh(\boldsymbol{x})cost(\boldsymbol{x})}] \approx \frac{1}{m} \sum_{i=1}^{m} \left[\mathbb{I}(y_i = +1)\, e^{-y_i h(\boldsymbol{x}_i) cost_+} + \mathbb{I}(y_i = -1) e^{-y_i h(\boldsymbol{x}_i) cost_-} \right], \tag{10.29}$$

where $y_i \in \{-1, +1\}$ is the ground-truth label of $\boldsymbol{x}_i$, $cost_+$ ($cost_-$) denotes the cost of misclassifying a positive (negative) example to the negative (positive) class, and h is the learner. The optimal solution minimizing ℓ_{cost} is

$$h^* = \frac{1}{cost_+ + cost_-} \ln \frac{p(y=+1 \mid \boldsymbol{x})cost_+}{p(y=-1 \mid \boldsymbol{x})cost_-} , \tag{10.30}$$

which is consistent with the Bayes optimal classifier because

$$\mathtt{sign}(h^*(\boldsymbol{x})) = \mathop{\arg\max}_{y \in \{+1,-1\}} p(y \mid \boldsymbol{x})cost_{\mathtt{sign}(y)} . \tag{10.31}$$

Note that it is difficult to minimize ℓ_{cost} directly by fitting an additive model, and therefore, as the general principle for minimizing convex loss with AdaBoost, Asymmetric Boosting uses gradient descent optimization instead. Figure 10.5 shows the Asymmetric Boosting algorithm.

A number of other cost-sensitive Boosting methods tried to minimize the expected cost. In contrast to Asymmetric Boosting which is derived directly from the Bayes decision theory, most of those cost-sensitive Boosting methods use heuristics to achieve cost sensitivity, and therefore, their optimal solution cannot guarantee to be consistent with the Bayes optimal solution. Some of them change the weight update rule of Adaboost by increasing the weights of high-cost examples, such as CSB0, CSB1, CSB2 [Ting, 2000], and Asymmetric AdaBoost [Viola and Jones, 2002]; Some of them change the weight update rule as well as α, the weight of base learners, by associating a cost with the weighted error rate of each class, such as AdaC1, AdaC2, AdaC3 [Sun et al., 2005], and AdaCost [Fan et al., 1999]. Table 10.1 summarizes the major modifications made by these methods on AdaBoost.

10.6 Class-Imbalance Ensemble

As mentioned before, cost-sensitive methods can be naturally applicable to class-imbalance learning, and thus, many cost-sensitive ensemble methods can be converted to class-imbalance ensemble methods. Considering the overfitting/underfitting risk of resampling, many ensemble methods have been carefully designed for smart rather than simply random resampling.

10.6.1 Bagging-Based Methods

Bagging-based class-imbalance learning methods use diverse training samples (we call them *bags* for convenience) to train multiple base learners in parallel, like Bagging. The difference lies in the fact that, Bagging-based class-imbalance learning methods try to construct a balanced data sample to train a base learner capable of handling imbalanced data in each iteration, whereas Bagging uses a bootstrap sample to train a base learner maximizing accuracy. Different bag construction strategies leads to different methods. Some methods employ under-sampling to reduce the majority class examples in a bag, such as UnderBagging [Wang et al., 2009]; some methods adopt over-sampling to increase the minority class examples, such as OverBagging [Wang et al., 2009]; some methods use

Table 10.1: Summary of cost-sensitive Boosting methods modified from AdaBoost.

Methods	Weight Update Rule	α_t (the Weight of h_t)
AdaCost	$w_{t+1}(i) = w_t(i)e^{-\alpha_t y_i h_t(\boldsymbol{x}_i)\beta_{\delta_i}}$ $\beta_{+1} = (1 - cost_i)/2$ $\beta_{-1} = (1 + cost_i)/2$	$\alpha_t = \frac{1}{2}\ln\frac{1+e_t}{1-e_t}$ with $e_t = \sum_{i=1}^{m} w_t(i) y_i h_t(\boldsymbol{x}_i)\beta_{\delta_i}$
CSB0	$w_{t+1}(i) = c_{\delta_i}(i) w_t(i)$ $c_{-1}(i) = cost_i,\ \ c_{+1}(i) = 1$	unchanged
CSB1	$w_{t+1}(i) = c_{\delta_i}(i) w_t(i) e^{-y_i h_t(\boldsymbol{x}_i)}$	unchanged
CSB2	$w_{t+1}(i) =$ $C_{\delta_i}(i) w_t(i) e^{-\alpha_t y_i h_t(\boldsymbol{x}_i)}$	unchanged
Asymmetric AdaBoost	$w_{t+1}(i) =$ $w_t(i) e^{-\alpha_t y_i h_t(\boldsymbol{x}_i)} e^{y_i \log \sqrt{K}}$ $K = \frac{cost_+}{cost_-}$ is cost ratio	unchanged
AdaC1	$w_{t+1}(i) =$ $w_t(i) e^{-\alpha_t y_i h_t(\boldsymbol{x}_i) cost_i}$	$\alpha_t = \frac{1}{2}\ln\frac{1+\sum_{i=1}^{m} cost_i w_t(i)\delta_i}{1-\sum_{i=1}^{m} cost_i w_t(i)\delta_i}$
AdaC2	$w_{t+1}(i) =$ $cost_i w_t(i) e^{-\alpha_t y_i h_t(\boldsymbol{x}_i)}$	$\alpha_t = \frac{1}{2}\ln\frac{\sum_{y_i = h_t(\boldsymbol{x}_i)} cost_i w_t(i)}{\sum_{y_i \neq h_t(\boldsymbol{x}_i)} cost_i w_t(i)}$
AdaC3	$w_{t+1}(i) =$ $cost_i w_t(i) e^{-\alpha_t y_i h_t(\boldsymbol{x}_i) cost_i}$	$\alpha_t = \frac{1}{2}\ln\frac{\sum_{i=1}^{m} w_t(i)(cost_i + cost_i^2 \delta_i)}{\sum_{i=1}^{m} w_t(i)(cost_i - cost_i^2 \delta_i)}$

‡ In the table, $\delta_i = +1$ if $h_t(\boldsymbol{x}_i) = y_i$ and –1 otherwise; $cost_i$ is the misclassification cost of $\boldsymbol{x}_i$; $cost_+$ ($cost_-$) denotes the cost of mistakenly classifying a positive (negative) example to the negative (positive) class. For clarity, in weight update rules, we omit the normalization factor Z_t, which is used to make w_{t+1} a distribution.

the hybrid of under- and/or over-sampling methods to balance the data, such as SMOTEBagging [Wang et al., 2009]. There are also methods that partition the majority class into a set of disjoint subsets of size m_+, and let each subset to be used together with all the minority class examples to construct a bag, such as Chan and Stolof's method [Chan and Stolfo, 1998].

UnderBagging/OverBagging [Wang et al., 2009]. Both construct a bag by obtaining two samples of the same size $m_- \cdot a\%$ from the minority class and the majority class separately by sampling with replacement, where $a\%$ varies from m_+/m_- to 100%. When $a\% = m_+/m_-$, under-sampling is conducted to remove the majority class examples, leading to UnderBagging; when $a\% = 100\%$, over-sampling is conduced to increase the minority examples, leading to OverBagging; otherwise, both under- and over-sampling are conduced, leading to a hybrid Bagging-based ensemble. The base learners are combined by majority voting.

SMOTEBagging [Wang et al., 2009]. Similar to OverBagging, a sample of m_- majority class examples are sampled with replacement. The difference lies in how the sample of minority examples is obtained. SMOTEBagging samples $m_- \cdot b\%$ minority class examples from the minority class, then generates $m_- \cdot (1 - b\%)$ synthetic minority class examples by SMOTE Chawla et al. [2002].

ChSt (Chan and Stolof's method) [Chan and Stolfo, 1998]. It partitions the majority class into a set of non-overlapping subsets, with each subset having approximately m_+ examples. Each of the majority class subset and all the minority class examples form a bag. The base learners are ensembled by stacking.

BRF (Balanced Random Forests) [Chen et al., 2004]. It adapts RF (Random Forest) [Breiman, 2001] to imbalanced data. To learn a single tree in each iteration, it firstly draws a bootstrap sample of size m_+ from the minority class, and then draws the same number of examples with replacement from the majority class. Thus, each training sample is a balanced data sample. Then, BRF induces a tree from each of the balanced training sample with maximum size, without pruning. The tree is generated by CART [Breiman et al., 1984] with the modification of a random feature subset to split on. The random tree learning procedure and the combination method are as same as in RF. Note that, RF can be applied directly after balancing training data by under- or over-sampling; in this way, however, it is not adapted to handle imbalanced data and thus is different from BRF.

10.6.2 Boosting-Based Methods

Boosting-based class-imbalance learning methods focus more on the minority class examples by increasing the number of minority class examples or decreasing the number of the majority class examples in each Boosting round, such as SMOTEBoost [Chawla et al., 2003] and RUSBoost [Seiffert et al., 2010], and/or by balancing the weight distribution directly, such as DataBoost-IM [Guo and Viktor, 2004].

SMOTEBoost [Chawla et al., 2003]. This method adopts Boosting architecture (AdaBoost.M2) to improve SMOTE [Chawla et al., 2002]. In each round of Boosting, SMOTE is used to generate synthetic examples for the minority class, then the weight distribution is adjusted accordingly. Thus, the weights of the minority class examples become higher. It can be used in multi-class problem. The algorithm is shown in Figure 10.6.

RUSBoost [Seiffert et al., 2010]. The difference between this method and SMOTEBoost lies in the fact that it uses random under-sampling to remove the majority class examples in each Boosting round.

Input: Data set $D = \{(\boldsymbol{x}_i, y_i)\}_{i=1}^m$ with $y \in \{1, ..., c\}$ and minority class c_m;
The number of synthetic examples to be generated in iteration N;
The number of iterations T.

Process:
1. Let $B = \{(i, y) : i = 1, ..., m, y \neq y_i\}$;
2. $\mathcal{D}_1(i, y) = 1/|B|$ for $(i, y) \in B$;
3. **for** $i = 1, \ldots, T$:
4. Modify $\mathcal{D}_t$ by creating N synthetic examples from c_m via SMOTE;
5. Train a weak learner using distribution $\mathcal{D}_t$;
6. Compute weak hypothesis $h_t : \mathcal{X} \times \mathcal{Y} \to [0, 1]$;
7. Compute the pseudo-loss of hypothesis h_t:
$e_t = \sum_{(i,y)\in B} \mathcal{D}_t(i, y)(1 - h_t(\boldsymbol{x}_i, y_i) + h_t(\boldsymbol{x}_i, y))$;
8. Set $\alpha_t = \ln \frac{1-e_t}{e_t}$;
9. Set $d_t(y) = \frac{1}{2}(1 - h_t(\boldsymbol{x}_i, y) + h_t(\boldsymbol{x}_i, y_i))$;
10. Update $\mathcal{D}_t : \mathcal{D}_{t+1}(i, y) = \frac{\mathcal{D}_t(i,y)}{Z_t} e^{-\alpha_t d_t(y)}$;
%% Z_t is a normalization constant such that $\mathcal{D}_{t+1}$ is a distribution
11. **end**

Output: $H(\boldsymbol{x}) = \arg\max_{y\in\mathcal{Y}} \sum_{t=1}^T \alpha_t h_t(\boldsymbol{x}, y)$

Figure 10.6: The SMOTEBoost algorithm.

DataBoost-IM Guo and Viktor [2004]. It designs two strategies to focus on not only the misclassified examples but also the minority class examples. One is selecting "hard" examples (examples easier to be misclassified) from the majority class and the minority class separately and generating synthetic examples to add into the training data; the other is balancing the total weights of the majority and minority classes. In detail, in each round, firstly $m_h = m \times err$ examples with the highest weights in current training data are selected, containing m_{hmaj} majority class examples and m_{hmin} minority class examples. From these hard examples, $m_l = \min(m_-/m_+, m_{hmaj})$ majority class examples and $m_s = \min((m_- \times m_l)/m_+, m_{hmin})$ minority class examples are selected as seed examples. Then, synthetic examples are generated from the seed examples for the majority class and the minority class separately, each with an initial weight equals the seed example's weight divided by the number of synthetic examples it generates. The synthetic examples are then added into the training data. Thus, there are more hard minority class examples than hard majority class examples. Finally, the total weights of the majority class and minority class are balanced; this increases the individual weights of all minority class examples.

10.6.3 Hybrid Ensemble Methods

It is well-known that, Boosting mainly reduces *bias*, whereas Bagging mainly reduces *variance*. There are efforts attempted to combine different ensemble

---

Input: Data set: $D = \{(\boldsymbol{x}_i, y_i)\}_{i=1}^m$ with minority class D_+ and majority class D_-;
The number of iterations: T;
The number of iterations to train an AdaBoost ensemble H_i: s_i.

Process:
1. **for** $i = 1, \ldots, T$:
2. Randomly sample a subset D_i of m_+ examples from the majority class;
3. Learn H_i using D_+ and D_i. H_i is an AdaBoost ensemble with s_i weak classifiers $h_{i,j}$ and corresponding weights $\alpha_{i,j}$. The ensemble's threshold is θ_i, i.e., $H_i(x) = \texttt{sign}\left(\sum_{j=1}^{s_i} \alpha_{i,j} h_{i,j}(\boldsymbol{x}) - \theta_i\right)$;
4. **end**

Output: $H(\boldsymbol{x}) = \texttt{sign}\left(\sum_{i=1}^{T} \sum_{j=1}^{s_i} \alpha_{i,j} h_{i,j}(\boldsymbol{x}) - \sum_{i=1}^{T} \theta_i\right)$

Figure 10.7: The EasyEnsemble algorithm.

strategies to achieve stronger generalization [Friedman, 2002, Webb, 2000, Webb and Zheng, 2004, Yu et al., 2007]. Such a hybrid ensemble strategy has also be exploited in class-imbalance learning, such as EasyEnsemble and BalanceCascade [Liu et al., 2009b], both trying to improve under-sampling by adopting Boosting and Bagging-based ensemble strategies.

EasyEnsemble [Liu et al., 2009b]. The motivation is to reduce the possibility of ignoring potentially useful information contained in the majority class examples while keeping the high efficiency of under-sampling. Firstly, it generates a set of balanced data samples, with each bag containing all minority class examples and a subset of the majority class examples with size m_+. This step is similar to Bagging-based methods for class-imbalance learning. Then an AdaBoost ensemble is trained from each bag. The final ensemble is formed by combining all base learners in all AdaBoost ensembles. The algorithm is shown in Figure 10.7. Note that it does not simply combine the AdaBoost ensembles' predictions; instead, it combines the base learners of the AdaBoost ensembles, which can be viewed as treating the base learners as binary features.

BalanceCascade [Liu et al., 2009b]. It tries to remove majority class examples in a guided way. In contrast to EasyEnsemble which generates subsamples of the majority class in an unsupervised parallel manner, BalanceCascade works in a supervised sequential manner. The basic idea is to shrink the majority class step-by-step in a cascade style. In each iteration, a subset D_i of m_+ examples is sampled from the majority class. Then, an AdaBoost ensemble H_i is trained from the union of D_i and D_+. After that, the majority class examples which are correctly classified by H_i are considered as redundant information and are removed from the majority class. The final ensemble is formed by combining

---

Input: Data set: $D = \{(\boldsymbol{x}_i, y_i)\}_{i=1}^m$ with minority class D_+ and majority class D_-;
The number of iterations: T;
The number of iterations to train an AdaBoost ensemble H_i: s_i.
Process:
1. $fpr \leftarrow (\frac{m_+}{m_-})^{1/(T-1)}$, fpr is the false positive rate that H_i should achieve;
2. **for** $i = 1, \ldots, T$:
3. Randomly sample a subset D_i of m_+ examples from the majority class;
4. Learn H_i using D_+ and D_i. H_i is an AdaBoost ensemble with s_i weak classifiers $h_{i,j}$ and corresponding weights $\alpha_{i,j}$. The ensemble's threshold is θ_i, i.e., $H_i(x) = \mathbf{sign}\left(\sum_{j=1}^{s_i} \alpha_{i,j} h_{i,j}(\boldsymbol{x}) - \theta_i\right)$;
5. Adjust θ_i such that H_i's false positive rate is fpr;
6. Remove from D_- all examples that are correctly classified by H_i;
7. **end**
Output: $H(\boldsymbol{x}) = \mathbf{sign}\left(\sum_{i=1}^{T} \sum_{j=1}^{s_i} \alpha_{i,j} h_{i,j}(\boldsymbol{x}) - \sum_{i=1}^{T} \theta_i\right)$

Figure 10.8: The BalanceCascade algorithm.

all the base learners in all the AdaBoost ensembles, like in EasyEnsemble. The algorithm is shown in Figure 10.8.

There are also ensemble methods that combine different class-imbalance learning methods; e.g., Zhou and Liu [2006a] combined neural networks generated by over-sampling, under-sampling and threshold-moving via *hard ensemble* or *soft ensemble*. Some ensemble methods combine classifiers trained from data with different imbalance levels; e.g., Estabrooks et al. [2004] generated multiple versions of training data with different imbalance levels, and then trained base classifiers from each of them by over- and under-sampling to be combined into an ensemble.

10.7 Further Readings

ROC curve and AUC can be used to study class-imbalance learning as well as cost-sensitive learning, and can be extended to multi-class problems [Hand and Till, 2001, Fawcett, 2006]. Discussion on the relationship between the PR and ROC curves can be found in [Davis and Goadrich, 2006].

Maloof [2003] indicated that, learning from imbalanced data sets and learning with unequal costs can be handled in a similar manner. On one hand, cost-sensitive learning has been deemed as a good solution to class-imbalance problem [Weiss, 2004, Chawla et al., 2004]; on the other hand, methods designed for class-imbalance problem can also help in cost-sensitive learning [Zhou and Liu, 2006a]. Thus, it is feasible to treat unequal misclassification costs and class-imbalance in a unified framework as in this book.

Various cost-sensitive learning methods [Domingos, 1999, Elkan, 2001, Ting, 2002, Zadrozny et al., 2003, Zhou and Liu, 2006a, Li et al., 2010b] have been developed to handle unequal misclassification costs, and various applications have been reported, such as cost-sensitive face recognition [Zhang and Zhou, 2010b], microRNA-binding prediction [Wu and Zhou, 2013], etc. In addition to class-dependent cost, there are many studies on example-dependent cost [Zadrozny and Elkan, 2001, Zadrozny et al., 2003, Brefeld et al., 2003], where some representative methods e.g., the costing method [Zadrozny et al., 2003], are also ensemble methods.

Abundant class-imbalance studies focused on binary classification, as can be seen in the survey [He and Garcia, 2009]. There are also studies concerning about multi-class imbalance learning, e.g., Tan et al. [2003], Sun et al. [2006], Hoens et al. [2012], Wang and Yao [2012], Fernández et al. [2013], Lin et al. [2013], Liu et al. [2013]; many of them are ensemble methods.

Rather than assuming that crisp cost values can be obtained in advance, there are also studies attempting to handle imprecise cost information appearing as *cost intervals* and *cost distributions* [Liu and Zhou, 2010, Zhou and Zhou, 2016], which may be more suitable to tasks where human experts can only provide rough cost estimates rather than precise cost values.

Chapter 11

Deep Learning and Deep Forest

11.1 Deep Neural Networks and Ensemble

Since AlexNet won the ImageNet competition [Krizhevsky et al., 2012], we have entered the era of **deep learning** [Goodfellow et al., 2016]. Nevertheless, ensemble methods are still very helpful.

On one hand, there are many studies trying to build ensembles of **Deep Neural Networks (DNNs)**, where the major effort was devoted to the reduction of training cost for generating multiple DNNs. For example, instead of independently training N number of DNNs from scratch, Huang et al. [2017a] proposed SE (Snapshot Ensembling), which leverages a cosine cyclical learning rate [Loshchilov and Hutter, 2017] to make the **Stochastic Gradient Descent (SGD)** process converge N times to local minima along its optimization path, and adds the current DNN to the ensemble at each time when SGD converges. Thus, the training time cost for the entire ensemble is identical to the time cost required for training a single DNN. Based on the insight that local optima found by SGD can be connected by simple curves of near constant loss [Draxler et al., 2018], Garipov et al. [2018] showed that by using a cyclical learning rate, it is possible to gather models that are spatially close to each other but produce diverse predictions, leading to FGE (Fast Geometric Ensembling) which exploits the gathered models to form ensembles without additional computational overhead compared to training a single model.

Wang et al. [2022] conducted a comprehensive evaluation and comparison of the efficiency of DNN ensembles with commonly used DNN architectures, and found that even the most simple methods for building ensembles can match or exceed the accuracy of state-of-the-art models while being more efficient. These findings hold true for several kinds of tasks, including image classification, video classification and semantic segmentation, and for various state-of-the-art DNN architectures, such as ViT [Dosovitskiy et al., 2021], EfficientNet [Tan and Le, 2019], ResNet [He et al., 2016] and MobileNetV2 [Sandler et al., 2018].

DOI: 10.1201/9781003587774-11

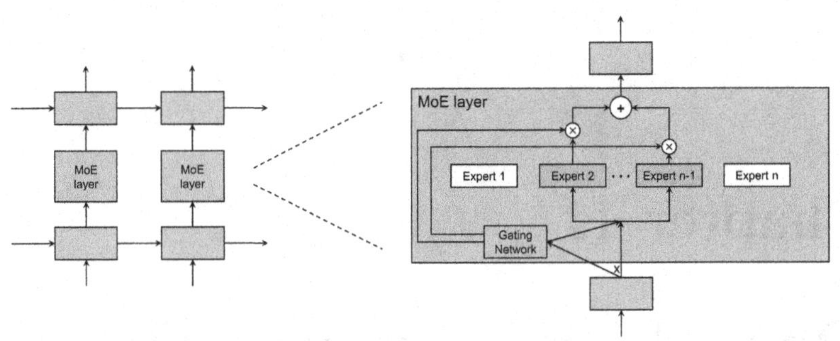

Figure 11.1: A Mixture of Experts (MoE) layer embedded within a recurrent neural network [Shazeer et al., 2017].

Similar results were also achieved in [Lobacheva et al., 2020, Kondratyuk et al., 2020]. These findings show that ensemble methods provide a simple complementary paradigm to achieve superior efficiency without tuning the architecture, and one can often improve accuracy while reducing inference and training cost by building ensembles of existing networks.

On the other hand, ensemble mechanisms have been well exploited in DNNs. For example, by recognizing that the most important ability of DNNs is **representation learning**, i.e., learning a feature representation that makes it easier than learning with the original representation, there are studies trying to combine the representation ability of DNNs with the generalization ability of ensemble methods, e.g., it has been shown that using ensembles such as **random forest** facilitated with features learned by DNNs, the performance can be even better than simply using DNNs [Kontschieder et al., 2015]. Many works have tried to connect random forest with neural networks, such as converting cascaded random forest to CNNs [Richmond et al., 2015] and exploiting random forest to help initialize neural networks [Welbl, 2014]. These works are typically based on early studies, e.g., mapping of trees to networks, tree-structured neural networks, as discussed in [Zhou and Chen, 2002].

In addition to the *external* exploitation of ensemble mechanisms like the aforementioned combination of random forest and DNNs, there is also *internal* exploitation of ensemble mechanisms in DNNs. The combination of **Mixture of Experts (MoE)** within DNNs is an example. Eigen et al. [2014] extended the MoE to a stacked model, which increases the number of effective experts by introducing an exponential number of paths through different combinations of experts at each layer. Shazeer et al. [2017] introduced a sparsely-gated MoE layer, as shown in Figure 11.1, which consists of up to thousands of feed-forward sub-networks embedded in a recurrent neural network, and a trainable gating network is employed for a sparse combination of these experts. Ma et al. [2018] proposed MMoE (Multi-gate Mixture-of-Experts), which adapts the MoE structure to multi-task learning by sharing the expert sub-models across all tasks and employing a gating network trained to optimize each task. The MoE mechanism has been successfully applied in large models such as GPT-4.

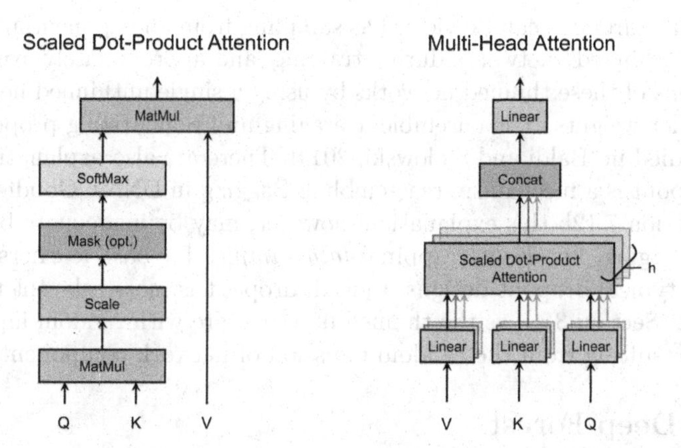

Figure 11.2: Scaled dot-product attention (left) and multi-head attention (right) [Vaswani et al., 2017].

Transformer [Vaswani et al., 2017] has achieved great success in tasks such as natural language processing [Devlin et al., 2019] and computer vision [Dosovitskiy et al., 2021]. Specifically, transformer was designed to process sequential data, but unlike recurrent neural networks, it processes the entire input sequence all at once, based on the **attention** mechanism. In particular, the transformer building blocks are scaled dot-product attention units, as shown in Figure 11.2 (left). When a sentence, for example, is passed into the transformer model, attention weights are calculated between every *token* simultaneously, and thus, the attention unit produces embeddings for every token in context that contain information about the token itself along with a weighted combination of other relevant tokens each weighted by its attention weight. Figure 11.2 (right) shows the **multi-head attention**, which is crucial for the performance of transformer. It runs through the scaled dot-product attention units several times in parallel, concatenates the independent attention outputs and transforms them linearly into the expected dimension. The idea behind multi-head attention is to allow the attention function to extract information from different representation subspaces, which would otherwise be impossible with a single attention head. It is evident that the multi-head attention is in essence an ensemble mechanism.

Ensemble mechanisms have also been exploited to explain the usefulness of DNN's key ingredients, e.g., **dropout**. The main idea of dropout is to randomly omit some components of the neural network, such as some hidden units or connection weights, with a certain probability in the forward propagation of the training phase, while the remaining components of the network are updated in backpropagation. It is evidently related to overfitting control, and extensive empirical studies [Hinton et al., 2012, Krizhevsky et al., 2012, Li et al., 2013b] verified that dropout is able to improve the performance and reduce overfitting risk. Great efforts have been devoted to understanding why dropout works.

Specifically, dropout can be viewed as sampling from an exponential number of different "thinned" networks during training, and approximately averaging the predictions of these thinned networks by using a single unthinned network that has smaller weights. The ensemble averaging and regularizing properties have been studied in [Baldi and Sadowski, 2014]. There are also explanations saying that dropout is a mechanism reassembling Bagging in DNNs [Goodfellow et al., 2016, Section 7.12]; this explanation, however, may be inadequate because the key of Bagging, i.e., bootstrapping *data samples* for base learners, does not occur in typical dropout designs. Indeed, dropout is more relevant to Random Subspace (Section 3.4), as the thinned networks are with random input feature subsets resulting from the random omission of network components.

11.2 Deep Forest

What is deep learning? Answers from the crowd are very likely to be that "*deep learning is a subfield of machine learning that uses deep neural networks*" (Sirignano [2017]). Actually, the great success of DNNs led to the rise of deep learning, and almost all deep learning applications were built upon neural network models, or more technically, multiple layers of parameterized *differentiable* nonlinear modules that can be trained by backpropagation. Considering that not all properties in the physical world are differentiable or can be best modeled by differentiable modules, it is interesting to answer the question "*Can deep learning be realized with non-differentiable modules?*"

The answer to the question may help understand important issues such as (1) Do deep models have to be DNNs, or, must deep models be constructed with differentiable modules? There were researches involving non-differentiable activation functions in DNNs; however, they usually use differentiable functions that upper-bound the non-differentiable ones for relaxation in the optimization/learning process, and thus, actually they still work with differentiable modules. (2) Is it possible to train deep models without **Backpropagation (BP)**? Note that backpropagation and gradient-based adjustment require differentiability. The community has developed many learning modules, whereas many are non-differentiable and can hardly be tuned by gradient-based adjustment; it would be interesting to know whether it is possible to construct deep models based on these modules. (3) Is it possible to enable deep models to win tasks on which other models such as RF or XGBoost exhibit superior performance?

The first deep model based on non-differentiable modules, **Deep Forest (DF)** [Zhou and Feng, 2019], offers positive answers to the above questions. DF relies on neither backpropagation nor gradient-based optimization, and the model can adaptively grow according to data. The inspiration for its development came from the conjecture that behind the mystery of DNNs there are three crucial characteristics, i.e., *layer-by-layer processing*, *in-model feature transformation*, and *sufficient model complexity* [Zhou and Feng, 2019].

To realize layer-by-layer processing, the seminal DF algorithm, gcForest, utilizes a cascade structure, as illustrated in Figure 11.3, where each level of cascade receives feature information processed by its preceding level.

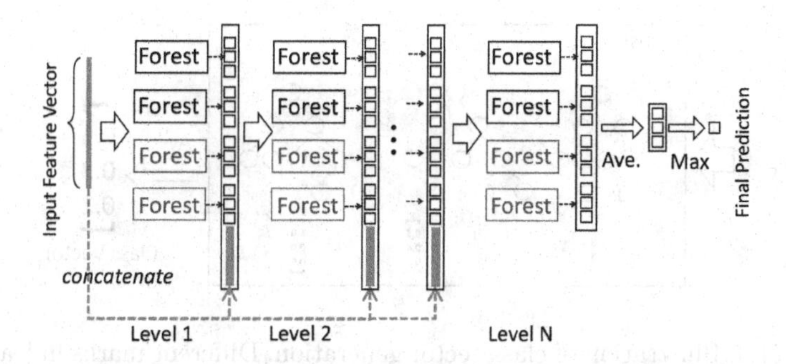

Figure 11.3: Illustration of the cascade forest structure. Suppose that each level of the cascade consists of two random forests (black) and two completely random forests (blue). Suppose that there are three classes to predict; thus, each forest will output a three-dimensional class vector, which is then concatenated for re-representation of the input.

Each level is an ensemble of decision tree forests, i.e., an **ensemble of ensembles**. Here, we include different types of forests to encourage the **diversity**. For simplicity, suppose that we use two **completely random forests** and two **random forests**. Each completely random forest contains 500 completely-random trees, generated by randomly assigning a feature for the split at each node, and growing the tree till pure leaf, i.e., each leaf node contains only the same class of instances. Similarly, each random forest contains 500 trees, by randomly picking $\sqrt{d}$ number of features as candidate (d is the number of input features) and selecting the one with the best *Gini* (see Section 1.2.1) value for split. The number of trees in each forest is a hyper-parameter.

Given an instance, each forest can produce an estimate of class distribution, by counting the percentage of different classes of training examples at the leaf node where the concerned instance falls, and then averaging across all trees in the same forest, as illustrated in Figure 11.4. The estimated class distribution forms a class vector, which is then concatenated with the original feature vector to input to the next level. For example, suppose that there are three classes, and each of the four forests will produce a three-dimensional class vector; consequently, the next level will receive $12 = 3 \times 4$ augmented features.

The above description adopts the simplest form of class vectors, i.e., the class distribution at the leaf nodes into which the concerned instance falls. It is evident that such a small number of augmented features may deliver very limited augmented information, and it is very likely to be drowned out when the original feature vectors are high-dimensional. It is expectable that more profit can be obtained if more augmented features are involved.

To reduce the risk of overfitting, class vector produced by each forest can be generated by k-fold cross validation. In detail, each instance will be used as training data for $k - 1$ times, resulting in $k - 1$ class vectors, which are then averaged to produce the final class vector as augmented features

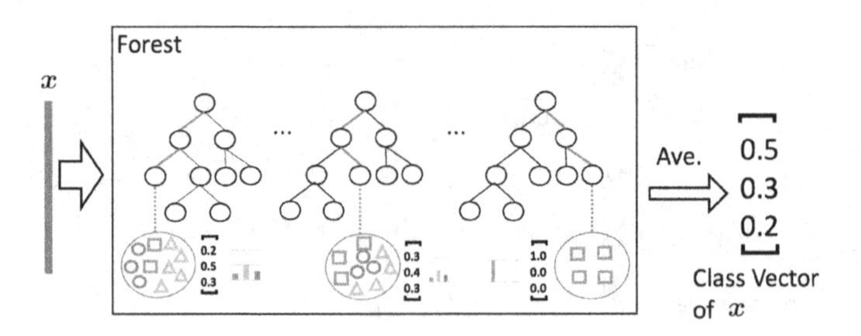

Figure 11.4: Illustration of class vector generation. Different marks in leaf nodes imply different classes; red color highlights paths along which the concerned instance traverses to leaf nodes.

for the next level of cascade. After expanding a new level, the performance of the whole cascade can be estimated on validation set, and the training procedure will terminate if there is no significant performance gain; thus, the number of cascade levels can be automatically determined. Note that the training error rather than cross validation error can also be used to control the cascade growth when there are abundant training data, or the training cost is concerned, or limited computation resource available. In contrast to most deep neural networks whose model complexities are fixed, deep forest can adaptively decide its model complexity by terminating training when adequate.

The design of gcForest was facilitated with a procedure called **multi-grained scanning**, inspired by the recognition that DNNs are powerful in handling feature relationships, e.g., convolutional neural networks are effective on image data where spatial relationships among the raw pixels are critical, recurrent neural networks are effective on sequence data where sequential relationships are critical.

As Figure 11.5 illustrates, sliding windows are used to scan the raw features. Suppose that there are 400 raw features and a window size of 100 features. For sequence data, a 100-dimensional feature vector will be generated by sliding the window for one feature; in total 301 feature vectors are produced. If the raw features are with spacial relationships, such as a 20×20 panel of 400 image pixels, then a 10×10 window will produce 121 feature vectors (i.e., 121 10×10 panels). All feature vectors extracted from positive/negative training examples are regarded as positive/negative instances, which will then be used to generate class vectors: instances extracted from the same size of windows will be used to train a completely random forest and a random forest, and then the class vectors are generated and concatenated as transformed features. As illustrated in Figure 11.5, for three classes, 301 three-dimensional class vectors are produced by each forest, leading to an 1,806-dimensional transformed feature vector corresponding to each 400-dimensional raw feature vector.

For instances extracted from the sliding windows, gcForest simply assigns them with the label of the original training example. Some label assignments are inherently incorrect. For example, suppose the original training example

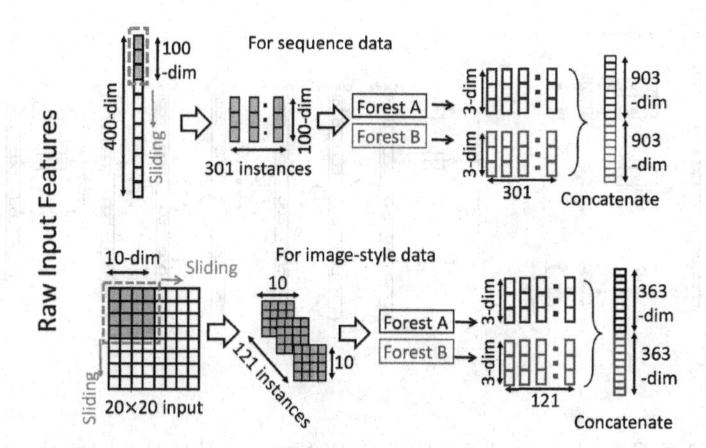

Figure 11.5: Illustration of feature re-representation using sliding window scanning. Suppose that there are three classes, 400-dimensional raw features, and 100-dimensional sliding window.

is a positive image about "car"; it is clear that many extracted instances do not contain a car, and therefore, they are incorrectly labeled as positive. This is actually related to **Flipping Output** [Breiman, 2000b], an approach for ensemble diversity enhancement. Note that when transformed feature vectors are too long to be accommodated, feature sampling can be performed, e.g., by subsampling the instances generated by sliding window scanning, as completely-random trees do not rely on feature split selection, whereas random forests are quite insensitive to feature split selection. The feature sampling process is also related to **Random Subspace** [Ho, 1998].

Figure 11.5 shows only one size of the sliding window. By using multiple sizes of sliding windows, multi-grained feature vectors will be generated, as shown in Figure 11.6, which summarizes the overall procedure of gcForest. Suppose the original input is of 400 raw features, and three window sizes are used for multi-grained scanning. For m training examples, a window with size of 100 features will generate a data set of $301 \times m$ 100-dimensional training examples. These data will be used to train a completely random forest and a random forest, each containing 500 trees. If there are three classes to be predicted, an 1,806-dimensional feature vector will be obtained. The transformed training set will then be used to train the 1st-grade of cascade forest.

Similarly, sliding windows with sizes of 200 and 300 features will generate 1,206-dimensional and 606-dimensional feature vectors, respectively, for each original training example. The transformed feature vectors, augmented with the class vector generated by the previous grade, will then be used to train the 2nd-grade and 3rd-grade of cascade forests, respectively. This procedure will be repeated till convergence of validation performance. In other words, the final model is actually a **cascade of cascades**, where each cascade consists of multiple levels each corresponding to a grain of scanning, e.g., the 1st cascade

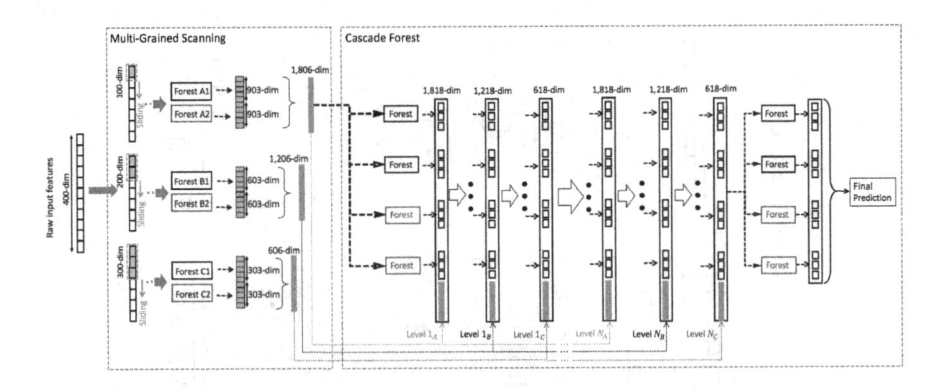

Figure 11.6: Overall procedure of gcForest. Suppose that there are three classes, 400-dimensional raw features, and three sizes of sliding windows.

consists of Level 1_A to Level 1_C in Figure 11.6. For difficult tasks, more grains can be used when computational resource allows.

Given a test instance, the multi-grained scanning procedure will go through to get the corresponding transformed feature representation, and then the cascade will go through till the last level. The final prediction will be obtained by aggregating the four 3-dimensional class vectors at the last level and will output the class with the maximum aggregated value.

It is evident that passing outputs of one level of learners as input to another level of learners is related to **stacking** [Wolpert, 1992, Breiman, 1996b]. However, stacking is easy to overfit with more than two levels, and can hardly enable a deep model by itself. The key of building a deep forest lies in the enhancement of diversity during model growth. Actually, gcForest exploits all major categories of diversity enhancement strategies described in Section 5.5. It is worth mentioning that the diversity plays the central role in the construction of deep forest. It is critical to avoid **diversity vanish** in constructing DFs, just like it is critical to avoid **gradient vanish** in constructing DNNs.

Zhou and Feng [2019] conjectured that numeric modeling tasks such as image/audio data are more suitable to DNNs because their operations, such as convolution, fit well with numeric signal modeling. Deep forest was not developed to replace DNNs for such tasks; instead, it offers an alternative when DNNs are not superior. There are plenty of tasks, especially categorical/symbolic or mixed modeling tasks, where deep forests have been found useful. Empirical study shows that the gcForest is able to achieve a performance highly competitive with DNNs on a broad range of tasks except large-scale image tasks, possibly because that more augmented features than that shown in Figure 11.4 need to be augmented for tasks involving high-dimensional data. Moreover, larger models tend to offer better performance on large-scale tasks, while computational facilities are crucial for enabling the training of larger models. Remind that the success of DNNs owes much to the acceleration offered by GPUs, but forest structure is unfortunately uncomfortable for GPUs. One possibility is to wait for adequate new hardwares, and another possibility is to resort to distributed computing implementations, like what has been done in a real-world application to automatic detection of cash-out fraud [Zhang et al., 2019].

Note that **Deep Forest** is a name in parallel to **Deep Neural Networks**. In addition to the seminal gcForest algorithm, a number of deep forest algorithms have been developed. In the following two sections we will show that forest models have some important characteristics that were believed to be specialty of neural networks only.

11.3 Forest and Auto-Encoder

Auto-encoder is a class of models aiming to map the input to a latent space and map it back to the original space, with reconstruction error as low as possible. It is fundamentally important for representation learning, and has been regarded as a key ingredient of deep learning [Goodfellow et al., 2016, Bengio et al., 2013a]. In fact, the hot wave of deep learning started with training a stack of auto-encoders in a greedy layer-wised fashion [Hinton et al., 2006].

Previously almost all auto-encoders were implemented based on neural networks, and the auto-encoder ability was thought as a speciality of neural networks. Feng and Zhou [2018] showed that forest models can also be used as auto-encoders.

An auto-encoder has two basic functions: **encoding** and **decoding**. There is no difficulty for a forest to do encoding since at least the leaf nodes information can be regarded as a kind of encoding; needless to say, the subsets of nodes or even the branch of paths may be able to offer more information for encoding. Feng and Zhou [2018] described a simple encoding procedure EncoderForest. Given a trained forest model of T trees and an input instance to be encoded, the forward encoding procedure sends the instance to each tree in the forest, and identifies the leaf nodes in which the instance falls. Thus, the indices of the T leaf nodes consist a T-dimensional vector, which is the encoding result. Note that this encoding procedure is independent to the tree building process, and thus, the trees can be learned in a supervised setting such as random forest, or in an unsupervised setting such as completely random tree forest.

The decoding function is not that obvious. In fact, forests are generally used for forward prediction, by going from the root of each tree to the leaves, whereas it is unknown how to do backward reconstruction, i.e., inducing the original samples from information obtained at the leaves. Feng and Zhou [2018] presented a forest decoding procedure as follows.

For simplicity of discussion, consider a binary classification task with four attributes. The first and second attributes are numerical ones; the third is a triple-valued attribute with values {RED, BLUE, GREEN}; the fourth is a boolean

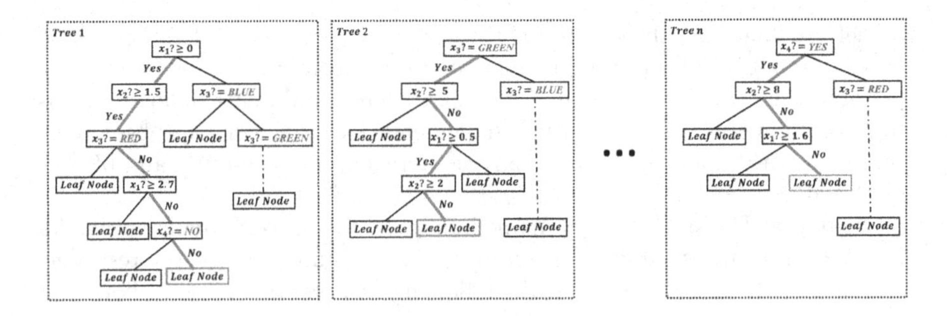

Figure 11.7: Traversing backward along decision paths.

attribute with values {YES, NO}. Given an instance $\boldsymbol{x}$, let x_i denote the value of $\boldsymbol{x}$ on the i-th attribute. Suppose in the encoding step a forest has been generated as shown in Figure 11.7, and the leaf nodes on which the instance $\boldsymbol{x}$ falling into are known and shown in Figure 11.7 as the red nodes. The goal is to reconstruct instance $\boldsymbol{x}$.

An effective yet simple, possibly the simplest, strategy for backward reconstruction in forest is to achieve the above goal as follows. First, each leaf node actually corresponds to a path coming from the root, and the path can be identified based on the leaf node without uncertainty. For example, the identified paths are highlighted in red in Figure 11.7.

Second, each path corresponds to a symbolic rule. For example, the highlighted tree paths correspond to the following rule set, where the i-th rule corresponds to the path of the i-th tree in the forest, and $\neg$ denotes negation:

1. $(x_1 \geq 0) \wedge (x_2 \geq 1.5) \wedge \neg(x_3 == \texttt{RED}) \wedge \neg(x_1 \geq 2.7) \wedge \neg(x_4 == \texttt{NO})$
2. $(x_3 == \texttt{GREEN}) \wedge \neg(x_2 \geq 5) \wedge (x_1 \geq 0.5) \wedge \neg(x_2 \geq 2)$
3. $\cdots$
4. $(x_4 == \texttt{YES}) \wedge \neg(x_2 \geq 8) \wedge \neg(x_1 \geq 1.6)$

The above rule set can be further adjusted into a more succinct form as follows:

1. $(2.7 \geq x_1 \geq 0) \wedge (x_2 \geq 1.5) \wedge \neg(x_3 == \texttt{RED}) \wedge (x_4 == \texttt{YES})$
2. $(x_1 \geq 0.5) \wedge \neg(x_2 \geq 2) \wedge (x_3 == \texttt{GREEN})$
3. $\cdots$
4. $\neg(x_1 \geq 1.6) \wedge \neg(x_2 \geq 8) \wedge (x_4 == \texttt{YES})$

Third, the Maximal-Compatible Rule (MCR) can be derived. MCR is such a rule that each of its component coverage cannot be enlarged, otherwise incompatible issue will occur. For example, from the above rule set the

Input: A path rule list *Rule_List* consists of T rules defined by a forest with T trees.
Process:
1. Initialize $MCR \leftarrow initialize\_list()$.
2. **for** i in range(T) **do**:
3. $\quad path\_rule \leftarrow rule\_list[i]$;
4. $\quad$ **for** *node_rule* in *path_rule.node_rule_list* **do**:
5. $\quad\quad j \leftarrow node\_rule.get\_attribute()$;
6. $\quad\quad bound \leftarrow node\_rule.get\_bound()$;
7. $\quad\quad MCR[j] \leftarrow intersect(MCR[j], bound)$;
8. $\quad$ **end**
9. **end**

Output: *MCR*

Figure 11.8: The MCR algorithm.

corresponding MCR can be obtained as follows:

$$(1.6 \geq x_1 \geq 0.5) \wedge (2 \geq x_2 \geq 1.5) \wedge (x_3 == \texttt{GREEN}) \wedge (x_4 == \texttt{YES})$$

For each component of this MCR, such as $(2 \geq x_2 \geq 1.5)$, its coverage cannot be enlarged. For example, if it was enlarged to $(3 \geq x_2 \geq 1.5)$, it would have conflict with the condition in $\neg(x_2 \geq 2)$ in the 2nd rule. The algorithm for identifying the MCR is shown in Figure 11.8. It can be proved that the original sample must reside in the input region defined by the MCR.

Finally, after obtaining the MCR, the original sample can be reconstructed. For categorical attributes such as x_3 and x_4, the original sample must take these values in the MCR; for numerical attributes, such as x_2, one can take a representative value, such as the mean value in the interval $[1.5, 2]$. Thus, the reconstructed sample is $\boldsymbol{x} = [0.55, 1.75, \texttt{GREEN}, \texttt{YES}]$. Note that for numerical value, there are many alternative ways for the reconstruction, such as the median, max, min, or even the histograms.

Given the above description, one can get a summary for conducting backward decoding of eForest. Concretely, given a trained forest with T trees along with the forward encoding x_{enc} in R^T for a particular instance, the backward decoding will first locate the individual leaf nodes via each element of x_{enc}, and then obtain T decision rules for the corresponding decision paths. After that, by calculating the MCR and taking a point estimate, one can get a reconstruction from x_{enc} back to x_{dec} in the input region. The algorithm is shown in Figure 11.9.

By enabling the eForest to conduct the forward encoding and backward decoding procedures, auto-encoder can thus be realized. Empirical studies demonstrate that eForest has good performance in terms of accuracy and speed, as well as the ability of fault tolerance and model re-usability. In particular, on text data, by using only 10% of the input bits, the model is still able

Input: x_{enc}, trained eForest F with T trees.
Process:
1. Initialize rule_list $\leftarrow$ *initialize_list*().
2. **for** i in range(T) **do**:
3. *path* $\leftarrow$ *F.tree*[i].*get_path*($x_{enc}[i]$);
4. *path_rule* $\leftarrow$ *calculate_rules*(*path*);
5. *path_rule* $\leftarrow$ *simplify*(*path_rule*);
6. *rule_list.append*(*path_rule*);
7. **end**
8. $MCR \leftarrow$ *calculate_MCR*(*rule_list*).
9. $x_{dec} \leftarrow$ *sample*(MCR,method='minimum').
Output: x_{dec}

Figure 11.9: The backward decoding algorithm.

to reconstruct the original data with high accuracy. Another advantage of eForest lies in the fact that it can be applied to symbolic attributes or mixed attributes directly, without transforming the symbolic attributes to numerical ones, especially when considering that the transforming procedure generally either loses information or introduces additional bias.

11.4 Forest and Hierarchical Distributed Representation

Hierarchical distributed representation [Hinton et al., 1986] is believed to be a key ingredient of deep neural networks [Bengio et al., 2013a], and it is believed that multi-layered distributed representation is only possible for neural networks or differentiable systems in general. However, Feng et al. [2018] showed that hierarchical distributed representation can also be realized with forests.

Consider a multi-layered feed-forward structure with $M-1$ intermediate layers and one final output layer. For $i \in \{0, 1, 2, \ldots, M\}$, denote by $\boldsymbol{o}_i$ the output for each layer including the input layer $\boldsymbol{o}_0$ and the output layer $\boldsymbol{o}_M$. For an input instance $\boldsymbol{x}$, the corresponding output at each layer is in R^{d_i}, where d_i is the number of units in the i-th layer. The learning task is therefore to learn the mappings $F_i : R^{d_{i-1}} \to R^{d_i}$ for each layer $i > 0$, such that the final output $\boldsymbol{o}_M$ minimizes the empirical loss ℓ on the training set. Mean squared errors and cross-entropy with extra regularization terms are common choices for the empirical loss ℓ. In an unsupervised setting, the desired output $\boldsymbol{y}$ can be the training data itself, leading to an auto-encoder where the loss function is the reconstruction error between the output and original input.

When each F_i is parametric and differentiable as in neural networks, such a learning task can be accomplished in an efficient way using backpropagation. The basic routine is to calculate the gradients of the loss function with respect to each parameter at each layer using the chain rule, and then perform gradient descent for parameter updates. Once the training is accomplished, the output for the intermediate layers can be regarded as the new representation learned by the model. Such a hierarchical representation can be interpreted as a multi-layered abstraction of the original input and is believed to be critical for the success of deep learning models.

When F_i is non-parametric as in decision trees and forests, backpropagation is no longer applicable since there is no parameter for calculating the derivatives of loss function. Feng et al. [2018] presented a process to address this problem with forest model of multi-layered GBDT, without relying on backpropagation.

First, at the t-th iteration, the F_i^{t-1}'s are obtained from the previous iteration, and a *pseudo-inverse* mapping G_i^t paired with each F_i^{t-1} can be obtained such that $G_i^t(F_i^{t-1}(\boldsymbol{o}_{i-1})) \approx \boldsymbol{o}_{i-1}$. This is achievable by minimizing the expected value of the reconstruction loss function as

$$G_i^t = \arg\min_{\hat{G}_i^t} \mathbb{E}_x[\ell^{inverse}(\boldsymbol{o}_{i-1}, \hat{G}_i^t(F_i^{t-1}(\boldsymbol{o}_{i-1})))] \ , \tag{11.1}$$

where the loss $\ell^{inverse}$ can be the reconstruction loss. Like an auto-encoder, random noise injection is often exploited; that is, instead of using a pure reconstruction error measure, it is good in practice to set

$$\ell^{inverse} = \|G_i(F_i(\boldsymbol{o}_{i-1} + \varepsilon)) - (\boldsymbol{o}_{i-1} + \varepsilon)\|, \varepsilon \sim \mathcal{N}(\boldsymbol{0}, \, diag(\sigma^2)) \ . \tag{11.2}$$

Thus, the model can be more robust in the sense that the inverse mapping is forced to learn how to map the neighboring training data to the right manifold. In addition, such randomness injection helps to attain a generative model by treating the inverse mapping direction as a generative path.

Second, once G_i^t has been updated, it can be used in forward mapping for the previous layer F_{i-1}. The key here is to assign pseudo-labels $\boldsymbol{z}_{i-1}^t$ for F_{i-1} where $i \in \{2, \ldots, M\}$, and the pseudo-labels of each layer are generated according to $\boldsymbol{z}_{i-1}^t = G_i(\mathbf{z}_i^t)$. That is, at the t-th iteration, for all the intermediate layers, the pseudo-labels for each layer can be *aligned* and propagated from the output layer to the input layer. Then, once the pseudo-labels for each layer are computed, each F_i^{t-1} can follow a step towards the pseudo-residuals $-\frac{\partial \ell(F_i^{t-1}(\boldsymbol{o}_{i-1}), \boldsymbol{z}_i^t)}{\partial F_i^{t-1}(\boldsymbol{o}_{i-1})}$ just like a typical regression GBDT.

It remains the only issue to set the pseudo-label $\boldsymbol{z}_M^t$ for the final layer to make the whole structure ready for update. Note that at layer M, one can always use the ground-truth label $\boldsymbol{y}$ as the output layer's pseudo-label. For instance, it is natural to define the pseudo-label of the output layer as

$$\boldsymbol{z}_M^t = \boldsymbol{o}_M - \alpha \frac{\partial \ell(\boldsymbol{o}_M, \boldsymbol{y})}{\partial \boldsymbol{o}_M} \ . \tag{11.3}$$

Then, F_M^t can be set to fit towards the pseudo-residuals $-\frac{\partial \ell(F_M^{t-1}(\boldsymbol{o}_{M-1}), \boldsymbol{z}_M^t)}{\partial F_M^{t-1}(\boldsymbol{o}_{M-1})}$. In other words, at the t-th iteration, the output layer F_M computes its pseudo-label $\boldsymbol{z}_M^t$ and produces the pseudo-labels for all the other layer via the inverse functions, and each F_i can thus be updated accordingly. Once all the F_i's get updated, the procedure can move to the next iteration to update G_i's. In practice, a bottom up update is suggested (update F_i before F_j for $i < j$) and each F_i can go several rounds of additive Boosting steps towards its current pseudo-label.

When training neural networks, the initialization can be achieved by assigning random Gaussian noise to each parameter, and then the procedure can move on to the next stage for parameter update. For tree models, it is non-trivial to draw a random tree structure from the distribution of all possible tree configurations. Therefore, instead of initializing the tree structure at random, some Gaussian noise is introduced to the output of intermediate layers, and some very tiny trees are trained to obtain F_i^0 for the initialization. Then, the training procedure moves on to iterative update forward mappings and inverse mappings. The procedure is illustrated in Figure 11.10.

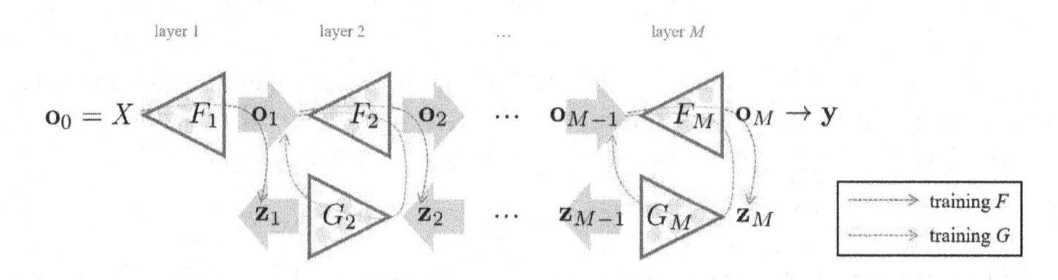

Figure 11.10: Illustration of the training process of mGBDT.

In classification tasks, one can set the forward mapping in the output layer as a linear classifier. On one hand, this will force the lower layers to learn a feature re-representation that is as linear separable as possible. On the other hand, the dimensionality of the output layer and that of the layer below are often very different, and therefore, it is generally difficult to get an accurate inverse mapping. By using a linear classifier for the forward mapping at the output layer, there is no need to calculate that particular corresponding inverse mapping since the pseudo-label for the layer below can be obtained by considering the global loss with respect to the output of the last hidden layer. It was shown that, under certain conditions, an update in the intermediate layer towards its pseudo-label helps to reduce the loss of the layer above, and thus helps to reduce the global loss [Feng et al., 2018].

Figure 11.11 visualizes the output of each intermediate layers via T-SNE [van der Maaten and Hinton, 2008]. It can be seen that the forest model offers multi-layered distributed representation, which was believed to be a speciality of neural network models only.

11.5 Deep Forest Extensions

11.5.1 Acceleration

Pang et al. [2018] attempted to reduce the computational and storage costs of gcForest by explicitly considering two aspects. First, gcForest processes all

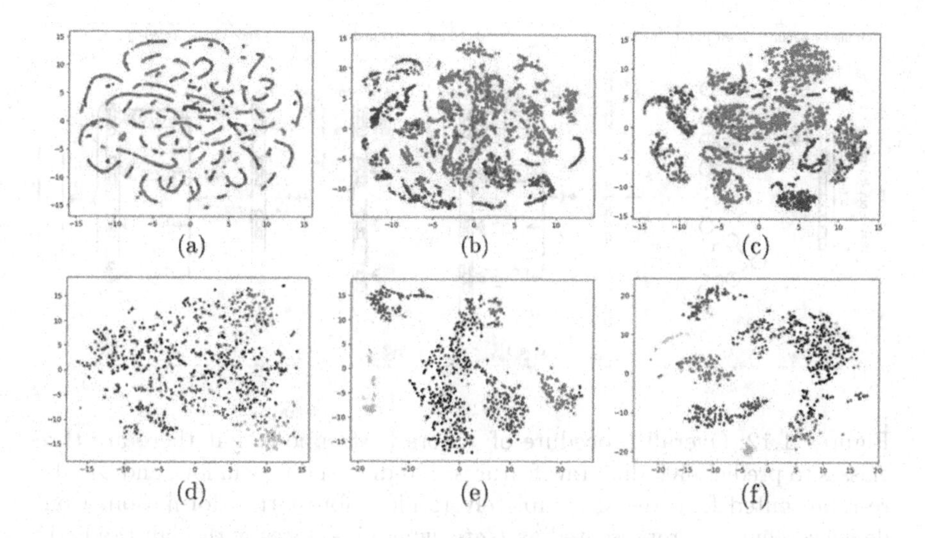

Figure 11.11: mGBDT forest feature visualization of (a) original representation, (b) 1st layer representation and (c) 2nd layer representation on *incomes* data set, and (d) original representation, (e) 1st layer representation, and (f) 2nd layer representation on *protein* data set.

instances through all levels of the cascade, and uses all features for learning, resulting in a linear increase of time complexity as the number of levels grows. Second, multi-grained scanning typically transforms one (original) instance into hundreds or even thousands of new instances, substantially increasing the number of training instances, and generating a high-dimensional input for the cascade process. Their proposed gcForest$_\mathsf{S}$ utilizes confidence screening, feature screening, and unsupervised feature transformation mechanisms to improve the efficiency of deep forests.

Confidence screening refers to that at each level of deep forest, instances with predictive confidences lower than a pre-set threshold will be passed to the next level, whereas other instances will get their final predictions at the current level. Thus, the number of instances to be passed to the next level will be significantly decreased, leading to significant reduction of computational cost.

Feature screening is a process of selecting features that are important for improving the performance at each level, rather than simply concatenating all the original features and transformed features of its preceding level. Pang et al. [2018] took both feature redundancy and nonlinear feature importance into consideration for the selection, formulated as:

$$\hat{\boldsymbol{\beta}} = \arg\min_{\boldsymbol{\beta}} \left\| y - \sum_{j=1}^{d} x_j \beta_j \right\|_2^2 + \lambda \sum_{j=1}^{d} (w^{\max} - w_j) |\beta_j| \,, \tag{11.4}$$

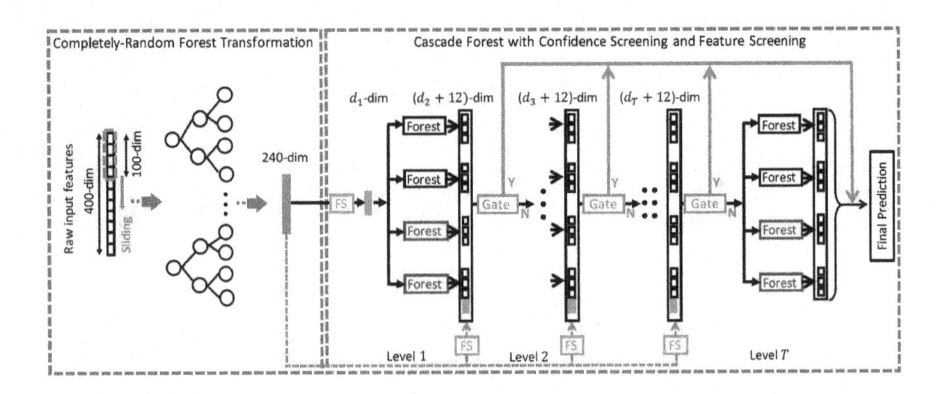

Figure 11.12: Overall procedure of gcForest$_\mathsf{S}$. Suppose that there are three classes to predict, 400-dim. raw features, 100-dim. sliding window, and 240-dim. re-represented features of completely random forest transformation. Confidence screening is represented as *Gate*, where instances with high predictive confidence (Y) at the i-th level are predicted directly, whereas only instances with low predictive confidence (N) traverse to the next level. Feature screening is abbreviated as *FS* and d_i is the selection size of the features at the i-th level.

where w_j is the feature importance of feature x_j obtained by simply averaging over trees, $w^{\max}$ is the maximum value of $\{w_1, w_2, \ldots, w_d\}$, and $\lambda \geq 0$. At each level of the cascade, features with non-zero coefficients of $\hat{\boldsymbol{\beta}}$ will be selected. The objective function aims to minimize the squared loss with a weighted ℓ_1 regularization, solved by least angle regression which can compute the solutions for all the values of λ extremely efficiently, with computational complexity in the same order as a single least squares.

Furthermore, considering that the multi-grained scanning used in gcForest results in high memory requirement and time cost, Pang et al. [2018] replaced it with an unsupervised feature transformation method, completely random forest transformation, which combines completely random forest with a variant of random subspace for feature transformation, resulting in linear time complexity with low memory requirements.

The overall procedure of gcForest$_\mathsf{S}$ is shown in Figure 11.12. Empirical studies show that it achieves highly competitive predictive performance with reduced time cost and memory requirement by one to two orders of magnitude, compared to the original gcForest.

hiDF [Chen et al., 2021c] leveraged stable **high-order interactions** of input features to generate informative and diverse feature representations. Specifically, a generalized version of Random Intersection Trees (gRIT) is designed to discover stable high-order interactions and Activated Linear Combination (ACL) is applied to transform these interactions into new feature representations, which can interact with input features across multiple layers. Thus, some high-order interactions between input features can be exploited to improve predictive performance. Moreover, hiDF provides hierarchical distributed representations from low-order to high-order interactions, enhancing the effectiveness and diversity of feature representation. These representations help to reduce the size of forests in the front layers, leading to the reduction of predictive time cost as well as memory requirement by one order of magnitude in experiments.

11.5.2 Metric Learning

Metric learning, or **distance metric learning** [Zhou, 2021, Section 10.6] attempts to learn an appropriate distance metric to measure the distance between instances, leading to an appropriate feature space in which the learning performance can be better than that in the original feature space. The basic idea is to learn a metric such that the distance between similar instances should be smaller than that between dissimilar instances.

Rather than a specific distance metric which assumes a linear structure of data, Utkin and Ryabinin [2018] exploited the deep forest in-model feature transformation to capture some nonlinear structure of data. Their proposed SDF (Siamese Deep Forest) utilizes the concatenation of the augmented features generated at each level of deep forest to re-represent instances and evaluates the distances between instances based on the re-representation. In contrast to gcForest where the class vectors are generated by averaging the percentage of different classes of training examples falling into the leaf nodes, as shown in Figure 11.4, Utkin and Ryabinin [2018] employed a weighted average where the weights can be determined to decrease/increase distances between similar/dissimilar instance pairs, as illustrated in Figure 11.13. To adapt the weights layer by layer, Utkin and Ryabinin [2018] took a greedy algorithm to train the SDF, where the weights are successively calculated for each level of the forest cascade.

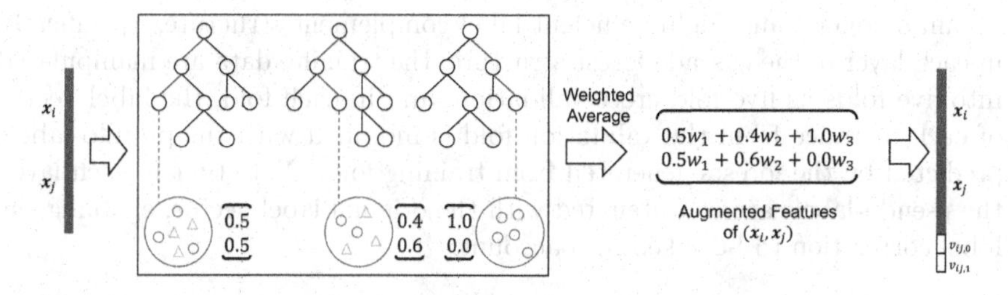

Figure 11.13: An illustration of the weights that can be determined to decrease/increase distances between similar/dissimilar instance pairs in Siamese Deep Forest.

Utkin and Ryabinin [2018] showed that the weights can be obtained by solving a quadratic optimization problem. Later, Utkin and Ryabinin [2019] proposed DisDF that combines Euclidean and Manhattan distances and simplifies the optimization problem, leading to a better computational efficiency than SDF.

11.5.3 Multi-Label Learning

Multi-label learning deals with tasks where each instance can be associated with multiple class labels simultaneously [Zhou and Zhang, 2017]. Yang et al. [2020] extended deep forest to multi-label learning and proposed MLDF (Multi-Label Deep Forest).

As mentioned in Section 2.6.2, there are many evaluation measures for multi-label learning [Wu and Zhou, 2017], such as *hamming loss*, *ranking loss* and *coverage*. Considering that deep forest can control model growth by evaluating different measures on the validation set, Yang et al. [2020] utilized measure-aware mechanisms to optimize the performance measure, catering to the needs of different users.

In detail, MLDF has two measure-aware mechanisms, i.e., *measure-aware feature reuse* and *measure-aware layer growth*. The measure-aware feature reuse mechanism can choose whether to reuse the feature representation of the previous layer in the next layer based on different evaluation measures. Figure 11.14 shows a comparison of MLDF with/without this mechanism. The measure-aware layer growth mechanism can control the model complexity based on different measures. Figure 11.15 shows the performance curves of MLDF by employing six different measures to control the model complexity. It can be seen that by considering different measures for validation, the growth of forests is terminated at different depths, while all with performance significantly better than RF-PCT, a traditional multi-label random forest.

There are multi-label learning tasks where the multiple labels are associated with each training example partially. This can happen, for example, in image tasks when there are lots of labels while only a subset of them have been annotated for training data. Wang et al. [2020] proposed the LCForest (Label Complement cascade Forest) which exploits the cascade forest structure to obtain a concise and highly efficient label complement structure. Specifically, in each layer of the cascade forest structure, the training data are manipulated into five folds as five-fold cross-validation, and in each fold, the label vector of each instance from the validation fold is modified with the pseudo-labels predicted by the forests generated from training folds. Note that in each layer, the pseudo-labels are concatenated with the original label vector, enabling the label correlation to be taken into account.

11.6 Theoretical Exploration

11.6.1 Generalization

The **cascade forest** structure shown in Figure 11.3 is fundamental to making the forest model go deep. Suppose that f_1 denotes the function of the first-layer forests, then given the input $\boldsymbol{x}$ to the first layer, the input to the second layer will be $[\boldsymbol{x}, f_1(\boldsymbol{x})]$, where $[\boldsymbol{a}, \boldsymbol{b}]$ denotes the concatenation of $\boldsymbol{a}$ and $\boldsymbol{b}$ to form a feature vector. Consider that the $f_1(\boldsymbol{x})$ is the prediction from the preceding layer, whereas $[\boldsymbol{x}, f_1(\boldsymbol{x})]$ is the input to the current layer in deep forest; this process

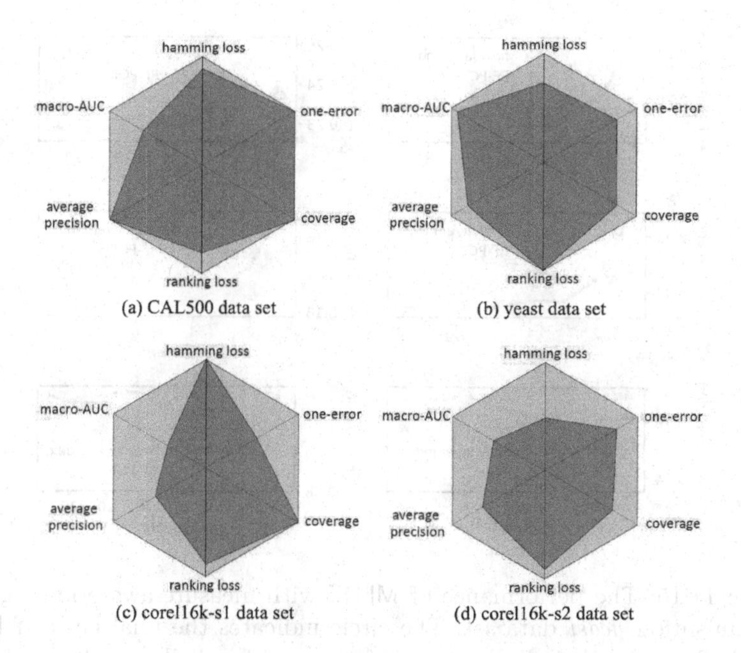

Figure 11.14: The light/dark hexagons represents the performance of MLDF with/without the measure-aware feature reuse mechanism on six performance measures. The larger the hexagons area, the better the performance.

is called **prediction concatenation** (abbr. preconc), which is crucial for the feature learning process in deep forest. Preconc is different from the well-known stacking operation in ensemble learning [Wolpert, 1992, Breiman, 1996b], where the second-level learners work in a feature space composed of only outputs of first-level learners. It is clear that preconc and the layer-by-layer processing, where the preceding level prediction is used as the augmented features for the next level, are two fundamental factors for the cascade forest structure.

Lyu et al. [2019] provided a simple theoretical explanation to the usefulness of the layer-by-layer processing in deep forest, inspired by Gao and Zhou [2013]'s **margin distribution** theory about Boosting (see Section 2.4.3), without considering the effect of preconc. By slightly modifying the learning process of gcForest to enable the forest models of the preceding layer to be included in the ensemble corresponding to the current layer via weighted combination, the following theorem has been proved:

Theorem 11.1 ([Lyu et al., 2019]). *Let $\mathcal{D}$ be a distribution over $\mathcal{X} \times \mathcal{Y}$ and D be a training set of m samples i.i.d. drawn from $\mathcal{D}$. For any $r, \delta > 0$, with probability at least $1 - \delta$, the T-level cascade forest model $F(\boldsymbol{x})$ satisfies*

$$\epsilon_{\mathcal{D}} \leq \inf_{r \in (0,1]} \left[P_{\boldsymbol{x} \sim D}[yF(\boldsymbol{x}) < r] + \frac{1}{m^d} + \frac{3\sqrt{\mu}}{m^{3/2}} + \frac{7\mu}{3m} + \lambda \sqrt{\frac{3\mu}{m}} \right], \tag{11.5}$$

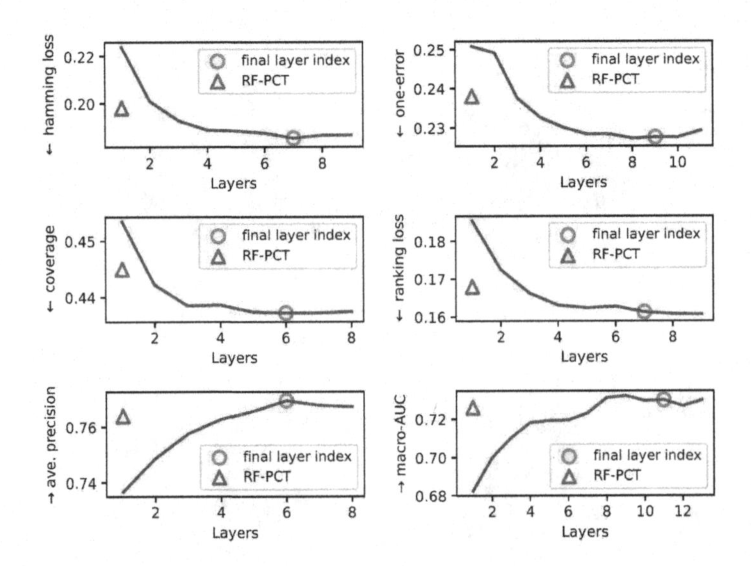

Figure 11.15: The performance of MLDF with measure-aware layer growth mechanism on *yeast* data set. The circle indicates the final layer of MLDF growth. The triangle indicates the performance of a shallow multi-label forest. ↓ / ↑ means the smaller/larger the value of the measure, the better the performance.

where $d = 2/(1 - \mathbb{E}^2_{\boldsymbol{x}\sim D}[yF(\boldsymbol{x})] + r/9) > 2$, $\mu = (1/r^2)\ln m \ln(2\sum_{t=1}^{T}\alpha_t|\mathcal{H}_t|) + \ln(2/\delta)$ *and* $\lambda = \sqrt{\mathrm{Var}_{\boldsymbol{x}\sim D}[yF(\boldsymbol{x})]/\mathbb{E}^2_{\boldsymbol{x}\sim D}[yF(\boldsymbol{x})]}$.

Note that $yF(\boldsymbol{x})$ corresponds to the margin on $\boldsymbol{x}$. Thus, this above result shows that the gap between the generalization error and the empirical margin loss is generally bounded by the term $O(\lambda\sqrt{\ln m/m} + \ln m/m)$, which is controlled by the ratio related to the margin standard deviation against the margin mean λ. It implies that the larger the *margin mean* and the smaller the *margin variance*, the better the generalization performance.

It is much more challenging to theoretically analyze the effect of **prediction concatenation**. Lyu et al. [2022] presented the attempt to regard the splits along new features and original features as a *region selector* and a *region classifier*, respectively, and their region-based generalization bound reveals the trade-off between **Rademacher complexity**[Zhou, 2021, Section 12.5] of the two-stage structure and the fraction of instances correctly classified in the selected region.

Suppose that the cascade forest has T layers, and let $\boldsymbol{f} = \{f_1, \ldots, f_T\}$ denote the forest modules corresponding to the 1st layer to the T-th layer, respectively. For the t-th layer, the forest module can be decomposed into two stages:

- **Region selector:** Let $r_i \in \mathcal{R}_i$ denote the i-th new feature learned in the previous layers. The region selector is defined as $s(\boldsymbol{x}, j) = \prod_{i\in C_j} r_i(\boldsymbol{x})$, where C_j is the learned decision rules of new features in the region j, and the family of all decision rules in the t-th layer is denoted by $\mathcal{C}_t$.

- **Region classifier:** For each selected region j in $\mathcal{X}$, the classifier $h_j \in H_j$ is learned by the samples satisfying $s(\boldsymbol{x}, j) > 0$.

Let $\mathcal{H}_j$ denote the family composed of products of a region j selector and a region j classifier, i.e.,

$$\mathcal{H}_j = \left\{ \boldsymbol{x} \mapsto s(\boldsymbol{x}, j) h_j(\boldsymbol{x}) \mid s(\boldsymbol{x}, j) \in \prod_{i \in C_j} \mathcal{R}_i, h_j \in H_j \right\} . \tag{11.6}$$

The number of training examples that not only fall into the sub-region j but also are correctly classified is

$$m_j^+ = \left| \{ i \colon y_i h_j(\boldsymbol{x}_i) > 0, s(\boldsymbol{x}_i, j) > 0 \} \right| . \tag{11.7}$$

The forest function in the t-th layer $f_t \colon \mathcal{X} \mapsto [-1, +1]$ is

$$f_t(\boldsymbol{x}) = \sum_{j \colon C_j \in \mathcal{C}_t} s(\boldsymbol{x}, j) h_j(\boldsymbol{x}) \quad \text{for every} \quad \boldsymbol{x} \in \mathcal{X} . \tag{11.8}$$

Let $\mathcal{F}_t$ denote the family of forest functions f_t in t-th level, and $\widehat{\mathfrak{R}}_D(\mathcal{H}_j)$ the Rademacher complexities of the two-stage structure.

Theorem 11.2 ([Lyu et al., 2022]). *Assume that for all decision rules of new features $C_j \in \mathcal{C}_t$, the two-stage functions in $\mathcal{H}_j$ take values in $[-1, 1]$. Then, for any $\delta > 0$, with probability at least $1 - \delta$ over the choice of a sample D of size $m \geq 1$, the following holds for all $C_j \in \mathcal{C}_t$ and all $f_t \in \mathcal{F}_t$:*

$$\epsilon_{\mathcal{D}} \leq \hat{\epsilon}_D + \sum_{j \colon C_j \in \mathcal{C}_t} \min \left(4\widehat{\mathfrak{R}}_D(\mathcal{H}_j), \frac{m_j^+}{m} \right) + C(m, \rho) + \sqrt{\frac{\log \frac{4}{\delta}}{2m}} , \tag{11.9}$$

where $C(m, \rho) = \frac{2}{\rho} \sqrt{\frac{\log T}{m}} + \sqrt{\frac{\log T}{\rho^2 m} \log \left(\frac{\rho^2 m}{\log T} \right)}$.

The above result provides a data-dependent generalization bound for the learning model of new features. It shows that the overfitting risk of each region j activated by the decision rules C_j is bounded by the minimum of Rademacher complexity of the two-stage function and m_j^+/m, the fraction of instances reaching each region that is correctly classified. It is possible to choose a region classifier from $\mathcal{H}_j$ with a relatively large complexity, as the fraction of training sample points reaching that region is small compared to the complexity of $\mathcal{H}_j$. Lyu et al. [2022] further showed that the complexity $\widehat{\mathfrak{R}}_D(\mathcal{H}_j)$ consists of two components, i.e., the complexity of the new feature sets $\mathcal{R}_i$ and the complexity of the region classifier set H_j. If $\mathcal{R}_i = \mathcal{R}$ is fixed, the sum of representation complexity is proportional to the number of new features $|C_j|$.

Lyu et al. [2022] also showed that interaction-based feature concatenation can select regions with a small fraction of samples to alleviate the overfitting risk due to high complexity, which explains why interaction-based feature concatenation usually outperforms prediction-based ones as reported in [Chen et al., 2021c].

Pang et al. [2018] proposed an approach to improve the efficiency of deep forest as introduced in Section 11.5.1, where the key idea is to pass the instances with high confidence directly to the final stage rather than passing through all the levels. They also presented the following generalization error bound.

Theorem 11.3. *Assume that the t-th level function in $\mathcal{H}_t$ takes values in $[-1,+1]$ for all $t \in \{1,\ldots,T\}$, and the training sample D is of size m drawn i.i.d. from underlying distribution $\mathcal{D}$. Then, for any $\delta > 0$, with probability at least $1-\delta$, the following holds for all h with T levels cascade forest:*

$$\epsilon_{\mathcal{D}} \leq \hat{\epsilon}_D + \sum_{t=1}^{T} \min\left(4\hat{\mathfrak{R}}_D\left(\mathcal{H}_t\right), \frac{m_t}{m}\right) + \tilde{O}\left(T\sqrt{\frac{\log T}{m}}\right) , \tag{11.10}$$

where $\hat{\mathfrak{R}}_D(\cdot)$ is the empirical Rademacher complexity, and m_t is the number of screened instances (i.e., instances of high confidence) at the t-th level.

This theorem sheds some lights on the design of cascade structure. In particular, the second term at the righthand side of (11.10) is to minimize the screening ratio m_t/m and complexity term $4\hat{\mathfrak{R}}_D(\mathcal{H}_t)$; this implies that, to make the generalization error bound tighter, one should try to reduce the complexity in the first few levels, because most instances will be screened in those first few levels and the screening ratio is large. Thus, this result suggests to exploit varied complexity at different levels in the cascade, from low to high (e.g., by increasing the ensemble size) as the level t increases.

11.6.2 Tree-Layer Structure

Arnould et al. [2021] presented a theoretical analysis of a simplified deep forest to exhibit the benefit of the tree-layer structure of deep forest over single trees. Specifically, they focused on regression problem $r(\boldsymbol{x}) = \mathbb{E}[y \mid X = \boldsymbol{x}]$, and considered quadratic risk $R(f) = \mathbb{E}_{(\boldsymbol{x},y)\sim\mathcal{D}}[(f(\boldsymbol{x}) - r(\boldsymbol{x}))^2]$ w.r.t. function f.

Let $D = \{(\boldsymbol{x}_1, y_1), (\boldsymbol{x}_2, y_2), \ldots, (\boldsymbol{x}_m, y_m)\}$ be *i.i.d.* copies of the generic pair $(\boldsymbol{x}, y)$ with $\boldsymbol{x} \in [0,1]^d$ and $y \in \{0,1\}$. Given a decision tree, denote by $L_m(\boldsymbol{x})$ the leaf node containing $\boldsymbol{x}$, and $N_m\left(L_m(\boldsymbol{x})\right)$ the number of data points falling into $L_m(\boldsymbol{x})$. The prediction of such a tree at point $\boldsymbol{x}$ is given by

$$\hat{r}_m(\boldsymbol{x}) = \frac{1}{N_m\left(L_m(\boldsymbol{x})\right)} \sum_{\boldsymbol{x}_i \in L_m(\boldsymbol{x})} y_i , \tag{11.11}$$

with the convention $0/0 = 0$, i.e., the prediction for $\boldsymbol{x}$ in a leaf with no observations is arbitrarily set to zero.

A shallow centered tree network, which can be viewed as a simplified deep forest, consists of two trees in cascade as follows:

- **Encoding layer**. The first-layer tree is a cycling centered tree of depth k built independently of the data by splitting recursively on each variable, at the center of the cells. The first cut is made along the first coordinate, the second along the second coordinate, and so on. The tree construction is terminated when exactly k cuts have been made. For each instance $\boldsymbol{x}$, empirical mean $\bar{y}_{L_m(\boldsymbol{x})}$ of the outputs y_i falling into the leaf $L_m(\boldsymbol{x})$ is extracted and passed as new feature to the next layer, together with the original features $\boldsymbol{x}$.

- **Output layer**. The second-layer tree is a centered tree of depth k' for which a cut can be performed at the center of a cell along a raw feature (as done by the encoding tree) or along the new feature $\bar{y}_{L_m(\boldsymbol{x})}$. In this case, two cells corresponding to $\bar{y}_{L_m(\boldsymbol{x})} < 1/2$ and $\bar{y}_{L_m(\boldsymbol{x})} \geq 1/2$ are created.

The resulting predictor is denoted by $\hat{r}_{k,k',m}(\boldsymbol{x})$, which is composed of a cascade of two trees with depth k and k', respectively, trained from the data D. Particularly, $\hat{r}_{k,0,m}(\boldsymbol{x})$ is the prediction given by the first encoding tree only, which outputs the mean of the y_i's falling into the leaf node containing $\boldsymbol{x}$.

The instance $\boldsymbol{x}$ is assumed to be uniformly distributed over $[0,1]^d$ and $y \in \{0,1\}$. Let $k^\star$ be multiple of d and let $p \in (1/2, 1]$. Consider a regular partition of the space with cells $C_1, \ldots, C_{2^{k^\star}}$ of generic form $\prod_{k=1}^{d}\left[\frac{i_k}{2^{k^\star/d}}, \frac{i_k+1}{2^{k^\star/d}}\right)$ for $i_1, \ldots, i_d \in \{0, \ldots, 2^{k^\star/d} - 1\}$. Assign arbitrarily a color (black or white) to each cell, which has a direct influence on the distribution of y in the cell, and for instance $\boldsymbol{x}$ in a given cell C,

$$\mathbb{P}[y = 1 \mid X = \boldsymbol{x}] = \begin{cases} p & \text{if } C \text{ is a black cell,} \\ 1-p & \text{if } C \text{ is a white one.} \end{cases} \tag{11.12}$$

Define $\mathcal{BC}$ and $\mathcal{WC}$ as the union of black and white cells, respectively, and $N_{\mathcal{BC}}$ and $N_{\mathcal{WC}}$ denote their respective number of black and white cells with $N_{\mathcal{BC}} + N_{\mathcal{WC}} = 2^{k^\star}$. The location and the numbers of the black and white cells are arbitrary. This distribution can be viewed as a *generalized chessboard* structure, and the whole distribution is parameterized by $k^\star$ ($2^{k^\star}$ is the total number of cells), p and $N_{\mathcal{BC}}$. Examples of this distribution are depicted in Figures 11.16 and 11.17 for different configurations and $d = 2$.

Arnould et al. [2021] studied a shallow network whose second-layer tree is of depth one, and whose first cut is performed along the new feature $\bar{y}_{L_m(\boldsymbol{x})}$ at 1/2. Two main regimes of training can be therefore identified when the first tree is either shallow ($k < k^\star$) or deep ($k \geq k^\star$).

Consider the balanced chessboard distribution in Figure 11.17. For $k < k^\star$, each leaf contains the same number of black and white cells, and hence the

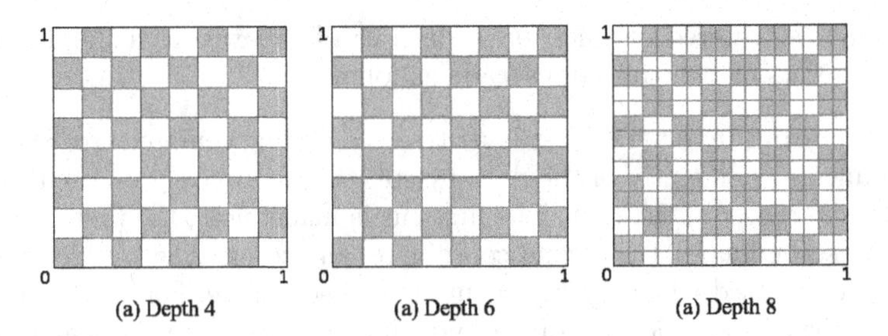

Figure 11.16: Arbitrary chessboard data distribution for $k^\star = 6$ and $N_{\mathcal{BC}} = 40$ black cells (p is not displayed here). Partition of the (first) encoding tree of depth $4, 6, 8$ is displayed in red color. The optimal depth of a single centered tree for this chessboard distribution is 6. (Plot based on a similar figure in [Arnould et al., 2021])

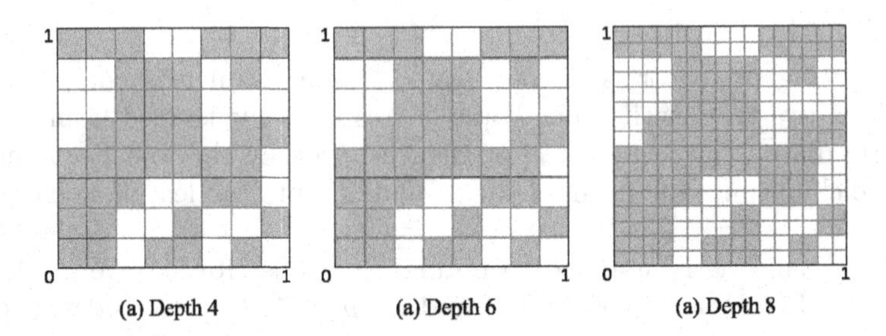

Figure 11.17: Chessboard data distribution for $k^\star = 6$ and $N_{\mathcal{BC}} = 2^{k^\star - 1}$. Partition of the (first) encoding tree of depth $4, 6, 8$ is displayed in red color. The optimal depth of a single centered tree for this chessboard distribution is 6. (Plot based on a similar figure in [Arnould et al., 2021])

mean value of the leaf is 1/2 in expectation, which is non-informative. The following theorem gives the risk of a single tree and a shallow tree network as $k < k^\star$.

Theorem 11.4 ([Arnould et al., 2021]). *Assume that the data is drawn from a balanced chessboard distribution (Figure 11.17) of parameters $k^\star, N_{\mathcal{BC}} = 2^{k^\star - 1}$ and $p > 1/2$. For a single tree $\hat{r}_{k,0,m}$ of depth k ($1 \le k < k^\star$), we have*

$$R(\hat{r}_{k,0,m}) \le \left(p - \frac{1}{2}\right)^2 + \frac{2^k}{2(m+1)} + \frac{\left(1 - 2^{-k}\right)^m}{4}, \tag{11.13}$$

$$R(\hat{r}_{k,0,m}) \ge \left(p - \frac{1}{2}\right)^2 + \frac{2^k + (m + 1 - 2^k)(1 - 2^{-k})^m}{4(m+1)}. \tag{11.14}$$

For the shallow tree network $\hat{r}_{k,1,m}$ ($1 \leq k < k^\star$), we have

$$\left(p - \frac{1}{2}\right)^2 \leq R(\hat{r}_{k,1,m}) \leq \left(p - \frac{1}{2}\right)^2 + \frac{2^{k/2+3}\left(p - \frac{1}{2}\right)}{\sqrt{\pi m}} + \frac{7 \cdot 2^{2k+2}}{\pi^2(m+1)}(1 + \varepsilon_{k,p}) + \frac{p^2 + (1-p)^2}{2}\left(1 - 2^{-k}\right)^m , \quad (11.15)$$

where $\varepsilon_{k,p} = o\left(2^{-k/2}\right)$ uniformly in p.

This theorem exhibits that the bias is not reduced for a shallow tree with depth $k < k^\star$, even for infinite samples. The term $(p - 1/2)^2$ appears in both the lower and upper bounds, i.e., no matter how large the training set is, the risk of the tree does not tend to zero. The shallow tree suffers from the same bias term so long as the first-layer tree is not deep enough. In all bounds, the term $(1 - 2^{-k})^m$ corresponding to the probability of $\boldsymbol{x}$ falling into an empty cell cannot be eliminated, whose splitting strategy is independent of the training data. However, the tree network can be improved with tree depth $k \geq k^\star$ in the first layer, as proved in the following theorem.

Theorem 11.5 ([Arnould et al., 2021]). *Assume that the data is drawn from a generalized chessboard with parameters $k^\star, N_{\mathcal{BC}}$ and $p > 1/2$. For a single tree $\hat{r}_{k,0,m}$ of depth k ($k \geq k^\star$), we have*

$$R(\hat{r}_{k,0,m}) \leq \frac{2^k p(1-p)}{m+1} + \Delta\frac{(1 - 2^{-k})^m}{2} , \quad (11.16)$$

$$R(\hat{r}_{k,0,m}) \geq \frac{2^{k-1} p(1-p)}{m+1} + \left(\Delta - \frac{2^k p(1-p)}{m+1}\right)\frac{(1-2^{-k})^m}{2} . \quad (11.17)$$

where $\Delta = p^2 + (1-p)^2$. For the shallow tree network $\hat{r}_{k,1,m}$ ($k \geq k^\star$), we have

$$R(\hat{r}_{k,1,m}) \leq 2\frac{p(1-p)}{m+1} + 2^{k+1}\left(1 - \frac{1 - e^{-2(p-1/2)^2}}{2^k}\right)^m + \bar{p}^2_{\mathcal{BC}} ; \quad (11.18)$$

and for $m \geq 2^{k+1}(k+1)$, we also have

$$R(\hat{r}_{k,1,m}) \geq \frac{2p(1-p)}{m} - \frac{2^{k+3}(1 - \rho_{k,p})^m}{m} + \bar{p}^2_{\mathcal{BC}} , \quad (11.19)$$

where $0 < \rho_{k,p} < 1$ depends only on p and k, and

$$\bar{p}^2_{\mathcal{BC}} = \left(\frac{N_{\mathcal{BC}}}{2^{k^\star}}p^2 + \frac{2^{k^\star} - N_{\mathcal{BC}}}{2^{k^\star}}(1-p)^2\right)\left(1 - 2^{-k}\right)^m . \quad (11.20)$$

This theorem shows a benefit when the first-layer tree is deep. In this case, the risk of the shallow tree network is $O(1/m)$, whereas that of a single tree is $O(2^k/m)$. In presence of complex and highly structured data (large $k^\star$ and similar distribution in different areas of the input space), the shallow tree benefits from a variance reduction phenomenon by a factor 2^k.

Note that the above analysis is based on the assumption that the first-layer tree is built through uniformly splitting each variable recursively, independently of training data; this is apparently very different from the tree-growing mechanism of deep forest. Thus, the results are relevant but not directly applicable to understanding the tree-layer structure of deep forest.

11.7 Further Readings

There are many studies combining ensemble methods with DNNs for better performance. For example, Deng and Platt [2014] combined ensemble methods and DNNs to improve speech recognition performance; Dvornik et al. [2019] designed an ensemble of DNNs to address the high-variance issue of few-shot classification; Lakshminarayanan et al. [2017] employed ensemble of DNNs to quantify predictive uncertainty; Zhu et al. [2019] presented BENN (Binary Ensemble Neural Network) which leverages ensemble to improve binary neural networks. The *multi-head attention*, which is crucial for the success of *transformer* [Vaswani et al., 2017], is also an ensemble mechanism, which tries to extract information from different representation subspaces and then combine to the expected dimension; a relevant idea was developed in MIML (*Multi-Instance Multi-Label learning*) [Zhou et al., 2012] and realized in a neural network where attention mechanism was achieved by *sub-concept* layer [Feng and Zhou, 2017].

Dropout, an important mechanism extensively exploited in DNNs, has been explained as an implicit ensemble mechanism as mentioned in Section 11.1. Besides, there are some significant theoretical efforts. Wager et al. [2013] showed that dropout is a first-order regularizer equivalent to an ℓ_2 regularizer applied after scaling the features by an estimate of the inverse diagonal Fisher information matrix. Generalization bounds have been presented to consider the effect of dropout in [McAllester, 2013, Li et al., 2013b]. Gao and Zhou [2016] proved that dropout is able to reduce the Rademacher complexity exponentially for DNNs.

In addition to heuristically designing approaches embedding neural networks into decision trees and cascades, which can be traced back to early studies described in [Zhou and Chen, 2002], there are some theoretical studies about the flexibility of selecting node or leaf functions from unions of complex hypothesis sets such as SVMs and kernel functions [DeSalvo et al., 2015].

The study of auto-encoder can date back to Bourlard and Kamp [1988], of which the goal is to learn associations from data. Almost all previous approaches for auto-encoders were based on neural networks [Hinton and Salakhutdinov, 2006, Hinton and Ranzato, 2010, Bengio et al., 2013c]. Applications of auto-encoders range from computer vision [Masci et al., 2011] to natural language processing [Mikolov et al., 2013] and semantic hashing for information retrieval tasks [Ruslan et al., 2007].

Though there is not yet a universal theory explaining why a deep model works better than a shallow one, many attempts at this question were based on the conjecture that it is the hierarchical distributed representations learned from data playing a vital role behind the effectiveness of deep models [Bengio et al., 2013a]. Bengio et al. [2013b] conjectured that better representations can be exploited to produce faster-mixing Markov chains, and therefore, a deeper model always helps. Tishby and Zaslavsky [2015] treated the hidden layers as a successive refinement of relevant information, where a deeper structure helps to speed up such process exponentially. As shown in this chapter, though both the auto-encoder ability and hierarchical distributed representation were thought as specialities of neural networks, forest models can accomplish those functions.

Chapter 12

Advanced Topics

12.1 Weakly Supervised Learning

Weakly supervised learning is an umbrella covering a variety of studies which attempt to construct predictive models by learning with weak supervision, mainly including learning with *incomplete*, *inexact* and *inaccurate* supervision [Zhou, 2018a].

12.1.1 Incomplete Supervision

Incomplete supervision concerns about the situation where we are given a small amount of labeled data, and it is insufficient to train a good learner, while abundant unlabeled data are available. Formally, the task is to learn $f : \mathcal{X} \mapsto \mathcal{Y}$ from a training data set $D = \{(\boldsymbol{x}_1, y_1), \ldots, (\boldsymbol{x}_l, y_l), \boldsymbol{x}_{l+1}, \ldots, \boldsymbol{x}_m\}$, where there are l labeled training examples (i.e., those given with y_i) and $u = m - l$ unlabeled instances. There are two major paradigms for this purpose, i.e., **semi-supervised learning** and **active learning**. The former has been introduced in Chapter 9, and thus, here we focus on the latter.

Active learning assumes that the ground-truth labels of unlabeled instances can be queried from an *oracle* [Settles, 2010]. For simplicity, assume that the labeling cost depends only on the number of queries. Thus, the goal of active learning is to minimize the number of queries such that the labeling cost for training a good model can be minimized. Given a small set of labeled data and abundant unlabeled data, active learning attempts to select the most valuable unlabeled instance to query.

A well-known active learning approach, **query-by-committee** or called **committee-based sampling**, is based on ensembles. This approach was proposed by Seung et al. [1992] and then implemented by many researchers for different tasks [Dagan and Engelson, 1995, Liere and Tadepalli, 1997, McCallum and Nigam, 1998, Kee et al., 2018]. In this approach, multiple learners are generated, and then the unlabeled instance on which the learners disagree the most is selected to query. For example, suppose that there are

 DOI: 10.1201/9781003587774-12

five learners, among which three learners predict positive and two learners predict negative for an instance $\boldsymbol{x}_i$, while four learners predict positive and one learner predicts negative for the instance $\boldsymbol{x}_j$; these learners disagree more on $\boldsymbol{x}_i$ than on $\boldsymbol{x}_j$, and therefore $\boldsymbol{x}_i$ will be selected to query.

One of the key issues of query-by-committee is how to generate the multiple learners in the committee. Freund et al. [1997] proved that when the Gibbs algorithm, a randomized learning algorithm is used to generate the learners by picking a hypothesis from a given hypothesis class according to *posterior* distribution, query-by-committee can exponentially improve the sample complexity compared to passive learning. The Gibbs algorithm, however, is computationally intractable. Abe and Mamitsuka [1998] showed that popular ensemble methods can be used to generate committee. Similar to other ensemble methods, the learners in the committee should be *diverse.* Abe and Mamitsuka [1998] developed the Query-by-Bagging and Query-by-Boosting methods. Query-by-Bagging employs Bagging to generate the committee. In each round, it re-samples the labeled training data by bootstrap sampling and trains a learner on each sample; then, the unlabeled instance on which the learners disagree the most is queried. Query-by-Boosting uses AdaBoost to generate the committee. In each round, it constructs a Boosted ensemble; then, the unlabeled instance with the minimum margin predicted by the Boosted ensemble is selected to query.

The use of ensemble provides the feasibility of combining active learning with semi-supervised learning. With multiple learners, given a set of unlabeled instances, in each round the unlabeled instance on which the learners disagree the most can be selected to query, while some other unlabeled instances can be exploited by the *majority teaching minority* strategy as that in semi-supervised parallel ensemble methods such as Tri-Training and Co-Forest (see Section 9.4). Zhou et al. [2006] proposed the SSAIRA method based on such an idea, and applied this method to improve the performance of *relevance feedback* in image retrieval. Later, Wang and Zhou [2008] theoretically analyzed the sample complexity of the combination of active learning and semi-supervised learning, and proved that the combination further decreases the sample complexity compared to using only semi-supervised learning or only active learning.

12.1.2 Inexact Supervision

Inexact supervision studies the situation where some supervision information is given, but not as exact as desired. A typical scenario is when only coarse-grained label information is available. Formally, the task is to learn $f : \mathcal{X} \mapsto \mathcal{Y}$ from a training data set $D = \{(X_1, y_1), \ldots, (X_m, y_m)\}$, where $X_i = \{\boldsymbol{x}_{i1}, \ldots, \boldsymbol{x}_{i,m_i}\} \subseteq \mathcal{X}$ is called a *bag*, $\boldsymbol{x}_{ij} \in \mathcal{X}$ $(j \in \{1, \ldots, m_i\})$ is an instance, m_i is the number of instances in X_i, and $y_i \in \mathcal{Y} = \{+1, -1\}$. X_i is a *positive* bag, i.e., $y_i = +1$, if there exists some unknown positive instance $\boldsymbol{x}_{ij}$ for $j \in \{1, \ldots, m_i\}$. The goal is to predict labels for unseen bags. This is called **multi-instance learning** Dietterich et al. [1997], Foulds and Frank [2010].

Ensemble methods have been found very useful in multi-instance learning [Zhou and Zhang, 2003], and many ensemble methods have been developed. Zhou and Zhang [2003] applied bootstrap sampling to bags, and then trained and combined multi-instance learners, resembling the Bagging approach. After that, many AdaBoost style multi-instance ensemble methods have been developed [Xu and Frank, 2004, Auer and Ortner, 2004, Viola et al., 2006].

Many methods try to improve the performance of multi-instance ensemble learning by the delicate design of diverse and discriminative training sets. Yuan et al. [2012] proposed a *hierarchical sampling* method called HSMILE, which performs both instance-level and bag-level sampling to construct diverse training sets for training the base learners. Initially, bag-level sampling is performed using bootstrap sampling, and then instance-level sampling is applied to each sampled bag. For negative bags, bootstrap sampling is directly applied to instance sampling; for positive bags, the most likely positive instance is selected by estimating the probable positive instance distribution according to *maximum a posteriori*, and then bootstrap sampling is applied to remaining instances. Yang et al. [2021b] proposed the ELDB to gradually construct the set of discriminative bags for training base learners in ensemble. Initially, it calculates a distinguishability score for each bag, and selects a set of bags with the highest scores. Then, a *self-reinforcement* mechanism is employed to update the initial set with more discriminative bags iteratively. In this way, different sets of discriminative bags can be generated in different iterations, leading to diverse base learners in ensemble. This process resembles AdaBoost process and thus, the final prediction is made by weighted voting rather than majority voting.

Rather than building an ensemble in the original feature space, Zhou and Zhang [2007] proposed CCE to convert the original multi-instance representation to single-instance representation through a feature transformation process, called **constructive clustering**. In detail, all instances of all bags are collected together and clustered into d groups. Then, each bag is re-represented by d binary features where the value of the i-th feature is set to one if the concerned bag has instances falling into the i-th group and zero otherwise. Thus, each bag is represented by a single feature vector such that single-instance classifiers can be trained to distinguish different classes of bags. By repeating the process with different d values, diverse classifiers can be built and combined into an ensemble for prediction. The constructive clustering is actually a **representation learning** process, which has been exploited later in other tasks [Zhou et al., 2012].

Wei et al. [2017] further extended the representation transformation strategy of CCE by proposing the miVLAD approach, which considers the number of instances of each bag falling into each group, based on the vector of locally aggregated descriptors representation. They also introduced the miFV approach to consider not only the mean and co-variance, but also the relations between instances based on the Fisher vector representation. The new feature representation keeps essential bag-level information, and simultaneously lead to excellent learning performances even when linear classifiers are used. Owing to the low computational cost in the mapping step and the scalability of linear classifiers, miVLAD and miFV can handle large-scale multi-instance data efficiently, with hundreds or even up to thousands of times faster than many previous multi-instance learning approaches.

12.1.3 Inaccurate Supervision

Inaccurate supervision studies the situation where the supervision information is not always ground-truth; that is, some label information may suffer from errors.

An interesting scenario of inaccurate supervision occurs with **crowdsourcing** [Brabham, 2008], a well-known paradigm to outsource work to individuals. In machine learning, crowdsourcing is commonly used as a cost-saving way to collect labels for training data. Specifically, the *user* outsources unlabeled instances to a large group of labelers to label. The labelers usually come from a large society and each of them is presented with multiple tasks. They are usually independent and relatively inexpensive, and provide labels based on their own judgments. Among the labelers, some may be more reliable than others; however, the user usually does not know this in advance because the identities of labelers are protected. There may exist "spammers" who assign almost random labels on the tasks (e.g., robots pretend to be a human for the monetary payment), or "adversaries" who give incorrect answers deliberately. Moreover, some tasks may be too difficult to many labelers. Thus, it is non-trivial to maintain learning performance using the inaccurate supervision information returned by the crowd.

In **crowdsourcing learning**, each data instance receives a set of noisy labels from different labelers. Many studies attempt to infer ground-truth labels from the crowd. The *majority voting* mechanism is widely used in practice with good performance [Sheng et al., 2008, Snow et al., 2008], where the aggregated label of an instance is determined by the votes of multiple labelers with identical or different weights. Wang and Zhou [2015] theoretically analyzed the error bound of the label inference by majority voting for binary classification, and showed that the error rate decreases exponentially with the number of involved labelers if the label quality is uniformly distributed. The *Dawid-Skene* (DS) model is a popular generative method to infer the ground-truth labels from the crowd. It simultaneously estimates the quality of labelers and infers the true label for each instance. The label inference error bounds for DS model have also been analyzed [Gao et al., 2016].

The multiple inaccurate labels of an instance in crowdsourcing enable the feasibility of training multiple weak learners for ensemble. Zhang et al. [2018] proposed a Bagging-style ensemble method for crowdsourcing learning. Instead of inferring the true label from the noisy label set, they directly trained multiple weak learners from the noisy labels. Specifically, bootstrap sampling is employed to generate different training sets, and multiple copies of each instance is generated with a specific weight. Given an instance $\boldsymbol{x}_i$, its corresponding noisy label set is denoted by $\{y_{i1}, \dots, y_{i,l_i}\}$, $y_{ik} \in \mathcal{Y}$ $(k = 1, \dots, l_i)$. This method generates $\{(\boldsymbol{x}_i, y_1, w_1), (\boldsymbol{x}_i, y_2, w_2), \dots, (\boldsymbol{x}_i, y_{|\mathcal{Y}|}, w_{|\mathcal{Y}|})\}$, where each weight is given by $w_j = (1 + \sum_{k=1}^{l_i} \mathbb{I}(y_{ik} = j))/(l_i + |\mathcal{Y}|)$. Laplace smoothing is adopted to avoid zero weights. A base learner with a weighted loss can be trained from the extended training set. Once the ensemble is constructed, a grouped prediction scheme via maximum likelihood is employed for the final prediction.

12.2 Open-Environment Learning

Conventional machine learning studies generally assume *close-environment* scenarios where important factors of the learning process hold invariant. With the great success of machine learning, nowadays, more and more practical tasks, particularly those involving *open-environment* scenarios where important factors are subject to change, called **open-environment learning** (abbr. **Open ML**) [Zhou, 2022], are present to the community. There are four major issues [Zhou, 2022], learning with *emerging new classes*, *changing data distributions*, *decremental/incremental features*, and *varied learning objectives*, where learning with emerging new classes has been introduced in Section 8.6, and thus, here we will focus on the three other issues.

12.2.1 Changing Data Distributions

In conventional machine learning, it is often assumed explicitly or implicitly that the testing and training data are drawn from the same data distribution, and the target concept, i.e., a posterior probability of class membership $p(y \mid \mathbf{x})$ is unchanged. With these assumptions, a learner, which fits the target concept well on the training data, generalizes well on the testing data. However, in real-world applications, this assumption is often violated, and the connotation of the target concept may change as time goes by. To learn a model capable of making accurate predictions, the evolution of concept must be considered.

In general, learning with changing data distributions is not always possible, e.g., if data distribution changes arbitrarily in every moment without knowledge about how it can change. Fortunately, in many real tasks, it is reasonable to assume that *current observation has close relation with recent observations*; in other words, the current instance and the most recent ones are usually from similar or even identical distribution, and the farther the less similar. Thus, we can try to exploit some recent data to help.

Ensemble methods have been well exploited for this purpose. Generally, individual learners are added/removed adaptively corresponding to different time steps, and their weights can also be adjusted dynamically for incoming instances [Beygelzimer et al., 2015, Gomes et al., 2017]. For example, Kolter and Maloof [2003] proposed the DWM (Dynamic Weighted Majority) method, which creates and deletes base learners dynamically in response to changes in performance, and makes prediction by a weighted-majority voting of these base learners. Sun et al. [2018] proposed the DTEL (Diversity and Transfer-based Ensemble Learning) approach, which maintains a fixed size model pool with the selection criteria based on diversity, and builds a new base tree by fine-tuning previous models.

Note that in some tasks we are given only one data set (i.e., a *single snapshot*) instead of a series of training data sets collected at different time points. To handle future data distribution change based on such single snapshot data, Yu and Zhou [2010] formulated the PCES (i.e., Positive Class Expansion with single Snapshot) problem, and proposed the SGBDota (Stochastic Gradient Boosting with Double Target) method based on the assumption that the target concept is in *expansion* and that positive training examples become positive ahead of negative ones. This method achieved champion of a data mining competition on the task of *potential custom prediction.*

12.2.2 Decremental/Incremental Features

Conventional machine learning generally assumes that all possible instances, including unseen ones, reside in the same feature space. Unfortunately, this does not always hold in many real applications.

Consider the following setting of learning with decremental/incremental features. A learning model is trained from some initial training data and then deployed to handle unseen data coming like a *stream*, with decremental and/or incremental features. For incoming testing data, the model should be able to make correct predictions; for incoming additional training data, the model should be able to be refined accordingly. Ideally, it is desired that the whole process does not require retraining based on holding *all data* received.

In general, it is not always possible to build a learning model which is able to benefit from $\boldsymbol{x} \in \mathcal{X}$ for $\hat{\boldsymbol{x}} \in \hat{\mathcal{X}} \neq \mathcal{X}$, because machine learning is to learn from experience to improve performance, whereas in most cases there might be little helpful experience from the learning in $\mathcal{X}$ to the learning in $\hat{\mathcal{X}}$ when $\hat{\mathcal{X}} \cap \mathcal{X} = \emptyset$. For example, as illustrated in Figure 12.1, if the feature spaces of phase$_1$ data (i.e., $\{(\boldsymbol{x}_1, y_1), (\boldsymbol{x}_2, y_2), \ldots, (\boldsymbol{x}_{T_1}, y_{T_1})\}$) and phase$_2$ data (i.e., $\{(\boldsymbol{x}_{T_1+1}, y_{T_1+1}), (\boldsymbol{x}_{T_1+2}, y_{T_1+2}), \ldots, (\boldsymbol{x}_{T_2}, y_{T_2})\}$) are totally different, then the model trained in phase$_1$ is helpless for phase$_2$, and a new model has to be trained from scratch based on feature set S_2 for phase$_2$.

Fortunately, it is often the case $\hat{\mathcal{X}} \cap \mathcal{X} \neq \emptyset$ in many real tasks. In other words, there are features of phase$_1$ survived to be active in phase$_2$, though many other features vanish, as illustrated in Figure 12.2.

For example, in sensor network applications, different sensors may have different battery lifetime, and thus, some old sensors are still working after new sensors being deployed. Formally, in phase$_1$, $\mathcal{X} = \mathcal{X}^{de} \cup \mathcal{X}^{s}$, where $\mathcal{X}^{de}$ and $\mathcal{X}^{s}$ denote the decremental and survived feature spaces, respectively; in phase$_2$, $\hat{\mathcal{X}} = \mathcal{X}^{s} \cup \mathcal{X}^{in}$, where $\mathcal{X}^{in}$ denotes the incremental feature space. As $\mathcal{X}^{s}$ is shared in both phases, Hou and Zhou [2018] trained not only a model$_1$

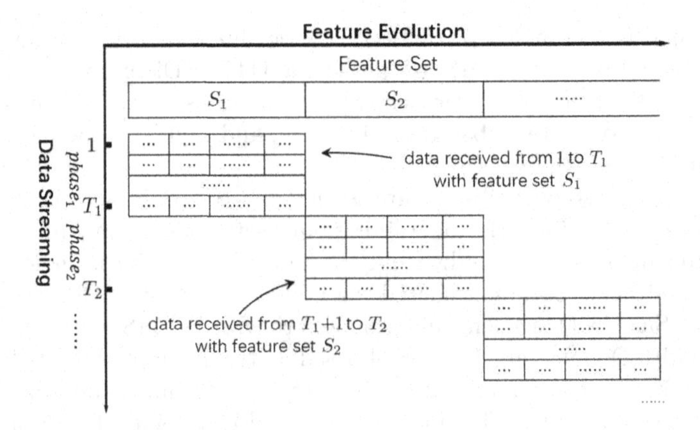

Figure 12.1: Illustration of feature evolution, where phase$_1$ is helpless to phase$_2$.

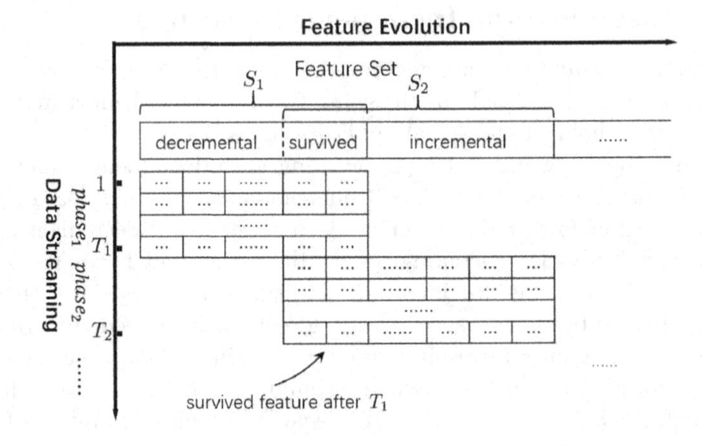

Figure 12.2: Illustration of the feature evolution, where phase$_1$ is helpful to phase$_2$ through survived features.

from $\mathcal{X}$, but also a model$_2$ based on $\mathcal{X}_s$ in phase$_1$, i.e.,

$$\min_{\boldsymbol{w},\boldsymbol{w}^s} \left\{ \sum_{i=1}^{T_1} \left(\langle \boldsymbol{w}, \boldsymbol{x}_i \rangle - y_i \right)^2 + \sum_{i=1}^{T_1} \left(\langle \boldsymbol{w}^s, \boldsymbol{x}_i^s \rangle - y_i \right)^2 \right.$$
$$\left. + \alpha \sum_{i=1}^{T_1} \left(\langle \boldsymbol{w}, \boldsymbol{x}_i \rangle - \langle \boldsymbol{w}^s, \boldsymbol{x}_i^s \rangle \right)^2 + \gamma \left(\|\boldsymbol{w}\|^2 + \|\boldsymbol{w}^s\|^2 \right) \right\}, \quad (12.1)$$

where $\langle \cdot, \cdot \rangle$ is inner product, and $\boldsymbol{w}$ and $\boldsymbol{w}^s$ are parameters of model$_1$ and model$_2$, respectively, while $\alpha, \gamma > 0$ are the regularization coefficients. Such a process works like *compressing* helpful predictive information from model$_1$ in

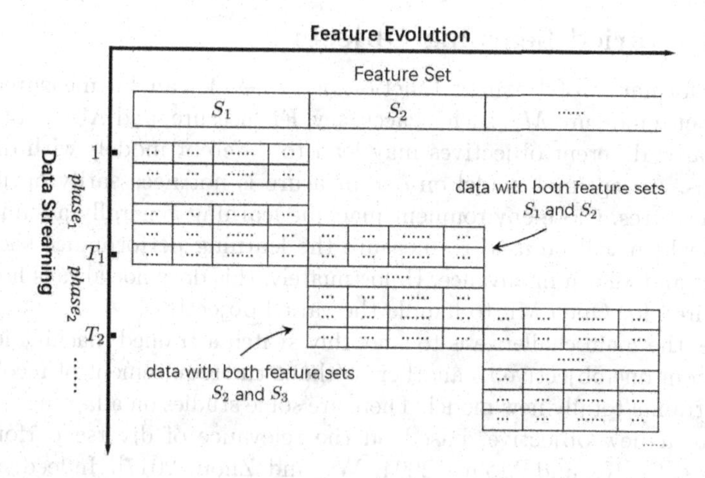

Figure 12.3: Illustration of the feature evolution, where phase_1 is helpful to phase_2 through shared instances.

$\mathcal{X}$ to model_2 in $\mathcal{X}^s$. Then, in phase_2, in addition to the model_3 trained based on $\hat{\mathcal{X}}$, the model_2 trained in phase_1 can still be used. Thus, the prediction in phase_2 can be made by combining model_3 fed with $\hat{\boldsymbol{x}}$ and model_2 fed with the $\mathcal{X}^s$ part of $\hat{\boldsymbol{x}}$. In this way, some experience learned from phase_1 can be exploited in phase_2 through the use of model_2.

Interestingly, even when $\hat{\mathcal{X}} \cap \mathcal{X} = \emptyset$, there are cases where it is possible to enable phase_1 learning to be helpful to phase_2; in particular, when feature increment occurs earlier than feature decrement [Hou et al., 2017], e.g., new sensors are deployed slightly before old sensors' batteries are exhausted. As illustrated in Figure 12.3, in this situation there exists a small set of data with both sets of features that can help build a mapping $\psi : \hat{\mathcal{X}} \mapsto \mathcal{X}$. Thus, though $\hat{\boldsymbol{x}}$ received in phase_2 comes with only features of $\hat{\mathcal{X}}$, model_1 learned in phase_1 can still be exploited by feeding it with $\psi(\hat{\boldsymbol{x}})$. Then, phase_2 prediction can be made by combining model_1 with model_2 trained from $\hat{\mathcal{X}}$, either through weighted selection or weighted combination. It has been proved that the cumulative loss of the weighted combination is comparable to the minimum loss between the two models, and the cumulative loss of the weighted selection is comparable to the loss of optimal selection.

The model training can be accomplished by online learning techniques such as online gradient descent, and thus, the above strategies can be naturally applied to stream data. It is noticeable that the above strategies can be naturally extended to more phases, and predictions can be made by the combination of multiple models from different feature spaces. Thus, the performance of later phases can be even enhanced by exploiting ensemble learning.

12.2.3 Varied Learning Objects

The performance of learning function $f\colon \mathcal{X} \mapsto \mathcal{Y}$ can be measured by a performance measure M_f, such as accuracy, F1 measure, and AUC, etc. Learning towards different objectives may lead to different models with different strengths. An optimal model on one measure is not necessarily optimal on other measures. Close-environment machine learning generally assumes that the M_f which will be used to measure the learning performance should be invariant and known in advance. Unfortunately, this does not always hold, and it is desired for Open ML to handle the varied objectives.

Here, the main challenge is to smoothly switch a trained machine learning model from one objective to another, without the requirement of recollecting data to train a totally new model. There are some studies on adapting a trained model to a new objective, based on the relevance of diverse performance measures [Cortes and Mohri, 2004, Wu and Zhou, 2017]. Indeed, a large variety of performance measures can be optimized by exploiting nonlinear auxiliary classifiers while keeping high computational efficiency, where ensemble mechanisms offer some advantages.

For example, [Li et al., 2013a] proposed the CAPO (Classifier Adaptation for Performance measure Optimization) method, which assumes that the final designed classifier $f(\boldsymbol{x})$ can be obtained for new measure by adding a delta function $f_\delta(\boldsymbol{x})$ to the current existing classifier $f'(\boldsymbol{x})$, i.e.,

$$f(\boldsymbol{x}) = \mathtt{sign}\left[f'(\boldsymbol{x}) + f_\delta(\boldsymbol{x})\right] . \tag{12.2}$$

Note that $f'(\boldsymbol{x})$ and $f_\delta(\boldsymbol{x})$ construct an ensemble, where $f'(\boldsymbol{x})$ can be of any type because it is treated as a black-box, and $f_\delta(\boldsymbol{x})$ is a real-valued function and the goal is to adjust the decision of $f'(\boldsymbol{x})$ such that $f(\boldsymbol{x})$ can achieve good performance. Li et al. [2013a] showed that the **classifier adaptation** problem can be reduced to a quadratic program problem with an efficient solution. By exploiting existing nonlinear classifiers, CAPO can generate nonlinear classifier which optimizes a large variety of performance measures including all the performance measure based on the contingency table and AUC, while keeping high computational efficiency. Furthermore, Li et al. [2013a] showed that an ensemble of auxiliary classifiers can be exploited to further improve the robustness of performance measure adaptation.

12.3 Reinforcement Learning

Reinforcement leaning [Sutton and Barto, 2018] is a branch of machine leaning. In contrast to supervised learning which produces predictors from labeled examples, reinforcement learning produces policies to maximize long-term rewards in interaction with environment.

12.3.1 Learning to Maximize Long-Term Rewards

In the reinforcement learning setting, an **environment** is commonly modeled as a **Markov Decision Process (MDP)**, with state space S, action space A, reward function R and transition function P. An agent uses a **policy** π to interact with the environment by observing the state $s \in S$ and producing an action $a = \pi(s) \in A$. The action is executed in the environment, producing an immediate reward $r = R(s, a)$ and leading to the next state $s' = P(s, a)$. This process is illustrated in Figure 12.4. Note that the transition to the next state is commonly stochastic, represented as the probability distribution $P(s' \mid s, a)$, and the policy can also be stochastic, distributed as $\pi(a \mid s)$.

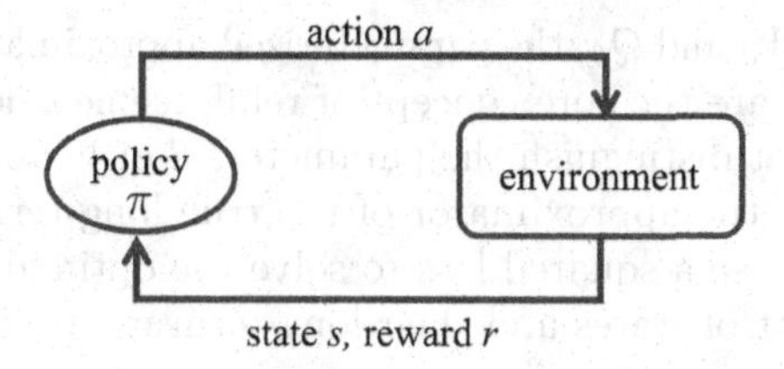

Figure 12.4: Reinforcement learning process.

By alternating the policy output and the environment transition, we can observe an interaction sequence as

$$s_0, a_0, r_0, s_1, a_1, r_1, \ldots, s_t, a_t, r_t, \cdots$$

where the subscript denotes the time step. The sequence may be infinitely long. The long-term reward, with a discount factor $\gamma < 1$, is then calculated as

$$V^{\pi}(s_0) = \mathbb{E}\left[\sum_{t=0}^{\infty} \gamma^t r_t\right], \tag{12.3}$$

where the long-term reward is denoted by the value function V, associated with the policy π starting from state s_0.

Reinforcement learning agent learns from interaction sequences to find the policy with maximum long-term rewards, that is,

$$\pi^* = \arg\max_{\pi} V^{\pi}(s_0)\ . \tag{12.4}$$

To solve the optimal policy, reinforcement learning algorithms generally apply a trial-and-error principle: Evaluate the policy by calculating V^{π} and then update the policy. Note that calculating V^{π} every time from interaction sequences requires to run the policy in the environment. Classical reinforcement learning that actively samples interaction sequences is called **online reinforcement learning**, while **offline reinforcement learning** works with only historically collected interaction sequences and no further sampling is allowed.

The sampling in the environment is often considered costly. It is possible to learn an approximate **environment model**, in which sampling is free. From this perspective, reinforcement learning algorithms that learn from the interaction sequences of the real environment are called **model-free** methods, whereas those who learn from interaction sequences from both the real environment and the environment model are called **model-based** methods.

There are a wide range of research topics in reinforcement learning, in which ensemble methods have been found well helpful. The following subsections will present some examples.

12.3.2 Critic Estimation

Critic functions, V_θ and Q_θ, the parameterized approximator of the long-term reward of a policy, are the core concept of reinforcement learning algorithms. Note that we do not distinguish the parameters θ of V and Q for simplicity.

The critic V_θ is the approximator of the true long-term reward V^π. It is straightforward to use a squared loss to solve the optimal parameters for V_θ, when observed a set of states and their long-term rewards, that is,

$$\theta^* = \arg\min_\theta \sum_s \left(V_\theta(s) - V^\pi(s)\right)^2 . \tag{12.5}$$

The critic Q_θ is the approximator of the one-step expansion of the true long-term reward $R(s,a) + \sum_{s' \in S} P(s' \mid s,a)V^\pi(s')$, where a is the fixed first step action. The learning objective is

$$\theta^* = \arg\min_\theta \sum_s (Q_\theta(s,a) - y(s,a))^2 , \tag{12.6}$$

where

$$y(s,a) = R(s,a) + \gamma \sum_{s' \in S} P(s' \mid s,a)V^\pi(s') . \tag{12.7}$$

Intuitively, $Q_\theta(s,a)$ approximates the long-term reward starting from the state s that executes the action a.

The critics are in the core of reinforcement learning algorithms. In classical **Q-learning** [Sutton and Barto, 2018] and its variants such as DQN [Mnih et al., 2015], the policy greedily selects the action according to Q function, i.e.,

$$\pi(s) = \arg\max_{a \in A} Q_\theta(s,a) . \tag{12.8}$$

Such methods are **critic-only** methods. State-of-the-art **actor-critic** methods search for high long-term reward policies with the help of critic functions. A typical approach is the **policy gradient** [Williams, 1992]. Note that for the policy parameterized as π_η, the gradient with regard to the parameter η leading to long-term reward increase and variance reduction is

$$\mathbb{E}\left[\nabla_\eta \log \pi_\eta(a \mid s) Q_\theta(s,a)\right] , \tag{12.9}$$

and

$$\mathbb{E}\left[\nabla_\eta \log \pi_\eta(a \mid s)(Q_\theta(s,a) - V_\theta(s))\right] , \tag{12.10}$$

respectively [Sutton et al., 1999]. Updating the parameter η along with this gradient forms the basic actor-critic policy gradient approach.

Hence, accurate critics help improve reinforcement learning performance. Using an ensemble for V and Q can reduce variance and improve the accuracy of the critics [Agarwal et al., 2020]. Besides, estimating critic functions has been a specific issue on which ensemble is useful.

Though the critic function tries to approximate the expected long-term reward, it is estimated through the Bellman equation. For every transition pair (s, a, r, s') in the interaction sequences, the approximation target is

$$y(s,a) = r + \gamma Q_\theta(s', \pi(s')) , \tag{12.11}$$

and we update $Q_\theta(s,a)$ to approach $y(s,a)$. This equation is a booststrap implementation of the mathematical expectation. However, when the policy is also derived from the critic, i.e., $\pi(s) = \arg\max_a Q(s,a)$, this equation can drive the critic function to be overestimated [van Hasselt, 2010]. Intuitively, this is because the max operator usually biases to the largest value caused by variance, whereas the booststrap estimation can be accumulated for such bias.

To solve **critic value overestimation**, van Hasselt [2010] proposed the double Q-learning method to maintain two critics, Q_θ and Q'_θ. When calculating the approximation target for the greedy policy $\pi(s) = \arg\max_a Q(s,a)$, the evaluation critic should be the different one, that is,

$$y(s,a) = r + \gamma Q'_\theta(s', \pi(s')) . \tag{12.12}$$

Double DQN also adopts such idea [van Hasselt et al., 2016], with Q'_θ being a delayed version of Q_θ. Though Double DQN achieves significant performance improvement against DQN through alleviating the overestimation, it usually underestimates the critic values.

Chen et al. [2021b] proposed REDQ, an ensemble critic method for better estimation of critic function, which maintains N critics $Q_1, \ldots, Q_N$. When calculating the approximation target, a random subset of critics $\mathcal{M}$ is picked out, and the approximation target is

$$y(s,a) = r + \gamma \min_{Q \in \mathcal{M}} Q_\theta(s', \pi(s')) . \tag{12.13}$$

The target is used to update all critics, and averaged critics are used to update policy. In this way, REDQ achieves highly accurate critic value.

The estimation of critic functions is more tricky in offline reinforcement learning, because there are only previously collected interaction sequences and many transition pairs are out of data. On unseen transition pairs, if the Q_θ function gives a high value, the policy will shift away from data and lose data support. The EDAC method exploits ensemble mechanism [An et al., 2021], which maintains N critic functions and uses the minimum Q value to alleviate the policy shift. The target is then calculated according to

$$y(s,a) = r + \gamma \min_{i=1,\ldots,N} Q_\theta(s', \pi(s')) \ . \tag{12.14}$$

12.3.3 Uncertainty Estimation

The disagreement among ensemble components can be viewed as a measure of uncertainty, which has been exploited in active learning [Abe and Mamitsuka, 1998, Zhou et al., 2006]. It is also useful in reinforcement learning to determine whether a state has been visited. In particular, uncertainty estimation is crucial for **curiosity-driven exploration** and offline reinforcement learning.

Reinforcement learning generally employs random action perturbations to explore state space; this can be inefficient as some states may be visited repeatedly. *Curiosity-driven exploration* encourages to visit *novel* states that have rarely been visited before, leading to improved efficiency. Suppose that a novelty measure $u(s,a)$ is added to the environmental reward, i.e., $r + u(s,a)$ is used as the new reward, and then, an agent maximizing the new reward is motivated to explore novel states.

To implement curiosity-driven exploration, the agent needs to remember the visited states/actions. For discrete state spaces, this is straightforward by taking $u(s,a) = 1/(1 + \text{count}(s,a))$, i.e., counting the times of the visited states/actions. For continuous state spaces, this is difficult as the agent may never visit an exactly same state twice. Thus, the key issue is how to measure the novelty of a state during exploration.

In [Pathak et al., 2019], a set of transition models is learned, i.e., $\hat{P}_1, \ldots, \hat{P}_N$. At each step, the transition models are used to predict the next state $\hat{s}_1, \ldots, \hat{s}_N$. The variance of the predictions is used as the novelty measure, that is,

$$u(s,a) = var_{i=1,\ldots,N}[\hat{P}_i(s,a)] \ . \tag{12.15}$$

In offline reinforcement learning where only a set of historical trajectories are available, the *conservatism principle* is commonly employed [Kumar et al., 2019], where the policy training is restricted within data support and not allowed to states far from data. For *model-based* approaches that construct transition models to train the policy, the conservatism principle can be implemented by avoiding transition to out-of-data states.

MOPO is a model-based offline reinforcement learning algorithm [Yu et al., 2020]. To implement the conservatism principle, it learns, by maximum likelihood, a set of transition models $\hat{P}_1, \ldots, \hat{P}_N$, and each model outputs mean and variance simultaneously. The variance of a model, $\hat{P}_i(s,a).var$, can be served as a novelty measure. MOPO takes the largest variance among the N models as the novelty measure, i.e.,

$$u(s,a) = \max_{i=1,\ldots,N} \hat{P}_i(s,a).var \ . \tag{12.16}$$

Unlike exploration that encourages large novelty, the conservatism principle minimizes novelty; this can be implemented by taking $r = R(s,a) - \alpha u(s,a)$, i.e., subtracting the novelty from the environmental rewards, such that a policy maximizing the rewards avoids visiting out-of-data states.

MOBILE [Sun et al., 2023] argues that the novelty should be about the long-term rewards rather than the current state/action as in MOPO, and the novelty in MOPO is replaced by

$$u(s,a) = var_{i=1,\dots,N}[r + V(\hat{P}_i(s,a))] , \tag{12.17}$$

where the critic V also takes the minimum value of two independently trained critic functions to avoid overestimation.

12.4 Online Learning

Online learning is about learning with online accumulated data [Cesa-Bianchi and Lugosi, 2006, Hazan, 2016]. This is important because data in many real-world applications are often accumulated over time, like a *stream*. Therefore, it is generally desired to learn models that can update in an online fashion.

12.4.1 Learning with Non-Stationary Data Streams

Consider the standard supervised online learning scenario for simplicity. It can be modeled as a T-round procedure, where T is the length of the data stream that can be potentially infinite. At the t-th round, the learner receives a data instance $\boldsymbol{x}_t \in \mathcal{X} \subseteq \mathbb{R}^d$ and makes a prediction as $\hat{y}_t \in \mathcal{Y}$ with the learning model parameterized by $\boldsymbol{w}_t \in \mathcal{W}$. For example, considering the simplest linear model, one has $\hat{y}_t = \boldsymbol{w}_t^{\boldsymbol{T}} \boldsymbol{x}_t$ with the model space $\mathcal{W} = \{\boldsymbol{w} \in \mathbb{R}^d \mid \|\boldsymbol{w}\|_2 \leq \Lambda\}$ for some constant $\Lambda > 0$. Subsequently, the model receives the truth $y_t \in \mathcal{Y}$, suffers from a loss $\ell(y_t, \hat{y}_t)$, receives some information from loss function as feedback and updates model parameter to $\boldsymbol{w}_{t+1}$. The loss $\ell(\cdot,\cdot)$ is generally different for different tasks, e.g., it can be chosen as $\ell(y_t, \hat{y}_t) = |y_t - \hat{y}_t|$ for classification $\mathcal{Y} = \{0, 1\}$, and it can also be set as $\ell(y_t, \hat{y}_t) = (y_t - \hat{y}_t)^2$ for regression $\mathcal{Y} = \mathbb{R}$. To simplify notation, let $f_t : \mathcal{W} \mapsto \mathbb{R}$ denote the online function, defined as $f_t(\boldsymbol{w}) = \ell(y_t, \hat{y}_t(\boldsymbol{w}, \boldsymbol{x}_t))$, where $\hat{y}_t(\boldsymbol{w}, \boldsymbol{x}_t)$ is used to highlight that the prediction depends on the model parameter $\boldsymbol{w}$ as well as the input instance $\boldsymbol{x}_t$.

It is noteworthy that real tasks often exhibit non-stationary characteristics, for example, the data distribution may vary over time, also referred to as distribution change [Zhou, 2022] or concept drift [Tsymbal, 2004]. This makes online learning even more challenging, especially when a theoretical guarantee is desired to be pursued. Ensemble methods have been found very helpful in online learning, particularly for online learning with non-stationary data streams with some theoretical guarantees.

12.4.2 Drifting Ensembles

A category of early ensemble methods for online learning was designed mostly for handling concept drift, where an ensemble is maintained and adjusted by adding/removing some models such that the ensemble is *drifted* according to concept drift, hence we call them **drifting ensembles**. It can be seen that after adding suitable models, the remaining effort is to select a subset of models for the final ensemble, which is actually an online fashion of ensemble pruning (see Chapter 6).

For example, SEA (Streaming Ensemble Algorithm) [Street and Kim, 2001] adds models trained from a sequential data batches, and then prunes the ensemble by excluding the weakest model. DWM (Dynamic Weighted Majority) [Kolter and Maloof, 2003, 2007] dynamically adds models and prunes the ensemble based on model performance and the global ensemble performance. AddExp (Additive Expert ensemble) [Kolter and Maloof, 2005] generalizes DWM to regression tasks, and enhances it with improved pruning mechanisms to cap the number of models. Learn^{++}.NSE [Elwell and Polikar, 2011] trains a new model for each batch of received data, and combines the models through dynamically weighted majority voting, based on each model's time-adjusted accuracy across current and past environments. DTEL [Sun et al., 2018] and Condor [Zhao et al., 2020a] add to ensemble a new model trained with help of earlier models.

Many drifting ensemble methods are practically effective for online learning, though they are primarily heuristic in nature. Next section will introduce a new category of online ensemble methods with strong theoretical foundations.

12.4.3 Online Ensemble

Online Ensemble is a new category of ensemble methods, which explicitly minimizes **regret** [Cesa-Bianchi and Lugosi, 2006] by ensemble mechanisms. Note that, online learning generally refers to learning with online data through regret minimization [Hazan, 2016], hence the name of online ensemble.

Regret is a common measure for online learning performance, which aims to depict learner's excess loss compared to the best comparator in hindsight. Formally,

$$\mathbf{Reg}_T \triangleq \sum_{t=1}^{T} f_t(\boldsymbol{w}_t) - \min_{\boldsymbol{w}\in\mathcal{W}} \sum_{t=1}^{T} f_t(\boldsymbol{w}) \ . \tag{12.18}$$

This notion is often referred to as **static regret** to emphasize the comparator with fixed rounds, i.e., the comparator $\boldsymbol{w}^* \in \arg\min_{\boldsymbol{w}\in\mathcal{W}} \sum_{t=1}^{T} f_t(\boldsymbol{w})$.

For non-stationary situations, the static regret is not suitable because the best fixed comparator may also perform poorly in changing environments, and instead, the following **dynamic regret** [Zinkevich, 2003] is often employed:

$$\mathbf{Reg}_T^{\mathbf{d}}(\boldsymbol{u}_1, \ldots, \boldsymbol{u}_T) \triangleq \sum_{t=1}^{T} f_t(\boldsymbol{w}_t) - \sum_{t=1}^{T} f_t(\boldsymbol{u}_t) , \tag{12.19}$$

where $\boldsymbol{u}_1, \ldots, \boldsymbol{u}_T \in \mathcal{W}$ is a sequence of time-varying comparators within the model space. The generality of the arbitrary comparators makes the dynamic regret encompass many other regrets; for example, the dynamic regret recovers the static regret by choosing $\boldsymbol{u}_1 = \cdots = \boldsymbol{u}_T \in \arg\min_{\boldsymbol{w} \in \mathcal{W}} \sum_{t=1}^{T} f_t(\boldsymbol{w})$, i.e., the best fixed comparator in hindsight.

In online learning, typically the regret is minimized through **online convex optimization** [Zinkevich, 2003, Hazan, 2016], where $f_t : \mathcal{W} \mapsto \mathbb{R}$ is supposed to be convex with respect to the model parameter $\boldsymbol{w}$, and the model space $\mathcal{W} \subseteq \mathbb{R}^d$ is compact and convex.

For non-stationary online learning with provably dynamic regret minimization, an online ensemble is usually deployed with two primary considerations. First, the model should be capable of handling potential changes manifested in the incoming data, which often arise due to the non-stationary nature of environments. Second, the model should adaptively incorporate the experience learned from historical data for online prediction. In essence, a desired online algorithm should be able to achieve *adaptivity* and handle *non-stationarity* simultaneously.

Since a sublinear dynamic regret is impossible unless restricting the non-stationarity level [Zhao and Zhang, 2021], the path length of comparators, $P_T = \sum_{t=2}^{T} \|\boldsymbol{u}_t - \boldsymbol{u}_{t-1}\|_2$, is often employed in the dynamic regret bound to reflect the non-stationarity level. To capture the adaptivity, the *problem-dependent* quantity $A_T = \sum_{t=1}^{T} \|\nabla f_t(\boldsymbol{w}_t) - M_t\|_2^2$ is introduced to encode the experience learned from historical data, where *optimistic gradient* M_t is an external input, serving as an estimate of the actual gradient $\nabla f_t(\boldsymbol{w}_t)$. If the algorithm knows nothing in advance, simply setting $M_t = \mathbf{0}$ corresponds to the worst-case scenario. If the algorithm learns from past data, proper setting of $\{M_t\}_{t=1}^{T}$ can improve performance. For instance, if the data stream exhibits a gradually evolving pattern, it is beneficial to set $M_t = \nabla f_{t-1}(\boldsymbol{w}_{t-1})$ as the last-round information to serve as a warmup. Generally speaking, the optimistic gradient offers the algorithm with capability of using what it learned from past data to make better future predictions.

To attain such dual capability, Zhao et al. [2024] proposed an adaptive algorithm for non-stationary online learning with an $O(\sqrt{A_T(1 + P_T)})$ dynamic regret, where A_T and P_T represent the adaptivity and non-stationarity terms introduced above, respectively. Zhao et al. [2024] proposed an online ensemble framework to tackle the uncertainty of the non-stationary environments while attaining the adaptivity. The basic idea is to maintain multiple base learners to explore environments, alongside a meta-algorithm by using an expert-tracking technique to track the most effective base learner on the fly. It is crucial for these base learners to exhibit a certain level of diversity, allowing them to approximately accommodate the unknown non-stationarity while minimizing the number of maintained models. Another essential idea is to facilitate effective *collaboration* between the meta and base learners, making the online ensemble framework significantly differ from the classic problem of *prediction with expert advice* [Littlestone and Warmuth, 1994, Cesa-Bianchi and Lugosi, 2006].

Figure 12.5 presents the online ensemble framework, which is general to encompass many situations. Instantiating the framework with specific surrogate losses and optimizations can result in various guarantees. For example, choosing a general optimism for both meta and base learners $h_t^{\text{meta}}(\boldsymbol{w}) = h_t^{\text{base}}(\boldsymbol{w}) = \langle M_t, \boldsymbol{w}\rangle$ yields the aforementioned $O(\sqrt{A_T(1+P_T)})$ dynamic regret. Finally, we mention that the online ensemble methods usually require $O(\log T)$ base learners to achieve the desired dynamic regret guarantees, which makes the computational efficiency an important issue [Zhao et al., 2022b].

Input: Step size pool $\mathcal{H} = \{\eta_1, \dots, \eta_N\}$;
Learning rate of meta algorithm ε;
Base learners $\{\mathcal{B}_i\}_{i=1}^N$;
Number of learning rounds T.

Process:

1. **Initialization:** $p_{0,i} = 1/N$, $\hat{\boldsymbol{w}}_{1,i}, \boldsymbol{w}_1$ be any point in $\mathcal{W}$
3. **for** $t = 1, \dots, T$:
4. Receive $\boldsymbol{w}_{t,i}$ from base learner $\mathcal{B}_i$;
5. Submit the model $\boldsymbol{w}_t = \sum_{i=1}^N p_{t,i}\boldsymbol{w}_{t,i}$;
6. Receive the gradient feedback $\nabla f_t(\boldsymbol{w}_t)$;
7. Construct the meta feedback loss $\ell_{t,i}$ and optimism $m_{t,i}$ via
$\ell_{t,i} = g_t^{\text{meta}}(\boldsymbol{w}_{t,i}) + \lambda c_{t,i}$, and $m_{t,i} = h_t^{\text{meta}}(\boldsymbol{w}_{t,i}) + \lambda c_{t,i}$;
8. Update the weight to $\boldsymbol{p}_{t+1}$ via $p_{t+1,i} \propto \exp(-\varepsilon(\sum_{s=1}^t \ell_{s,i} + m_{t+1,i}))$;
9. **for** $i = 1, \dots, N$:
10. $\mathcal{B}_i$ updates the model by
$$\hat{\boldsymbol{w}}_{t+1,i} = \Pi_{\mathcal{W}}[\hat{\boldsymbol{w}}_{t,i} - \eta_i \nabla g_t^{\text{base}}(\boldsymbol{w}_{t,i})],$$
$$\boldsymbol{w}_{t+1,i} = \Pi_{\mathcal{W}}[\hat{\boldsymbol{w}}_{t+1,i} - \eta_i \nabla h_{t+1}^{\text{base}}(\boldsymbol{w}_{t,i})];$$
11. **end for**
12. **end for**

Figure 12.5: The Online Ensemble framework.

Note that online ensemble can be also applied beyond the scope of non-stationary online learning. For example, the ensemble structure proves beneficial for universal online learning [van Erven and Koolen, 2016, Wang et al., 2019b, Zhang et al., 2022a, Yan et al., 2023c], which aims to devise a single algorithm that is agnostic to the curvature information of the online functions (convex/exponential concave/strongly convex) while achieving the same regret guarantees as if those information were known. In addition, online ensemble can be used to effectively handle an unknown level of corruptions in the scenarios where the learning environments might be corrupted [Wei et al., 2022].

12.5 Improving Understandability

In many real-world tasks, the **understandability** or **comprehensibility** of the learned model is important, in addition to attaining strong generalization ability. It is usually required that the learned model and its predictions are understandable and interpretable. Symbolic rules and decision trees are usually deemed as understandable models. For example, every decision made by a decision tree can be explained by the tree branches it goes through.

Understandability is an inherent deficiency of ensemble methods as well as many other complicated learning models such as deep neural networks. Ensemble lacks understandability even when understandable models such as decision trees are used as base learners because of model aggregation. This section introduces some techniques for improving ensemble understandability.

12.5.1 Ensemble Reduction to Single Model

Considering that the understandability of an ensemble is lost mainly because of multiple aggregated models, one possible approach for the improvement of understandability is to reduce the ensemble to a single model.

CMM [Domingos, 1998]. This method uses the ensemble to label some artificially generated instances, and then applies the base learning algorithm, which was used to train the base learners for the ensemble, to generate a single learner on the artificial data together with the original training data. By adding the artificial data, it is expected that the final single learner can mimic the behavior of ensemble. Note that the final single learner is trained using the same base learning algorithm. Though this avoids the conflict of different biases of different types of learners, the performance of the final single learner has high risk of overfitting because it can strengthen peculiar patterns in the training data that affect the base learning algorithm. Also, CMM will not improve understandability if the base learners of the ensemble are not comprehensible.

Archetype Selection [Ferri et al., 2002]. This method calculates the similarity between each base learner and the ensemble by comparing their predictions on an artificial data set, and then selects the single base learner that is the most similar to the ensemble. Note that this method may fail in some cases, e.g., there may not exist a base learner that is very close to the ensemble, or the base learners themselves are not comprehensible.

Twice Learning [Zhou and Jiang, 2004, Zhou, 2005]. This method uses the ensemble to generate an artificial data set, and then exploits the artificial data set together with the original training set to generate a single simpler learner.

Note that the learning algorithm for the final single learner is different from the base learning algorithm of the ensemble; this difference reduces the risk of overfitting, and the final single learner can even be more accurate than the ensemble itself. Hence, the task is learned twice, leading to the name **twice learning** [Zhou, 2005]. NeC4.5 [Zhou and Jiang, 2004], an implementation of twice learning, employs a neural network ensemble to generate a C4.5 decision tree, with much better understandability and comparable or superior generalization performance. It is theoretically explained that the procedure can be beneficial when the original training data set does not capture the whole distribution or contains noise, and the first-stage learner (e.g., the ensemble) is more accurate than the second-stage learner (e.g., the C4.5 decision tree) [Zhou and Jiang, 2004].

ISM [Assche and Blockeel, 2007]. This method tries to learn a single decision tree from a tree ensemble without generating an artificial data set, by considering that it is difficult to generate artificial data in some domains such as those involving *relational* data. The basic idea is to construct a single tree, where each split is decided by the utility of this split in similar paths of the trees in the ensemble. Roughly speaking, for each candidate split of a node, a path of feature tests can be obtained from the root to the node. Then, similar paths in the trees of the ensemble will be identified, and the utility of the split in each path can be calculated, e.g., according to information gain. The utility values are aggregated from all the similar paths, and finally the candidate split is selected with the largest aggregated utility for the current node.

12.5.2 Rule Extraction from Ensemble

Improving ensemble understandability by rule extraction was inspired by studies on rule extraction from single neural networks [Andrews et al., 1995, Tickle et al., 1998, Zhou, 2004], with the goal of using a set of symbolic *if-then* rules to represent the ensemble.

REFNE [Zhou et al., 2003]. This method uses the ensemble to generate an artificial data set, and then tries to identify a feature-value pair such as '*color = red*', which is able to make correct prediction on some artificial examples. If there exists such a feature-value pair, then a rule with one antecedent is generated, e.g., *if 'color = red' then positive*, and it removes the artificial examples classified correctly by rule. REFNE searches for other one-antecedent rules on the remaining artificial data, and if there is no more, it starts to search for two-antecedent rules such as *if 'color = blue' and 'shape = round' then positive*, and so on. Numeric features are discretized adaptively, and sanity checks are executed based on statistical tests before each rule is accepted. Note that, REFNE generates *priority rules*, also called *decision list*, which must be applied in the order that the earlier generated, the earlier applied. This method suffers from efficiency and can only be applied to small or medium scale data sest.

C4.5Rule-PANE [Zhou and Jiang, 2003]. This method improves REFNE by using C4.5 Rule [Quinlan, 1993] to replace the complicated rule generation procedure in REFNE. Though it is named as *C4.5 Rule Preceded by Artificial Neural Ensemble*, similar to REFNE, this method can be applied to extract rules from any type of ensembles comprising any types of base learners.

Note that, though in most cases the ensemble is more accurate than the extracted rules, there are also cases where the extracted rules are even more accurate than the ensemble. In such cases, there is a conflict between attaining a high *accuracy* and high *fidelity*. If the goal is to explain the ensemble or mimic behaviors of the ensemble, then the higher accuracy of the extracted rules has to be sacrificed. However, if the goal is to achieve an accurate and comprehensible model, then it is not necessary to care about whether the behaviors of the ensemble can be correctly mimicked; actually this recognition motivated the *twice learning* method. This is the **fidelity-accuracy dilemma** [Zhou, 2004].

12.5.3 Visualization of Ensemble

Visualization is an important approach to help people understand the behaviors of learned models. One of the most straightforward ways is to plot the decision boundary of an ensemble after each learning round. In such a plot, the x-axis and y-axis correspond to any pair of features, while each point corresponds to an instance. For example, Figures 12.6 and 12.7 provide illustrations of the visualization results of Boosted decision stumps and Bagged decision stumps on the *three-Gaussians* data set, respectively.

Note that visualization with dimensions higher than three is generally difficult. For data with more than three dimensions, dimension reduction can be performed. Furthermore, visualization can be performed on some important feature combinations.

12.6 Future Directions of Ensembles

There are many interesting research directions in ensemble for future work. In addition to those mentioned before, we highlight two directions, that is, *structural diversity* and *ensembles in learnware*.

It is well-accepted that understanding diversity is the holy grail problem in ensemble research. Though some advances have been attained as introduced in Chapter 5, it is still a long way for a complete understanding of diversity. For example, it is not yet known whether diversity is really a driving force, or actually a trap, since it might be just another appearance of accuracy. Particularly, most studies only consider behavioral diversity, i.e., how the learners behave when making predictions, and neglect that learners can be potentially different even when making the same predictions. An important

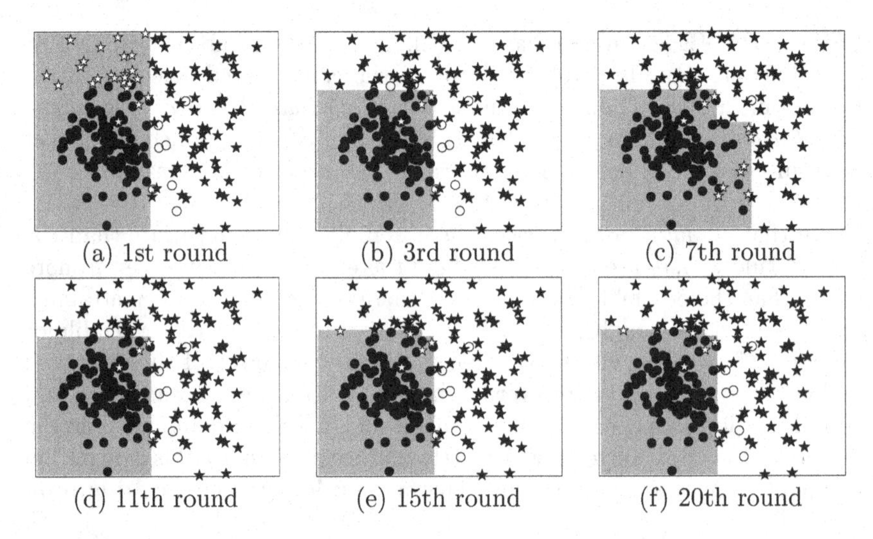

Figure 12.6: Boosted decision stumps on *three-Guassians*, where circles/stars denote positive/negative examples, and solid/empty mark correctly/incorrectly classified examples, respectively.

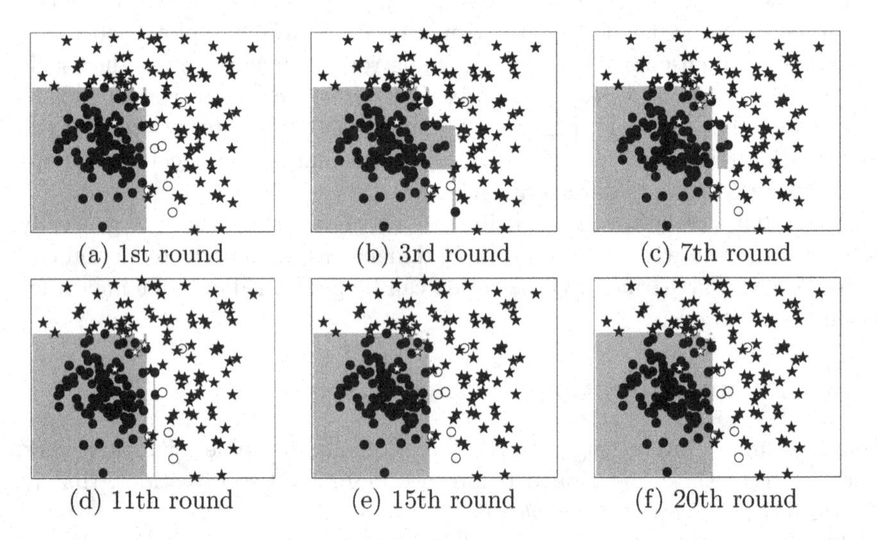

Figure 12.7: Bagged decision stumps on *three-Guassians*, where circles/stars denote positive/negative examples, and solid/empty mark correctly/incorrectly classified examples, respectively.

direction is to see whether **structural diversity** offers some fundamental insights (see Section 5.6).

A **learnware** [Zhou, 2016, Zhou and Tan, 2024] is a well-performed trained machine learning model with a **specification** which enables it to be adequately

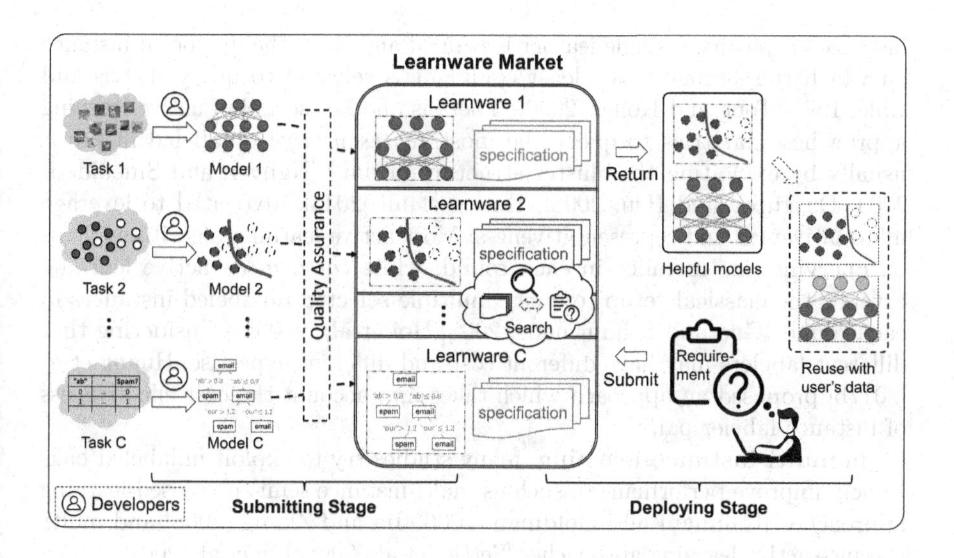

Figure 12.8: The learnware market and the submitting/deploying stages.

identified to reuse according to the requirement of future users who know nothing about the learnware in advance. The learnware paradigm attempts to enable users to reuse models developed by other people, rather than building machine learning models from scratch, with the hope of reusing models to do things even beyond their original purposes, where the training data of developers and users are protected. The *learnware market* (also called *learnware dock system*) may accommodate millions of well-performed models submitted by different developers, on different tasks, using different data, optimizing different objectives, etc. Each model will be assigned a *specification* when it is accepted by the learnware market. As illustrated in Figure 12.8, once the learnware market has been built, when a user is going to tackle a machine learning task, she can submit her *requirement*, and then the learnware market will identify and return to her some helpful learnware(s) that can be reused in various ways such as to constitute an ensemble. There are many interesting issues to be explored, such as how to identify helpful learnwares without examining all models held in the learnware market, how to reuse models trained on relevant but different tasks to solve the current user task, etc., where ensemble mechanisms may play vital roles in many places.

12.7 Further Readings

Besides query-by-committee, **uncertainty sampling** is another well-known active learning approach which tries to query the most *informative* unlabeled instance. Typically, a single learner is trained and then, the unlabeled instance on which the learner is the least confident is selected to query [Lewis and Gale, 1994, Tong and Koller, 2000]. There is another school of active learning approaches that tries to query the most *representative* unlabeled instance, usually by exploiting the cluster structure of data [Nguyen and Smeulders, 2004, Dasgupta and Hsu, 2008]. Huang et al. [2014] advocated to leverage informativeness and representativeness. Most active learning algorithms focus on querying one instance in each round, while *batch mode* active learning extends the classical setup to query multiple selected unlabeled instances in each round [Guo and Schuurmans, 2008, Hoi et al., 2009]. Considering that different labelers may have different cost and different expertise, Huang et al. [2017b] proposed an approach which takes into account the cost-effectiveness of instance-labeler pairs.

In **multi-instance learning**, many studies try to exploit unlabeled bags to help improve performances, such as multi-instance semi-supervised learning approaches [Rahmani and Goldman, 2006, Jia and Zhang, 2008] and multi-instance active learning approaches [Settles et al., 2008, Liu et al., 2009a]. Zhou and Xu [2007] indicated that if instances in multi-instance bags were assumed *i.i.d.*, then multi-instance learning can be treated as a special case of semi-supervised learning. Indeed, it is often unreasonable to assume independent instances because the instances in the same multi-instance bag were generally extracted from the same object. Later, Zhou et al. [2009] initialized the research line which does not assume *i.i.d.* instances in multi-instance learning.

More about weakly supervised learning can be found in [Zhou, 2018a], while more about open-environment learning can be found in [Zhou, 2022]. It is worth mentioning that ensemble methods have also been found helpful in **multi-label learning**, where one data instance can be associated with multiple labels simultaneously [Zhou and Zhang, 2017, Zhang and Zhou, 2014] (See Section 2.6.2).

When reinforcement learning occurs in environments that contain another agent with the opposite reward function, the learning problem becomes a *game*. For *zero-sum games*, the agent seeks a policy to approximate an *Nash equilibrium*. Such a policy is hard to obtain at once and is usually an average of a set of models. In *fictitious self-play* [Heinrich et al., 2015], an agent iteratively finds the best response opponent to the current policy, which is extended from the *fictitious play* [Brown, 1951] for normal-form games. When a best response opponent is well trained by reinforcement learning, this opponent policy is averaged into the agent's current policy. Note that the averaging operator here is not to sum over the output of each base policy, but a probabilistic mixing of the policies; this is evidently an ensemble method. Model averaging is common in reinforcement learning based game playing methods such as [Lanctot et al., 2017]. Averaging many models can be a problem with increasing number of base policies. For this purpose, Heinrich et al. [2015] tried to reduce the behavior of the average model to a single model; this is similar to *twice learning*.

Comprehensive surveys about **drifting ensemble** methods can be found in [Gama et al., 2014, Gomes et al., 2017]. In addition to online supervised learning, online ensemble methods have also been developed for online label shift [Bai et al., 2022], covariate shift [Zhang et al., 2023], online bandit feedback [Zhao et al., 2020b, 2021], online non-stochastic control [Zhao et al., 2023, Yan et al., 2023b], online Markov decision processes [Zhao et al., 2022a], as well as time-varying games [Zhang et al., 2022b, Yan et al., 2023a].

Twice Learning [Zhou and Jiang, 2004, Zhou, 2005] was proposed to improve understandability of complicated learning systems. Ten years later, a similar idea was presented under the name **knowledge distillation** [Hinton et al., 2015], which has been recognized as a fundamentally important technique and widely used in deep learning, where the first-stage and second-stage learners are generally called *teacher* and *student* models, respectively. The student models are usually chosen to be with fewer layers and fewer channels in each layer [Wang et al., 2018], or a quantized network [Polino et al., 2018], or a small network with efficient operators [Howard et al., 2017], or a small network with optimized structure [Liu et al., 2020]. It ia also regarded as an effective approach for the compression and acceleration of DNNs, e.g., to generate lightweight, efficient and effective language models [Sanh et al., 2019, Jiao et al., 2020].

There are abundant studies about **model reuse** under different scenarios, and many of them exploited ensemble mechanisms. For example, Segev et al. [2017] exploited random forest in model transfer learning, and Ding and Zhou [2020] proposed the MoreBoost to conduct model reuse with the guidance of a reusability indicator constructed based on unlabeled data. There are also studies about *on-site ensemble* [Li et al., 2010a], which tries to use ensemble methods as tools to exploit *remote* resources scattered over internet without merging the data to a single site.

References

N. Abe and H. Mamitsuka. Query learning strategies using boosting and bagging. In *Proceedings of the 15th International Conference on Machine Learning*, pages 1–9, Madison, WI, 1998.

A. A. Aburomman and M. B. I. Reaz. A survey of intrusion detection systems based on ensemble and hybrid classifiers. *Computers & Security*, 65:135–152, 2017.

S. Affeldt, L. Labiod, and M. Nadif. Spectral clustering via ensemble deep autoencoder learning (SC-EDAE). *Pattern Recognition*, 108:107522, 2020.

R. Agarwal, D. Schuurmans, and M. Norouzi. An optimistic perspective on offline reinforcement learning. In *Proceedings of the 37th International Conference on Machine Learning*, pages 104–114, Virtual Event, 2020.

C. C. Aggarwal and S. Sathe. *Outlier Ensembles: An Introduction.* Springer, 2017.

R. Agrawal, T. Imieliński, and A. Swami. Mining association rules between sets of items in large databases. *ACM SIGMOD Record*, 22(2):207–216, 1993.

R. Agrawal, J. Gehrke, D. Gunopulos, and P. Raghavan. Automatic subspace clustering of high dimensional data for data mining applications. In *Proceedings of the 24th ACM SIGMOD International Conference on Management of Data*, pages 94–105, Seattle, WA, 1998.

M. R. Ahmadzadeh and M. Petrou. Use of Dempster-Shafer theory to combine classifiers which use different class boundaries. *Pattern Analysis and Application*, 6(1):41–46, 2003.

A. Al-Ani and M. Deriche. A new technique for combining multiple classifiers using the Dempster-Shafer theory of evidence. *Journal of Artificial Intelligence Research*, 17:333–361, 2002.

K. M. Ali and M. J. Pazzani. Error reduction through learning multiple descriptions. *Machine Learning*, 24(3):173–202, 1996.

E. L. Allwein, R. E. Schapire, and Y. Singer. Reducing multiclass to binary: A unifying approach for margin classifiers. *Journal of Machine Learning Research*, 1: 113–141, 2000.

E. Alpaydin. *Introduction to Machine Learning.* MIT Press, 4th edition, 2020.

Y. Amit and D. Geman. Shape quantization and recognition with randomized trees. *Neural Computation*, 9(7):1545–1588, 1997.

G. An, S. Moon, J. Kim, and H. O. Song. Uncertainty-based offline reinforcement learning with diversified Q-ensemble. In *Advances in Neural Information Processing Systems 34*, pages 7436–7447, Virtual Event, 2021.

M. R. Anderberg. *Cluster Analysis for Applications.* Academic, 1973.

R. Andrews, J. Diederich, and A. B. Tickle. Survey and critique of techniques for extracting rules from trained artificial neural networks. *Knowledge-Based Systems*, 8(6):373–389, 1995.

M. Ankerst, M. Breunig, H.-P. Kriegel, and J. Sander. OPTICS: Ordering points to identify the clustering structure. In *Proceedings of the 25th ACM SIGMOD International Conference on Management of Data*, pages 49–60, Philadelphia, PA, 1999.

M. Anthony and N. Biggs. *Computational Learning Theory.* Cambridge University Press, 1992.

M. B. Araújo and M. New. Ensemble forecasting of species distributions. *Trends in Ecology & Evolution*, 22(1):42–47, 2007.

L. Arnould, C. Boyer, and E. Scornet. Analyzing the tree-layer structure of deep forests. In *Proceedings of the 38th International Conference on Machine Learning*, pages 342–350, Virtual Event, 2021.

R. Arriaga and S. Vempala. An algorithmic theory of learning: Robust concepts and random projection. *Machine Learning*, 63(2):161–182, 2006.

S. Aryal, K. M. Ting, J. R. Wells, and T. Washio. Improving iForest with relative mass. In *Proceedings of the 18th Pacific-Asia Conference on Knowledge Discovery and Data Mining*, pages 510–521, Tainan, China, 2014.

J. A. Aslam and S. E. Decatur. General bounds on statistical query learning and PAC learning with noise via hypothesis boosting. In *Proceedings of the 35th IEEE Annual Symposium on Foundations of Computer Science*, pages 282–291, Palo Alto, CA, 1993.

E. Asmis. *Epicurus' Scientific Method.* Cornell University Press, 1984.

A. V. Assche and H. Blockeel. Seeing the forest through the trees: Learning a comprehensible model from an ensemble. In *Proceedings of the 18th European Conference on Machine Learning*, pages 418–429, Warsaw, Poland, 2007.

P. Auer and R. Ortner. A boosting approach to multiple instance learning. In *Proceedings of the 15th European Conference on Machine Learning*, pages 63–74, Pisa, Italy, 2004.

R. Avogadri and G. Valentini. Fuzzy ensemble clustering based on random projections for DNA microarray data analysis. *Artificial Intelligence in Medicine*, 45(2-3): 173–183, 2009.

H. Ayad and M. Kamel. Finding natural clusters using multi-clusterer combiner based on shared nearest neighbors. In *Proceedings of the 4th International Workshop on Multiple Classifier Systems*, pages 166–175, Guilford, UK, 2003.

Y. Bai, Y.-J. Zhang, P. Zhao, M. Sugiyama, and Z.-H. Zhou. Adapting to online label shift with provable guarantees. In *Advances in Neural Information Processing Systems 35*, pages 29960–29974, New Orleans, LA, 2022.

B. Bakker and T. Heskes. Clustering ensembles of neural network models. *Neural Networks*, 16(2):261–269, 2003.

P. Baldi and P. J. Sadowski. The dropout learning algorithm. *Artificial Intelligence*, 210:78–122, 2014.

T. R. Bandaragoda, K. M. Ting, D. Albrecht, F. T. Liu, Y. Zhu, and J. R. Wells. Isolation-based anomaly detection using nereast-neighbor ensembles. *Computational Intelligence*, 34(4):968–998, 2018.

R. E. Banfield, L. O. Hall, K. W. Bowyer, and W. P. Kegelmeyer. Ensemble diversity measures and their application to thinning. *Information Fusion*, 6(1):49–62, 2005.

J. F. Banzhaf. Weighted voting doesn't work: A mathematical analysis. *Rutgers Law Review*, 19:317, 1964.

D. Barbará, J. Couto, and Y. Li. COOLCAT: An entropy-based algorithm for categorical clustering. In *Proceedings of the 11th ACM International Conference on Information and Knowledge Management*, pages 582–589, McLean, VA, 2002.

D. Barbará, Y. Li, J. Couto, J.-L. Lin, and S. Jajodia. Bootstrapping a data mining intrusion detection system. In *Proceedings of the 18th ACM Symposium on Applied Computing*, pages 421–425, Melbourne, FL, 2003.

P. Bartlett. The sample complexity of pattern classification with neural networks: The size of the weights is more important than the size of the network. *IEEE Trans. Neural Networks*, 44(2):525–536, 1998.

P. L. Bartlett and M. H. Wegkamp. Classification with a reject option using a hinge loss. *Journal of Machine Learning Research*, 9(59):1823–1840, 2008.

P. L. Bartlett, M. I. Jordan, and J. D. McAuliffe. Convexity, classification, and risk bounds. *Journal of the American Statistical Association*, 101(473):138–156, 2006.

S. Basu, A. Banerjee, and R. J. Mooney. Semi-supervised clustering by seeding. In *Proceedings of the 19th International Conference on Machine Learning*, pages 19–26, Sydney, Australia, 2002.

E. Bauer and R. Kohavi. An empirical comparison of voting classification algorithms: Bagging, boosting, and variants. *Machine Learning*, 36(1-2):105–139, 1999.

Y. Bengio, A. Courville, and P. Vincent. Representation learning: A review and new perspectives. *IEEE Trans. Pattern Analysis and Machine Intelligence*, 35(8): 1798–1828, 2013a.

Y. Bengio, G. Mesnil, Y. Dauphin, and S. Rifai. Better mixing via deep representations. In *Proceedings of the 30th International Conference on Machine Learning*, pages 552–560, Atlanta, GA, 2013b.

Y. Bengio, L. Yao, G. Alain, and P. Vincent. Generalized denoising auto-encoders as generative models. In *Advances in Neural Information Processing Systems 26*, pages 899–907, Lake Tahoe, NV, 2013c.

K. Bennett, A. Demiriz, and R. Maclin. Exploiting unlabeled data in ensemble methods. In *Proceedings of the 8th ACM SIGKDD International Conference on Knowledge Discovery and Data Mining*, pages 289–296, Edmonton, Canada, 2002.

J. Bergstra, N. Casagrande, D. Erhan, D. Eck, and B. Kégl. Aggregate features and AdaBoost for music classification. *Machine Learning*, 65(2-3):473–484, 2006.

V. Berikov and I. Pestunov. Ensemble clustering based on weighted co-association matrices: Error bound and convergence properties. *Pattern Recognition*, 63:427–436, 2017.

A. Beygelzimer, S. Kale, and H. Luo. Optimal and adaptive algorithms for online boosting. In *Proceedings of the 32nd International Conference on Machine Learning*, pages 2323–2331, Lille, France, 2015.

Y. Bi, J. Guan, and D. Bell. The combination of multiple classifiers using an evidential reasoning approach. *Artificial Intelligence*, 172(15):1731–1751, 2008.

Y. Bian, Y. Wang, Y. Yao, and H. Chen. Ensemble pruning based on objection maximization with a general distributed framework. *IEEE Trans. Neural Networks and Learning Systems*, 31(9):3766–3774, 2019.

G. Biau. Analysis of a random forests model. *Journal of Machine Learning Research*, 13:1063–1095, 2012.

G. Biau, L. Devroye, and G. Lugosi. Consistency of random forests and other averaging classifiers. *Journal of Machine Learning Research*, 9:2015–2033, 2008.

P. J. Bickel, Y. Ritov, and A. Zakai. Some theory for generalized boosting algorithms. *Journal of Machine Learning Research*, 7:705–732, 2006.

M. Bilenko, S. Basu, and R. J. Mooney. Integrating constraints and metric learning in semi-supervised clustering. In *Proceedings of the 21st International Conference on Machine Learning*, pages 81–88, Banff, Canada, 2004.

J. A. Bilmes. A gentle tutorial of the EM algorithm and its applications to parameter estimation for Gaussian mixture and hidden Markov models. Technical Report TR-97-021, Department of Electrical Engineering and Computer Science, University of California, Berkeley, CA, 1998.

C. M. Bishop. *Pattern Recognition and Machine Learning*. Springer, 2006.

C. M. Bishop and M. Svensén. Bayesian hierarchical mixtures of experts. In *Proceedings of the 19th Conference in Uncertainty in Artificial Intelligence*, pages 57–64, Acapulco, Mexico, 2003.

A. Blum and S. Chawla. Learning from labeled and unlabeled data using graph mincuts. In *Proceedings of the 18th International Conference on Machine Learning*, pages 19–26, Williamstown, MA, 2001.

A. Blum and T. Mitchell. Combining labeled and unlabeled data with co-training. In *Proceedings of the 11th Annual Conference on Computational Learning Theory*, pages 92–100, Madison, WI, 1998.

N. Bonettini, E. D. Cannas, S. Mandelli, L. Bondi, P. Bestagini, and S. Tubaro. Video face manipulation detection through ensemble of CNNs. In *Proceedings of the 25th International Conference on Pattern Recognition*, pages 5012–5019, Milan, Italy, 2020.

H. Bourlard and Y. Kamp. Auto-association by multilayer perceptrons and singular value decomposition. *Biological Cybernetics*, 59(4):291–294, 1988.

D. C. Brabham. Crowdsourcing as a model for problem solving: An introduction and cases. *Convergence*, 14(1):75–90, 2008.

J. K. Bradley and R. E. Schapire. FilterBoost: Regression and classification on large datasets. In *Advances in Neural Information Processing Systems 20*, pages 185–192, Vancouver, Canada, 2007.

U. Brefeld, P. Geibel, and F. Wysotzki. Support vector machines with example dependent costs. In *Proceedings of the 14th European Conference on Machine Learning*, pages 23–34, Cavtat-Dubrovnik, Croatia, 2003.

L. Breiman. Bias, variance, and arcing classifiers. Technical Report 460, Statistics Department, University of California, Berkeley, CA, 1996a.

L. Breiman. Stacked regressions. *Machine Learning*, 24(1):49–64, 1996b.

L. Breiman. Out-of-bag estimation. Technical report, Department of Statistics, University of California, Berkeley, CA, 1996c.

L. Breiman. Bagging predictors. *Machine Learning*, 24(2):123–140, 1996d.

L. Breiman. Prediction games and arcing algorithms. *Neural Computation*, 11(7): 1493–1517, 1999.

L. Breiman. Some infinity theory for predictor ensembles. Technical report, Department of Statistics, University of California, Berkeley, CA, 2000a.

L. Breiman. Randomizing outputs to increase prediction accuracy. *Machine Learning*, 40(3):229–242, 2000b.

L. Breiman. Random forests. *Machine Learning*, 45(1):5–32, 2001.

L. Breiman. Population theory for boosting ensembles. *Annals of Statistics*, 32(1): 1–11, 2004a.

L. Breiman. Consistency for a simple model of random forests. Technical report, Department of Statistics, University of California, Berkeley, CA, 2004b.

L. Breiman, J. Friedman, C. J. Stone, and R. A. Olshen. *Classification and Regression Trees.* Taylor & Francis, 1984.

M. M. Breunig, H.-P. Kriegel, R. T. Ng, and J. Sander. LOF: Identifying density-based local outliers. In *Proceedings of the 26th ACM SIGMOD International Conference on Management of Data*, pages 93–104, Dallas, TX, 2000.

F. P. Brooks. Three great challenges for half-century-old computer science. *Journal of the ACM*, 50(1):25–26, 2003.

G. Brown. An information theoretic perspective on multiple classifier systems. In *Proceedings of the 8th International Workshop on Multiple Classifier Systems*, pages 344–353, Reykjavik, Iceland, 2009.

G. Brown. Some thoughts at the interface of ensemble methods and feature selection. In *Proceedings at the 9th International Workshop on Multiple Classifier Systems*, page 314, Cairo, Egypt, 2010.

G. Brown, J. L. Wyatt, R. Harris, and X. Yao. Diversity creation methods: A survey and categorisation. *Information Fusion*, 6(1):5–20, 2005a.

G. Brown, J. L. Wyatt, and P. Tino. Managing diversity in regression ensembles. *Journal of Machine Learning Research*, 6(55):1621–1650, 2005b.

G. W. Brown. Iterative solution of games by fictitious play. *Activity Analysis of Production and Allocation*, 13(1):374–376, 1951.

P. Büchlmann and B. Yu. Analyzing bagging. *Annals of Statistics*, 30(4):927–961, 2002.

P. Bühlmann and B. Yu. Boosting with the L_2-loss: Regression and classification. *Journal of the American Statistical Association*, 98(462):324–339, 2003.

A. Buja and W. Stuetzle. The effect of bagging on variance, bias, and mean squared error. Technical report, AT&T Labs-Research, 2000a.

A. Buja and W. Stuetzle. Smoothing effects of bagging. Technical report, AT&T Labs-Research, 2000b.

A. Buja and W. Stuetzle. Observations on bagging. *Statistica Sinica*, 16(2):323–351, 2006.

Y. Cao, T. A. Geddes, J. Y. H. Yang, and P. Yang. Ensemble deep learning in bioinformatics. *Nature Machine Intelligence*, 2(9):500–508, 2020.

M. A. Carreira-Perpinan and R. S. Zemel. Proximity graphs for clustering and manifold learning. In *Advances in Neural Information Processing System 17*, pages 225–232, Vancouver, Canda, 2004.

R. Caruana, A. Niculescu-Mizil, G. Crew, and A. Ksikes. Ensemble selection from libraries of models. In *Proceedings of the 21st International Conference on Machine Learning*, pages 18–23, Banff, Canada, 2004.

V. Castelli and T. M. Cover. On the exponential value of labeled samples. *Pattern Recognition Letters*, 16(1):105–111, 1995.

P. D. Castro, G. P. Coelho, M. F. Caetano, and F. J. V. Zuben. Designing ensembles of fuzzy classification systems: An immune-inspired approach. In *Proceedings of the 4th International Conference on Artificial Immune Systems*, pages 469–482, Banff, Canada, 2005.

N. Cesa-Bianchi and G. Lugosi. *Prediction, Learning, and Games.* Cambridge University Press, 2006.

P. Chan and S. Stolfo. Toward scalable learning with non-uniform class and cost distributions: A case study in credit card fraud detection. In *Proceeding of the 4th International Conference on Knowledge Discovery and Data Mining*, pages 164–168, New York, NY, 1998.

P. K. Chan, W. Fan, A. L. Prodromidis, and S. J. Stolfo. Distributed data mining in credit card fraud detection. *IEEE Intelligent Systems*, 14(6):67–74, 1999.

V. Chandola, A. Banerjee, and V. Kumar. Anomaly detection: A survey. *ACM Computing Surveys*, 41(3):1–58, 2009.

O. Chapelle and A. Zien. Semi-supervised learning by low density separation. In *Proceedings of the 10th International Workshop on Artificial Intelligence and Statistic*, pages 57–64, Bridgetown, Barbados, 2005.

O. Chapelle, B. Schölkopf, and A. Zien, editors. *Semi-Supervised Learning.* MIT Press, 2006.

N. V. Chawla, K. W. Bowyer, L. O. Hall, and W. P. Kegelmeyer. SMOTE: Synthetic minority over-sampling technique. *Journal of Artificial Intelligence Research*, 16: 321–357, 2002.

N. V. Chawla, A. Lazarevic, L. O. Hall, and K. W. Bowyer. SMOTEBoost: Improving prediction of the minority class in boosting. In *Proceedings of the 7th European Conference on Principles and Practice of Knowledge Discovery in Databases*, pages 107–119, Cavtat-Dubrovnik, Croatia, 2003.

N. V. Chawla, N. Japkowicz, and A. Kotcz. Editorial to the special issue on learning from imbalanced data sets. *ACM SIGKDD Explorations*, 6(1):1–6, 2004.

C. Chen, A. Liaw, and L. Breiman. Using random forest to learn imbalanced data. Technical Report 666, Department of Statistics, University of California, Berkeley, CA, 2004.

D. Chen, W. Wang, W. Gao, and Z.-H. Zhou. Tri-net for semi-supervised deep learning. In *Proceedings of the 27th International Joint Conference on Artificial Intelligence*, pages 2014–2020, Stockholm, Sweden, 2018a.

H. Chen, P. Tiňo, and X. Yao. A probabilistic ensemble pruning algorithm. In *Proceedings of the 6th IEEE International Conference on Data Mining-Workshops*, pages 878–882, Hong Kong, China, 2006.

H. Chen, P. Tiňo, and X. Yao. Predictive ensemble pruning by expectation propagation. *IEEE Trans. Knowledge and Data Engineering*, 21(7):999–1013, 2009.

H. Chen, B. Jiang, and X. Yao. Semisupervised negative correlation learning. *IEEE Trans. Neural Networks and Learning Systems*, 29(11):5366–5379, 2018b.

J. Chen, S. Sathe, C. C. Aggarwal, and D. S. Turaga. Outlier detection with autoencoder ensembles. In *Proceedings of the 17th SIAM International Conference on Data Mining*, pages 90–98, Houston, TX, 2017.

J. Chen, Y. Geng, Z. Chen, I. Horrocks, J. Z. Pan, and H. Chen. Knowledge-aware zero-shot learning: Survey and perspective. In *Proceedings of the 30th International Joint Conference on Artificial Intelligence*, pages 4366–4373, Virtual Event, 2021a.

K. Chen and S. Wang. Semi-supervised learning via regularized boosting working on multiple semi-supervised assumptions. *IEEE Trans. Pattern Analysis and Machine Intelligence*, 33(1):129–143, 2011.

T. Chen and C. Guestrin. XGBoost: A scalable tree boosting system. In *Proceedings of the 22nd ACM SIGKDD International Conference on Knowledge Discovery and Data Mining*, pages 785–794, San Francisco, CA, 2016.

X. Chen, C. Wang, Z. Zhou, and K. W. Ross. Randomized ensembled double Q-learning: Learning fast without a model. In *Proceedings of the 9th International Conference on Learning Representations*, Virtual Event, 2021b.

Y.-H. Chen, S.-H. Lyu, and Y. Jiang. Improving deep forest by exploiting high-order interactions. In *Proceedings of the 21st IEEE International Conference on Data Mining*, pages 1030–1035, Auckland, New Zealand, 2021c.

B. Clarke. Comparing Bayes model averaging and stacking when model approximation error cannot be ignored. *Journal of Machine Learning Research*, 4:683–712, 2003.

S. Clémençon and J. Jakubowicz. Scoring anomalies: A M-estimation formulation. In *Proceedings of the 16th International Conference on Artificial Intelligence and Statistics*, pages 659–667, Scottsdale, AZ, 2013.

A. L. V. Coelho, C. A. M. Lima, and F. J. V. Zuben. GA-based selection of components for heterogeneous ensembles of support vector machines. In *Proceedings of the Congress on Evolutionary Computation*, pages 2238–2245, Canbera, Australia, 2003.

J. Cohen. A coefficient of agreement for nominal scales. *Educational and Psychological Measurement*, 20(1):37–46, 1960.

T. H. Cormen, C. E. Leiserson, and R. L. Rivest, editors. *Introduction to Algorithms*. MIT Press, 1990.

I. Corona, G. Giacinto, C. Mazzariello, F. Roli, and C. Sansone. Information fusion for computer security: State of the art and open issues. *Information Fusion*, 10(4): 274–284, 2009.

C. Cortes and M. Mohri. AUC optimization vs. error rate minimization. In *Advances in Neural Information Processing Systems 16*, pages 313–320, Vancouver, Canada, 2004.

C. Cortes, M. Mohri, and U. Syed. Deep boosting. In *Proceedings of the 31st International Conference on Machine Learning*, pages 1179–1187, Beijing, China, 2014.

T. M. Cover and P. E. Hart. Nearest neighbor pattern classification. *IEEE Trans. Information Theory*, 13(1):21–27, 1967.

T. M. Cover and J. A. Thomas. *Elements of Information Theory.* Wiley, 1991.

M. Coyle and B. Smyth. On the use of selective ensembles for relevance classification in case-based web search. In *Proceedings of the 8th European Conference on Case-Based Reasoning*, pages 370–384, Fethiye, Turkey, 2006.

F. G. Cozman and I. Cohen. Unlabeled data can degrade classification performance of generative classifiers. In *Proceedings of the 15th International Florida Artificial Intelligence Research Society Conference*, pages 327–331, Pensacola, FL, 2002.

K. Crammer and Y. Singer. On the learnability and design of output codes for multiclass problems. *Machine Learning*, 47(2-3):201–233, 2002.

N. Cristianini and J. Shawe-Taylor. *An Introduction to Support Vector Machines and Other Kernel-Based Learning Methods.* Cambridge University Press, 2000.

P. Cunningham and J. Carney. Diversity versus quality in classification ensembles based on feature selection. Technical Report TCD-CS-2000-02, Department of Computer Science, Trinity College Dublin, Dublin, Ireland, 2000.

A. Cutler and G. Zhao. PERT - perfect random tree ensembles. In *Proceedings of the 33rd Symposium on the Interface of Computing Science and Statistics*, pages 490–497, Costa Mesa, CA, 2001.

Q. Da, Y. Yu, and Z.-H. Zhou. Learning with augmented class by exploiting unlabeled data. In *Proceedings of the 28th AAAI Conference on Artificial Intelligence*, pages 1760–1766, Québec, Canada, 2014.

I. Dagan and S. P. Engelson. Committee-based sampling for training probabilistic classifiers. In *Proceedings of the 12th International Conference on Machine Learning*, pages 150–157, San Francisco, CA, 1995.

F. d'Alché-Buc, Y. Grandvalet, and C. Ambroise. Semi-supervised MarginBoost. In *Advances in Neural Information Processing Systems 14*, pages 553–560, Vancouver, Canada, 2001.

M. Darnstädt, H. U. Simon, and B. Szörényi. Supervised learning and co-training. *Theoretical Computer Science*, 519:68–87, 2014.

S. Das, W.-K. Wong, T. G. Dietterich, A. Fern, and A. Emmott. Incorporating expert feedback into active anomaly discovery. In *Proceedings of the 16th IEEE International Conference on Data Mining*, pages 853–858, Barcelona, Spain, 2016.

S. Das, W.-K. Wong, A. Fern, T. G. Dietterich, and M. A. Siddiqui. Incorporating feedback into tree-based anomaly detection. In *Proceedings of the ACM SIGKDD Workshop on Interactive Data Exploration and Analytics*, pages 25–34, Nova Scotia, Canada, 2017.

B. V. Dasarathy. *Nearest Neighbor (NN) Norms: NN Pattern Classification Techniques.* IEEE Computer Society Press, 1991.

S. Dasgupta and D. Hsu. Hierarchical sampling for active learning. In *Proceedings of the 25th International Conference on Machine Learning*, pages 208–215, Helsinki, Finland, 2008.

I. Davidson. An ensemble technique for stable learners with performance bounds. In *Proceedings of the 19th National Conference on Artificial Intelligence*, pages 330–335, San Jose, CA, 2004.

J. Davis and M. Goadrich. The relationship between Precision-Recall and ROC curves. In *Proceedings of the 23rd International Conference on Machine Learning*, pages 233–240, Pittsburgh, PA, 2006.

W. H. E. Day and H. Edelsbrunner. Efficient algorithms for agglomerative hierarchical clustering methods. *Journal of Classification*, 1(1):7–24, 1984.

N. C. de Concorcet. *Essai sur l'Application de l'Analyze à la Probabilité des Décisions Rendues à la Pluralité des Voix.* Imprimérie Royale, Paris, France, 1785.

A. Demiriz, K. P. Bennett, and J. Shawe-Taylor. Linear programming boosting via column generation. *Machine Learning*, 46(1-3):225–254, 2002.

A. P. Dempster. Upper and lower probabilities induced by a multivalued mapping. *Annals of Mathematical Statistics*, 38(2):325–339, 1967.

A. P. Dempster, N. M. Laird, and D. B. Rubin. Maximum likelihood from incomplete data via the EM algorithm. *Journal of the Royal Statistical Society, Series B*, 39 (1):1–22, 1977.

J. Demšar. Statistical comparisons of classifiers over multiple data sets. *Journal of Machine Learning Research*, 7:1–30, 2006.

L. Deng and J. Platt. Ensemble deep learning for speech recognition. In *Proceedings of the 15th Annual Conference of the International Speech Communication Association*, pages 231–238, Singapore, 2014.

M. Denil, D. Matheson, and N. De Freitas. Narrowing the gap: Random forests in theory and in practice. In *Proceedings of the 31st International Conference on Machine Learning*, pages 665–673, Beijing, China, 2014.

G. DeSalvo, M. Mohri, and U. Syed. Learning with deep cascades. In *Proceedings of the 26th International Conference on Algorithmic Learning Theory*, pages 254–269, Banff, Canada, 2015.

J. Devlin, M.-W. Chang, K. Lee, and K. Toutanova. BERT: Pre-training of deep bidirectional transformers for language understanding. In *Proceedings of the 2019 Conference of the North American Chapter of the Association for Computational Linguistics: Human Language Technologies*, pages 4171–4186, Minneapolis, MN, 2019.

I. Diakonikolas, R. Impagliazzo, D. M. Kane, R. Lei, J. Sorrell, and C. Tzamos. Boosting in the presence of Massart noise. In *Proceedings of the 34th Annual Conference on Learning Theory*, pages 1585–1644, Boulder, CO, 2021.

L. Didaci, G. Giacinto, F. Roli, and G. L. Marcialis. A study on the performances of dynamic classifier selection based on local accuracy estimation. *Pattern Recognition*, 38(11):2188–2191, 2005.

T. G. Dietterich. Approximate statistical tests for comparing supervised classification learning algorithms. *Neural Computation*, 10(7):1895–1923, 1998.

T. G. Dietterich. Ensemble methods in machine learning. In *Proceedings of the 1st International Workshop on Multiple Classifier Systems*, pages 1–15, Sardinia, Italy, 2000a.

T. G. Dietterich. An experimental comparison of three methods for constructing ensembles of decision trees: Bagging, boosting, and randomization. *Machine Learning*, 40(2):139–157, 2000b.

T. G. Dietterich and G. Bakiri. Solving multiclass learning problems via error-correcting output codes. *Journal of Artificial Intelligence Research*, 2:263–286, 1995.

T. G. Dietterich, R. H. Lathrop, and T. Lozano-Pérez. Solving the multiple-instance problem with axis-parallel rectangles. *Artificial Intelligence*, 89(1-2):31–71, 1997.

T. G. Dietterich, G. Hao, and A. Ashenfelter. Gradient tree boosting for training conditional random fields. *Journal of Machine Learning Research*, 9:2113–2139, 2008.

Y.-X. Ding and Z.-H. Zhou. Boosting-based reliable model reuse. In *Proceedings of The 12th Asian Conference on Machine Learning*, pages 145–160, Bangkok, Thailand, 2020.

C. Domingo and O. Watanabe. MadaBoost: A modification of AdaBoost. In *Proceedings of the 13th Annual Conference on Computational Learning Theory*, pages 180–189, Palo Alto, CA, 2000.

P. Domingos. Knowledge discovery via multiple models. *Intelligent Data Analysis*, 2 (1-4):187–202, 1998.

P. Domingos. MetaCost: A general method for making classifiers cost-sensitive. In *Proceedings of the 5th ACM SIGKDD International Conference on Knowledge Discovery and Data Mining*, pages 155–164, San Diego, CA, 1999.

P. Domingos and M. Pazzani. On the optimality of the simple Bayesian classifier under zero-one loss. *Machine Learning*, 29(2-3):103–130, 1997.

A. V. Dorogush, V. Ershov, and A. Gulin. CatBoost: Gradient boosting with categorical features support. arXiv:1810.11363, 2018.

A. Dosovitskiy, L. Beyer, A. Kolesnikov, D. Weissenborn, X. Zhai, T. Unterthiner, M. Dehghani, M. Minderer, G. Heigold, S. Gelly, J. Uszkoreit, and N. Houlsby. An image is worth 16x16 words: Transformers for image recognition at scale. In *Proceedings of the 9th International Conference on Learning Representations*, Virtual Event, 2021.

F. Draxler, K. Veschgini, M. Salmhofer, and F. Hamprecht. Essentially no barriers in neural network energy landscape. In *Proceedings of the 35th International Conference on Machine Learning*, pages 1308–1317, Stockholm, Sweden, 2018.

C. Drummond and R. C. Holte. Exploiting the cost of (in)sensitivity of decision tree splitting criteria. In *Proceedings of the 17th International Conference on Machine Learning*, pages 239–246, San Francisco, CA, 2000.

C. Drummond and R. C. Holte. Cost curves: An improved method for visualizing classifier performance. *Machine Learning*, 65(1):95–130, 2006.

R. O. Duda, P. E. Hart, and D. G. Stork. *Pattern Classification.* Wiley, 2nd edition, 2000.

B. Durrant and N. Lim. A diversity-aware model for majority vote ensemble accuracy. In *Proceedings of the 23rd International Conference on Artificial Intelligence and Statistics*, pages 4078–4087, Palermo, Italy, 2020.

R. Durrant and A. Kabán. Sharp generalization error bounds for randomly-projected classifiers. In *Proceedings of the 30th International Conference on Machine Learning*, pages 693–701, Atlanta, GA, 2013.

N. Dvornik, J. Mairal, and C. Schmid. Diversity with cooperation: Ensemble methods for few-shot classification. In *Proceedings of the 17th IEEE/CVF International Conference on Computer Vision*, pages 3722–3730. Seoul, Korea, 2019.

B. Efron and R. Tibshirani. *An Introduction to the Bootstrap.* Chapman & Hall, 1993.

D. Eigen, M. Ranzato, and I. Sutskever. Learning factored representations in a deep mixture of experts. In *Proceeding of the 2nd International Conference on Learning Representations*, Banff, Canada, 2014.

J. Elith, J. R. Leathwick, and T. Hastie. A working guide to boosted regression trees. *Journal of Animal Ecology*, 77(4):802–813, 2008.

C. Elkan. The foundations of cost-senstive learning. In *Proceedings of the 17th International Joint Conference on Artificial Intelligence*, pages 973–978, Seattle, WA, 2001.

R. Elwell and R. Polikar. Incremental learning of concept drift in nonstationary environments. *IEEE Trans. Neural Networks*, 22(10):1517–1531, 2011.

S. Escalera, O. Pujol, and P. Radeva. Boosted landmarks of contextual descriptors and Forest-ECOC: A novel framework to detect and classify objects in clutter scenes. *Pattern Recognition Letters*, 28(13):1759–1768, 2007.

S. Escalera, O. Pujol, and P. Radeva. Error-correcting ouput codes library. *Journal of Machine Learning Research*, 11:661–664, 2010a.

S. Escalera, O. Pujol, and P. Radeva. On the decoding process in ternary error-correcting output codes. *IEEE Trans. Pattern Analysis and Machine Intelligence*, 32(1):120–134, 2010b.

E. Eskin. Anomaly detection over noisy data using learned probability distributions. In *Proceedings of the 17th International Conference on Machine Learning*, pages 255–262, Stanford, CA, 2000.

E. Eskin, A. Arnold, M. Prerau, L. Portnoy, and S. Stolfo. A geometric framework for unsupervised anomaly detection. In D. Barbará and S. Jajodia, editors, *Applications of Data Mining in Computer Security*, pages 77–101. Springer, 2002.

A. Estabrooks, T. Jo, and N. Japkowicz. A multiple resampling method for learning from imbalanced data sets. *Computational Intelligence*, 20(1):18–36, 2004.

M. Ester, H.-P. Kriegel, J. Sander, and X. Xu. A density-based algorithm for discovering clusters in large spatial databases with noise. In *Proceedings of the 2nd International Conference on Knowledge Discovery and Data Mining*, pages 226–231, Portland, OR, 1996.

V. Estivill-Castro. Why so many clustering algorithms - A position paper. *SIGKDD Explorations*, 4(1):65–75, 2002.

W. Fan. On the optimality of probability estimation by random decision trees. In *Proceedings of the 19th National Conference on Artificial Intelligence*, pages 336–341, San Jose, CA, 2004.

W. Fan, S. J. Stolfo, J. Zhang, and P. K. Chan. AdaCost: Misclassification cost-sensitive boosting. In *Proceedings of the 16th International Conference on Machine Learning*, pages 97–105, Bled, Slovenia, 1999.

W. Fan, F. Chu, H. Wang, and P. S. Yu. Pruning and dynamic scheduling of cost-sensitive ensembles. In *Proceedings of the 18th National Conference on Artificial intelligence*, pages 146–151, Edmonton, Canada, 2002.

W. Fan, H. Wang, P. S. Yu, and S. Ma. Is random model better? On its accuracy and efficiency. In *Proceedings of the 3rd IEEE International Conference on Data Mining*, pages 51–58, Melbourne, FL, 2003.

R. Fano. *Transmission of Information: Statistical Theory of Communications.* MIT Press, 1961.

T. Fawcett. ROC graphs with instance varying costs. *Pattern Recognition Letters*, 27(8):882–891, 2006.

J. Feng and Z.-H. Zhou. Deep MIML network. In *Proceedings of the 31st AAAI Conference on Artificial Intelligence*, pages 1884–1890, San Francisco, CA, 2017.

J. Feng and Z.-H. Zhou. Autoencoder by forest. In *Proceedings of the 32nd AAAI Conference on Artificial Intelligence*, pages 2967–2973, New Orleans, LO, 2018.

J. Feng, Y. Yu, and Z.-H. Zhou. Multi-layered gradient boosting decision trees. In *Advances in Neural Information Processing Systems 31*, pages 3555–3565, Montréal, Canada, 2018.

X. Z. Fern and C. E. Brodley. Random projection for high dimensional data clustering: A cluster ensemble approach. In *Proceedings of the 20th Internaiontal Conference on Machine Learning*, pages 186–193, Washington, DC, 2003.

X. Z. Fern and C. E. Brodley. Solving cluster ensemble problems by bipartite graph partitioning. In *Proceedings of the 21st International Conference on Machine Learning*, page 36, Alberta, Canada, 2004.

X. Z. Fern and W. Lin. Cluster ensemble selection. In *Proceedings of the 8th SIAM International Conference on Data Mining*, pages 787–797, Atlanta, GA, 2008.

A. Fernández, V. López, M. Galar, M. José del Jesus, and F. Herrera. Analysing the classification of imbalanced data-sets with multiple classes: Binarization techniques and ad-hoc approaches. *Knowledge-Based Systems*, 42:97–110, 2013.

M. Fernández-Delgado, E. Cernadas, S. Barro, and D. Amorim. Do we need hundreds of classifiers to solve real world classification problems? *Journal of Machine Learning Research*, 15:3133–3181, 2014.

C. Ferri, J. Hernández-Orallo, and M. J. Ramírez-Quintana. From ensemble methods to comprehensible models. In *Proceedings of the 5th International Conference on Discovery Science*, pages 165–177, Lübeck, Germany, 2002.

D. Fisher. Improving inference through conceptual clustering. In *Proceedings of the 6th National Conference on Artificial Intelligence*, pages 461–465, Seattle, WA, 1987.

R. A. Fisher. The use of multiple measurements in taxonomic problems. *Annals of Eugenics*, 7(2):179–188, 1936.

J. L. Fleiss. *Statistical Methods for Rates and Proportions.* John Wiley & Sons, 2nd edition, 1981.

J. Foulds and E. Frank. A review of multi-instance learning assumptions. *Knowledge Engineering Review*, 25(1):1–25, 2010.

A. Fred and A. K. Jain. Data clustering using evidence accumulation. In *Proceedings of the 16th International Conference on Pattern Recognition*, pages 276–280, Quebec, Canada, 2002.

A. Fred and A. K. Jain. Combining multiple clusterings using evidence accumulation. *IEEE Trans. Pattern Analysis and Machine Intelligence*, 27(6):835–850, 2005.

J. H. Freidman and W. Stuetzle. Projection pursuit regression. *Journal of American Statistical Association*, 76(376):817–823, 1981.

Y. Freund. Boosting a weak learning algorithm by majority. *Information and Computation*, 121(2):256–285, 1995.

Y. Freund. An adaptive version of the boost by majority algorithm. *Machine Learning*, 43(3):293–318, 2001.

Y. Freund. A more robust boosting algorithm. arXiv:0905.2138, 2009.

Y. Freund and R. E. Schapire. A decision-theoretic generalization of on-line learning and an application to boosting. In *Proceedings of the 2nd European Conference on Computational Learning Theory*, pages 23–37, Barcelona, Spain, 1995.

Y. Freund and R. E. Schapire. A decision-theoretic generalization of on-line learning and an application to boosting. *Journal of Computer and System Sciences*, 55(1): 119–139, 1997.

Y. Freund, H. S. Seung, E. Shamir, and N. Tishby. Selective sampling using the query by committee algorithm. *Machine Learning*, 28(2-3):133–168, 1997.

J. Friedman and J. Meulman. Multiple additive regression trees with application in epidemiology. *Statistics in Medicine*, 22:1365–1381, 2003.

J. Friedman, T. Hastie, and R. Tibshirani. Additive logistic regression: A statistical view of boosting (with discussions). *Annals of Statistics*, 28(2):337–407, 2000.

J. Friedman, T. Hastie, and R. Tibshirani. Regularization paths for generalized linear models via coordinate descent. *Journal of Statistical Software*, 33(1):1–22, 2010.

J. H. Friedman. Greedy function approximation: A gradient boosting machine. *Annals of Statistics*, 29(5):1189–1232, 2001.

J. H. Friedman. Stochastic gradient boosting. *Computational Statistics & Data Analysis*, 38(4):367–378, 2002.

J. H. Friedman and P. Hall. On bagging and nonlinear estimation. *Journal of Statistical Planning and Inference*, 137(3):669–683, 2007.

J. Frost. *Hypothesis Testing: An Intuitive Guide for Making Data Driven Decisions.* Statistics by Jim Publishing, State College, PA, 2020.

A. Fujino, N. Ueda, and K. Saito. A hybrid generative/discriminative approach to semi-supervised classifier design. In *Proceedings of the 20th National Conference on Artificial Intelligence*, pages 764–769, Pittsburgh, PA, 2005.

G. Fumera and F. Roli. A theoretical and experimental analysis of linear combiners for multiple classifier systems. *IEEE Trans. Pattern Analysis and Machine Intelligence*, 27(6):942–956, 2005.

G. Fumera, F. Roli, and G. Giacinto. Reject option with multiple thresholds. *Pattern Recognition*, 33(12):2099–2101, 2000.

J. Gama, I. Zliobaite, A. Bifet, M. Pechenizkiy, and A. Bouchachia. A survey on concept drift adaptation. *ACM Computing Surveys*, 46(4):44:1–44:37, 2014.

Y. Ganin and V. Lempitsky. Unsupervised domain adaptation by backpropagation. In *Proceedings of the 32nd International Conference on Machine Learning*, pages 1180–1189, Lille, France, 2015.

C. Gao, Y. Lu, and D. Zhou. Exact exponent in optimal rates for crowdsourcing. In *Proceedings of the 33rd International Conference on Machine Learning*, pages 603–611, New York, NY, 2016.

J. Gao and P.-N. Tan. Converting output scores from outlier detection algorithms to probability estimates. In *Proceedings of the 6th IEEE International Conference on Data Mining*, pages 212–221, Hong Kong, China, 2006.

W. Gao and Z.-H. Zhou. Approximation stability and boosting. In *Proceedings of the 21st International Conference on Algorithmic Learning Theory*, pages 59–73, Canberra, Australia, 2010a.

W. Gao and Z.-H. Zhou. The kth, median and average margin bounds for AdaBoost. arXiv:1009.3613, 2010b.

W. Gao and Z.-H. Zhou. On the doubt about margin explanation of boosting. *Artificial Intelligence*, 203:1–18, 2013.

W. Gao and Z.-H. Zhou. Dropout Rademacher complexity of deep neural networks. *Science China Information Sciences*, 59(7):072104:1–072104:12, 2016.

W. Gao, F. Xu, and Z.-H. Zhou. Towards convergence rate analysis of random forests for classification. *Artificial Intelligence*, 313:103788, 2022.

C. W. Gardiner. *Handbook of Stochastic Methods.* Springer, 3rd edition, 2004.

T. Garipov, P. Izmailov, D. Podoprikhin, D. P. Vetrov, and A. G. Wilson. Loss surfaces, mode connectivity, and fast ensembling of DNNs. In *Advances in Neural Information Processing Systems 31*, pages 8803–8812, Montréal, Canada, 2018.

Y. Geifman and R. El-Yaniv. SelectiveNet: A deep neural network with an integrated reject option. In *Proceedings of the 36th International Conference on Machine Learning*, pages 2151–2159, Long Beach, CA, 2019.

S. Geman, E. Bienenstock, and R. Doursat. Neural networks and the bias/variance dilemma. *Neural Computation*, 4(1):1–58, 1992.

C. Geng, S.-J. Huang, and S. Chen. Recent advances in open set recognition: A survey. *IEEE Trans. Pattern Analysis and Machine Intelligence*, 43(10):3614–3631, 2020.

P. Germain, A. Lacasse, F. Laviolette, M. March, and J.-F. Roy. Risk bounds for the majority vote: From a PAC-Bayesian analysis to a learning algorithm. *Journal of Machine Learning Research*, 16(26):787–860, 2015.

P. Geurts, D. Ernst, and L. Wehenkel. Extremely randomized trees. *Machine Learning*, 63(1):3–42, 2006.

B. Ghojogh and M. Crowley. The theory behind overfitting, cross validation, regularization, bagging, and boosting: tutorial. arXiv:1905.12787, 2019.

G. Giacinto and F. Roli. Adaptive selection of image classifiers. In *Proceedings of the 9th International Conference on Image Analysis and Processing*, pages 38–45, Florence, Italy, 1997.

G. Giacinto and F. Roli. A theoretical framework for dynamic classifier selection. In *Proceedings of the 15th International Conference on Pattern Recognition*, pages 2008–2011, Barcelona, Spain, 2000a.

G. Giacinto and F. Roli. Dynamic classifier selection. In *Proceedings of the 1st International Workshop on Multiple Classifier Systems*, pages 177–189, Cagliari, Italy, 2000b.

G. Giacinto and F. Roli. Design of effective neural network ensembles for image classification purposes. *Image and Vision Computing*, 19(9-10):699–707, 2001.

G. Giacinto, F. Roli, and G. Fumera. Design of effective multiple classifier systems by clustering of classifiers. In *Proceedings of the 15th International Conference on Pattern Recognition*, pages 160–163, Barcelona, Spain, 2000.

G. Giacinto, F. Roli, and L. Didaci. Fusion of multiple classifiers for intrusion detection in computer networks. *Pattern Recognition Letters*, 24(12):1795–1803, 2003.

G. Giacinto, R. Perdisci, M. D. Rio, and F. Roli. Intrusion detection in computer networks by a modular ensemble of one-class classifiers. *Information Fusion*, 9(1): 69–82, 2008.

C. Giraud-Carrier. A note on the utility of incremental learning. *AI Communications*, 13(4):215–223, 2000.

T. Gneiting and A. E. Raftery. Weather forecasting with ensemble methods. *Science*, 310(5746):248–249, 2005.

K. Goebel, M. Krok, and H. Sutherland. Diagnostic information fusion: Requirements flowdown and interface issues. In *Proceedings of the IEEE Aerospace Conference*, volume 6, pages 155–162, Big Sky, MT, 2000.

N. Goix, A. Sabourin, and S. Clémençon. On anomaly ranking and excess-mass curves. In *Proceedings of the 18th International Conference on Artificial Intelligence and Statistics*, pages 287–295, San Diego, CA, 2015.

N. Goix, N. Drougard, R. Brault, and M. Chiapino. One class splitting criteria for random forests. In *Proceedings of the 9th Asian Conference on Machine Learning*, pages 343–358, Seoul, Korea, 2017.

D. E. Goldberg. *Genetic Algorithm in Search, Optimization and Machine Learning.* Addison-Wesley, 1989.

H. M. Gomes, J. P. Barddal, F. Enembreck, and A. Bifet. A survey on ensemble learning for data stream classification. *ACM Computing Surveys*, 50(2):23:1–23:36, 2017.

I. Goodfellow, Y. Bengio, and A. Courville. *Deep Learning.* MIT Press, 2016.

D. M. Green and J. M. Swets. *Signal Detection Theory and Psychophysics.* John Wiley & Sons, 1966.

G. Grimmett and D. Stirzaker. *Probability and Random Processes.* Oxford University Press, 4th edition, 2020.

A. Grønlund, L. Kamma, K. Green Larsen, A. Mathiasen, and J. Nelson. Margin-based generalization lower bounds for boosted classifiers. In *Advances in Neural Information Processing Systems 32*, pages 11940–11949, Vancouver, Canada, 2019.

A. Grønlund, L. Kamma, and K. Green Larsen. Margins are insufficient for explaining gradient boosting. In *Advances in Neural Information Processing Systems 33*, pages 1902–1912, Virtual Event, 2020.

A. J. Grove and D. Schuurmans. Boosting in the limit: Maximizing the margin of learned ensembles. In *Proceedings of the 15th National Conference on Artificial Intelligence*, pages 692–699, Madison, WI, 1998.

S. Guha, R. Rastogi, and K. Shim. ROCK: A robust clustering algorithm for categorical attributes. In *Proceedings of the 15th International Conference on Data Engineering*, pages 512–521, Sydney, Australia, 1999.

H. Guo and H. Viktor. Learning from imbalanced data sets with boosting and data generation: The DataBoost-IM approach. *ACM SIGKDD Explorations*, 6(1):30–39, 2004.

Y. Guo and D. Schuurmans. Discriminative batch mode active learning. In *Advances in Neural Information Processing Systems 20*, pages 593–600, Vancouver, Canada, 2008.

I. Guyon and A. Elisseeff. An introduction to variable and feature selection. *Journal of Machine Learning Research*, 3:1157–1182, 2003.

S. T. Hadjitodorov and L. I. Kuncheva. Selecting diversifying heuristics for cluster ensembles. In *Proceedings of the 7th International Workshop on Multiple Classifier Systems*, pages 200–209, Prague, Czech, 2007.

S. T. Hadjitodorov, L. I. Kuncheva, and L. P. Todorova. Moderate diversity for better cluster ensembles. *Information Fusion*, 7(3):264–275, 2006.

M. Halkidi, Y. Batistakis, and M. Vazirgiannis. On clustering validation techniques. *Journal of Intelligent Information Systems*, 17(2-3):107–145, 2001.

J. Han, J. Pei, and H. Tong. *Data Mining: Concepts and Techniques.* Morgan Kaufmann, 4th edition, 2022.

X. Han, X. Chen, and L.-P. Liu. GAN ensemble for anomaly detection. In *Proceedings of the 35th AAAI Conference on Artificial Intelligence*, pages 4090–4097, Virtual Event, 2021.

D. J. Hand and R. J. Till. A simple generalization of the area under the ROC curve to multiple classification problems. *Machine Learning*, 45(2):171–186, 2001.

D. J. Hand, H. Mannila, and P. Smyth. *Principles of Data Mining.* MIT Press, 2001.

J. A. Hanley and B. J. McNeil. A method of comparing the areas under receiver operating characteristic curves derived from the same cases. *Radiology*, 148(3): 839–843, 1983.

L. K. Hansen and P. Salamon. Neural network ensembles. *IEEE Trans. Pattern Analysis and Machine Intelligence*, 12(10):993–1001, 1990.

D. R. Hardoon, S. Szedmak, and J. Shawe-Taylor. Canonical correlation analysis: An overview with application to learning methods. *Neural Computation*, 16(12): 2639–2664, 2004.

S. Hariri, M. C. Kind, and R. J. Brunner. Extended isolation forest. *IEEE Trans. Knowledge and Data Engineering*, 33(4):1479–1489, 2021.

M. Harries. Boosting a strong learner: Evidence against the minimum margin. In *Proceedings of the 16th International Conference on Machine Learning*, pages 171–179, Bled, Slovenia, 1999.

T. Hastie and R. Tibshirani. Classification by pairwise coupling. *Annals of Statistics*, 26(2):451–471, 1998.

T. Hastie, R. Tibshirani, and J. Friedman. *Elements of Statistical Learning.* Springer, 2nd edition, 2016.

V. Hautamaki, I. Karkkainen, and P. Franti. Outlier detection using k-nearest neighbour graph. In *Proceedings of the 17th International Conference on Pattern Recognition*, pages 430–433, Cambridge, UK, 2004.

S. Haykin. *Neural Networks: A Comprehensive Foundation.* Prentice-Hall, 2nd edition, 1998.

E. Hazan. Introduction to online convex optimization. *Foundations and Trends in Optimization*, 2(3-4):157–325, 2016.

H. He and E. Garcia. Learning from imbalanced data. *IEEE Trans. Knowledge and Data Engineering*, 21(9):1263–1284, 2009.

H. He, S. Chen, K. Li, and X. Xu. Incremental learning from stream data. *IEEE Trans. Neural Networks*, 22(12):1901–1914, 2011.

K. He, X. Zhang, S. Ren, and J. Sun. Deep residual learning for image recognition. In *Proceedings of the 29th IEEE Conference on Computer Vision and Pattern Recognition*, pages 770–778, Las Vegas, NV, 2016.

X. He, J. Pan, O. Jin, T. Xu, B. Liu, T. Xu, Y. Shi, A. Atallah, R. Herbrich, S. Bowers, and J. Q. Candela. Practical lessons from predicting clicks on ads at Facebook. In *Proceedings of the 8th International Workshop on Data Mining for Online Advertising*, pages 1–9, New York, NY, 2014.

Z. He, X. Xu, and S. Deng. A cluster ensemble method for clustering categorical data. *Information Fusion*, 6(2):143–151, 2005.

M. Hein and M. Maier. Manifold denoising. In *Advances in Neural Information Processing System 19*, pages 561–568, Vancouver, Canda, 2006.

J. Heinrich, M. Lanctot, and D. Silver. Fictitious self-play in extensive-form games. In *Proceedings of the 32nd International Conference on Machine Learning*, pages 805–813, Lille, France, 2015.

M. Hellman and J. Raviv. Probability of error, equivocation, and the Chernoff bound. *IEEE Trans. Information Theory*, 16(4):368–372, 1970.

D. Hernández-Lobato, G. Martínez-Muñoz, and A. Suárez. Statistical instance-based pruning in ensembles of independent classifiers. *IEEE Trans. Pattern Analysis and Machine Intelligence*, 31(2):364–369, 2008.

D. Hernández-Lobato, G. Martínez-Muñoz, and A. Suárez. Empirical analysis and evaluation of approximate techniques for pruning regression bagging ensembles. *Neurocomputing*, 74(12-13):2250–2264, 2011.

A. Hinneburg and D. A. Keim. An efficient approach to clustering in large multimedia databases with noise. In *Proceedings of the 4th International Conference on Knowledge Discovery and Data Mining*, pages 58–65, New York, NY, 1998.

G. Hinton, O. Vinyals, and J. Dean. Distilling the knowledge in a neural network. arXiv:1503.02531, 2015.

G. E. Hinton and M. A. Ranzato. Modeling pixel means and covariances using factorized third-order Boltzmann machines. In *Proceedings of the 23rd IEEE Conference on Computer Vision and Pattern Recognition*, pages 2551–2558, San Francisco, CA, 2010.

G. E. Hinton and R. Salakhutdinov. Reducing the dimensionality of data with neural networks. *Science*, 313(5786):504–507, 2006.

G. E. Hinton, J. L. McClelland, and D. E. Rumelhart. Distributed representations. In M. A. Boden, editor, *Parallel Distributed Processing: Explorations in the Microstructure of Cognition*, pages 77–109. MIT Press, 1986.

G. E. Hinton, S. Osindero, and Y.-W. Simon. A fast learning algorithm for deep belief nets. *Neural Computation*, 18(7):1527–1554, 2006.

G. E. Hinton, N. Srivastava, A. Krizhevsky, I. Sutskever, and R. R. Salakhutdinov. Improving neural networks by preventing co-adaptation of feature detectors. *arXiv:1207.0580*, 2012.

T. K. Ho. Random decision forests. In *Proceedings of the 3rd International Conference on Document Analysis and Recognition*, pages 278–282, Montréal, Canada, 1995.

T. K. Ho. The random subspace method for constructing decision forests. *IEEE Trans. Pattern Analysis and Machine Intelligence*, 20(8):832–844, 1998.

T. K. Ho, J. J. Hull, and S. N. Srihari. Decision combination in multiple classifier systems. *IEEE Trans. Pattern Analysis and Machine Intelligence*, 16(1):66–75, 1994.

V. Hodge and J. Austin. A survey of outlier detection methodologies. *Artificial Intelligence Review*, 22(2):85–126, 2004.

T. R. Hoens, Q. Qian, N. Chawla, and Z.-H. Zhou. Building decision trees for the multi-class imbalance problem. In *Proceedings of the 16th Pacific-Asia Conference on Knowledge Discovery and Data Mining*, pages 122–134, Kuala Lumpur, Malaysia, 2012.

S. C. H. Hoi, R. Jin, J. Zhu, and M. R. Lyu. Semisupervised SVM batch mode active learning with applications to image retrieval. *ACM Trans. Information Systems*, 27(3):1–29, 2009.

Y. Hong, S. Kwong, H. Wang, and Q. Ren. Resampling-based selective clustering ensembles. *Pattern Recognition Letters*, 30(3):298–305, 2009.

P. Hore, L. Hall, and D. Goldgof. A cluster ensemble framework for large data sets. In *Proceedings of the 19th IEEE International Conference on Systems, Man and Cybernetics*, pages 3342–3347, Taipei, 2006.

P. Hore, L. O. Hall, and D. B. Goldgof. A scalable framework for cluster ensembles. *Pattern Recognition*, 42(5):676–688, 2009.

D. W. Hosmer, S. Lemesbow, and R. X. Sturdivant. *Applied Logistic Regression*. Wiley, 3rd edition, 2013.

H. Hotelling. Relations between two sets of variates. *Biometrika*, 28(3-4):321–377, 1936.

B.-J. Hou, L. Zhang, and Z.-H. Zhou. Learning with feature evolvable streams. In *Advances in Neural Information Processing Systems 30*, pages 1417–1427, Long Beach, CA, 2017.

C. Hou and Z.-H. Zhou. One-pass learning with incremental and decremental features. *IEEE Trans. Pattern Analysis and Machine Intelligence*, 40(11):2776–2792, 2018.

A. G. Howard, M. Zhu, B. Chen, D. Kalenichenko, W. Wang, T. Weyand, M. Andreetto, and H. Adam. MobileNets: Efficient convolutional neural networks for mobile vision applications. arXiv:1704.04861, 2017.

C.-W. Hsu and C.-J. Lin. A comparison of methods for multi-class support vector machines. *IEEE Trans. Neural Networks*, 13(2):415–425, 2002.

X. Hu, E. K. Park, and X. Zhang. Microarray gene cluster identification and annotation through cluster ensemble and EM-based informative textual summarization. *IEEE Trans. Information Technology in Biomedicine*, 13(5):832–840, 2009.

F.-J. Huang, Z.-H. Zhou, H.-J. Zhang, and T. Chen. Pose invariant face recognition. In *Proceedings of the 4th IEEE International Conference on Automatic Face and Gesture Recognition*, pages 245–250, Grenoble, France, 2000.

G. Huang, Y. Li, G. Pleiss, Z. Liu, J. E. Hopcroft, and K. Q. Weinberger. Snapshot ensembles: Train 1, get M for free. In *Proceedings of the 5th International Conference on Learning Representations*, Toulon, France, 2017a.

S.-J. Huang, Y. Yu, and Z.-H. Zhou. Multi-label hypothesis reuse. In *Proceedings of the 18th ACM SIGKDD International Conference on Knowledge Discovery and Data Mining*, pages 525–533, Beijing, China, 2012.

S.-J. Huang, R. Jin, and Z.-H. Zhou. Active learning by querying informative and representative examples. *IEEE Trans. Pattern Analysis and Machine Intelligence*, 36(10):1936–1949, 2014.

S.-J. Huang, J.-L. Chen, X. Mu, and Z.-H. Zhou. Cost-effective active learning from diverse labelers. In *Proceedings of the 26th International Joint Conference on Artificial Intelligence*, pages 1879–1885, Melbourne, Australia, 2017b.

Y. S. Huang and C. Y. Suen. A method of combining multiple experts for the recognition of unconstrained handwritten numerals. *IEEE Trans. Pattern Analysis and Machine Intelligence*, 17(1):90–94, 1995.

Z. Huang. Extensions to the k-means algorithm for clustering large data sets with categorical values. *Data Mining and Knowledge Discovery*, 2(3):283–304, 1998.

R. A. Hutchinson, L.-P. Liu, and T. G. Dietterich. Incorporating boosted regression trees into ecological latent variable models. In *Proceedings of the 25th AAAI Conference on Artificial Intelligence*, pages 1343–1348, San Francisco, CA, 2011.

F. Idrees, M. Rajarajan, M. Conti, T. M. Chen, and Y. Rahulamathavan. PIndroid: A novel Android malware detection system using ensemble learning methods. *Computers & Security*, 68:36–46, 2017.

R. A. Jacobs, M. I. Jordan, S. J. Nowlan, and G. E. Hinton. Adaptive mixtures of local experts. *Neural Computation*, 3(1):79–87, 1991.

A. K. Jain and R. C. Dubes. *Algorithms for Clustering Data.* Prentice Hall, 1988.

A. K. Jain, M. N. Murty, and P. J. Flynn. Data clustering: A review. *ACM Computing Surveys*, 31(3):264–323, 1999.

G. M. James. Variance and bias for general loss functions. *Machine Learning*, 51(2): 115–135, 2003.

Y. Jia and C. Zhang. Instance-level semisupervised multiple instance learning. In *Proceedings of the 23rd AAAI Conference on Artificial Intelligence*, pages 640–645, Chicago, IL, 2008.

X. Jiao, Y. Yin, L. Shang, X. Jiang, X. Chen, L. Li, F. Wang, and Q. Liu. Tinybert: Distilling BERT for natural language understanding. In *Findings of the Association for Computational Linguistics: EMNLP 2020*, pages 4163–4174, Virtual event, 2020.

T. Joachims. Transductive inference for text classification using support vector machines. In *Proceedings of the 16th International Conference on Machine Learning*, pages 200–209, Bled, Slovenia, 1999.

I. T. Jolliffe. *Principal Component Analysis.* Springer, 2nd edition, 2002.

M. I. Jordan and R. A. Jacobs. Hierarchies of adaptive experts. In *Advances in Neural Information Processing Systems 4*, pages 985–992, Denver, CO, 1991.

M. I. Jordan and L. Xu. Convergence results for the EM approach to mixtures of experts architectures. *Neural Networks*, 8(9):1409–1431, 1995.

P. Karczmarek, A. Kiersztyn, W. Pedrycz, and E. Al. K-Means-based isolation forest. *Knowledge-Based Systems*, 195:105659, 2020.

P. Karczmarek, A. Kiersztyn, W. Pedrycz, and D. Czerwiński. Fuzzy C-Means-based isolation forest. *Applied Soft Computing*, 106:107354, 2021.

G. Karypis and V. Kumar. A fast and high quality multilevel scheme for partitioning irregular graphs. *SIAM Journal on Scientific Computing*, 20(1):359–392, 1998.

G. Karypis, R. Aggarwal, V. Kumar, and S. Shekhar. Multilevel hypergraph partitioning: Application in VLSI domain. In *Proceedings of the 34th Annual Design Automation Conference*, pages 526–529, Anaheim, CA, 1997.

L. Kaufman and P. J. Rousseeuw, editors. *Finding Groups in Data: An Introduction to Cluster Analysis.* John Wiley & Sons, 1990.

V. Kazemi and J. Sullivan. One millisecond face alignment with an ensemble of regression trees. In *Proceedings of the IEEE Conference on Computer Vision and Pattern Recognition*, Columbus, OH, 2014.

G. Ke, Q. Meng, T. Finley, T. Wang, W. Chen, W. Ma, Q. Ye, and T.-Y. Liu. LightGBM: A highly efficient gradient boosting decision tree. In *Advances in Neural Information Processing Systems 30*, pages 3149–3157, Long Beach, CA, 2017.

M. Kearns. Efficient noise tolerant learning from statistical queries. *Journal of the ACM*, 45(6):983–1006, 1998.

M. Kearns and L. Valiant. Cryptographic limitations on learning boolean formulae and finite automata. In *Proceedings of the 21st Annual ACM Symposium on Theory of Computing*, pages 433–444, Seattle, WA, 1989.

M. J. Kearns and U. Vazirani. *An Introduction to Computational Learning Theory*. MIT Press, 1994.

S. Kee, E. Del Castillo, and G. Runger. Query-by-committee improvement with diversity and density in batch active learning. *Information Sciences*, 454:401–418, 2018.

F. Keller, E. Müller, and K. Böhm. HiCS: High contrast subspaces for density-based outlier ranking. In *Proceedings of the 28th IEEE International Conference on Data Engineering*, pages 1037–1048, Washington, DC, 2012.

D. J. Ketchen Jr and C. L. Shook. The application of cluster analysis in strategic management reserach: An analysis and critique. *Strategic Management Journal*, 17(6):441–458, 1996.

T. Kieu, B. Yang, C. Guo, and C. S. Jensen. Outlier detection for time series with recurrent autoencoder ensembles. In *Proceedings of the 28th International Joint Conference on Artificial Intelligence*, pages 2725–2732, Macao, China, 2019.

J. Kittler and F. M. Alkoot. Sum versus vote fusion in multiple classifier systems. *IEEE Trans. Pattern Analysis and Machine Intelligence*, 25(1):110–115, 2003.

J. Kittler, M. Hatef, R. Duin, and J. Matas. On combining classifiers. *IEEE Trans. Pattern Analysis and Machine Intelligence*, 20(3):226–239, 1998.

D. Klein, S. D. Kamvar, and C. Manning. From instance-level constraints to space-level constraints: Making the most of prior knowledge in data clustering. In *Proceedings of the 19th International Conference on Machine Learning*, pages 307–314, Sydney, Australia, 2002.

J. Klusowski and P. Tian. Large scale prediction with decision trees. *Journal of the American Statistical Association*, 119:525–537, 2024.

D. E. Knuth. *The Art of Computer Programming, Volume 3: Sorting and Searching*. Addison-Wesley, 2nd edition, 1997.

A. H. Ko, R. Sabourin, and J. A. S. Britto. From dynamic classifier selection to dynamic ensemble selection. *Pattern Recognition*, 41(5):1718–1731, 2008.

R. Kohavi and D. H. Wolpert. Bias plus variance decomposition for zero-one loss functions. In *Proceeding of the 13th International Conference on Machine Learning*, pages 275–283, Bari, Italy, 1996.

T. Kohonen. *Self-Organization and Associative Memory*. Springer, 1989.

J. F. Kolen and J. B. Pollack. Back propagation is sensitive to initial conditions. In *Advances in Neural Information Processing Systems 3*, pages 860–867, Denver, CO, 1990.

J. Z. Kolter and M. A. Maloof. Dynamic weighted majority: A new ensemble method for tracking concept drift. In *Proceedings of the 3rd IEEE International Conference on Data Mining*, pages 123–130, Melbourne, FL, 2003.

J. Z. Kolter and M. A. Maloof. Using additive expert ensembles to cope with concept drift. In *Proceedings of the 22nd International Conference on Machine Learning*, pages 449–456, Bonn, Germany, 2005.

J. Z. Kolter and M. A. Maloof. Learning to detect and classify malicious executables in the wild. *Journal of Machine Learning Research*, 7:2721–2744, 2006.

J. Z. Kolter and M. A. Maloof. Dynamic weighted majority: An ensemble method for drifting concepts. *Journal of Machine Learning Research*, 8:2755–2790, 2007.

D. Kondratyuk, M. Tan, M. Brown, and B. Gong. When ensembling smaller models is more efficient than single large models. arXiv:2005.00570, 2020.

E. B. Kong and T. G. Dietterich. Error-correcting output coding corrects bias and variance. In *Proceedings of the 12th International Conference on Machine Learning*, pages 313–321, Tahoe City, CA, 1995.

Y. Kong and T. Yu. A deep neural network model using random forest to extract feature representation for gene expression data classification. *Scientific Reports*, 8: 16477, 2018.

P. Kontschieder, M. Fiterau, A. Criminisi, and S. R. Bulò. Deep neural decision forests. In *Proceedings of the 15th IEEE International Conference on Computer Vision*, pages 1467–1475, Santiago, Chile, 2015.

H.-P. Kriegel, P. Kröger, E. Schubert, and A. Zimek. Interpreting and unifying outlier scores. In *Proceedings of the 11th SIAM International Conference on Data Mining*, pages 13–24, Mesa, AZ, 2011.

A. Krizhevsky, I. Sutskever, and G. E. Hinton. Imagenet classification with deep convolutional neural networks. In *Advances in Neural Information Processing Systems 25*, pages 1106–1114, Lake Tahoe, NV, 2012.

A. Krogh and J. Vedelsby. Neural network ensembles, cross validation, and active learning. In *Advances in Neural Information Processing Systems 7*, pages 231–238, Denver, CO, 1994.

M. Kubat and S. Matwin. Addressing the curse of imbalanced training sets: One sided selection. In *Proceedings of the 14th Intemational Conference on Machine Learning*, pages 179–186, Nashville, TN, 1997.

H. W. Kuhn. The Hungarian method for the assignment problem. *Naval Research Logistics Quarterly*, 2(1-2):83–89, 1955.

M. Kukar and I. Kononenko. Cost-sensitive learning with neural networks. In *Proceedings of the 13th European Conference on Artificial Intelligence*, pages 445–449, Brighton, UK, 1998.

A. Kumar, J. Fu, M. Soh, G. Tucker, and S. Levine. Stabilizing off-policy Q-learning via bootstrapping error reduction. In *Advances in Neural Information Processing Systems 32*, pages 11761–11771, Vancouver, Canada, 2019.

L. Kuncheva. Getting lost in the wealth of classifier ensembles? In *Proceedings of the 5th International Conference on Pattern Recognition Applications and Method*, page 7, Rome, Italy, 2016.

L. I. Kuncheva. A theoretical study on six classifier fusion strategies. *IEEE Trans. Pattern Analysis and Machine Intelligence*, 24(2):281–286, 2002.

L. I. Kuncheva. *Combining Pattern Classifiers: Methods and Algorithms.* John Wiley & Sons, 2004.

L. I. Kuncheva. Classifier ensembles: Facts, fiction, faults and future. In *Plenary Talk at the 19th International Conference on Pattern Recognition*, Tampa, Florida, 2008.

L. I. Kuncheva. *Combining Pattern Classifiers: Methods and Algorithms*. John Wiley & Sons, 2nd edition, 2014.

L. I. Kuncheva and S. T. Hadjitodorov. Using diversity in cluster ensembles. In *Proceedings of the 17th IEEE International Conference on Systems, Man and Cybernetics*, pages 1214–1219, Hague, Netherlands, 2004.

L. I. Kuncheva and D. P. Vetrov. Evaluation of stability of k-means cluster ensembles with respect to random initialization. *IEEE Trans. Pattern Analysis and Machine Intelligence*, 28(11):1798–1808, 2006.

L. I. Kuncheva and C. J. Whitaker. Measures of diversity in classifier ensembles and their relationship with the ensemble accuracy. *Machine Learning*, 51(2):181–207, 2003.

L. I. Kuncheva, J. C. Bezdek, and R. P. Duin. Decision templates for multiple classifier fusion: An experimental comparison. *Pattern Recognition*, 34(2):299–314, 2001.

L. I. Kuncheva, C. J. Whitaker, C. Shipp, and R. Duin. Limits on the majority vote accuracy in classifier fusion. *Pattern Analysis and Applications*, 6(1):22–31, 2003.

L. I. Kuncheva, S. T. Hadjitodorov, and L. P. Todorova. Experimental comparison of cluster ensemble methods. In *Proceedings of the 9th International Conference on Information Fusion*, pages 1–7, Florence, Italy, 2006.

S. Kutin and P. Niyogi. Almost-everywhere algorithmic stability and generalization error. In *Proceedings of the 18th Conference on Uncertainty in Artificial Intelligence*, pages 275–282, Edmonton, Canada, 2002.

S. W. Kwok and C. Carter. Multiple decision trees. In *Proceedings of the 4th International Conference on Uncertainty in Artificial Intelligence*, pages 327–338, Minneapolis, MN, 1988.

G. Kyriakides and K. G. Margaritis. *Hands-On Ensemble Learning with Python*. Packt Publishing, Birmingham, UK, 2019.

A. Lacasse, F. Laviolette, M. Marchand, P. Germain, and N. Usunier. PAC-Bayes bounds for the risk of the majority vote and the variance of the Gibbs classifier. In *Advances in Neural Information Processing Systems 19*, pages 769–776, Vancouver, Canada, 2006.

B. Lakshminarayanan, D. M. Roy, and Y. W. Teh. Mondrian forests: Efficient online random forests. In *Advances in Neural Information Processing Systems 27*, pages 3140–3148, Montréal, Canada, 2014.

B. Lakshminarayanan, A. Pritzel, and C. Blundell. Simple and scalable predictive uncertainty estimation using deep ensembles. In *Advances in Neural Information Processing Systems 30*, pages 6402–6413, Long Beach, CA, 2017.

L. Lam and S. Y. Suen. Application of majority voting to pattern recognition: An analysis of its behavior and performance. *IEEE Trans. Systems, Man and Cybernetics - Part A: Systems and Humans*, 27(5):553–568, 1997.

M. Lanctot, V. F. Zambaldi, A. Gruslys, A. Lazaridou, K. Tuyls, J. Pérolat, D. Silver, and T. Graepel. A unified game-theoretic approach to multiagent reinforcement learning. In *Advances in Neural Information Processing Systems 30*, pages 4190–4203, Long Beach, CA, 2017.

J. Langford and J. Shawe-Taylor. PAC-Bayes & margins. In *Advances in Neural Information Processing Systems 15*, pages 439–446, Vancouver, Canada, 2002.

A. Lazarevic and V. Kumar. Feature bagging for outlier detection. In *Proceedings of the 11th ACM SIGKDD Conference on Knowledge Discovery and Data Mining*, pages 157–166, Chicago, IL, 2005.

A. Lazarevic and Z. Obradovic. Effective pruning of neural network classifier ensembles. In *Proceedings of the 11th International Joint Conference on Neural Networks*, pages 796–801, Washington, DC, 2001.

Y. Lee, H. Yao, and C. Finn. Diversify and disambiguate: Out-of-distribution robustness via disagreement. In *Proceedings of the 10th International Conference on Learning Representations*, Virtual Event, 2022.

D. Lewis and W. Gale. A sequential algorithm for training text classifiers. In *Proceedings of the 17th Annual International ACM SIGIR Conference on Research and Development in Information Retrieval*, pages 3–12, Dublin, Ireland, 1994.

F. Li, Y. Qian, J. Wang, C. Dang, and L. Jing. Clustering ensemble based on sample's stability. *Artificial Intelligence*, 273:37–55, 2019.

M. Li and Z.-H. Zhou. Improve computer-aided diagnosis with machine learning techniques using undiagnosed samples. *IEEE Trans. Systems, Man and Cybernetics - Part A: Systems and Humans*, 37(6):1088–1098, 2007.

M. Li, W. Wang, and Z.-H. Zhou. Exploiting remote learners in Internet environment with agents. *Science China Information Sciences*, 53(1):64–76, 2010a.

N. Li and Z.-H. Zhou. Selective ensemble under regularization framework. In *Proceedings of the 8th International Workshop Multiple Classifier Systems*, pages 293–303, Reykjavik, Iceland, 2009.

N. Li, Y. Yu, and Z.-H. Zhou. Diversity regularized ensemble pruning. In *Proceedings of the 2012 European Conference on Machine Learning and Principles and Practice of Knowledge Discovery in Databases*, pages 330–345, Bristol, UK, 2012.

N. Li, I. W. Tsang, and Z.-H. Zhou. Efficient optimization of performance measures by classifier adaptation. *IEEE Trans. Pattern Analysis and Machine Intelligence*, 35(6):1370–1382, 2013a.

S. Z. Li, Q. Fu, L. Gu, B. Schölkopf, and H. J. Zhang. Kernel machine based learning for multi-view face detection and pose estimation. In *Proceedings of the 8th IEEE International Conference on Computer Vision*, pages 674–679, Vancouver, Canada, 2001.

W. Li, M. D. Zeiler, S. Zhang, Y. LeCun, and R. Fergus. Regularization of neural networks using DropConnect. In *Proceedings of the 30th International Conference on Machine Learning*, pages 1058–1066, Atlanta, GA, 2013b.

Y.-F. Li and Z.-H. Zhou. Towards making unlabeled data never hurt. *IEEE Trans. Pattern Analysis and Machine Intelligence*, 37(1):175–188, 2015.

Y.-F. Li, J. T. Kwok, and Z.-H. Zhou. Cost-sensitive semi-supervised support vector machine. In *Proceedings of the 24th AAAI Conference on Artificial Intelligence*, pages 500–505, Atlanta, GA, 2010b.

Y.-F. Li, I. W. Tsang, J. T. Kwok, and Z.-H. Zhou. Convex and scalable weakly labeled SVMs. *Journal of Machine Learning Research*, 14(7):2151–2188, 2013c.

R. Liere and P. Tadepalli. Active learning with committees for text categorization. In *Proceedings of the 14th National Conference on Artificial Intelligence*, pages 591–596, Providence, RI, 1997.

J. S. Lim. *Ensemble Learning of High Dimension Datasets.* PhD thesis, University of Waikato, 2020.

H.-T. Lin and L. Li. Support vector machinery for infinite ensemble learning. *Journal of Machine Learning Research*, 9(9):285–312, 2008.

M. Lin, K. Tang, and X. Yao. Dynamic sampling approach to training neural networks for multiclass imbalance classification. *IEEE Trans. Neural Networks and Learning Systems*, 24(4):647–660, 2013.

X. Lin, S. Yacoub, J. Burns, and S. Simske. Performance analysis of pattern classifier combination by plurality voting. *Pattern Recognition Letters*, 24(12):1959–1969, 2003.

Y. Lin and Y. Jeon. Random forests and adaptive nearest neighbors. *Journal of the American Statistical Association*, 101(474):578–590, 2006.

Y. M. Lin, Y. Lee, and G. Wahba. Support vector machines for classification in nonstandard situations. *Machine Learning*, 46(1):191–202, 2002.

N. Littlestone and M. K. Warmuth. The weighted majority algorithm. *Information and Computation*, 108(2):212–261, 1994.

B. Liu and R. Mazumder. ForestPrune: Compact depth-pruned tree ensembles. In *Proceedings of the 26th International Conference on Artificial Intelligence and Statistics*, pages 9417–9428, Valencia, Spain, 2023.

D. Liu, X. Hua, L. Yang, and H. Zhang. Multiple-instance active learning for image categorization. In *Proceedings of the 15th International Conference on Multimedia Modeling*, pages 239–249, Sophia-Antipolis, France, 2009a.

F. T. Liu, K. M. Ting, and W. Fan. Maximizing tree diversity by building complete-random decision trees. In *Proceedings of the 9th Pacific-Asia Conference on Knowledge Discovery and Data Mining*, pages 605–610, Hanoi, Vietnam, 2005.

F. T. Liu, K. M. Ting, Y. Yu, and Z.-H. Zhou. Spectrum of variable-random trees. *Journal of Artificial Intelligence Research*, 32:355–384, 2008a.

F. T. Liu, K. M. Ting, and Z.-H. Zhou. Isolation forest. In *Proceedings of the 8th IEEE International Conference on Data Mining*, pages 413–422, Pisa, Italy, 2008b.

F. T. Liu, K. M. Ting, and Z.-H. Zhou. On detecting clustered anomalies using SCiForest. In *Proceedings of the 21st European Conference on Machine Learning and 14th European Conference on Principles of Data Mining and Knowledge Discovery*, pages 274–290, Barcelona, Spain, 2010.

F. T. Liu, K. M. Ting, and Z.-H. Zhou. Isolation-based anomaly detection. *ACM Trans. Knowledge Discovery in Data*, 6(1):3:1–3:39, 2012.

L.-P. Liu, Y. Yu, Y. Jiang, and Z.-H. Zhou. TEFE: A time-efficient approach to feature extraction. In *Proceedings of the 8th IEEE International Conference on Data Mining*, pages 423–432, Pisa, Italy, 2008c.

X.-Y. Liu and Z.-H. Zhou. The influence of class imbalance on cost-sensitive learning: An empirical study. In *Proceedings of the 6th IEEE International Conference on Data Mining*, pages 970–974, Hong Kong, China, 2006.

X.-Y. Liu and Z.-H. Zhou. Learning with cost intervals. In *Proceedings of the 16th ACM SIGKDD Conference on Knowledge Discovery and Data Mining*, pages 403–412, Washington, DC, 2010.

X.-Y. Liu, J. Wu, and Z.-H. Zhou. Exploratory undersampling for class-imbalance learning. *IEEE Trans. Systems, Man, and Cybernetics - Part B: Cybernetics*, 39 (2):539–550, 2009b.

X.-Y. Liu, Q.-Q. Li, and Z.-H. Zhou. Learning imbalanced multi-class data with optimal dichotomy weights. In *Proceedings of the 13th IEEE International Conference on Data Mining*, pages 478–487, Dallas, TX, 2013.

Y. Liu and X. Yao. Ensemble learning via negative correlation. *Neural Networks*, 12 (10):1399–1404, 1999.

Y. Liu, X. Jia, M. Tan, R. Vemulapalli, Y. Zhu, B. Green, and X. Wang. Search to distill: Pearls are everywhere but not the eyes. In *Proceeding of the IEEE/CVF Conference on Computer Vision and Pattern Recognition*, pages 7536–7545, Seattle, WA, 2020.

S. P. Lloyd. Least squares quantization in PCM. *IEEE Trans. Information Theory*, 28(2):129–136, 1982.

E. Lobacheva, N. Chirkova, M. Kodryan, and D. P. Vetrov. On power laws in deep ensembles. In *Advances in Neural Information Processing Systems 33*, pages 2375–2385, Virtual Event, 2020.

B. Long, Z. Zhang, and P. S. Yu. Combining multiple clusterings by soft correspondence. In *Proceedings of the 4th IEEE International Conference on Data Mining*, pages 282–289, Houston, TX, 2005.

I. Loshchilov and F. Hutter. SGDR: stochastic gradient descent with warm restarts. In *Proceeding of the 5th International Conference on Learning Representations*, Toulon, France, 2017.

S.-H. Lyu, L. Yang, and Z.-H. Zhou. A refined margin distribution analysis for forest representation learning. In *Advances in Neural Information Processing Systems 32*, pages 5531–5541, Vancouver, Canada, 2019.

S.-H. Lyu, Y.-H. Chen, and Z.-H. Zhou. A region-based analysis for the feature concatenation in deep forests. *Chinese Journal of Electronics*, 31(6):1072–1080, 2022.

H. Ma, B. Ghojogh, M. N. Samad, D. Zheng, and M. Crowley. Isolation Mondrian forest for batch and online anomaly detection. In *Proceedings of the IEEE International Conference on Systems, Man, and Cybernetics*, pages 3051–3058, Toronto, Canada, 2020.

J. Ma, Z. Zhao, X. Yi, J. Chen, L. Hong, and E. H. Chi. Modeling task relationships in multi-task learning with multi-gate mixture-of-experts. In *Proceedings of the 24th ACM SIGKDD International Conference on Knowledge Discovery and Data Mining*, pages 1930–1939, London, UK, 2018.

P. K. Mallapragada, R. Jin, A. K. Jain, and Y. Liu. SemiBoost: Boosting for semi-supervised learning. *IEEE Trans. Pattern Analysis and Machine Intelligence*, 30 (11):2000–2014, 2009.

M. A. Maloof. Learning when data sets are imbalanced and when costs are unequal and unknown. In *Proceedings of the Workshop on Learning from Imbalanced Data Sets at the 20th International Conference on Machine Learning*, pages 1–2, Washington, DC, 2003.

I. Maqsood, M. R. Khan, and A. Abraham. An ensemble of neural networks for weather forecasting. *Neural Computing & Applications*, 13(2):112–122, 2004.

D. D. Margineantu. *Methods for Cost-Sensitive Learning*. PhD thesis, Department of Computer Science, Oregon State University, Corvallis, OR, 2001.

D. D. Margineantu and T. G. Dietterich. Pruning adaptive boosting. In *Proceedings of the 14th International Conference on Machine Learning*, pages 211–218, Nashville, TN, 1997.

H. Markowitz. Portfolio selection. *Journal of Finance*, 7(1):77–91, 1952.

G. Martínez-Muñoz and A. Suárez. Aggregation ordering in bagging. In *Proceedings of the 3rd International Conference on Artifical Intelligence and Applications*, pages 258–263, Innsbruck, Austria, 2004.

G. Martínez-Muñoz and A. Suárez. Pruning in ordered bagging ensembles. In *Proceedings of the 23rd International Conference on Machine Learning*, pages 609–616, Pittsburgh, PA, 2006.

G. Martínez-Muñoz and A. Suárez. Using boosting to prune bagging ensembles. *Pattern Recognition Letters*, 28(1):156–165, 2007.

G. Martínez-Muñoz, D. Hernández-Lobato, and A. Suárez. An analysis of ensemble pruning techniques based on ordered aggregation. *IEEE Trans. Pattern Analysis and Machine Intelligence*, 31(2):245–259, 2009.

M. Masana, X. Liu, B. Twardowski, M. Menta, A. D. Bagdanov, and J. van de Weijer. Class-incremental learning: Survey and performance evaluation on image classification. *IEEE Trans. Pattern Analysis and Machine Intelligence*, 45(5): 5513–5533, 2023.

J. Masci, U. Meier, D. Cireşan, and J. Schmidhuber. Stacked convolutional auto-encoders for hierarchical feature extraction. In *Proceedings of the 21st International Conference on Artificial Neural Networks*, pages 52–59, 2011.

H. Masnadi-Shirazi and N. Vasconcelos. Asymmetric Boosting. In *Proceeding of the 24th International Conference on Machine Learning*, pages 609–616, Corvallis, OR, 2007.

L. Mason, J. Baxter, P. Bartlett, and M. Frean. Boosting algorithms as gradient descent. In *Advances in Neural Information Processing Systems 12*, pages 512–518, Denver, CO, 1999.

L. Mason, J. Baxter, P. L. Bartlett, and M. Frean. Functional gradient techniques for combining hypotheses. In P. J. Bartlett, B. Schölkopf, D. Schuurmans, and A. J. Smola, editors, *Advances in Large-Margin Classifiers*, pages 221–246. MIT Press, 2000.

A. Maurer and M. Pontil. Empirical Bernstein bounds and sample-variance penalization. In *Proceedings of the 22nd Conference on Learning Theory*, Montréal, Canada, 2009.

D. McAllester. A PAC-Bayesian tutorial with a dropout bound. *arXiv:1307.2118*, 2013.

A. McCallum and K. Nigam. Employing EM and pool-based active learning for text classification. In *Proceedings of the 15th International Conference on Machine Learning*, pages 350–358, Madison, WI, 1998.

R. A. McDonald, D. J. Hand, and I. A. Eckley. An empirical comparison of three boosting algorithms on real data sets with artificial class noise. In *Proceedings of the 4th International Workshop on Multiple Classifier Systems*, pages 35–44, Guilford, UK, 2003.

W. McGill. Multivariate information transmission. *IEEE Trans. Information Theory*, 4(4):93–111, 1954.

D. Mease and A. Wyner. Evidence contrary to the statistical view of boosting (with discussions). *Journal of Machine Learning Research*, 9:131–201, 2008.

N. Meinshausen and G. Ridgeway. Quantile regression forests. *Journal of Machine Learning Research*, 7:983–999, 2006.

P. Melville and R. J. Mooney. Creating diversity in ensembles using artificial data. *Information Fusion*, 6(1):99–111, 2005.

A. Mensi and M. Bicego. Enhanced anomaly score for isolation trees. *Pattern Recognition*, 120:108115, 2021.

C. E. Metz. Basic principles of ROC analysis. *Seminars in Nuclear Medicine*, 8(4): 283–298, 1978.

T. Mikolov, I. Sutskever, K. Chen, G. S. Corrado, and J. Dean. Distributed representations of words and phrases and their compositionality. In *Advances in Neural Information Processing Systems 26*, pages 3111–3119, Lake Tahoe, NV, 2013.

D. J. Miller and H. S. Uyar. A mixture of experts classifier with learning based on both labelled and unlabelled data. In *Advances in Neural Information Processing System 9*, pages 571–577, Denver, CO, 1996.

Y. Mirsky, T. Doitshman, Y. Elovici, and A. Shabtai. Kitsune: An ensemble of autoencoders for online network intrusion detection. In *Proceedings of the 25th Annual Network and Distributed System Security Symposium*, San Diego, CA, 2018.

B. Mirzasoleiman, A. Karbasi, R. Sarkar, and A. Krause. Distributed submodular maximization. *Journal of Machine Learning Research*, 17(235):1–44, 2016.

V. Mnih, K. Kavukcuoglu, D. Silver, A. A. Rusu, J. Veness, M. G. Bellemare, A. Graves, M. A. Riedmiller, A. Fidjeland, G. Ostrovski, S. Petersen, C. Beattie, A. Sadik, I. Antonoglou, H. King, D. Kumaran, D. Wierstra, S. Legg, and D. Hassabis. Human-level control through deep reinforcement learning. *Nature*, 518(7540):529–533, 2015.

X. Mu, P. Watta, and M. H. Hassoun. Analysis of a plurality voting-based combination of classifiers. *Neural Processing Letters*, 29(2):89–107, 2009.

X. Mu, K. M. Ting, and Z.-H. Zhou. Classification under streaming emerging new classes: A solution using completely-random trees. *IEEE Trans. Knowledge and Data Engineering*, 29(8):1605–1618, 2017a.

X. Mu, F. Zhu, J. Du, E.-P. Lim, and Z.-H. Zhou. Streaming classification with emerging new class by class matrix sketching. In *Proceedings of the 31st AAAI Conference on Artificial Intelligence*, pages 2373–2379, San Francisco, CA, 2017b.

K. Muandet, K. Fukumizu, B. Sriperumbudur, and B. Schölkopf. Kernel mean embedding of distributions: A review and beyond. *Foundations and Trends in Machine Learning*, 10(1-2):1–141, 2017.

I. Mukherjee and R. Schapire. A theory of multiclass boosting. In *Advances in Neural Information Processing Systems 23*, pages 1714–1722, Vancouver, Canada, 2010.

E. Müller, M. Schiffer, and T. Seidl. Statistical selection of relevant subspace projections for outlier ranking. In *Proceedings of the 27th IEEE International Conference on Data Engineering*, pages 434–445, Hannover, Germany, 2011.

S. K. Murthy, S. Kasif, and S. Salzberg. A system for the induction of oblique decision trees. *Journal of Artificial Intelligence Research*, 2:1–33, 1994.

L. Nanni, Y. M. Costa, A. Lumini, M. Y. Kim, and S. R. Baek. Combining visual and acoustic features for music genre classification. *Expert Systems with Applications*, 45:108–117, 2016.

A. Narasimhamurthy. Theoretical bounds of majority voting performance for a binary classification problem. *IEEE Trans. Pattern Analysis and Machine Intelligence*, 27(12):1988–1995, 2005.

A. M. Narasimhamurthy. A framework for the analysis of majority voting. In *Proceedings of the 13th Scadinavian Conference on Image Analysis*, pages 268–274, Halmstad, Sweden, 2003.

S. Nash and A. Sofer. *Linear and Nonlinear Programming.* McGraw-Hill, 1996.

R. Ng and J. Han. Efficient and effective clustering method for spatial data mining. In *Proceedings of the 20th International Conference on Very Large Data Bases*, pages 144–155, Santiago, Chile, 1994.

H. T. Nguyen and A. W. M. Smeulders. Active learning using pre-clustering. In *Proceedings of the 21st International Conference on Machine Learning*, pages 623–630, Banff, Canada, 2004.

K. Nigam, A. K. McCallum, S. Thrun, and T. Mitchell. Text classification from labeled and unlabeled documents using EM. *Machine Learning*, 39(2-3):103–134, 2000.

N. J. Nilsson. *Learning Machines: Foundations of Trainable Pattern-Classifying Systems.* New York: McGraw-Hill, 1965.

D. Opitz and R. Maclin. Popular ensemble methods: An empirical study. *Journal of Artificial Intelligence Research*, 11:169–198, 1999.

M. J. Osborne and A. Rubinstein. *A Course in Game Theory.* MIT Press, 1994.

M. E. Otey, A. Ghoting, and S. Parthasarathy. Fast distributed outlier detection in mixed-attribute data sets. *Data Mining and Knowledge Discovery*, 12(2-3): 203–228, 2006.

M. Pagliardini, M. Jaggi, F. Fleuret, and S. P. Karimireddy. Agree to disagree: Diversity through disagreement for better transferability. In *Proceedings of the 11th International Conference on Learning Representations*, Kigali, Rwanda, 2023.

S. J. Pan and Q. Yang. A survey on transfer learning. *IEEE Trans. Knowledge and Data Engineering*, 22(10):1345–1359, 2009.

M. Pang, K.-M. Ting, P. Zhao, and Z.-H. Zhou. Improving deep forest by confidence screening. In *Proceedings of the 18th IEEE International Conference on Data Mining*, pages 1194–1199, Singapore, 2018.

S. Panigrahi, A. Kundu, S. Sural, and A. K. Majumdar. Credit card fraud detection: A fusion approach using Dempster-Shafer theory and Bayesian learning. *Information Fusion*, 10(4):354–363, 2009.

I. Partalas, G. Tsoumakas, and I. Vlahavas. Pruning an ensemble of classifiers via reinforcement learning. *Neurocomputing*, 72(7-9):1900–1909, 2009.

D. Partridge and W. J. Krzanowski. Software diversity: Practical statistics for its measurement and exploitation. *Information & Software Technology*, 39(10): 707–717, 1997.

A. Passerini, M. Pontil, and P. Frasconi. New results on error correcting output codes of kernel machines. *IEEE Trans. Neural Networks*, 15(1):45–54, 2004.

D. Pathak, D. Gandhi, and A. Gupta. Self-supervised exploration via disagreement. In *Proceedings of the 36th International Conference on Machine Learning*, pages 5062–5071, Long Beach, CA, 2019.

M. Pawlik and N. Augsten. Tree edit distance: Robust and memory-efficient. *Information Systems*, 56:157–173, 2016.

R. Perdisci, G. Gu, and W. Lee. Using an ensemble of one-class SVM classifiers to harden payload-based anomaly detection systems. In *Proceedings of the 6th IEEE International Conference on Data Mining*, pages 488–498, Hong Kong, China, 2006.

M. P. Perrone and L. N. Cooper. When networks disagree: Ensemble method for hybird neural networks. In L. N. Cooper, editor, *How We Learn; How We Remember: Toward an Understanding of Brain and Neural Systems*, pages 342–358. World Scientific, 1995.

A. Platanios, A. Blum, and T. M. Mitchell. Estimating accuracy from unlabeled data. In *Proceedings of the 30th Conference on Uncertainty in Artificial Intelligence*, pages 682–691, Quebec, Canada, 2014.

J. C. Platt. Probabilities for SV machines. In A. J. Smola, P. L. Bartlett, B. Schölkopf, and D. Schuurmans, editors, *Advances in Large Margin Classifiers*, pages 61–74. MIT Press, 2000.

R. Polikar, A. Topalis, D. Parikh, D. Green, J. Frymiare, J. Kounios, and C. M. Clark. An ensemble based data fusion approach for early diagnosis of Alzheimer's disease. *Information Fusion*, 9(1):83–95, 2008.

A. Polino, R. Pascanu, and D. Alistarh. Model compression via distillation and quantization. In *Proceeding of the 6th International Conference on Learning Representations*, Vancouver, Canada, 2018.

B. R. Preiss. *Data Structures and Algorithms with Object-Oriented Design Patterns in Java.* Wiley, 1999.

O. Pujol, P. Radeva, and J. Vitrià. Discriminant ECOC: A heuristic method for application dependent design of error correcting output codes. *IEEE Trans. Pattern Analysis and Machine Intelligence*, 28(6):1007–1012, 2006.

O. Pujol, S. Escalera, and P. Radeva. An incremental node embedding technique for error correcting output codes. *Pattern Recognition*, 41(2):713–725, 2008.

C. Qian, Y. Yu, and Z. Zhou. Pareto ensemble pruning. In *Proceedings of the 19th AAAI Conference on Artificial Intelligence*, pages 2935–2941, Austin, TX, 2015a.

C. Qian, Y. Yu, and Z.-H. Zhou. Subset selection by Pareto optimization. In *Advances in Neural Information Processing Systems 28*, pages 1774–1782, Montréal, Canada, 2015b.

C. Qian, J.-C. Shi, Y. Yu, K. Tang, and Z.-H. Zhou. Subset selection under noise. In *Advances in Neural Information Processing Systems 30*, pages 3560–3570, Long Beach, CA, 2017.

S. Qiao, W. Shen, Z. Zhang, B. Wang, and A. Yuille. Deep co-training for semi-supervised image recognition. In *Proceedings of the 15th European Conference on Computer Vision*, pages 135–152, Munich, Germany, 2018.

R. Qin, M. Li, and H. Ding. Solving soft clustering ensemble via k-sparse discrete Wasserstein barycenter. In *Advances in Neural Information Processing Systems 34*, pages 900–913, Virtual Event, 2021.

J. R. Quinlan. Induction of decision trees. *Machine Learning*, 1(1):81–106, 1986.

J. R. Quinlan. *C4.5: Programs for Machine Learning.* Morgan Kaufmann, 1993.

R. Rahmani and S. A. Goldman. MISSL: Multiple-instance semi-supervised learning. In *Proceedings of the 23rd International Conference on Machine Learning*, pages 705–712, Pittsburgh, PA, 2006.

S. Rajbhandari, C. Li, Z. Yao, M. Zhang, R. Y. Aminabadi, A. A. Awan, J. Rasley, and Y. He. DeepSpeed-MoE: Advancing mixture-of-experts inference and training to power next-generation AI scale. In *Proceedings of the 39th International Conference on Machine Learning*, pages 18332–18346, Baltimore, MD, 2022.

S. Ramaswamy, R. Rastogi, and K. Shim. Efficient algorithms for mining outliers from large data sets. *ACM SIGMOD Record*, 29(2):427–438, 2000.

Š. Raudys and F. Roli. The behavior knowledge space fusion method: Analysis of generalization error and strategies for performance improvement. In *Proceedings of the 4th International Workshop on Multiple Classifier Systems*, pages 55–64, Guildford, UK, 2003.

S. Rayana and L. Akoglu. Less is more: Building selective anomaly ensembles. *ACM Trans. Knowledge Discovery from Data*, 10(4):Article 42, 2016.

S. Rayana, W. Zhong, and L. Akoglu. Sequential ensemble learning for outlier detection: A bias-variance perspective. In *Proceedings of the 16th IEEE International Conference on Data Mining*, pages 421–425, Barcelona, Spain, 2016.

R. A. Redner and H. F. Walker. Mixture densities, maximum likelihood and the EM algorithm. *SIAM Review*, 26(2):195–239, 1984.

L. Reyzin and R. E. Schapire. How boosting the margin can also boost classifier complexity. In *Proceedings of the 23rd International Conference on Machine Learning*, pages 753–760, Pittsburgh, PA, 2006.

D. L. Richmond, D. Kainmueller, M. Y. Yang, E. W. Myers, and C. Rother. Relating cascaded random forests to deep convolutional neural networks for semantic segmentation. arXiv:1507.07583, 2015.

M. Robnik-Šikonja. Improving random forests. In *Proceedings of the 15th European Conference on Machine Learning*, pages 359–370, Pisa, Italy, 2004.

J. J. Rodriguez, L. I. Kuncheva, and C. J. Alonso. Rotation forest: A new classifier ensemble method. *IEEE Trans. Pattern Analysis and Machine Intelligence*, 28 (10):1619–1630, 2006.

G. Rogova. Combining the results of several neural network classifiers. *Neural Networks*, 7(5):777–781, 1994.

L. Rokach. *Pattern Classification Using Ensemble Methods.* World Scientific, 2010.

L. Rokach. *Ensemble Learning: Pattern Classification Using Ensemble Methods.* World Scientific, 2nd edition, 2019.

A. Ross, W. Pan, L. Celi, and F. Doshi-Velez. Ensembles of locally independent prediction models. In *Proceedings of the 34th AAAI Conference on Artificial Intelligence*, pages 5527–5536, New York, NY, 2020.

D. M. Roy and Y. W. Teh. The Mondrian process. In *Advances in Neural Information Processing Systems 21*, pages 1377–1384, Vancouver, Canada, 2008.

D. E. Rumelhart, G. E. Hinton, and R. J. Williams. Learning internal representations by error propagation. In D. E. Rumelhart and J. L. McClelland, editors, *Parallel Distributed Processing: Explorations in the Microstructure of Cognition*, volume 1, pages 318–362. MIT Press, 1986.

S. Ruslan, A. Mnih, and G. E. Hinton. Restricted Boltzmann machines for collaborative filtering. In *Proceedings of the 24th International Conference on Machine Learning*, pages 791–798, Corvallis, OR, 2007.

D. Ruta and B. Gabrys. Application of the evolutionary algorithms for classifier selection in multiple classifier systems with majority voting. In *Proceedings of the 2nd International Workshop on Multiple Classifier Systems*, pages 399–408, Cambridge, UK, 2001.

K. Saito, Y. Ushiku, and T. Harada. Asymmetric tri-training for unsupervised domain adaptation. In *Proceedings of the 34th International Conference on Machine Learning*, pages 2988–2997, Sydney, Australia, 2017.

L. Saitta and N. Lavrac. Machine learning - a technological roadmap. Technical report, University of Amsterdam, Amsterdam, Netherland, 2000.

M. Sandler, A. G. Howard, M. Zhu, A. Zhmoginov, and L.-C. Chen. Mobilenetv2: Inverted residuals and linear bottlenecks. In *Proceedings of the 31st IEEE Conference on Computer Vision and Pattern Recognition*, pages 4510–4520, Salt Lake City, UT, 2018.

V. Sanh, L. Debut, J. Chaumond, and T. Wolf. Distilbert, a distilled version of BERT: Smaller, faster, cheaper and lighter. arXiv:1910.01108, 2019.

R. E. Schapire. The strength of weak learnability. *Machine Learning*, 5(2):197–227, 1990.

R. E. Schapire and Y. Singer. Improved boosting algorithms using confidence-rated predictions. *Machine Learning*, 37(3):297–336, 1999.

R. E. Schapire, Y. Freund, P. Bartlett, and W. S. Lee. Boosting the margin: A new explanation for the effectiveness of voting methods. *Annals of Statistics*, 26(5): 1651–1686, 1998.

W. J. Scheirer, A. R. Rocha, A. Sapkota, and T. E. Boult. Towards open set recognition. *IEEE Trans. Pattern Analysis and Machine Intelligence*, 35(7):1757–1772, 2013.

J. Schiffers. A classification approach incorporating misclassification costs. *Intelligent Data Analysis*, 1(1):59–68, 1997.

B. Schölkopf and A. J. Smola. *Learning with Kernels.* MIT Press, Cambridge, MA, 2002.

M. G. Schultz, E. Eskin, E. Zadok, and S. J. Stolfo. Data mining methods for detection of new malicious executables. In *Proceedings of the IEEE Symposium on Security and Privacy*, pages 38–49, Oakland, CA, 2001.

E. Scornet, G. Biau, and J.-P. Vert. Consistency of random forests. *Annals of Statistics*, 43(4):1716–1741, 2015.

A. K. Seewald. How to make stacking better and faster while also taking care of an unknown weakness. In *Proceedings of the 19th International Conference on Machine Learning*, pages 554–561, Sydney, Australia, 2002.

N. Segev, M. Harel, S. Mannor, K. Crammer, and R. El-Yaniv. Learn on source, refine on target: A model transfer learning framework with random forests. *IEEE Trans. Pattern Analysis and Machine Intelligence*, 39(9):1811–1824, 2017.

C. Seiffert, T. Khoshgoftaar, J. V. Hulse, and A. Napolitano. RUSBoost: A hybrid approach to alleviating class imbalance. *IEEE Trans. Systems, Man, and Cybernetics - Part A: Systems and Humans*, 40(1):185–197, 2010.

K. Sen and A. Mishra. A generalised Polya-Eggenberger model generating various discrete probability distributions. *Sankhyā: The Indian Journal of Statistics, Series A*, 58(2):243–251, 1996.

B. Settles. Active learning literature survey. Technical Report 1648, Department of Computer Sciences, University of Wisconsin at Madison, Wisconsin, WI, 2010. http://pages.cs.wisc.edu/~bsettles/pub/settles.activelearning.pdf.

B. Settles, M. Craven, and S. Ray. Multiple-instance active learning. In *Advances in Neural Information Processing Systems 20*, pages 1289–1296, Vancouver, Canada, 2008.

H. S. Seung, M. Opper, and H. Sompolinsky. Query by committee. In *Proceedings of the 5th Annual ACM Conference on Computational Learning Theory*, pages 287–294, Pittsburgh, PA, 1992.

G. Shafer. *A Mathematical Theory of Evidence.* Princeton University Press, 1976.

N. Shazeer, A. Mirhoseini, K. Maziarz, A. Davis, Q. V. Le, G. E. Hinton, and J. Dean. Outrageously large neural networks: The sparsely-gated mixture-of-experts layer. In *Proceedings of the 5th International Conference on Learning Representations*, Toulon, France, 2017.

G. Sheikholeslami, S. Chatterjee, and A. Zhang. WaveCluster: A multi-resolution clustering approach for very large spatial databases. In *Proceedings of the 24th International Conference on Very Large Data Bases*, pages 428–439, New York, NY, 1998.

H. B. Shen and K. C. Chou. Ensemble classifier for protein fold pattern recognition. *Bioinformatics*, 22(14):1717–1722, 2006.

V. S. Sheng, F. J. Provost, and P. G. Ipeirotis. Get another label? improving data quality and data mining using multiple, noisy labelers. In *Proceedings of the 14th ACM SIGKDD International Conference on Knowledge Discovery and Data Mining*, pages 614–622, Las Vegas, NV, 2008.

J. Shi and J. Malik. Normalized cuts and image segmentation. *IEEE Trans. Pattern Analysis and Machine Intelligence*, 22(8):888–905, 2000.

C. A. Shipp and L. I. Kuncheva. Relationships between combination methods and measures of diversity in combining classifiers. *Information Fusion*, 3(2):135–148, 2002.

L. Shoemaker and L. O. Hall. Anomaly detection using ensembles. In *Proceedings of the 10th International Workshop on Multiple Classifier Systems*, pages 6–15, Naples, Italy, 2011.

B. Silverman. *Density Estimation for Statistics and Data Analysis*. Chapman and Hall, 1986.

J. Sirignano. Deep learning models in finance. *SIAM News*, 50(5):1, 2017.

D. B. Skalak. The sources of increased accuracy for two proposed boosting algorithms. In *Proceeding of the AAAI'96 Workshop on Integrating Multiple Learned Models*, page 1133, Portland, OR, 1996.

N. Slonim, N. Friedman, and N. Tishby. Multivariate information bottleneck. *Neural Computation*, 18(8):1739–1789, 2006.

A. Smola, A. Gretton, L. Song, and B. Schölkopf. A Hilbert space embedding for distributions. In *Proceedings of the 18th International Conference on Algorithmic Learning Theory*, pages 13–31, Sendai, Japan, 2007.

P. Smyth and D. Wolpert. Stacked density estimation. In *Advances in Neural Information Processing Systems 10*, pages 668–674, Denver, CO, 1998.

P. H. A. Sneath and R. R. Sokal. *Numerical Taxonomy: The Principles and Practice of Numerical Classification*. W. H. Freeman, 1973.

R. Snow, B. O'Connor, D. Jurafsky, and A. Y. Ng. Cheap and fast - but is it good? evaluating non-expert annotations for natural language tasks. In *Proceedings of Conference on Empirical Methods in Natural Language Processing*, pages 254–263, Honolulu, HI, 2008.

R. Socher, M. Ganjoo, C. D. Manning, and A. Y. Ng. Zero-shot learning through cross-modal transfer. In *Advances in Neural Information Processing Systems 26*, pages 935–943, Lake Tahoe, NV, 2013.

Y. Song, C.-T. Li, J.-Y. Nie, M. Zhang, D. Zhao, and R. Yan. An ensemble of retrieval-based and generation-based human-computer conversation systems. In *Proceedings of the 27th International Joint Conference on Artificial Intelligence*, pages 4382–4388, Stockholm, Sweden, 2018.

V. Soto, G. Martínez-Muñoz, D. Hernández-Lobato, and A. Suárez. A double pruning algorithm for classification ensembles. In *Proceedings of 9th International Workshop Multiple Classifier Systems*, pages 104–113, Cairo, Egypt, 2010.

K. A. Spackman. Signal detection theory: Valuable tools for evaluating inductive learning. In *Proceedings of the 6th International Workshop on Machine Learning*, pages 160–163, Ithaca, NY, 1989.

G. Staerman, P. Mozharovskyi, S. Clémençon, and F. d'Alché-Buc. Functional isolation forest. In *Proceedings of the 11th Asian Conference on Machine Learning*, pages 332–347, Nagoya, Japan, 2019.

M. Stephens. Use of the Kolmogorov-Smirnov, Cramer-von Mises and related statistics without extensive tables. *Journal of the Royal Statistical Society: Series B*, 32(1):115–122, 1970.

W. N. Street and Y. Kim. A streaming ensemble algorithm (SEA) for large-scale classification. In *Proceedings of the 7th ACM SIGKDD International Conference on Knowledge Discovery & Data Mining*, pages 377–382, San Francisco, CA, 2001.

A. Strehl and J. Ghosh. Cluster ensembles - A knowledge reuse framework for combining multiple partitions. *Journal of Machine Learning Research*, 3:583–617, 2002.

A. Strehl, J. Ghosh, and R. J. Mooney. Impact of similarity measures on webpage clustering. In *Proceedings of the 17th National Conference on Artificial Intelligence*, page 64, Austin, TX, 2000.

M. Studeny and J. Vejnarova. The multi-information function as a tool for measuring stochastic dependence. In M. I. Jordan, editor, *Learning in Graphical Models*, pages 261–297. Springer, 1998.

H.-I. Suk, S.-W. Lee, and D. Shen. Deep ensemble learning of sparse regression models for brain disease diagnosis. *Medical Image Analysis*, 37:101–113, 2017.

T. Sun and Z.-H. Zhou. Structural diversity for decision tree ensemble learning. *Frontiers of Computer Science*, 12(3):560–570, 2018.

Y. Sun, A. K. C. Wong, and Y. Wang. Parameter inference of cost-sensitive boosting algorithms. In *Proceedings of the 4th International Conference Machine Learning and Data Mining in Pattern Recognition*, pages 21–30, Leipzig, Germany, 2005.

Y. Sun, M. S. Kamel, and Y. Wang. Boosting for learning multiple classes with imbalanced class distribution. In *Proceedings of the 6th International Conference on Data Mining*, pages 592–602, Hong Kong, China, 2006.

Y. Sun, K. Tang, Z. Zhu, and X. Yao. Concept drift adaptation by exploiting historical knowledge. *IEEE Trans. Neural Networks and Learning Systems*, 29 (10):4822–4832, 2018.

Y. Sun, J. Zhang, C. Jia, H. Lin, J. Ye, and Y. Yu. Model-Bellman inconsistency for model-based offline reinforcement learning. In *Proceedings of the 40th International Conference on Machine Learning*, pages 33177–33194, Honolulu, HA, 2023.

R. S. Sutton and A. G. Barto. *Reinforcement Learning: An Introduction.* MIT Press, 2nd edition, 2018.

R. S. Sutton, D. A. McAllester, S. Singh, and Y. Mansour. Policy gradient methods for reinforcement learning with function approximation. In *Advances in Neural Information Processing Systems 12*, pages 1057–1063, Denver, CO, 1999.

H. Takeda, Y. Tamura, and S. Sato. Using the ensemble Kalman filter for electricity load forecasting and analysis. *Energy*, 104:184–198, 2016.

C. Tamon and J. Xiang. On the boosting pruning problem. In *Proceedings of the 11th European Conference on Machine Learning*, pages 404–412, Barcelona, Spain, 2000.

A. C. Tan, D. Gilbert, and Y. Deville. Multi-class protein fold classification using a new ensemble machine learning approach. In *Proceedings of the 14th International Conference on Genome Informatics*, pages 206–217, Yokohama, Japan, 2003.

M. Tan and Q. V. Le. EfficientNet: Rethinking model scaling for convolutional neural networks. In *Proceedings of the 36th International Conference on Machine Learning*, pages 6105–6114, Long Beach, CA, 2019.

P.-N. Tan, M. Steinbach, and V. Kumar. *Introduction to Data Mining.* Pearson, 2018.

C. Tang, D. Garreau, and U. von Luxburg. When do random forests fail? In *Advances in Neural Information Processing Systems 31*, pages 2987–2997, Montréal, Canada, 2018.

E. K. Tang, P. N. Suganthan, and X. Yao. An analysis of diversity measures. *Machine Learning*, 65(1):247–271, 2006.

J. Tang, Z. Chen, A. W.-C. Fu, and D. W.-L. Cheung. Enhancing effectiveness of outlier detections for low density patterns. In *Proceedings of the 6th Pacific-Asia Conference on Knowledge Discovery and Data Mining*, pages 535–548, Taipei, 2002.

Z. Tao, H. Liu, S. Li, Z. Ding, and Y. Fu. Marginalized multiview ensemble clustering. *IEEE Trans. Neural Network and Learning Systems*, 31(2):600–611, 2020.

J. W. Taylor and R. Buizza. Neural network load forecasting with weather ensemble predictions. *IEEE Trans. Power Systems*, 17(3):626–632, 2002.

S. Theodoridis and K. Koutroumbas. *Pattern Recognition.* Academic Press, New York, NY, 4th edition, 2008.

R. Tibshirani. Bias, variance and prediction error for classification rules. Technical report, Department of Statistics, University of Toronto, Toronto, Canada, 1996.

A. B. Tickle, R. Andrews, M. Golea, and J. Diederich. The truth will come to light: Directions and challenges in extracting the knowledge embedded within trained artificial neural networks. *IEEE Trans. Neural Networks*, 9(6):1057–1067, 1998.

K. M. Ting. A comparative study of cost-sensitive boosting algorithms. In *Proceedings of the 17th International Conference on Machine Learning*, pages 983–990, San Francisco, CA, 2000.

K. M. Ting. An instance-weighting method to induce cost-sensitive trees. *IEEE Trans. Knowledge and Data Engineering*, 14(3):659–665, 2002.

K. M. Ting and I. H. Witten. Issues in stacked generalization. *Journal of Artificial Intelligence Research*, 10:271–289, 1999.

K.-M. Ting, J. R. Wells, S. C. Tan, S. W. Teng, and G. I. Webb. Feature-subspace aggregating: Ensembles for stable and unstable learners. *Machine Learning*, 82(3): 375–397, 2011.

K. M. Ting, G. T. Zhou, F. T. Liu, and S. C. Tan. Mass estimation. *Machine Learning*, 90(1):127–160, 2013.

K. M. Ting, Y. Zhu, and Z.-H. Zhou. Isolation kernel and its effect on SVM. In *Proceedings of the 24th ACM SIGKDD International Conference on Knowledge Discovery and Data Mining*, pages 2329–2337, London, UK, 2018.

K. M. Ting, B.-C. Xu, T. Washio, and Z.-H. Zhou. Isolation distributional kernel: A new tool for kernel based anomaly detection. In *Proceedings of the 26th ACM SIGKDD International Conference on Knowledge Discovery and Data Mining*, pages 198–206, Virtual Event, 2020.

K. M. Ting, B.-C. Xu, T. Washio, and Z.-H. Zhou. Isolation distributional kernel: A new tool for point and group anomaly detections. *IEEE Trans. Knowledge and Data Engineering*, 35(3):2697–2710, 2023.

N. Tishby and N. Zaslavsky. Deep learning and the information bottleneck principle. In *2015 IEEE Information Theory Workshop*, pages 1–5, Jerusalem, Israel, 2015.

I. O. Tolstikhin, S. Gelly, O. Bousquet, C.-J. Simon-Garriel, and B. Schölkopf. AdaGAN: Boosting generative models. In *Advances in Neural Information Processing Systems 30*, Long Beach, CA, 2017.

I. Tomek. Two modifications of CNN. *IEEE Trans. Systems, Man and Cybernetics*, 6(11):769–772, 1976.

S. Tong and D. Koller. Support vector machine active learning with applications to text classification. In *Proceedings of the 17th International Conference on Machine Learning*, pages 999–1006, San Francisco, CA, 2000.

A. Topchy, A. K. Jain, and W. Punch. Combining multiple weak clusterings. In *Proceedings of the 3rd IEEE International Conference on Data Mining*, pages 331–338, Melbourne, FL, 2003.

A. Topchy, A. K. Jain, and W. Punch. A mixture model for clustering ensembles. In *Proceedings of the 4th SIAM International Conference on Data Mining*, pages 379–390, Lake Buena Vista, FL, 2004a.

A. Topchy, B. Minaei-Bidgoli, A. K. Jain, and W. F. Punch. Adaptive clustering ensembles. In *Proceedings of the 17th International Conference on Pattern Recognition*, pages 272–275, Cambridge, UK, 2004b.

A. P. Topchy, M. H. C. Law, A. K. Jain, and A. L. Fred. Analysis of consensus partition in cluster ensemble. In *Proceedings of the 4th IEEE International Conference on Data Mining*, pages 225–232, Brighton, UK, 2004c.

G. Tsoumakas, I. Katakis, and I. Vlahavas. Effective voting of heterogeneous classifiers. In *Proceedings of the 15th European Conference on Machine Learning*, pages 465–476, Pisa, Italy, 2004.

G. Tsoumakas, L. Angelis, and I. P. Vlahavas. Selective fusion of heterogeneous classifiers. *Intelligent Data Analysis*, 9(6):511–525, 2005.

G. Tsoumakas, I. Partalas, and I. Vlahavas. An ensemble pruning primer. In O. Okun and G. Valentini, editors, *Applications of Supervised and Unsupervised Ensemble Methods*, pages 155–165. Springer, 2009.

A. Tsymbal. The problem of concept drift: definitions and related work. *Computer Science Department, Trinity College Dublin*, 106(2):58, 2004.

Z. Tu, Z.-H. Zhou, W. Wang, J. Jiang, and B. Wang. Unsupervised metric fusion by cross diffusion. In *Proceedings of 2012 IEEE Conference on Computer Vision and Pattern Recognition*, pages 2997–3004, Providence, RI, 2012.

K. Tumer. *Linear and Order Statistics Combiners for Reliable Pattern Classification*. PhD thesis, The University of Texas at Austin, 1996.

K. Tumer and J. Ghosh. Theoretical foundations of linear and order statistics combiners for neural pattern classifiers. Technical Report TR-95-02-98, Computer and Vision Research Center, University of Texas, Austin, TX, 1995.

K. Tumer and J. Ghosh. Analysis of decision boundaries in linearly combined neural classifiers. *Pattern Recognition*, 29(2):341–348, 1996.

P. D. Turney. Types of cost in inductive concept learning. In *Proceedings of the Workshop on Cost-Sensitive Learning at the 17th International Conference on Machine Learning*, pages 217–225, New Brunswick, NJ, 1994.

N. Ueda and R. Nakano. Generalization error of ensemble estimators. In *Proceedings of International Conference on Neural Networks*, pages 90–95, Washington, DC, 1996.

P. E. Utgoff. Incremental induction of decision trees. *Machine Learning*, 4(2):161–186, 1989.

L. V. Utkin and M. A. Ryabinin. A Siamese deep forest. *Knowledge-Based Systems*, 139:13–22, 2018.

L. V. Utkin and M. A. Ryabinin. Discriminative metric learning with deep forest. *International Journal on Artificial Intelligence Tools*, 28(2):1950007:1–1950007:19, 2019.

W. Utschick and W. Weichselberger. Stochastic organization of output codes in multiclass learning problems. *Neural Computation*, 13(5):1065–1102, 2004.

L. G. Valiant. A theory of the learnable. *Communications of the ACM*, 27(11): 1134–1142, 1984.

H. Valizadegan, R. Jin, and A. K. Jain. Semi-supervised boosting for multi-class classification. In *Proceedings of the 19th European Conference on Machine Learning*, pages 522–537, Antwerp, Belgium, 2008.

L. J. P. van der Maaten and G. E. Hinton. Visualizing high-dimensional data using t-SNE. *Journal of Machine Learning Research*, 9(86):2579–2605, 2008.

M. Van ErP, L. Vuurpijl, and L. Schomaker. An overview and comparison of voting methods for pattern recognition. In *Proceedings of the 8th International Workshop on Frontiers in Handwriting Recognition*, pages 195–200, Niagara-on-the-Lake, Canada, 2002.

T. van Erven and W. M. Koolen. Metagrad: Multiple learning rates in online learning. In *Advances in Neural Information Processing Systems 29*, pages 3666–3674, Barcelona, Spain, 2016.

H. van Hasselt. Double Q-learning. In *Advances in Neural Information Processing Systems 23*, pages 2613–2621, Vancouver, Canada, 2010.

H. van Hasselt, A. Guez, and D. Silver. Deep reinforcement learning with double Q-learning. In *Proceedings of the 30th AAAI Conference on Artificial Intelligence*, pages 2094–2100, Phoenix, AZ, 2016.

C. van Rijsbergen. *Information Retrieval.* Butterworths, 1979.

V. N. Vapnik. *Statistical Learning Theory.* Wiley, 1998.

A. Vaswani, N. Shazeer, N. Parmar, J. Uszkoreit, L. Jones, A. N. Gomez, L. Kaiser, and I. Polosukhin. Attention is all you need. In *Advances in Neural Information Processing Systems 30*, pages 5998–6008, Long Beach, CA, 2017.

P. Viola and M. Jones. Rapid object detection using a boosted cascade of simple features. In *Proceedings of the IEEE Computer Society Conference on Computer Vision and Pattern Recognition*, pages 511–518, Kauai, HI, 2001.

P. Viola and M. Jones. Fast and robust classification using asymmetric AdaBoost and a detector cascade. In *Advances in Neural Information Processing Systems 14*, pages 1311–1318, Vancouver, Canada, 2002.

P. Viola and M. J. Jones. Robust real-time face detection. *International Journal of Computer Vision*, 57(2):137–154, 2004.

P. Viola, J. Platt, and C. Zhang. Multiple instance boosting for object detection. In *Advances in Neural Information Processing Systems 18*, pages 1419–1426, Vancouver, Canada, 2006.

S. Wager, S. Wang, and P. Liang. Dropout training as adaptive regularization. In *Advances in Neural Information Processing Systems 26*, pages 351–359, Lake Tahoe, NV, 2013.

K. Wagstaff, C. Cardie, S. Rogers, and S. Schrödl. Constrained k-means clustering with background knowledge. In *Proceedings of the 18th International Conference on Machine Learning*, pages 577–584, Williamstown, MA, 2001.

M. Wainberg, B. Alipanahi, and B. J. Frey. Are random forests truly the best classifiers? *Journal of Machine Learning Research*, 17(110):1–5, 2016.

B. Wang, J. Lu, Z. Yan, H. Luo, T. Li, Y. Zheng, and G. Zhang. Deep uncertainty quantification: A machine learning approach for weather forecasting. In *Proceedings of the 25th ACM SIGKDD International Conference on Knowledge Discovery and Data Mining*, pages 2087–2095, Anchorage, AK, 2019a.

F. Wang and C. Zhang. Label propagation through linear neighborhoods. In *Proceedings of the 23rd International Conference on Machine Learning*, pages 985–992, Pittsburgh, PA, 2006.

G. Wang, S. Lu, and L. Zhang. Adaptivity and optimality: A universal algorithm for online convex optimization. In *Proceedings of the 35th Conference on Uncertainty in Artificial Intelligence*, pages 659–668, Tel Aviv, Israel, 2019b.

H. Wang, H. Zhao, X. Li, and X. Tan. Progressive blockwise knowledge distillation for neural network acceleration. In *Proceedings of the 27th International Joint Conference on Artificial Intelligence*, pages 2769–2775, Stockholm, Sweden, 2018.

L. Wang, M. Sugiyama, C. Yang, Z.-H. Zhou, and J. Feng. On the margin explanation of boosting algorithm. In *Proceedings of the 21st Annual Conference on Learning Theory*, pages 479–490, Helsinki, Finland, 2008.

Q.-W. Wang, L. Yang, and Y.-F. Li. Learning from weak-label data: A deep forest expedition. In *Proceedings of the 34th AAAI Conference on Artificial Intelligence*, pages 6251–6258, New York, NY, 2020.

S. Wang and X. Yao. Multiclass imbalance problems: Analysis and potential solutions. *IEEE Trans. Systems, Man, and Cybernetics, Part B - Cybernetics*, 42(4):1119–1130, 2012.

S. Wang, K. Tang, and X. Yao. Diversity exploration and negative correlation learning on imbalanced data sets. In *Proceedings of the 20th International Joint Conference on Neural Networks*, pages 3259–3266, Atlanta, GA, 2009.

W. Wang and Z.-H. Zhou. Analyzing co-training style algorithms. In *Proceedings of the 18th European Conference on Machine Learning*, pages 454–465, Warsaw, Poland, 2007.

W. Wang and Z.-H. Zhou. On multi-view active learning and the combination with semi-supervised learning. In *Proceedings of the 25th International Conference on Machine Learning*, pages 1152–1159, Helsinki, Finland, 2008.

W. Wang and Z.-H. Zhou. A new analysis of co-training. In *Proceedings of the 27th International Conference on Machine Learning*, pages 1135–1142, Haifa, Israel, 2010.

W. Wang and Z.-H. Zhou. Crowdsourcing label quality: A theoretical analysis. *Science China Information Sciences*, 58(11):1–12, 2015.

W. Wang and Z.-H. Zhou. Theoretical foundation of co-training and disagreement-based algorithms. arXiv:1708.04403, 2017.

W. Wang, J. Yang, and R. Muntz. STING: A statistical information grid approach to spatial data mining. In *Proceedings of the 23rd International Conference on Very Large Data Bases*, pages 186–195, Athens, Greece, 1997.

X. Wang, D. Kondratyuk, E. Christiansen, K. M. Kitani, Y. Movshovitz-Attias, and E. Eban. Wisdom of committees: An overlooked approach to faster and more accurate models. In *Proceedings of the 10th International Conference on Learning Representations*, Virtual Event, 2022.

M. K. Warmuth, K. A. Glocer, and S. V. Vishwanathan. Entropy regularized LPBoost. In *Proceedings of the 19th International Conference on Algorithmic Learning Theory*, pages 256–271, Budapest, Hungary, 2008.

S. Watanabe. Information theoretical analysis of multivariate correlation. *IBM Journal of Research and Development*, 4(1):66–82, 1960.

S. Waterhouse, D. Mackay, and T. Robinson. Bayesian methods for mixtures of experts. In *Advances in Neural Information Processing Systems 8*, pages 351–357, Denver, CO, 1995.

S. R. Waterhouse and A. J. Robinson. Constructive algorithms for hierarchical mixtures of experts. In *Advances in Neural Information Processing Systems 8*, pages 584–590, Denver, CO, 1995.

C. Watkins and P. Dayan. Q-learning. *Machine Learning*, 8(3):279–292, 1992.

G. I. Webb. MultiBoosting: A technique for combining boosting and wagging. *Machine Learning*, 40(2):159–196, 2000.

G. I. Webb and Z. Zheng. Multistrategy ensemble learning: Reducing error by combining ensemble learning techniques. *IEEE Trans. Knowledge and Data Engineering*, 16(8):980–991, 2004.

G. I. Webb, J. R. Boughton, and Z. Wang. Not so naïve Bayes: Aggregating one-dependence estimators. *Machine Learning*, 58(1):5–24, 2005.

C.-Y. Wei, C. Dann, and J. Zimmert. A model selection approach for corruption robust reinforcement learning. In *Proceedings of the 33rd International Conference on Algorithmic Learning Theory*, pages 1043–1096, 2022.

X.-S. Wei, J. Wu, and Z.-H. Zhou. Scalable algorithms for multi-instance learning. *IEEE Trans. Neural Networks and Learning Systems*, 28(4):975–987, 2017.

G. M. Weiss. Mining with rarity: A unifying framework. *SIGKDD Explorations Newsletter*, 6(1):7–19, 2004.

J. Welbl. Casting random forests as artificial neural networks (and profiting from it). In *Proceedings of the 36th German Conference on Pattern Recognition*, pages 765–771, Münster, Germany, 2014.

P. Werbos. *Beyond Regression: New Tools for Prediction and Analysis in the Behavior Science*. PhD thesis, Harvard University, 1974.

D. West, S. Dellana, and J. Qian. Neural network ensemble strategies for financial decision applications. *Computers & Operations Research*, 32(10):2543–2559, 2005.

R. J. Williams. Simple statistical gradient-following algorithms for connectionist reinforcement learning. *Machine Learning*, 8(3-4):229–256, 1992.

T. Windeatt and R. Ghaderi. Coding and decoding strategies for multi-class learning problems. *Information Fusion*, 4(1):11–21, 2003.

W. H. Wolberg and O. L. Mangasarian. Multisurface method of pattern separation for medical diagnosis applied to breast cytology. *Proceedings of the National Academy of Sciences*, 87(23):9193–9196, 1990.

D. H. Wolpert. Stacked generalization. *Neural Networks*, 5(2):241–260, 1992.

D. H. Wolpert. The lack of a priori distinctions between learning algorithms. *Neural Computation*, 8(7):1341–1390, 1996.

D. H. Wolpert and W. G. Macready. No free lunch theorems for optimization. *IEEE Trans. Evolutionary Computation*, 1(1):67–82, 1997.

D. H. Wolpert and W. G. Macready. An efficient method to estimate bagging's generalization error. *Machine Learning*, 35(1):41–55, 1999.

D. Wood, T. Mu, A. Webb, H. Reeve, M. Lujan, and G. Brown. A unified theory of diversity in ensemble learning. *Journal of Machine Learning Research*, 24(359): 1–49, 2023.

K. Woods, W. P. Kegelmeyer, and K. Bowyer. Combination of multiple classifiers using local accuracy estimates. *IEEE Trans. Pattern Analysis and Machine Intelligence*, 19(4):405–410, 1997.

J.-S. Wu and Z.-H. Zhou. Sequence-based prediction of microRNA-binding residues in proteins using cost-sensitive Laplacian support vector machines. *IEEE/ACM Trans. Computational Biology and Bioinformatics*, 10(3):752–759, 2013.

X.-Z. Wu and Z.-H. Zhou. A unified view of multi-label performance measures. In *Proceedings of the 34th International Conference on Machine Learning*, pages 3780–3788, Sydney, Australia, 2017.

Y.-C. Wu, Y.-X. He, C. Qian, and Z.-H. Zhou. Multi-objective evolutionary ensemble pruning guided by margin distribution. In *Proceedings of the 17th International Conference on Parallel Problem Solving from Nature*, pages 427–441, Dortmund, Germany, 2022.

Y. Xian, C. H. Lampert, B. Schiele, and Z. Akata. Zero-shot learning - a comprehensive evaluation of the good, the bad and the ugly. *IEEE Trans. Pattern Analysis and Machine Intelligence*, 41(9):2251–2265, 2019.

E. P. Xing, A. Y. Ng, M. I. Jordan, and S. Russell. Distance metric learning, with applications to clustering with side-information. In *Advances in Neural Information Processing Systems 15*, pages 505–512, Vancouver, Canada, 2002.

B.-C. Xu, K. M. Ting, and Z.-H. Zhou. Isolation set-kernel and its application to multi-instance learning. In *Proceedings of the 25th ACM SIGKDD International Conference on Knowledge Discovery and Data Mining*, pages 941–949, Anchorage, AK, 2019.

B.-C. Xu, K. M. Ting, and Y. Jiang. Isolation graph kernel. In *Proceedings of the 35th AAAI Conference on Artificial Intelligence*, pages 10487–10495, Virtual Event, 2021a.

L. Xu and S. Amari. Combining classifiers and learning mixture-of-experts. In *Encyclopedia of Artificial Intelligence*, pages 318–326. IGI, 2009.

L. Xu and M. I. Jordan. On convergence properties of the EM algorithm for Gaussian mixtures. *Neural Computation*, 8(1):129–151, 1996.

L. Xu, A. Krzyzak, and C. Y. Suen. Methods of combining multiple classifiers and their applications to handwriting recognition. *IEEE Trans. Systems Man and Cybernetics*, 22(3):418–435, 1992.

L. Xu, M. I. Jordan, and G. E. Hinton. An alternative model for mixtures of experts. In *Advances in Neural Information Processing Systems 7*, pages 633–640, Denver, CO, 1994.

L. Xu, W. Li, and D. Schuurmans. Fast normalized cut with linear constraints. In *Proceedings of the 22nd IEEE Conference on Computer Vision and Pattern Recognition*, pages 2866–2873, Miami, FL, 2009.

L. Xu, B. Li, and E. Chen. Ensemble pruning via constrained eigen-optimization. In *Proceedings of the 12th IEEE International Conference on Data Mining*, pages 715–724, Brussels, Belgium, 2012.

X. Xu and E. Frank. Logistic regression and boosting for labeled bags of instances. In *Proceedings of the 8th Pacific-Asia Conference on Knowledge Discovery and Data Mining*, pages 272–281, Sydney, Australia, 2004.

Y.-X. Xu, M. Pang, J. Feng, K. M. Ting, Y. Jiang, and Z.-H. Zhou. Reconstruction-based anomaly detection with completely random forest. In *Proceedings of the 21st SIAM International Conference on Data Mining*, pages 127–135, Virtual Event, 2021b.

L. Yan, R. H. Dodier, M. Mozer, and R. H. Wolniewicz. Optimizing classifier performance via an approximation to the Wilcoxon-Mann-Whitney statistic. In *Proceedings of the 20th International Conference on Machine Learning*, pages 848–855, Washington, DC, 2003.

R. Yan, J. Tesic, and J. R. Smith. Model-shared subspace boosting for multi-label classification. In *Proceedings of the 13th ACM SIGKDD International Conference on Knowledge Discovery and Data Mining*, pages 834–843, San Jose, CA, 2007.

W. Yan and F. Xue. Jet engine gas path fault diagnosis using dynamic fusion of multiple classifiers. In *Proceedings of the International Joint Conference on Neural Networks*, pages 1585–1591, Hong Kong, China, 2008.

Y.-H. Yan, P. Zhao, and Z.-H. Zhou. Fast rates in time-varying strongly monotone games. In *Proceedings of the 40th International Conference on Machine Learning*, pages 39138–39164, Honolulu, HI, 2023a.

Y.-H. Yan, P. Zhao, and Z.-H. Zhou. Online non-stochastic control with partial feedback. *Journal of Machine Learning Research*, 24(273):1–50, 2023b.

Y.-H. Yan, P. Zhao, and Z.-H. Zhou. Universal online learning with gradual variations: A multi-layer online ensemble approach. In *Advances in Neural Information Processing Systems 36*, pages 37682–37715. New Orleans, LA, 2023c.

L. Yang, X.-Z. Wu, Y. Jiang, and Z.-H. Zhou. Multi-label learning with deep forest. In *Proceedings of the 24th European Conference on Artificial Intelligence*, pages 1634–1641, Santiago de Compostela, Spain, 2020.

L. Yang, Y. Wang, M. Gao, A. Shrivastava, K. Weinberger, W.-L. Chao, and S.-N. Lim. Deep co-training with task decomposition for semi-supervised domain adaptation. In *Proceedings of the 19th IEEE/CVF International Conference on Computer Vision*, pages 8886–8896, Montréal, Canada, 2021a.

M. Yang, Y.-X. Zhang, X. Wang, and F. Min. Multi-instance ensemble learning with discriminative bags. *IEEE Trans. Systems, Man, and Cybernetics: Systems*, 52(9): 5456–5467, 2021b.

H.-J. Ye, D.-C. Zhan, Y. Jiang, and Z.-H. Zhou. What makes objects similar: A unified multi-metric learning approach. *IEEE Trans. Pattern Analysis and Machine Intelligence*, 41(5):1257–1270, 2019.

D.-Y. Yeung and C. Chow. Parzen-window network intrusion detectors. In *Proceedings of 2002 International Conference on Pattern Recognition*, volume 4, pages 385–388, Quebec, Canada, 2002.

H. Ykhlef and D. Bouchaffra. An efficient ensemble pruning approach based on simple coalitional games. *Information Fusion*, 34:28–42, 2017.

D. Yu, G. Sheikholeslami, and A. Zhang. FindOut: Finding outliers in very large datasets. *Knowledge and Information Systems*, 4(4):387–412, 2002.

T. Yu, G. Thomas, L. Yu, S. Ermon, J. Y. Zou, S. Levine, C. Finn, and T. Ma. MOPO: Model-based offline policy optimization. In *Advances in Neural Information Processing Systems 33*, pages 14129–14142, Vritual Event, 2020.

Y. Yu and Z.-H. Zhou. A framework for modeling positive class expansion with single snapshot. *Knowledge and Information Systems*, 25(2):211–227, 2010.

Y. Yu, Z.-H. Zhou, and K. M. Ting. Cocktail ensemble for regression. In *Proceedings of the 7th IEEE International Conference on Data Mining*, pages 721–726, Omeha, NE, 2007.

Y. Yu, Y.-F. Li, and Z.-H. Zhou. Diversity regularized machine. In *Proceedings of the 22nd International Joint Conference on Artificial Intelligence*, pages 1603–1608, Barcelona, Spain, 2011.

Z. Yu and H.-S. Wong. Class discovery from gene expression data based on perturbation and cluster ensemble. *IEEE Trans. NanoBioscience*, 8(2):147–160, 2009.

H. Yuan, M. Fang, and X. Zhu. Hierarchical sampling for multi-instance ensemble learning. *IEEE Trans. Knowledge and Data Engineering*, 25(12):2900–2905, 2012.

G. Yule. On the association of attributes in statistics: with illustrations from the material of the childhood society. *Philosophical Transactions of the Royal Society A*, 194:257–319, 1900.

B. Zadrozny and C. Elkan. Obtaining calibrated probability estimates from decision trees and naive Bayesian classifiers. In *Proceedings of the 18th International Conference on Machine Learning*, pages 609–616, Williamstown, MA, 2001.

B. Zadrozny, J. Langford, and N. Abe. Cost-sensitive learning by cost-proportionate example weighting. In *Proceedings of the 3rd IEEE International Conference on Data Mining*, page 435, Melbourne, FL, 2003.

J. Zhang, M. Wu, and V. S. Sheng. Ensemble learning from crowds. *IEEE Trans. Knowledge and Data Engineering*, 31(8):1506–1519, 2018.

L. Zhang, G. Wang, J. Yi, and T. Yang. A simple yet universal strategy for online convex optimization. In *Proceedings of the 39th International Conference on Machine Learning*, pages 26605–26623, Baltimore, MD, 2022a.

M. Zhang, P. Zhao, H. Luo, and Z.-H. Zhou. No-regret learning in time-varying zero-sum games. In *Proceedings of the 39th International Conference on Machine Learning*, pages 26772–26808, Baltimore, MD, 2022b.

M.-L. Zhang and Z.-H. Zhou. Exploiting unlabeled data to enhance ensemble diversity. In *Proceedings of the 9th IEEE International Conference on Data Mining*, pages 609–618, Sydney, Australia, 2010a.

M.-L. Zhang and Z.-H. Zhou. A review on multi-label learning algorithms. *IEEE Trans. Knowledge and Data Engineering*, 26(8):1819–1837, 2014.

T. Zhang. Analysis of regularized linear functions for classification problems. Technical Report RC-21572, IBM Thomas J. Watson Research Division, Albany, NY, 1999.

T. Zhang. Covering number bounds of certain regularized linear function classes. *Journal of Machine Learning Research*, 2:527–550, 2002.

T. Zhang and B. Yu. Boosting with early stopping: Convergence and consistency. *Annals of Statistics*, 33(4):1538–1579, 2005.

T. Zhang, R. Ramakrishnan, and M. Livny. BIRCH: An efficient data clustering method for very large databases. In *Proceedings of the ACM SIGMOD International Conference on Management of Data*, pages 103–114, Montréal, Canada, 1996.

X. Zhang, S. Wang, T. Shan, and L. Jiao. Selective SVMs ensemble driven by immune clonal algorithm. In *Proceedings of the 6th EvoWorkshop on Applications of Evolutionary Computing*, pages 325–333, Lausanne, Switzerland, 2005.

X. Zhang, L. Jiao, F. Liu, L. Bo, and M. Gong. Spectral clustering ensemble applied to SAR image segmentation. *IEEE Trans. Geoscience and Remote Sensing*, 46(7): 2126–2136, 2008.

Y. Zhang and Z.-H. Zhou. Cost-sensitive face recognition. *IEEE Trans. Pattern Analysis and Machine Intelligence*, 32(10):1758–1769, 2010b.

Y. Zhang, S. Burer, and W. N. Street. Ensemble pruning via semi-definite programming. *Journal of Machine Learning Research*, 7:1315–1338, 2006.

Y.-J. Zhang, P. Zhao, L. Ma, and Z.-H. Zhou. An unbiased risk estimator for learning with augmented classes. In *Advances in Neural Information Processing Systems 33*, pages 10247–10258, Virtual Event, 2020.

Y.-J. Zhang, Z.-Y. Zhang, P. Zhao, and M. Sugiyama. Adapting to continuous covariate shift via online density ratio estimation. In *Advances in Neural Information Processing Systems 36*, pages 29074–29113, New Orleans, LA, 2023.

Y.-L. Zhang, J. Zhou, W. Zheng, J. Feng, L. Li, Z. Liu, M. Li, Z. Zhang, C. Chen, X. Li, Y. Qi, and Z.-H. Zhou. Distributed deep forest and its application to automatic detection of cash-out fraud. *ACM Trans. Intelligent Systems and Technology*, 10(5):55:1–55:19, 2019.

P. Zhao and L. Zhang. Improved analysis for dynamic regret of strongly convex and smooth functions. In *Proceedings of the 3rd Conference on Learning for Dynamics and Control*, pages 48–59, Virtual Event, 2021.

P. Zhao, L.-W. Cai, and Z.-H. Zhou. Handling concept drift via model reuse. *Machine Learning*, 109(3):533–568, 2020a.

P. Zhao, L. Zhang, Y. Jiang, and Z.-H. Zhou. A simple approach for non-stationary linear bandits. In *Proceedings of the 23rd International Conference on Artificial Intelligence and Statistics*, pages 746–755, Palermo, Italy, 2020b.

P. Zhao, G. Wang, L. Zhang, and Z.-H. Zhou. Bandit convex optimization in non-stationary environments. *Journal of Machine Learning Research*, 22(125):1–45, 2021.

P. Zhao, L.-F. Li, and Z.-H. Zhou. Dynamic regret of online Markov decision processes. In *Proceedings of the 39th International Conference on Machine Learning*, pages 26865–26894, Baltimore, MD, 2022a.

P. Zhao, Y.-F. Xie, L. Zhang, and Z.-H. Zhou. Efficient methods for non-stationary online learning. In *Advances in Neural Information Processing Systems 35*, pages 11573–11585, New Orleans, LA, 2022b.

P. Zhao, Y.-H. Yan, Y.-X. Wang, and Z.-H. Zhou. Non-stationary online learning with memory and non-stochastic control. *Journal of Machine Learning Research*, 24(206):1–70, 2023.

P. Zhao, Y.-J. Zhang, L. Zhang, and Z.-H. Zhou. Adaptivity and non-stationarity: Problem-dependent dynamic regret for online convex optimization. *Journal of Machine Learning Research*, 25(98):1–52, 2024.

Q.-C. Zheng, S.-H. Lyu, S.-Q. Zhang, Y. Jiang, and Z.-H. Zhou. On the consistency rate of decision tree learning algorithms. In *Proceedings of the 26th International Conference on Artificial Intelligence and Statistics*, pages 7824–7848, Valencia, Spain, 2023.

D. Zhou, O. Bousquet, T. N. Lal, J. Weston, and B. Schölkopf. Learning with local and global consistency. In *Advances in Neural Information Processing Systems 16*, pages 321–328, Vancouver, Canada, 2002a.

Y.-H. Zhou and Z.-H. Zhou. Large margin distribution learning with cost interval and unlabeled data. *IEEE Trans. Knowledge and Data Engineering*, 28(7):1749–1763, 2016.

Z.-H. Zhou. Rule extraction: Using neural networks or for neural networks? *Journal of Computer Science and Technology*, 19(2):249–253, 2004.

Z.-H. Zhou. Comprehensibility of data mining algorithms. In J. Wang, editor, *Encyclopedia of Data Warehousing and Mining*, pages 190–195. IGI, Hershey, PA, 2005.

Z.-H. Zhou. When semi-supervised learning meets ensemble learning. In *Proceedings of the 8th International Workshop on Multiple Classifier Systems*, pages 529–538, Reykjavik, Iceland, 2009.

Z.-H. Zhou. Ensemble learning. In *Encyclopedia of Biometrics*, pages 411–416. Springer, 2nd edition, 2015.

Z.-H. Zhou. Learnware: On the future of machine learning. *Frontiers of Computer Science*, 10(4):589–590, 2016.

Z.-H. Zhou. A brief introduction to weakly supervised learning. *National Science Review*, 5(1):44–53, 2018a.

Z.-H. Zhou. Ensemble. In *Encyclopedia of Database Systems*. Springer, 2nd edition, 2018b.

Z. H. Zhou. *Machine Learning*. Springer, 2021.

Z.-H. Zhou. Open-environment machine learning. *National Science Review*, 9(8): nwac123, 2022.

Z.-H. Zhou and Z. Chen. Hybrid decision tree. *Knowledge-Based Systems*, 15(8): 515–528, 2002.

Z.-H. Zhou and J. Feng. Deep forest. *National Science Review*, 6(1):74–86, 2019.

Z.-H. Zhou and Y. Jiang. Medical diagnosis with C4.5 rule preceded by artificial neural network ensemble. *IEEE Trans. Information Technology in Biomedicine*, 7 (1):37–42, 2003.

Z.-H. Zhou and Y. Jiang. NeC4.5: Neural ensemble based C4.5. *IEEE Trans. Knowledge and Data Engineering*, 16(6):770–773, 2004.

Z.-H. Zhou and M. Li. Tri-training: Exploiting unlabeled data using three classifiers. *IEEE Trans. Knowledge and Data Engineering*, 17(11):1529–1541, 2005.

Z.-H. Zhou and M. Li. Semi-supervised learning by disagreement. *Knowledge and Information Systems*, 24(3):415–439, 2010a.

Z.-H. Zhou and N. Li. Multi-information ensemble diversity. In *Proceedings of the 9th International Workshop on Multiple Classifier Systems*, pages 134–144, Cairo, Egypt, 2010b.

Z.-H. Zhou and X.-Y. Liu. Training cost-sensitive neural networks with methods addressing the class imbalance problem. *IEEE Trans. Knowledge and Data Engineering*, 18(1):63–77, 2006a.

Z.-H. Zhou and X.-Y. Liu. On multi-class cost-sensitive learning. In *Proceeding of the 21st National Conference on Artificial Intelligence*, pages 567–572, Boston, WA, 2006b.

Z.-H. Zhou and Z.-H. Tan. Learnware: Small models do big. *Science China Information Sciences*, 67(1):112102, 2024.

Z.-H. Zhou and W. Tang. Selective ensemble of decision trees. In *Proceedings of the 9th International Conference on Rough Sets, Fuzzy Sets, Data Mining and Granular Computing*, pages 476–483, Chongqing, China, 2003.

Z.-H. Zhou and W. Tang. Clusterer ensemble. *Knowledge-Based Systems*, 19(1): 77–83, 2006.

Z.-H. Zhou and J.-M. Xu. On the relation between multi-instance learning and semi-supervised learning. In *Proceeding of the 24th International Conference on Machine Learning*, pages 1167–1174, Corvallis, OR, 2007.

Z.-H. Zhou and Y. Yu. Ensembling local learners through multimodal perturbation. *IEEE Trans. Systems, Man, and Cybernetics - Part B: Cybernetics*, 35(4):725–735, 2005.

Z.-H. Zhou and M.-L. Zhang. Ensembles of multi-instance learners. In *Proceedings of the 14th European Conference on Machine Learning*, pages 492–502, Cavtat-Dubrovnik, Croatia, 2003.

Z.-H. Zhou and M.-L. Zhang. Solving multi-instance problems with classifier ensemble based on constructive clustering. *Knowledge and Information Systems*, 11(2):155–170, 2007.

Z.-H. Zhou and M.-L. Zhang. Multi-label learning. In C. Sammut and G. I. Webb, editors, *Encyclopedia of Machine Learning and Data Mining*, pages 875–881. Springer, 2017.

Z.-H. Zhou, Y. Jiang, Y.-B. Yang, and S.-F. Chen. Lung cancer cell identification based on artificial neural network ensembles. *Artificial Intelligence in Medicine*, 24(1):25–36, 2002b.

Z.-H. Zhou, J. Wu, and W. Tang. Ensembling neural networks: Many could be better than all. *Artificial Intelligence*, 137(1-2):239–263, 2002c.

Z.-H. Zhou, Y. Jiang, and S.-F. Chen. Extracting symbolic rules from trained neural network ensembles. *AI Communications*, 16(1):3–15, 2003.

Z.-H. Zhou, K.-J. Chen, and H.-B. Dai. Enhancing relevance feedback in image retrieval using unlabeled data. *ACM Trans. Information Systems*, 24(2):219–244, 2006.

Z.-H. Zhou, D.-C. Zhan, and Q. Yang. Semi-supervised learning with very few labeled training examples. In *Proceedings of the 22nd AAAI Conference on Artificial Intelligence*, pages 675–680, Vancouver, Canada, 2007.

Z.-H. Zhou, Y.-Y. Sun, and Y.-F. Li. Multi-instance learning by treating instances as non-i.i.d. samples. In *Proceeding of the 26th International Conference on Machine Learning*, pages 1249–1256, Montréal, Canada, 2009.

Z.-H. Zhou, M.-L. Zhang, S.-J. Huang, and Y.-F. Li. Multi-instance multi-label learning. *Artificial Intelligence*, 176(1):2291–2320, 2012.

Z.-H. Zhou, Y. Yu, and C. Qian. *Evolutionary Learning: Advances in Theories and Algorithms.* Springer, 2019.

J. Zhu, S. Rosset, H. Zou, and T. Hastie. Multi-class AdaBoost. Technical report, Department of Statistics, University of Michigan, Ann Arbor, MI, 2006.

S. Zhu, X. Dong, and H. Su. Binary ensemble neural network: More bits per network or more networks per bit? In *Proceedings of the 32nd IEEE Conference on Computer Vision and Pattern Recognition*, pages 4923–4932, Long Beach, CA, 2019.

X. Zhu. Semi-supervised learning literature survey. Technical Report 1530, Department of Computer Sciences, University of Wisconsin at Madison, Madison, WI, 2006. http://www.cs.wisc.edu/~jerryzhu/pub/ssl_survey.pdf.

X. Zhu, Z. Ghahramani, and J. Lafferty. Semi-supervised learning using Gaussian fields and harmonic functions. In *Proceedings of the 20th International Conference on Machine Learning*, pages 912–919, Washington, DC, 2003.

X. Zhu, X. Wu, and Y. Yang. Dynamic classifier selection for effective mining from noisy data streams. In *Proceedings of the 14th IEEE International Conference on Data Mining*, pages 305–312, Brighton, UK, 2004.

Y. Zhu, K. M. Ting, and Z.-H. Zhou. New class adaptation via instance generation in one-pass class incremental learning. In *Proceeding of the 17th IEEE International Conference on Data Mining*, pages 1207–1212, New Orleans, LA, 2017a.

Y. Zhu, K. M. Ting, and Z.-H. Zhou. Discover multiple novel labels in multi-instance multi-label learning. In *Proceedings of the 31st AAAI Conference on Artificial Intelligence*, pages 2977–2983, San Francisco, CA, 2017b.

A. Zimek, M. Gaudet, R. J. G. B. Campello, and J. Sander. Subsampling for efficient and effective unsupervised outlier detection ensembles. In *Proceedings of the 19th ACM SIGKDD International Conference on Knowledge Discovery and Data Mining*, pages 428–436, Chicago, IL, 2013.

A. Zimek, R. J. G. B. Campello, and J. Sander. Ensembles for unsupervised outlier detection: Challenges and research questions. *SIGKDD Explorations*, 15(1):11–22, 2014.

M. Zinkevich. Online convex programming and generalized infinitesimal gradient ascent. In *Proceedings of the 20th International Conference on Machine Learning*, pages 928–936, Washington, DC, 2003.

Index

Printed in the United States
by Baker & Taylor Publisher Services

Printed in the United States
by Baker & Taylor Publisher Services